ACTIVE LEARNING

In order to understand economic concepts, it is important to practice and develop your skills in reading and interpreting graphs. Prentice Hall has developed two levels of interactive graphing tools to help you achieve these goals. Go to the text Web site, www.prenhall.com/OSULLIVAN, for access to these valuable interactive tools along with other important active learning Web resources.

Active Graphs Level One are interactive graph exercises and problems that require you to consider several key concepts in sequence. Below is a list of Level One Active Graphs to accompany *Survey of Economics: Principles and Tools*, Second Edition.

CHAPTER	FIGURE / TEXT REFERENCE	GRAPH TITLE
Chapter 1	Figures 1.1, 1.2	Scarcity and the Production Possibilities Curve
	The Principle of Opportunity Cost	Opportunity Costs
	Think Marginal	The Marginal Principle
	Figure 1.4	The Principle of Diminishing Returns
	The Reality Principle	The Reality Principle
	The Reality Principle	Real vs. Nominal
	Figure 1A.2	Shifting a Curve
	Figure 1A.4	Nonlinear Relationships
	Chapter 1, Appendix	Curves, Which Way Do They Shift?
	Chapter 1, Appendix	Adjacent or Stacked Graphs
Chapter 2	Figure 2.1	The Demand Curve and the Law of Demand
	Figure 2.2	The Market Demand Curve
	Figure 2.4	The Supply Curve and the Law of Supply
	Figure 2.5	Market Equilibrium
Chapter 3	Predicting Changes in Total Revenue	Predicting Changes in Total Revenue
	Figure 3.3	Predicting Changes in Price and Quantity
Chapter 4	Figure 4.3	The Relationship Between Marginal Cost and Average Total Cost
	Chapter 4, Text	Average Cost Curves
	Figure 4.7	Long-Run Average Cost
Chapter 5	Figure 5.2	The Marginal Principle and the Output Decision
	Figure 5.3	The Shutdown Decision
	Figures 5.5, 5.7	Market Effects in Changes of Demand and Supply
	Increase in Demand and the Incentive to Enter	The Increase in Demand for Video Rentals
	Figure 5.8	Short-Run vs. Long-Run Supply Curves
Chapter 6	Figures 6.5, 6.6	The Price and Quantity Decision for a Monopolist
	Figure 6.7	Regulation of a Natural Monopolist
Chapter 7	Figure 7.8	Entry Deterrence by an Insecure Monopolist
Chapter 9	Figure 9.1	The Short-Run Labor Demand Curve
	Figure 9.5	Supply and Demand for Labor
	Figure 9.6	Occupational Licensing
	Labor Unions and Wages	Labor Unions and Wages

continues next page

continued

CHAPTER	FIGURE / TEXT REFERENCE	GRAPH TITLE
Chapter 13	Figure 13.6	Shifts of Aggregate Demand and the Long-Run Aggregate Supply Curve
	Figure 13.8	Shifts of Aggregate Demand and the Short-Run Aggregate Supply Curve
Chapter 14	Figure 14.6	The Multiplier
	Figure 14.7	Government Spending and Taxation
	Figure 14.1	Exports and Imports
Chapter 16	Figure 16.4	The Demand for Money
	Figure 16.5	Interest Rate Determination
	Figures 16.7, 16.8	Monetary Policy
Chapter 17	Figure 17.1	Quotas, Voluntary Export Restraints, and Tariffs
	Figure 17.2	The Determination of Exchange Rates

Active Graphs Level Two are interactive graph exercises and problems that allow you to manipulate variables and shift curves based on an economic scenario. Students can assess their understanding of a concept before moving on. Below is the list of Level Two Active Graphs to accompany *Survey of Economics: Principles and Tools*, Second Edition.

CHAPTER	FIGURE / TEXT REFERENCE	GRAPH TITLE
Chapter 1	Figure 1.2	Production Possibilities Frontier: Understanding Growth
	Using the Principle: Warships, Security, Collectibles	Production Possibilities Frontier: Understanding Opportunity Costs
	Chapter 1, Appendix	Understanding Graphs
Chapter 2	Market Effects of Changes in Demand	Supply and Demand: Market Equilibrium
	Decreases in Demand	Supply and Demand: Shifting Curves I
	Market Effects of Changes in Supply	Supply and Demand: Shifting Curves II
	Decreases in Supply	Supply and Demand: Shifting Curves III
	Market Effects of Simultaneous Changes in Market Demand and Supply	Supply and Demand: Shifting Curves IV
Chapter 3	Chapter 3, Appendix	Calculating Elasticity
Chapter 5	Economic Profit	Maximizing Profit at the Perfectly Competitive Firm
	Figure 5.5	Perfect Competition in the Long Run
	Figure 5.10	Long-Run Supply
Chapter 6	Table 6.1 and Figure 6.2	Marginal Revenue for a Single-Price Monopoly
	Figure 6.3	Maximizing Profit for a Single-Price Monopoly
	Figure 6.7	Regulating a Natural Monopoly
Chapter 7	Figure 7.3	Monopolistic Competition
Chapter 8	Bicycle Theft Insurance	Moral Hazard
Chapter 9	Figure 9.2	The Market for Labor
Chapter 13	The Short-Run Aggregate Supply Curve	Aggregate Supply and Aggregate Demand: Demand-Side Inflation and Deflation
	The Short-Run Aggregate Supply Curve	Aggregate Supply and Aggregate Demand: Supply-Side Inflation and Deflation
	Output and Price in the Short-Run and in the Long-Run	Aggregate Supply and Aggregate Demand: The Slope of the Aggregate Supply Curve
Chapter 14	Government Spending and Taxation	Aggregate Expenditures
Chapter 17	Rationales for Protectionist Policies	Understanding Tariffs and Quotas

Survey of Economics
Principles and Tools

Second Edition

Prentice Hall Series in Economics

Adams/Brock, *The Structure of American Industry*, Tenth Edition

Ayers/Collinge, *Economics: Explore & Apply*

Ayers/Collinge, *Macroeconomics: Explore & Apply*

Ayers/Collinge, *Microeconomics: Explore & Apply*

Blanchard, *Macroeconomics*, Third Edition

Blau/Ferber/Winkler, *The Economics of Women, Men, and Work*, Fourth Edition

Boardman/Greenberg/Vining/Weimer, *Cost Benefit Analysis: Concepts and Practice*, Second Edition

Bogart, *The Economics of Cities and Suburbs*

Case/Fair, *Principles of Economics*, Seventh Edition

Case/Fair, *Principles of Macroeconomics*, Seventh Edition

Case/Fair, *Principles of Microeconomics*, Seventh Edition

Caves, *American Industry: Structure, Conduct, Performance*, Seventh Edition

Colander/Gamber, *Macroeconomics*

Collinge/Ayers, *Economics by Design: Principles and Issues*, Third Edition

DiPasquale/Wheaton, *Urban Economics and Real Estate Markets*

Eaton/Eaton/Allen, *Microeconomics*, Fifth Edition

Folland/Goodman/Stano, *Economics of Health and Health Care*, Fourth Edition

Fort, *Sports Economics*

Froyen, *Macroeconomics: Theories and Policies*, Seventh Edition

Greene, *Econometric Analysis*, Fifth Edition

Heilbroner/Milberg, *The Making of Economic Society*, Eleventh Edition

Hess, *Using Mathematics in Economic Analysis*

Heyne/Boetke/Prychitko, *The Economic Way of Thinking*, Tenth Edition

Keat/Young, *Managerial Economics*, Fourth Edition

Lynn, *Economic Development: Theory and Practice for a Divided World*

Mathis/Koscianski, *Microeconomic Theory: An Integrated Approach*

Milgrom/Roberts, *Economics, Organization, and Management*

O'Sullivan/Sheffrin, *Economics: Principles and Tools*, Third Edition

O'Sullivan/Sheffrin, *Macroeconomics: Principles and Tools*, Third Edition

O'Sullivan/Sheffrin, *Microeconomics: Principles and Tools*, Third Edition

O'Sullivan/Sheffrin, *Survey of Economics: Principles and Tools*, Second Edition

Petersen/Lewis, *Managerial Economics*, Fifth Edition

Pindyck/Rubinfeld, *Microeconomics*, Fifth Edition

Reynolds/Masters/Moser, *Labor Economics and Labor Relations*, Eleventh Edition

Roberts, *The Choice: A Fable of Free Trade and Protectionism*, Revised Edition

Sawyer/Sprinkle, *International Economics*

Schiller, *The Economics of Poverty and Discrimination*, Ninth Edition

Weidenbaum, *Business and Government in the Global Marketplace*, Seventh Edition

Survey of
Economics
Principles and Tools
Second Edition

Arthur O'Sullivan

Lewis & Clark College

Steven M. Sheffrin

University of California, Davis

PEARSON

Prentice
Hall

Upper Saddle River, New Jersey 07458

Library of Congress Cataloging-in-Publication Data

O'Sullivan, Arthur.
   Survey of economics: principles and tools / Arthur O'Sullivan, Steven M. Sheffrin.—2nd ed.
      p. cm.—(Prentice-Hall series in economics)
   Includes bibliographical references and index.
   ISBN 0-13-143969-3 (pbk.)
   1. Economics. I. Sheffrin, Steven M. II. Title. III. Series.
HB171.5.O843 2004
330—dc22   2003058208

Executive Editor: Rod Banister
Editor-in-Chief: P. J. Boardman
Managing Editor (Editorial): Gladys Soto
Project Manager: Marie McHale
Editorial Assistant: Joy Golden
Media Project Manager: Victoria Anderson
Executive Marketing Manager: Kathleen McLellan
Marketing Assistant: Melissa Owens
Managing Editor (Production): Cynthia Regan
Production Editor: Michael Reynolds
Production Assistant: Joe DeProspero
Permissions Supervisor: Suzanne Grappi
Manufacturing Buyer: Diane Peirano
Design Manager: Maria Lange
Designer: Steve Frim
Interior Design: Lee Goldstein
Cover Design: Steve Frim
Cover Illustration/Photo: Jerry McDaniel
Manager, Print Production: Christy Mahon
Composition/Full-Service Project Management: UG / GGS Information Services, Inc.
Printer/Binder: Quebecor World Book Services, Dubuque
Cover Printer: Phoenix Color

Credits and acknowledgments borrowed from other sources and reproduced, with permission, in this textbook appear on appropriate page within text (or on page 429).

Pearson Education LTD.
Pearson Education Australia PTY, Limited
Pearson Education Singapore, Pte. Ltd
Pearson Education North Asia Ltd
Pearson Education, Canada, Ltd
Pearson Educaci;aaon de Mexico, S.A. de C.V.
Pearson Education–Japan
Pearson Education Malaysia, Pte. Ltd

10 9 8 7 6 5 4 3 2
ISBN 0-13-143969-3

To Our Children: Conor, Maura, Meera, and Kiran

About the Authors

Arthur O'Sullivan

Arthur O'Sullivan is a professor of economics at Lewis and Clark College in Portland, Oregon. After receiving his B.S. degree in economics at the University of Oregon, he spent two years in the Peace Corps, working with city planners in the Philippines. He received his Ph.D. degree in economics from Princeton University in 1981 and has taught at the University of California, Davis, and Oregon State University, winning several teaching awards at both schools. He recently accepted an endowed professorship at Lewis and Clark College, where he teaches microeconomics and urban economics. He is the author of the best-selling textbook, *Urban Economics*, currently in its fifth edition.

Professor O'Sullivan's research explores economic issues concerning urban land use, environmental protection, and public policy. His articles appear in many economics journals, including *Journal of Urban Economics, Journal of Environmental Economics and Management, National Tax Journal, Journal of Public Economics*, and *Journal of Law and Economics*.

Professor O'Sullivan lives with his family in Lake Oswego, Oregon. He enjoys outdoor activities, including tennis, rafting, and hiking. Indoors, he plays chess, foosball, and Ping-Pong with his two kids and is lucky to win one of five games.

Steven M. Sheffrin

Steven M. Sheffrin is dean of the division of social sciences and professor of economics at the University of California, Davis. He has been a visiting professor at Princeton University, Oxford University, and the London School of Economics and has served as a financial economist with the Office of Tax Analysis of the United States Treasury Department. He has been on the faculty at Davis since 1976 and served as the chairman of the department of economics. He received his B.A. from Wesleyan University and his Ph.D. in economics from the Massachusetts Institute of Technology.

Professor Sheffrin is the author of eight other books and monographs and over 100 articles in the fields of macroeconomics, public finance, and international economics. His most recent books include *Rational Expectations* (Second Edition) and *Property Taxes and Tax Revolts: The Legacy of Proposition 13* (with Arthur O'Sullivan and Terri Sexton), both from Cambridge University Press.

Professor Sheffrin has taught macroeconomics at all levels, from large lectures of principles (classes of 400) to graduate classes for doctoral students. He is the recipient of the Thomas Mayer Distinguished Teaching Award in economics.

He lives with his wife Anjali (also an economist) and his two children in Davis, California. In addition to a passion for current affairs and travel, he plays a tough game of tennis.

Brief Contents

Contents

3 Elasticity: A Measure of Responsiveness   63

4 Production and Cost   81

5 Perfect Competition: Short Run and Long Run   105

A CLOSER LOOK

Preface

Our Story

When we set out to write an economics text, we were driven by the vision of the sleeping student. A few years ago, one of the authors was in the middle of a fascinating lecture on monopoly pricing when he heard snoring. It wasn't the first time a student had fallen asleep in one of his classes, but this was the loudest snoring he had ever heard—it sounded like a sputtering chain saw. The instructor turned to Bill, who was sitting next to the sleeping student and asked, "Could you wake him up?" Bill looked at the sleeping student and then gazed theatrically around the room at the other students. He finally looked back at the instructor and said, "Well professor, I think you should wake him up. After all, you put him to sleep."

That experience changed the way we taught economics. It highlighted for us a basic truth—for many students, economics isn't exactly exciting. We took this as a challenge—to get first-time economics students to see the *relevance* of economics to their *lives*, their *careers*, and their *futures*.

In order to get students to see the relevance of economics we knew that we had to *engage* them. With the first three editions of *Economics: Principles and Tools*, we helped professors to do that by emphasizing an active learning approach. We engaged students by teaching them how to do something—economic analysis. We kept the book brief, lively, and to the point, and used the five key principles of economics as an organizing theme.

One-Semester Book

Our full-length text was a success in classrooms across the country. But many schools and universities teach a one-semester course in economics, which covers both microeconomics and macroeconomics. Although instructors can successfully choose material from our full-length text for a one-semester course, it would be much more valuable to the instructors and students if there were a dedicated one-semester book to meet their needs.

Our objective was to develop a one-semester book that preserved the key features of *Economics: Principles and Tools*. We knew we had the right ingredients. Our book was unified by the repeated use of key principles of economics, which stressed the unity of economic thinking. Our style was also right: The text was brief, lively, and fully accessible to students.

In creating a one-semester book, we remained true to our basic teaching philosophy: An introductory course in economics should be taught as if it were the last economics class a student will ever take. Because this is true for most students, we just have an opportunity to teach them how to do economics. The best way to teach economics is to focus on a few key concepts and ideas and apply them repeatedly in different circumstances.

In designing the one-semester book, we knew we had to focus on just the absolute essentials. In microeconomics, we start with the five key principles of economics and move quickly into the heart of microeconomics—supply and demand. We then turn to production and cost, competition and market structure, market failures, and the labor market. Macroeconomics begins with chapters that introduce national income, unemployment, and inflation. We then focus on the importance of long-run economic growth and introduce economic fluctuations. We cover monetary and fiscal policy, both in the long run and the short run. The book concludes with international trade and finance.

We worked hard to make every explanation of key ideas and key concepts as simple as possible. In a one-semester course, the student will be introduced to a wide range of ideas. It is important that these ideas be as straightforward and transparent as possible.

Key Changes

Although the first edition was a big success, we decided that we could do better. In revising the book, we found several opportunities to reduce the technical detail of the presentation in favor of more intuitive explanations. In the introductory chapter, we expanded the discussion of the economic way of thinking, adding material on positive versus normative statements, marginal decision making, and the notion of ceteris paribus. We also updated all the data and added many new applications of economic analysis. We rewrote the chapter dealing with pollution, public goods, and imperfect information to emphasize the theme of market failure. The expanded chapter also explores the bargaining solution to environmental problems and marketable pollution permits. For the macroeconomic chapters, we updated all the data, examples, and analysis to reflect the economic downturn of the beginning of this century. We redesigned the chapters on fiscal and monetary policy to fully integrate them with aggregate demand and supply analysis.

Principles and Tools

In keeping with the themes of relevance and student accessibility, we have once again organized our text around the **five key principles** of economics. Throughout the text, every point of theory is tied back to the five key principles and is indicated by the lock-and-key symbol.

1. **The Principle of Opportunity Cost.** The opportunity cost of something is what you sacrifice to get it.
2. **The Marginal Principle.** Pick the level of an activity at which the marginal benefit equals the marginal cost.
3. **The Principle of Diminishing Returns.** If we increase one input while holding the other inputs fixed, output will increase, but at a decreasing rate.
4. **The Spillover Principle.** In some circumstances, decision-makers do not bear all the costs or experience all the benefits from their decision
5. **The Reality Principle.** What matters to people is the real value of money or income—its purchasing power—not the face value of money or income.

We use these principles to explain the logic underpinning the most important tools of economics. By using these five principles repeatedly, we reveal the logic of economic reasoning and demystify the tools of economics. Students see the big picture and also learn how to use the tools of economics properly.

"What I Do, I Understand"—Confucius

Our book is based on **Active Learning**, a teaching approach based on the idea that students learn best by doing. Our book engages students by letting them do activities as they read. We implement **Active Learning** with the following features:

Economic Detective exercises provide a few clues and then ask the student to solve the economic mystery.

Using the Tools questions at the end of each chapter give students opportunities to do their own economic analysis. Complete answers appear at the end of each chapter.

Economic experiments actively involve the student in role-playing as consumers, producers, and policymakers. All these activities are designed to be fun for students and easy for professors, who decide when and how to use them.

Test Your Understanding questions help students determine whether they understand the preceding material before continuing. These are straightforward questions that ask students to review and synthesize what they have read. Complete answers appear at the end of each chapter.

Economic Detective

The Video Elasticity Mystery

The manager of a video-rental store has asked you to solve a mystery. According to national studies of the video-rental market, the price elasticity of demand for video rentals is 0.8: A 10% increase in price decreases the quantity of videos demanded by about 8%. In other words, the demand for videos is inelastic. Based on this information, the manager of the video store increased her price by 20%, expecting her total revenue to increase. She expected the good news (more money per rental) to dominate the bad news (fewer rentals). When her total revenue decreased instead of increasing, she was puzzled. Your job is to solve this mystery.

The key to solving this mystery is to recognize that the manager can't use the results of ~~~~~ ~redict th~ ~sing her ~~~~~ ~~~~al

Using the **TOOLS**

We've explained the five key principles of economics, which provide the foundation of economic analysis. Here are some opportunities to use the principles to do your own economic analysis.

1. ECONOMIC EXPERIMENT: PRODUCING FOLDITS

Here is a simple economic experiment that takes about 15 minutes to run. The instructor places a single stapler and a stack of paper on a table. Students produce "foldits" by folding a page of paper in thirds and stapling both ends of the folded page. There is an inspector who checks each foldit to be sure that it is produced correctly. The experiment starts with a single worker, who has one minute to produce as many foldits as possible. After the i~~~~~ ~records the number of foldits p~~~~~ the process is repeated with

TEST Your Understanding

1. List the three basic questions about a society's economy.
2. Which of these three questions does the production possibilities curve help answer?
3. How would a large earthquake affect a country's production possibilities curve?

Chapter-Opening Stories begin each chapter and motivate the chapter's subject matter.

Each chapter starts with a list of **practical questions** that are answered in the chapter.

Lively examples are integrated throughout the text and help bring economic concepts to life. We have hundreds of fresh, new examples in this edition.

A Closer Look boxes are featured throughout the text and provide brief, interesting examples of the tools and concepts discussed in the text.

A CLOSER LOOK — HOW TO CUT TEEN SMOKING BY 60%

Under the 1997 Tobacco Settlement, if smoking by teenagers does not decline by 60% by the year 2007, cigarette makers will face a fine of $2 billion. The settlement is expected to increase cigarette prices by about 62 cents per pack, a percentage increase of about 25%. Will that be enough to reduce teen smoking by the target percentage? The answer depends on the price elasticity of demand for cigarettes.

The demand for cigarettes by teenagers is elastic: The teen elasticity is 1.3, meaning that a 10% increase in the price of cigarettes will decrease teen cigarette consumption by 13%. About half the reduction results from fewer teen smokers, and the other half results from fewer cigarettes for each teen smoker. Although the teen demand for cigarettes is relatively elastic, a 25% ~~~~~ ~will not be enough t~ ~moking

by the target amount. Given an elasticity of 1.3, the price of cigarettes must increase by about 46% (equal to 60% divided by 1.3).

The Teaching and Learning Package

Print Supplements

Test Bank

We've assembled a team of dedicated educators to edit, write, review, and accuracy check the questions available in the test bank. The test bank, prepared by Cheryl McGaughey of Angelo State University, offers multiple-choice, true/false, short-answer, and problem questions. The questions in the test bank are presented in sequential order and are centered around the topics in the text itself. Each question is keyed by degree of difficulty as easy, moderate, or difficult (labeled 1, 2, or 3). *Easy* questions involve straightforward recall of information in the text. *Moderate* questions require some analysis on the student's part. *Difficult* questions usually entail more complex analysis. To help instructors select questions quickly and efficiently, we have used the skill descriptors of fact, definition, conceptual, and analytical (labeled F, D, C, or A). A question labeled *fact* tests a student's knowledge of factual information presented in the text. A *definition* question asks the student to define an economic term or concept. *Conceptual* questions test a student's understanding of a concept. *Analytical* questions require the student to apply an analytical procedure to answer the question. The test bank includes questions with tables that provide students with the numbers that they need to use in solving for numerical answers. It also contains questions based on the graphs that appear in the book. The questions ask students to interpret the information presented in the graph. The test bank is available in a computerized format using TestGen-EQ test generating software. This software is available on the Instructor's Resource CD-ROM.

Instructor's Manuals

The Instructor's Manual, prepared by Murat Kara of Angelo State University, reflects the textbook's organization, incorporating policy problems in extended examples, exercises, extra questions, and useful Internet links. The manuals also provide detailed outlines (suitable for use as lecture notes) and solutions to all questions in the textbook.

The Instructor's Manual contains by chapter a summary, objectives, an outline, examples for class discussion, teaching tips, extended examples, Internet exercises, and tips for classroom experiments. Solutions to the Using the Tools, Problems and Discussion Questions, and Test Your Understanding sections are also provided.

Study Guide

The Study Guide, revised by Deborah J. Bauer of University of Oregon, emphasizes the practical application of theory. It is a practicum designed to promote comprehension of economic principles and develop each student's ability to apply them to different problems.

The Study Guide contains by chapter an overview of the corresponding chapter in the textbook, a checklist to provide a quick summary of material covered in the textbook, a list of key terms, and practice exams with detailed answer keys. Integrated throughout the Study Guide are Performance Enhancing Tips (PETs), which are designed to help students understand economics by applying the principles and promoting analytical thinking.

Two practice exams, featuring both multiple-choice and essay questions, are included at the end of each chapter. Both exams require students to apply one or more economic principles to arrive at each correct answer. Full solutions to the multiple-choice questions are included, not only listing each correct answer but also explaining in detail why one answer is correct and the others are not. Detailed answers to the essay questions are also provided.

Technology Supplements

New TestGen-EQ Software

The print test bank is designed for use with the TextGen-EQ test-generating software. This computerized computerized package allows instructors to custom design, save, and generate classroom tests. The test program permits instructors to edit, add, or delete questions from the test bank; edit existing graphics and create new graphics; analyze test results; and organize a database of tests and student results. This new software allows for greater flexibility and ease of use. It provides many options for organizing and displaying tests, along with a search and sort feature. This software may be found on the Instructor's Resource CD-ROM to accompany the text.

PowerPoint Presentation

This lecture presentation tool, revised by Jamal Husein of Angelo State University, offers outlines and summaries of important text material, tables and graphs that build, and additional exercises. The PowerPoint presentation is downloadable from the O'Sullivan/Sheffrin Web site at *www.prenhall.com/osullivan* and also available on the Instructor's Resource CD-ROM.

Instructor's Resource CD-ROM

The Instructor's Resource CD-ROM allows instructors to easily access all the resources available with the text and edit the Instructor's Manual, test bank, and PowerPoint presentations.

Internet Resources

Prentice Hall's Internet Resources provide students with a variety of interactive graphing and self-assessment tools. It also supplies numerous current news articles and supporting exercises.

Companion Web Site: *www.prenhall.com/osullivan*

The Companion Web Site is a content-rich, multidisciplinary Web site with Internet exercises, activities, and resources related specifically to *Survey of Economics: Principles and Tools*, Second Edition. The site contains:

In the News articles and Internet Exercises are available related to topics in each chapter. These articles, from news publications such as *The Wall Street Journal* and *The New York Times,* help show students the relevance of economics in today's world. They are fully supported by activities and discussion questions.

The Online Study Guide offers students another opportunity to sharpen their problem-solving skills and to assess their understanding of the text material. The Online Study Guide for O'Sullivan/Sheffrin contains two levels of quizzes. Each level includes 20–25 multiple-choice and essay questions per chapter. The Online Study Guide grades each question submitted by the student, provides immediate feedback for correct and incorrect answers, and allows students to e-mail results to up to four e-mail addresses.

For Instructors

- **Syllabus Manager.** This feature allows instructors to enhance their lectures with all the resources available with this text. Instructors can post their own syllabus and link to any of the material on the site.

- **Downloadable Supplements.** These features allow instructors to access the book's PowerPoint presentations, Instructor's Manual, and other materials.

Companion Web Site PLUS for Instructors and Students

Available by using the access code packaged with every new text, Companion Web Site PLUS uses all of the content of the Companion Web site listed previously as well as the following additional interactive resources:

- **Active Graphs Level One.** These Active Graphs support key graphs and concepts in the text. They invite students to change the value of variables and curves and see the effects in the movement of the graph.

- **Active Graphs Level Two.** These Active Graphs ask students to modify graphs based on an economic scenario and questions. Students receive an instant response to their answers. If their answer is incorrect, the response will detail how they should have changed the graph.

- **eGraph and Graphing Questions.** This electronic tool allows students to create precise, colorful graphs, using Flash technology.

Research Navigator™

Research Navigator™ is an online academic research service that helps students learn and master the skills needed to write effective papers and complete research assignments. Students and faculty can access Research Navigator™ through an access code found in front of *The Prentice Hall Guide to Evaluating Online Resources with Research Navigator.* This guide can be shrinkwrapped, at no additional cost, with our text. Once you register, you have access to all the resources in Research Navigator™ for six months.

Research Navigator™ includes three databases of credible and reliable source material:

- EBSCO's ContentSelect™ Academic Journal database gives you instant access to thousands of academic journals and periodicals. You can search these online journals by keyword, topic, or multiple topics. It also guides students step-by-step through the writing of a research paper.

- *The New York Times* Search-by-Subject™ Archive allows you to search by subject and by keyword.

- Link Library is a collection of links to Web sites, organized by academic subject and key terms. The links are monitored and updated each week.

The Econ Tutor Center

Staffed with experienced economics instructors, the Prentice Hall Econ Tutor Center provides students with one-to-one tutoring on concepts and problems in the book. Students can access the Tutor Center via toll-free phone, fax, e-mail, or interactive web. Please contact your Prentice Hall representative for information on how to make this service available to your students.

Online Course Offerings

Faculty resources, including converted test banks for WebCT and Blackboard, can be downloaded for instructors to create online courses. Contact your local Prentice Hall sales representative for further information.

Subscription Offers

Analyzing current events is an important skill for economics students to develop. To sharpen this skill and further support the book's theme of exploration and application, Prentice Hall offers you and your students three *news subscription* offers:

The Wall Street Journal Print and Interactive Editions Subscription

Prentice Hall has formed a strategic alliance with the *Wall Street Journal*, the most respected and trusted daily source of information on business and economics. For a small additional charge, Prentice Hall offers your students a 10- or 15-week subscription to the *Wall Street Journal* print edition and the *Wall Street Journal Interactive Edition*. Upon adoption of a special book with the subscription package, professors will receive a free one-year subscription of the print and interactive version as well as weekly subject-specific *Wall Street Journal* educators' lesson plans.

The Financial Times

We are pleased to announce a special partnership with *The Financial Times*. For a small additional charge, Prentice Hall offers your students a 15-week subscription to *The Financial Times*. Upon adoption of a special book with the subscription package, professors will receive a free one-year subscription. Please contact your Prentice Hall representative for details and ordering information.

Economist.com

Through a special arrangement with *Economist.com*, Prentice Hall offers your students a 12-week subscription to *Economist.com* for a small additional charge. Upon adoption of a special book with the subscription package, professors will receive a free six-month subscription. Please contact your Prentice Hall representative for further details and ordering information.

A Word of Thanks

There is a long distance between the initial vision of an innovative text and the final product. Along the way we participated in a structured process to reach our goal.

We would like to extend a special thanks to those who contributed to this second edition revision by providing detailed reviewer comments:

Peter Boelman-Lopez, Riverside Community College

Jeff Davis, ITT Technical Institute

Nirmalendu Debnath, Lane College

Frank Garland, Tri-County Technical College

Marlene Kim, University of Massachusetts, Boston

Denise Kummer, St. Louis Community College

Theodore Larsen, University of Nebraska, Kearney

Stephen Morrell, Barry University

Quenton Pulliam, Nashville State Technical College

Rose Rubin, University of Memphis

Carl Schmertmann, Florida State University

Chuck Sicotte, Rock Valley College

Diane Tyndall, Craven Community College

Mark Wylie, Spokane Falls Community College

We also wish to acknowledge the assistance of the many individuals who participated in reviews and focus groups for the first three editions of *Economics: Principles and Tools:*

Carlos Aquilar, El Paso Community College

Jim Bradley, University of South Carolina

Thomas Collum, Northeastern Illinois University

David Craig, Westark College

Jeff Holt, Tulsa Junior College

Thomas Jeitschko, Texas A & M University

Gary Langer, Roosevelt University

Mark McCleod, Virginia Polytechnic Institute and State University

Tom McKinnon, University of Arkansas

Amy Meyers, Parkland Community College

Hassan Mohammadi, Illinois State University

John Morgan, College of Charleston

Norm Paul, San Jancinto Community College

Nampeang Pingkaratwat, Chicago State University

Scanlan Romer, Delta Community College

Barbara Ross-Pfeiffer, Kapiolani Community College

Virginia Shingleton, Valparaiso University

Zahra Saderion, Houston Community College

Jim Swofford, University of South Alabama

Linda Wilson, University of Texas–Arlington

Janet West, University of Nebraska–Omaha

Michael Youngblood, Rock Valley Community College

Many people read all or parts of the manuscript at various stages. For their helpful criticisms, we thank:

Christine Amsler, Michigan State University

Karijit K. Arora, Le Moyne College

Alex Azarchs, Pace University

Kevin A. Baird, Montgomery County Community College

Donald Balch, University of South Carolina

Sheryl Ball, Virginia Polytechnic Institute and State University

Mahamudu Bawumia, Baylor University

Charles Scott Benson Jr. Idaho State University

John Payne Bigelow, Louisiana State University

Scott Bloom, North Dakota State University

Janice Boucher Breuer, University of South Carolina

Kathleen K. Bromley, Monroe Community College

Cindy Cannon, North Harris College

Katie Canty, Cape Fear Community College

David L. Coberly, Southwest Texas State University

John L. Conant, Indiana State University

Ana-Maria Conley, DeVry Institute of Technology

Ed Coulson, Penn State University

Lee Craig, North Carolina State University

Peggy Crane, Southwestern College

Albert B. Culver, California State University, Chico

Norman Cure, Macomb Community College

Irma de Alonso, Florida International University

Sel Dibooglu, Southern Illinois University

Martine Duchatelet, Barry University

Mousumi Duttaray, Indiana University

Ghazi Duwaji, University of Texas, Arlington

David Eaton, Murray State University

Duane Eberhardt, Missouri Southern State College

Carl Enomoto, New Mexico State University
David Figlio, University of Florida
E.B. Gendel, Woodbury University
Dan Georgianna, University of Massachusetts–Dartmouth
Linda Ghent, East Carolina University
Hossein Gholami, Fayetteville Tech Community College
Randy R. Grant, Linfield College
Paul C. Harris, Jr., Camden County College
James E. Hartley, Mount Holyoke College
Rowland Harvey, DeVry Institute of Technology
John Henry, California State University, Sacramento
Robert Herman, Nassau Community College
Charles W. Haase, San Francisco State University
Charlotte Denise Hixson, Midlands Technical College
Jeff Holt, Tulsa Community College
Brad Hoppes, Southwest Missouri State University
Calvin Hoy, County College of Morris
Jonathan O. Ikoba, Scott Community College
John A. Jascot, Capital Community Technical College
Thomas Jeitschko, Texas A & M University
George Jensen, California State University, Los Angeles
Taghi T. Kermani, Youngstown State University
Rose Kilburn, Modesto Junior College
Philip King, San Francisco State University
James T. Kyle, Indiana State University
Gary Langer, Roosevelt University
Susan Linz, Michigan State University
Marianne Lowery, Erie Community College
Melanie Marks, Longwood College
Jessica McCraw, University of Texas, Arlington
Thomas J. Meeks, Virginia State University
Jeannette Mitchell, Rochester Institute of Technology
Rahmat Mozayan, Heald College
William Neilson, Texas A & M University

Alex Obiya, San Diego City College
Paul Okello, University of Texas, Arlington
Charles M. Oldham, Jr., Fayetteville Technical Community College
Jack W. Osman, San Francisco State University
Carl Parker, Fort Hays State University
Randall Parker, East Carolina University
Stephen Perez, Washington State University
Stan Peters, Southeast Community College
Chirinjev Peterson, Greenville Technical College
Nampeang Pingkarawat, Chicago State University
L. Wayne Plumly, Jr., Valdosta State University
Dan Rickman, Oklahoma State University
John Robertson, University of Kentucky
Barbara Ross-Pfeiffer, Kapiolani Community College
George Schatz, Maine Maritime Academy
Kurt Schwabe, University of California, Riverside
Mark Siegler, Williams College
Terri Sexton, California State University, Sacramento
Dennis Shannon, Belleville Area College
Virginia Shingleton, Valparaiso University
Ed Sorensen, San Francisco State University
Abdulwahab Sraiheen, Kutztown University
James Swofford, University of South Alabama
Evan Tanner, Thunderbird, The American Graduate School of International Management
Robert Tansky, St. Clair County Community College
Denise Turnage, Midlands Technical College
Fred Tyler, Fordham University
James R. VanBeek, Blinn College
Daniel Villegas, Cal Polytechnic State University
Chester Waters, Durham Technical Community College, Shaw University
Irvin Weintraub, Towson State University
Donald Wells, University of Arizona
James Wheeler, North Carolina State University
Gilbert Wolfe, Middlesex Community College

A special acknowledgment goes to the instructors who were willing to class-test drafts of the manuscript in different stages of development. They provided us with instant feedback on parts that worked and parts that needed changes:

John Constantine, University of California, Davis
John Farrell, Oregon State University
James Hartley, Mt. Holyoke College
Kailash Khandke, Furman College

Peter Lindert, University of California, Davis
Louis Makowski, University of California, Davis
Stephen J. Perez, Washington State University
Barbara Ross-Pfeiffer, Kapiolani Community College

From the start, Prentice Hall provided us with first-class support and advice. PJ Boardman, Kathleen McLellan, Marie McHale, Gladys Soto, and Joy Golden of Prentice Hall contributed in myriad ways to the project. We want to single out two people for special mention. Our Development Editor, Mike Elia, worked with us patiently to make our prose clean and lively, and our presentation utterly clear. Finally, we are deeply indebted to Rod Banister, Economics Editor at Prentice Hall, who used a combination of great organizational skill and a good sense of humor to guide the project from start to finish.

Last but not least, we must thank our families, who have seen us disappear, sometimes physically and other times mentally, to spend hours wrapped up in our own world of principles of economics. A project of this magnitude is very absorbing, and our families have been particularly supportive in this endeavor.

ARTHUR O'SULLIVAN

STEVEN SHEFFRIN

Principles of Economics

It was the end of the month, and Frieda was broke. When she saw a billboard announcing a free lunch at a downtown hotel, she acted immediately, calling the toll-free number to sign up for a "healthy and tasty free lunch." The operator told Frieda to show up at 10:30 for a 90-minute presentation on "Timeless Time-Shares," a program offering time-share condominiums in Florida. The operator told Frieda that after she sat through the presentation, she could have her free lunch. Is the lunch really free?

n this chapter, we explain what economics is all about, introducing five key principles that provide a foundation for economic analysis. The dictionary defines a **principle** as a simple, self-evident truth that most people readily understand and accept. For example, most people readily accept the principle of gravity. The five principles of economics provide the underlying logic of economic analysis and also help explain the tools of economic analysis. As you go through this book, you will see these principles again and again as you do your own economic analysis. Before we discuss these principles, we'll provide an overview of economics.

Principle: A simple truth that most people understand and accept.

What Is Economics?

Economics: The study of the choices made by people who are faced with scarcity.

Scarcity: A situation in which resources are limited and can be used in different ways, so one good or service must be sacrificed for another.

Economics is the study of the choices made by people when there is scarcity, that is, when there are limits to what they can get. Scarcity is a situation in which resources—the things we use to produce goods and services—are limited in quantity and can be used in different ways. Because resources are limited, we must sacrifice one good or service for another. Here are some examples of scarcity:

- Like everyone else, you have a limited amount of time today. If you play video games for an hour, you have one less hour to spend on other activities such as studying, exercising, or working.
- A city has a limited amount of land. If the city uses an acre of land to build a park, there is one less acre for apartments, office buildings, or factories.
- A nation has a limited number of people, so if it builds a space station, it has fewer people to serve as teachers, software developers, and police officers.

Because of scarcity, people must make choices. You must decide how to spend your time; the city must decide how to use its land; and we as a nation must decide how to divide our people among teaching, science, law enforcement, and the military.

Decisions are made at every level in society. Individuals decide what products to buy, what occupation to pursue, and how much money to save. Firms decide what products to produce and how to produce them. Governments decide what projects and programs to complete and how to pay for them. The choices made by individuals, firms, and governments answer three basic questions:

1. What products do we produce? There are trade-offs in the choice among alternative products. For example, if a hospital devotes its resources to producing more heart transplants, it has fewer resources for caring for premature infants.
2. How do we produce these products? There are alternative ways to produce the products we desire. For example, utility companies can produce electricity with oil, solar power, or nuclear power. Professors can teach college students in large lectures or in small sections.
3. Who consumes the products? We must decide how the products of society are distributed among people. If some people earn more money than others, should they consume more goods? How much money should be taken from the rich and given to the poor?

Resources—The Factors of Production

Factors of production: The resources that are used to produce goods and services.

Let's take a closer look at the first question, What products do we produce? The resources that are used to produce products are known as the **factors of production**. Economists have identified five factors of production:

1. **Natural resources** are created by acts of nature. Natural resources—for example, arable land, mineral deposits, oil and gas deposits, and water—are used to produce goods and services. Some economists refer to all types of natural resources as land.

2. **Labor** is the human effort—including both physical and mental effort—used to produce goods and services. Labor is scarce because there are only 24 hours in each day: If we spend time in one activity, such as work, we have less time for other activities, such as recreation.

3. **Physical capital** is made by human beings and is used to produce goods and services; some examples of physical capital are machines, buildings, equipment, roads, pencils, computers, and trucks.

4. **Human capital** is the knowledge and skills a worker acquires through education and experience; human capital, like physical capital, is used to produce goods and services, although not in the same way. Every job requires some human capital: To be a surgeon, you must learn anatomy and acquire surgical skills; to be an accountant, you must learn the rules of accounting and acquire computer skills; to be a taxi driver, you must know the city's streets; to be a musician, you must know how to play an instrument well enough to be paid for doing so. One of the reasons for getting a college degree is to increase your human capital, widening your employment opportunities.

5. **Entrepreneurship** is the effort used to coordinate the production and sale of goods and services. An entrepreneur comes up with an idea for a good or a service and decides how to produce it. The entrepreneur takes risks, committing money and time without any guarantee of profit, hoping, of course, for success and big profits.

Natural resources: Things created by acts of nature and used to produce goods and services.

Labor: Human effort, including both physical and mental effort, used to produce goods and services.

Physical capital: Objects made by human beings to produce goods and services.

Human capital: The knowledge and skills acquired by a worker through education and experience and used to produce goods and services.

Entrepreneurship: Effort used to coordinate the production and sale of goods and services.

Production Possibilities

Before we can decide what products to produce, we must determine which combinations of products are possible, given our productive resources and our technological know-how. A production possibilities graph shows an economy's production options—the different combinations of products the economy can produce. The two-dimensional graph can show the production options with two general categories of goods, such as farm goods and factory goods or capital goods and consumer goods. The graph can also show the production options for any pair of specific goods, such as guns and butter, computers and space missions, or houses and automobiles.

Figure 1.1 shows a **production possibilities curve** for an economy that produces farm goods and factory goods. The possible or feasible combinations of these two types of goods are shown on the curve and in the shaded area. For example, one option is point *b*, with 700 tons of factory goods and 10 tons of farm goods. Another option is point *i*, with 300 tons of factory goods and 20 tons of farm goods. The set of points on the border between the shaded and unshaded areas is called the production possibilities curve (or production possibilities frontier) because it separates the combinations that are attainable (the shaded area within the curve and the curve itself) from the combinations that are not attainable (the unshaded area outside the curve).

What is the difference between points inside the curve and points on the curve? For any point inside the curve, we can find a point on the curve that generates more of both goods. For example, at point *i* the economy can produce 300 tons of factory goods and 20 tons of farm goods. But we know from point *d* that the economy could produce more of both products: 400 tons of factory goods and 50 tons of farm goods. Producing at point *i* is clearly inferior to producing at point *d*. In general, an economy that is producing at a point inside the production possibilities curve could do better: It could produce more of both goods.

Production possibilities curve: A curve that shows the possible combinations of goods and services available to an economy, given that all productive resources are fully employed and efficiently used.

Figure 1.1

Scarcity and the Production Possibilities Curve

The production possibilities curve (or frontier) illustrates the notion of scarcity: With a given amount of resources, an increase in farm goods comes at the expense of factory goods. The curve is bowed outward because resources are not perfectly adaptable to the production of the two goods.

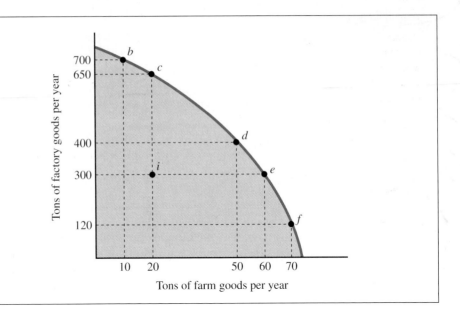

Tons of factory goods per year

Tons of farm goods per year

An economy might reach a point below the curve for two reasons. First, the economy's resources are not fully employed. For example, some workers could be idle, or some production facilities could be idle or underused. Second, the economy's resources are used inefficiently. Products can be produced with different mixtures of inputs, and some mixtures produce more output than others. If businesses pick the wrong input mixture, the economy won't produce as much output as it could. In contrast, when an economy reaches a point on the production possibilities curve, it would be impossible to increase the production of both goods. For every point on the curve, the society's resources are fully employed and used in an efficient manner.

The production possibilities curve illustrates the notion of scarcity. At a given time, an economy has a fixed amount of each factor of production. That means we can produce more of one product only if we produce less of another product. To produce more farm goods, we take resources away from factories. As we move resources out of factory production, the quantity of factory goods will decrease. For example, if we move from point *b* to point *c* on the production possibilities curve in Figure 1.1, we sacrifice 50 tons of factory goods (700 tons − 650 tons) to get 10 more tons of farm goods (20 tons − 10 tons).

Compare the move from point *b* to point *c* with the move from point *e* to point *f*. Starting at point *b*, a 10-ton increase in farm goods decreases factory goods by 50 tons. Starting at point *e*, a 10-ton increase in farm goods decreases factory goods by 180 tons. On the lower part of the curve, we sacrifice more factory goods to get the same 10-ton increase in farm goods. Why?

The answer is that resources are not perfectly adaptable for the production of both goods. Some resources are more suitable for factory production, while others are more suitable for farming. Starting at point *b*, the economy uses its most fertile land to produce farm goods. A 10-ton increase in farm goods reduces the quantity of factory goods by only 50 tons because plenty of fertile land is available for conversion to farming. As the economy moves downward along the production possibilities curve, farmers will be forced to use land that is progressively less fertile. To increase farm output by 10 tons, farmers will need more land and more of the other inputs. As progressively larger quantities of resources are diverted from factory goods, the sacrifice of factory goods becomes larger and larger. In the move from point *e* to *f*, the land converted to farming is so poor that to increase farm output by 10 tons, the diversion of land to farming decreases factory output by 180 tons.

What sort of changes would shift the entire production possibilities curve? The curve shows the production options available with a given set of productive resources, so <u>an increase in an economy's resources will shift the entire curve outward</u>. If an economy acquires more resources—natural resources, labor, physical capital, human capital, or entrepreneurial ability—the economy can produce more of both products. As a result, the production possibilities curve will shift outward, as shown in Figure 1.2. For example, if we start at point *d* and the economy's resources increase, we can produce more factory goods (point *g*), more farm goods (point *h*), or more of both goods (points between *g* and *h*). The curve will also shift outward as a result of technological innovations that allow us to produce more output with a given quantity of resources.

The production possibilities frontier could shift inward as well. Suppose a hurricane destroys factories, roads, and train tracks. The economy will have fewer resources available for production, so the production possibilities curve will shift inward. That means the nation will produce fewer factory goods, fewer farm goods, or fewer of both. Similarly, wars in Iraq and Kosovo—which caused widespread destruction of roads, factories, bridges, electricity generation facilities, and housing—shifted the production possibilities frontiers of those economies inward.

Markets and the Invisible Hand

Let's look at how a market-based economy answers the three basic economic questions. A **market** is an arrangement that allows buyers and sellers to exchange things. According to Adam Smith, the Scotsman who wrote *Wealth of Nations* (1776) and is considered the founder of modern economics,

> *Man is the only animal that makes bargains; one dog does not exchange bones with another dog.*

We use markets to make our bargains, exchanging what we have for what we want. If each person were self-sufficient, producing everything he or she consumed, there would

Market: An arrangement that allows buyers and sellers to exchange things: A buyer exchanges money for a product; a seller exchanges a product for money.

Figure 1.2

Shifting the Production Possibilities Curve

The production possibilities curve will shift outward as a result of an increase in the economy's resources (natural resources, labor, physical capital, human capital, and entrepreneurship) or a technological innovation that increases the output from a given amount of resources.

be no need for markets. Markets exist because we aren't self-sufficient—we consume many products produced by others. To get the money to pay for these products, each of us produces something to sell: Some people grow food, others produce goods such as clothing and bicycles, and still others provide services such as medical care or legal advice. Because each of us specializes in producing one or two products, we need markets to sell what we have produced and to buy what we don't produce.

For example, the labor market allows workers and firms to exchange time and money. A software firm has money and wants workers to design programs, while the worker has time and wants income to support a family. Similarly, the car market allows consumers and producers to exchange cars and money. A consumer has money and wants a car, while a producer has a car and wants money. By providing opportunities to trade goods and services, markets help society answer the three basic questions—what to produce, how to produce it, and who gets the products produced.

Markets determine the prices of goods and services, and these prices guide decisions about what and how much to buy and sell. Consider a hurricane in Florida that disrupts the electric power supply and disables refrigerators, so people must use ice to preserve their food. The sudden increase in the demand for ice will increase its price. The higher price will cause consumers to use ice wisely and to switch to foods that don't require refrigeration. At the same time, the higher price will encourage profit-seeking firms to produce more ice to accommodate the greater demand. On both sides of the market, the higher price helps the state deal with the power disruption caused by the hurricane.

The decisions made in markets result from the interactions of millions of people, each acting in his or her own self-interest. Adam Smith used the metaphor of the invisible hand to explain that people acting in their own self-interest may actually promote the interest of society as a whole.

It is not from the benevolence of the butcher, the brewer, or the baker that we expect our dinner, but from their regard to their own interest. We address ourselves, not to their humanity but to their self-love, and never talk to them of our own necessities but of their advantages. [Man is] led by an invisible hand to promote an end which was no part of his intention. . . . By pursuing his own interest he frequently promotes that of the society more effectually than when he really intends to promote it.

Adam Smith, *Wealth of Nations* (New York: Modern Library, 1994)

In the last sentence, Smith said "frequently," not "always." Smith recognized that individuals pursuing their own self-interest will not necessarily promote the social interest. Later in the book, we'll discuss situations in which the pursuit of self-interest will be contrary to the interest of society as a whole. In these cases, it is sensible for the government to guide people's decisions to promote the social interest.

In modern economies, most of the decisions about how much to produce, how to produce it, and who gets the products are made in markets. Of course, no economy relies exclusively on markets to make these economic decisions. Later in the book, we'll look at how government regulates markets, provides goods and services, imposes taxes to pay for the goods and services it provides, and redistributes income.

The Economic Way of Thinking

How do economists think about problems and decision making? This economic way of thinking is best summarized by noted economist John Maynard Keynes: "The Theory of Economics does not furnish a body of settled conclusions immediately applicable to policy. It is a method rather than a doctrine, an apparatus of the mind, a technique of thinking which helps its possessor to draw correct conclusions." Let's look at some of the elements of the economic way of thinking.

Positive and Normative Economics

The focus of most modern economic reasoning is on positive analysis. **Positive economics** concerns the forces that affect economic activity and predicts the consequences of alternative actions. Here are some questions answered by positive economics:

Positive economics: Analysis that answers the question, What is or what will be?

- How will an increase in the price of Internet access affect the number of subscribers?

- How will an increase in the wage for fast-food workers affect the number of workers hired?

- What fraction of an income tax cut will be spent on consumer goods, and what fraction will be saved?

- How will an increase in interest rates affect investment in factories?

In other words, positive economics answers the question, What is or what will be?

A second type of economic reasoning is normative in nature. **Normative economics** answers the question, What ought to be? Here are some examples of normative questions:

Normative economics: Analysis that answers the question, What ought to be?

- Should the government increase the minimum wage?

- Should a commuter who drives to work during the rush hour pay a congestion tax of $5 per day?

- Should the government provide free prescription drugs to senior citizens?

- Should NASA stage a manned mission to Mars?

Although most economists shy away from normative questions and instead focus on positive analysis, economic reasoning is an important part of most policy debates. Economists contribute to the debates by doing positive economic analysis about the consequences of alternative actions. For example, an economist could predict how a $5 congestion tax would affect the number of rush-hour vehicles and then tell us how much faster traffic would flow. This positive analysis sets the stage for citizens and policymakers to decide whether or not to impose the congestion tax. Similarly, an economist would remind us that a mission to Mars would use resources that could be used for other programs such as college loans and tell us how a cut in student-loan programs would affect the number of people attending college. After an economist quantifies the trade-offs, citizens and policymakers can make a choice.

To summarize, most modern economic analysis is positive in nature but is often focused on the question relevant for normative concerns. Nassau Senior, the first professor of political economy at Oxford, summarizes the role of economic analysis in public policy.

But the economists' conclusions, whatever be their generality and their truth, do not authorize him in adding a single syllable of advice. That privilege belongs to the writer and statesman who has considered all the causes which may promote or impede the general welfare of those whom he addresses, not to the theorist who has considered only one, though among the most important, of those causes. The business of a Political Economist is neither to recommend nor to dissuade, but to state general principle.

As you go through this book, you'll find plenty of positive economic analysis relevant to today's policy debates.

Use Assumptions to Simplify

Economists use assumptions to make things simpler and to focus on what really matters. Most people use simplifying assumptions in their everyday thinking and decision making. For example, suppose you want to travel from Seattle to San Francisco by automobile. If you use a road map to pick a travel route, you are using two assumptions to simplify your decision making:

- The earth is flat: The flat road map does not show the curvature of the earth.
- The highways are flat: The standard road map does not show hills and mountains.

These two assumptions are abstractions from reality. But they are useful because they simplify your decision making without affecting your choice of a travel route. You could plan your trip with a globe that shows all the topographical features of the alternative travel routes between Seattle and San Francisco, but you would probably pick the same travel route because the curvature of the earth and the topography of the highways are irrelevant for your trip. In this case, the assumptions underlying the standard road map are harmless.

What if you decide to travel by bicycle instead of by automobile? Now the two assumptions are not harmless unless you want to pedal up mountains. If you use the standard road map and assume that there are no mountains between Seattle and San Francisco, you are likely to pick a mountainous route instead of a flat one. In this case, the simplifying assumption makes a difference. The lesson from this example is that we must think carefully about whether an assumption is truly harmless.

In this book, we use simplifying assumptions to help make it easier to learn a concept or to analyze something. Most of the assumptions will be harmless in the sense that they simplify the analysis by eliminating irrelevant details. Although many of the assumptions are unrealistic, that does not mean that the analysis based on the assumption is incorrect. Just as we can use an unrealistic road map to plan a trip, we can use unrealistic assumptions to do economic analysis. When we use an assumption that actually affects the analysis, we'll alert you to this fact and explore the implications of alternative assumptions.

Most of the economic analysis in this book is based on two assumptions, both of which are realistic in most circumstances:

- **Self-interest.** We'll assume that people act in their own self-interest, without considering the effects of their actions on other people. We assume that a pizza consumer doesn't care about other people who might want to buy the pizza but only about his or her own well-being. Similarly, we assume that a pizzeria owner doesn't care about how his or her decisions affect other people but only about the owner's profit. There is solid evidence that most people act in their own self-interest in most situations, so the economic analysis in this book is relevant for a wide range of decisions.

- **Informed decisions.** We'll assume that people make informed decisions. We assume that a consumer deciding what to eat for lunch knows the price of pizza, the prices of alternative foods, and the relevant characteristics of the foods (taste, amount of fat, number of calories). With this information, the consumer can make an informed decision about what to eat. Similarly, the manager of a pizzeria knows the cost of producing pizza, and this information leads to an informed decision about how many pizzas to produce and what price to charge. In most cases, consumers and producers have enough information to make informed decisions. Later in the book, we'll discuss situations in which one side of the market is poorly informed.

Explore the Relationship Between Two Variables

Economic analysis often involves variables and how they affect each other. A **variable** is a measure of something that can have different values. For example, consider a student who has a part-time job and also receives a fixed weekly allowance from her parents. Her weekly income is a variable whose value is determined by the values of the other variables: the number of hours she works, the hourly wage she is paid, and the weekly allowance she gets from her parents.

To explore the relationship between any two variables, such as the hours worked and weekly income, we must assume that the other variables do not change. For example, the student might say, "If I work one more hour this week, my income will increase by $8." In making this statement, the student is exploring the relationship between two variables (work time and income), assuming that the other two variables (wage and allowance) do not change. To be complete, the statement must say, "If I work one more hour this week, my income will increase by $8, assuming that my wage and my allowance do not change."

This book contains many statements about the relationship between two variables. For example, the number of pizzas a person eats depends on the price of pizza, the price of burgers, and that person's income. Suppose we say, "A decrease in the price of pizzas increases the quantity of pizzas consumed." This is a statement about the relationship between two variables—the price of pizzas and the quantity of pizzas—implicitly assuming that the other two variables, the price of burgers and the person's income, do not change in value. Sometimes we will make this assumption explicit by adding a warning label: "A decrease in the price of pizzas increases the quantity of pizzas consumed, **ceteris paribus**." The Latin words mean "other things being equal to what they were before." In the present context, the phrase means "other variables being fixed." From now on, whenever we refer to a relationship between two variables, we assume that the other relevant variables are held fixed.

> **Variable:** A measure of something that can take on different values.

> **Ceteris paribus:** Latin, meaning "other things being equal." In economics, the phrase indicates that all other variables are held fixed.

Think Marginal

Economists often need to consider how a small change in one variable causes a change in another variable. A small change in value is called a **marginal change**. The marginal question is, If we increase one variable by one unit, by how much will the other variable change? The key feature of this marginal question is that one variable increases by a single unit. For the student who is concerned about income, the marginal question is, If I work one more hour per week, by how much will my income increase?

You will encounter marginal thinking throughout this book. Here are some other marginal questions:

> **Marginal change:** A small change in value.

- If I spend one more year in school, by how much will my lifetime income increase?
- If I buy one more CD, how many tapes will I sacrifice?
- If a table producer hires one more carpenter, how many more tables will be produced?
- If national income increases by $1 billion, by how much will spending on consumer goods increase?

Answering a marginal question like any of these is the first step in deciding whether or not to pursue a particular activity. You will see more about this as we move along in this book.

Microeconomics and Macroeconomics

There are two types of economic analysis: microeconomics and macroeconomics. **Microeconomics** is the study of the choices made by households, firms, and government and of how these choices affect the markets for goods and services. Let's look at three ways that we can use microeconomic analysis:

Microeconomics: The study of the choices made by consumers, firms, and government and of how their choices affect the market for a particular good or service.

1. Understand markets and predict changes. One reason for studying microeconomics is to understand better how markets work. Once you know how markets operate, you can use economic analysis to predict changes in the price of a particular good and changes in the quantity of the good sold.
2. Make personal and managerial decisions. We use economic analysis, on the personal level, to decide how to spend our time, what career to pursue, and how to spend and save the money we earn. As workers, we use economic analysis to decide how to produce goods and services, how much to produce, and how much to charge for them.
3. Evaluate public policies. Although modern societies use markets to make most of the decisions concerning production and consumption, the government has several important roles in a market-based society. We can use economic analysis to determine how well the government performs its roles in the market economy. We can also explore the trade-offs associated with various public policies.

Macroeconomics: The study of the nation's economy as a whole.

Macroeconomics is the study of the nation's economy as a whole. In macroeconomics, we learn about important topics that are regularly discussed in newspapers and on television, including unemployment, inflation, the budget deficit, and the trade deficit. Macroeconomics explains why economies grow and change, and why economic growth is sometimes interrupted. Let's look at three ways we can use macroeconomic analysis:

1. Understand how a national economy operates. One purpose of studying macroeconomics is to understand how the entire economy works. We can use macroeconomic analysis to explain why some countries grow much faster than others.
2. Understand the grand debates over economic policy. Macroeconomics developed as a separate branch of economics during the 1930s, when the entire world suffered from massive unemployment. With a knowledge of macroeconomics, you can make sense of all sorts of policy debates, including the debate over the wisdom of policies designed to reduce the unemployment rate.
3. Make informed business decisions. A manager who understands how the national economy operates will make better decisions involving interest rates, exchange rates, the inflation rate, and the unemployment rate. A manager who intends to borrow money for a new production facility, for instance, could use her knowledge of macroeconomics to predict the effects of current public policies on interest rates and then decide whether to borrow the money now or later. Similarly, a manager must keep an eye on the inflation rate to help decide how much to charge for his firm's products and how much to pay workers. A manager who studies macroeconomics will be better equipped to understand the complexities of unemployment, interest rates, and inflation.

Now that we've seen what economics is all about, we're ready to discuss the five key principles of economics. These key principles are self-evident truths that most people readily accept, and they provide the logical foundation for economic reasoning. We'll use these principles throughout the book to explain the tools of economic analysis.

TEST Your Understanding

1. List the three basic questions about a society's economy.
2. Which of these three questions does the production possibilities curve help answer?
3. How would a large earthquake affect a country's production possibilities curve?

The Principle of Opportunity Cost

The principle of **opportunity cost** incorporates the notion that no matter what we do, there is always a trade-off. We must trade off one thing for another because resources are limited and can be used in different ways: By acquiring something, we use up resources that could have been used to acquire something else. The notion of opportunity cost allows us to measure this trade-off.

Opportunity cost: A measure of something that can take on different values.

PRINCIPLE of Opportunity Cost

The opportunity cost of something is what you sacrifice to get it.

Most decisions involve several alternatives. For example, if you spend an hour studying for an economics exam, you have one less hour to pursue other activities. To determine the opportunity cost of something, we look at what you consider the best of these other activities. Suppose the alternatives to studying economics are studying for a history exam and playing a video game. If you consider studying for history a better use of your time than video play, then the opportunity cost of studying economics is what you sacrifice by not studying history. We ignore the video game because that is not the best alternative use of your time.

How can we measure the opportunity cost of an hour spent studying for an economics exam? Suppose an hour of studying history—instead of economics—would increase your grade on a history exam by four points. In this case, the opportunity cost of an hour studying economics is four points lost on the history exam. If the best alternative to studying economics were playing video games, then the opportunity cost would be the pleasure you would get from an hour in the video arcade.

The production possibilities curve illustrates the principle of opportunity cost for an entire economy. The curve in Figure 1.1 shows all the possible combinations of goods and services available to an economy, assuming that all its productive resources are fully employed. The principle of opportunity cost explains why the production possibilities curve is negatively sloped. At a given time, an economy has fixed amounts of productive resources, so the production of one product comes at the expense of another product.

The principle of opportunity cost can be applied to decisions about how to spend a fixed money budget. For example, suppose that you have a fixed budget to spend on recorded music, and CDs cost twice as much as audiotapes. If you buy a CD, you must sacrifice two tapes: The opportunity cost of one CD is two audiotapes. A hospital with a fixed salary budget can increase the number of doctors only at the expense of nurses or physician's assistants. If a doctor costs five times as much as a nurse, the opportunity cost of a doctor is five nurses.

In some cases, a good that appears to be free actually has a cost. That's why economists are fond of saying, "There's no such thing as a free lunch." Suppose someone offers to buy you lunch if you agree to listen to a sales pitch for a time-share condominium.

Although you don't pay any money for the lunch, there is an opportunity cost because you could spend that time in another way. The lunch isn't free: You sacrifice an hour of your time to get it.

Using the Principle: Warships, Security, Collectibles

We can use the principle of opportunity cost to explore the cost of military spending. Malaysia bought two warships in 1992, paying a price equal to the cost of providing safe drinking water for the 5 million Malaysians who lacked it.[1] In other words, the opportunity cost of the warships was safe drinking water for 5 million people.

What's the cost of greater airport security in response to threats of international terror? A recent study estimates the following annual costs of various security measures: $6 billion to put a sky marshal on each plane, $1 billion to put federal employees in charge of airport security, and $2.5 billion to equip airports and aircraft with antiterror devices (reinforced cockpit doors, sophisticated 3D baggage scanners, and biometric identity devices such as retinal and fingerprint scanners.[2] These costs add up to about $18 per airline ticket. Another cost of security is the opportunity cost of the time spent going through security checks. If the typical passenger arrives at the airport 90 minutes earlier and values his or her time at $20 per hour, the time cost is $30 per passenger. For another example of opportunity cost, read "A Closer Look: Plowshares, Pruning Hooks, and Ecotels?"

What is the cost of buying a collectible good such as a baseball card, an antique Barbie doll, a Beanie Baby, or a work of art? Suppose you buy an antique Barbie doll for $1,000, intending to resell it for more money a year later. If the price doesn't change and you resell it for $1,000, does that mean having the doll for a year didn't cost you anything? Applying the principle of opportunity cost, you could have invested the $1,000 in a bank account earning 5% interest, so the cost of having the Barbie doll for the year is the $50 you could have earned in a bank account during the year.

A CLOSER LOOK   PLOWSHARES, PRUNING HOOKS, AND ECOTELS?

The prophet Isaiah predicted, "They will beat their swords into plowshares, and their spears into pruning hooks." All over Central America, old military facilities are being transformed to give eco-tourists a close look at the region's flora and fauna. In the middle of Panama's rain forest, a radar tower used earlier by the U.S. military has been transformed into a seven-room eco-lodge, giving tourists from around the world the opportunity to watch king vultures soar above the forest and view howler monkeys swing from the trees. The Canopy Tower was selected by *Audubon* magazine as one of the world's nine "ultimate outposts" for bird lovers. On the Atlantic side of Panama, the infamous School of the Americas—where the U.S. military educated Latin American military dictators in the arts of war—has been converted into a 310-room hotel. The concrete amphitheater that hosted military briefings will now be used as a vantage point for tourists viewing monkeys and tropical birds.

Using the Principle: The Opportunity Cost of a College Degree

What is the opportunity cost of a college degree? Consider a student who spends four years in college, paying $10,000 per year for tuition and books. Part of the opportunity cost of college is the $40,000 worth of other goods the student must sacrifice to pay for tuition and books. Instead of going to college, the student could spend this money on a car, stereo equipment, or ski trips. If instead of going to college, the student could have worked as a bank clerk for $20,000 per year, the other part of the opportunity cost of college is $80,000 that could have been earned during the four years. That makes the total opportunity cost of the student's college degree $120,000:

Tuition and books (4 years at $10,000 per year)	$40,000
Opportunity cost of college time (4 years at $20,000 per year)	$80,000
Total opportunity cost	$120,000

We haven't included the costs of food or housing in our computations of opportunity cost. That's because a student must eat and live somewhere even if he or she doesn't go to college. But if housing and food are more expensive in college, then we would include the extra costs of housing and food in our calculations of opportunity cost.

There are other factors to consider in a person's decision to attend college. As we'll see later, a college degree can increase a person's earning power, so there are benefits from a college degree. In addition, there is the thrill of learning and the pleasure of meeting new people. To make an informed decision about whether to attend college, we must compare the benefits to the opportunity costs.

The Marginal Principle

The marginal principle provides a simple decision-making rule that helps individuals, firms, and governments make decisions. Economists think in marginal terms, considering how a one-unit change in one variable affects the value of another variable. When we say marginal, we're considering a small change or an incremental change.

Marginal **PRINCIPLE**

> **Increase the level of an activity if its marginal benefit exceeds its marginal cost; reduce the level of an activity if its marginal cost exceeds its marginal benefit. If possible, pick the level at which the activity's marginal benefit equals its marginal cost.**

The marginal principle enables us to fine-tune our decisions. We can use the principle to determine whether a one-unit increase in a variable would make us better off. For example, a barber could decide whether to keep his or her shop open for one more hour. You could decide whether to study one more hour for a psychology midterm.

The marginal principle is based on a comparison of the marginal benefits and marginal costs of a particular activity. The **marginal benefit** of some activity is the extra benefit resulting from a small increase in the activity, for example, the extra revenue generated by keeping a barbershop open for one more hour. Similarly, the **marginal cost** is the additional cost resulting from a small increase in the activity, for example, the additional costs incurred by keeping a shop open for one more hour. According to the marginal principle, you should continue to increase the activity as long as the marginal benefit is greater than the marginal cost. When you've reached the level where the marginal benefit equals the marginal cost, your fine tuning is done. It's worth emphasizing

Marginal benefit: The extra benefit resulting from a small increase in some activity.

Marginal cost: The additional cost resulting from a small increase in some activity.

that the marginal principle is based on marginal benefits and costs, not total benefits and total costs.

Example: Pedaling for Television Time

To illustrate the marginal principle, consider an experiment conducted by researchers at St. Luke's Roosevelt Hospital in New York City.[3] The researchers addressed the following question, "If a child must pedal a stationary bicycle to run a television set, will he watch less TV, and if so, how much less?"

The researchers randomly assigned sedentary children, ages 8 to 12, to two types of TVs. The first had a stationary bicycle in front of the TV, but the TV operated independently of the bicycle: No pedaling was required to operate the TV. In contrast, the second type of TV worked only if the child pedaled a bike facing the TV. The kids in the control group (no pedaling required) watched an average of 20 hours of TV per week, while the kids in the treatment group (pedaling required) watched just a few hours per week.

We can use the marginal principle to explain the results of the experiment. Figure 1.3 shows the marginal benefit of TV time for the control group. The marginal benefit curve is negatively sloped, reflecting the idea that each hour of TV is worth less than the previous hour: The first hour of TV time is worth more than the second hour; the second hour is worth more than the third; and so on. Specifically, the first hour generates a benefit of $1.30 (shown by point *b*), while the second hour generates a benefit of $1.20 (point *m*). The marginal benefit decreases by $0.05 for each additional hour, reaching $0.35 for 20 hours of TV time (point *n*).

To determine the marginal cost of TV time, we can use the notion of opportunity cost. Suppose that for the typical kid, the value of the next-best alternative use of time is $0.35 per hour. This could be the value of an hour spent playing with friends, reading, studying, or playing videogames. In Figure 1.3, the marginal cost of TV time is constant at $0.35 per hour. Using the marginal principle, we would predict that the typical kid in the control group (no pedaling) would choose point *n*, watching 20 hours of TV per week. It is not sensible to watch the twenty-first hour because the extra benefit exceeds the opportunity cost.

Figure 1.3

The Marginal Principle and TV Time

If the opportunity cost of TV time is $0.35 per hour and pedaling is not required for TV time, the marginal principle is satisfied at point *n*, and the child will watch 20 hours of TV per week. If pedaling is required and the discomfort of pedaling is $0.85 per hour, the marginal cost of TV time is $1.20 (equal to $0.35 + $0.85), and the marginal principle is satisfied at point *m*, with only 3 hours of TV time per week.

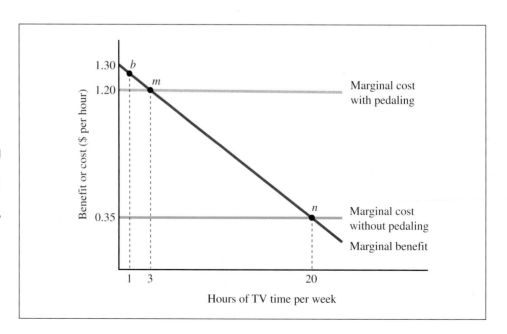

In Figure 1.3, the marginal cost of TV time is higher for the treatment group because pedaling requires effort. To compute the marginal cost of TV for the treatment group, we must add the discomfort of pedaling to the opportunity cost of TV time. In Figure 1.3, we assume that the discomfort is measured as $0.85 per hour of pedaling, so the marginal cost curve is horizontal at $1.20 (equal to $0.35 + $0.85). The marginal principle is satisfied at point m, with only 3 hours of TV time. For a pedaling kid, the first hour of TV has a benefit of $1.30 and a cost of $1.20, so it is worthwhile. Similarly, the benefit of the second hour of TV exceeds the marginal cost. For the third hour, the marginal benefit equals the marginal cost, so the marginal principle is satisfied with 3 hours. For the fourth hour of TV time, the marginal benefit is only $1.15, which is less than the marginal cost. Therefore, it would not be sensible to pedal for the fourth hour of TV time.

Using the Marginal Principle: Renting College Facilities

Many colleges rent their facilities to student groups for events such as film showings, dances, and musical performances. Suppose that your student film society is looking for an auditorium to use for an all-day Hitchcock film festival. Your college has a new auditorium that would be perfect for your event. According to the campus facility manager, "The daily rent on the auditorium is $450, an amount that includes $300 to help pay for the cost of building the auditorium, $50 to help pay for insurance, and $100 to cover the extra costs of electricity and janitorial services for a one-day event." Your society is willing to offer up to only $200 for the auditorium. How should you convince the facility manager to accept this offer?

You might point out that in its decision the college should determine the marginal cost of renting out the auditorium. The marginal cost equals the extra costs the college incurs by allowing the student group to use an otherwise vacant auditorium. In our example, the extra cost is $100 for extra electricity and janitorial service. It would be sensible for the college to rent the auditorium because the marginal benefit ($200 from the student group) exceeds the marginal cost ($100). In fact, the college should be willing to rent the facility for any amount greater than $100.

Most colleges do not use this sort of logic. Instead, they use complex formulas to compute the perceived cost of renting out a facility. In most cases, the perceived cost includes some of the fixed costs of the college, costs that are unaffected by renting out the facility for the day. In our example, the facility manager included $300 worth of construction cost and $50 worth of insurance cost as part of the cost of the auditorium, computing a cost of $450 instead of $100. Because many colleges include costs that aren't affected by the use of a facility, they overestimate the actual cost of renting out their facilities, missing opportunities to serve student groups and make some money at the same time.

TEST Your Understanding

4. The cost of a master's degree in engineering equals the tuition plus the cost of books. True or false? Explain.

5. Suppose a nation picks 1,000 young adults at random to serve in the army. What information do you need to determine the cost of using these people in the army?

6. Explain the logic behind the economist's quip, "There is no such thing as a free lunch."

7. If a bus company adds a third daily bus between two cities, the company's total costs will increase from $500 to $600 per day and its total revenue will increase by $150 per day. Should the company add the third bus?

8. Suppose you can save $50 by purchasing your new car in a different city. If the trip requires only $10 in gasoline, is the trip worthwhile?

The Principle of Diminishing Returns

Diminishing returns: As one input increases while the other inputs are held fixed, output increases but at a decreasing rate.

Xena had a small copy shop with one copying machine and one worker. When a backlog of orders piled up, she decided to hire a second worker, expecting that doubling her workforce would double the output of her copy shop, from 500 pages per hour to 1,000. She was surprised when output increased only to 800 pages per hour. If she had known about the principle of **diminishing returns**, she would not have been surprised.

PRINCIPLE of Diminishing Returns

Suppose output is produced with two or more inputs and we increase one input while holding the other input or inputs fixed. Beyond some point—called the point of diminishing returns— output will increase at a decreasing rate.

Xena added a worker (one input) while holding the number of copying machines (the other input) fixed. Because the two workers shared a single copying machine, each worker spent some time waiting for the machine to be available. As a result, although adding the second worker increased the output of the copy shop, output did not double. With a single worker and a single copy machine, Xena had reached the point of diminishing returns: As she increased the number of workers, output increased but at a decreasing rate. The first worker increased output by 500 pages (from zero to 500), but the second worker increased output by only 300 pages (from 500 to 800).

The principle of diminishing returns is relevant when we try to produce more output in an existing production facility (a factory, a store, an office, or a farm) by increasing the number of workers sharing the facility. When we add a worker to the facility, each worker becomes less productive because he or she works with a smaller piece of the facility: There are more workers to share the machinery, equipment, and factory space. As we pack more and more workers into the factory, total output increases but at a decreasing rate.

Table 1.1 shows fictitious but convenient data for representing the production of pizza at a particular facility. The production facility is the pizzeria premises, the pizza oven, and all the machines and equipment used to produce pizza. If the pizzeria has a

Table 1.1 Diminishing Returns for Pizza

Number of Workers	Total Product: Pizzas Produced	Marginal Product
1	12	12
2	18	6
3	21	3
4	22	1

single worker, the single worker assembles 12 uncooked pizzas per hour and pops them into the oven as soon as they are assembled. Suppose he is joined by a second worker, who could also assemble 12 pizzas per hour. Because this second worker shares the pizza oven with the first worker, he will occasionally have to wait before he can pop his assembled pizzas into the oven. Similarly, once the second worker's pizzas are in the oven, the first worker will have to wait to get another batch of his assembled pizzas into that oven. Therefore, we wouldn't expect output to double just because the number of workers has doubled. If total output is only 18 pizzas, adding workers increases output but at a decreasing rate: Hiring the first worker increased output by 12 pizzas (from zero to 12); hiring the second increased output by only six pizzas.

Figure 1.4 shows the pizzeria's **total product curve**, which shows how many pizzas are produced with different quantities of labor. As the pizzeria adds workers, total product increases but at a decreasing rate. Hiring a second worker increases output by six pizzas, whereas hiring a third worker increases output by only three pizzas, and hiring a fourth worker increases output by only one pizza. It's possible that hiring a fifth worker would not increase output at all or may even reduce output because the workers will get into each other's way.

The **marginal product of labor** is defined as the change in output from one additional worker. As shown in the third column in Table 1.1, the marginal product of the first pizza worker is 12 pizzas, and the marginal product of the second worker is six pizzas. In a three-worker pizzeria, even more time would be spent waiting for an empty oven, and the marginal product of the third worker is only three pizzas. When there are diminishing returns, the marginal product of labor decreases as the number of workers increases.

Diminishing Returns in the Short Run

Later in the book, we use the principle of diminishing returns to explore the decisions made by a firm in the short run. The **short run** is a period of time over which one or more factors of production is fixed. In most cases, the short run is defined as a period of time over which a firm cannot modify an existing facility or build a new one. The length of the short run varies across industries, depending on how long it takes to build a production facility. The short run for a hot-dog stand lasts just a few days: That's how long it takes to get another hot-dog cart. In contrast, if it takes a year to build a computer factory, the

Total product curve: A curve showing the relationship between the quantity of labor and the quantity of output.

Marginal product of labor: The change in output from one additional worker.

Short run: A period of time over which one or more factors of production is fixed; in most cases, a period of time over which a firm cannot modify an existing facility or build a new one.

Figure 1.4
Total Product Curve and Diminishing Returns
As the number of workers increases, the number of pizzas produced per hour increases, but at a decreasing rate. The second worker increases output by 6 pizzas (from 12 pizzas to 18 pizzas), but the fourth worker increases output by only 1 pizza (from 21 pizzas to 22 pizzas). Diminishing returns occurs because workers share a pizza oven.

short run for a computer manufacturer is one year. Diminishing returns occur in the short run because adding workers to an existing facility means that each worker gets a smaller piece of the facility, and each becomes less productive.

What About the Long Run?

Long run: A period of time long enough that a firm can change all the factors of production, meaning that a firm can modify its existing production facility or build a new one.

The principle of diminishing returns is not relevant in the **long run**. The long run is defined as a period of time long enough for a firm to change all its factors of production, meaning that it can modify its existing facility or build a new one. To increase output in the long run, a firm can build an additional production facility and hire workers to staff it. In the long run, the firm will not suffer from diminishing returns because workers won't have to share a production facility with more and more other workers. For example, if the firm builds a second factory that is identical to the first and hires the same number of workers, the firm's output will double. Because firms can duplicate or replicate their production facilities in the long run, the principle of diminishing returns is irrelevant for long-run decisions.

The Spillover Principle

Earlier in this chapter, we discussed the role of markets in determining what goods are produced, how they are produced, and who gets what is produced. The metaphor of the invisible hand suggests that the decisions of millions of consumers and producers, each acting in his or her own self-interest, will frequently promote the interests of society as a whole. Let's consider some cases when we cannot rely on individuals to make choices that are socially desirable.

Spillover: A cost or benefit experienced by people who are external to the decision about how much of a good to produce or consume.

The spillover principle suggests that the costs or benefits of some decisions "spill over" onto people who are not involved in making those decisions. A **spillover** occurs when people who are external to a decision are affected by the decision. Another word for spillover is *externality*.

Spillover **PRINCIPLE**

For some goods, the costs or benefits associated with producing or consuming those goods are not confined to the person or organization producing or consuming them.

Let's examine spillover costs first and then turn to spillover benefits. Consider a paper mill that dumps chemical wastes into a river—wastes that make the water unhealthy for drinking. The manager of the paper firm decides how much paper to produce, but some of the costs of producing paper are incurred by people who live in a city downstream from the mill. For example, the city might spend extra money to clean the water before citizens can safely drink it. Suppose for each ton of paper produced, the city's water-treatment costs increase by $10. In this case, the spillover cost of paper is $10 per ton. In deciding how much paper to produce, the paper firm will consider the cost of the inputs it buys—for example, it may pay $30 per ton for labor and raw materials—but won't consider the $10 spillover cost incurred by people downstream.

Here are some other examples of spillover costs:

- When Freon leaks from a car air conditioner, it is released into the atmosphere, where it depletes the protective ozone layer and increases the number of cases of skin cancer. A person deciding whether to repair a leaky air conditioner might not consider the effects of releasing Freon on the number of cancer cases.

- Your neighbor throws a loud party while you are trying to study. In deciding whether to have the party, the neighbor doesn't consider the consequences for your exam grade.

- Secondhand smoke from cigarettes is bothersome and causes health problems for people who breathe it in.

In each example, the decision maker incurs some—but not all—of the costs associated with the decision. As we'll see later in the book, the challenge for policymakers is to ensure that everyone who bears the costs of a decision is involved in the decision-making process.

Some goods generate spillover benefits instead of spillover costs. Suppose a farmer is thinking about building a dike or small flood-control dam on a river at a cost of $100,000. If the farmer's benefit from the dike is only $40,000, he or she won't build it. If three other farmers would experience the same benefit, the total benefit would be $160,000, and it would be sensible for them to get together and build the dike. To make the right decision, we must get all the potential beneficiaries to participate in the decision-making process. If each of the four farmers contributed $25,000 to a dike-building fund, the dike could be built.

There are many goods that generate spillover benefits. Here are some examples:

- If a person contributes money to public television, everyone who watches public television benefits from that contribution. A person deciding whether to contribute doesn't necessarily consider the benefits experienced by others.

- If a scientist discovers a new way to treat a common disease, everyone suffering from the disease will benefit. In deciding what problem to work on, the scientist doesn't necessarily consider the benefits experienced by society as a whole.

- If you get a college degree, you may become a better team worker, so your fellow workers will be more productive and earn more income. In your decision to complete college, you probably didn't consider the benefits to be experienced by your fellow workers.

- If you buy a fire extinguisher, it is less likely that a fire that starts in your apartment will spread to other apartments. In deciding whether to buy an extinguisher, you probably don't consider the benefits to your neighbors.

There are spillover benefits from scientific research. In considering what problems to work on, scientists don't necessarily consider the spillover benefits from their research.

In each case, some of the benefits spill over onto people who are not involved in the decision-making process, so a decision maker might decide against taking an action that would be beneficial to society. For example, scientists might not spend their time on a project that could reduce disease. Your high school friends might decide to forgo college because the costs they incur exceed the benefits they will experience.

If people do not face the full costs and benefits of their actions—including the spillover costs and spillover benefits—we cannot rely on unregulated markets to make decisions that are in the general interests of society. But there are ways for the government to intervene in markets to ensure that decision makers bear the full costs or experience the full benefits of their actions. Later in the book, we'll discuss some of the ways in which government can solve spillover problems.

TEST Your Understanding

9. When a table producer hired its 20th worker, the output of its factory increased by five tables per month. If the firm hires 2 more workers—a 21st and a 22nd worker—would you expect output to increase by 10 tables per month?

10. According to the principle of diminishing returns, an additional worker decreases total output. True or false? Explain.

11. For each of the following examples, is there a spillover benefit or a spillover cost?
   a. Your roommate plays loud, obnoxious music.
   b. Strip mining causes oil and gas to enter the underground water system, making smoking in your bathtub hazardous to your health.
   c. A person in a residential neighborhood collects and restores old cars on his front lawn.
   d. A family contributes $5,000 to an organization that provides holiday meals to the poor.
   e. A landowner preserves a large stand of ancient trees and thus provides a habitat for the spotted owl (an endangered species).

The Reality Principle

One of the key ideas in economics is that people are interested not just in the amount of money they have but also in how much their money will buy.

Reality PRINCIPLE

What matters to people is the real value of money or income—its purchasing power—not the face value of money or income.

To illustrate this principle, suppose you work in the college bookstore to earn extra money to pay for movies and newspapers. If your take-home pay is $10 per hour, is this a high wage or a low wage? The answer depends on the prices of the goods you buy. If a movie costs $4 and a newspaper costs $1, with one hour of work you could afford to see two movies and buy two papers. The wage may seem high enough for you. But if a movie costs $8 and a newspaper costs $2, an hour of work would buy only one movie and one paper, and the same $10 wage doesn't seem so high. This is the reality principle in action: What matters is not how many dollars you earn but what those dollars will purchase.

The reality principle can explain how people choose the amount of money to carry around with them. Suppose you typically withdraw $40 per week from an ATM to cover your normal expenses. If the prices of all the goods you purchase during the week double, you would have to withdraw $80 per week to make the same purchases. The amount of money people carry around depends on the prices of the goods and services they buy.

Economists use special terms to express the ideas behind the reality principle:

- The **nominal value** of an amount of money is simply its face value. For example, the nominal wage paid by the bookstore is $10 per hour.

- The **real value** of an amount of money is measured in terms of the quantity of goods the money can buy. For example, the real value of your bookstore wage would fall as the prices of movies and newspapers increased even though your nominal wage stayed the same.

Nominal value: The face value of an amount of money.

Real value: The value of an amount of money in terms of the quantity of goods the money can buy.

Using the Reality Principle: Government Programs and Statistics

Government officials use the reality principle when they design public programs. For example, Social Security payments are increased each year to ensure that the checks received by the elderly and other recipients will purchase the same amount of goods and services even if prices have increased.

The government also uses the reality principle when it publishes statistics about the economy. For example, when the government issues reports about changes in "real wages" in the economy over time, these statistics take into account the prices of the goods purchased by workers. Therefore, the real wage is stated in terms of its buying power rather than its face value, or nominal value.

TEST Your Understanding

12. Average hourly earnings in the United States increased between 1970 and 1993, but real wages fell. How could this occur?

13. Suppose your wage doubles and so do the prices of all consumer goods. Are you better off, worse off, or about the same?

14. Suppose your bank pays you 4% per year on your savings account: Each $100 in the bank grows to $104 over a one-year period. If prices increase by 3% per year, how much do you really gain by keeping $100 in the bank for a year?

Using the TOOLS

We've explained the five key principles of economics, which provide the foundation of economic analysis. Here are some opportunities to use the principles to do your own economic analysis.

1. ECONOMIC EXPERIMENT: PRODUCING FOLDITS

Here is a simple economic experiment that takes about 15 minutes to run. The instructor places a single stapler and a stack of paper on a table. Students produce "foldits" by folding a page of paper in thirds and stapling both ends of the folded page. There is an inspector who checks each foldit to be sure that it is produced correctly. The experiment starts with a single worker, who has one minute to produce as many foldits as possible. After the instructor records the number of foldits produced, the process is repeated with two workers, then three, then four, and so on. The question is, How does the number of foldits produced change as the number of workers increases?

2. What's the Cost?

Consider the following statements about costs. Are they correct? If not, provide a correct statement about the relevant cost.

- One year ago, I loaned $100 to a friend, and she just paid me back the whole $100. The loan didn't cost me anything.
- Our sawmill bought five truckloads of logs a year ago for $20,000. Today we'll use the logs to make picnic tables. The cost of using the logs is $20,000.
- Our new football stadium was built on land that was donated to our university by a wealthy alum. The university didn't have to buy the land, so the cost of the stadium equals the amount the university pays to the construction company that builds the stadium.

3. How Much RAM?

You are about to buy a personal computer and must decide how much random-access memory (RAM) to have in the computer, which comes in "blocks" of 32 megabytes. Suppose each block of RAM costs $40. For example, a computer with two blocks of memory (64 MB) costs $40 more than a computer with one block (32 MB). The marginal benefit of memory is $320 for the first block and decreases by half for each additional block, to $160 for the second block, $80 for the third block, and so on. How many blocks of memory should you get in your computer? Illustrate your answer with a graph.

Summary

This chapter explains what economics is and introduces the five key principles of economics. If you understand these principles, you are ready for the rest of the book, which will show you how to do your own economic analysis. In fact, if you've done the exercises in this chapter, you're already doing economic analysis. Here are the main points of the chapter.

1. Economics is the study of the choices made by people who are faced with scarcity. Microeconomics is the study of the choices made by consumers, firms, and government and of how their choices affect the market for a particular good or service. Macroeconomics is the study of the nation's economy as a whole.

2. The production possibilities curve shows the combinations of goods and services available to an economy and illustrates the notion of scarcity.

3. Principle of opportunity cost. The opportunity cost of something is what you sacrifice to get it.

4. Marginal principle. Increase the level of an activity if its marginal benefit exceeds its marginal cost; reduce the level if its marginal cost exceeds its marginal benefit. If possible, pick the level at which the marginal benefit equals the marginal cost.

5. Principle of diminishing returns. Suppose that output is produced with two or more inputs and that we increase one input while holding the other inputs fixed. Beyond some point—called the point of diminishing returns—output will increase at a decreasing rate.

6. Spillover principle. For some goods, the costs or benefits associated with the good are not confined to the person or organization that decides how much of the good to produce or consume.

7. Reality principle. What matters to people is the real value of money or income—its purchasing power—not the face value of money or income.

Key Terms

ceteris paribus, 9
diminishing returns, 16
economics, 2
entrepreneurship, 3
factors of production, 2
human capital, 3
labor, 3
long run, 18
macroeconomics, 10
marginal benefit, 13

marginal change, 9
marginal cost, 13
marginal product of labor, 17
market, 5
microeconomics, 10
natural resources, 3
nominal value, 21
normative economics, 7
opportunity cost, 11
physical capital, 13

positive economics, 7
principle, 2
production possibilities curve, 3
real value, 21
scarcity, 2
short run, 17
spillover, 18
total product curve, 17
variable, 9

Problems and Discussion Questions

1. Suppose another year of college will increase your lifetime earnings by $30,000. The costs of tuition and books add up to only $8,000 for the additional year. Comment on the following statement: Because the benefit of $30,000 exceeds the $8,000 cost, you should complete another year of college.

2. To celebrate its 50th anniversary, a gas station sells gasoline at the price it charged on its first day of operation: $0.10 per gallon. As you drive by the gas station, you notice a long line of people waiting to buy gasoline. What types of people would you expect to join the line?

3. You are the mayor of a large city, and you must decide how many police officers to hire. Explain how you could use the marginal principle to help make the decision.

4. Consider a city that must decide how many mobile cardiac arrest units (specially equipped ambulances designed to treat people immediately after a heart attack) to deploy. Explain how you could use the marginal principle to help make the decision.

5. Explain why the principle of diminishing returns does not occur in the long run.

6. You are the manager of a firm that makes computers. If you had to decide how much output to produce in the next week, would you use the principle of diminishing returns? If you had to decide how much output to produce 10 years from now, would you use the principle of diminishing returns?

7. Your coffee shop has a single espresso machine. As the firm adds more and more workers, would you expect output (espressos per hour) to increase at a constant rate? Why or why not?

8. Use the spillover principle to discuss the following examples. Are there spillover costs or spillover benefits?

   a. Logging causes soil erosion and stream degradation, harming fish.

   b. An environmental group buys 50 acres of wetlands to provide a habitat for migrating birds.

   c. Your office mate smokes cigarettes.

   d. A person buys a dilapidated house in your neighborhood and fixes it up.

9. Explain this statement: The salaries of baseball players have increased in both real and nominal terms.

10. Web Exercise. Visit the Web site for the CIA's World Fact Book (*www.odci.gov/cia/publications/factbook/*). Pick a country and get some data about its factors of production (labor, human capital, natural resources).

11. Web Exercise. Visit the Web site of the IndUS Entrepreneurs, a nonprofit organization for entrepreneurs (*www.tie.org*). Access the page describing the organization's programs (*www.tie.org/prog.html*). What does this organization do and how might it be helpful for aspiring entrepreneurs?

12. Web Exercise. Visit the Web site of the U.S. Environmental Protection Agency (EPA), accessing the page with answers to frequently asked questions (*www.epa.gov/history/faqs/index.htm*). What is the EPA's mission, what are its goals, and how does it try to achieve these goals? Why do we need an organization like the EPA?

13. Web Exercise. The price of a gallon of gasoline was $0.42 in 1973 and had risen to $1.33 by 1999. How does the change in the price of gasoline compare to the cost of other goods? To answer, go to the Web site of the Bureau of Labor Statistics (*www.bls.gov/cpihome.htm*) and get information on the consumer price index (CPI). The CPI measures the cost

of a standard market basket of goods in different years. The value of the CPI is 100 in the base year; as prices increase, the value of the CPI increases. For example, a value of 123 means that prices have risen to the point where the cost of the standard market basket of goods is 23% higher than it was in the base year. How does the CPI figure for 1973 compare to that of 1999? Has the price of gasoline increased or decreased compared to the cost of other consumer goods?

Take It to the Net

We invite you to visit the O'Sullivan/Sheffrin page on the Prentice Hall Web site at: **www.prenhall.com/osullivan/** for this chapter's World Wide Web exercise.

Model Answers to Questions

Test Your Understanding

1. What goods and services do we produce? How do we produce the goods and services we select? Who consumes the goods and services we produce?

2. The production possibilities curve shows the combinations of goods that are available to the economy, so it helps us answer the first question.

3. If the earthquake destroys some of the country's buildings, roads, and bridges, the country will have less physical capital and will be able to produce less. The production possibilities curve will shift inward.

4. False. This statement ignores the opportunity cost of time spent in school.

5. We need the opportunity cost of using the people in the army instead of in the civilian economy. One measure of the opportunity cost is the wages the people could have earned as engineers, teachers, doctors, lawyers, or factory workers.

6. One of the costs of a lunch is the time spent eating it. Even if someone else pays for your lunch, it is not truly free.

7. The marginal benefit is $150, and the marginal cost is only $100 (equal to $600 − $500), so it would be sensible to add the third bus.

8. It will be worthwhile if the opportunity cost of the time spent traveling is less than $40.

9. No. If the factory experiences diminishing returns, the additional output from the 21st worker will be smaller than the output from the additional output from the 20th worker, and the extra output from the 22nd worker will be even smaller than the output from the 21st worker. Therefore, hiring two more workers will increase total output by less than 10 tables.

10. False. The principle says that output increases but at a decreasing rate. It does not say that hiring another worker decreases output, although this is a possibility with a very crowded factory.

11. Cost or Benefit?
    a. Spillover cost: You must listen to what you consider awful music chosen by your roommate.
    b. Spillover cost: People who bathe in the contaminated water risk being burned.
    c. Spillover cost: For most people, a bunch of partly restored cars (cars jacked up on the street or on the front lawn) is an eyesore.
    d. Spillover benefit: Even people who don't contribute are happy if the poor receive holiday meals.
    e. Spillover benefit: Many people like the idea of preventing a species from becoming extinct.

12. The price of consumer goods increased faster than wages.

13. Your real wage hasn't changed, so you are just as well off.

14. A set of goods that cost you $100 will cost you $103 today, so you must use $3 of your $4 interest earnings to cover the higher costs, leaving you with only $1 as actual interest earnings.

Using the Tools

2. What's the Cost? The opportunity cost of the loan to the friend is the interest the person could have earned if the $100 were in a bank account instead. The oppor-

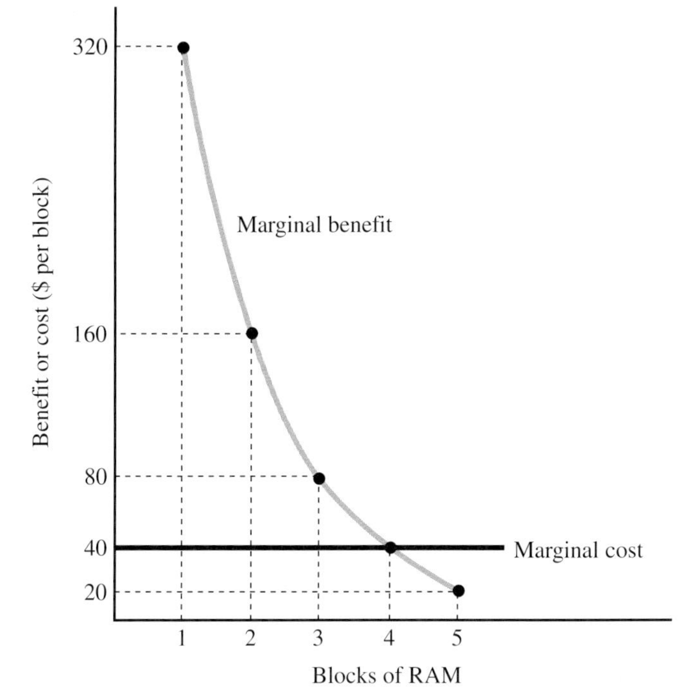

Figure 1.A
How Much RAM?

[Graph: Y-axis labeled "Benefit or cost ($ per block)" with values 20, 40, 80, 160, 320. X-axis labeled "Blocks of RAM" with values 1, 2, 3, 4, 5. A downward-sloping curve labeled "Marginal benefit" passes through points (1, 320), (2, 160), (3, 80), (4, 40), (5, 20). A horizontal line at 40 is labeled "Marginal cost."]

tunity cost of the logs is the amount of money the firm could get by selling the logs on the log market today. The opportunity cost of the land is the value of land in its next-best alternative—for example, a classroom building, a library, or a student center.

3. How much RAM? See Figure 1.A. The marginal benefit of RAM equals the marginal cost at four blocks (128 MB).

Notes

1. United Nations Development Program, *Human Development Report 1994* (New York: Oxford University Press, 1994).

2. Peter Navarro and Aron Spencer, "Assessing the Cost of Terrorism," *Milken Institute Review*, Fourth Quarter 2001, pp. 17–28.

3. *USA Today*, April 19, 1999, p. 1.

APPENDIX

Using Graphs and Formulas

In this appendix, we review the mechanics of graphing. You'll recognize most of the simple graphs and formulas in this appendix because they were covered in your high school mathematics. We'll review them here to prepare you to use them as you begin your own economic analysis.

Table 1A.1 Relationship Between Work Time and Income

Hours worked per week	0	10	22	30
Income per week	$40	$120	$216	$280

Using Graphs to Show Relationships

A graph is a visual representation of the relationship between two variables. As we saw earlier in Chapter 1, a variable is a measure of something that can take on different values. For example, suppose that you have a part-time job and you are interested in the relationship between the number of hours you work and your weekly income. The relevant variables are the hours you work per week and your weekly income.

We can use a table of numbers such as Table 1A.1 to show the relationship between time worked and income. Let's assume that your weekly allowance from your parents is $40 and your part-time job pays $8 per hour. If you work 10 hours per week, for example, your weekly income is $120 ($40 from your parents and $80 from your job). The more you work, the higher your weekly income: If you work 22 hours, your weekly income is $216; if you work 30 hours, it is $280.

Drawing a Graph

A graph makes it easier to see the relationship between time worked and income. To draw a graph, we perform seven simple steps:

1. Draw a horizontal line to represent the first variable. In Figure 1A.1, we measure time worked along the horizontal axis (also known as the *x* axis). As we move to the right along the horizontal axis, the number of hours worked increases, from zero to 30 hours. The numbers along the horizontal axis are spaced equally.

2. Draw a vertical line intersecting the first line to represent the second variable. In Figure 1A.1, we measure income along the vertical axis (also known as the *y* axis). As we move up along the vertical axis, income increases from zero to $280.

3. Pick a combination of time worked and income from the table of numbers. From the second column, for instance, time worked is 10 hours and income is $120.

Figure 1A.1

Relationship Between Hours Worked and Total Income

There is a positive relationship between the amount of work time and income. The slope of the curve is $8: Each additional hour of work increases income by $8.

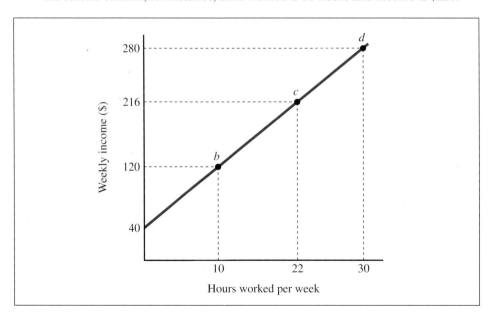

4. Find the point on the horizontal axis with that number of hours worked—10 hours worked—and draw a dashed line vertically straight up from that point.

5. Find the point on the vertical axis with the income corresponding to those hours worked ($120) and draw a dashed line horizontally straight to the right from that point.

6. The intersection of the dashed lines shows the combination of those hours worked and the income for working those hours. Point *b* shows the combination of 10 hours worked and $120 income.

7. Repeat steps 3 through 6 for different combinations of work time and income from the table of numbers. Once you have a series of points on the graph (*b*, *c*, and *d*), you can connect them to draw a curve that shows the relationship between hours worked and income.

There is a **positive relationship** between two variables if an increase in the value of one variable increases the value of the other variable. An increase in the time you work increases your income, so there is a positive relationship between the two variables. As you increase the time you work, you move upward along the curve shown in Figure 1A.1 to higher income levels.

There is a **negative relationship** between two variables if an increase in the value of one variable decreases the value of the other variable. For example, there is a negative relationship between the amount of time you work and your performance in school. Some people refer to a positive relationship as a direct relationship and to a negative relationship as an inverse relationship.

Positive relationship: A relationship in which an increase in the value of one variable increases the value of another variable.

Negative relationship: A relationship in which an increase in the value of one variable decreases the value of another variable.

Computing the Slope

How sensitive is one variable to changes in the other variable? We can use the slope of the curve to measure this sensitivity. The **slope of a curve** is the change in the variable on the vertical axis resulting from a one-unit increase in the variable on the horizontal axis. Once we pick two points on a curve, we can compute the slope as follows:

Slope of a curve: The change in the variable on the vertical axis resulting from a one-unit increase in the variable on the horizontal axis.

$$\text{slope} = \frac{\text{vertical difference between two points}}{\text{horizontal difference between two points}}$$

To compute the slope of a curve, we take four steps:

1. Pick two points on the curve: for example, points *b* and *c* in Figure 1A.1.
2. Compute the vertical distance between the two points (also known as the rise). For points *b* and *c*, the vertical distance between the points is $96 ($216 − $120).
3. Compute the horizontal distance between the same two points (also known as the run). For points *b* and *c*, the horizontal distance between the points is 12 hours (22 hours − 10 hours).
4. Divide the vertical distance by the horizontal distance to get the slope. The slope between points *b* and *c* is $8 per hour:

$$\text{slope} = \frac{\text{vertical difference}}{\text{horizontal difference}} = \frac{96}{12} = 8$$

In this case, a 12-hour increase in time worked increases income by $96, so the increase in income per hour of work is $8, which makes sense because this is the hourly wage.

Because the curve is a straight line, the slope is the same at all points along the curve. You can check this yourself by using the values between points *c* and *d* to calculate the slope.

Moving Along the Curve Versus Shifting the Curve

Up to this point, we've explored the effect of changes in variables that cause movement along a given curve. In Figure 1A.1, we see the relationship between a student's hours of work (on the horizontal axis) and her income (on the vertical axis). The student's income also depends on her allowance and her wage; so we can make two observations about the curve in Figure 1A.1:

1. To draw this curve, we must specify the weekly allowance ($40) and the hourly wage ($8).

2. The curve shows that an increase in time worked increases the student's income, ceteris paribus. In this case, we are assuming that her allowance and her wage are fixed.

A change in the student's weekly allowance will shift the curve showing the relationship between time worked and income. In Figure 1A.2, when the allowance increases from $40 to $70, the curve shifts upward by $30. For a given time worked, the student's income increases by $30. Now the income associated with 10 hours of work and the higher allowance is $150 (point z), compared to $120 with 10 hours of work and the original allowance (point b). In general, an increase in the allowance shifts the curve upward and leftward: For a given amount of time worked, the student will have more income (an upward shift as a result of the increased allowance). To reach a given amount of income, the student needs fewer hours of work (a leftward shift).

This book uses dozens of two-dimensional curves, each of which shows the relationship between only two variables. That is all a single curve can show. A common error is to forget that a single curve tells only part of the story. In Figure 1A.2, we needed two curves to show what happened when we looked at three variables (work time, allowance, and income). Here are some simple rules that will help us avoid this error:

- A change in one of the variables shown on the graph causes movement along the curve. In Figure 1A.2, an increase in work time causes movement along the curve from point b to point c.

- A change in one of the variables that is not shown on the graph (one of the variables held fixed in drawing the curve) shifts the entire curve. In Figure 1A.2, an increase in the allowance causes the entire curve to shift upward.

Figure 1A.2

Shifting the Curve

To draw a curve showing the relationship between hours worked and total income, we assume that the weekly allowance ($40) and the wage ($8) are fixed. An increase in the weekly allowance from $40 to $70 shifts the curve upward by $30: For each quantity of work hours, income is $30 higher.

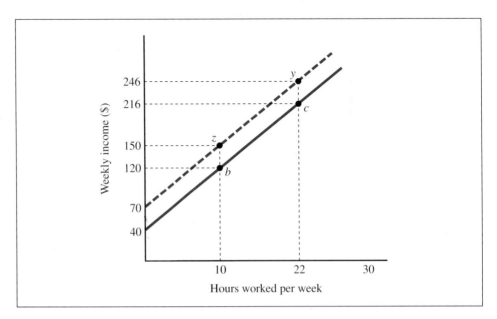

Table 1A.2 Relationship Between CDs and Tapes

Number of CDs purchased	0	5	10	15
Number of tapes purchased	30	20	10	0

Negative and Nonlinear Relationships

We can use a graph to show a negative relationship between two variables. Consider a consumer who has a monthly budget of $300 to spend on CDs (at a price of $20 per CD) and cassette tapes (at a price of $10 per tape). Table 1A.2 shows the relationship between the number of CDs purchased and the number of tapes purchased. If the consumer buys five CDs in a certain month, he will spend a total of $100 on CDs, leaving $200 to spend on tapes. With the $200, he can buy 20 tapes at a price of $10 per tape. As the number of CDs increases, the number of tapes decreases, from 20 tapes and 5 CDs, to 10 tapes and 10 CDs, to zero tapes and 15 CDs.

Using the seven-step process outlined earlier, we can use the numbers in Table 1A.2 to draw a curve showing this negative relationship. In Figure 1A.3, the curve is negatively sloped: The more the consumer spends on CDs, the fewer tapes he can buy. We can use points e and f to compute the slope of the curve. The slope is -2 tapes per CD: A five-unit increase in CDs (the horizontal difference, or the run) decreases the number of tapes by 10 (the vertical difference, or the rise):

$$\text{slope} = \frac{\text{vertical difference}}{\text{horizontal difference}} = \frac{-10}{5} = -2$$

The curve is a straight line with a constant slope of -2 tapes per CD.

We can use a graph to show a nonlinear relationship between two variables. Panel A of Figure 1A.4 shows the relationship between study time and the exam grade that results from study time. Although the exam grade increases as study time increases, the grade increases at a decreasing rate; that means the increase in grade is smaller and smaller for each additional hour of study. For example, the second hour of study increases the grade by 4 points (from 6 points to 10 points), but the ninth hour of study

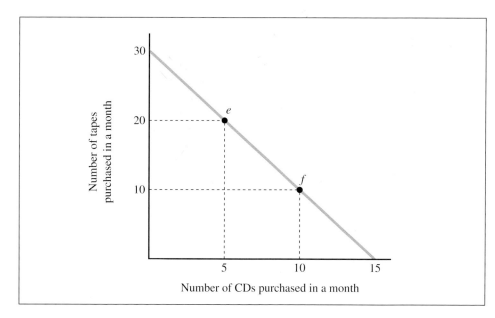

Figure 1A.3

A Negative Relationship Between CD Purchases and Tape Purchases

There is a negative relationship between the number of CDs purchased and the number of cassette tapes purchased. Because the price of CDs is $20 and the price of tapes is $10, the slope of the curve is -2 tapes per CD: Each additional CD decreases the number of tapes by 2.

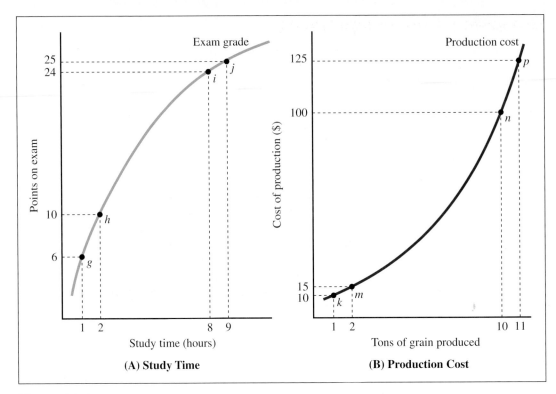

Figure 1A.4

Nonlinear Relationships

(A) Study time. There is a positive and nonlinear relationship between study time and the grade on an exam. As study time increases, the exam grade increases at a decreasing rate. For example, the second hour of study increases the grade by 4 points (from 6 points to 10 points), but the ninth hour of study increases the grade by only 1 point (from 24 points to 25 points).

(B) Production cost. There is a positive and nonlinear relationship between the quantity of grain produced and total production cost. As the quantity increases, total cost increases at an increasing rate. For example, to increase production from 1 ton to 2 tons, production cost increases by $5 (from $10 to $15), but to increase production from 10 to 11 tons, total cost increases by $25 (from $100 to $125).

increases the grade by only 1 point (from 24 points to 25 points). This is a nonlinear relationship: The slope of the curve changes as we move along the curve. In Figure 1A.4, the slope decreases as we move to the right along the curve: The slope is 4 between points *g* and *h* but only 1 between points *i* and *j*.

Another possibility for a nonlinear curve is that the slope increases (the curve becomes steeper) as we move to the right along the curve. This is shown in panel B of Figure 1A.4. The slope of the curve increases as the amount of grain increases, meaning that total production cost increases at an increasing rate. If the producer increases production from 2 tons to 3 tons, the total cost increases by $5 (from $10 to $15). On the upper portion of the curve, if the producer increases production from 10 to 11 tons, the total cost increases by $25 (from $100 to $125).

Using Formulas to Compute Values

Economists often use formulas to compute the values of the relevant variables. Here is a brief review of the mechanics of formulas.

Computing Percentage Changes

In many cases, the formulas that economists use involve percentage changes. In this book, we use the simple approach to computing percentage changes: We divide the change in the variable by the initial value of the variable and then multiply by 100. For example, if the price of pizzas increases from $20 to $22, the percentage change is 10%: The change ($2) divided by the initial value ($20) is 0.10; multiplying this number by 100 generates a percentage change of 10%:

$$\text{percentage change} \; = \; \frac{\text{absolute change}}{\text{initial value}} = \frac{2}{20} = 0.10 = 10\%$$

Going in the other direction, if the price decreases from $20 to $19, the percentage change is −5%: The change (−$1) divided by the initial value ($20) is −0.05, or −5%. The alternative to the simple approach is the midpoint approach, under which the percentage change equals the absolute change in the variable divided by the average value or the midpoint of the variable. For example, if the price of pizza increases from $20 to $22, the computed percentage change under the midpoint approach would be 9.52381%:

$$\text{percentage change} = \frac{\text{absolute change}}{\text{average value}} = \frac{2}{(20 + 22) \,/\, 2}$$

$$= \frac{2}{21} = 0.0952381 = 9.52381\%$$

If the change in the variable is relatively small, the extra precision associated with the midpoint approach is usually not worth the extra effort. The simple approach allows us to spend less time doing tedious arithmetic and more time doing economic analysis. In this book, we use the simple approach to compute percentage changes: If the price increases from $20 to $22, the price has increased by 10%.

If we know a percentage change, we can translate it into an absolute change. For example, if a price has increased by 10% and the initial price is $20, then we add 10% of the initial price ($2 is 10% of $20) to the initial price ($20), for a new price of $22. If the price decreases by 5%, we subtract 5% of the initial price ($1 is 5% of $20) from the initial price ($20) for a new price of $19.

Using Formulas to Compute Missing Values

It will often be useful to compute the value of the numerator or the denominator of a formula. To do so, we use simple algebra to rearrange the formula to put the missing variable on the left side of the equation. For example, consider the relationship between time worked and income. The formula for the slope is

$$\text{slope} = \frac{\text{difference in income}}{\text{difference in work time}}$$

If we're interested in how much more income you'll earn from more work hours, we rearrange the formula by multiplying both sides of the equation by the difference in work time:

$$\text{slope} \times \text{difference in work} = \text{difference in income}$$

Then swapping sides, we get:

$$\text{difference in income} = \text{slope} \times \text{difference in work time}$$

For example, if the slope is $8 and you work 7 extra hours, your increase in income will be $56, computed as $8 per hour times 7 hours.

We can use the same process to compute the difference in work time required to achieve a target change in income. In this case, we multiply both sides of the slope formula by the difference in work time and then divide both sides by the slope. The result is:

$$\text{difference in work time} = \frac{\text{difference in income}}{\text{slope}}$$

For example, to achieve a target of $56 more income, you need to work 7 hours, computed as $56/$8 per hour.

Key Terms

negative relationship, 27   positive relationship, 27   slope of a curve, 27

Problems and Discussion Questions

1. Suppose you belong to a tennis club that has a monthly fee of $100 and a charge of $5 per hour for court time to play tennis.
   a. Use a curve to show the relationship between the monthly bill from the club and the hours of tennis played.
   b. What is the slope of the curve?
   c. If you increase your monthly tennis time by three hours, by how much will your monthly bill increase?

2. Suppose that to make pizza, Terry uses three ingredients: tomato sauce, dough, and cheese. Terry initially uses 100 gallons of tomato sauce per day, and the cost of the other ingredients (dough, cheese) is $500 per day.
   a. Draw a curve to show the relationship between the price of tomato sauce and the daily cost of producing pizza (for prices between $1 and $5).
   b. To draw the curve, what variables are assumed to be fixed?
   c. What sort of changes would cause movement upward along the curve?
   d. What is the slope of the curve?

   e. What sort of changes would cause the entire curve to shift upward?

3. Compute the percentage changes for the following changes:

Initial Value	New Value	Percentage Change
10	11	_____
100	98	_____
50	53	_____

4. The price of jeans decreases by 15%. If the original price was $20, what is the new price?

5. Suppose the slope of a curve showing the relationship between the number of burglaries per month (on the vertical axis) and the number of police officers (on the horizontal axis) is −0.5 burglaries per police officer. Use the slope formula to compute the change in the number of burglaries resulting from hiring eight additional police officers.

6. Complete the statement: A change in one of the variables shown on a graph causes movement _____ a curve, while a change in one of the variables that is not shown on the graph _____ the curve.

Supply, Demand, and Market Equilibrium

2

Between 2000 and 2002, the price of vanilla beans quadrupled, from $50 to $200 per kilo. Was this good news for vanilla growers in Madagascar, the world's leading producer? The soaring price was actually bad news for the growers. The price hike was caused by tropical storms that reduced harvests, so the growers sold a smaller quantity at the higher price. The higher price unleashed the forces of supply and demand, to the detriment of Madagascar growers. On the demand side of the market, many consumers and food manufacturers switched to synthetic vanilla, which sells for as little as $15 per kilo. On the supply side, the high price encouraged people in other countries to enter the lucrative market. In India, 10,000 hectares are expected to be cultivated in the next few years. In East Timor, the world's newest nation, many coffee growers switched to vanilla beans and harvested their first crop in 2002.

We know that a market is an arrangement that allows buyers and sellers to exchange money and products. In this chapter, we use a model of supply and demand—the most important tool of economic analysis—to see how markets work. We can use the model of supply and demand to see how the prices of goods and services are affected by all sorts of changes in the economy, such as bad weather, higher income, technological innovation, taxes, regulation, and changes in consumer preferences. This chapter will prepare you for the applications of supply and demand you'll see in this book. You'll also learn how to be an economic detective, using clues from the market to explain past changes in market prices.

We will use the model of supply and demand to explain how a perfectly competitive market operates. A **perfectly competitive market** has a very large number of firms, each of which produces the same standardized product and is so small that it does not affect the market price of the good it produces. The classic example of a perfectly competitive firm is a wheat farm that produces a tiny fraction of the total supply of wheat. No matter how much wheat the farm produces, the market price of wheat won't change.

This chapter includes many applications of supply and demand analysis. Here are some practical questions we answer:

Perfectly competitive market: A market with a very large number of firms, each of which produces the same standardized product and is so small that it does not affect the market price of the good it produces.

1. Ted Koppel, host of the ABC news program *Nightline*, once suggested that the prices of illegal drugs had fallen because the supply of illegal drugs had increased. Was he correct?
2. Some data published in your local newspaper seem to suggest that gasoline consumers violate the law of demand, buying more gasoline at higher prices. Should you be skeptical about the data?
3. Over the last few decades, the consumption of chicken and turkey has increased. Why?

The Demand Curve

On the demand side of a product market, consumers buy products from firms. The main question concerning the demand side of the market is, How much of a particular product are consumers willing to buy during a particular period? A consumer who is "willing to buy" a particular product is willing to sacrifice enough money to purchase it. The consumer doesn't merely have a desire to buy the good but is also willing to sacrifice something to get it. Notice that demand is defined for a particular period—for example, a day, a month, or a year.

We'll start our discussion of demand with the individual consumer. How much of a particular product is an individual willing to buy? It depends on a number of variables. Here is a list of the variables that affect a consumer's decision, using the pizza market as an example:

- The price of the product, for example, the price of a pizza
- Consumer income
- The price of substitute goods such as tacos or sandwiches
- The price of complementary goods such as beer or lemonade
- Consumer tastes and advertising
- Consumer expectations about future prices

Together these variables determine how much of a particular product an individual consumer is willing to buy. We'll start our discussion of demand with the relationship between the price and quantity demanded, a relationship that is represented graphically by the demand curve.

The Individual Demand Curve and the Law of Demand

The starting point for a discussion of individual demand is a **demand schedule**, a table of numbers that shows the relationship between price and quantity demanded, ceteris paribus (the Latin phrase for "everything else held fixed"). The variables that are held fixed in the demand schedule are the other determinants of demand: income, the prices of substitutes and complements, consumer tastes, advertising, and expectations about future prices. Table 2.1 shows Al's demand schedule for pizza. At a price of $2, Al buys 13 pizzas per month. As the price rises, he buys fewer pizzas: 10 pizzas at a price of $4, 7 pizzas at a price of $6, and so on, down to only 1 pizza at a price of $10.

The **individual demand curve** shows the relationship between the price and the quantity demanded by a consumer, ceteris paribus. To draw the curve, we assume that everything else that affects a consumer's choice (income, prices of substitutes, prices of complementary goods, tastes, advertising, expectations about future prices) does not change. The only variable that changes is the price of pizza, and we use the numbers from the demand schedule to draw the individual demand curve. Figure 2.1 shows Al's demand curve for pizza.

The demand curve is negatively sloped, reflecting the **law of demand**. This law is not a legal restriction that sends violators to jail, but it is a pattern of behavior that we observe in most consumers.

Law of Demand

The higher the price, the smaller the quantity demanded, ceteris paribus (everything else held fixed).

The words *ceteris paribus* provide a reminder that to isolate the relationship between price and quantity demanded, we assume that the other variables that influence consumers are unchanged. In Al's case, we see that as the price of pizza increases, he consumes fewer pizzas. A movement along the demand curve is called a **change in quantity demanded**, a change in the quantity a consumer is willing to buy when the price of the good changes. For example, if the price increases from $8 to $10, we move along the demand curve from point *c* to point *b*, and the quantity demanded decreases from four pizzas per month to one pizza per month.

To see why the law of demand is sensible, think about how Al might react to an increase in the price of pizza:

Demand schedule: A table of numbers that shows the relationship between price and quantity demanded by a consumer, ceteris paribus (everything else held fixed).

Individual demand curve: A curve that shows the relationship between price and quantity demanded by a consumer, ceteris paribus (everything else held fixed).

Law of demand: The higher the price, the smaller the quantity demanded, ceteris paribus (everything else held fixed).

Change in quantity demanded: A change in the amount of a good demanded resulting from a change in the price of the good; represented graphically by movement along the demand curve.

Table 2.1   Al's Demand Schedule for Pizzas

Price ($)	Quantity of Pizzas per Month
2	13
4	10
6	7
8	4
10	1

Figure 2.1

The Individual Demand Curve

According to the law of demand, the higher the price, the smaller the quantity demanded, everything else being equal. Therefore, the demand curve is negatively sloped: When the price increases from $6 to $8, the quantity demanded decreases from seven pizzas per month (point *d*) to four pizzas per month (point *c*).

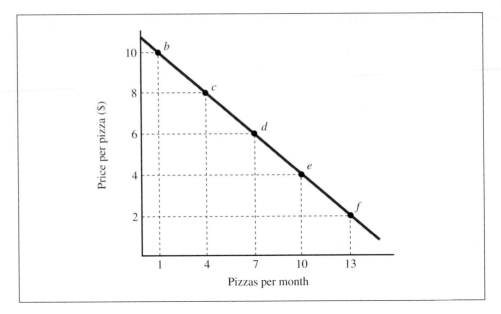

Substitution effect: The change in consumption resulting from a change in the price of one good relative to the price of other goods.

Income effect: The change in consumption resulting from a change in the consumer's real income.

- **Substitution effect.** The more money Al spends on pizza, the less he has to spend on other products such as tacos, music, books, and travel. The price of pizza determines exactly how much of these other goods he sacrifices to get a pizza. If the price of pizza is $6 and the price of tacos is $1, Al will sacrifice six tacos for each pizza he buys. If the price of pizza increases to $8, he'll now sacrifice eight tacos for each pizza. Given the larger sacrifice associated with buying pizza, he is likely to buy fewer pizzas, substituting tacos for pizza.

- **Income effect.** Suppose Al has a food budget of $100 per month and buys 10 pizzas at a price of $6 each (a total cost of $60), spending $40 on other food. If the price of pizza rises to $7 each, the cost of his original food choices will be $110 ($70 for pizza and $40 on other items), well above his $100 food budget. To avoid exceeding his budget, Al must cut back on something and will probably cut back on pizza as well as other items. This is called the income effect because when the price of pizza increases, the purchasing power of Al's income (or budget) decreases, forcing him to consume smaller quantities.

From Individual to Market Demand

Market demand curve: A curve showing the relationship between price and quantity demanded by all consumers together, ceteris paribus (everything else held fixed).

The **market demand curve** shows the relationship between the price of the good and the quantity that all consumers together are willing to buy, ceteris paribus. As in the case of the individual demand curve, when we draw the market demand curve, we assume that the other variables that affect individual demand (income, the prices of substitute and complementary goods, tastes, and price expectations) are fixed. In addition, we assume that the number of consumers is fixed. The market demand curve shows the relationship between price and the quantity demanded by all consumers, everything else being equal.

Figure 2.2 shows how to derive the market demand curve when there are only two consumers. Panel A shows Al's demand curve for pizza, and panel B shows Bea's demand curve for pizza. At a price of $8, Al will buy four pizzas (point *c*) and Bea will buy two pizzas (point *g*), so the total quantity demanded at this price is six pizzas (4 + 2). In panel C, point *j* shows the point on the market demand curve associated with a price of $8; at this price, the market quantity demanded is six pizzas. At a price of only $4, Al buys 10 pizzas and Bea buys 6 pizzas, for a total of 16 pizzas (shown by point *k* on the market demand curve).

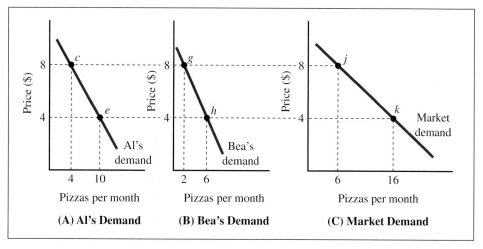

Figure 2.2

From Individual to Market Demand
The market demand equals the sum of the demands of all consumers. In this case, there are only two consumers, so at each price, the market quantity demanded equals the quantity demanded by Al plus the quantity demanded by Bea. At a price of $8, Al's quantity is four pizzas (point *c*) and Bea's quantity is two pizzas (point *g*), so the market quantity demanded is six pizzas (point *j*). Each consumer obeys the law of demand, so the market demand curve is negatively sloped.

The market demand is negatively sloped, reflecting the law of demand. If each consumer obeys the law of demand, consumers as a group will too. When the price increases from $4 to $8, there is a change in quantity demanded as we move along the demand curve from point *k* to *j*. The movement along the demand curve occurs if the price of pizza is the only variable that has changed.

The Supply Curve

On the supply side of a perfectly competitive market, firms sell their products to consumers. The main question for the supply side of the market is how much of a particular product firms are willing to sell.

Here are the variables that affect the decisions of sellers, using the market for pizza as an example:

- The price of the product, such as the price of pizza
- The cost of the inputs used to produce the product, such as the wage paid to workers, the cost of electricity, and the cost of equipment
- The state of production technology, such as the knowledge used in making pizza
- The number of producers, such as the number of pizzerias
- Producer expectations about future prices
- Taxes or subsidies from the government

Together these variables determine how much of a particular product producers are willing to sell. We'll start our discussion of market supply with the relationship between the price of a good and the quantity of that good supplied, a relationship that is represented graphically by the supply curve.

The Marginal Principle and the Output Decision

A perfectly competitive market has dozens or perhaps hundreds of firms, and we'll start our discussion of the supply curve with an individual firm. Nora's supply curve shows how many pizzas she is willing to produce at each price. Her decision about how many pizzas to produce is based on the marginal principle.

Marginal **Principle**

Increase the level of an activity if its marginal benefit exceeds its marginal cost; reduce the level of an activity if its marginal cost exceeds its marginal benefit. If possible, pick the level at which the activity's marginal benefit equals its marginal cost.

Nora's activity is producing pizzas. If the price of pizza is $8, the marginal benefit of producing a pizza is the $8 Nora gets from selling it. In Figure 2.3, when the price is $8, the marginal benefit curve for pizza is horizontal at $8. Recall that marginal cost is the increase in total cost resulting from one more unit. In Figure 2.3, the marginal cost curve for pizza is positively sloped, indicating that the more pizzas Nora produces, the higher the marginal cost of production. Later in the book, we'll explain the rationale for the positive slope.

When the price of pizza is $8, Nora satisfies the marginal principle at point p. She produces exactly 300 pizzas because that's the quantity at which the $8 marginal benefit equals the marginal cost of producing pizza. She stops at 300 pizzas because the marginal cost of producing the 301st pizza exceeds the $8 she could get from selling it. For example, if the marginal cost of the 301st pizza is $8.02, she would lose $0.02 on the 301st pizza.

How would Nora react to an increase in the price of pizza? If the price of pizza increased to $10, the marginal benefit of pizza production will increase to $10. At the higher price, it makes sense to produce the 301st pizza because the $10 benefit exceeds the $8.02 cost of producing it. In fact, when Nora applies the marginal principle with the higher price, she will increase production to 400 pizzas because that's the quantity at

Figure 2.3

The Marginal Principle and the Output Decision

The marginal benefit curve is horizontal at the market price. To satisfy the marginal principle, the firm produces the quantity at which the marginal benefit equals the marginal cost. An increase in the price shifts the marginal benefit curve upward and increases the quantity at which the marginal benefit equals the marginal cost.

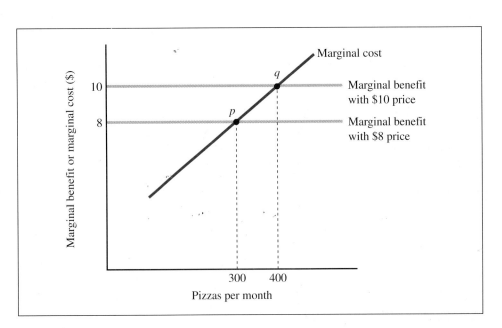

which the $10 marginal benefit equals the marginal cost. In Figure 2.3 the marginal benefit curve for a price of $10 intersects the marginal cost curve at 400 pizzas (point q).

Individual Supply and the Law of Supply

A firm's **supply schedule** is a table of numbers that shows the relationship between price and the quantity supplied by the individual firm, ceteris paribus. The other variables that are held fixed are input costs, technology, expectations, and government taxes or subsidies. Table 2.2 shows Nora's supply schedule for pizza. At a price of $4, she supplies 100 pizzas per month. As the price rises, she supplies more pizza: 200 pizzas at a price of $6; 300 pizzas at a price of $8; and so on, up to 500 pizzas at a price of $12.

The **individual supply curve** shows the relationship between the price and the quantity supplied by a single firm, ceteris paribus. The only variable that changes is the price of pizza, and we use the numbers from the supply schedule to draw a supply curve. Panel A of Figure 2.4 shows Nora's supply curve for pizza.

Nora's supply curve is positively sloped, reflecting the **law of supply**, a pattern of behavior that we observe in producers.

Law of Supply

The higher the price, the larger the quantity supplied, ceteris paribus (everything else held fixed).

The words *ceteris paribus* remind us that to isolate the relationship between price and quantity supplied, we assume that the other determinants of supply are unchanged. As the price of pizza increases, Nora produces a larger quantity of pizza. A movement along the supply curve is called a **change in quantity supplied**, a change in the quantity a producer is willing to sell when the price of the good changes. For example, if the price increases from $8 to $10, Nora moves upward along her supply curve from point p to point q, and the quantity supplied increases from 300 pizzas per month to 400 pizzas per month.

Individual Supply to Market Supply

The **market supply curve** for a particular good shows the relationship between the price of the good and the quantity that all producers together are willing to sell, ceteris paribus. To draw the market supply curve, we assume that the other variables that influence individual suppliers are fixed. In addition, we assume that the number of producers is fixed.

Panel B of Figure 2.4 shows the market supply curve when there are 100 producers, each of which has the same individual supply curve as Nora. At a price of $8, Nora supplies 300 pizzas per month (point p), so the 100 firms together produce 30,000 piz-

Supply schedule: A table of numbers that shows the relationship between price and quantity supplied, ceteris paribus (everything else held fixed).

Individual supply curve: A curve that shows the relationship between price and quantity supplied by a producer, ceteris paribus (everything else held fixed).

Law of supply: The higher the price, the larger the quantity supplied, ceteris paribus (everything else held fixed).

Change in quantity supplied: A change in the quantity supplied resulting from a change in the price of the good; represented graphically by movement along the supply curve.

Market supply curve: A curve showing the relationship between price and quantity supplied by all producers together, ceteris paribus (everything else held fixed).

Table 2.2 Nora's Supply Schedule for Pizza

Price ($)	Quantity of Pizzas per Month
4	100
6	200
8	300
10	400
12	500

Figure 2.4

Individual and Market Supply Curve

(A) Supply of individual firm. Nora supplies 300 pizzas at a price of $8 (point p) but 400 pizzas at a price of $10 (point q). **(B) Market supply.** There are 100 identical pizzerias, so the market quantity equals 100 times the quantity supplied by Nora, the typical pizzeria. At a price of $8, Nora supplies 300 pizzas (point p), so the market quantity supplied is 30,000 pizzas (point u).

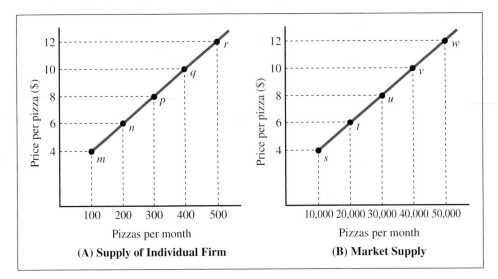

(A) Supply of Individual Firm   **(B) Market Supply**

zas (300 pizzas per firm × 100 firms), as shown by point u. If the price increases to $10, Nora supplies 400 pizzas (point q), so the quantity supplied by the market is 40,000 (point v).

The market supply curve is positively sloped, reflecting the law of supply. If each firm obeys the law of supply, firms as a group will too. When the price increases from $8 to $10, there is a change in quantity supplied as we move along the market supply curve from point u to point v. The movement along the supply curve occurs if the price of pizza is the only variable that has changed.

TEST Your Understanding

1. Complete the statement with *increase* or *decrease*: When a price increases, the law of demand suggests that the quantity demanded will _____, while the law of supply suggests that the quantity supplied will _____.

2. List the variables that are held fixed in drawing a market demand curve.

3. List the variables that are held fixed in drawing a market supply curve.

Market Equilibrium

Market equilibrium: A situation in which the quantity of a product demanded equals the quantity supplied, so there is no pressure to change the price.

When the quantity of a product demanded equals the quantity supplied, this is called a **market equilibrium**. When a market reaches an equilibrium, there is no pressure to change the price. For example, if pizza firms produce exactly the quantity of pizza consumers are willing to buy, there will be no pressure for the price of pizza to change. The equilibrium price is shown by the intersection of the supply and demand curves. In Figure 2.5, at a price of $8, the supply curve shows that firms will produce 30,000 pizzas, which is exactly the quantity that consumers are willing to buy at that price.

Excess Demand Causes the Price to Rise

Excess demand: A situation in which, at the prevailing price, consumers are willing to buy more than producers are willing to sell.

If the price is below the equilibrium price, there will be **excess demand** for the product. Excess demand (sometimes called a shortage) occurs when consumers are willing to buy more than producers are willing to sell. In Figure 2.5, at a price of $6, there is an excess

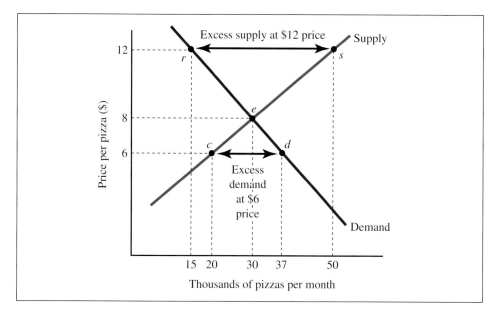

Excess supply at $12 price

Figure 2.5

Supply, Demand, and Market Equilibrium
At the market equilibrium (point *e*, with price = $8 and quantity = 30,000), the quantity supplied equals the quantity demanded. At a price lower than the equilibrium price ($6), there is excess demand (the quantity demanded exceeds the quantity supplied). At a price above the equilibrium price ($12), there is excess supply (the quantity supplied exceeds the quantity demanded).

demand equal to 17,000 pizzas: Consumers are willing to buy 37,000 pizzas (point *d*), but producers are willing to sell only 20,000 pizzas (point *c*). This mismatch between supply and demand will cause the price of pizza to rise. Firms will increase the price they charge for their limited supply of pizza, and anxious consumers will pay the higher price to get one of the few pizzas that are available.

An increase in price eliminates excess demand by changing both the quantity demanded and quantity supplied. As the price increases:

• The market moves upward along the demand curve (from point *d* toward point *e*), *decreasing* the quantity demanded.

• The market moves upward along the supply curve (from point *c* toward point *e*), *increasing* the quantity supplied.

Because quantity demanded decreases while quantity supplied increases, the gap between the quantity demanded and the quantity supplied narrows. The price will continue to rise until excess demand is eliminated. In Figure 2.5, at a price of $8, the quantity supplied equals the quantity demanded.

In some cases, government creates an excess demand for a good by setting a maximum price (sometimes called a price ceiling). If the government sets a maximum price that is less than the equilibrium price, the result is a permanent excess demand for the good. The most prominent example in the United States is rent control, a maximum price for apartments. During World War II, the federal government instituted a national system of rent controls. Although New York City was the only city to retain rent control after the war, rent control returned to dozens of cities in the 1970s. Since then, several states have passed laws that have weakened rent control.

Excess Supply Causes the Price to Drop

What happens if the price is above the equilibrium price? **Excess supply** (sometimes called a surplus) occurs when producers are willing to sell more than consumers are willing to buy. This is shown by points *r* and *s* in Figure 2.5. At a price of $12, the excess supply is 35,000 pizzas: producers are willing to sell 50,000 pizzas (point *s*), but consumers are

Excess supply: A situation in which, at the prevailing price, producers are willing to sell more than consumers are willing to buy.

willing to buy only 15,000 pizzas (point *r*). This mismatch will cause the price of pizza to fall as firms cut the price to sell their pizza. As the price drops:

- The market moves downward along the demand curve, *increasing* the quantity demanded.
- The market moves downward along the supply curve, *decreasing* the quantity supplied.

Because the quantity demanded increases while the quantity supplied decreases, the gap between quantity supplied and demanded narrows. The price will continue to drop until excess supply is eliminated. In Figure 2.5, at price of $8, the quantity supplied equals the quantity demanded.

The government sometimes creates an excess supply of a good by setting a minimum price (sometimes called a price floor). If the government sets a minimum price that is greater than the equilibrium price, the result is a permanent excess supply. For several decades, the U.S. government has set minimum prices for dozens of agricultural products such as corn and dairy products. The European Community has price supports (minimum prices) for grains, dairy products, livestock, and sugar, and Japan has price supports for dairy products and sugar.

TEST Your Understanding

4. Complete the statement: The market equilibrium is shown by the intersection of the _____ curve and the _____ curve.

5. Complete the statement with *less* or *greater*: Excess demand occurs when the price is _____ than the equilibrium price; excess supply occurs when the price is _____ than the equilibrium price.

6. Complete the statement with *supply* or *demand*: A maximum price below the equilibrium price causes excess _____, while a minimum price above the equilibrium price causes excess _____.

Market Effects of Changes in Demand

We've seen that a market equilibrium occurs when the quantity supplied equals the quantity demanded, shown graphically by the intersection of the supply curve and the demand curve. In this part of the chapter, we'll see how changes on the demand side of the market affect the equilibrium price and equilibrium quantity.

Change in Quantity Demanded Versus Change in Demand

Earlier in the chapter, we listed the variables that determine how much of a particular product consumers are willing to buy. One of the variables is the price of the product, and the law of demand summarizes the negative relationship between price and quantity demanded. We're ready to take a closer look at the other variables that affect demand—income, the prices of related goods, tastes, advertising, and the number of consumers—and see how changes in these variables affect the demand for the product and the market equilibrium.

If any of these other variables change, the relationship between price and quantity—shown numerically in the demand schedule and graphically in the demand curve—will change. That means we will have an entirely different demand schedule and a different demand curve. To convey the idea that changes in these other variables change the demand schedule and the demand curve, a change in any of these variables causes a **change in demand**. In contrast, a change in the price of the good causes a *change in quantity demanded*.

Change in demand: A change in the amount of a good demanded resulting from a change in something other than the price of the good; represented graphically by a shift of the demand curve.

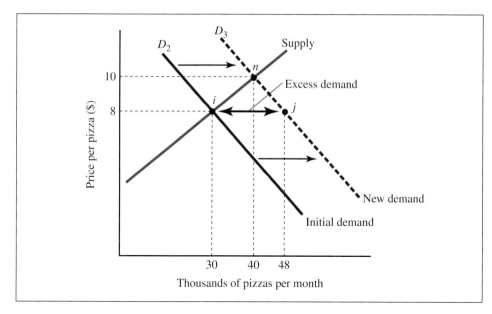

Figure 2.6

Market Effects of an Increase in Demand
An increase in demand shifts the demand curve to the right: At each price, the quantity demanded increases. At the initial price ($8), the shift of the demand curve causes excess demand, causing the price to rise. Equilibrium is restored at point *n*, with a higher equilibrium price ($10, up from $8) and a larger equilibrium quantity (40,000 pizzas, up from 30,000 pizzas).

Increase in Demand

We'll start with changes in the pizza market that increase the demand for pizza. An increase in demand means that at each price, consumers are willing to buy a larger quantity. In Figure 2.6, an increase in demand shifts the market demand curve from D_2 to D_3. At the initial price of $8, the quantity demanded increases from 30,000 pizzas (point *i*) to 48,000 (point *j*). An increase in demand like the one represented in Figure 2.6 can occur for several reasons, which are listed in the first column of Table 2.3:

- **Increase in income.** Consumers use their income to buy products, and the more money they have, the more money they spend. For a **normal good**, there is a positive relationship between consumer income and the quantity consumed.

Normal good: A good for which an increase in income increases demand.

Table 2.3 Shifting the Demand Curve

An increase in demand shifts the demand curve to the right when	A decrease in demand shifts the demand curve to the left when
The good is normal and income increases	The good is normal and income decreases
The good is inferior and income decreases	The good is inferior and income increases
The price of a substitute good increases	The price of a substitute good decreases
The price of a complementary good decreases	The price of a complementary good increases
Population increases	Population decreases
Consumer tastes shift in favor of the product	Consumer tastes shift away from the product
Successful advertising increases demand	
Consumers expect a higher price in the future	Consumers expect a lower price in the future

Substitutes: Two goods that are related in such a way that an increase in the price of one good increases the demand for the other good.

Complements: Two goods that are related in such a way that an increase in the price of one good decreases the demand for the other good.

- **Increase in price of a substitute good.** When two goods are **substitutes**, an increase in the price of the first good causes some consumers to switch to the second good. Tacos and pizzas are substitutes, so an increase in the price of tacos increases the demand for pizzas as some consumers substitute pizza for tacos, which are now more expensive relative to pizza.

- **Decrease in price of a complementary good.** When two goods are **complements**, they are consumed together as a package, and a decrease in the price of one good decreases the cost of the entire package. As a result, consumers buy more of both goods. Pizza and beer are complementary goods, so a decrease in the price of beer decreases the cost of a beer and pizza meal, increasing the demand for pizza.

- **Increase in population.** An increase in the number of people means that there are more pizza consumers—more individual demand curves to add up to get the market demand curve—so market demand increases.

- **Shift in consumer tastes.** Consumers' preferences or tastes change over time, and when consumers' preferences shift in favor of pizza, the demand for pizza increases.

- **Favorable advertising.** The purpose of an advertising campaign is to shift consumers' preferences in favor of a product, so a successful pizza advertising campaign will increase the demand for pizza.

- **Expectations of higher future prices.** If consumers think next month's pizza price will be higher than they had initially expected, they may buy a larger quantity today (and a smaller quantity next month). That means that the demand for pizza today will increase.

Market Effects of an Increase in Demand

We can use Figure 2.6 to show the effects of an increase in demand on the equilibrium price and equilibrium quantity. An increase in the demand for pizza shifts the demand curve to the right, from D_2 to D_3. At the initial price of $8 (the equilibrium price with the initial demand curve), there will be an excess demand, as indicated by points i and j: Consumers are willing to buy 48,000 pizzas (point j), but producers are willing to sell only 30,000 pizzas (point i). Consumers want to buy 18,000 more pizzas than producers are willing to supply, so there is pressure to increase the price.

As the price rises, the excess demand shrinks because the quantity demanded decreases while the quantity supplied increases.

- The market moves upward along the supply curve to a larger quantity supplied.
- The market moves upward along the new demand curve to a smaller quantity demanded.

The supply curve intersects the new demand curve at point n, so the new equilibrium price is $10 (up from $8), and the new equilibrium quantity is 40,000 pizzas (up from 30,000).

Decrease in Demand

What sort of changes in the pizza market will decrease the demand for pizza? A decrease in demand means that at each price, consumers are willing to buy a smaller quantity. In Figure 2.7, a decrease in demand shifts the market demand curve from D_2 to D_1. At the initial price of $8, the quantity demanded decreases from 30,000 pizzas (point i) to

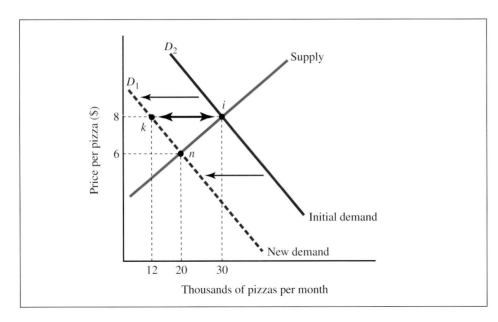

Figure 2.7
Market Effects of a Decrease in Demand
A decrease in demand shifts the demand curve to the left: At each price, the quantity demanded decreases. At the initial price ($8), the leftward shift of the demand curve causes excess supply, causing the price to fall. Equilibrium is restored at point *n*, with a lower equilibrium price ($6, down from $8) and a smaller equilibrium quantity (20,000 pizzas, down from 30,000 pizzas).

12,000 pizzas (point *k*). A decrease in demand like the one represented in Figure 2.7 can occur for several reasons, which are listed in the second column of Table 2.3:

- **Decrease in income.** A decrease in income means that consumers have less to spend, so they buy a smaller quantity of each normal good.

- **Decrease in price of a substitute good.** A decrease in the price of a substitute good such as tacos makes pizza more expensive relative to tacos, causing consumers to demand less pizza.

- **Increase in price of a complementary good.** An increase in the price of a complementary good such as beer increases the cost of a beer and pizza meal, decreasing the demand for pizza.

- **Decrease in population.** A decrease in the number of people means that there are fewer pizza consumers, so the market demand for pizza decreases.

- **Shift in consumer tastes.** When consumers' preferences shift away from pizza in favor of other products, the demand for pizza decreases.

- **Expectations of lower future prices.** If consumers think next month's pizza price will be lower than they had initially expected, they may buy a smaller quantity today, meaning the demand for pizza today will decrease.

Market Effects of a Decrease in Demand

We can use Figure 2.7 to show the effects of a decrease in demand on the equilibrium price and equilibrium quantity. A decrease in the demand for pizza shifts the demand curve to the left, from D_2 to D_1. At the initial price of $8 (the equilibrium price with the initial demand curve), there will be an excess supply, as indicated by points *i* and *k*: Producers are willing to sell 30,000 pizzas (point *i*), but given the lower demand, consumers are willing to buy only 12,000 pizzas (point *k*). Producers want to sell 18,000 more pizzas than consumers are willing to buy, so there is pressure to decrease the price.

The excess supply means that there is pressure to reduce prices, and as the price falls, the excess supply shrinks because the quantity demanded increases while the quantity supplied decreases.

- The market moves downward along the supply curve to a smaller quantity supplied.
- The market moves downward along the new demand curve to a larger quantity demanded.

The supply curve intersects the new demand curve at point *n*, so the new equilibrium price is $6 (down from $8), and the new equilibrium quantity is 20,000 pizzas (down from 30,000 pizzas).

Normal Versus Inferior Goods

Inferior good: A good for which an increase in income decreases demand.

Up to this point, we've assumed that there is a positive relationship between income and the demand for a particular product such as pizza. The label for such a good is a *normal good*, a label indicating that for most products there is a positive relationship between income and demand. For some goods, however, there is a negative rather than a positive relationship between income and consumption. For an **inferior good**, an increase in income decreases demand, shifting the demand curve to the left. In most cases, an inferior good is an inexpensive good such as margarine that has an expensive alternative (butter). As income increases, some consumers switch from the inexpensive good to the expensive one—for example, buying less margarine and more butter. As a result, the demand for margarine decreases and the demand curve shifts to the left. Some other examples of inferior goods are intercity bus travel and used clothing.

TEST Your Understanding

7. Which of the following go together?
   a. Change in demand
   b. Change in quantity demanded
   c. Change in price
   d. Movement along the demand curve
   e. Shifting the demand curve
   f. Change in income

8. What's wrong with the following statement? Demand increased because the demand curve shifted.

9. Complete the statement with *right* or *left*: An increase in the price of cassette tapes will shift the demand curve for CDs to the _____; an increase in the price of CD players will shift the demand curve for CDs to the _____.

10. In the following list of variables, circle the ones that change as we move along the demand curve for pencils, and cross out the ones that are assumed to be fixed: quantity of pencils demanded, number of consumers, price of pencils, price of pens, consumer income.

Market Effects of Changes in Supply

We've seen that changes in demand shift the demand curve and change the equilibrium price and quantity. In this part of the chapter, we'll see how changes on the supply side of the market affect the equilibrium price and quantity.

Change in Quantity Supplied Versus Change in Supply

Earlier in the chapter, we listed the variables that determine how much of a particular product firms are willing to sell. One of the variables is the price of the product, and the relationship between price and quantity supplied is shown by the law of supply. We're ready to take a closer look at the other variables that affect supply—input costs, technology, the number of firms, and price expectations—and see how changes in these variables affect the supply of the product and the market equilibrium.

If any of these other variables change, the relationship between price and quantity—shown numerically in the supply schedule and graphically in the supply curve—will change. That means that we will have an entirely different supply schedule and a different supply curve. To convey the idea that changes in these other variables change the supply schedule and the supply curve, a change in any of these variables causes a **change in supply**. In contrast, a change in the price of the good causes a *change in quantity supplied* (defined earlier in the chapter).

Change in supply: A change in the amount of a good supplied resulting from a change in something other than the price of the good; represented graphically by a shift of the supply curve.

Increase in Supply

We'll start with changes in the pizza market that increase the supply of pizza. An increase in supply means that at each price, producers are willing to sell a larger quantity. In Figure 2.8, an increase in supply shifts the market supply curve from S_2 to S_3. At the initial price of $8, the quantity demanded increases from 30,000 pizzas (point i) to 45,000 (point m). An increase in supply like the one represented in Figure 2.8 can occur for several reasons, which are listed in the first column of Table 2.4:

- **Decrease in input costs.** A decrease in the cost of labor or some other input will make pizza production less costly and more profitable at a given price, so producers will supply more.

- **Advance in technology.** A technological advance that makes it possible to produce pizza at a lower cost will make pizza production more profitable, so producers will supply more.

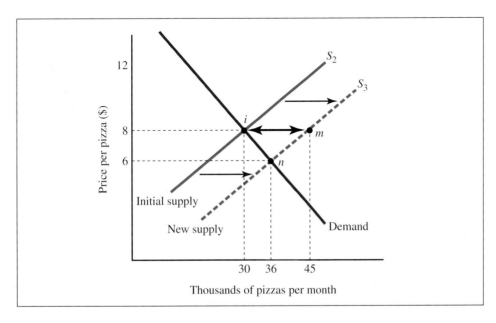

Figure 2.8
Market Effects of an Increase in Supply
An increase in supply shifts the supply curve to the right: At each price, the quantity supplied increases. At the initial price ($8), the rightward shift of the supply curve causes excess supply, causing the price to drop. Equilibrium is restored at point n, with a lower equilibrium price ($6, down from $8) and a larger equilibrium quantity (36,000 pizzas, up from 30,000 pizzas).

Table 2.4 Shifting the Supply Curve

An increase in supply shifts the supply curve to the right when	A decrease in supply shifts the supply curve to the left when
The cost of an input decreases	The cost of an input increases
A technological advance decreases production costs	
The number of firms increases	The number of firms decreases
Producers expect a lower price in the future	Producers expect a higher price in the future
The item is subsidized	The item is taxed

- **An increase in the number of producers.** The market supply is the sum of the supplies of all producers, so the larger the number of producers, the greater the supply.

- **Expectations of lower future prices.** If firms think next month's pizza price will be lower than they had initially expected, they may be willing to sell a larger quantity today (and a smaller quantity next month). That means that the supply of pizza today will increase.

- **Subsidy.** If the government subsidizes the production of the product (pays firms some amount for each unit produced), the subsidy will make the product more profitable, so firms will produce more.

Market Effects of an Increase in Supply

We can use Figure 2.8 to show the effects of an increase in supply on the equilibrium price and equilibrium quantity. An increase in the supply of pizza shifts the supply curve to the right, from S_2 to S_3. At the initial price of $8 (the equilibrium price with the initial supply curve), there will be an excess supply, as indicated by points i and m: Producers are willing to sell 45,000 pizzas (point m), but consumers are willing to buy only 30,000 (point i). Producers want to sell 15,000 more pizzas than consumers are willing to buy, so there is pressure to decrease the price.

As the price decreases, the excess supply shrinks because the quantity supplied decreases while the quantity demanded increases.

- The market moves downward along the new supply curve to a smaller quantity supplied.

- The market moves downward along the demand curve to a larger quantity demanded.

The new supply curve intersects the demand curve at point n, so the new equilibrium price is $6 (down from $8) and the new equilibrium quantity is 36,000 pizzas (up from 30,000).

Decrease in Supply

What sort of changes in the pizza market will decrease the supply of pizza? A decrease in supply means that at each price, producers are willing to supply a smaller quantity. In Figure 2.9, a decrease in supply shifts the market supply curve from S_2 to S_1. At the initial price of $8, the quantity supplied decreases from 30,000 pizzas (point i) to 14,000

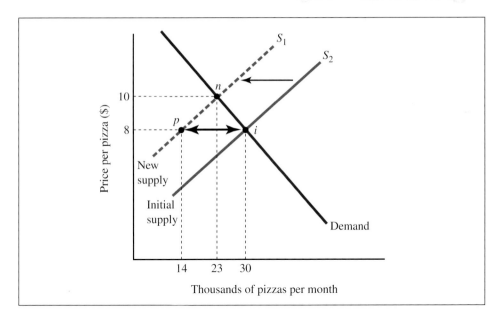

Figure 2.9
Market Effects of a Decrease in Supply
A decrease in supply shifts the supply curve to the left: At each price, the quantity supplied decreases. At the initial price ($8), the leftward shift of the supply curve causes excess demand, causing the price to rise. Equilibrium is restored at point n, with a higher equilibrium price ($10, up from $8) and a smaller equilibrium quantity (23,000 pizzas, down from 30,000 pizzas).

pizzas (point p). A decrease in supply like the one represented in Figure 2.9 can occur for several reasons, which are listed in the second column of Table 2.4:

- **Increase in input costs.** An increase in the cost of labor or some other input will make pizza production more costly and less profitable at a given price, so producers will supply less.

- **Decrease in the number of producers.** The market supply is the sum of the supplies of all producers, so a decrease in the number of producers decreases supply.

- **Expectations of higher future prices.** If firms think next month's pizza price will be higher than they had initially expected, they may be willing to sell a smaller quantity today (and a larger quantity next month). That means that the supply of pizza today will decrease.

- **Tax.** If the government imposes a tax on producers (a firm pays the government some amount for each unit produced), the tax will make the product more costly and less profitable, so firms will supply less.

Market Effects of a Decrease in Supply

We can use Figure 2.9 to show the effects of a decrease in supply on the equilibrium price and equilibrium quantity. A decrease in the supply of pizza shifts the supply curve to the left, from S_2 to S_1. At the initial price of $8 (the equilibrium price with the initial supply curve), there will be an excess demand, as indicated by points i and p: Consumers are willing to buy 30,000 pizzas (point i), but producers are willing to sell only 14,000 pizzas (point p). Consumers want to buy 16,000 more pizzas than producers are willing to sell, so there is pressure to increase the price.

As the price increases, the excess demand shrinks because the quantity demanded decreases while the quantity supplied increases.

- The market moves upward along the demand curve to a smaller quantity demanded.

- The market moves upward along the new supply curve to a larger quantity supplied.

The new supply curve intersects the demand curve at point *n*, so the new equilibrium price is $10 (up from $8), and the new equilibrium quantity is 23,000 pizzas (down from 30,000).

Market Effects of Simultaneous Changes in Demand and Supply

What happens to the equilibrium price and quantity when both supply and demand increase? It depends on which change is larger. In panel A of Figure 2.10, the increase in demand is larger than the increase in supply, meaning the demand curve shifts by a larger amount than the supply curve. The market equilibrium moves from point *i* to point *d*, and the equilibrium price increases from $8 to $9. This is sensible because an increase in demand tends to pull the price up, while an increase in supply tends to push the price down. If demand increases by a larger amount, the upward pull will be stronger than the downward push, and the price will rise.

We can be certain that when supply and demand both increase, the equilibrium quantity will increase. That's because both changes tend to increase the equilibrium quantity. In panel A of Figure 2.10, the equilibrium quantity increases from 30,000 to 44,000 pizzas.

Panel B of Figure 2.10 shows what happens when the increase in supply is larger than the increase in demand. The equilibrium moves from point *i* to *s*, meaning that the price falls from $8 to $7. This is sensible because the downward pull on the price resulting from the increase in supply is stronger than the upward pull from the increase in demand. As expected, the equilibrium quantity rises from 30,000 to 45,000 pizzas.

What about simultaneous *decreases* in supply and demand? In this case, the equilibrium quantity will certainly fall because both changes tend to decrease the equilibrium quantity. The effect on the equilibrium price depends on which change is larger, the decrease in demand, which pushes the price downward, or the decrease in supply,

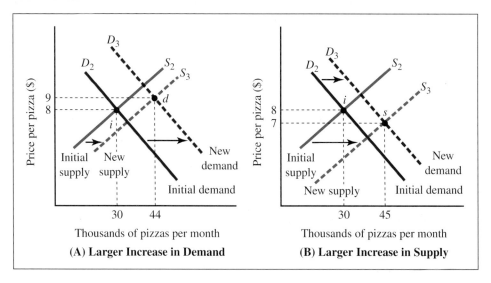

Figure 2.10

Market Effects of Simultaneous Changes in Supply and Demand

(A) Larger increase in demand. If the increase in demand is larger than the increase in supply (if the shift of the demand curve is larger than the shift of the supply curve), both the equilibrium price and the equilibrium quantity will increase.

(B) Larger increase in supply. If the increase in supply is larger than the increase in demand (if the shift of the supply curve is larger than the shift of the demand curve), the equilibrium price will decrease and the equilibrium quantity will increase.

which pulls the price upward. If the change in demand is larger, the price will fall because the force pushing the price down will be stronger than the force pulling it up. In contrast, if the decrease in supply is larger, the price will rise because the force pulling the price up will be stronger than the force pushing it down.

TEST Your Understanding

11. Which of the following items go together?
   a. Change in quantity supplied
   b. Change in input cost
   c. Change in price
   d. Shifting the supply curve
   e. Movement along the supply curve
   f. Change in supply

12. An increase in the wage of computer workers will shift the supply curve for computers to the left. True or false? Explain.

13. In the following list, circle the variables that change as we move along the market supply curve for housing, and cross out the variables that are assumed to be fixed: quantity of housing supplied, number of potential consumers, price of wood, price of houses, consumer income.

Applications

We can use the lessons from the pizza market to explore the effects of changes in other markets on equilibrium prices and quantities. Table 2.5 summarizes the effects of changes in demand and supply on equilibrium prices and quantities. When demand changes and the demand curve shifts, price and quantity change in the same direction.

- **Increase in demand.** Both the equilibrium price and the equilibrium quantity increase.
- **Decrease in demand.** Both the equilibrium price and the equilibrium quantity decrease.

When supply changes and the supply curve shifts, price and quantity change in opposite directions.

- **Increase in supply.** The equilibrium price decreases, but the equilibrium quantity increases.

Table 2.5   Market Effects of Changes in Demand or Supply

Change in Demand or Supply	Change in Price	Change in Quantity
Increase in demand	Increase	Increase
Decrease in demand	Decrease	Decrease
Increase in supply	Decrease	Increase
Decrease in supply	Increase	Decrease

• Decrease in supply. The equilibrium price increases, but the equilibrium quantity decreases.

Changes in Demand: Product Safety, Population Growth

How does public information about the safety of products affect equilibrium prices and quantities? In 1999, a controversial report suggested that pesticide residue on apples made them unsafe for infants and small children. Although many experts disputed the report, it decreased the demand for apples. In Figure 2.11, the initial equilibrium is shown by point i, with a price of $0.60 per pound and a quantity of 26,000 pounds per month. The pesticide report shifted the demand curve to the left, leading to excess supply at the original price ($0.60). The new equilibrium is shown by point n, with a lower equilibrium price ($0.50) and a smaller equilibrium quantity (20,000 pounds). The decrease in demand decreased the equilibrium price and the equilibrium quantity of apples.

How would an increase in enrollment at a university affect the equilibrium price of apartments in the university town? An increase in enrollment will increase the number of students seeking apartments. In the next set of "Test Your Understanding" exercises, you'll have an opportunity to draw supply and demand curves for the apartment market and predict the effect of an increase in enrollment on the equilibrium price and quantity.

Changes in Supply: Weather, Technology

How does poor weather affect equilibrium prices? In 1992, several events combined to decrease the world supply of coffee and increase its price. Poor weather and insect infestations in Brazil and Colombia decreased the coffee-bean harvest by about 40%. In addition, a slow-down by dockworkers at Santos, Brazil's main coffee port, decreased the amount supplied to the world market. In Figure 2.12, the initial equilibrium is shown by point i, with a price of $0.60 per pound. The poor weather, insect infestations, and other supply disruptions shifted the supply curve to the left, causing excess demand at the original price. The new equilibrium is shown by point n. The equilibrium price of coffee increased to $0.72 per pound, and the equilibrium quantity decreased from 30 million to 22 million pounds per month.

Figure 2.11

Market Effects of Pesticide Residue

A report of pesticide residue on apples decreases the demand for apples, shifting the demand curve to the left. Equilibrium is restored at point n, with a lower price ($0.50, down from $0.60) and a smaller quantity (20,000 pounds, down from 26,000 pounds).

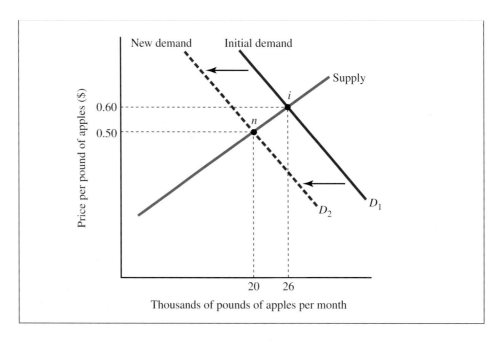

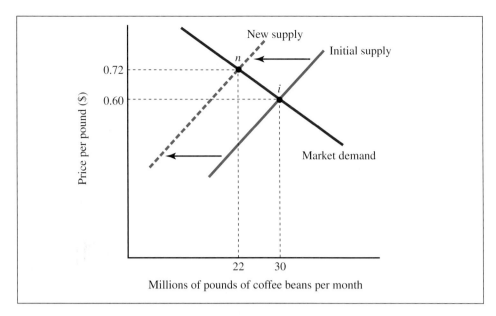

Figure 2.12
Bad Weather and the Coffee Market
Bad weather decreases the supply of coffee beans, shifting the supply curve to the left. Equilibrium is restored at point *n*, with a higher price ($0.72, up from $0.60) and a smaller quantity (22 million pounds, down from 30 million pounds).

How do technological innovations affect equilibrium prices? Recent innovations in electronics have decreased the cost of producing personal computers. In the next set of "Test Your Understanding" exercises, you'll have an opportunity to draw supply and demand curves for personal computers and predict the effects of technological innovation on the equilibrium price and quantity.

The Economic Detective

Economic Detective

We can use the information in Table 2.5 to play economic detective. Suppose we observe changes in the equilibrium price and quantity of a particular good, but we don't know what caused these changes. It could have been a change in demand or a change in supply. We can use the information in Table 2.5 to work backward, using what we observe about changes in prices and quantities to discover the reason for the changes. We discuss two cases for the economic detective: an increase in the consumption of poultry products and a decrease in the price of illegal drugs.

The Mystery of Increasing Poultry Consumption

Why has the consumption of poultry (chicken and turkey) increased so much over the last several decades? One possibility is that consumers have become more health conscious and have switched from red meat to poultry as part of an effort to eat healthier food. In other words, the demand curve for poultry may have shifted to the right, increasing the equilibrium quantity of poultry. Of course, an increase in demand will increase the price, too, so if this explanation is correct, we should also observe higher prices for poultry.

According to the U.S. Department of Agriculture, this popular explanation is incorrect.[1] In fact, the increase in poultry consumption was caused by an increase in supply, not an increase in demand. This conclusion is based on the fact that poultry prices have been decreasing, not increasing. Between 1950 and 1990, the real price of poultry (adjusted for inflation) decreased by about 75%. As shown in Figure 2.13, an increase in supply causes the market equilibrium to shift from point *i* (price = $2 and quantity = 50 million pounds) to point *n* (price = $0.80 and quantity = 90 million pounds). The increase in supply decreases the equilibrium price. The supply of poultry increased because innovations in

INCREASING THE SUPPLY OF WIND POWER

Every few weeks in 2001, newspapers announced the development of another huge wind farm, a collection of turbines propelled by the wind and hooked up to the electric power system or electric grid. According to the United States Energy Department, the supply of electricity from wind doubled in just one year.

The explosion in wind electricity resulted from technological innovations that decreased the cost of producing electricity from the wind. In the 1980s, the cost of wind electricity was about 50 cents per kilowatt-hour. Several design innovations—including the replacement of small rapid rotors with large slow-moving blades and the development of monitoring systems that permit the turbines to change their direction and blade angle to more efficiently harness the wind—have decreased the cost of maintaining the turbines and increased the electricity output per hour. By 2001, the cost of wind power had dropped to about 4 cents per kilowatt-hour, compared with 2.5 to 3 cents for electricity generated by conventional sources (natural gas and coal). Because the producers of wind power receive a federal tax credit of 1.5 cents per kilowatt-hour, wind power is often competitive with conventional power sources.

In graphical terms, the technological innovations in the design of wind turbines decreased production costs, shifting the supply curve for wind electricity to the right, increasing the equilibrium quantity and decreasing the price. The federal tax credit amplified the rightward shift of the supply curve, leading to an even larger increase in quantity and decrease in price.

Figure 2.13
The Mystery of Increasing Poultry Consumption

Because the price of poultry decreased at the same time that the quantity of poultry consumed increased, we know that the increase in consumption resulted from an increase in supply, not an increase in demand. Innovations in poultry processing decreased production costs, shifting the supply curve to the right.

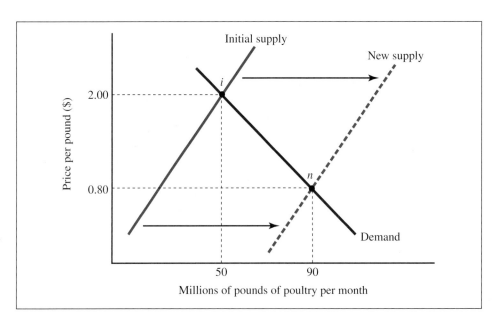

poultry processing decreased the cost of producing poultry products. The lesson here is that we shouldn't jump to conclusions based on limited information. A change in the equilibrium quantity could result from either a change in supply or a change in demand. To draw any conclusions, we need information about both price and quantity.

There may be a grain of truth in the popular explanation. It is possible that both demand and supply increased, shifting both curves to the right. Because the price of poultry decreased, however, we know that the shift of the supply curve (which tends to decrease the price) overwhelmed any shift of the demand curve (which tends to increase the price). Although changes in consumer preferences might contribute to increasing poultry consumption, the changes in consumption were caused largely by changes on the supply side of the market.

The Mystery of Falling Cocaine Prices

Ted Koppel, host of the ABC news program *Nightline*, once said, "Do you know what's happened to the price of drugs in the United States? The price of cocaine, way down, the price of marijuana, way down. You don't have to be an expert in economics to know that when the price goes down, it means more stuff is coming in. That's supply and demand."[2] According to Koppel, the price of drugs dropped because the government's efforts to control the supply of illegal drugs had failed. In other words, the lower price resulted from an increase in supply. According to the U.S. Department of Justice, however, the quantity of drugs consumed actually decreased during the period of dropping prices.[3] Is Koppel's economic detective work sound?

In this case, both the price and the quantity decreased. As shown in the second row of Table 2.5, when both the price and the quantity decrease, that means demand has decreased. In Figure 2.14, a decrease in demand shifts the demand curve to the left, and the market moves from point *i* (price = $15 and quantity = 400 units per day) to point *n* (price = $10 and quantity = 300 units per day). Koppel's explanation (an increase in supply) would be correct if the quantity of drugs increased at the same time that the price decreased. Because the quantity of drugs consumed actually decreased during the period of dropping prices, Koppel's explanation is incorrect. Lower demand—not a failure of the government's drug policy and an increase in supply—was responsible for the decrease in drug prices.

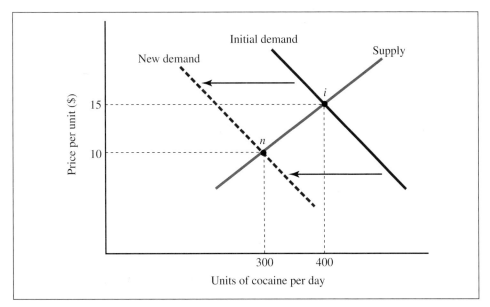

Figure 2.14

The Mystery of Lower Drug Prices
Because the quantity of cocaine consumed decreased at the same time that the price of cocaine decreased, we know that the decrease in price resulted from a decrease in demand, not an increase in supply. A decrease in the demand for cocaine decreased the price and decreased the quantity consumed.

14. Complete the statement with *supply* or *demand*: If the price and quantity change in the same direction, _____ is changing; if the price and quantity change in opposite directions, _____ is changing.

15. Use a supply and demand graph to predict the effects of an increase in university enrollment on the equilibrium price and quantity of apartments in the university town.

16. Use a supply and demand graph to predict the effects of a technological innovation in electronics on the equilibrium price and quantity of personal computers.

Market Equilibrium, the Invisible Hand, and Efficiency

In this chapter, we've seen that the market equilibrium reflects the forces of the "invisible hand." The actions of individual buyers and sellers, each acting in his or her own self-interest, lead to a market equilibrium: The quantity demanded equals the quantity supplied. Does the market equilibrium promote the social interest, or could society do better?

Recall that Adam Smith said that the pursuit of individual interest "frequently" promotes the social interest. The market equilibrium will be efficient from the social perspective if four conditions are met:

1. **Informed buyers and sellers.** Both buyers and sellers have enough information to make informed decisions about buying and selling.

2. **Perfect competition.** A perfectly competitive market has a very large number of firms, each of which is so small that it takes the market price as given. Firms are free to enter or exit the market, so whenever there is an opportunity to make a profit—that is, whenever the price of a product exceeds the cost of producing it—firms will enter the market and supply more of the product. The quantity supplied will continue to increase until the opportunity for profit is eliminated, which happens when the price is just high enough to cover the cost of providing the product, but no higher.

3. **No spillover benefit.** There is a spillover benefit when part of the benefits from some product go to someone who does not decide how much of the product to consume. For example, if your farm is on a floodplain and another farmer builds a dike to protect low-lying areas, you benefit from that farmer's decision to build a dam.

4. **No spillover cost.** There is a spillover cost when part of the cost of producing some product is borne by someone who does not decide how much of the product to produce. For example, if you live downstream from a paper mill that dumps chemical waste into the river, you bear some of the cost of paper production because it makes the river unsafe for swimming and drinking.

If these conditions are met—and they are met in many, if not most, markets—the individual decisions underlying the market supply and demand curves will promote the social interest. In other words, society as a whole can do no better than the market equilibrium.

Later in the book, we'll explore markets in which one or more of these conditions are not met. Chapter 6 explores markets with a small number of sellers: In this case, prices will be too high and the quantities sold will be too low. In Chapter 8, we'll see that if buyers and sellers are not well informed, markets may collapse. Chapter 8 also looks at markets with spillover benefits and costs. When a good generates spillover benefits, the market will provide too few of it. When there are spillover costs, the market will produce too much of the good.

Using the **Tools**

In this chapter, you learned how to use two tools of economics—the supply curve and the demand curve—to find equilibrium prices to predict changes in prices and quantities. Here are some opportunities to use these tools to do your own economic analysis.

1. ECONOMIC EXPERIMENT: MARKET EQUILIBRIUM

The simple experiment takes about 20 minutes. We start by dividing the class into two equal groups: consumers and producers.

a. The instructor provides each consumer with a number indicating the maximum amount he or she is willing to pay (WTP) for a bushel of apples: The WTP is a number between $1 and $100. Each consumer has the opportunity to buy one bushel of apples per trading period. The consumer's score for a single trading period equals the gap between his or her WTP and the price actually paid for apples. For example, if the consumer's WTP is $80 and he or she pays only $30 for apples, the consumer's score is $50. Each consumer has the option of not buying apples. This will be sensible if the best price the consumer can get exceeds his or her WTP. If the consumer does not buy apples, his or her score will be zero.

b. The instructor provides each producer with a number indicating the cost of producing a bushel of apples (a number between $1 and $100). Each producer has the opportunity to sell one bushel per trading period. The producer's score for a single trading period equals the gap between the selling price and the cost of producing apples. So if a producer sells apples for $20 and his or her cost is only $15, the producer's score is $5. Producers have the option of not selling apples, which is sensible if the best price the producer can get is less than his or her cost. If the producer does not sell apples, his or her score is zero.

Once everyone understands the rules, consumers and producers meet in a trading area to arrange transactions. A consumer may announce how much he or she is willing to pay for apples and wait for a producer to agree to sell apples at that price. Alternatively, a producer may announce how much he or she is willing to accept for apples and wait for a consumer to agree to buy apples at that price. Once a transaction has been arranged, the consumer and producer inform the instructor of the trade, record the transaction, and leave the trading area.

There are several trading periods, each of which lasts a few minutes. After the end of each trading period, the instructor lists the prices at which apples sold during that period. Then another trading period starts, providing consumers and producers another opportunity to buy or sell one bushel of apples. After all the trading periods have been completed, each participant computes his or her score by adding the scores from each trading period.

2. Using Data to Draw a Demand Curve

The following table shows data on gasoline prices and gasoline consumption in a particular city. Is it possible to use these data to draw a demand curve? If so, draw the demand curve. If not, why not?

Year	Gasoline Price (per Gallon)	Quantity Consumed (Millions of Gallons)
1999	1.20	400
2000	1.40	300
2001	1.60	360

3. Foreign Farm Workers and the Price of Berries

Current law allows thousands of Mexican workers to work on farms in the United States during harvest season. Suppose a new law outlaws the use of foreign farm workers. Assume that the resulting excess demand for labor increases the wage paid to farm workers by 20%. Use a supply–demand graph to predict the effects of the higher wage on the price of berries.

4. Market Effects of an Import Ban on Shoes

Consider a nation that initially imports half the shoes it consumes. Use a supply–demand graph to predict the effect of a ban on shoe imports on the equilibrium price and quantity of shoes.

5. The Mystery of Free Used Newspapers

In 1987, you could sell a ton of used newspapers for $60. Five years later, you could not sell them at any price. In other words, the price of used newspapers dropped from $60 to zero in just five years. Over this period, the quantity of used newspapers bought and sold increased. What caused the drop in price? Defend your answer with a supply–demand graph.

Summary

In this chapter, we've seen how supply and demand determine prices. And we saw how to predict the effects of changes in demand or supply on prices. Here are the main points of the chapter.

1. To draw a market demand curve, we must be certain the other determinants of demand (consumer income, prices of related goods, tastes, expectations, and number of consumers) are held fixed.

2. To draw a market supply curve, we must be certain the other determinants of supply (input costs, technology, the number of producers, expectations, taxes and subsidies) are held fixed.

3. An equilibrium in a market is shown by the intersection of the demand curve and the supply curve. When a market reaches an equilibrium, there is no pressure to change the price.

4. A change in demand changes price and quantity in the same direction: An increase in demand increases the equilibrium price and quantity; a decrease in demand decreases the equilibrium price and quantity.

5. A change in supply changes price and quantity in opposite directions: An increase in supply decreases price and increases quantity; a decrease in supply increases price and decreases quantity.

Key Terms

change in demand, 42
change in quantity demanded, 35
change in quantity supplied, 39
change in supply, 47
complements, 44
demand schedule, 35
excess demand, 40
excess supply, 41

income effect, 36
individual demand curve, 35
individual supply curve, 39
inferior good, 46
law of demand, 35
law of supply, 39
market demand curve, 36
market equilibrium, 40

market supply curve, 39
normal good, 43
perfectly competitive market, 34
substitutes, 44
substitution effect, 36
supply schedule, 39

Problems and Discussion Questions

1. Figure 2.A shows the supply and demand curves for CD players. Complete the following statements.
   a. At the market equilibrium (shown by point _____), the price of CD players is _____ and the quantity of CD players is _____.
   b. At a price of $100, there would be excess _____, so we would expect the price to _____ (fill in with *increase* or *decrease*).
   c. At a price exceeding the equilibrium price, there would be excess _____ so we would expect the price to _____ (fill in with *increase* or *decrease*).

2. The following table shows the quantities of corn supplied and demanded at different prices:

Price per Ton	Quantity Supplied	Quantity Demanded	Excess Demand or Excess Supply
$ 80	600	1,200	_____
$ 90	800	1,100	_____
$100	1,000	1,000	_____
$110	1,200	900	_____

   a. Complete the table.
   b. Draw the demand curve and the supply curve.
   c. What is the equilibrium price of corn?

3. Consider the market for personal computers. Suppose that the demand is stable: The demand curve doesn't change. Predict the effects of the following changes on the equilibrium price of computers. Illustrate your answer with a supply and demand diagram.
   a. The cost of memory chips (one component of a computer) decreases.
   b. The government imposes a $100 tax on personal computers.

4. Draw a supply–demand diagram to illustrate the effect of an increase in income on the market for restaurant meals.

5. Suppose that the tuition charged by public universities increases. Draw a supply–demand diagram to illustrate the effects of the tuition hike on the market for private college education.

6. Suppose that the government imposes a tax of $1 per pound of fish and collects the tax from fish producers. Draw a supply–demand diagram to illustrate the market effects of the tax.

7. As summer approaches, the equilibrium price of rental cabins increases and the equilibrium quantity of cabins rented increases. Draw a supply–demand diagram that explains these changes.

8. Suppose that the initial price of a pocket phone is $100 and that the initial quantity demanded is 500 phones per day. Depict graphically the effects of a technological innovation that decreases the cost of

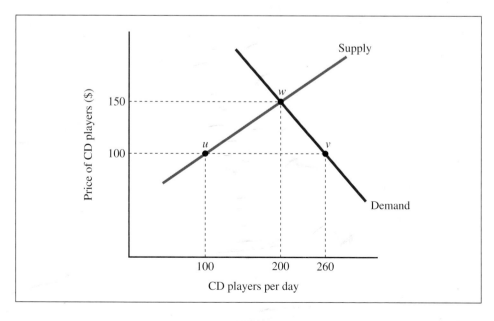

Figure 2.A
Supply and Demand for CD Players

producing pocket phones. Label the starting point with an *i* and the new equilibrium with an *n*.

9. You've been hired as an economic consultant to evaluate the nation's airport security systems (metal detectors and machines that allow security people to see what's inside carry-on luggage). Suppose these security systems add $5 to the typical airplane ticket and require 10 minutes of extra time for each passenger. List the questions you will answer in your evaluation.

10. Suppose a freeze in Florida wipes out 20% of the orange crop. How will this affect the equilibrium price of California oranges? Defend your answer with a graph.

11. The Multifiber Agreement sets import quotas for various apparel products—including shirts—coming into the United States. Use a supply–demand graph to show the effects of the shirt quota on the equilibrium price of shirts in the United States.

12. **Web Exercise.** Visit the Web site of the National Association of Realtors (*www.realtor.com*). Follow the "Find a Home" instructions and check housing prices for a three-bedroom, two-bath house in several cities—for example, San Francisco, California; Topeka, Kansas; Dallas, Texas; Concord, Massachusetts; and Seattle, Washington. Use supply and demand diagrams to explain why housing prices vary from city to city.

13. **Web Exercise.** Visit the Web site of eBay, a company that provides online auctions (*www.ebay.com*). Suppose you want to buy a traditional 35-mm camera. Access the listing of cameras being auctioned and check the most recent bids. Suppose someone develops a digital camera that takes better pictures than the traditional 35-mm camera at half the cost. Predict the effects of the new camera on the supply of traditional 35-mm cameras and the prices for cameras auctioned on the eBay site.

Take It to the Net

We invite you to visit the O'Sullivan/Sheffrin page on the Prentice Hall Web site at: **www.prenhall.com/osullivan/** for additional World Wide Web exercises for this chapter.

Model Answers to Questions

Chapter-Opening Questions

1. As is explained in one of the "Economic Detective" exercises, a lower price doesn't necessarily mean that supply has increased. The equilibrium quantity decreased at the same time, so the price drop was caused by a decrease in demand.

2. As is explained in one of the "Using the Tools" exercises, we can't draw a demand curve from a table of price and quantity data unless we know that the other determinants of demand (income, population, prices of substitute and complementary goods, tastes, advertising) are fixed over the period covered by the data.

3. Innovations in poultry processing decreased the cost of producing poultry products. The resulting increase in supply decreased the equilibrium price, causing consumers to buy more poultry products.

Test Your Understanding

1. Decrease, increase.

2. Consumer income, the prices of substitute goods, the prices of complementary goods, consumer tastes, advertising, the number of consumers, and price expectations.

3. Input costs, technology, price expectations, number of producers, taxes and subsidies.

4. Supply, demand.

5. Less, greater.

6. Demand, supply.

7. One group is a, e, and f; another group is b, c, and d.

8. The statement is incorrect because it confuses the direction of causality. The correct statement is: The demand curve shifted because demand increased. When something other than the price of the product changes, the relationship between price and quantity changes, causing the demand curve to shift.

9. Right, left.

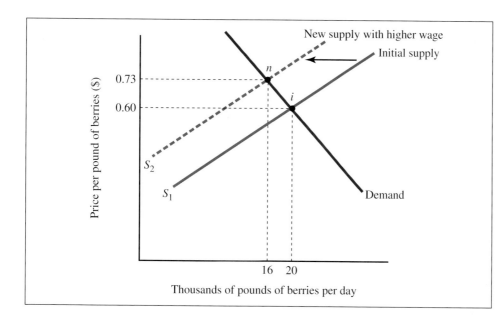

Figure 2.B
Market Effects of Higher Farm Wages
Reducing the number of foreign farm workers will increase the wage of farm workers, increasing the production costs of berry producers. The supply curve shifts to the left: At each price, a smaller quantity is supplied. Equilibrium is restored at point *n*, with a higher price ($0.73, up from $0.60) and a smaller quantity (16,000 pounds, down from 20,000 pounds).

10. Circle quantity of pencils demanded and price of pencils. Cross out number of consumers, price of pens, and consumer income.

11. One group is a, c, and e; another group is b, d, and f.

12. True. An increase in the wage increases production cost, so fewer computers will be supplied at each price.

13. Circle quantity of housing supplied and price of houses. Cross out number of consumers, price of wood, and consumer income.

14. Demand, supply.

15. An increase in enrollment will increase the number of students seeking apartments, increasing the demand for apartments and shifting the demand curve to the right. The resulting excess demand for apartments will increase the equilibrium price and the equilibrium quantity.

16. The innovations will decrease the cost of producing personal computers, shifting the supply curve to the right. The resulting excess supply of computers will decrease the equilibrium price and increase the equilibrium quantity.

Using the Tools

2. **Using Data to Draw a Demand Curve.** It's tempting to use the data in the table to plot three combinations of price and quantity, connect the points with a curve, call it a demand curve. That is not appropriate because we don't know what happened to the other determinants of the demand for gasoline over this period (consumer income, prices of substitutes and complements, tastes, advertising, price expectations). To draw a demand curve with these data, we must have additional data showing that these other variables did not change. If any of these other variables changed, we cannot draw a demand curve.

3. **Foreign Farm Workers and the Price of Berries.** The higher wage caused by the elimination of foreign farm workers will increase the production costs of berry farmers. The resulting decrease in supply of berries will shift the supply curve to the left. In Figure 2.B, the equilibrium price of berries increases from $0.60 to $0.73.

4. **Market Effects of an Import Ban.** An import ban has the same effect as a decrease in the number of firms in the market: Supply decreases, shifting the market supply curve to the left. In Figure 2.C, the free-trade equilibrium is shown by point *f*, and the equilibrium with an import ban is shown by point *b*. The ban on imported shoes increases the price of shoes from $25 to $34.

5. **The Mystery of Free Used Newspapers.** Between 1987 and 1992, the price and quantity moved in opposite directions, meaning that the decrease in price was caused by an increase in supply. Over this five-year period, hundreds of communities adopted curbside recycling programs. These programs increased the supply of used newspapers, generating an excess supply of used newspapers that decreased the equilibrium price. In Figure 2.D, the increase in supply was so large that the equilibrium price fell to zero.

Figure 2.C
The Market Effects of an Import Ban

A ban on shoe imports decreases the supply of shoes, shifting the supply curve to the left. The free-trade equilibrium is shown by point *f*, and the equilibrium under the import ban is shown by point *b*. The import ban increases the price from $25 to $34 and decreases the quantity from 12 million to 9 million pairs of shoes.

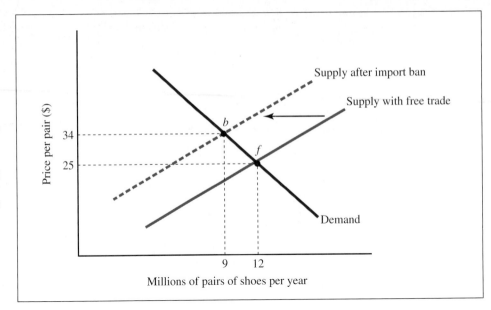

Figure 2.D
The Mystery of Free Used Newspapers

Between 1987 and 1992, the price of used newspapers decreased from $60 per ton to zero, a result of increases in supply caused by the expansion of curbside recycling programs.

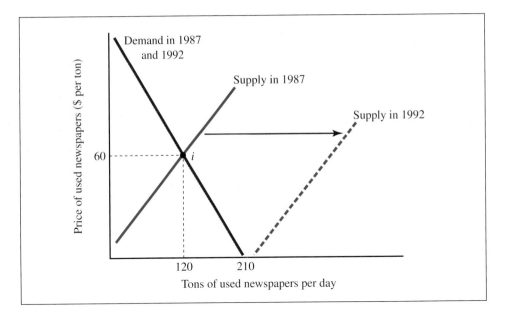

Notes

1. Mark R. Weimar and Richard Stillman, *Market Trends Driving Broiler Consumption, Livestock and Poultry Situation and Outlook Report LPS-44* (Washington, DC: U.S. Department of Agriculture, Economic Research Service, November 1990).

2. Kenneth R. Clark, "Legalize Drugs. A Case for Koppel," *Chicago Tribune*, August 30, 1988, sec. 5, p. 8.

3. U.S. Department of Justice, *Drugs, Crime, and the Justice System* (Washington, DC: U.S. Government Printing Office, 1992), p. 30.

Elasticity: A Measure of Responsiveness

In every large city in the United States, the public bus system runs a deficit: The total revenue from passenger fares is less than the cost of operating the bus system. Suppose your city wants to reduce its bus deficit and has decided to increase bus fares by 10%. Consider the following exchange between two city officials:

- Buster: A fare increase is a great idea. We'll collect more money from bus riders, so revenue will increase and the deficit will shrink.
- Bessie: Wait a minute, Buster. Haven't you heard about the law of demand? The increase in the bus fare will decrease the number of passengers taking buses, so we'll collect less money, not more, and the deficit will grow.

Who is right? As we'll see in this chapter, we can't predict how an increase in price will affect total revenue unless we know just how responsive consumers are to an increase in price. Like other consumers, bus riders obey the law of demand, but that doesn't necessarily mean that total fare revenue will fall.

Price elasticity of demand: A measure of the responsiveness of the quantity demanded to changes in price; computed by dividing the percentage change in quantity demanded by the percentage change in price.

Price elasticity of supply: A measure of the responsiveness of the quantity supplied to changes in price; computed by dividing the percentage change in quantity supplied by the percentage change in price.

From Chapter 2, we know that the quantity of a product demanded is affected by the price of the product. The **price elasticity of demand** measures the responsiveness of quantity demanded to changes in the price of the product. We say that demand is elastic if a small change in price causes a large change in quantity demanded. Demand is inelastic if the quantity does not change very much as price changes. We can also use the concept of elasticity to measure the responsiveness of consumer demand to changes in the other variables that affect demand: consumer income, the price of substitute goods, and the price of complementary goods.

Switching to the supply side of the market, we can use elasticity to measure the responsiveness of the quantity supplied to changes in price. We know from Chapter 2 that an increase in price will increase the quantity supplied, but sometimes the question is, How much more will be supplied at the higher price? The **price elasticity of supply** measures the responsiveness of quantity supplied to changes in price. We say that supply is elastic if a small change in price causes a large change in the quantity supplied. In contrast, if producers are not very responsive, we say that supply is inelastic.

This chapter contains many applications of the concept of elasticity. Here are some practical questions that we answer:

1. How would a tax on beer affect the number of highway deaths among young adults?
2. Why is a bumper crop bad news for farmers?
3. If a firm wants to increase its total revenue, should it raise or lower its price?
4. Why do policies that limit the supply of illegal drugs increase the number of burglaries and robberies?
5. If the demand for a product increases, what information do we need to predict the resulting change in the equilibrium price?

The Price Elasticity of Demand

When the price of a good decreases, consumers will buy more of it, but how much more will they buy? The price elasticity of demand (E_d) measures the responsiveness of consumers to changes in price. We compute the price elasticity of demand by dividing the percentage change in the quantity demanded by the percentage change in price:

$$E_d = \frac{\text{percentage change in quantity demanded}}{\text{percentage change in price}}$$

As we saw in the appendix to Chapter 1, the simple way to compute the percentage change in a variable is to divide the change in the variable by the initial value of the variable. Suppose the price of milk increases from $2 to $2.20. (The appendix to this chapter shows how to compute the price elasticity with the more precise midpoint formula described in the appendix to Chapter 1.)

We can use the numbers shown in Figure 3.1 to compute the price elasticity of demand for milk as follows:

- The percentage change in price equals the change in price (+$0.20) divided by the initial price ($2), or +10% (equal to +$0.20/$2).
- The percentage change in quantity demanded equals the change in quantity (−15 million) divided by the initial quantity (100 million), or −15% (equal to −15 million /100 million).

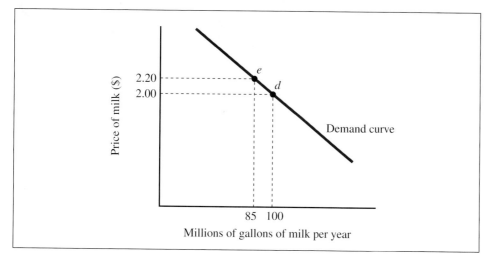

Figure 3.1

Market Demand Curve and Price Elasticity of Demand

A 10% rise in the price of milk (from $2 to $2.20) decreases the quantity demanded by 15% (from 100 to 85), so the price elasticity of demand is 1.5 = 15%/10%.

The conventional practice is to ignore any minus signs and compute the price elasticity as follows:

$$E_d = \frac{\text{percentage change in quantity demanded}}{\text{percentage change in price}} = 1.5$$

In this example, the price elasticity of demand E_d is equal to 1.5.

Why do we ignore the minus sign? The law of demand tells us that price and quantity move in opposite directions, so the percentage change in quantity will always have the opposite sign (+ or −) of the percentage change in price (− or +). In our example, a +10% change in price results in a −15% change in quantity. So to be absolutely precise, the price elasticity should be reported as a negative number. The conventional approach is to report all price elasticities as positive numbers. This means that a large number indicates that the quantity demanded is very elastic, or highly responsive to changes in price. As long as we remember the law of demand, there is no harm in dropping minus signs and reporting all price elasticities of demand as positive numbers.

The responsiveness of consumers to price changes varies from one good to another. An increase in the price of table salt doesn't change the quantity of salt demanded very much, but an increase in the price of a specific brand of cornflakes causes a large reduction in the quantity demanded. We can use the concept of price elasticity of demand to divide goods into three groups:

1. **Elastic.** If the price elasticity of demand for a particular good is greater than 1.0, we say that demand is elastic. This is sensible because if the elasticity is greater than 1.0, the percentage change in quantity demanded exceeds the percentage change in price, meaning that consumers are very responsive to changes in price.

2. **Inelastic.** If the price elasticity of demand is less than 1.0, consumers are not very responsive to changes in price, and we say that demand is inelastic.

3. **Unitary elastic.** If the elasticity equals 1.0, the percentage change in quantity demanded equals the percentage change in price, and we say that demand is unitary elastic.

Elastic demand: The price elasticity of demand is greater than 1.0.

Inelastic demand: The price elasticity of demand is less than 1.0.

Elasticity and Substitutes

The price elasticity of demand for a particular good depends on the availability of substitutes. Consider two goods: insulin (a medicine for diabetics) and cornflakes. There are no good substitutes for insulin, so consumers are not very responsive to changes in price: An increase in price doesn't cause a large reduction in the quantity of insulin demanded. In other words, the lack of substitutes for insulin means that the demand is inelastic. In contrast, there are many substitutes for cornflakes, including different types of corn cereal and cereals made from other grains (wheat, rice, and oats). Therefore, a small increase in the price of cornflakes will cause a large decrease in quantity demanded as consumers switch to other types of cereal whose price has not changed. In other words, if substitutes are plentiful, demand is relatively elastic.

Table 3.1 shows the price elasticities of demand for various products. The different elasticities illustrate the importance of substitutes in determining the price elasticity of demand. Because there are no good substitutes for water and salt, it's not surprising that the elasticities are small. For example, the price elasticity of demand for water (0.2) means that a 10% increase in the price of water would decrease the quantity demanded by only 2%:

$$E_d = \frac{\text{percentage change in quantity demanded}}{\text{percentage change in price}} = \frac{2\%}{10\%} = 0.2$$

The demand for cigarettes, an addictive good, is also inelastic. The elasticity of 0.3 means that a 10% increase in price would cause a 3% decrease in quantity demanded. Because there are no good substitutes for coffee, the demand for coffee is inelastic (0.3). But because different brands of coffee are substitutes for one another, the demand for a specific brand of coffee is very elastic (between 5.6 and 8.9). An elasticity of 5.6 means that a 10% increase in price of a specific brand would decrease the quantity demanded

Table 3.1   Price Elasticities of Demand for Selected Products

Product	Price Elasticity of Demand
Salt	0.1
Water	0.2
Coffee	0.3
Cigarettes	0.3
Shoes and footwear	0.7
Housing	1.0
Automobiles	1.2
Foreign travel	1.8
Restaurant meals	2.3
Air travel	2.4
Motion pictures	3.7
Specific brands of coffee	5.6

Sources: Frank Chaloupka, "Rational Addictive Behavior and Cigarette Smoking," *Journal of Political Economy*, August 1991, pp. 722–742; Gregory Chow, *Demand for Automobiles in the United States* (Amsterdam: North-Holland, 1957); David Ellwood and Mitchell Polinski, "An Empirical Reconciliation of Micro and Grouped Estimates of the Demand for Housing," *Review of Economics and Statistics*, vol. 61, 1979, pp. 199–205; H. F. Houthakker and Lester B. Taylor, *Consumer Demand in the United States: Analysis and Projections*, 2nd ed. (Cambridge, MA: Harvard University Press, 1970); John R. Nevin, "Laboratory Experiments for Estimating Consumer Demand: A Validation Study," *Journal of Marketing Research*, vol. 11, August 1974, pp. 261–268; Herbert Scarf and John Shoven, *Applied General Equilibrium Analysis* (New York: Cambridge University Press, 1984).

by 56%. The change in quantity is large because consumers can easily switch to other brands.

For another example of the price elasticity of demand, consider the demand for trash disposal. Until recently, most cities charged a fixed monthly fee for trash collection. Under an alternative approach, called pay-to-throw, the more trash a household generates, the higher is its trash bill. In 1991, Charlottesville, Virginia, switched 75 households from a fixed monthly fee to a price of $0.80 per 32-gallon bag of trash. The new pricing plan caused the following changes among the households participating in the experiment[1]:

- The volume of trash collected decreased by 37%, to 0.46 bag per person per week. The price elasticity of demand with respect to the volume of trash was 0.23.

- The weight of trash collected decreased by 14%, to 9.37 pounds per person per week. The weight decreased by a small amount because of the "Seattle stomp," a technique that allows a person to pack more trash into each bag. (Seattle conducted an early experiment in pay-to-throw pricing.) The price elasticity of demand with respect to the weight of trash was 0.08.

- The weight of recyclable materials (collected at no cost to the household) increased by 16%, to 4.27 pounds per person per week.

- Illegal dumping (littering and dumping household trash in commercial dumpsters) is difficult to measure. It appears that it may have increased by about 0.5 pound per person per week.

This study has some lessons for other communities that are considering a pay-to-throw plan: Although the total volume of trash would decrease, the total weight would decrease by a small amount, and illegal dumping would increase.

Other Determinants of Elasticity

We've seen that the availability of substitute goods affects the price elasticity of demand. Several other factors affect the price elasticity of demand:

- **Time.** Because it takes time to change consumption habits and find substitute goods, the more time we give consumers to respond to a price change, the larger their response. When the price of gasoline increases, consumers' immediate response is limited by their inability to immediately buy more fuel-efficient cars or move closer to their workplaces. Eventually, consumers can change cars and relocate, so we would expect a much larger reduction in gasoline consumption in the long run. As time passes, demand becomes more elastic because consumers have more options.

- **Importance in budget.** If a good represents a small part of the budget of the typical consumer, demand for it is relatively inelastic. If the price of pencils increases by 10% (from $0.50 to $0.55), there will be a relatively small decrease in the quantity demanded because the price change is trivial relative to the income of the typical consumer. In contrast, a 10% increase in the price of cars (from $20,000 to $22,000) will generate a much larger response because the change in price is large relative to consumer income. International comparisons of the price elasticity of demand for food suggest that demand is more price elastic when the good represents a large part of the budget. In wealthy countries such as the United States, Canada, and Germany, the price elasticity of demand for food is around 0.15.[2] In poor countries

Under the 1997 Tobacco Settlement, if smoking by teenagers does not decline by 60% by the year 2007, cigarette makers will face a fine of $2 billion. The settlement is expected to increase cigarette prices by about 62 cents per pack, a percentage increase of about 25%. Will that be enough to reduce teen smoking by the target percentage? The answer depends on the price elasticity of demand for cigarettes.

The demand for cigarettes by teenagers is elastic: The teen elasticity is 1.3, meaning that a 10% increase in the price of cigarettes will decrease teen cigarette consumption by 13%. About half the reduction results from fewer teen smokers, and the other half results from fewer cigarettes for each teen smoker. Although the teen demand for cigarettes is relatively elastic, a 25% price hike will not be enough to cut teen smoking

by the target amount. Given an elasticity of 1.3, the price of cigarettes must increase by about 46% (equal to 60% divided by 1.3).

such as India, Nigeria, and Bolivia, people spend a larger fraction of their budget on food, so they are more responsive to changes in food prices: In these countries, the price elasticity is around 0.34.

TEST Your Understanding

1. Complete the statement: To compute the price elasticity of demand, we divide the percentage change in _____ by the percentage change in _____.

2. Complete the statement: If a 10% increase in price decreases the quantity demanded by 12%, the price elasticity of demand is _____.

3. Explain why the demand for prerecorded audiotapes is more elastic in the long run than in the short run.

Using the Price Elasticity of Demand

The price elasticity of demand is a very useful tool for economic analysis. We know from the law of demand that a decrease in price will increase the quantity demanded, ceteris paribus. If we know the elasticity of demand for a particular good, we can predict how much more of that good will be sold at the lower price. We can also predict whether an increase in price will increase or decrease total spending on the good.

Predicting Changes in Quantity Demanded

As we saw in the Appendix to Chapter 1, we can use simple algebra to rearrange a formula to compute the value of the numerator. Rearranging the formula for price elasticity, we get:

$$\text{percentage change in quantity demanded} = E_d \times \text{percentage change in price}$$

For example, suppose you run a campus film series, and you know that the price elasticity of demand is 2.0. If you decide to increase your ticket price by 15%, you can use the rearranged formula to predict that the quantity demanded will decrease by 30%:

$$\text{percentage change in quantity demanded} = 2 \times 15\% = 30\%$$

Applications: College Education, Highway Deaths, Medical Care

How could university officials use the price elasticity of demand? Suppose a university increases its tuition from $4,000 to $4,400 and wants to predict how many fewer students will enroll in the university as a result of the higher price. The price elasticity of demand for higher education is about 1.4, so a 10% increase in tuition will decrease enrollment by 14%:

$$\text{percentage change in quantity demanded} = 1.4 \times 10\% = 14\%$$

How would a tax on beer affect highway deaths among young adults? The price elasticity of demand for beer among young adults is about 1.3, and the number of highway deaths is roughly proportional to the group's beer consumption.[3] If a state imposes a beer tax that increases the price of beer by 20%, what will happen to the number of highway deaths among young adults? Using the elasticity formula, we predict that beer consumption will decrease by 26%:

$$\text{percentage change in quantity demanded} = 1.3 \times 20\% = 26\%$$

If the number of highway deaths among young adults is proportional to their beer consumption, the number of highway deaths will also decrease by 26%. Of course, some adults will switch from beer to other alcoholic beverages. The larger the number that simply switch, the smaller the effect of the beer tax on highway deaths.

If the price of medical care increases, how will consumers respond? The rising cost of medical care has forced many nations to take a closer look at programs that subsidize medical care for their citizens. If prices are increased to cover more of the costs of providing medical care, how will this affect poor and wealthy households? For an answer, read "A Closer Look: Pricing Medical Care in Developing Countries."

Predicting Changes in Total Revenue

If a firm increases the price of its product, will total sales revenue increase or decrease? The answer depends on the price elasticity of demand for the product. If we know the price elasticity, we can determine whether a price hike will increase or decrease the firm's total revenue.

Let's return to the example of the campus film series. Suppose you are thinking about increasing the price of tickets from $4 to $4.40. An increase in the ticket price brings good news and bad news:

- **Good news.** You get more money for each ticket sold.
- **Bad news.** You sell fewer tickets.

Your total revenue will decrease if the bad news (fewer tickets sold) dominates the good news (more money per ticket). The elasticity of demand tells us how the good news compares to the bad news. If demand is elastic, consumers will respond to the higher price by purchasing many fewer tickets, so although you will collect more money per ticket, you'll sell so few tickets that your total revenue will decrease. For example, as Table 3.2

PRICING MEDICAL CARE IN DEVELOPING COUNTRIES

Many developing nations subsidize medical care, charging consumers a small fraction of the cost of providing the services. If a nation increased its price of medical care, how would the higher price affect its poor and wealthy households? In Câote d'Ivoire in Africa, the price elasticity of demand for hospital services is 0.47 for poor households and 0.29 for wealthy households. This means that a 10% increase in the price of hospital services would cause poor households to cut back their hospital care by 4.7%, while wealthy households would cut back by only 2.9%. In Peru, the differences between poor and wealthy households are even larger: The price elasticity is 0.67 for poor households but only 0.03 for wealthy households. The same pattern occurs in the demand for the medical services provided by physicians and health clinics. The poor are much more sensitive to price, so when prices increase, they suffer much larger reductions in medical care.

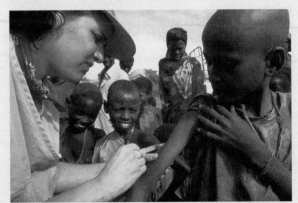

In developing nations, the poor are relatively sensitive to changes in the price of medical care.

Source: Paul Gertler and Jacques van der Gaag, *The Willingness to Pay for Medical Care: Evidence from Two Developing Countries* (Baltimore: Johns Hopkins University Press, 1990).

shows, if the price elasticity of demand is 2.0, a 10% increase in price will decrease the quantity demanded by 20%, from 100 to 80 tickets. Because the percentage decrease in quantity (the bad news) exceeds the percentage increase in price (the good news), total revenue decreases, from $400 to $352.

In general, an elastic demand means that the percentage change in quantity (the bad news from a price hike) will exceed the percentage change in price (the good news), so an increase in price will decrease total revenue.

We get the opposite result if the demand for the good is inelastic: An increase in price increases total revenue. If demand is inelastic, consumers are not very responsive to an increase in price, so the good news (more money per unit sold) dominates the bad news (fewer units sold). For example, suppose that the campus bookstore starts with a textbook price of $50 and a quantity of 100 books. If the bookstore increases its price by 10% (from $50 to $55 per book) and the elasticity of demand for textbooks is 0.4, the quantity of textbooks sold will decrease by only 4% (from 100 to 96). Therefore, the store's total revenue will be $5,280 ($55 × 96), compared to only $5,000 at the lower price ($50 × 100). In general, an inelastic demand means that the percentage change in quantity will be smaller than the percentage change in price, so an increase in price will increase total revenue.

Table 3.2 Price and Total Revenue with Elastic Demand

Price	Quantity of Tickets Sold	Total Revenue
4.00	100	$400
4.40	80	$352

Table 3.3 summarizes the revenue effects of changes in prices for different types of goods:

- **Elastic demand.** There is a negative relationship between price and total revenue: An increase in price decreases total revenue; a decrease in price increases total revenue.

- **Inelastic demand.** There is a positive relationship between price and total revenue: An increase in price increases total revenue; a decrease in price decreases total revenue.

- **Unitary elastic demand.** Total revenue does not vary with price.

The relationship between elasticity and total revenue provides a simple test of whether demand is elastic or inelastic. Suppose that when a music store increases the price of its CDs, its total revenue from CDs drops. The negative relationship between price and total revenue means that demand for the store's CDs is elastic: Total revenue decreases because consumers are very responsive to an increase in price, buying a much smaller quantity. In contrast, suppose that when a city increases the price it charges for water, the total revenue from water sales increases. The positive relationship between price and total revenue suggests that the demand for the city's water is inelastic: Total revenue increases because consumers are not responsive to an increase in price.

Applications: Transit Deficits, Property Crime

At the beginning of the chapter, we considered the question of whether increasing the price of bus rides would reduce a city's transit deficit. Now we know that to answer the question, we need to know the price elasticity of demand for bus service. The price elasticity in the typical city is 0.33, meaning that a 10% increase in fares will decrease ridership by about 3.3%.[4] Because demand for bus travel is inelastic, the good news associated with a fare hike (more revenue per rider) will dominate the bad news (fewer riders), and total fare revenue will increase. In other words, an increase in fares will reduce the transit deficit.

What's the connection between antidrug policies and property crimes such as robbery, burglary, and auto theft? The government uses search-and-destroy tactics to restrict the supply of illegal drugs. If this approach succeeds, drugs become scarce and the price of drugs increases. Because the demand for illegal drugs is inelastic, the increase in price will increase total spending on illegal drugs. Many drug addicts support their habits by stealing personal property—robbing people, stealing cars, and burglarizing homes—so the increase in total spending on drugs means that drug addicts will

Table 3.3   Elasticity and Total Revenue

Type of Demand	Value of Price Elasticity of Demand	Change in Quantity Versus Change in Price	Effect of Higher Price on Total Revenue	Effect of Lower Price on Total Revenue
Elastic	Greater than 1.0	Larger percentage change in quantity	Decreases	Increases
Inelastic	Less than 1.0	Smaller percentage change in quantity	Increases	Decreases
Unitary elastic	1.0	Same percentage changes in quantity and price	Does not change	Does not change

commit more property crimes.[5] To support their more expensive drug habits, addicts will commit more burglaries, robberies, and auto thefts.

Economic Detective

The Video Elasticity Mystery

The manager of a video-rental store has asked you to solve a mystery. According to national studies of the video-rental market, the price elasticity of demand for video rentals is 0.8: A 10% increase in price decreases the quantity of videos demanded by about 8%. In other words, the demand for videos is inelastic. Based on this information, the manager of the video store increased her price by 20%, expecting her total revenue to increase. She expected the good news (more money per rental) to dominate the bad news (fewer rentals). When her total revenue decreased instead of increasing, she was puzzled. Your job is to solve this mystery.

The key to solving this mystery is to recognize that the manager can't use the results of a national study to predict the effects of increasing her own price. The national study suggests that if all video stores in the nation increased their prices by 10%, the nationwide quantity of videos demanded would drop by 8%. But when a single video store in a city increases its price, consumers can easily switch to other video stores in the city. As a result, a 10% increase in the price of video rentals at one store will decrease the quantity sold by that store by much more than 8%. The demand facing an individual store is elastic, so an increase in price will decrease total revenue.

TEST Your Understanding

4. Complete the statement: If the price elasticity of demand is 0.6, a 10% increase in price will _____ (fill in with *increase* or *decrease*) the quantity demanded by _____%.

5. If an increase in the price of accordions does not change total revenue from accordion sales, what can we infer about the price elasticity of demand for accordions?

6. Suppose the price elasticity of demand for vanity license plates in the state of Ohio is 2.6. If the state's objective is to maximize its revenue from vanity plates, should it pick a higher price or a lower one?

The Price Elasticity of Supply

Let's look at elasticity on the supply side of the market. The price elasticity of supply measures the responsiveness of producers to changes in price. We compute this elasticity by dividing the percentage change in quantity supplied by the percentage change in price:

$$E_s = \frac{\text{percentage change in quantity supplied}}{\text{percentage change in price}}$$

In Figure 3.2, when the price of milk increases from $2 to $2.20, the quantity supplied increases from 100 million gallons to 120 million gallons. In other words, a 10% increase in price increases the quantity supplied by 20%, so the price elasticity of supply is 2.0:

$$E_s = \frac{\text{percentage change in quantity supplied}}{\text{percentage change in price}} = \frac{20\%}{10\%} = 2.0$$

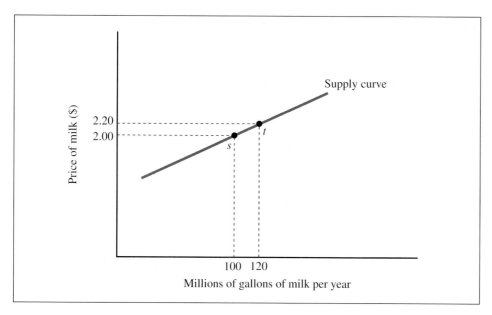

Figure 3.2

Market Supply Curve and Price Elasticity of Supply
A 10% increase in the price of milk (from $2 to $2.20) increases the quantity supplied by 20% (from 100 to 120 million gallons), so the price elasticity of supply is $2.0 = 20\%/10\%$.

Time is an important factor in determining the price elasticity of supply for a product. When the price of a particular product increases, the immediate response is that current producers produce more of the product in their existing production facilities (for example, factories, stores, offices, or restaurants). Although a higher price will certainly induce firms to produce more, the response is limited by the limited capacity of the firms' production facilities. Over time, however, new firms can enter the market and old firms can build new production facilities, so there will be a larger response in the long run. As time passes, supply becomes more elastic because more and more firms have the time to build production facilities and produce more output.

The milk industry provides a good example of the difference between short-run and long-run supply elasticities. The price elasticity of supply over a one-year period is 0.12: If the price of milk increases by 10% and stays there for a year, the quantity of milk supplied will rise by only 1.2%.[6] In the short run, dairy farmers can squeeze a little more output from their existing production facilities. Over a 10-year period, the price elasticity is 2.5: The same 10% rise in price will increase the quantity supplied by 25%. In the long run, dairy farmers can expand existing facilities and build new ones, so in the long run, there is a larger response to a higher price.

We can use the price elasticity of supply to predict the effect of price changes on the quantity supplied. For example, suppose that the elasticity of supply is 0.8 and the price increases by 5%. Rearranging the elasticity formula, we would predict a 4% increase in quantity supplied:

percentage change in quantity supplied = E_s × percentage change in price
percentage change in quantity supplied = $0.80 \times 5\% = 4\%$

As we saw in Chapter 2, many governments establish minimum prices for agricultural products. The higher the minimum price, the larger the quantity supplied, consistent with the law of supply. If we know the price elasticity of supply, we can predict just how much more will be supplied at the higher price. For example, if the minimum price of cheese increases by 10% and the price elasticity is 0.6, the quantity of cheese supplied will rise by 6%:

percentage change in quantity supplied = $0.60 \times 10\% = 6\%$

Predicting Price Changes Using Price Elasticities

When supply or demand changes—when the supply curve or demand curve shifts—we can draw a supply and demand diagram to predict whether the equilibrium price will increase or decrease. In many cases, the simple diagram will show all we need to know about the effects of a change in supply or demand. But what if we want to predict how much a price will increase or decrease? We can use a simple formula to predict the change in the equilibrium price resulting from a change in supply or a change in demand.

In Figure 3.3, an increase in demand shifts the demand curve to the right and increases the equilibrium price. We explained in Chapter 2 that a demand curve shifts as a result of a change in something other than the price of the product—for example, a change in income, tastes, or the price of a related good. When demand increases, the immediate effect is excess demand: At the original price ($2), the quantity demanded exceeds the quantity supplied by 35 million gallons (135 million − 100 million). As the price increases, both consumers and producers help eliminate the excess demand: Consumers buy less (the law of demand), and firms produce more (the law of supply). If both consumers and producers are very responsive to changes in price, it will take a small increase in price to eliminate the excess demand. In other words, an increase in demand will cause a small increase in price if both demand and supply are elastic.

Price-change formula: A formula that shows the percentage change in equilibrium price resulting from a change in demand or supply, given values for the price elasticity of supply and price elasticity of demand.

We can use the following **price-change formula** to predict the change in the equilibrium price resulting from a change in demand. We divide the percentage change in demand by the sum of the price elasticities of supply and demand:

$$\text{percentage change in equilibrium price} = \frac{\text{percentage change in demand}}{E_s + E_d}$$

The numerator is the rightward shift of the demand curve in percentage terms. In Figure 3.3, the initial quantity demanded at a price of $2 is 100 million gallons (shown

Figure 3.3

Increase in Demand Increases the Equilibrium Price

An increase in demand shifts the demand curve to the right, increasing the equilibrium price. In this case, a 35% increase in demand increases the price by 10%. Using the price-change formula, we have 10% = 35%/(2.0 + 1.5).

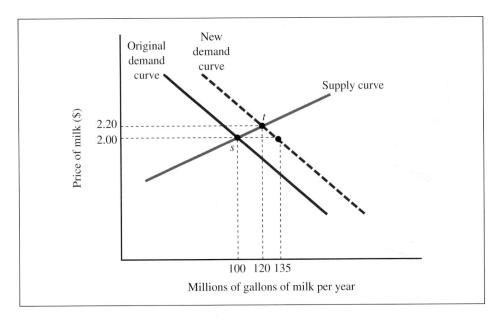

by the initial demand curve), while the new quantity demanded at the same price is 135 million gallons (shown by the new demand curve). The change in demand is 35 percent (35/100). The two price elasticities appear in the denominator, which means that the larger the elasticities, the smaller the increase in price for a given increase in demand. If consumers and producers are very responsive to changes in price (the elasticities are large numbers), excess demand will be eliminated with a relatively small increase in the equilibrium price.

We can use a simple example to see how the price-change formula works. Suppose that demand increases by 35% (the demand curve shifts to the right by 35%). If the supply elasticity is 2.0 and the demand elasticity is 1.5, the predicted change in the equilibrium price is 10%:

$$\text{percentage change in equilibrium price} = \frac{\text{percentage change in demand}}{E_s + E_d}$$

$$= \frac{35\%}{2.0 + 1.5} = 10\%$$

In Figure 3.3, the equilibrium price increases by 10%, from $2 to $2.20. If either demand or supply were less elastic (if either of the elasticity numbers were smaller), the predicted change in price would be larger. For example, if the supply elasticity were 0.25 instead of 2.0, we would predict a 20% increase in price (35%/1.75). The price change is larger because with less elastic supply it takes a larger price hike to eliminate the excess demand.

What about the direction of the price change? We know from Chapter 2 that an increase in demand increases the equilibrium price and a decrease in demand decreases the equilibrium price. Therefore, the percentage change in price is positive when the change in demand is positive (when demand increases and the demand curve shifts to the right), and negative when the change in demand is negative (when demand decreases and the demand curve shifts to the left). For example, suppose the demand for a product decreases by 15% (the demand curve shifts to the left by 15%). If the supply elasticity is 1.0 and the demand elasticity is 0.5, the price-change formula shows that the equilibrium price will decrease by 10%:

$$\text{percentage change in equilibrium price} = \frac{\text{percentage change in demand}}{E_s + E_d}$$

$$= \frac{-15\%}{1.0 + 0.5} = -10\%$$

We can use a slightly different version of the price-change formula to predict the change in the equilibrium price resulting from a change in supply. As explained in Chapter 2, a change in supply results from changes in something other than the price of the product—for example, a change in the cost of labor or raw materials, a change in production technology, or a change in the number of firms. The immediate effect of an increase in supply is excess supply: At the original price, the quantity supplied exceeds the quantity demanded. As the price drops, consumers respond by purchasing more, and producers respond by producing less, so the gap between quantity supplied and demanded narrows. If both consumers and producers are very responsive to changes in price, it will take a small decrease in price to eliminate the excess supply. In other words, an increase in supply will cause a small decrease in price if both demand and supply are elastic.

To predict the change in price resulting from a change in supply, we just substitute supply for demand in the numerator of the price-change formula and add a minus sign. The minus sign indicates that there is a negative relationship between the equilibrium price and supply: When supply increases—when the supply curve shifts to the right—the price drops; when supply decreases, the price rises:

$$\text{percentage change in equilibrium price} = \frac{\text{percentage change in supply}}{E_s + E_d}$$

For example, suppose the supply of milk increases by 10%. If the price elasticity of demand is 0.6 and the price elasticity of supply is 1.4, the equilibrium price will decrease by 5%:

$$\text{percentage change in equilibrium price} = \frac{\text{percentage change in supply}}{E_s + E_d}$$
$$= -\frac{10\%}{1.4 + 0.6} = -5\%$$

TEST Your Understanding

7. Complete the statement: If a 10% increase in price increases the quantity supplied by 15%, the price elasticity of supply is _____.

8. Suppose the price elasticity of a supply of cheese is 0.8. If the price of cheese rises by 20%, by what percentage will the quantity supplied change?

9. Suppose that the elasticity of demand for chewing tobacco is 0.7 and the elasticity of supply is 2.3. If an antichewing campaign decreases the demand for chewing tobacco by 30%, in what direction and by what percentage will the price of chewing tobacco change?

10. Suppose that the elasticity of demand for motel rooms in a town near a ski area is 1.0 and the elasticity of supply is 0.5. If the population of the surrounding area increases by 30%, in what direction and by what percentage will the price of motel rooms change?

Using the Tools

This chapter introduced several new tools of economics, including four different elasticities and a formula that can be used to predict the change in price resulting from a change in supply or demand. Here are some opportunities to use these tools to do your own economic analysis.

1. Projecting Transit Ridership

As a transit planner, you must predict how many people ride commuter trains and how much money is generated from train fares. According to a recent study,[7] the short-run price elasticity of demand for commuter rail is 0.62 and the long-run elasticity is 1.59. The current ridership is 100,000 people per day. Suppose fares increase by 10%.

a. Predict the changes in train ridership over a one-month period (short run) and a five-year period (long run).

b. Over the one-month period, will total revenue increase or decrease? What will happen in the five-year period?

2. Bumper Crops

Your job is to predict the total revenue generated by the nation's corn crop. Last year's crop was 100 million bushels, and the price was $4 per bushel. This year's weather was favorable throughout the country, and this year's crop will be 110 million bushels, or 10% larger than last year's. The price elasticity of demand for corn is 0.5.

a. Predict the effect of the bumper crop on the price of corn, assuming that the entire crop is sold this year.

b. Predict the total revenue from this year's corn crop.

c. Did the favorable weather increase or decrease the total revenue from corn? Why?

3. Washington, D.C., Gas Tax

You are a tax analyst for Washington, D.C., and have been asked to predict how much revenue will be generated by the city's gasoline tax. The initial quantity of gasoline is 100 million gallons per month, and the price elasticity of demand for gasoline in the typical large city is 4.0. The tax, which is $0.10 per gallon, will increase the price of gasoline by 5%.

a. How much revenue will the gasoline tax generate?

b. In 1980, tax analysts in Washington, D.C., based their revenue predictions for a gasoline tax on the elasticity of demand for gasoline in the United States as a whole, which is 1.0. Would you expect the national elasticity to be larger or smaller than the elasticity for the typical large city? Would you expect the analysts to overestimate or underestimate the revenue from the gasoline tax?

4. College Enrollment and Housing

Consider a college town where the initial price of apartments is $400 and the initial quantity is 1,000 apartments. The price elasticity of demand for apartments is 1.0, and the price elasticity of supply of apartments is 0.5.

a. Use supply and demand curves to show the initial equilibrium, and label the equilibrium point *i*.

b. Suppose an increase in college enrollment is expected to increase the demand for apartments in a college town by 15%. Use your graph to show the effects of the increase in demand on the apartment market. Label the new equilibrium point *f*.

c. Predict the effect of the increase in demand on the equilibrium price of apartments.

Summary

This chapter deals with the numbers behind the laws of demand and supply. The law of demand tells us that an increase in the price of a product will decrease the quantity demanded, ceteris paribus. If we know the price elasticity of demand for that good, we can determine just how much less of it will be sold at the higher price. Similarly, if we know the price elasticity of supply for a product, we can determine just how much more of it will be supplied at a higher price. Here are the main points of the chapter.

1. The price elasticity of demand—defined as the percentage change in quantity demanded divided by the percentage change in price—measures the responsiveness of consumers to changes in price.

2. Demand is relatively elastic if there are good substitutes.

3. If demand is elastic, there is a negative relationship between price and total revenue. If demand is inelastic, there is a positive relationship between price and total revenue.

4. The price elasticity of supply—defined as the percentage change in quantity supplied divided by the percentage change in price—measures the responsiveness of producers to changes in price.

5. If we know the elasticities of supply and demand, we can predict the percentage change in price resulting from a change in demand or supply.

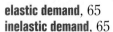

Key Terms

elastic demand, 65   price-change formula, 74   price elasticity of supply, 64
inelastic demand, 65   price elasticity of demand, 64

Problems and Discussion Questions

1. When the price of CDs increased from $10 to $11, the quantity of CDs demanded decreased from 100 to 87. What is the price elasticity of demand for CDs? Is demand elastic or inelastic?

2. Explain why the demand for residential natural gas (gas used for heating, cooling, and cooking) is more elastic than the demand for residential electricity.

3. Would you expect the demand for a specific brand of running shoes to be more elastic or less elastic than the demand for running shoes in general? Why?

4. For each of the following goods, indicate whether you expect demand to be inelastic or elastic, and explain your reasoning: opera, foreign travel, local telephone service, video rentals, and eggs.

5. You observe a positive relationship between the price your store charges for CDs and the total revenue from CDs. Is the demand for your CDs elastic or inelastic?

6. Suppose the price elasticity of demand for a campus film series is 1.4. If the objective of the film society is to maximize its total revenue (price times the number of tickets sold), should it increase or decrease its price?

7. As the head of a state chapter of Mothers Against Drunk Driving (MADD), you are to speak in support of policies that discourage drunk driving. The number of highway deaths among young adults, which is roughly proportional to the group's beer consumption, is initially 100 deaths per year. You

have scheduled a news conference to express your support for a beer tax that will increase the price of beer by 10%. The price elasticity of demand for beer is 1.3. Complete the following statement: "The beer tax will decrease the number of highway deaths among young adults by about _____ per year."

8. When the price of paper increases from $100 to $104 per ton, the quantity supplied increased from 200 to 220 tons per day. What is the price elasticity of supply?

9. Suppose that the government restricts logging to protect an endangered species. The restrictions increase the price of wood products and shift the supply curve for new housing to the left by 4%. The initial price of new housing is $100,000, the elasticity of demand is 1.0, and the elasticity of supply is 3.0. Predict the effect of the logging restriction on the equilibrium price of new housing. Illustrate your answer with a graph that shows the initial point (i) and the new equilibrium (f).

10. Web Exercise. Visit the Web site of Roll Back the Beer Tax (*www.beertax.com*). What are the arguments against beer taxes? Does this site ignore some of the benefits associated with beer taxes? What do you think about beer taxes?

11. Web Exercise. Visit the Web site of the Centers for Disease Control (*www.cdc.gov*). Search for the facts on the price elasticity of demand for cigarettes. How are the estimated elasticities used by policy analysts?

Take It to the Net

We invite you to visit the O'Sullivan/Sheffrin page on the Prentice Hall Web site at: **www.prenhall.com/osullivan/** for additional World Wide Web exercises for this chapter.

Model Answers to Questions

Chapter-Opening Questions

1. A beer tax will increase the price of beer, decreasing beer consumption. Highway deaths are roughly proportional to beer consumption, so the tax will also decrease highway deaths. The actual change in highway deaths depends on the price elasticity of demand for beer.

2. As shown in "Using the Tools: Bumper Crops," a bumper crop of corn decreases the equilibrium price of corn by a relatively large amount because the demand for corn is inelastic. Although corn farmers will sell more bushels, they will receive much less per bushel, so total revenue will drop.

3. If demand is elastic, the firm should lower its price. If demand is inelastic, the firm should raise its price.

4. The policies increase the price of the illegal drug, which increases total spending on the drug because demand is inelastic. If drug addicts support their habits with property crime, they must commit more crime to support their more expensive habits.

5. The percentage change in demand, the price elasticity of supply, and the price elasticity of demand.

Test Your Understanding

1. Quantity, price.

2. 1.2.

3. An increase in the price of tapes will cause some consumers to buy CD players and switch from tapes to CDs, but this takes some time.

4. Decrease, 6.

5. The price elasticity is 1.0 (neither elastic nor inelastic).

6. Demand is elastic, so a decrease in price would increase total revenue.

7. 1.5 = 15%/10%.

8. The quantity supplied will increase by 16%.

9. Using the price-change formula, the price will decrease by 10% = 30%/3.

10. Using the price-change formula, the price will increase by 20% = 30%/1.5.

Using the Tools

1. Projecting Transit Ridership

a. According to the elasticity formula, ridership will decrease by 6.2% in the short run (a loss of 6,200 riders) and 15.9% in the long run (a loss of 15,900 riders).

b. Demand is inelastic in the short run, so total revenue will increase. Demand is elastic in the long run, so total revenue will eventually decrease.

2. Bumper Crops

a. Using the price elasticity formula, to sell an additional 10% of corn, the price must decrease by 20%, to $3.20.

b. Total revenue is 110 million $3.20, or $352 million.

c. Total revenue last year was $400 million, so the bumper crop decreased total revenue. This occurs because demand is inelastic, so the price decreases by a large amount.

3. Washington, D.C., Gas Tax

a. Using the price elasticity formula, the 5% increase in price will decrease the quantity demanded by 20%, from 100 million gallons to 80 million gallons. The revenue is the tax per gallon ($0.10) × the quantity (80 million gallons), or $8 million.

b. They will overestimate the revenue from the tax because they will underestimate the change in quantity demanded by the tax. Specifically, they will predict a quantity of 95 million gallons instead of 80 million gallons and revenue of $9.5 million instead of $8 million. Because it is relatively easy to buy gasoline in a nearby city, the demand for gasoline will be relatively elastic at the city level.

4. College Enrollment and Housing

c. Use the price-change formula to compute the change in the equilibrium price. The price increases by 10% = 15%/(0.50 + 1.0).

Notes

1. Don Fullerton and Thomas Kinnaman, "Household Responses to Pricing Garbage by the Bag," *American Economic Review*, vol. 86, no. 4, 1996, pp. 971–984.

2. Chin-Fun Cling and James Peale Jr., "Income and Price Elasticities," in *Advances in Econometrics Supplement*, edited by Henri Theil (Greenwich, CT: JAI Press, 1989).

3. Henry Saffer and Michael Grossman, "Beer Taxes, the Legal Drinking Age, and Youth Motor Vehicle Fatalities," *Journal of Legal Studies*, vol. 41, June 1987.

4. Kenneth A. Small, *Urban Transportation Economics* (Philadelphia, PA: Harwood Academic Publishers, 1992).

5. L. P. Silverman and N. L. Sprull, "Urban Crime and the Price of Heroin," *Journal of Urban Economics*, vol. 4, 1977, pp. 80–103.

6. Richard Klemme and Jean-Paul Chavas, "The Effects of Changing Milk Price on Milk Supply and National Dairy Herd Size," *Economic Issues*, University of Wisconsin, June 1985.

7. Richard Voith, "The Long Run Elasticity of Demand for Commuter Rail Transportation," *Journal of Urban Economics*, vol. 30, 1991, pp. 360–372.

APPENDIX

Using the Midpoint Formula to Compute Price Elasticity

The midpoint formula (Appendix, Chapter 1) provides a more precise way to compute percentage changes than the formula used in this chapter. Using the midpoint approach, we divide the change in a variable (for example, the change in price) by the average value of the variable (the average price). We can use this approach to compute the price elasticity associated with points *d* and *e* in Figure 3.1.

The percentage change in price equals the change (0.20) divided by the average price ($2.10), or 9.52%:

$$\text{percentage change in price} = \frac{\text{change}}{\text{average value}} = \frac{0.20}{(2.00 + 2.20)/2}$$
$$= \frac{0.20}{2.10} = 0.0952 = 9.52\%$$

The percentage change in quantity equals the change (−15) divided by the average quantity (92.5), or −16.22%:

$$\text{percentage change in quantity} = \frac{\text{change}}{\text{average value}} = \frac{-15}{(100 + 85)/2}$$
$$= \frac{-15}{92.5} = -0.1622 = 16.22\%$$

If we plug these percentage changes into the formula for the price elasticity of demand, the computed price elasticity is 1.7:

$$E_d = \frac{\text{percentage change in demand}}{\text{percentage change in price}} = \frac{16.22}{9.52} = 1.7$$

Why is this elasticity different from the elasticity we computed with the simple approach (1.5)? The midpoint approach measures the percentage changes more precisely, so we get a more precise measure of price elasticity. In this case, the percentage changes are relatively small, so the two elasticity numbers aren't too far apart. If the percentage changes were larger, however, the elasticity numbers generated by the two approaches would be quite different, and it would be wise to use the midpoint approach.

Production and Cost

Consider a nation that regulates entry into the trucking industry, limiting the number of trucking firms to just one. The nation is considering the elimination of these entry restrictions. At a public hearing on the issue, the manager of the regulated trucking firm issued a grim warning to the regulatory authorities. "If you deregulate this market, four firms will enter it, and the average cost of truck freight will at least triple. A single large firm is much more cost-efficient than five small firms. If you want firms in your nation to pay three times as much for their truck freight, go ahead and deregulate this market."

T his chapter is about how production cost varies with the size of a given production facility. Before a nation decides whether to deregulate its trucking industry, for example, it should take a careful look at how the average cost of trucking services varies with the number of trucking firms. Similarly, before a firm builds a computer chip factory, it should compare the production cost per chip in a large factory to the cost per chip in a small one. This chapter also explores how the cost of production varies with the quantity of output produced in a given facility. Before a computer firm decides how many chips to produce in its chip factory, it should take a careful look at the cost of producing different quantities of chips.

In later chapters, we'll use the cost curves discussed in this chapter to explain firms' decisions about whether to enter a market and how much output to produce once they enter. In this chapter, we'll see how to use cost curves to answer the following practical questions:

1. If the government breaks up a large aluminum producer into two smaller firms, by how much will the average cost of producing a given quantity of aluminum increase?
2. Are large hospitals more efficient than smaller hospitals? If so, how much more efficient?
3. Why is the typical short-run average cost curve shaped like the letter *U*, while the typical long-run average cost curve is shaped like the letter *L*?
4. Suppose that one electric utility has three times as many customers as another electric utility. Which utility has a higher unit cost of electricity, and how large is the cost difference?

Introduction

This chapter is about production cost in the short run and long run. Let's start with some definitions of cost and then review the difference between the short run and the long run.

Economic Profit Versus Accounting Profit

Explicit cost: The firm's actual cash payments for its inputs.

Our discussion of the firm's cost is based on the notion of economic cost. You may be surprised to hear that accountants and economists differ in the way they compute the cost of production. As we see in Table 4.1, a firm's total accounting cost equals the firm's **explicit cost**, defined as actual cash payments for inputs. For example, if the firm spends a total of $60,000 per year on labor, materials, rent, and machinery, its explicit cost would be $60,000, and this is the firm's total accounting cost.

The key principle underlying the computation of economic cost is the principle of opportunity cost.

Principle of Opportunity Cost

The opportunity cost of something is what you sacrifice to get it.

Implicit cost: The opportunity cost of nonpurchased inputs.

The firm's total economic cost equals explicit cost plus **implicit cost**. The firm's implicit cost is defined as the opportunity cost of nonpurchased inputs such as the entrepreneur's time or money.

- Opportunity cost of the entrepreneur's time. An entrepreneur has less time to pursue other activities, and economic cost includes the opportunity cost of the time

Table 4.1 Accounting Versus Economic Cost

	Accounting Approach	Economic Approach
Explicit cost (purchased inputs)	$60,000	$ 60,000
Implicit: opportunity cost of entrepreneur's time	30,000	
Implicit: opportunity cost of funds	10,000	
Total cost	$60,000	$100,000

spent running the firm. If an entrepreneur could earn $30,000 per year in another job, the opportunity cost of his or her time is $30,000 per year.

- Opportunity cost of funds. Many entrepreneurs use their own funds to set up and run their businesses, and economic cost includes the opportunity cost of these funds. If an entrepreneur starts a business with some money withdrawn from his or her bank account, sacrificing $10,000 of interest income per year, the opportunity cost of the funds invested in the firm is $10,000 per year.

In this case, the implicit cost is $40,000 per year, and the **economic cost**—defined as the sum of the explicit and implicit cost—is $100,000. The economic cost is higher because the economist includes implicit cost, but the accountant does not. When we refer to the firm's production cost, we mean the economic cost of production, including both implicit and explicit cost.

Economic cost: Explicit cost plus implicit cost.

Short-Run Versus Long-Run Decisions

In later chapters, we'll see how firms use their cost curves to make two types of decisions:

1. A firm that already has a production facility must decide how much output to produce in that facility. This is a **short-run** decision because one of the factors of production (the facility) is fixed.
2. A firm that has decided to enter a market must decide how large a facility to build. Such a firm is making a **long-run** decision because none of the factors of production is fixed. The firm starts from scratch and can choose a production facility of any size.

Short run: A period of time over which one or more factors of production are fixed.

Long run: A period of time long enough that a firm can change all factors of production.

In most cases, the long run is the time required for a firm to build a production facility and start producing output. For example, if it takes a firm in the garden tool business one year to build a factory, the long run for that firm is one year, and the short run is any time less than a year. The long run varies across industries. If it takes one day to get a hot-dog cart and start selling hot dogs, the long run is a day. In contrast, it takes several years to design and build a computer chip factory, so the long run in that industry is several years.

Production and Cost in the Short Run

The short run is defined as a period of time over which at least one input to the production process is fixed. For most firms, the fixed input is its production facility, for example, a factory, store, office, or farm. In the short run, the firm cannot modify its production facility or build a new facility.

As we saw in Chapter 1, the key principle for short-run decision making is the principle of diminishing returns.

Principle of Diminishing Returns

Suppose that output is produced with two or more inputs and we increase one input while holding the other inputs fixed. Beyond some point—called the point of diminishing returns—output will increase at a decreasing rate.

A pizzeria experiences diminishing returns because its workers share a fixed production facility: a pizza oven. When the pizzeria adds a worker, each worker becomes less productive because he or she works with a smaller piece of the production facility. As the pizzeria adds more and more workers, output increases at a decreasing rate, meaning the marginal product of labor decreases.

Production and Marginal Product

Consider a firm that produces lawn rakes in a factory equipped with machines and other equipment. The firm's variable input is labor, and the firm's fixed input is its production facility, the equipped factory. As the number of workers increases—and the production facility doesn't change—what happens to the quantity of rakes produced?

Table 4.2 shows the hypothetical relationship between the number of workers and the number of rakes produced per minute. The firm needs 8 workers to produce 1 rake per minute, 12 workers to produce 2 rakes per minute, and so on up to 130 workers to produce 10 rakes per minute. Figure 4.1 uses the numbers in Table 4.2 to show the firm's **total product curve**, the relationship between the quantity of labor and the quantity of output produced. Let's look at two different parts of the total product curve, starting with the part between points *d* and *e*.

The shape of the total product curve between points *d* and *e* is explained by diminishing returns. As the number of workers increases beyond 15, the curve becomes flatter; that is, output increases at a decreasing rate. The rake workers share the factory and

Total product curve: A curve showing the relationship between the quantity of labor and the quantity of output produced.

Table 4.2   Labor Input and Output

Output: Rakes per Minute	Labor: Number of Workers
0	0
1	8
2	12
3	15
4	20
5	27
6	36
7	48
8	65
9	90
10	130

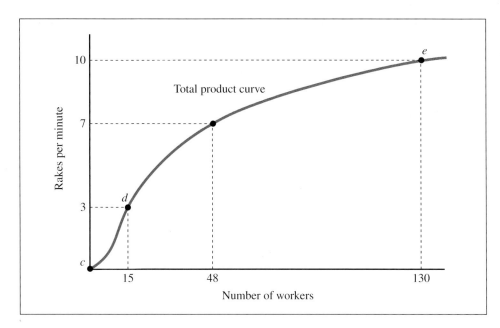

Figure 4.1

Total Product Curve
The total product curve shows the relationship between the quantity of labor and the quantity of output, given a fixed production facility. For the first 15 workers, output increases at an increasing rate: a result of labor specialization. Point *d* is the point of diminishing returns. Beyond this point, adding workers increases output at a decreasing rate.

all the machinery for making rakes, and as the number of workers increases, each worker has a smaller share of the facility. Eventually, adding a worker makes each worker in the factory less productive, so the marginal product of labor decreases and the total product curve becomes flatter. In Figure 4.1, this happens at point *d*, the point of diminishing returns.

To illustrate the notion of diminishing returns, consider the amounts of labor required to produce between three and five rakes per minute. In Table 4.2, to increase output from three to four rakes, the firm must increase its workforce from 15 to 20 workers, hiring five additional workers. To increase output from four to five rakes per minute, the firm must increase its workforce from 20 to 27 workers, hiring seven additional workers. Because of diminishing returns resulting from sharing the production facility, it takes progressively more workers to increase output by one more rake.

What about the total product curve between points *c* and *d*? For a small workforce and a small quantity of output, the slope of the curve increases as the number of workers increases. In other words, the marginal product of labor increases for the first 15 workers. Although this may seem to be contrary to the principle of diminishing returns, remember that the principle says that *eventually* output will increase at a decreasing rate. So what's different when the firm produces a small quantity of output?

The difference is the possibility of labor specialization. Suppose there are 15 distinct tasks associated with making a rake. If the firm hires only eight workers, some of the workers will be forced to perform more than one of these tasks. Together, the eight workers will produce one rake per minute. Adding four more workers would allow some workers to specialize, each doing one of the 15 tasks. A worker with a single task will spend less time switching between tasks and also will become more skillful in the assigned task. In other words, specialization increases output per worker, so the firm can increase output from one to two rakes by adding only four workers. Adding three more workers—bringing the workforce to 15 workers—allows each worker to specialize in a single task, and increases output from two to three rakes per minute. In this example, there are benefits from specialization for the first 15 workers, so the firm's marginal product increases for the first 15 workers.

Short-Run Total Cost and Short-Run Marginal Cost

Now that we know about the relationship between the quantities of labor and output, we're ready to introduce several of the firm's short-run cost curves. Table 4.3 shows some hypothetical cost data for the rake producer whose total product curve is shown in Figure 4.2. The question is, How does the cost of producing rakes vary as the number of rakes produced *per minute* increases?

There are two types of production cost in the short run: fixed cost and variable cost.

Fixed cost (FC): Cost that does not depend on the quantity produced.

1. **Fixed cost (FC)** is defined as the cost that does not vary with the quantity produced. In our example, the fixed cost is the cost of the rake factory, including the cost of the building and all the machinery and equipment inside. We're interested not in the total output of the rake factory over its 30-year life but in its output per minute. Therefore, we must translate the one-time $100 million expense for the factory into a cost per minute—for example, $36 per minute. As shown in the second column in Table 4.3, the fixed cost is $36 per minute, regardless of how much output is produced.

Total variable cost (TVC): Cost that varies as the firm changes its output.

2. Variable cost is defined as a cost that varies with the quantity produced. For example, to produce more rakes, the firm must hire more workers. If we assume that the firm pays each of its workers $1 per minute, the **total variable cost (TVC)** per minute is the same as the number of workers, $8 for one rake, $12 for two rakes, and so on. To simplify matters, we'll ignore the cost of the materials needed to make rakes.

Short-run total cost (STC): The total cost of production in the short run, when one or more inputs (for example, the production facility) is fixed; equal to fixed cost plus variable cost.

The **short-run total cost (STC)** equals the sum of fixed and variable costs. Figure 4.2 shows the three cost curves. The horizontal line shows the fixed cost of $36, and the lower of the two positively sloped curves shows the total variable cost. The third curve shows short-run total cost as the sum of fixed cost and total variable cost. The vertical distance between the STC curve and the TVC curve equals the firm's fixed cost.

Table 4.3 Short-Run Production Costs

(1) Output: Rakes per Minute	(2) Fixed Cost (FC)	(3) Total Variable Cost (TVC)	(4) Short-Run Total Cost (STC)	(5) Short-Run Marginal Cost (SMC)	(6) Average Fixed Cost (AFC)	(7) Short-Run Average Variable Cost (SAVC)	(8) Short-Run Average Total Cost (SATC)
0	36	0	36	—	—	—	—
1	36	8	44	8.00	36.00	8.00	44.00
2	36	12	48	4.00	18.00	6.00	24.00
3	36	15	51	3.00	12.00	5.00	17.00
4	36	20	56	5.00	9.00	5.00	14.00
5	36	27	63	7.00	7.20	5.40	12.60
6	36	36	72	9.00	6.00	6.00	12.00
7	36	48	84	12.00	5.14	6.86	12.00
8	36	65	101	17.00	4.50	8.13	12.63
9	36	90	126	25.00	4.00	10.00	14.00
10	36	130	166	40.00	3.60	13.00	16.60

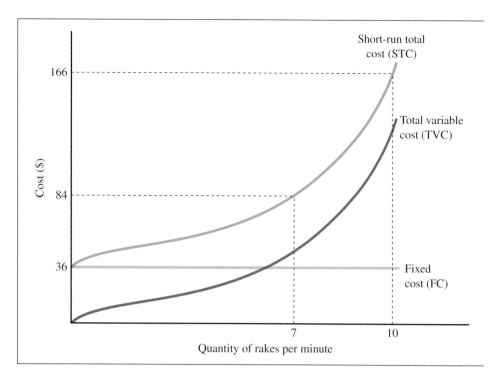

Figure 4.2
Short-Run Cost: Fixed Cost, Variable Cost, and Total Cost
The short-run total cost curve shows the relationship between the quantity of output and production costs given a fixed production facility. Short-run total cost equals fixed cost (the cost that does not vary with the quantity produced) plus total variable cost (the cost that varies with the quantity produced).

Economists like to think on the margin, and marginal cost is part of marginal thinking. The **short-run marginal cost (SMC)** is defined as the change in short-run total cost resulting from producing one more unit of the good. As shown in the fourth column of Table 4.3, if the firm decides to produce just one rake, its short-run total cost increases from $36 (the fixed cost) to $44, so the marginal cost of the first rake is $8. For the first three rakes, the marginal cost gets smaller and smaller, a result of the benefits of labor specialization. The firm needs eight workers to produce the first rake (a marginal cost of $8), but only four more workers to produce the second rake (marginal cost = $4), and only three more workers to produce the third rake. We saw earlier that specialization leads to increasing marginal productivity; now we know that it also leads to decreasing marginal cost. In Figure 4.3, the short-run marginal cost curve is negatively sloped for the first three rakes.

Starting with the fourth rake, the short-run marginal cost increases as the number of rakes increases, a result of diminishing returns. Once the benefits of labor specialization are exhausted, diminishing returns set in, and it takes more and more workers to increase output by one rake. To increase output from three to four rakes, the firm needs five additional workers (marginal cost = $5, shown by point *c*). To increase output from four to five rakes, the firm needs seven additional workers (marginal cost = $7, shown by point *d*). Because the firm requires more and more workers to increase production by one unit, the marginal cost of production increases. In Table 4.3 and Figure 4.3, marginal cost increases to $12 for the seventh rake, to $25 for the ninth rake, and so on.

Our example has two assumptions that simplify the calculations of marginal cost. First, we ignore the material cost of producing rakes (for example, the cost of plastic). Second, Table 4.3 shows output and costs in increments of one rake, so we can read the marginal cost by looking at two successive rows in the table. In more realistic cases, we can use a simple formula to compute marginal cost:

short-run marginal cost = change in total cost/change in quantity produced

Short-run marginal cost (SMC): The change in short-run total cost resulting from producing one more unit of the good.

Figure 4.3

Short-Run Marginal Cost and Short-Run Average Cost

The positively sloped portion of the short-run marginal cost (SMC) curve results from diminishing returns. The short-run average total cost (SATC) curve is U shaped, a result of spreading fixed cost (which pulls down the average total cost) and diminishing returns (which pulls up the average total cost). The SMC curve intersects each average cost (SAVC and SATC) curve at the minimum point of the average curve.

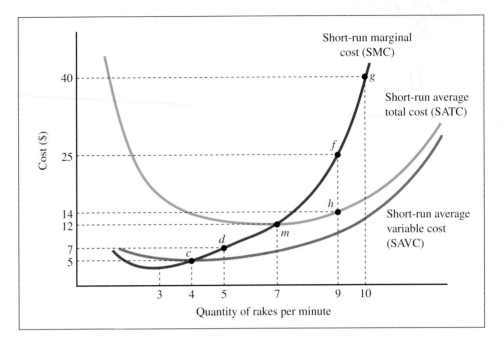

For example, suppose the total cost of producing 4 rakes is $61 (including $5 for materials) and the total cost of producing 7 units is $91 (including $7 for materials). In this case, the marginal cost (the change in total cost per unit change in quantity produced) in this interval is, on average, $10:

$$\text{short-run marginal cost} = (\$91 - \$61)/3 \text{ rakes} = \$30/3 \text{ rakes} = \$10$$

Short-Run Average Cost Curves

It will often be useful to express a firm's cost of production as average cost. There are three types of short-run average cost:

Average fixed cost (AFC): Fixed cost divided by the quantity produced.

Short-run average variable cost (SAVC): Total variable cost divided by the quantity produced.

Short-run average total cost (SATC): Short-run total cost divided by the quantity of output; equal to AFC plus SAVC.

1. **Average fixed cost (AFC):** fixed cost divided by the quantity produced.
2. **Short-run average variable cost (SAVC):** total variable cost divided by the quantity produced.
3. **Short-run average total cost (SATC):** total cost divided by the quantity produced; equal to the sum of AFC and SAVC.

The last three columns of Table 4.3 show these three types of average cost for our rake producer. To compute AFC, we simply divide the fixed cost by the quantity of rakes produced. In our example, AFC decreases from $36 per rake, to $18 per rake for two rakes, and so on. As output increases, the fixed cost ($36) is spread over more units, so AFC decreases.

To compute SAVC, we divide the total variable cost by the quantity of rakes produced. In Figure 4.3, the SAVC curve is negatively sloped for small quantities of output but positively sloped for larger quantities. The negative slope reflects the benefits of labor specialization when the firm produces a small quantity of output. Adding workers to a small workforce makes workers more productive on average, so the average cost of labor per rake drops. The SAVC curve is positively sloped for large quantities of output, a result of diminishing returns: Adding more workers to a large workforce makes workers less productive on average, so the average cost of labor per rake rises.

Why is the SATC curve shaped like a U? At very small quantities of output, the curve is negatively sloped, a result of two forces that work together to pull SATC down as output increases:

1. **Spreading the fixed cost.** For small quantities of output, a one-unit increase in output reduces AFC by a large amount because the fixed cost is pretty "thick," being spread over just a few units of output. For example, going from one rake to two rakes decreases AFC from $36 per rake to $18 per rake.

2. **Labor specialization.** For small quantities of output, SAVC decreases as output increases, a result of labor specialization that increases worker productivity.

These two forces both pull SATC downward as output increases, so the curve is negatively sloped for small quantities of output.

What happens once the firm reaches the point at which the benefits of labor specialization are exhausted? As the firm continues to increase output, the average variable cost increases, a result of diminishing returns. There is a tug-of-war between two forces; the spreading of fixed cost continues to pull SATC down, while diminishing returns and rising SAVC pushes SATC up. In other words, the SATC curve could be negatively sloped or positively sloped, depending on the relative strengths of the two forces.

The outcome of the tug-of-war depends on the quantity produced, giving the SATC curve its U shape.

- **Intermediate quantities of output** (between three and seven rakes per minute). The tug-of-war is won by the spreading of fixed cost, so SATC decreases as output increases. In this case, the decrease in AFC is larger than the increase in SAVC largely because the fixed cost isn't too "thin" and diminishing returns are not too strong. As a result, short-run average total cost decreases as output increases.

- **Large quantities of output** (eight rakes per minute or more). The tug-of-war is won by diminishing returns and rising SAVC, so SATC increases as output increases. In this case, the reductions in AFC are relatively small because the fixed cost is so "thin" already, and diminishing returns are severe. As a result, short-run average total cost increases as output increases.

The Relationship Between Marginal and Average Curves

Figure 4.3 shows the relationship between short-run marginal cost and short-run average total cost. Whenever the marginal cost is less than the average total cost (for fewer than seven rakes), the average total cost is falling. In contrast, whenever the marginal cost exceeds the average total cost (for more than seven rakes), the average total cost is rising. Finally, when the marginal cost equals the average total cost, the average cost is neither rising nor falling (for seven rakes). In other words, the marginal cost curve intersects the short-run average total cost curve at its minimum point.

We can use some simple logic to explain the relationship between average cost and marginal cost. Suppose that you start the semester with a cumulative grade-point average (GPA) of 3.0 (a B average) and enroll in a single course this semester—a history course. If you receive a grade of C in history (2.0 for computing your GPA), your GPA will drop below 3.0. Your GPA decreases because the grade in the "marginal" course (the history course) is less than the "average" grade (the starting GPA), so the marginal grade pulls down your GPA. Suppose that you take an economics class the following semester and get a grade of A (4.0 for computing your GPA). In this case, your GPA will increase because the marginal grade (in economics) is higher than your average (your GPA), so the marginal grade pushes up your GPA. If you were to take a course the following semester and your grade in the course is the same as your GPA, your GPA wouldn't change. To summarize, whenever the marginal grade is less than the average grade, the average will fall; whenever the marginal grade exceeds the average grade, the average will rise; whenever the marginal grade equals the average grade, the average will not change.

In Figure 4.3, the SATC curve is negatively sloped for the first six rakes. Using the arithmetic of averages, the fact that the average cost is decreasing means that the marginal cost is lower than the average cost: The lower marginal cost pulls down the average. In contrast, the SATC curve is positively sloped for eight or more rakes, which means that the marginal cost exceeds the average total cost: The higher marginal cost pulls up the average. If the average total cost is neither increasing nor decreasing, the marginal cost must equal the average total cost. In Figure 4.3, this happens at point m, the minimum point of the SATC curve. Using the same logic, the marginal cost equals the average variable cost at the minimum point of the SAVC curve (point c).

What is the relationship between average variable cost and average total cost? The total cost is the sum of fixed cost and variable cost, so the difference between the average total cost and the average variable cost is the average fixed cost. As output increases, the average fixed cost decreases because the fixed cost is spread over more and more rakes, decreasing the vertical distance between average total cost and average variable cost. In Figure 4.3, as output increases, the vertical distance between SAVC and SATC decreases.

Economic Detective

The Cost of Pencils

Mr. Big wants to enter the pencil-making business. He gathered some information from two existing pencil manufacturers: Sharp, Inc., and Pointy, Inc. The two firms have identical production facilities—identical factories and equipment. The two firms also pay the same wage to their workers and pay the same prices for materials. Although Sharp produces 1,000 pencils per minute and Pointy produces 2,000 per minute, each firm has a short-run average total cost of $0.10 per pencil. After building a production facility identical to the ones used by Sharp and Pointy, Mr. Big hired enough workers and bought enough materials to produce 2,500 pencils per minute. Based on the experience of Sharp and Pointy, he expected to produce at an average cost of $0.10 per pencil. After all, he thought, that's the average cost for 1,000 pencils and 2,000 pencils, so it should also be the average cost for 2,500 pencils. Much to his dismay, his average cost was $0.14 per pencil.

We can solve this mystery with a quick look at a typical short-run average total cost curve. In Figure 4.4, the U-shaped SATC curve shows an average cost of $0.10 for both Sharp (1,000 pencils) and Pointy (2,000 pencils). Sharp produces on the negatively sloped portion of the average cost curve, while Pointy produces on the positively sloped portion. In contrast, Mr. Big produces 2,500 pencils at an average cost of $0.14. Mr. Big thought that because Sharp and Pointy had the same average cost, the average cost curve must be horizontal. He didn't realize that the short-run average cost curve is U shaped. Along a U-shaped curve, it is possible to have the same average cost for two different quantities of output. Unfortunately for Mr. Big, it's not possible to have the same average cost for three different quantities.

TEST Your Understanding

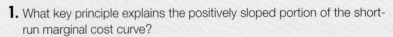

1. What key principle explains the positively sloped portion of the short-run marginal cost curve?

2. Comment on the following statement: "We're planning on increasing the output of our rubber-chicken factory by 10%. It's obvious that our short-run average total cost will decrease because we'll spread our fixed costs over more chickens."

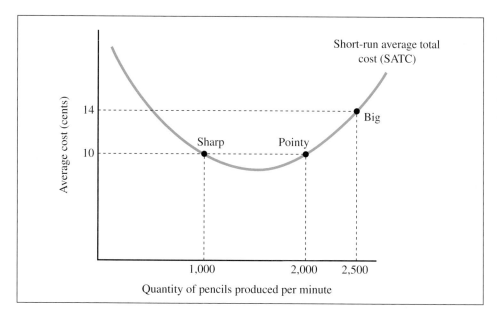

Figure 4.4
The Cost Mystery
Because the short-run average total cost curve is U shaped, it is possible to have the same short-run average cost at two—but not three—different quantities of output.

3. According to the foreman in your chair factory, the short-run marginal cost of chairs is less than the short-run average cost. If you increase your output of chairs, will your short-run average cost increase or decrease?

4. Complete the statement with *average* or *marginal*: The short-run marginal cost curve intersects the short-run average cost curve at the minimum point of the _____ cost curve.

Production and Cost in the Long Run

Up to this point, we've been exploring short-run cost curves, which show the cost of producing different quantities of output in a given production facility. Let's turn next to long-run cost curves, which show the production costs in facilities of different sizes. The long run is defined as the period of time over which a firm is perfectly flexible in its choice of all inputs. In the long run, a firm can build a new production facility (factory, store, office, or restaurant) or modify an existing facility.

The key difference between the short run and the long run is that there are no diminishing returns in the long run. Remember that diminishing returns occur because workers share a fixed production facility, so the more workers in the facility, the smaller the piece of the facility available for each worker. In the long run, the firm can expand its production facility as its workforce grows.

Expansion and Replication

Continuing the example of rake production, consider a rake producer that has decided to replace its existing factory with a new one. The firm has been producing seven rakes per minute at a total cost of $84 per minute, or an average cost of $12 per rake. If the firm wants to produce twice as much output per minute in its new facility, what should it do?

One possibility is to simply double the original operation. The firm could build two factories that are identical to the original factory and hire two workforces, each identical to the original workforce. In this case, the firm's total cost will double with its output: Each new factory will produce 7 rakes per minute at a cost of $84 per minute, so the firm

Table 4.4 Long-Run Costs: Total and Average Cost

Output: Rakes per Minute	Long-Run Total Cost	Long-Run Average Cost
3.5	$ 70	$20
7	$ 84	$12
14	$168	$12
28	$336	$12

Long-run total cost: The total cost of production in the long run when a firm is perfectly flexible in its choice of all inputs and can choose a production facility of any size.

Long-run average cost of production (LAC): Long-run total cost divided by the quantity of output produced.

can produce a total of 14 rakes per minute at twice the cost, $168 per minute. The firm's **long-run total cost** is defined as the total cost of production when the firm is perfectly flexible in its choice of all inputs and can choose a production facility of any size. Table 4.4 shows the firm's long-run total cost for several different quantities, including 7, 14, and 28 rakes per minute. The replication process means that the long-run total cost increases proportionately with the quantity produced, from $84 for 7 rakes per minute to $168 for 14 rakes per minute to $336 for 28 rakes per minute.

The firm's **long-run average cost of production (LAC)** is defined as long-run total cost divided by the quantity of output produced. In Table 4.4, the long-run average cost is $12 per rake for seven or more rakes per minute. Because long-run total cost is proportional to the quantity produced, the long-run average cost doesn't change as output increases. In Figure 4.5, the long-run average cost curve is horizontal for seven or more rakes per minute.

For a firm that wants to double its output in the long run, replication is one option. Another possibility is to build a single larger factory, one that can produce the target quantity of output at a lower cost than would be possible by simply building two factories identical to the original. If so, the long-run average cost of producing the larger quantity (for example, 14 rakes per minute) would be less than $12.

Figure 4.5
Long-Run Average Cost Curve
The long-run average cost curve is negatively sloped for up to seven rakes per minute, a result of indivisible inputs and the effects of labor specialization. If the firm replicates the operation that produces seven rakes per minute, the long-run average cost curve will be horizontal beyond seven rakes per minute.

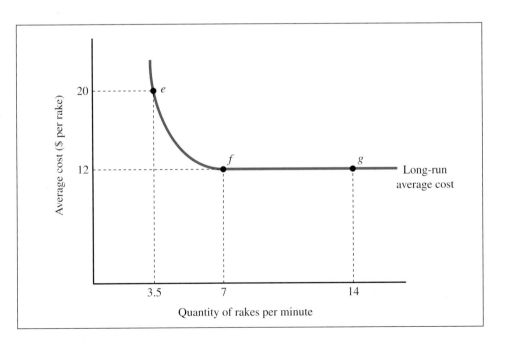

Decrease in Output and Indivisible Inputs

Suppose that instead of expanding its operation, a rake producer wants to reduce its operation, producing half as many rakes per minute as it did in its original operation. Could the firm simply hire half as many workers, build a factory with half the floor area, and fill the factory with half as much machinery and equipment? Perhaps, but there may be a problem with indivisible inputs.

An input is **indivisible** if it cannot be scaled down to produce a smaller quantity of output. For example, firms use industrial molds to make multiple copies of the same item, and a firm needs a mold regardless of how many copies it produces. Suppose the rake factory uses an industrial mold to shape plastic into the fan-shaped end of the rake. The firm needs the standard mold, regardless of how many rakes it produces, so cutting back from 7 rakes per minute to 3.5 rakes per minute won't affect the cost of the mold; cutting output in half won't cut the firm's long-run total costs in half.

Table 4.4 shows the implications of indivisible inputs for total and average cost. In the first row, the long-run total cost of producing 3.5 rakes per minute is $70, compared to $84 for 7 rakes per minute. That means the long-run average cost of 3.5 rakes is $20 per rake ($70/3.5), compared to $12 per rake for 7 rakes per minute. In Figure 4.5, the long-run average cost is negatively sloped between points e and f. In general, if there are indivisible inputs, the long-run average total cost curve will be negatively sloped.

Most production processes have at least one indivisible input. Here are some other examples of firms and their indivisible inputs:

- A railroad company providing freight service between two cities must lay a set of tracks between them. The company cannot scale down the tracks by laying a half set of tracks (a single rail).

- A cable TV firm uses a cable running throughout its territory.

- A computer chip factory uses "clean rooms" and complex machines and testing equipment.

Indivisible input: An input that cannot be scaled down to produce a smaller quantity of output.

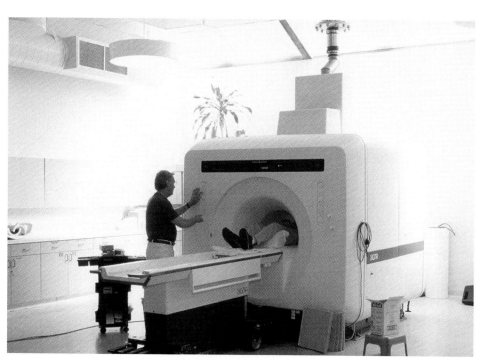

The production of many goods and services involves indivisible inputs, such as this imaging machine for medical diagnosis.

- A shipping firm uses a large ship to carry TV sets from Japan to the United States.
- A steel producer uses a large blast furnace.
- A hospital uses imaging machines (for X rays, CAT scans, and MRIs).
- A pizzeria uses a pizza oven.

These indivisible inputs cannot be scaled down to produce a smaller quantity of output. For example, it is impractical to produce a small quantity of steel in a factory with a small blast furnace, just as it is impractical to transport a single TV set across the ocean in a rowboat. For another example of indivisible inputs, read "A Closer Look: Indivisible Inputs and the Cost of Fake Killer Whales."

Decrease in Output and Labor Specialization

As we saw earlier in the chapter, labor specialization increases productivity and decreases cost. A second reason for higher average long-run costs in a smaller operation is that labor will be less specialized in the small operation. As the number of workers decreases, each worker will be forced to take on more production tasks. Labor productivity will be lower because workers spend more time switching between tasks and will be less proficient because they have less experience at each task. The workers in the smaller rake firm will be less specialized and, thus, less productive, so the workforce required to produce 3.5 rakes per minute will be more than half the workforce required to produce 7 rakes per minute. When the firm cuts back to only 3.5 rakes per minute, the firm's labor costs will not be cut in half, so the long-run average cost will increase to some amount greater than $12.

A CLOSER LOOK   INDIVISIBLE INPUTS AND THE COST OF FAKE KILLER WHALES

Sea lions off the Washington coast eat steelhead and other fish, depleting some species threatened with extinction and decreasing the harvest of the commercial fishing industry. Rick Funk, a plastics manufacturer, thinks that a variation on the scarecrow would solve the sea lion problem. Killer whales love to eat sea lions, and Funk says that he could build a life-sized fiberglass killer whale, mount it on a rail like a roller coaster, and then send the whale diving through the water to scare off the sea lions. According to Funk, it would cost about $16,000 to make the first whale. Once the mold is made, however, each additional whale would cost an additional $5,000: It would cost a total of $21,000 for two whales, $26,000 for three whales, and so on.

This little story illustrates the effects of indivisible inputs on the firm's cost curves. The cost of the first whale ($16,000) includes the cost of the mold (the indivisible input). Once the firm has the mold, the additional cost for each whale is only $5,000, so the average cost per whale decreases as the number of whales increases.

How much would it cost to make fake killer whales to scare away sea lions that feast on steelhead and other fish?

Source: Sandi Doughton, "Killer Whale Latest Idea on Sea Lions," *The Oregonian*, January 7, 1995.

Two centuries ago, Adam Smith used the making of sewing pins to illustrate the benefits from specialization.[1]

> *A workman . . . could scarce, perhaps with his utmost industry, make one pin a day, and certainly could not make twenty. But the way in which this business is now carried on . . . one man draws out the wire, another straightens it, a third cuts it, a fourth points it, a fifth grinds the top for receiving the head; to make the head requires two or three distinct operations. . . . The . . . making of a pin is, in this manner, divided into about eighteen distinct operations. . . . I have seen a small manufactory of this kind where ten men . . . make among them . . . upward of forty eight thousand pins in a day.*

The idea of specialization is summarized in the old saying that a person who is a jack of all trades is a master of none. In a small operation, each worker is a jack of many tasks and is not very productive at any particular one. In a large operation, each worker concentrates on just a few tasks and becomes a master at them.

Economies of Scale

A firm experiences **economies of scale** if an increase in the quantity produced decreases the long-run average production cost. When there are economies of scale, the long-run average cost curve is negatively sloped. In Figure 4.5, the rake producer experiences economies of scale between points *e* and *f*. For example, at point *e*, the long-run average cost of producing 3.5 rakes per minute is $20, compared to $12 for 7 rakes per minute (point *f*). An increase in output from 3.5 to 7 rakes per minute decreases the long-run average cost of production, so there are some economies (that is, cost savings) associated with scaling up the firm's operation. The economies of scale result from indivisible inputs and the benefits from labor specialization.

Recent technological innovations have decreased the cost of producing electricity from the wind, leading to the development of wind farms. There are scale economies in the production of electricity from wind because although large wind turbines are more costly than small ones, the higher cost is somewhat offset by greater generating capacity. For the details, read "A Closer Look: Scale Economies in Wind Power."

Economies of scale: A situation in which an increase in the quantity produced decreases the long-run average cost of production.

Actual Long-Run Average Cost Curves

What does the typical long-run average cost curve look like? Figures 4.6 through 4.9 show the actual long-run average cost curves for several products: electricity generation, aluminum production, truck freight, and hospital services. Each long-run average cost curve is negatively sloped for small quantities of output and relatively flat (almost horizontal) over a large range of output. In addition, each curve has a slight positive slope for large quantities of output. In other words, these curves are L shaped. Other studies suggest that the long-run cost curves of a wide variety of goods and services have the same shape.[2]

Why is the typical long-run average cost curve L shaped? The average cost curves are negatively sloped for small quantities of output because there are economies of scale resulting from indivisible inputs and labor specialization. The long-run average cost curves are horizontal over a wide range of output because once a firm reaches a certain scale, long-run total cost increases proportionally with output, reflecting the ability to increase inputs and outputs proportionally.

SCALE ECONOMIES IN WIND POWER

There are scale economies in the production of electricity from wind because the cost of purchasing, installing, and maintaining a wind turbine increases less than proportionately with the generating capacity of the turbine. This table shows the various costs of a small turbine (150-kilowatt capacity) and a large turbine (600-kilowatt capacity), each with an assumed lifetime of 20 years.

Costs of Wind Turbines

	Small Turbine (150 kilowatt)	Large Turbine (600 kilowatt)
Purchase price of turbine	$150,000	$420,000
Installation cost	$100,000	$100,000
Operating and maintenance cost	$75,000	$126,000
Total cost	$325,000	$646,000
Electricity generated (kilowatt-hours)	5 million	20 million
Average cost (per kilowatt-hour)	$0.065	$0.032

The large turbine has four times the generation capacity, but its purchase price is less than three times as large, its installation cost is the same, and its operating and maintenance costs are less than twice as large. Under typical wind conditions, the large turbine would produce about 20 million kilowatt-hours over its lifetime, compared to 5 million kilowatt-hours for the smaller turbine. The average cost per kilowatt-hour is $0.032 for the large turbine, compared to $0.065 for the small turbine.

Figure 4.6
Long-Run Average Cost Curve for Electricity Generation

Source: Laurits Christensen and William H. Greene, "Economies of Scale in U.S. Electric Power Generation," *Journal of Political Economy*, vol. 84, 1976, pp. 655–676. Reprinted by permission of The University of Chicago Press.

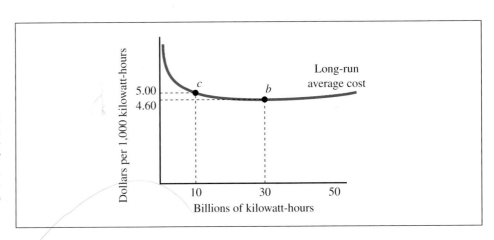

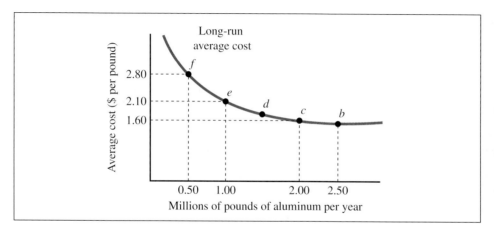

Figure 4.7

Long-Run Average Cost Curve for Aluminum Production

Source: Joel P. Clark and Merton C. Flemings, "Advanced Materials and the Economy," *Scientific American*, vol. 255, October 1986, pp. 51–60. Copyright © 1986 by Scientific American, Inc. All rights reserved.

Minimum Efficient Scale

One way to quantify the extent of scale economies in the production of a particular good is to determine the minimum efficient scale for producing the good. The **minimum efficient scale** is defined as the output at which scale economies are exhausted. In graphical terms, the minimum efficient scale is the quantity at which the long-run average cost curve becomes horizontal, for example, point *f* in Figure 4.5. If a firm starts out with a quantity of output below the minimum efficient scale, an increase in output will decrease its long-run average cost. Once the minimum efficient scale has been reached, an increase in output no longer decreases the long-run average cost.

> **Minimum efficient scale:** The output at which scale economies are exhausted.

Economists have estimated the minimum efficient scale for various industries. In Britain, the minimum efficient scale is 1 million tons of sulfuric acid per year (about 30% of the British market), 9 million tons for steel (about 33% of the British market), 10 million tons of oil per year (10% of the British market), and 300,000 tons of ethylene per year (9% of the British market).[3] In the United States, the minimum efficient scale for automobiles is between 200,000 and 400,000 autos per year.[4] This means that a production facility serving between 3% and 6% of the U.S. market would be large enough to fully exploit the economies of scale in auto production.

The possibility of economies of scale provides one reason why two companies may consider merging into one. There may be cost savings from using production facilities more efficiently, as well as savings in operating cost from combining the purchases of inputs and coordinating shipping operations.

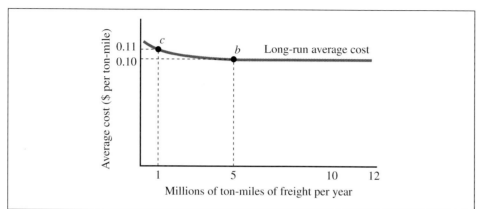

Figure 4.8

Long-Run Average Cost Curve for Truck Freight

Source: Roger Koenker, "Optimal Scale and the Size Distribution of American Trucking Firms," *Journal of Transport Economics and Policy*, January 1977, p. 62. *Courtesy of the Journal of Transport Economics and Policy.*

Figure 4.9
Long-Run Average Cost Curve for Hospital Services

Source: Harold A. Cohen, "Hospital Cost Curves with Emphasis on Measuring Patient Care Output," in *Empirical Studies in Health Economics*, edited by Herbert E. Klarman (Baltimore: Johns Hopkins University Press, 1970). © 1970. Reproduced with permission of Johns Hopkins University Press.

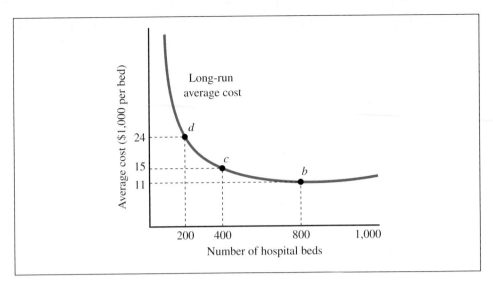

Diseconomies of Scale

If a firm's long-run average cost curve is positively sloped, the firm experiences **diseconomies of scale**, meaning that when the firm increases its output, the long-run average cost of production increases. Diseconomies of scale may arise for two reasons:

Diseconomies of scale: A situation in which an increase in the quantity produced increases the long-run average cost of production.

1. **Coordination problems.** One of the problems of a large organization is that it requires several layers of management (a bureaucracy) to coordinate the activities of the different parts of the organization. If an increase in the firm's output requires additional layers of management, the long-run average cost curve may be positively sloped.

2. **Increasing input costs.** When a firm increases its output, it will demand more of each of its inputs and may be forced to pay higher prices for some of these inputs. An increase in input prices will increase the long-run average cost of production, generating a positively sloped long-run average cost curve.

The long-run cost curves shown in Figures 4.6 through 4.9 suggest that diseconomies of scale are relatively mild. Once we reach a large quantity of output, the long-run average cost curves have a small positive slope. The studies of other goods and services generate the same sort of L-shaped curves, suggesting that diseconomies of scale are not very severe, at least in the range of outputs firms actually produce. This is sensible because if a firm experienced diseconomies of scale, it could decrease its long-run average cost by decreasing the quantity of output.

The experience of General Motors suggests there are diseconomies of scale in the production of automobiles, largely because of coordination problems.[5] General Motors, which is one-third bigger than Ford and larger than the two largest Japanese automakers (Toyota and Nissan) combined, produces automobiles at an average cost that is between $200 and $2,000 higher than the average cost of Ford, Chrysler, and the Japanese. The Saturn project—an independent manufacturing operation with its own production facilities and its own input suppliers—is General Motors' response to these diseconomies of scale. By dividing its production into smaller pieces, General Motors hopes to avoid the high costs resulting from diseconomies of scale.

Firms recognize the possibility of diseconomies of scale and adopt various strategies to avoid them. An example of a firm that adjusts its operations to avoid diseconomies of scale is Minnesota Mining & Manufacturing, also known as 3M. According to Gordon Engdahl, the company's vice president for human resources, "We made a conscious effort to keep our units as small as possible because it keeps them flexible and vital. When one gets too large, we break it apart. We like to say that our success in recent years amounts to multiplication by division."[6]

Application: Trucking Services

At the start of this chapter, the manager of a trucking firm suggested that the entry of four or five new trucking firms into the market would triple the average cost of trucking services. The cost curve for the trucking industry shown in Figure 4.8 suggests that the manager overstated the effects of deregulation on the average cost of trucking services. Suppose that the regulated firm provides 5 million ton-miles of trucking services per year at an average cost of $0.10 per ton-mile (point *b*). The entry of four firms would decrease the output per firm to 1 million ton-miles per year, increasing the cost per ton-mile to $0.11 (point *c*). In other words, deregulation would increase the average cost by only $0.01 per ton-mile.

Short-Run Versus Long-Run Cost

Why is the firm's short-run average cost curve U shaped, while the long-run average cost curve is L shaped? For large quantities of output, the short-run curve is positively sloped because of diminishing returns and the resulting increases in the labor cost per unit of output. In the long run, the firm can scale up its operation by building a larger production facility, so the firm does not suffer from diminishing returns. If there are no diseconomies of scale, the long-run average cost curve will be negatively sloped or horizontal. If the firm experiences some diseconomies of scale, the long-run average cost curve will eventually be positively sloped, but the short-run average cost curve will be much steeper.

TEST Your Understanding

5. Draw a line connecting each item on the left with the appropriate item on the right.

    a. Diseconomies of scale cost curve   1. Negatively sloped long-run average

    b. Economies of scale cost curve   2. Positively sloped long-run average

    c. Indivisible inputs

    d. Input specialization

    e. Coordination problems

6. When you mention that most firms have L-shaped long-run average cost curves, your new boss says, "You're wrong. Haven't you heard of the principle of diminishing returns?" How should you respond?

7. As a child, you recorded the costs of your lemonade stand and drew your long-run average cost curve. Now you work in a computer chip factory. Would you expect any similarities between the lemonade cost curve and the long-run average cost curve for the chip factory? Would you expect any differences?

Using the **Tools**

You've learned all about the firm's short- and long-run cost curves. Here are some opportunities to use those curves as graphical tools in your own economic analysis.

1. Production Consultant

A hammer manufacturer has just hired you to advise the firm on its production costs. In your first meeting with production managers, you hear the following statements. Are they true or false? Explain.

a. "If the production process is subject to diminishing returns, the long-run average cost curve will be positively sloped."

b. "At the current output level, this factory is subject to diminishing returns. Therefore, the firm is operating along the upward-sloping portion of its short-run marginal cost (SMC) curve."

c. "At the current output level, this factory is subject to diminishing returns. Therefore, the firm is operating along the upward-sloping portion of its short-run average total cost (SATC) curve."

d. "The short-run average total cost of producing 250 hammers is less than the short-run average cost of producing 260 hammers. Therefore, the short-run marginal cost of 260 hammers is less than the short-run average cost of 260 hammers."

2. Cost of Breaking Up an Aluminum Firm

Consider a large aluminum firm that initially produces 2 million pounds of aluminum per year. Suppose that an antitrust action breaks up the firm into two smaller firms, each of which produces half as much as the original firm. Use the information in Figure 4.7 to predict the effects on the long-run average cost of producing aluminum.

3. Cost of Hospital Services

A small city is about to replace its aging 800-bed hospital with either a new 800-bed hospital or two new 400-bed hospitals. In a public hearing before the city council, an economic consultant makes the following statement: "A big hospital is much more efficient than a small one, so it would be silly to build two 400-bed hospitals rather than a single 800-bed hospital. In fact, the cost per bed of an 800-bed hospital is about one-third of the cost per bed of a 400-bed hospital." Use the information in Figure 4.9 to comment on this statement.

Summary

In this chapter, we looked at the cost side of a firm, explaining the shapes of the firm's short-run cost curves and long-run cost curves. Here are the main points of the chapter.

1. The positively sloped portion of the short-run marginal cost (SMC) curve results from diminishing returns.

2. The short-run average total cost (SATC) curve is U shaped because of the conflicting effects of (a) fixed costs being spread over a larger quantity of output and (b) diminishing returns.

3. The long-run average cost (LAC) curve is horizontal over some range of output because replication is an option, so doubling output will no more than double long-run total cost.

4. The long-run average cost (LAC) curve is negatively sloped for small quantities of output because there are indivisible inputs that cannot be scaled down and a smaller operation has limited opportunities for labor specialization.

5. Diseconomies of scale arise if there are problems in coordinating a large operation or higher input costs in a larger organization.

Key Terms

average fixed cost (AFC), 88
diseconomies of scale, 98
economic cost, 83
economies of scale, 95
explicit cost, 82
fixed cost (FC), 86
implicit cost, 82
indivisible input, 93

long run, 83
long-run average cost of production (LAC), 92
long-run total cost, 92
minimum efficient scale, 97
short run, 83
short-run average total cost (SATC), 88

short-run average variable cost (SAVC), 88
short-run marginal cost (SMC), 87
short-run total cost (STC), 86
total product curve, 84
total variable cost (TVC), 86

Problems and Discussion Questions

1. Suppose that the indivisible inputs used in the production of shirts have a cost per day of $400. To produce one shirt per day, the firm must also spend a total of $5 on other inputs (labor, materials, and other capital). For each additional shirt, the firm incurs the same additional cost ($5). Compute the average cost for 40 shirts, 100 shirts, 200 shirts, and 400 shirts. Draw the long-run average cost curve for 40 to 400 shirts per day.

2. Consider a firm with the following short-run costs:

Quantity	Variable Cost	Total Cost
1	30	90
2	50	110
3	90	150
4	140	200
5	200	260

   a. What is the firm's fixed cost?
   b. Compute short-run marginal cost, short-run average variable cost, and short-run average total cost for the different quantities of output.
   c. Draw the three cost curves. Explain the relationship between the SMC curve and the SATC curve and the relationship between the SAVC curve and the SATC curve.

3. Given the following relationship between labor input and the quantity produced, compute the marginal product of labor for the different input levels. Then draw the total product curve and the marginal product curve.

Labor	Output
0	0
1	5
2	11
3	15
4	18
5	19

4. Consider a firm that has a fixed cost of $60 per minute. Complete the following table.

Output	FC	TVC	STC	SMC	AFC	SAVC	SATC
1	___	10	___	___	___	___	___
2	___	18	___	___	___	___	___
3	___	30	___	___	___	___	___
4	___	45	___	___	___	___	___
5	___	65	___	___	___	___	___
6	___	90	___	___	___	___	___

5. Consider a firm that has constant marginal returns. That means that the first worker is just as productive as the second, who is just as productive as the third, and so on. The same is true for all the firm's inputs.
   a. Draw the firm's short-run marginal cost curve.
   b. Explain why this firm's cost curve differs from the short-run marginal cost curve for rake production.

6. Beaverduck Bus Company wants to compute the cost of adding a third daily bus between Eugene

and Corvallis. Comment on the following statement of Abby Abacus, the company accountant: "If we add the third bus, our total cost would increase from $700 to $780. Therefore, the marginal cost of the third bus is $260 ($780/3)."

7. You want to know the short-run marginal cost of producing a Chevrolet Caprice. Comment on the following statement from an analyst in the production department: "The marginal cost of a Caprice, given our current volume, is $12,500. Of course, the actual marginal cost depends on the number of cars produced. The larger the number produced, the lower the unit cost because we will spread out our design and tooling costs over more cars."

8. Explain the difference between diseconomies of scale and diminishing returns. Based on the cost curves you've seen in this chapter, which is more pervasive?

9. Suppose that one firm generates 30 billion kilowatt-hours of electricity, which is about three times the output of a second electricity firm. Which firm will have a higher cost per kilowatt-hour? Use the information in Figure 4.6 to predict the difference in the average costs of the two firms.

10. Web Exercise. Visit the Web site of the Cooperative Administrative Support Unit (CASU), an organization that helps government agencies reduce their operating costs (*www.dol.gov/dol/casu/welcome.html*). What economic concept allows CASU to help government agencies reduce their costs? Check out the details of CASU's "cost per copy" program. Are there economies of scale in photocopying?

11. Web Exercise. Visit the Web site of the Bureau of Labor Statistics (*stats.bls.gov/*) and do a keyword search of the site for information on compensation costs. How does the hourly compensation of U.S. workers compare to the compensation of workers in other countries?

Take It to the Net

We invite you to visit the O'Sullivan/Sheffrin page on the Prentice Hall Web site at: **www.prenhall.com/osullivan/** for additional World Wide Web exercises for this chapter.

Model Answers to Questions

Chapter-Opening Questions

1. As shown in Figure 4.7, the average cost for the large firm is $1.60 per pound (point *c*), compared to an average cost of $2.10 for each of the small firms.

2. As shown in Figure 4.8, although a larger trucking firm has lower average costs than a small one, the difference is relatively small, except for very small firms.

3. The short-run curve reflects diminishing returns, which pulls up short-run average cost as output increases. There are no diminishing returns in the long run.

4. In Figure 4.6, the larger firm (30 billion kilowatt-hours) has an average cost that is 8% lower than the smaller firm (10 billion kilowatt-hours).

Test Your Understanding

1. The principle of diminishing returns.

2. It's not obvious that the short-run average cost will decrease because diminishing returns pull up average cost as the quantity of output increases. If the initial quantity of output is large enough, the bad news associated with increasing output (diminishing returns) will dominate the good news (spreading out the fixed costs), so average cost will increase.

3. If the marginal cost is less than the average cost, the marginal pulls down the average, so the average cost curve is negatively sloped. Therefore, average cost will decrease, at least for small increases in output.

4. Average.

5. Draw lines from "diseconomies of scale" and "coordination problems" to "positively sloped long-run average cost curve." Draw lines from "economies of scale," "indivisible inputs," and "input specialization" to "negatively sloped long-run average cost curve."

6. Diminishing returns occur when we increase output in an existing production facility. The principle of diminishing returns is applicable in the short run, not in the long run. To draw the long-run cost curve, we assume that we can change the size of the production facility.

7. There are some indivisible inputs for the lemonade stand (the pitcher and the sign), just as there are indivisible inputs for the chip factory (testing equipment, clean room). Therefore, both operations will have negatively sloped long-run average cost curves. Of course, the cost of these indivisible inputs is tiny for the lemonade stand and huge for the chip factory. Therefore, the average cost curve for the chip factory will be negatively sloped over a large range of output. If your lemonade stand was a one-person operation, you probably never experienced the benefits from input specialization. In contrast, input specialization will be important in the chip factory.

Using the Tools

1. Production Consultant

   a. False. The principle of diminishing returns is applicable to the short-run cost curves, not the long-run curves.

   b. True. Diminishing returns imply increasing short-run marginal cost.

   c. False. Diminishing returns imply increasing short-run marginal cost but do not imply increasing short-run average cost. If the output is small enough, the spreading of fixed costs will generate a negatively sloped short-run average cost curve even if there are diminishing returns.

   d. False. The first sentence implies that the short-run average cost curve is positively sloped. This means that the short-run marginal cost exceeds the short-run average cost.

2. Cost of Breaking Up an Aluminum Firm. In Figure 4.7, the average cost for the large firm is $1.60 per pound (point *c*), compared to an average cost of $2.10 for each of the small firms.

3. Cost of Hospital Services. At the start of this chapter, an economic consultant claims that the average cost per bed in an 800-bed hospital would be one-third the cost per bed in each 400-bed hospital. The long-run average cost curve shown in Figure 4.9 indicates that the consultant has overstated the scale economies in hospital services. For the 800-bed hospital, the long-run average cost is $11,000 per bed (point *b*), compared to a long-run average cost of $15,000 per bed for a 400-bed hospital (point *c*). Although the larger hospital is more efficient, the difference in cost is not as large as the consultant has suggested.

Notes

1. Adam Smith, *The Wealth of Nations* (New York: The Modern Library, 1937), pp. 4–5.
2. John Johnson, *Statistical Cost Analysis* (New York: McGraw-Hill, 1960).
3. Aubrey Silberson, "Economies of Scale in Theory and Practice," *Economic Journal*, vol. 82, 1972, pp. 369–391.
4. Walter Adams and James W. Brock, "Automobiles," Chapter 4 in *The Structure of the American Economy*, 9th ed., edited by Walter Adams and James W. Brock (Upper Saddle River, NJ: Prentice Hall, 1995).
5. Adams and Brock.
6. Frederick C. Klein, "At 3M Plants, Workers Have Flexibility, Involvement—And Their Own Radios," *Wall Street Journal*, February 5, 1982, p. 1.

5

Perfect Competition: Short Run and Long Run

In 1992, Hurricane Andrew struck the southeastern United States, leaving millions of people without electricity for several days. Refrigerators stopped working, and thousands of people suddenly needed a lot of ice to cool and preserve their food. The price of a bag of ice immediately rose from $1 to $5. The same sort of price hikes occurred for chain saws (for clearing downed trees), bottled water, tar paper (for repairing roofs), and plywood. If you had been the governor of Florida in 1992, what would you have done?

This is the first of three chapters exploring the decisions made by firms in different types of markets. Markets differ in the number of firms that compete against one another for customers. At one extreme is a monopoly: a market with a single seller. We'll explore the decisions of a monopolist in the next chapter. In this chapter, we'll look at the other extreme, a **perfectly competitive market**, a market with four features:

- There are many firms.
- The product is standardized or homogeneous.
- Firms can freely enter or leave the market in the long run.
- Each firm takes the market price as given.

Perfectly competitive market: A market with a very large number of firms, each of which produces the same standardized product and takes the market price as given.

The first three features of perfect competition imply the fourth. If there are many firms selling a standardized product, each firm has a tiny fraction of the market, and no matter how much any individual firm produces and sells, the market price won't change. There is no incentive for any firm to cut the price because any firm can sell as much as it wants at the market price. There is no incentive to raise the price because a firm doing so would lose all its customers to other firms selling the standardized product at the market price. A perfectly competitive firm is a price taker: It takes the market price as given. For example, each corn farmer produces a tiny fraction of the total supply of corn, and no matter how much corn one farmer produces, the price of corn won't change.

If you're thinking that the model of perfect competition is not very realistic, you're right. Most firms have some control over their prices. When a firm increases its price slightly, it will certainly sell less, but the quantity sold will probably not go to zero. Although perfect competition is rare, it's a good starting point for the analysis of firms' decisions because a price-taking firm's decision is easy to understand. The firm doesn't have to worry about picking a price; it just decides how much to produce, given the market price. Once you understand this simple case, you will be ready to tackle the more complex decisions of firms that have some control over their prices.

In this chapter, you will see how firms use information on revenues and costs to decide how much output to produce. We'll consider both the short-run and the long-run responses to an increase in price, showing that the law of supply works in both the short run and the long run. Here are some practical questions that we answer:

1. What information does the firm need to decide how much output to produce?
2. If your firm's accountant reports that you are losing money, should you close your business or continue to operate at a loss?
3. How did Hurricane Andrew affect prices in the short run and in the long run?
4. Health concerns decreased the demand for butter. The price initially dropped but then rose. Why?

The Short-Run Output Decision

Total revenue: The money the firm gets by selling its product; equal to the price times the quantity sold.

The firm's objective is to maximize its profit, equal to revenue minus cost. A firm's **total revenue** is the money the firm gets by selling its product and is equal to the price times the quantity sold. For example, the total revenue for a farmer who sells 100 bushels of corn at $2 per bushel is $200. We know from Chapter 4 that a firm's total economic cost is the sum of its explicit costs (the firm's actual cash payments for its inputs) and implicit costs (the opportunity costs of nonpurchased inputs such as the entrepreneur's time or money). A firm's **economic profit** equals its total revenue minus its total economic cost. If our corn farmer has an economic cost of $180, the farmer's profit would be $20.

Economic profit: Total revenue minus total economic cost.

The Total Approach: Computing Total Revenue and Total Cost

The first approach to deciding how much output to produce involves computing the total revenue and total cost of different quantities of output. Table 5.1 shows the total revenue and total cost of a hypothetical rake producer. As shown in the third column, if the price of rakes is $25 per rake, the firm's total revenue equals $25 times the number of rakes produced, so total revenue increases by $25 for each additional rake produced and sold. The fourth column shows the short-run total costs associated with different quantities of rakes produced. The fifth column shows economic profit, defined as total revenue minus total cost. In this example, profit is maximized when the firm produces either eight or nine rakes per minute. In either case, total revenue exceeds total cost by $99. We'll assume that whenever profit is highest for two quantities of output (eight and nine in this case), the firm produces the larger quantity.

Figure 5.1 shows how to choose the quantity of output that maximizes profit. We're looking for the largest profit, meaning the biggest gap between total revenue and total cost. In this case, profit is maximized when the firm produces either eight or nine rakes, with a profit equal to $99.

The Marginal Approach

The other way to decide how much output to produce involves the marginal principle, the general decision-making rule that is one of the key principles of economics.

Marginal **PRINCIPLE**

Increase the level of an activity if its marginal benefit exceeds its marginal cost, but reduce the level if the marginal cost exceeds the marginal benefit. If possible, pick the level at which the marginal benefit equals the marginal cost.

Table 5.1   Deciding How Much Output to Produce

Output: Rakes per Minute	Price	Total Revenue	Total Cost	Profit	Marginal Revenue (Price)	Marginal Cost
0	25	0	36	−36	25	0
1	25	25	44	−19	25	8
2	25	50	48	2	25	4
3	25	75	51	24	25	3
4	25	100	56	44	25	5
5	25	125	63	62	25	7
6	25	150	72	78	25	9
7	25	175	84	91	25	12
8	25	200	101	99	25	17
9	25	225	126	99	25	25
10	25	250	166	84	25	40

Figure 5.1

Using the Total Approach to Choose an Output Level

Economic profit is shown by the vertical distance between the total revenue curve and the total cost curve. To maximize profit, the firm chooses the quantity of output that generates the largest vertical difference between the two curves.

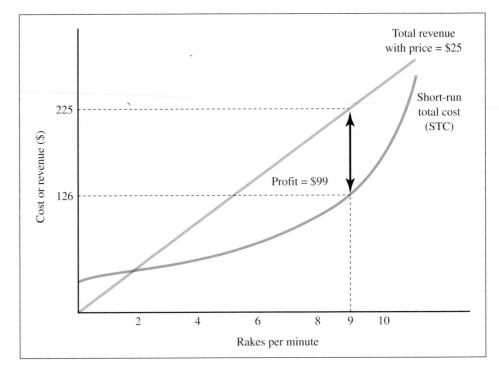

In our example, the firm's activity is producing rakes, so to use the marginal principle, the firm must compute the marginal benefit and the marginal cost of producing different quantities of rakes.

The benefit of producing and selling rakes is the revenue the firm collects. Therefore, the marginal benefit of producing rakes is the **marginal revenue** from rakes: the change in total revenue that results from selling one more rake.

Marginal revenue: The change in total revenue that results from selling one more unit of output.

$$\text{marginal benefit} = \text{marginal revenue}$$

As shown in columns two and three in Table 5.1, the perfectly competitive rake firm can sell as much as it wants at the $25 market price, so if the firm sells one more unit of output, its total revenue increases by $25. This means that

$$\text{marginal revenue} = \text{market price}$$

The marginal principle tells us that the firm will maximize its profit by choosing the quantity at which marginal revenue (the market price) equals marginal cost:

$$\text{price} = \text{marginal cost}$$

Figure 5.2 illustrates the use of the marginal principle for the firm's output decision. In panel A, the market supply and demand curves represent the collective choices of all rake producers and consumers. The market supply curve intersects the market demand curve at a price of $25. In panel B, the horizontal line shows the market price—the marginal revenue for the perfectly competitive firm. The marginal revenue line intersects the marginal cost curve at a quantity of nine rakes per minute, so that's the quantity that maximizes profit (where marginal revenue equals marginal cost).

To see that an output of nine rakes per minute maximizes the firm's profit, imagine that the firm produced only four rakes per minute. Could the firm make more profit by producing five rakes instead of four?

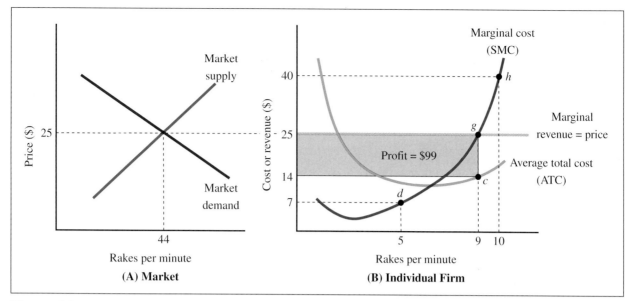

Figure 5.2
The Marginal Approach to Picking an Output Level
A perfectly competitive firm takes the market price as given. In panel A, the market supply curve intersects the market demand curve at a price of $25. In panel B, using the marginal principle, the typical firm will maximize profit at point *g*, where the market price ($25) equals the marginal cost. Economic profit equals the difference between price and average cost ($11 = $25 − $14) times the quantity produced (nine rakes per minute), or $99 per minute.

1. From the seventh row of numbers in Table 5.1 and point *d* in Figure 5.2, we know that the marginal cost of the fifth rake is $7.
2. The price of rakes is $25, so the marginal benefit (marginal revenue) is $25.

Because the extra revenue from the fifth rake (price = $25) exceeds the extra cost (marginal cost = $7), the production and sale of the fifth rake increases the firm's total profit by $18 (equal to $25 − $7). Therefore, it is sensible to produce the fifth rake. The same logic applies, with different numbers for marginal cost, for the sixth through the eighth rakes. For the ninth rake, marginal revenue equals marginal cost, so the firm's profit doesn't change. To be consistent with the marginal principle, we'll assume that the firm goes to the point at which marginal revenue equals marginal cost. In this case, the firm produces the ninth rake.

The same logic applies for producing any quantity greater than 9 rakes per minute. Imagine the firm produced 10 rakes. Would its profit be higher if it produced 1 fewer rake (9 rakes instead of 10)? From Table 5.1 and the marginal cost curve in Figure 5.2, we see that the marginal cost of the 10th rake is $40 (point *h*), which exceeds the marginal revenue (the market price) of $25. The 10th rake adds more to cost ($40) than it adds to revenue ($25), so producing the rake decreases the firm's profit by $15 (equal to $40 − $25). The marginal principle suggests that the firm should choose point *g*, with an output of 9 rakes.

Economic Profit

We've seen that the perfectly competitive firm maximizes its profit by producing the quantity at which its marginal revenue (price) equals its marginal cost. How much profit does the firm earn? The firm's economic profit equals its total revenue minus its total cost. The firm's average profit equals the difference between price and average cost. The easiest way to compute a firm's total economic profit is to multiply the average profit per unit produced by the quantity produced:

$$\text{economic profit} = (\text{price} - \text{average cost}) \times \text{quantity produced}$$

In Figure 5.2, the average cost of producing nine rakes is $14 (point c), so the economic profit is $99:

$$\text{economic profit} = (\$25 - \$14) \times 9 = \$99$$

In Figure 5.2, the firm's profit is shown by the area of the shaded rectangle. The height of the rectangle is the average profit ($11 per rake), and the width of the rectangle is the quantity produced (nine rakes).

Economic Detective

The Turnaround Artist

Emilio knows how to turn an unprofitable company into a profitable one. His latest project was a firm that was losing money producing and selling hammers. The firm sold 100 hammers per day at a price of $20 each and lost $500 per day. Emilio showed up at the factory on Monday and told the factory manager to increase production to 101 hammers on Tuesday. After a brief conversation with the factory manager on Wednesday, Emilio gave his advice, collected his fee, and disappeared. One week later, the firm was producing fewer hammers but making a profit of $2 on each hammer. What is Emilio's secret formula for success? What was his advice on Wednesday?

The key to answering these questions is the marginal principle. The purpose of Emilio's experiment was to compute the marginal cost of hammers. He compared the total cost of producing 101 hammers to the total cost of 100 hammers and must have discovered that the marginal cost of the 101st hammer was greater than the market price ($20). According to the marginal principle, if the marginal cost exceeds the marginal benefit (the price), a decrease in output will increase profit. Emilio's formula for success is the marginal principle.

TEST Your Understanding

1. Explain why a perfectly competitive firm takes prices as given.
2. Complete the statement: A perfectly competitive firm will produce the quantity of output at which _____ equals _____.
3. Suppose the market price of sugar is $0.22 per pound. If a sugar farmer produces 100,000 pounds, the marginal cost of sugar is $0.30 per pound. Is the farmer maximizing profit? If not, should the farmer produce more sugar or less sugar?

The Shut-Down Decision

Consider next the decisions faced by a firm that is losing money. Suppose the market price is so low that the firm's total revenue is less than its total cost, even though the firm used the marginal principle to decide how much to produce. For an unprofitable firm like this one, the question is, Should we continue to operate at a loss or should we shut down? This may seem like a silly question. Why would any firm continue to operate if it is losing money? As we'll see, it will be sensible to operate at a loss if the firm would lose even more money by shutting down.

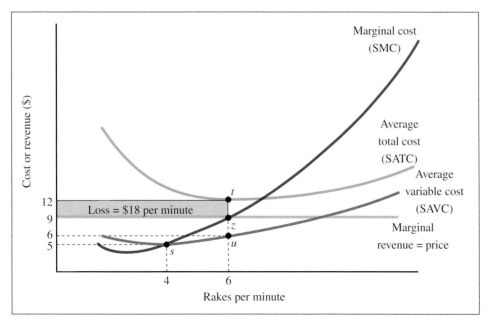

Figure 5.3

Shut-Down Decision

With a price of $9, the firm should pick point z, producing six rakes per minute. The average cost exceeds the price by $3, so the firm loses $18 per minute ($3 per rake × 6 rakes per minute). The average variable cost is $6 per rake, which is less than the $9 price, so total revenue exceeds total variable cost, and it is sensible to continue operating at a loss, rather than shut down.

Figure 5.3 shows the situation faced by an unprofitable firm. Suppose the market price of rakes drops to $9 per rake. If the firm continues to operate, it will produce six rakes per minute (shown by point z, where the marginal revenue—the price—equals marginal cost). The firm's problem is that the average total cost of production ($12, as shown by point t) is less than the price ($9), so economic profit is negative. The average cost exceeds the price by $3, so the firm will lose $18 per minute ($3 per rake × 6 rakes per minute). Should the firm continue to operate at a loss, or shut down?

Total Revenue versus Total Variable Cost

The firm should continue to operate if the benefit of operating exceeds the cost of operating. The benefit equals the firm's total revenue, or the price times the quantity produced. In Figure 5.3, the firm can sell six rakes at a price of $9 per rake, so the total revenue from operating is $54. The firm's cost of operating—as opposed to shutting down—equals the firm's total variable cost, defined earlier as the cost that varies with the amount produced. As shown by point u, when the firm produces six rakes, its average variable cost is $6 per rake. Therefore, its total variable cost is $36 ($6 per rake × 6 rakes). Because the benefit of operating (total revenue of $54) exceeds the variable cost ($36), it is sensible for the firm to continue to operate.

We can use a shortcut to determine whether total revenue exceeds the total variable cost. Total revenue is the price times the quantity produced, and total variable cost is the average variable cost times the quantity produced. Therefore, if the price exceeds the average variable cost, total revenue will exceed total variable cost. The firm should continue to operate if price exceeds the average variable cost; otherwise, it should shut down.

Operate:	price >	average variable cost
Shut down:	price <	average variable cost

In Figure 5.3, the price is $9 and the average variable cost of six rakes is $6 per rake, so it is sensible to continue operating, even at a loss.

The firm's **shut-down price** is defined as the price at which the firm is indifferent between operating and shutting down. In Figure 5.3, the shut-down price is $5 (shown

Shut-down price: The price at which the firm is indifferent between operating and shutting down.

A firm should shut down an unprofitable facility if its total revenue is less than its total variable cost.

by point *s*). If the market price of rakes drops below the shut-down price, the firm would be better off shutting down. At the shut-down price, marginal cost equals price (the marginal principle) and average variable cost also equals the price (for total revenue to equal total variable cost). Therefore, marginal cost equals average variable cost, and as we saw in Chapter 4, that happens at the minimum point of the average variable cost curve. That means that the shut-down price is the minimum average variable cost.

Why Operate an Unprofitable Facility?

Sunk cost: The cost a firm has already paid or has agreed to pay sometime in the future.

If the idea of operating an unprofitable facility is puzzling, think about what would happen if the firm shut down. Although the firm would no longer pay for labor and materials, it would still pay for its idle production facility, for example, a factory full of machinery and equipment. The cost of the production facility is a **sunk cost**, defined as a cost the firm has already paid or has agreed to pay sometime in the future. For example, a firm with a $1 million production facility has a sunk cost of $1 million, regardless of whether the firm paid for the facility in the past or will pay for it in the future. What matters is that the firm cannot do anything about this sunk cost.

If a firm shuts down its production facility, it will still pay its sunk cost—the cost of the production facility. In our example, the sunk cost is the same as the fixed cost, which is $36 per minute (see the first row of numbers in Table 5.1, where the total cost with zero output is $36). Therefore, the firm will lose $36 per minute if it shuts down. But if the firm operates, it will lose only $18 per minute. Because the firm loses less money if it operates, it is sensible to continue operating.

How long should a firm continue to operate at a loss? Let's think about what happens when the firm must decide whether to build a new production facility. The firm will build a new facility—and produce output to stay in the market—only if total revenue is high enough to cover all the costs of production, including the cost of a new facility. Although a firm may operate an existing facility at a loss, it won't replace it if the new facility would be unprofitable, too.

TEST Your Understanding

4. Complete the statement with a number: If a lamp producer can sell 40 lamps per day at a price of $20 per lamp, the benefit of operating its production facility is _____ per day.

5. Complete the statement with *operate* or *shut down*: Consider a firm with total revenue of $500, total cost of $700, and variable cost of $400. The firm should _____ its production facility.

Short-Run Supply Curves

Now that we've explored the output decision of a price-taking firm, we're ready to show how firms respond to changes in the market price of output. We'll represent the relationship between price and quantity supplied with two short-run supply curves, one for the individual firm and one for the entire market.

The Short-Run Supply Curve of the Firm

The firm's **short-run supply curve** shows the relationship between the market price and the quantity supplied by the firm over a period of time during which one input—the production facility—cannot be changed. In the case of rake producers, the firm's supply curve answers the following question: At a given price of rakes, how many rakes will the firm produce? We have already used the marginal principle and the marginal cost curve to answer this question for two different prices. At a price of $9, the marginal revenue (price) equals marginal cost when the firm produces six rakes per minute; at a price of $25, price equals marginal cost with nine rakes. In general, because the firm chooses the quantity at which price equals marginal cost, if we want to determine the quantity supplied at a particular price, we read it off the marginal cost curve.

    The firm's short-run supply curve is the part of the firm's short-run marginal cost curve above the shut-down price. The shut-down price for the rake firm is $5, so as shown in Figure 5.4, the short-run supply curve is the marginal cost curve starting at $5. For any price above the shut-down price, the firm will choose the quantity at which price equals marginal cost, so we can find the firm's quantity supplied from its marginal cost curve. If the price is $12, the firm will supply seven rakes per minute (point *m*). As the price increases, the firm responds by supplying more rakes: eight rakes when the price is $17 and nine rakes when the price is $25.

    What about prices below the shut-down price? If the price drops below the shut-down price, the firm's total revenue will not be high enough to cover its total variable

Short-run supply curve: A curve showing the relationship between the price of a product and the quantity of output supplied by a firm in the short run.

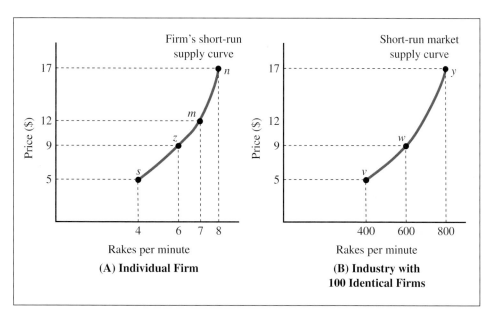

Figure 5.4
Short-Run Supply Curves
In panel A, the firm's short-run supply curve is the part of the marginal cost curve above the shut-down price ($5). For prices below the shut-down price, the firm shuts down, so the quantity supplied is zero. In panel B, there are 100 firms in the market, so the market supply at a given price is 100 times the quantity supplied by the typical firm. At a price of $9, each firm supplies 6 rakes per minute (point *z*), so the market supply is 600 rakes per minute (point *w*).

cost, so the firm will shut down and produce no output. In panel A of Figure 5.4, the firm's supply curve starts at point *s*, indicating that the quantity supplied is zero for any price less than $5.

In many parts of the developing world, people cannot afford their own phones and have traditionally relied on pay phones. The recent development of mobile phones has generated a new competitive industry in many developing nations. Read "A Closer Look: Wireless Women."

The Market Supply Curve

Short-run market supply curve: A curve showing the relationship between price and the quantity of output supplied by all firms in the short run.

The **short-run market supply curve** shows the relationship between the market price and the quantity supplied by all firms in the short run. Panel B of Figure 5.4 shows the short-run market supply curve when there are 100 identical rake firms. For each price, we get the quantity supplied for the entire market by multiplying the quantity supplied by the typical firm (from the individual supply curve) by 100. At a price of $9, each firm produces 6 rakes (point *z*), so the market supply is 600 rakes (point *w*). If the price increases to $17, each firm produces 8 rakes, so the market supply is 800 rakes (point *y*).

What happens if firms are not identical but instead have different individual supply curves? To compute the market supply in this case, we would add the quantities supplied by the dozens (or hundreds) of firms in the market. The assumption that firms are identical is harmless: It makes it easier to derive the market supply curve from the supply curve of the typical firm, but it does not change the analysis.

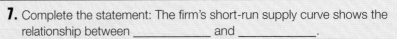

TEST Your Understanding

7. Complete the statement: The firm's short-run supply curve shows the relationship between _____ and _____.

8. Suppose that you want to draw the firm's short-run supply curve. What information do you need?

9. Suppose there are 100 identical firms in a perfectly competitive industry. At a price of $22, the typical firm supplies 50 units of output. What is the market quantity supplied at a price of $22?

The Long-Run Supply Curve for an Increasing-Cost Industry

In the long run, firms can enter or leave an industry, and existing firms can modify their facilities or build new facilities. A market reaches a long-run equilibrium when three conditions hold:

1. The quantity of the product supplied equals the quantity demanded.
2. Each firm in the market maximizes its profit, given the market price.
3. Each firm in the market earns zero economic profit, so there is no incentive for other firms to enter the market.

The first two conditions are actually the two conditions for short-run equilibrium, so the only difference between the short run and the long run is that in the long run, economic profit is zero. When a firm earns zero economic profit, its total revenue equals its total economic cost. The total economic cost includes the opportunity cost of all the

WIRELESS WOMEN

In Pakistan, many poor villagers cannot afford their own phones, and phone service is provided by thousands of "wireless women," entrepreneurs who invest $310 in a Village Phone package, which includes wireless phone equipment (transceiver, battery, charger), a signboard, a calculator, and a stopwatch.[1] Then they sell phone service to their neighbors, charging by the minute and second. On average, their net income is about $2 per day, about three times the average per-capital income in Pakistan.

firm's inputs, including the opportunity cost of the entrepreneur's time and the opportunity cost of the firm's capital (buildings and machinery). The entrepreneur is being paid just as well as he or she could be in the next-best alternative activity, and the firm's capital is receiving a rate of return comparable to the return earned by capital in other industries. When a firm earns zero economic profit, its total revenue is just high enough to cover all its costs—including the opportunity cost of all its inputs—but not high enough to cause additional firms to enter the industry.

Figure 5.5 shows a market in long-run equilibrium. The demand curve intersects the short-run market supply curve at a price of $12 and a quantity of 700 rakes per minute (condition 1). There are 100 firms, each of which produces seven rakes per minute. Each firm maximizes its profit by choosing the quantity at which the marginal revenue (the price) equals the marginal cost, producing seven rakes per minute (condition 2). At the quantity chosen by each firm, price equals short-run average total cost, so each firm makes zero economic profit (condition 3).

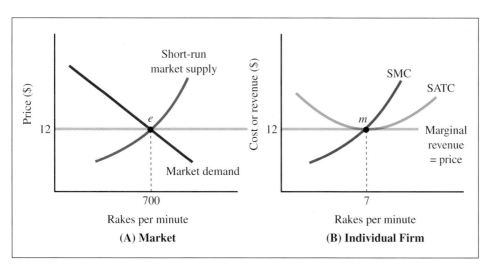

(A) Market

(B) Individual Firm

Figure 5.5
Long-Run Market Equilibrium
In panel A, the market demand curve intersects the short-run market supply curve at a price of $12. In panel B, given the market price, the typical firm satisfies the marginal principle at point *m*, producing seven rakes per minute. Because price equals the average cost at the chosen quantity, economic profit is zero, and no other firms will enter the market.

Production Costs and the Size of the Industry in the Long Run

Long-run market supply curve: A curve showing the relationship between the market price and quantity supplied by all firms in the long run.

Let's look at the **long-run market supply curve**, which shows the relationship between the market price and the quantity supplied by all firms in the long run, a period long enough that firms can enter or leave the market. Suppose the typical rake firm produces seven rakes per minute, using a standard set of inputs, including a factory, some workers, and raw materials (wood and plastic). In a perfectly competitive industry, there are no restrictions on entry, so anyone can use the standard set of inputs to produce seven rakes per minute.

Table 5.2 shows hypothetical data on the cost of producing rakes. Let's start with the first row, which shows the firm's production costs in an industry with 50 firms and a total of 350 rakes (with 7 rakes per firm). To compute the total cost for the typical firm, we add the cost of the firm's production facility (the cost of the rake factory), the cost of labor, and the cost of materials. In the first row, the total cost of the typical firm producing 7 rakes per minute is $70, and the average cost is $10 per rake ($70 divided by 7 rakes).

Increasing-cost industry: An industry in which the average cost of production increases as the total output of the industry increases; the long-run supply curve is positively sloped.

The rake industry is an example of an **increasing-cost industry**, defined as an industry in which the average cost of production increases as the total output of the industry increases. In the last column of Table 5.2, the average cost is $10 per rake in an industry that produces 350 rakes, $12 per rake in an industry that produces 700 rakes, and so on. The average cost increases as the industry grows for two reasons:

1. **Increasing input prices.** As an industry grows, it competes with other industries for limited amounts of various inputs, and this competition drives up the prices of these inputs. For example, suppose that the rake industry competes against other industries for a limited amount of special wood. To get more of that wood to produce more rakes, firms in the rake industry must outbid other industries for the limited amount available, and this competition drives up the price of wood.

2. **Less productive inputs.** A small industry will use only the most productive inputs, but as the industry grows, firms may be forced to use less productive inputs. For example, a small rake industry will use only the most skillful workers. As the industry grows, it will have to rely on less skillful workers. As the average skill level of the industry's workforce decreases, the average cost of production increases: In a large rake industry, it will take more hours of labor—and more money—to produce each rake. Another example is the production of agricultural products such as sugar. Because of variation in climate and soil conditions, it is cheaper to grow sugar in some areas than in others. As the quantity of sugar produced increases, growers are forced to produce sugar in areas with higher costs.

Drawing the Long-Run Market Supply Curve

The long-run supply curve tells us how much output will be produced at each price in the long run, when the number of firms in the market can change. Given a market price, we determine the total output of the industry by multiplying the output per

Table 5.2 Industry Output and Average Production Cost

Number of Firms	Industry Output	Rakes per Firm	Total Cost for Typical Firm	Average Cost per Rake
50	350	7	$70	$10
100	700	7	84	12
150	1,050	7	96	14

firm (seven rakes in our example) by the number of firms in the industry. So the key question for the long-run supply curve is, How many firms will be in the market at that price?

Let's think about the incentive for a firm to enter the market. Economic profit is positive when total revenue exceeds total cost or when price exceeds the average cost. Whenever there is an opportunity to make a profit in a market—whenever the price exceeds average cost—firms will enter the market. Firms will continue to enter a market until economic profit is zero, which happens when the price equals average cost. When economic profit is zero, the firm's revenue is high enough to cover all its costs—including the opportunity cost of all its inputs—but not high enough to cause additional firms to enter the market. Each firm that is already in the market makes just enough money to stay in business, so there is no incentive for new firms to enter the market, and no incentive for existing firms to leave.

As a starting point, suppose the price of rakes is $12. There are no restrictions on entry into the industry, so any firm can use the standard set of inputs to produce seven rakes per minute. The information in Table 5.2 suggests that there will be 100 firms in the market. To explain why 100 is the correct number, think about what would happen if there were either fewer firms or more firms:

- **Fewer firms.** If there were fewer than 100 firms, the average cost per rake would be less than the $12 price. If there were only 50 firms (producing a total of 350 rakes per minute), the average cost would be only $10 per rake. At that average cost, the profit per rake would be $2 (a price of $12 minus an average cost of $10). Firms would start to enter this profitable market, and entry would continue until the average cost reached the $12 market price. This occurs when there are 100 firms producing a total of 700 rakes.

- **More firms.** If there were more than 100 firms, the average cost per rake would exceed the $12 price. If there were 150 firms (producing a total of 1,050 rakes per minute), the average cost would be $14 per rake. Each firm would lose $2 per rake (an average cost of $14 minus a price of $12). Firms would start to leave this unprofitable market, and exit would continue until the average cost dropped to the $12 market price, which occurs when there are 100 firms producing a total of 700 rakes.

To find the number of firms in the market, we find the number of firms at which the average cost per rake equals the $12 market price. If the price equals the average cost, each of the 100 firms makes zero economic profit, so there is no incentive for new firms to enter the market and no incentive for existing firms to leave.

Each point on the long-run supply curve shows the quantity of rakes supplied at a particular price. To find a point on the supply curve, we pick a price and then determine how many rakes the industry will produce at that price. At a price of $12, there will be 100 firms producing 700 rakes, so one point on the supply curve shown in Figure 5.6 is point h. To find the other points on the long-run supply curve, we pick other prices and use the data in Table 5.2 to determine the quantity at which price equals the average cost of production. At a price of $10, the quantity is 350 rakes (point e), and at a price of $14, the quantity is 1,050 (point j).

The long-run supply curve in Figure 5.6 is positively sloped, as it will be for any increasing-cost industry. This is another example of the law of supply. The higher the price of rakes, the larger the quantity supplied. An increase in the price of rakes makes rake production more profitable, so firms enter the market, increasing the quantity supplied to the market. Firms will continue to enter the market until the average cost per rake reaches the market price. Each firm gets just enough revenue to cover its produc-

Figure 5.6

Long-Run Market Supply Curve

The long-run market supply curve shows the relationship between the price and quantity supplied in the long run, when firms can enter or leave the industry. At each point on the supply curve, the market price equals the long-run average cost of production. The market supply curve for an increasing-cost industry is positively sloped.

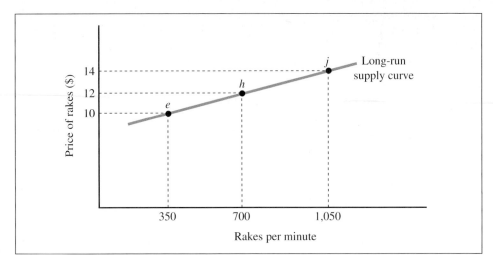

tion costs, so economic profit is zero. For another example of the law of supply, read "A Closer Look: The Supply of Wolfram During World War II."

Examples of Increasing-Cost Industries: Sugar, Rental Housing

The sugar industry is an example of an increasing-cost industry. If the price of sugar is only $0.11 per pound, sugar production is profitable in areas with relatively low production costs, including the Caribbean, Latin America, Australia, and South Africa.[2] At a price of $0.11, the world supply of sugar equals the amount produced in these areas. As the price increases, sugar production becomes profitable in areas where production costs are higher, increasing the quantity of sugar supplied as these other areas join the world market. For example, at a price of $0.14 per pound, sugar production is profitable in the European Union; at a price of $0.24, production is profitable even in the United States. The law of supply works in the world sugar market: The higher the price, the larger the number of areas that produce sugar, so the larger the quantity of sugar supplied.

Another example of an increasing-cost industry is rental housing. Local governments use land-use zoning to restrict the amount of land available for apartments. When housing producers decide to build more apartments, there is fierce competition for the small amount of land zoned for apartments, so the cost of land—and the cost per apartment—increases by a large amount.[3]

The supply of rental housing is relatively inelastic because most local governments restrict the amount of land available for building apartments.

TEST Your Understanding

10. Complete the statement: The long-run supply curve shows the relationship between _____ (on the horizontal axis) and _____ (on the vertical axis).

11. Use Table 5.2 to compute the average cost in a 75-firm industry, assuming that the total cost of the typical firm in such an industry is $70.

12. Circle the three items in the following list that go together: positively sloped supply curve, horizontal supply curve, increasing-cost industry, increasing average cost of production, constant average cost of production.

Market Equilibrium Revisited

We can use what we've learned about the short-run supply curve and the long-run supply curve to get a deeper understanding of perfectly competitive markets. Let's use the two supply curves to explore the short-run and the long-run effects of a change in demand.

Increase in Demand and the Incentive to Enter

Figure 5.7 shows the short-run effects of an increase in the demand for rakes. Panel A shows what's happening at the market level. Let's start with the initial equilibrium shown by point *e*: The original demand curve intersects the short-run market supply curve at a price of $12 per rake and a quantity of 700 rakes. When demand increases, the market demand curve shifts to the right, and it intersects the supply curve at a price of $17 and a quantity of 800 rakes. In panel B, an increase in price from $12 to $17 increases the output per firm from seven rakes to eight rakes. At this quantity, the $17 price now exceeds the average total cost, so the typical firm makes an economic profit (shown by the shaded rectangle). At the market level shown in panel A, the new short-run equilibrium has a price of $17 and a quantity of 800 rakes.

This is not a long-run equilibrium because each firm is making a positive economic profit. Firms will enter the profitable market and as they compete for customers, the

Figure 5.7

Short-Run Effects of an Increase in Demand

An increase in demand increases the market price to $17, causing the typical firm to produce eight rakes instead of seven. Price exceeds the short-run average total cost at the chosen quantity, so economic profit is positive. Firms will enter the profitable market.

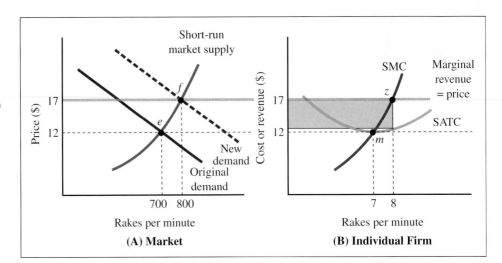

price of rakes will decrease. New firms will continue to enter the market until the price drops to the point at which economic profit is zero. The question is, How far does the price drop?

The Long-Run Effects of an Increase in Demand

We can use the long-run supply curve to determine the long-run price. In Figure 5.8, the short-run effect of the increase in demand is shown by the move from point *e* to point *f*: The price increases from $12 to $17, and the quantity increases from 700 to 800. The new long-run equilibrium is shown by point *s*, where the new demand curve intersects the long-run supply curve. Starting with a price of $17 (the new short-run equilibrium), firms will continue to enter the market until the price drops to $14 and the quantity is 1,050 rakes per minute. At this price and quantity, each of the 150 firms produces seven rakes per minute and earns zero economic profit.

Figure 5.8 shows how the price of rakes changes over time. An increase in demand causes a large upward jump in the price (from point *e* to point *f*), followed by a slide

Figure 5.8

Short-Run and Long-Run Effects of an Increase in Demand

The short-run supply curve is steeper than the long-run supply curve because there are diminishing returns in the short run. In the short run, an increase in demand increases the price from $12 (point *e*) to $17 (point *f*). In the long run, firms enter the industry, and the price drops to $14 (point *s*). The large upward jump in price is followed by a downward slide to the new long-run equilibrium price.

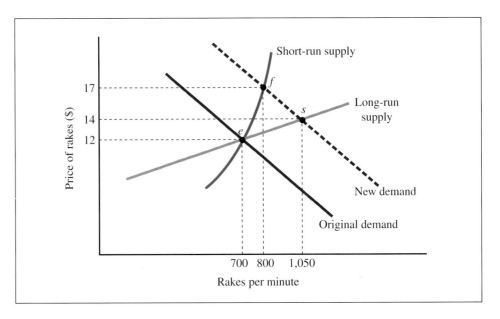

downward to the new long-run equilibrium price (from point *f* to point *s*). In the short run, firms respond to an increase in price by squeezing more output from their existing production facilities. Because of diminishing returns, it is costly to increase output in the short run, so the price increases by a large amount. The higher price causes new firms to enter the market, and as they enter, the price gradually drops to the point at which each firm makes zero economic profit. The long-run supply curve is relatively flat because firms enter the industry and build new factories, so there are no diminishing returns.

Long-Run Supply for a Constant-Cost Industry

As the rake industry expanded, the average cost of production increased, a result of higher input costs. In other words, the rake industry is an increasing-cost industry. In contrast, as a **constant-cost industry** grows, it continues to buy its inputs at the same prices. For this to happen, the industry must be a small part of the relevant input markets, meaning that the expansion of the industry doesn't have a big enough effect on the input market to affect input prices. As a result, the average cost of production for the typical firm doesn't change as the industry grows. In Table 5.2, the rake industry would be a constant-cost industry if the average cost of rakes were constant at $10, regardless of how many rakes were produced.

As an example of a constant-cost industry, consider the taxi industry in a city. As the taxi industry grows, it will use more gasoline, more workers, and more cars, but because the industry is such a small part of the markets for gasoline, labor, and cars, the prices of these inputs won't change. As a result, the average cost of production won't change as the industry grows.

The long-run supply curve for a constant-cost industry is horizontal at the constant average cost of production. If the average cost of taxi service is $3 per mile (including the cost of gasoline, the taxicab, and the driver), the long-run supply curve for taxi service is horizontal at $3, as shown in Figure 5.9. At any lower price, the quantity of taxi service supplied would be zero because no rational firm would provide taxi service at a price less than the average cost of providing the service. At any higher price, firms would enter the taxi industry in droves, and entry would continue until the price dropped to the constant average cost of taxi service ($3).

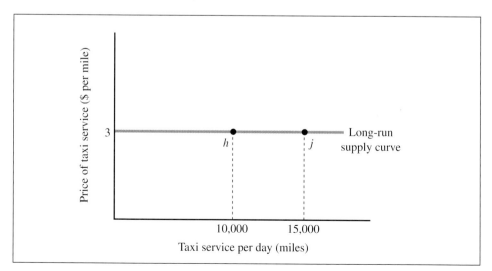

Figure 5.9

Long-Run Supply Curve for a Constant-Cost Industry
In a constant-cost industry, input prices do not change as the industry grows, so the average production cost is constant and the long-run supply curve is horizontal. For the taxi industry, the cost per mile of taxi service is constant at $3, so the supply curve is horizontal at $3 per mile of service.

Hurricane Andrew and the Price of Ice

For an example of the short-run and long-run effects of an increase in demand, let's look at the short-run and long-run effects of a hurricane. In 1992, Hurricane Andrew struck the southeastern United States, leaving millions of people without electricity for several days. Figure 5.10 shows the short- and long-run effects of the hurricane on the price of ice, which was used to cool and preserve food in areas without electricity. Before the hurricane, the market was at point *e*, with a price of $1 per bag of ice. The long-run supply curve is horizontal, indicating that the ice industry is a constant-cost industry.

In the short run (a day or two), the number of ice suppliers is fixed. The increase in demand caused by the hurricane moved the market from point *e* to point *f*, and the price rose to $5 per bag of ice. In the long run, firms responded to the higher price by entering the market. Many people trucked ice from distant locations and sold it from trucks parked on streets and highways. As these firms entered the ice market in the days after the hurricane, the price of ice gradually dropped, and the market eventually reached the intersection of the new demand curve and the long-run supply curve (point *s*), with a price equal to the prehurricane price.

This pattern of price changes following the hurricane was observed in other markets. Immediately after the hurricane, $200 chain saws were sold for $900, but the price dropped steadily as new roadside firms entered the market. The same sort of price changes occurred for bottled water, tar paper, and plywood. The basic pattern was a large upward jump in price followed by a downward slide to the long-run equilibrium price.

Public officials are often tempted to pass laws prohibiting what's called *price gouging*, charging high prices for scarce goods after a natural disaster. One effect of such laws is to slow the transition from the short run to the long run. The people who set up roadside stands to sell ice were motivated by the high price. If the price were controlled at $1 per bag, few people would have incurred the large expenses associated with trucking the ice from distant locations and setting up roadside stores. The result would have been less ice and more spoiled food. An alternative to a law regulating prices is to leave prices to

Figure 5.10
Hurricane Andrew and the Price of Ice
A hurricane increases the demand for ice, shifting the demand curve to the right. In the short run, the supply curve is steep, so the price rises by a large amount. In the long run, firms enter the industry, pulling down the price. Because this is a constant-cost industry, the supply curve is horizontal, and the large upward jump in price is followed by a downward slide back to the original price.

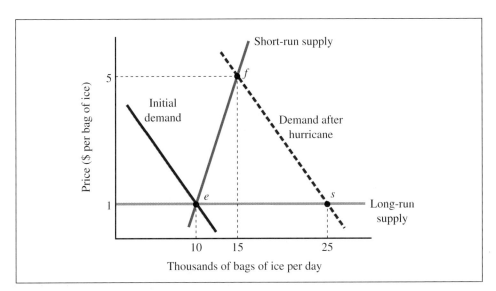

the market and help to ease the transition from short run to long run by making it easier for entrepreneurs to enter the market.

Butter Prices

Several years ago, people became concerned about the undesirable health effects of eating butter. The demand for butter dropped, decreasing its price. Some time later, the price of butter started rising steadily, although demand hadn't been changing. After several months of price hikes, the price of butter was getting close to the price observed before demand decreased. According to a consumer watchdog organization, the rising price of butter was evidence of a conspiracy on the part of butter producers. Is there some other explanation for the rising price of butter?

The key to solving this puzzle is the distinction between the short run and the long run. In Figure 5.11, the short-run effect of a decrease in demand is shown by the move from point e (price = $2.00) to point f (price = $1.44). In the short run, not many firms will leave the market when the price drops, so the decrease in demand will cause a large price drop. Although many of the remaining firms will lose money, they will stay in the market if their total revenue covers their total variable cost. In the long run, however, unprofitable firms will leave the market, causing the price to rise. In Figure 5.11, the new long-run equilibrium is shown by point s, with a price of $1.80. The pattern of a large price drop followed by a gradual increase in price is a normal pattern for a perfectly competitive market.

TEST Your Understanding

13. Explain why the short-run supply curve is steeper than the long-run supply curve.

14. Describe the short-run price effect and the long-run price effect of a decrease in the demand for rakes.

15. Under what circumstances would an increase in demand for a particular good not affect the price of the good in the long run?

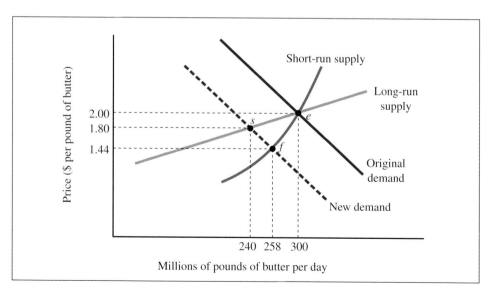

Figure 5.11
Short-Run and Long-Run Effects of a Decrease in the Demand for Butter
The short-run supply curve is steeper than the long-run supply curve because there are diminishing returns in the short run. In the short run, a decrease in demand decreases the price from $2 (point e) to $1.44 (point f). In the long run, firms leave the industry, and the price rises to the new equilibrium price of $1.80 (point s).

Using the TOOLS

We've seen how a perfectly competitive firm can use its cost curves to decide how much to produce and whether to continue operating an unprofitable operation. We've also explored the short- and long-run effects of changes in demand. Here are some opportunities to do your own economic analysis.

1. Advice for an Unprofitable Firm

You've been hired as an economic consultant to a price-taking firm that produces shirts. The firm already has a shirt factory, so it is operating in the short run. The price of shirts is $5, the hourly wage is $12, and each shirt requires $1 worth of material. At the current level of output (20 workers and 70 shirts per hour), the firm is losing money: Its total cost exceeds its total revenue. The firm has experimented with different numbers of workers and discovered that 21 workers would produce 72 shirts; 15 workers would produce 60 shirts; and 16 workers would produce 63 shirts. Your job is to tell the firm which of these four options to take:

- **Option 1.** Shut down the unprofitable operation.
- **Option 2.** Continue to produce 70 shirts per hour.
- **Option 3.** Produce more shirts.
- **Option 4.** Produce fewer shirts.

2. Maximizing the Profit Margin

According to the marginal principle, the firm should choose the quantity of output at which price equals marginal cost. A tempting alternative is to maximize the firm's profit margin, defined as the difference between price and short-run average total cost. Use the firm's short-run cost curves to evaluate this approach. Draw the firm's short-run supply curve and compare it to the supply curve of a firm that maximizes its profit.

3. Market Effects of an Increase in Housing Demand

Consider the market for apartments in a small city. In the initial equilibrium, the monthly rent (the price) is $500 and the quantity is 10,000 apartments. Suppose that the population of the city suddenly increases by 24%. The price elasticity of demand for apartments is 1.0. The short-run price elasticity of supply is 0.2, and the long-run price elasticity of supply is 0.5.

a. Depict graphically the short- and long-run effects of the increase in population.

b. By what percentage will the price increase in the short run? (Use the price-change formula from Chapter 3.)

c. By what percentage will the price increase in the long run?

Summary

In this chapter, we explored the decisions made by perfectly competitive firms and the implications of these decisions for the supply side of the market. In the short run, a firm uses the marginal principle to decide how much output to produce. In the long run, a firm will enter a market if the price exceeds the average cost of production. Here are the main points of this chapter:

1. A price-taking firm should produce the quantity of output at which the marginal revenue (the price) equals the marginal cost of production.

2. An unprofitable firm should continue to operate if its total revenue exceeds its total variable cost.

3. The long-run supply curve will be positively sloped if the average cost of production increases as the industry grows.

4. The long-run supply curve is flatter than the short-run supply curve because there are diminishing returns in the short run, but not in the long run.

5. An increase in demand causes a large upward jump in price, followed by a downward slide to the new long-run equilibrium price.

Key Terms

constant-cost industry, 121
economic profit, 106
increasing-cost industry, 116
long-run market supply curve, 116

marginal revenue, 108
perfectly competitive market, 106
short-run market supply curve, 114
short-run supply curve, 113

shut-down price, 111
sunk cost, 112
total revenue, 106

Problems and Discussion Questions

1. In the following table, provide the numbers for marginal cost. Then use the data to draw the short-run supply curve for tables.

Tables per Hour	Total Cost	Marginal Cost
3	120	—
4	155	—
5	200	—
6	270	—

2. The following table shows short-run marginal costs for a perfectly competitive firm:

Output	100	200	300	400	500
Marginal cost	\$5	\$10	\$20	\$40	\$70

a. Use this information to draw the firm's marginal cost curve.

b. Suppose the shut-down price is \$10. Draw the firm's short-run supply curve.

c. Suppose there are 100 identical firms with the same marginal cost curve. Draw the short-run industry supply curve.

3. You've been hired by an unprofitable firm to determine whether it should shut down its unprofitable operation. The firm currently uses 70 workers to produce 300 units of output per day. The daily wage (per worker) is \$100, and the price of the firm's output is \$30. Although you don't know the firm's fixed cost, you know that it is high enough that the firm's total cost exceeds its total revenue. Should the firm continue to operate at a loss?

4. Consider the choices facing an unprofitable (and perfectly competitive) firm. The firm currently pro-

duces 100 units per day and sells them at a price of \$22 each. At the current output quantity, the total cost is \$3,000 per day, the variable cost is \$2,500 per day, and the marginal cost is \$45.

a. Evaluate the following statement from the firm's accountant: "Given our current production level, our variable cost (\$2,500) exceeds our total revenue (\$2,200). We should shut down our production facility."

b. Illustrate your answer with a graph showing short-run cost curves and the revenue curve of a perfectly competitive firm.

5. Consider the following statement from a wheat farmer to his workers: "The price of wheat is very low this year, and the most I can get from the crop is \$35,000. If I paid you the same amount as I paid you last year (\$30,000), I'd lose money, because I also have to worry about the \$20,000 I paid three months ago for seed and fertilizer. I'd be crazy to pay a total of \$50,000 to harvest a crop I can sell for only \$35,000. If you are willing to work for half as much as last year (\$15,000), my total cost will be \$35,000, so I'll break even. If you don't take a pay cut, I won't harvest the wheat." Is the farmer bluffing, or will the farmworkers lose their jobs if they reject the proposed pay cut?

6. Consider a firm that uses the following rule to decide how much output to produce: If the profit margin (price minus short-run average total cost) is positive, the firm will produce more output. Use the firm's short-run cost curves to evaluate this approach. Draw the firm's short-run supply curve and compare it to the short-run supply curve of a profit-maximizing firm.

7. Consider the following data on the relationship between the price of gasoline (in real terms, adjusted for inflation) and the quantity of gasoline sold per day in the city of Ceteris Paribus:

Year	Price	Gallons per Day
1995	$1.00	50,000
1996	$1.10	53,000

If possible, draw the industry supply curve and compute the price elasticity of supply.

8. Between 1980 and 1990, the percentage of U.S. households with videocassette recorders (VCRs) increased from 1% to 70%. The rapid growth in the number of VCRs increased the demand for video rentals. Predict the effects of this increase in demand on the price of video rentals in the short run and the long run.

9. Suppose each lamp manufacturer produces 10 lamps per hour. In the following table, fill in a number wherever you see a _____. Then use the data in the table to draw the long-run supply curve for lamps.

Number of Firms	Industry Output	Total Cost for Typical Firm	Average Cost per Lamp
40	_____	$300	$_____
80	_____	$360	$_____
120	_____	$420	$_____

10. Suppose that a new technology decreases the amount of labor time required to produce a particular good. Would you expect all firms eventually to adopt the new technology?

11. Draw a long-run supply curve for haircutting that is consistent with the following statement: "The haircutting industry in our city uses a tiny fraction of the electricity, scissors, and commercial space available on the market. In addition, the industry uses only about 100 of the 50,000 people who could cut hair."

12. Draw a long-run supply curve for pencils and explain why you drew it as you did.

13. Web Exercise. Visit the Web site of Agricultural Weather Com (*www.agriculturalweather.com*). How might the information available at this Web site be useful to someone involved in the market for Florida orange juice?

14. Web Exercise. Visit the Web site of the Florida Agricultural Statistics Service (*www.nass.usda. gov/fl/*). Access the reports provided to get some data on recent trends in the price of some Florida citrus products. Draw a supply–demand graph consistent with the recent changes in prices and quantities.

Take It to the Net

We invite you to visit the O'Sullivan/Sheffrin page on the Prentice Hall Web site at: **www.prenhall.com/osullivan/** for additional World Wide Web exercises for this chapter.

Model Answers to Questions

Chapter-Opening Questions

1. To use the marginal principle, the firm needs the price (marginal benefit or marginal revenue) and the marginal cost of production for different levels of output.

2. It would be sensible to shut down if your total revenue is less than your variable cost. Otherwise, it would be sensible to continue operating.

3. Hurricane Andrew increased the demand for goods such as ice, chain saws, and plywood. In the short run, the supply curve for ice is steep, so the price increased by a relatively large amount. Over time, the price dropped as new firms entered the market to supply ice.

4. The large drop in price was a short-run effect, reflecting the steep short-run supply curve. As

firms dropped out of the market and production decreased, the price started to rise.

Test Your Understanding

1. The firm is such a tiny part of the market that no matter how much output it produces, it will not affect the market price.

2. Marginal revenue (or price), marginal cost.

3. The farmer is not maximizing profit because the marginal revenue (price) is less than the marginal cost. The farmer should produce less sugar.

4. $800 ($20 per lamp × 40 lamps).

5. Operate.

6. Average variable cost.

7. Price, quantity supplied.

8. You need the short-run marginal cost curve and the shut-down price. If you have the average variable cost curve and the marginal cost curve, you can figure out the shut-down price by finding the price at which the two curves intersect.

9. 5,000 units (50 units per firm × 100 firms).

10. Quantity supplied, price.

11. The average cost per rake is $10 ($70/7 rakes).

12. The related terms are positively sloped supply curve, increasing-cost industry, and increasing average cost of production.

13. There are diminishing returns in the short run, so production costs increase rapidly as a firm increases its output.

14. In the short run, the price would drop by a large amount. Then the price would start to rise. If the rake industry is an increasing-cost industry, the new long-run price would be less than the original price.

15. If the good is produced by a constant-cost industry, one with a horizontal long-run supply curve.

Using the Tools

1. **Advice for an Unprofitable Firm.** At the current output level (70 shirts), the marginal cost of production is $7 per shirt: To produce 1 more shirt, the firm must use half an hour of labor, which would cost $6 (half of the hourly wage) and $1 worth of material. Because the marginal cost exceeds the price ($5), the firm is not maximizing its profit.

   At an output level of 60 shirts, the marginal cost of production is only $5 per shirt: To produce 1 more shirt, the firm must use one-third of an hour of labor, which would cost $4 (one-third of the hourly wage) and $1 worth of material. At this quantity of output, the price equals marginal cost, so the firm is maximizing profit. Total revenue

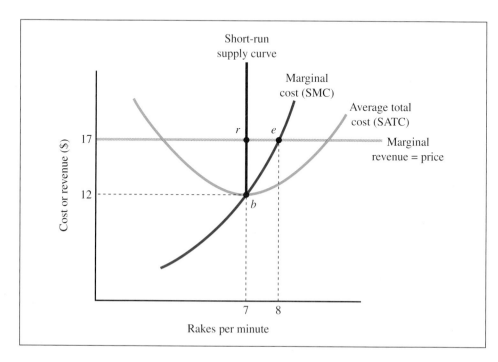

Figure 5.A

Short-Run Supply Curve with Maximizing the Profit Margin

A firm that maximizes its profit margin (the difference between price and average cost) will produce the quantity at which average cost is at its minimum. The supply curve is a vertical line starting at the minimum of the average cost curve.

($300 = $5 per shirt × 60 shirts) exceeds variable cost ($240 = $180 for labor [$12 per hour × 15 hours]) plus $60 for materials ($1 per shirt × 60 shirts), so it is sensible to continue to operate, even if total cost exceeds total revenue.

2. **Maximizing the Profit Margin.** To maximize the profit margin, the firm will choose the quantity that generates the largest possible gap between the price and average cost, and this occurs at the minimum point of the average cost curve. In Figure 5.A, the average total cost curve reaches its minimum point at point *b*, with a quantity of seven rakes and an average cost of $12. With a price of $17, the firm would produce seven rakes per minute and earn a profit of $5 per rake or $35 per minute.

As shown in Figure 5.A, at a price of $17, the firm would earn more profit by using the marginal principle. The price equals marginal cost with eight rakes, and profit is $38.40 (an average cost of $12.20 means profit per unit is $4.80). The profit margin approach is misguided because it looks at only one part of the profit picture: Total profit equals the profit margin times the quantity produced. Although the profit margin will be lower with eight rakes, total profit will be higher.

As shown in Figure 5.A, the supply curve is a vertical line starting at the minimum point of the average cost curve. Suppose the firm will shut down if the profit margin is negative. At any price less than $12, price will be less than average cost, so the profit margin will be negative and the firm will shut down. To maximize the gap between price and average cost, the firm will choose the quantity associated with the minimum point of the average cost curve (seven rakes), regardless of the price of rakes. Therefore, as long as the price exceeds $12, the firm will produce seven rakes. In contrast, the supply curve of a profit-maximizing firm is the marginal cost curve above the shut-down price.

3. **Market Effects of an Increase in Housing Demand**
   a. See Figure 5.B.
   b. Use the price-change formula from Chapter 3: percentage change in price = percentage change in demand/$(E_s + E_d)$ = 24/1.20 = 20%.
   c. Percentage change in price = 24/1.50 = 16%.

Figure 5.B
Short- and Long-Run Effects of Population Growth
The initial equilibrium is shown by point *i*. The increase in demand moves the market to point *s* in the short run and to point *f* in the long run.

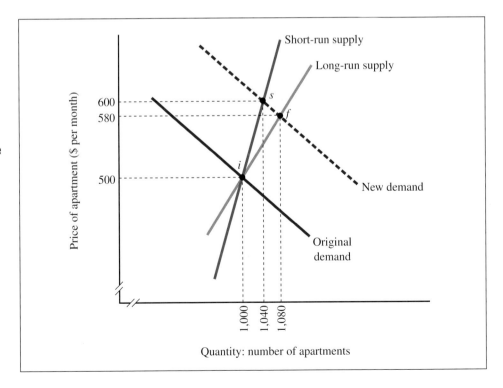

128   Chapter 5   Perfect Competition: Short Run and Long Run

Notes

1. TeleCommons Development Group, "Grameen Telecom's Village Phone Programme: A Multi-Media Case Study" (*http://www.telecommons. com/villagephone*).

2. Frederic L. Hoff and Max Lawrence, *Implications of World Sugar Markets, Policies, and Production Costs for U.S. Sugar*, Agricultural Economic Research Report 543 (Washington, DC: U.S. Department of Agriculture, Economic Research Service, November 1985).

3. Frank De Leeuw and Nkanta Ekanem, "The Supply of Rental Housing," *American Economic Review*, vol. 61, 1971, pp. 806–817.

4. D. I. Gordon and R. Dangerfield, *The Hidden Weapon* (New York: Harper & Brothers, 1947), pp. 105–116.

Monopoly

The Coca-Cola Company recently built a new football scoreboard for a large state university. Now football fans can enjoy the latest in scoreboard graphics as they watch the game. In addition, Coca-Cola gave $2.3 million to remodel the university's student center,[1] providing students with a comfortable place to meet, eat, talk, and relax. What explains this outburst of generosity? Does it have anything to do with the fact that Coca-Cola was recently given the exclusive right to sell beverages on campus—a monopoly? Who is really paying for the scoreboard and the student center?

I n Chapter 5, we explored the decisions made by firms in a perfectly competitive market, a market where there are dozens or perhaps hundreds of firms. This chapter deals with the opposite extreme: a **monopoly**, a market served by a single firm. In contrast with a perfectly competitive or price-taking firm, a monopolist can pick any price it wants. Of course, the higher the price it charges, the smaller the quantity it will sell, because consumers obey the law of demand.

Monopoly: A market in which a single firm serves the entire market.

A monopoly occurs when there is one firm and a barrier to entry—a barrier that prevents other firms from entering a market. Here is a list of possible barriers to entry:

- A **patent** is granted by the government, giving an inventor the exclusive right to sell a new product for some period of time. Under a General Agreement on Tariffs and Trade (GATT) agreement that took effect in 1995, patents in the United States and other GATT nations are now issued for 20 years from the time the inventor applies for a patent. To receive a patent, the inventor must prove the product is useful and novel (a true innovation, not just a slight modification of an existing product) and must provide a working model. Patent holders in many European countries pay an annual renewal fee for their patents, and the longer an inventor holds a patent, the higher the annual fee. In the United States, there are no renewal fees, so by paying a one-time fee, an inventor can prevent anyone else from selling the product for 20 years.

Patent: The exclusive right to sell a particular good for some period of time.

- In some cases, the government implicitly grants monopoly power by allowing industrial associations to restrict the number of firms in the market. For example, the U.S. government allows sports associations such as the major-league baseball leagues to restrict the number and location of teams.

Franchise or licensing scheme: A policy under which the government picks a single firm to sell a particular good.

- Under a **franchise or licensing scheme**, the government designates a single firm to sell a particular good. Here are some examples of franchise and licensing schemes:

  Some cities select a single firm to provide off-street parking.

  The National Park Service picks a single firm to sell food and other goods in Yosemite National Park.

Natural monopoly: A market in which the entry of a second firm would make the price less than the average cost, so a single firm serves the entire market.

- In some markets, there are large economies of scale in production (average cost decreases as the firm's output increases), so a single firm will be profitable, but a pair of firms would lose money. A **natural monopoly** occurs when the entry of a second firm would make price less than average cost, so a single firm serves the entire market.

- As we'll see later in the book, some firms use illegal means to exclude other firms from the market.

To explain how a monopoly works, we'll start with an example of a monopoly that results from a patent. We'll see that a monopolist can use the marginal principle to find the price that generates the highest possible profit. Later in this chapter, we'll explore the policy implications of a natural monopoly. Here are some of the practical questions relating to monopoly that we will answer:

1. What are the trade-offs associated with patents and other policies that grant monopoly power?
2. When the patent on a popular pharmaceutical drug expires, what happens to the price of the drug?
3. Should the government allow an electric utility (a monopolist in the market for electricity) to charge any price it wants?

The National Park Service picks a single firm to sell food and other goods in Yosemite National Park.

The Monopolist's Output Decision

A monopolist must decide what price to charge and how much output to produce. Like other firms, the monopoly's objective is to maximize profit, defined as the difference between total revenue and total cost. We learned about production costs in an earlier chapter, so we start our discussion with the revenue side of the monopolist's profit picture. Then we show how a monopolist picks a price and a quantity.

Total Revenue and Marginal Revenue

A firm's total revenue—the money it gets by selling its product—equals the price times the quantity sold. Table 6.1 shows how to use a demand schedule (in the first two columns) to compute a firm's total revenue (in the third column). At a price of $16, the firm doesn't sell anything, so its total revenue is zero. To sell one unit, the firm must cut

Table 6.1   Demand, Total Revenue, and Marginal Revenue

Price	Quantity Sold	Total Revenue	Marginal Revenue
$16	0	0	—
$14	1	$14	$ 14
$12	2	$24	$ 10
$10	3	$30	$ 6
$ 8	4	$32	$ 2
$ 6	5	$30	$−2
$ 4	6	$24	$−6

its price to $14, so its total revenue is $14. To get consumers to buy two units instead of just one, the firm must cut its price to $12. The total revenue associated with selling two units is $24. As the price continues to drop and the quantity sold increases, total revenue increases for a while but then starts falling. To sell five units instead of four, the firm cuts its price from $8 to $6, and total revenue decreases from $32 to $30. The total revenue associated with selling six units is even lower ($24). The top panel in Figure 6.1 shows the relationship between total revenue and the quantity sold.

Marginal revenue: The change in total revenue from selling one additional unit.

The firm's **marginal revenue** is defined as the change in total revenue that results from selling one more unit of output. In Table 6.1, we compute marginal revenue by taking the difference between the total revenue from selling a certain quantity of output (for example, three units), and the total revenue from selling one fewer unit of output (for example, two units). As shown in the fourth row in the table, the total revenue from selling three units is $30 and the total revenue from selling two units is $24, so the marginal revenue from selling the third unit is $6. As shown in the table and in the lower panel of Figure 6.1, marginal revenue is positive for the first four units sold. Beyond four units, selling an additional unit results in lower total revenue, so marginal revenue is negative. For example, the marginal revenue for the fifth unit is −$2, and the marginal revenue for the sixth unit is −$6.

Table 6.1 and Figure 6.1 illustrate the trade-offs associated with cutting a price to sell a larger quantity. When the firm cuts its price from $12 to $10, there is good news and bad news:

- **Good news.** The firm collects $10 from the new customer (the third), so revenue increases by $10.

Figure 6.1
Total Revenue and Marginal Revenue
As the firm cuts its price to sell more output, its total revenue rises for the first four units sold but then decreases for the fifth and sixth units. Therefore, marginal revenue (the change in total revenue from selling one more unit) is positive for the first four units and then becomes negative.

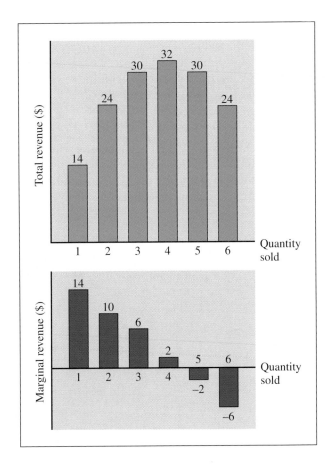

- **Bad news.** If the firm has the same price for all its customers, it cuts the price for everyone, so it gets less revenue from the customers who would have been willing to pay the higher price ($12). Specifically, the firm collects $2 less from each of the two original customers, so revenue decreases by $4.

The combination of good news and bad news leads to a net increase in total revenue of only $6, resulting from the $10 gained from the new customer minus the $4 lost on the first two customers. Because of the bad news associated with selling an additional unit of output, a firm's marginal revenue is always less than its price.

We can use a simple expression to show how marginal revenue is determined by the good news and bad news from selling one more unit of output.

$$\text{marginal revenue} = \text{new price} - \text{old quantity} \times \text{slope of demand curve}$$

The good news is the new price ($10 in our example) and the bad news is the old quantity (2 units in our example) times the slope of the demand curve (the change in price required to sell one more unit of output, which is $2 in our example):

$$\text{marginal revenue} = \$10 - 2 \text{ units} \times \$2 \text{ per unit} = \$6$$

Similarly, to sell the fifth unit, the firm would cut the price from $8 to $6, and marginal revenue is actually negative:

$$\text{marginal revenue} = \$6 - 4 \text{ units} \times \$2 \text{ per unit} = -\$2$$

Figure 6.2 shows the demand curve and marginal revenue curve for the data shown in Table 6.1. Because the firm must cut its price to sell more output, the marginal revenue curve lies below the demand curve. For example, the demand curve shows that the firm will sell three units at a price of $10 (point *d*), but the marginal revenue for this quantity is only $6 (point *i*). For quantities of five units and greater, marginal revenue is negative because when the firm cuts its price to sell one additional unit, the bad news

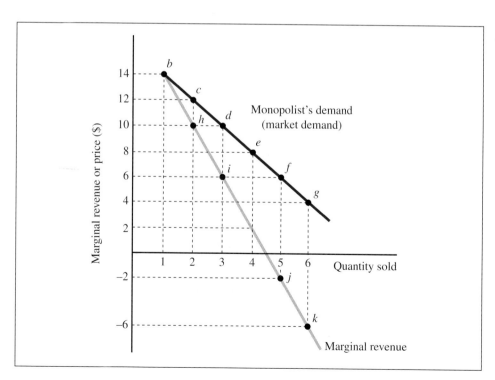

Figure 6.2

Demand Curve and Marginal Revenue Curve

Marginal revenue is equal to the price for the first unit sold but is less than the price for all other units sold. To increase the quantity sold, a firm cuts its price and receives less revenue on the units that could have been sold at the higher price. Therefore, beyond the first unit sold, the marginal revenue curve lies below the demand curve.

dominates the good news: The amount the firm loses on its original customers exceeds the amount it gains on the new one, so total revenue drops.

The Marginal Principle and the Output Decision

We use a simple example to explain how a monopolist decides how much output to produce. Sneezy, who holds a patent on a new drug that cures the common cold, must decide how much of the drug to produce and what price to charge for it. These two decisions are related because according to the law of demand, the higher the price, the smaller the quantity demanded. Sneezy can use the marginal principle to choose how much to produce and what price to charge.

 Marginal **PRINCIPLE**

Increase the level of an activity if its marginal benefit exceeds its marginal cost, but reduce the level if the marginal cost exceeds the marginal benefit. If possible, pick the level at which the marginal benefit equals the marginal cost.

Sneezy's activity is producing the cold drug, and he will pick the quantity at which the marginal revenue from selling one more unit (the marginal benefit) equals the marginal cost associated with that unit:

marginal revenue = marginal cost

The first two columns in Table 6.2 show the relationship between the price of the cold drug and the quantity demanded. We can use these numbers to draw the market demand curve, as shown in Figure 6.3. Because Sneezy is a monopolist—the only seller of the drug—the market demand curve shows how much he will sell at each price. The demand curve is negatively sloped, consistent with the law of demand. For example, at a price of $18 per dose, the quantity demanded is 600 doses per hour (point *h*), compared to 900 doses at a price of $15 (point *m*).

Like other monopolists, Sneezy must cut his price to sell a larger quantity, so marginal revenue is less than price. This is shown in the third column of Table 6.2 and in Figure 6.3. We can use the marginal revenue formula explained earlier to compute marginal revenue for different quantities of output. To simplify the arithmetic, rather than use the "new" price and "old" quantity, we can use a matched pair of price and quantity

Table 6.2   Using the Marginal Principle to Pick a Price and Quantity

Price (per Dose)	Quantity Sold (Doses)	Marginal Revenue	Marginal Cost	Total Revenue	Total Cost	Profit
$18	600	$12	$4.00	$10,800	$5,710	$5,090
$17	700	$10	$4.60	$11,900	$6,140	$5,760
$16	800	$ 8	$5.30	$12,800	$6,635	$6,165
$15	900	$ 6	$6.00	$13,500	$7,200	$6,300
$14	1,000	$ 4	$6.70	$14,000	$7,835	$6,165
$13	1,100	$ 2	$7.80	$14,300	$8,560	$5,740
$12	1,200	0	$9.00	$14,400	$9,400	$5,000

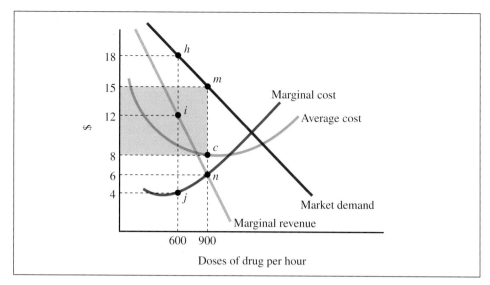

Figure 6.3
Monopolist Picks a Quantity and a Price
To maximize profit, the monopolist picks point *n*, where marginal revenue equals marginal cost. The monopolist produces 900 doses per hour at a price of $15 (point *m*). The average cost is $8 (point *c*), so the profit per dose is $7 (equal to the $15 price minus the $8 average cost) and the total profit is $6,300 (equal to $7 per dose times 900 doses).

from the demand curve to get an approximation of marginal revenue. The slope of the demand curve is $0.01 per dose. For example, at a price of $18, the quantity sold is 600 doses, so marginal revenue is

$$\text{marginal revenue} = \$18 - 600 \text{ doses} \times \$0.01 = \$12$$

Similarly, at a price of $15, the quantity is 900 doses and marginal revenue = $15 − 900 doses × $0.01 = $6.

Picking a Quantity and a Price

We're ready to show how a monopolist can use the marginal principle to pick a quantity and price. To maximize his profit, Sneezy should produce the quantity at which the marginal revenue equals marginal cost. By looking at the numbers in Table 6.2, we can see that this happens with a quantity of 900 doses and a price of $15, as shown in the fourth row. In Figure 6.3, the marginal revenue curve intersects the marginal cost curve at point *n* with a quantity of 900 doses, so that's the quantity that maximizes profit. To get consumers to buy this quantity, the price must be $15 (point *m* on the demand curve). The average cost of production is $8 per dose (shown by point *c*), so the profit per dose is $7 ($15 minus $8). Sneezy's profit equals the profit per dose ($7) times the quantity sold (900 doses), or $6,300 per hour.

To show that a price of $15 and a quantity of 900 doses maximizes Sneezy's profit, let's see what would happen if he picked some other quantity. Suppose he decided to produce 599 doses per hour at a price just above $18 (just above point *h* on the demand curve). Could he make more profit by cutting his price by enough to sell one more dose? Sneezy should answer two questions:

1. What is the extra cost associated with producing dose number 600? As shown by point *j* on the marginal cost curve, the marginal cost of the 600th dose is $4.
2. What is the extra revenue associated with dose number 600? As shown by point *i* on the marginal revenue curve, the marginal revenue is $12.

If Sneezy wants to maximize his profit, he should produce the 600th dose because the $12 extra revenue exceeds the $4 extra cost, so his total profit will increase by $8. The same argument applies, with different numbers for marginal revenue, and marginal cost, for doses 601, 602, and so on, up to 900 doses. Sneezy should continue to increase the quantity produced as long as the marginal revenue exceeds the marginal cost. The marginal principle is satisfied at point n, with a total of 900 doses.

Why should Sneezy stop at 900 doses? Beyond 900 doses, the marginal revenue from an additional dose will be less than the marginal cost associated with producing it. Although Sneezy could cut his price and sell a larger quantity, an additional dose would add less to revenue than it adds to cost, so his total profit would decrease. As shown in the fifth row in Table 6.2, Sneezy could sell 1,000 doses at a price of $14, but the marginal revenue at this quantity is only $4, while the marginal cost at this quantity is $6.70. Producing the 1,000th dose would decrease Sneezy's profit by $2.70. For any quantity exceeding 900 doses, the marginal revenue is less than the marginal cost, so Sneezy should produce exactly 900 doses.

The Costs of Monopoly

What are the trade-offs—the costs and benefits to society as a whole—associated with a monopoly? This is an important question because in many cases, a monopoly results from government policy. If the costs exceed the benefits, it may be sensible to remove the barriers to entry and allow other firms to enter the market. We discuss the costs of monopoly in this part of the chapter and explore the benefits in the next part. We'll start with a concept that quantifies the consumer benefits of a market.

The Demand Curve and Consumer Surplus

If you said "thank you" the last time you purchased a product, did you mean it? If you were willing to pay more than the price you actually paid, you received what's called **consumer surplus**. Consumer surplus is the difference between the maximum amount a consumer is willing to pay for a product and the price that he or she pays for the product. For example, if you are willing to pay $21 for a CD that you buy for $10, your consumer surplus is $11.

Let's start our discussion of consumer surplus with another look at the demand curve, which shows how much consumers are willing to pay for a product. Figure 6.4 shows the market demand curve for lawn cutting in a small town. The demand curve shows that no one will pay to have their lawn cut for $25 (point t), but the first consumer (Juan) will pay for a cut if the price drops to $22. This suggests that Juan is willing to pay up to $22 to have his lawn cut but no more. Moving down the demand curve, the second consumer (Tupak) will pay for lawn cutting when the price drops to $19, suggesting that he is willing to pay up to $19. As we continue to move downward along the demand curve, other consumers are willing to pay less and less for each additional lawn cut.

We can use the demand curve to measure just how much of a net benefit or surplus consumers get. Suppose that the price of a lawn cut is $10, and everyone pays this price. Juan's consumer surplus is $12, the amount he is willing to pay ($22) minus the price. Similarly, Tupak's consumer surplus is $9, equal to the difference between the amount he is willing to pay ($19) and the market price. To compute the total consumer surplus in the lawn-cutting market, we simply add up the surpluses for each of the five consumers who buy lawn cutting at a price of $10. In this example, the market consumer surplus is $30, equal to $12 (Juan) + $9 (Tupak) + $6 (Thurl) + $3 (Forest) + $0 (Fivola). The fifth consumer (Fivola) gets no consumer surplus because the price equals the amount she is willing to pay. The sixth person (Siggy) doesn't have his lawn cut because the amount he is willing to pay is less than the price. In general, the total consumer sur-

Consumer surplus: The difference between the maximum amount a consumer is willing to pay for a product and the price that he or she pays for the product.

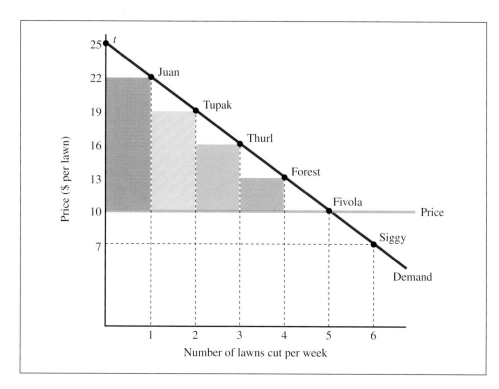

Figure 6.4

Demand Curve and Consumer Surplus
Consumer surplus equals the maximum amount a consumer is willing to pay (shown by the demand curve) minus the price paid. Juan is willing to pay $22, so if the price is $10, his consumer surplus is $12. The market consumer surplus equals the sum of the surpluses earned by all consumers in the market. In this case, the market consumer surplus is $30 = $12 + $9 + $6 + $3 + $0.

plus in a market is shown by the area between the demand curve and the horizontal price line.

Monopoly Versus Perfect Competition

How does a monopoly differ from a perfectly competitive market? To show the difference, let's consider an example of an arthritis drug that could be produced by a monopoly or a perfectly competitive industry. Let's take the long-run perspective, a period of time long enough that a firm is perfectly flexible in its choice of inputs and firms can enter or leave a perfectly competitive market.

Consider the monopoly outcome first. To simplify matters, let's assume that the long-run average cost of producing the arthritis drug is constant at $8 per dose. As we saw in Chapter 4, if average cost is constant, the marginal cost equals average cost. In panel A of Figure 6.5, the long-run marginal cost curve is the same as the long-run average cost curve. Given the demand and marginal revenue curves in panel A of Figure 6.5, the monopolist will maximize profit where marginal revenue equals marginal cost (point n), producing 200 doses per hour at a price of $18 per dose. The monopolist's profit is $2,000 per hour (a $10 profit per dose [$18 − $8] × 200 doses).

Consider next the market for the arthritis drug under perfect competition. We're assuming that the arthritis drug industry is a constant-cost industry: Input prices do not change as the industry grows, so the long-run market supply curve is horizontal at the long-run average cost of producing the drug ($8 per dose). In panel B of Figure 6.5, the horizontal long-run supply curve intersects the demand curve at point p, with an equilibrium price of $8 and an equilibrium quantity of 400 doses per hour. Compared to a monopoly outcome, the perfectly competitive outcome has a lower price ($8 instead of $18) and a larger quantity (400 doses instead of 200).

To examine the social cost of monopoly power, let's imagine that we start with a perfectly competitive market and then switch to a monopoly. Consumers will be worse off

Figure 6.5
Monopoly Versus Perfect Competition

(A) Monopoly. The monopolist picks the quantity at which long-run marginal cost equals marginal revenue (200 doses per hour, as shown by point n). As shown by point m on the demand curve, the price associated with this quantity is $18 per dose.

(B) Perfect competition. The long-run supply curve of a perfectly competitive, constant-cost industry intersects the demand curve at point p. The equilibrium price is $8, and the equilibrium quantity is 400 doses per hour.

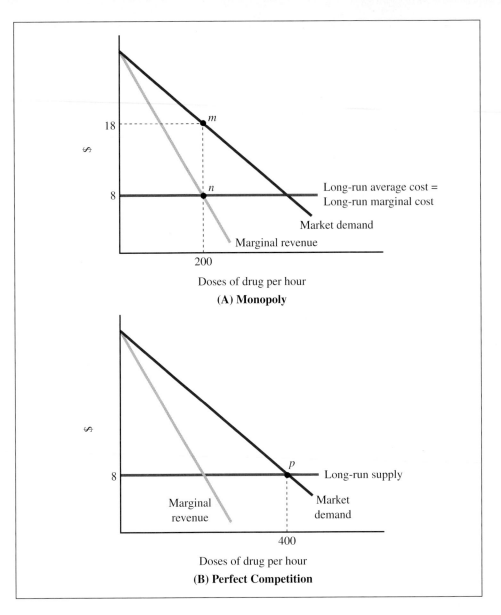

(A) Monopoly

Doses of drug per hour

(B) Perfect Competition

Doses of drug per hour

under monopoly, and we can use the concept of consumer surplus to determine just how much worse off they are. As we saw earlier in the chapter, consumer surplus is shown by the area between the demand curve and the horizontal price line. In Figure 6.6, the monopoly price is $18, so the consumer surplus associated with the monopoly is shown by triangle C. In contrast, the perfectly competitive price is $8, so the consumer surplus with perfect competition is shown by the larger triangle consisting of triangle C, rectangle R, and triangle D. In other words, a switch from perfect competition to monopoly decreases consumer surplus by the areas R and D.

Let's take a closer look at the loss of consumer surplus resulting from a switch to monopoly:

• **Rectangle R.** The switch to monopoly increases the price by $10 per dose. Consumers buy 200 doses from the monopolist and pay $10 extra on each of these doses, for a loss of $2,000 per hour.

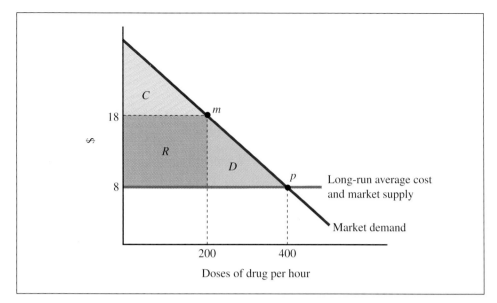

Figure 6.6
Deadweight Loss from Monopoly
A switch from perfect competition to monopoly increases the price from $8 to $18 and decreases the quantity sold from 400 to 200 doses. Consumer surplus decreases by an amount shown by the areas *R* and *D*, while profit increases by the amount shown by rectangle *R*. The net loss to society is shown by triangle *D* (the deadweight loss of monopoly).

- **Triangle *D*.** The switch to monopoly decreases the quantity consumed because the price increases and consumers obey the law of demand. Consumers lose consumer surplus on the doses they would have consumed at the lower price. This loss is shown by triangle *D*, with an area of $1,000 (one half the base of the triangle (200 doses) times the height ($10)).

The total loss of consumers is the sum of the areas of rectangle *R* and triangle *D*, or $3,000.

How much better off are firms under perfect competition? Under perfect competition, each firm makes zero economic profit, while a monopolist earns positive economic profit. In Figure 6.6, the monopolist's profit is shown by rectangle *R*: The profit margin is $10 (a price of $18 minus an average cost of $8) and the quantity is 200 doses per hour, for a total profit of $2,000 per hour. The switch to monopoly means that the monopolist gains rectangle *R* at the expense of consumers: They pay an additional $10 per dose, while the monopolist gets a profit of $10 per dose.

Only part of the loss experienced by consumers is recovered by the monopolist, so there is a net loss from switching to monopoly. Consumers lose rectangle *R* and triangle *D*, but the monopolist gains only rectangle *R*. That leaves triangle *D* as the net loss or **deadweight loss from monopoly**. The word *deadweight* indicates that this loss is not offset by a gain to anyone. In contrast, rectangle *R* is lost by consumers but gained by the monopolist. Consumers lose triangle *D* because in a perfectly competitive market, they would receive some consumer surplus from the 201st through 400th doses, which of course a monopolist would not produce. The lesson is that monopoly is inefficient because, compared to a perfectly competitive market, the monopolist produces less output.

Rent Seeking: Using Resources to Get Monopoly Power

Another source of inefficiency from a government-sanctioned monopoly is that firms use resources to acquire monopoly power. A firm that gets a monopoly on a particular product will earn a large profit, so firms are willing to spend large sums of money in an effort to persuade the government to erect barriers to entry (licenses, franchises, and industrial associations). One way to get monopoly power is to hire lobbyists to

Deadweight loss from monopoly: A measure of the inefficiency from monopoly; equal to the difference between the consumer-surplus loss from monopoly pricing and the monopoly profit.

Rent seeking: The process under which a firm spends money to persuade the government to erect barriers to entry and pick the firm as the monopolist.

persuade legislators and other policymakers to grant monopoly power. This is known as **rent seeking**.

Rent seeking is inefficient because it uses resources that could be used in other ways. For example, the people employed as lobbyists could instead produce goods and services. The classic study of rent seeking found that firms in some industries spent up to 30% of their total revenue to get monopoly power.[2]

At the beginning of this chapter, we saw that Coca-Cola helped a state university to build a new football scoreboard and remodel the student center. Was this an act of generosity? In return for the scoreboard and the remodeled student center, Coca-Cola earned the exclusive right to sell beverages on campus. Just like any monopolist, Coca-Cola will use its monopoly power to charge higher prices for beverages, so the cost of the scoreboard and student center actually comes out of the pockets of students.

TEST Your Understanding

1. Why is a monopolist's marginal revenue less than its price?

2. Complete the statement with a number: At a price of $15 per CD, a firm sells 80 CDs per day. If the slope of the demand curve is $0.10 per CD, marginal revenue is _____.

3. You want to determine the quantity of output produced by a monopolist. What information do you need, and how would you use it?

4. At a price of $18 per CD, the marginal revenue of a CD seller is $12. If the marginal cost of CDs is $9, should the firm increase or decrease the quantity produced? Should it increase or decrease its price?

Patents and Monopoly Power

Are there benefits associated with a government-sanctioned monopoly? As we'll see, a patent or another entry barrier encourages innovation because the innovator knows he or she will earn monopoly profits on a new product for some specific period of time. If the monopoly profits are large enough to offset the substantial research and development costs of a new product, a firm will develop the product and become a monopolist.

Incentives for Innovation

Let's use the arthritis drug to show why a patent encourages innovation. Suppose that Hanna hasn't yet developed the drug and she computes the potential benefits and costs of developing the drug as follows:

- The cost of research and development would be $14 million.

- The estimated annual profit from a monopoly would be $2 million (in today's dollars).

- Hanna's competitors will need three years to develop and produce their own versions of the drug, so if Hanna isn't protected by a patent, her monopoly will last only three years.

Based on these numbers, Hanna won't develop the drug unless she receives a patent that lasts at least seven years. That's the length of time she needs to recover her research and development costs ($2 million per year × 7 years = $14 million). If there is no patent and she loses her monopoly in three years, she will earn a profit of $6 million, which is less than her research and development costs. On the other hand, with a 20-year patent, she will earn $40 million, which is more than enough to recover her costs.

Trade-Offs from Patents

Is the patent for Hanna's drug beneficial from the social perspective? The patent grants monopoly power to Hanna, and she responds by charging a higher price and producing less than the quantity that would be produced in a perfectly competitive market (200 doses per hour instead of 400). From society's perspective, 400 doses would be better than 200 doses, but we don't have that choice: Hanna won't develop the drug unless a patent protects her from competition for at least seven years. Therefore, society's choice is between 200 doses (the patent and monopoly outcome) and zero doses. Because 200 doses is clearly better than none, the patent is beneficial from society's perspective.

What about a product that would be developed without the protection of a patent? Suppose Marcus could develop a new drug with a research and development project costing $5 million. If Marcus does not have a patent for his new drug, he would earn monopoly profits of $2 million per year for three years, a total of $6 million. Because his research and development costs are low relative to the monopoly profit, a three-year monopoly will generate enough profit to cover his costs, so he will develop the new drug even without a patent. Therefore, if the government issues a 20-year patent, the only effect is to prolong Marcus's monopoly, and that means the patent would be inefficient from society's perspective.

What are the general conclusions about the merits of the patent system? As usual, there are some trade-offs. It is sensible to grant a patent for a product that would otherwise not be developed but not sensible to grant one for a product that would be developed even without a patent. Unfortunately, no one knows in advance whether a particular product would be developed without a patent, so the government can't be selective in granting patents. Therefore, some patents will merely prolong a firm's monopoly power and generate higher prices. There is no consensus among economists on whether the benefits of patents (from the development of new products) exceed the costs (from prolonging monopoly power).

What happens when a patent expires? New firms will enter the market, and the resulting competition for consumers will decrease prices. The transition from monopoly to competition is not always a smooth one, as you'll see in "A Closer Look: Barriers to Generic Drugs."

There are trade-offs with patents: The monopoly power causes higher prices for consumers but encourages firms to invest in research and development to develop new drugs.

A CLOSER LOOK   BARRIERS TO GENERIC DRUGS

When the patent for a popular pharmaceutical drug expires, other firms introduce generic versions of the drug. The generics are virtually identical to the original branded drug, but they sell at a much lower price. The producers of branded drugs have an incentive to delay the introduction of generic drugs, and sometimes use illegal means to do so.

In 1999, the Federal Trade Commission (FTC) launched a probe of four large pharmaceutical companies to determine whether they unfairly stifled competition from generic producers. The FTC is investigating allegations that the makers of branded drugs made deals with generic suppliers to keep generics off the market. The alleged practices include cash payments and exclusive licenses for new versions of the branded drug.[3] Eli Lilly and Company announced a deal under which Sepracor, Inc., would have the exclusive right to

sell a purified version of Prozac (the antidepressant with annual sales of $2.8 billion). In effect, this deal would extend Lilly's monopoly over the drug for another 15 years. Abbott Laboratories was accused of paying $24 million per year to Ivax Corporation and an undisclosed amount to Novartis AG to delay the launch of their generic versions of Hytrin, Abbott's hypertension drug. Similar allegations of payoffs to generic suppliers have been levied against Hoechst AG in connection with its annual payment of $40 million to Andrx Corporation, which had produced—but not sold—a generic version of Cardizem, Hoechst's heart medication. Another tactic used by the producers of branded drugs is to claim that generics are not as good as the branded drug. DuPont has asserted that generic versions of its Coumadin (a blood thinner) are not equivalent to Coumadin and may pose risks to patients.

Do the Benefits Exceed the Costs?

From the efficiency perspective, we cannot make a clear-cut case for or against a government-sanctioned monopoly. As usual, there are both benefits and costs associated with using patents, licenses, franchises, and industrial associations to establish monopolies:

- On the cost side, a monopolist produces less output than a perfectly competitive market, and people also waste resources trying to get and keep monopoly power.

- On the benefit side, a patent or a license increases the payoff from research and development, and firms respond by developing new products.

In some cases—when research and development costs are substantial and other firms could quickly imitate a new product—the benefits will dominate the costs, and public policies that support a monopoly are sensible. In other cases, it would be more efficient to eliminate the artificial barriers to entry.

TEST Your Understanding

5. Your city will select a single firm to provide off-street parking. Your long-run average cost is $30 per parking space per day, and you would charge a price of $35 per space per day for a total of 500 spaces. How much would you be willing to pay for the monopoly?

6. Consider the arthritis example. Will Hanna develop the drug without a patent if she will have a monopoly for five years instead of just three years?

7. Critically appraise the following statement: "I just invented a new product. I could do the research and development required to bring the product to the market, but it would cost me $100 million. Once other firms develop imitations of my product, I will earn an annual profit of only $1 million. If I don't have a patent, I would be crazy to develop this product."

Natural Monopoly

Up to this point, we have considered a monopoly that results from artificial barriers to entry. In some monopolized markets, a second firm could enter a market, but if it did, both firms would lose money. That's why a single firm serves the entire market in what's called a natural monopoly. The classic examples of natural monopolies are public utilities (sewerage, water, and electricity generation) and transportation services (railroad freight and mass transit). We'll use the example of electricity generation to explain why a natural monopoly occurs.

Picking an Output Level

Figure 6.7 shows the long-run average cost curve for electricity generation, using real data from Chapter 4. The curve is negatively sloped and steep, reflecting the large economies of scale associated with generating electric power. These economies of scale occur because the indivisible inputs required to generate power (the power plant or hydroelectric dam) are very costly.

What about the long-run marginal cost of generating electricity? As we learned in Chapter 4, if the average cost of production is decreasing (if the average cost curve is negatively sloped), the marginal cost is less than the average cost. In Figure 6.7, the long-run marginal cost curve of electricity lies below the long-run average cost curve.

Figure 6.7 shows how to use the cost curves and revenue curves to pick the output level that maximizes profit. If a single firm—a monopolist—provides electricity, the

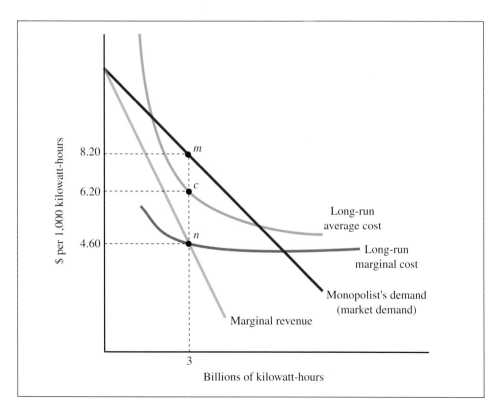

Figure 6.7

Natural Monopolist Uses the Marginal Principle to Pick a Price and Quantity
Because of scale economies in production (indivisible inputs), the long-run average cost curve is negatively sloped. The monopolist chooses point *n* (where marginal revenue equals marginal cost), supplying 3 billion units at a price of $8.20 per unit (point *m*) and an average cost of $6.20 per unit (point *c*). The profit per unit of electricity is $2.

monopolist's demand curve is the same as the market demand curve: To determine how much electricity the monopolist will sell at a particular price, we look at the market demand curve. The demand curve is negatively sloped, and the marginal revenue curve lies below the demand curve. The marginal principle is satisfied at point n, with 3 billion units of electricity (thousands of kilowatt-hours). The price associated with this quantity is $8.20 per unit of electricity (shown by point m), and the average cost is $6.20 per unit (shown by point c), so the profit per unit of electricity is $2. The price exceeds the average cost, so the electric company will earn a profit.

Will a Second Firm Enter?

If there are no artificial barriers to entry, a second firm could enter the electricity market. What would happen if a second firm entered the market? In Figure 6.8, the entry of a second firm would shift the demand curve facing the first firm—the former monopolist—to the left, from D_1 to D_2: At each price, the first firm will sell a smaller quantity of electricity because it now shares the market with another firm. For example, at a price of $8.20, the total quantity of electricity sold is 3 billion units, or 1.5 billion units for each firm. In general, the larger the number of firms, the lower the demand curve facing the typical firm. D_2 is the demand curve for the typical firm in a two-firm market, so it is also the demand curve for the potential entrant.

Will a second firm enter the electricity market? In this example, the demand curve of the typical firm in a two-firm market lies entirely below the long-run average cost curve, so there is no quantity at which the price exceeds the average cost of production. No matter what price the typical firm charges, it will lose money. The firm's demand curve lies below the average cost curve because the average cost curve is steep, reflecting the large economies of scale in generating electricity. A second firm—with half the market—would have a very high average cost and wouldn't be able to charge a price

Figure 6.8

Why Won't a Second Firm Enter the Market?
The entry of a second electricity firm would shift the demand curve facing the typical firm to the left. In this example, after entry, the firm's demand curve lies entirely below the long-run average cost curve. No matter what price the typical firm charges, it will lose money. Therefore, a second firm will not enter the market.

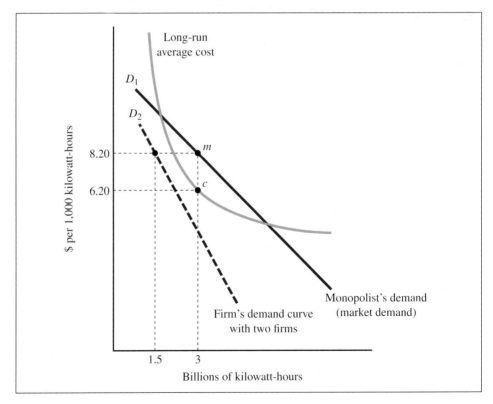

high enough to cover its high average cost. Therefore, the second firm will not enter the market, so there will be a single firm, a natural monopoly. For an example of a potential new natural monopoly, read "A Closer Look: Will Satellite Radio Be a Natural Monopoly?"

Price Controls for a Natural Monopoly

When a monopoly is inevitable—the case of natural monopoly—the government often sets a maximum price for the monopolist. There are many examples of natural monopolies that are subject to maximum prices. Local governments regulate utilities and firms that provide water, electricity, and local telephone service. State governments use public utility commissions (PUCs) to regulate the electric power industry.

Let's use the electricity market to explain the effects of government regulation of a natural monopoly. Suppose the government sets a maximum price for electricity and forces the electric company to serve all the consumers who are willing to pay the maximum price. In other words, the government—not the firm—picks a point on the market demand curve. Under an **average cost pricing policy**, the government picks the lowest price at which the market demand curve intersects the monopolist's long-run average cost curve. In Figure 6.9, the original average cost curve intersects the demand curve at

Average cost pricing policy: A regulatory policy under which the government picks the lowest price at which the market demand curve intersects the long-run average cost curve.

Figure 6.9
Regulation Using Average Cost Pricing
Under an average cost pricing policy, the government chooses the price at which the demand curve intersects the average cost curve. Regulation shifts the long-run average cost curve upward, so the government picks point *r*, with a price of $6 per unit.

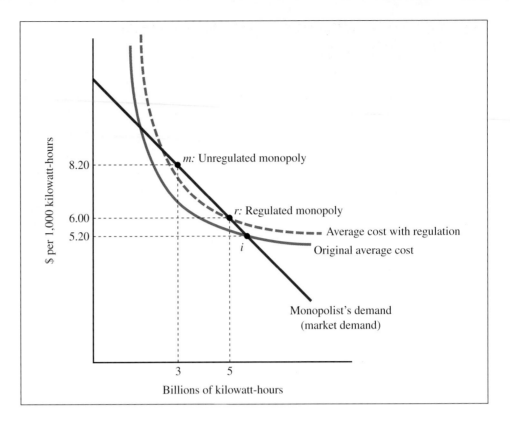

point *i*, with a price of $5.20 per unit of electricity. Although consumers would prefer a lower price, the electric company would lose money at any price less than $5.20, so lower prices are not feasible.

How will this regulatory policy affect the monopolist's production costs? Under average cost pricing, a change in the monopolist's production cost will not affect its profit because the government will adjust the regulated price to keep the price equal to the average cost. The government will increase the regulated price when the monopolist's cost increases, and decrease the price when its cost decreases. Because there is no reward for cutting its costs and no penalty for higher costs, the monopolist has little incentive to control its costs, so its costs will increase, pulling up the regulated price.

The average cost policy causes the market to move along the market demand curve in two steps:

1. **Downward slide.** Starting from the price and quantity resulting from an unregulated monopoly (point *m*), we slide down the demand curve to point *i*, the point that would occur if regulation did not increase the monopolist's cost.

2. **Upward climb.** As the monopolist's cost increases because of regulation, the regulator increases the price to cover the extra costs, so we climb part way back up the market demand curve, from point *i* to point *r*.

In this example, the net effect of this regulatory policy is a lower price of electricity ($6 instead of $8.20) and a larger quantity (5 billion units instead of 3 billion units). In other words, the regulatory policy moves the market downward along the market demand curve, from point *m* to point *r*.

Does a Decrease in Demand Decrease the Price?

When the population of Powerland decreased, the demand for all sorts of goods—including housing, clothing, and electricity—decreased as well. The decrease in the demand for housing decreased the price of housing, consistent with simple supply and demand analysis. In contrast, the price of electricity increased, a result that seems to defy the laws of supply and demand. What explains the puzzling increase in the price of electricity?

The key to solving this mystery is the fact that electricity is a regulated natural monopoly, with prices set by government regulators. The government of Powerland uses an average cost pricing policy to set the price of electricity: The regulated price equals the average cost of production. Any decrease in the quantity of electricity produced will lead to a higher average cost as the producer moves upward along the negatively sloped average cost curve. Under average cost pricing, the higher the average cost, the higher the regulated price. In graphical terms, the demand curve for electricity shifted to the left, so it intersected the negatively sloped average cost curve at a smaller quantity of electricity and a higher average cost. The regulated price is shown by the intersection of the demand curve and the average cost curve, so a leftward shift in demand increases the regulated price.

TEST Your Understanding

9. Complete the statement: A natural monopolist picks the quantity of output at which _____ equals _____.

10. Explain the effects of the entry of a second firm on the demand curve facing the original monopolist.

11. Complete the statement with above or below: A natural monopoly occurs when the long-run cost curve lies entirely _____ the demand curve of the typical firm in a two-firm market.

Using the TOOLS

1. Textbook Pricing: Publishers Versus Authors

Consider the problem of setting a price for an economics textbook. The marginal cost of production is constant at $20 per book. The publisher knows from experience that the slope of the demand curve is $0.20 per textbook: Starting with a price of $48, a price cut of $0.20 will increase the quantity demanded by one textbook. For example, here are some combinations of price and quantity:

Price per textbook	$44	$40	$36	$32	$30
Quantity of textbooks	80	100	120	140	150

a. What price will the publisher choose?

b. Suppose that the author receives a royalty payment equal to 10% of the total sales revenue from the book. If the author could choose a price, what would it be?

c. Why do the publisher and the author disagree about the price for the book?

d. Design an alternative author-compensation scheme under which the author and the publisher would choose the same price.

2. Payoff for Casino Approval

In 1996, developers interested in building an American Indian casino in Creswell, Oregon, placed a curious announcement in the local newspaper. If local voters approved the casino, the developers promised to give citizens $2 million per year. Given an adult population of about 1,600, each adult in Creswell would receive a cash payment of $1,250 per year.

a. Why did the developers propose this deal? Why aren't similar deals proposed for new clothing stores, music stores, or auto-repair shops?

b. If the deal goes through and you moved to Creswell, would you expect to get $1,250 per year?

3. Environmental Costs for Regulated Monopoly

The Bonneville Power Administration (BPA) is a regulated monopoly that uses dozens of hydroelectric dams to generate electricity. The dams block the path of migrating fish and, thus, contribute to the decline of several species of fish. Suppose that BPA spends $100 million to make its hydroelectric dams less hazardous for migrating fish. Who will bear the cost of this program?

Summary

In this chapter, we've seen some of the subtleties of monopolies and their pricing policies. Compared to a perfectly competitive market, a monopoly means a higher price, a smaller quantity, and resources wasted in the process of seeking monopoly power. On the positive side, some of the products we use today might never have been invented without the patent system and the monopoly power it grants. Here are the main points of the chapter:

1. Compared to a perfectly competitive market, a market served by a monopolist will have a higher price and a smaller quantity of output.

2. Some firms spend money and use resources to acquire monopoly power, a process known as rent seeking.

3. Patents protect innovators from competition, leading to higher prices for new products but a greater incentive to develop new products.

4. A natural monopoly occurs when there are large-scale economies in production, so the market can support only one firm.

5. Under an average cost pricing policy, the regulated price for a natural monopoly is equal to the average cost of production.

Key Terms

average cost pricing policy, 147
consumer surplus, 138
deadweight loss from monopoly, 141

franchise or licensing scheme, 132
marginal revenue, 134
monopoly, 132

natural monopoly, 132
patent, 132
rent seeking, 142

Problems and Discussion Questions

1. Consider a restaurant that charges $10 for all you can eat and has 30 customers at this price. The slope of the demand curve is $0.10 per meal, and the marginal cost of providing a meal is $3. What price will satisfy the marginal principle and maximize the restaurant's profit?

2. The National Park Service grants a single firm the right to sell food and other goods in Yosemite National Park. Discuss the trade-offs associated with this policy.

3. Since 1963, many state governments that outlaw commercial lotteries have introduced state lotter-

ies to raise revenue for state and local governments. In 1994, the net revenue from state lotteries was about $10 billion. Would you expect the state lotteries to have higher or lower paybacks (total prize money divided by the total amount of money collected) than commercial games of chance such as horse racing and slot machines? Explain.

4. Consider the Slappers, a hockey team that plays in an arena with 8,000 seats. The only cost associated with staging a hockey game is a fixed cost of $6,000: The team incurs this cost regardless of how many people attend a game. The demand curve for hockey tickets has a slope of $0.001 per ticket ($1 divided by 1,000 tickets): Each $1 increase in price decreases the number of tickets sold by 1,000. For example, here are some combinations of price and quantity:

Price per ticket	$4	$5	$6	$7
Quantity of tickets	8,000	7,000	6,000	5,000

The owner's objective is to maximize the profit per hockey game (total revenue minus the $6,000 fixed cost).

   a. What price will maximize profit?
   b. If the owner picks the price that maximizes profit, how many seats in the arena will be empty?
   c. Is it rational to leave some seats empty?

5. The government allows professional sports associations (collections of teams) to restrict the number of teams. How do these barriers to entry affect the price of tickets to professional sporting events and the number of tickets sold? If we eliminated these barriers to entry, what would happen to ticket prices and total attendance at sporting events?

6. Consider a natural monopolist. Here are some data on prices and quantities:

Price per unit	$20	$19	$18	$17	$16
Quantity (units)	100	120	140	160	180
Marginal revenue	—	—	—	—	—

   a. Complete the table: For each quantity, use the formula for marginal revenue to compute the marginal revenue.
   b. Draw the monopolist's demand curve and the monopolist's marginal revenue curve.
   c. Suppose that the monopolist's long-run marginal cost is $9. How much output should the monopolist produce?

7. Consider a regulated natural monopoly with an initial price (equal to average cost) of $3 per unit. Suppose the demand for the monopolist's product decreases. What will happen to the price? How does this differ from the effects of a decrease in demand for a product produced in a perfectly competitive market?

8. Consider a monopolist who owns a natural spring that produces water that, according to nearby residents, has a unique taste and healing properties. The monopolist has a fixed cost of installing plumbing to tap the water but no marginal cost. The demand curve for the springwater is linear. Depict graphically the monopolist's choice of a price and quantity. At the profit-maximizing quantity, what is the price elasticity of demand? If the spring were owned by the government, what price would it charge?

9. In the board game "Monopoly," when a player gets the third deed for a group of properties (for example, the third orange property: St. James, New York, and Tennessee Avenues), he or she doubles the rent charged on each property in the group. Similarly, a player who has a single railroad charges a rent of $25, while a player who has all four railroads charges a rent of $200 for each railroad. Are these rules consistent with the analysis of monopoly in this chapter?

10. Adam Smith predicted that a monopolist would charge "the highest price which can be got." Do you agree?

11. Suppose the drug company Bristol-Meyers-Squibb announces that it will increase the price of Taxol, the cancer-fighting drug, by 10%. According to a consumer advocate, "The price hike will increase Bristol's total revenue from Taxol by 10%." Do you agree? What is the advocate assuming about the price elasticity of demand for Taxol? Is this assumption realistic?

12. Web Exercise. How much does it cost to get a patent on an invention? To find out, visit the Web site of the U.S. Patent and Trademark Office (*www.uspto.gov*). A patent on an invention is called a utility patent. How much does it cost to file for a patent? How much do you pay when it is issued? How much do you pay to maintain your patent?

13. Web Exercise. Visit the Web site of the U.S. Postal Service, one of the world's largest government-sanctioned monopolies (*www.usps.gov*). If you access the part of the site with the title "Inside the Postal Service," you can get some facts and figures and read the annual performance plan. List some of the facts and some of the postal service's goals and objectives.

Take It to the Net

We invite you to visit the O'Sullivan/Sheffrin page on the Prentice Hall Web site at: **www.prenhall.com/osullivan/** for additional World Wide Web exercises for this chapter.

Model Answers to Questions

Chapter-Opening Questions

1. The bad news is that a monopolist charges a higher price. The good news is that monopoly profits encourage innovation.

2. In response to competition from generic equivalents, the producer of the branded drug usually decreases its price, but the price of the branded drug is still higher than the price of generic drugs.

3. An unregulated monopolist will charge a high price and earn a large profit, so the government often sets a maximum price.

Test Your Understanding

1. To sell one more unit, the monopolist must cut the price. The marginal revenue equals the price minus the revenue lost from selling goods at a lower price to the original customers.

2. MR = $15 − (80 units × $0.10 per unit) = $7.

3. You need the marginal revenue curve and the marginal cost curve. The monopolist will pick the quantity at which the two curves intersect.

4. Marginal revenue exceeds marginal cost, so the firm should increase the quantity produced. To increase the quantity, the firm must cut its price.

5. The profit per space is $5 ($35 − $30), so the daily profit is $2,500 ($5 per space × 500 spaces). You are willing to pay up to $2,500 per day for the monopoly.

6. If Hanna's monopoly profit lasts five years, she'll earn a total of $10 million, which is still less than the cost of the research and development project ($14 million). She won't develop the drug.

7. It will be sensible to develop the product even without a patent if the inventor maintains his or her monopoly position long enough. Suppose it takes other firms five years to develop an imitation product and the original inventor earns a profit of $30 million per year. In this case, the monopoly profit will more than cover the costs of research and development.

8. The absence of a patent will discourage innovation in gambling devices. Perhaps this is an indirect way of discouraging gambling.

9. Marginal revenue, marginal cost.

10. The firm's demand curve shifts to the left: At each price, the firm sells a smaller quantity.

11. Below.

Using the Tools

1. **Textbook Pricing: Publishers Versus Authors**

   a. To maximize profit, the publisher picks the quantity at which marginal revenue (MR) equals marginal cost. Using the marginal revenue formula, we can compute the marginal revenue at each price and quantity. Here are the numbers for marginal revenue:

Price	$44	$40	$36	$32	$30
Quantity	80	100	120	140	150
MR	$28	$20	$12	$ 4	$ 0

   If the marginal cost is $20, the publisher will pick a price of $40 and a quantity of 100 books.

   b. The author's objective is to maximize total revenue (price times quantity), not profit (total revenue minus total cost). From the author's perspective, the marginal cost of selling another textbook is zero, so to satisfy the marginal principle, the author will choose the price at which marginal revenue is zero. In this case, the author would choose a price of $30.

   c. They disagree because the author ignores production costs.

   d. If the author received a share of profits instead of a share of revenue, he or she would choose the same price as the publisher.

2. **Payoff for Casino Approval**

   a. The proposal to pay residents a total of $2 million per year is an example of rent seeking. The developers anticipate a profit of at least $2 million per year from their casino monopoly and are willing to pay at least this amount to get the monopoly. There are no such offers of cash for stores and repair shops because the city doesn't regulate entry into these other activities, so there are no monopoly profits and rent seeking.

b. The prospect for a big annual cash payment will attract people to Creswell, so we would expect the population to grow and the per capita payment to shrink.

3. Environmental Costs for a Regulated Monopoly. The environmental costs will increase the monopolist's costs, and the higher costs will result in a higher regulated price. In graphical terms, the long-run average cost curve will shift upward, and the demand curve will intersect the cost curve at a higher price. Consumers will bear the costs of environmental protection.

Notes

1. Jeannie Donnelly, "OSU Beverages Will Be Provided Exclusively by Coca-Cola," *The Daily Barometer*, May 27, 1994, p. 1.
2. Richard A. Posner, "The Social Costs of Monopoly and Regulation," *Journal of Political Economy*, vol. 83, 1975, pp. 807–827.
3. Ralph T. King, Jr., "FTC Widens Probe into Generic-Drug Barriers," *Wall Street Journal*, March 9, 1999, p. B8.
4. Tim Jones, "Satellite Radio Sends Signal," *Chicago Tribune*, January 18, 2001; Florida Today Space Online, September 18, 2000 (*www.flatoday.com/space/explore/stories/2000b/*); Richard McCaffery, "TMF Interview with XM Satellite Radio President and Chief Executive Officer Hugh Panero," The Motley Fool (*www.fool.com*); Hilary Chipba, "Sirius Satellite Radio Surges on Daimler Deal, Upcoming Deals and More," Stockhouse.com (*www.investorlinks.com*).

7

Monopolistic Competition, Oligopoly, and Antitrust

You've probably heard an advertisement that goes like this: "If you buy a stereo from us and find the same stereo at another store for a lower price, we'll pay you the difference in price." Does this sort of price-matching policy lead to higher or lower stereo prices for consumers? As we'll see in this chapter, the surprising answer is that price matching leads to higher prices.

n this chapter, we explore the middle ground of market structure, looking at markets ranging in size from a few firms to a few dozen firms. This contrasts with our earlier discussion of the two extremes of market structure—perfect competition, with so many firms that each firm takes the market price as a given, and monopoly, with a single firm that chooses a price knowing that it has no competitors. In markets that lie between these extremes, each firm picks its own price, knowing that consumers have the option of buying from other firms. Firms act strategically, recognizing that an action by one firm (for example, lowering the price) will trigger a reaction by other firms in the market.

This chapter explores two types of decisions by firms. The first is the decision to enter a market. The second decision is what price to charge—and, thus, how much to sell. We'll look at how firms sometimes compete with one another, cutting prices to attract customers. At other times, firms try to conspire to fix prices at an artificially high level. The final part of the chapter explores antitrust policy, a set of policies designed to encourage competition and lower prices. Here are some practical questions that we answer:

1. Hub owns the only bike shop in town, selling bikes at a price of $150 with an average cost of $120, earning a profit of $30 per bike. If Spoke opens a second bike shop, can she expect to earn the same profit per bike?

2. How did the deregulation of trucking services affect the prices and profits of trucking firms?

3. If you never buy a textbook online but instead buy all your books from the campus bookstore, do you benefit from the existence of online textbook sellers?

4. Why did the government prevent a proposed merger between Office Depot and Staples, two office supply chains?

The Effects of Market Entry

Consider a market served by a single profitable firm, a monopolist. We saw in Chapter 6 that if there are large economies of scale in production, the entry of a second firm would drive the market price below average cost, meaning that each firm would lose money: Its total cost would exceed its total revenue. Because no firm will enter a market where it will lose money, the market will remain a monopoly. In this chapter, we will see that if there are not large economies of scale, additional firms will enter the market, driving down prices and profit.

Output and Entry Decisions

As we saw earlier in the book, a firm in any market can use the marginal principle to decide how much output to produce.

Marginal **Principle**

Increase the level of an activity if its marginal benefit exceeds its marginal cost but reduce the level of the activity if the marginal cost exceeds the marginal benefit. If possible, pick the level of the activity at which the marginal benefit equals the marginal cost.

Consider a firm whose activity is producing toothbrushes. The marginal benefit of producing toothbrushes is the marginal revenue from selling one more brush. In Figure 7.1, if a single firm produces toothbrushes, the demand curve facing the firm is the mar-

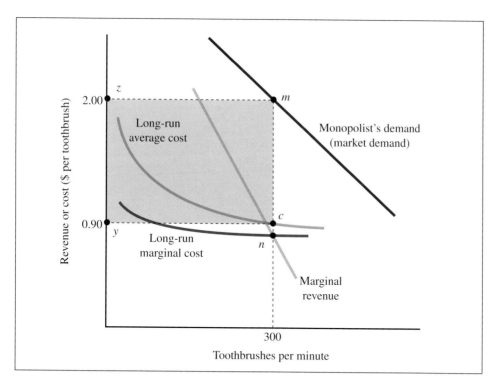

Figure 7.1

Short-Run Equilibrium in Monopolistic Competition: A Single Toothbrush Producer
The single toothbrush producer (a monopolist) picks point *n* (where marginal revenue equals marginal cost), supplying 300 toothbrushes per minute at a price of $2 (point *m*) and an average cost of $0.90 (point *c*). The profit per brush is $1.10.

ket demand curve. The marginal cost of producing toothbrushes is simply the marginal cost of production.

A firm that is considering entering the toothbrush market must make a long-run decision about what size and type of production facility to build. Therefore, the long-run cost curves—which show production costs for a firm that hasn't committed to a particular production facility—are relevant for the firm's entry decision. In Figure 7.1, the long-run average cost curve is L shaped, which, as we saw in Chapter 4, is consistent with empirical studies of production costs. If the average cost of production is decreasing (if the average cost curve is negatively sloped), the marginal cost is less than the average cost. In Figure 7.1, the marginal cost curve lies below the average cost curve.

As we saw in Chapter 6, the monopolist will maximize profit by picking the quantity at which marginal revenue equals marginal cost. In Figure 7.1, this happens at point *n*, with a quantity of 300 toothbrushes. From the market demand curve, the price associated with this quantity is $2. Given an average cost of $0.90 per toothbrush, the monopolist's profit per unit is $1.10 (equal to $2 − $0.90), so the total profit is $330 (shown by the shaded area). Given the large profits in the toothbrush market, will a second firm enter the market?

When a second firm enters a market, the demand curve facing the original firm shifts to the left. At any particular price, some consumers will patronize the new firm, so there will be fewer consumers who are willing to purchase toothbrushes from the first firm. In other words, the first firm will sell fewer brushes at each price. In Figure 7.2, the demand curve facing the first firm—the original monopolist—shifts to the left, and profit decreases for three reasons:

1. The market price drops. The marginal principle is satisfied at point *x*, so the first firm produces 200 toothbrushes at a price of $1.85 (point *e*). The competition between the two firms causes the price to drop, from $2 to $1.85.

2. The quantity produced by the first firm decreases. The first firm produces only 200 toothbrushes, down from 300 produced as a monopolist.

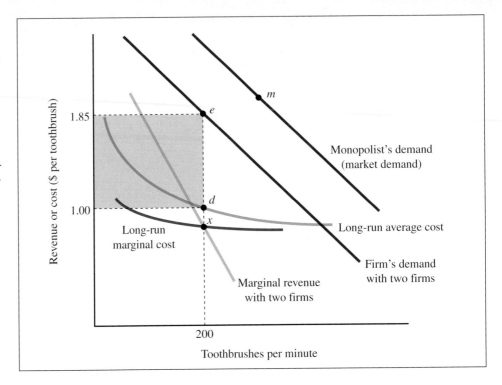

Figure 7.2

Entry Decreases Price and Increases Average Cost

The entry of a second tooth-brush producer shifts the demand curve for the original firm to the left: A smaller quantity is sold at each price. The marginal principle is satisfied at point *x*, so the firm produces a smaller quantity (200 instead of 300 toothbrushes) at a higher average cost ($1 instead of $0.90 per tooth-brush) and sells at a lower price ($1.85 instead of $2).

3. The first firm's average cost of production increases. The decrease in the quantity produced causes the firm to move upward along its negatively sloped average cost curve to a higher average cost (from $0.90 to $1).

The combination of a lower price, a higher average cost, and a smaller quantity means that the first firm earns less profit. The profit rectangle (shown by points *z, m, c,* and *y* in Figure 7.1) shrinks because the top of the rectangle (determined by the price) sinks, the bottom of the rectangle (determined by the average cost) rises, and the right side of the rectangle (determined by the quantity) moves to the left. In our example, the profit drops from $330 to $170.

What about the second firm? If we assume that the second firm has access to the same production technology as the first firm and pays the same prices for its inputs, the cost curves for the second firm will be identical to the cost curves for the first firm. If the second firm manufactures the same product as the first firm, the demand curve facing the second firm will be identical to the demand curve facing the first firm. As a result, we can use Figure 7.2 to represent both firms. Each firm produces 200 toothbrushes at an average cost of $1 per toothbrush and sells them at a price of $1.85.

Applications: Spoke's Entry, Tire Stores, Deregulation

As an example of the effects of entry on price, cost, and profit, consider Spoke's hypo-thetical decision about whether to enter the bike market. Hub—the monopolist—ini-tially sells bikes at a price of $150 with an average cost of $120 per bike, for a profit of $30 per bike. Suppose that Spoke enters the market, the price will drop to $140 and her average cost will be $125. In other words, Spoke could earn a profit of $15 per bike. Although Spoke's entry squeezes profit from both sides—decreasing the market price and increasing the average cost—there is still some profit to be made, so she will enter the market. Of course, other firms may also enter the market, so Spoke should not count on making a $15 profit per bike for very long.

Empirical studies of real markets provide overwhelming evidence that entry decreases market prices and firms' profit.[1] In one study of the retail pricing of tires, a market with only two tire stores had a price of $55 per tire, compared to a price of $53 in a market with three stores, $51 with four stores, and $50 with five stores. In other words, the larger the number of stores, the lower the price of tires. A study of the Motor Carrier Act of 1980, which eliminated the government's entry restrictions on the trucking industry, caused new firms to enter the trucking market, decreasing freight prices by about 22%. The deregulation of telecommunications markets in Western Europe is expected to increase the number of firms in the market and decrease the price of international calls by as much as 50%.

Monopolistic Competition

Now that we know the effects of entry into a monopolized market, let's think about how many firms will actually enter a particular market. In a market subject to **monopolistic competition**, dozens of firms enter the market. Here are the characteristics of such a market:

Monopolistic competition: A market served by dozens of firms selling slightly different products.

1. **Many firms.** Because there are relatively small economies of scale, small firms can produce at about the same average cost as large firms. Therefore, even a small firm can cover its costs, and the market can support many firms.

2. **Differentiated products.** The firms sell slightly different products, with differences in physical characteristics, services, or the aura or image associated with the product. Some products are differentiated by where they're sold, giving consumers the opportunity to buy a particular product (for example, gasoline, food, CDs, or hardware) at different locations.

3. **No artificial barriers to entry.** There are no patents or government regulations preventing firms from entering the market.

What's the logic behind the label *monopolistic competition*? Although it may seem like an oxymoron, there are good reasons for the label. Each firm differentiates its product in such a way that it has a *monopoly* for a narrowly defined good. For example, each firm in the toothbrush market uses a unique design for its toothbrushes, so each is a monopolist for its unique toothbrush. There is keen *competition* among firms for customers to buy products that are close but not perfect substitutes. When one firm increases its price, many of its consumers will switch to the products of other firms because they are close substitutes.

Let's take a closer look at the notion of product differentiation, one of the key features of monopolistic competition. Firms in such a market differentiate their products in several ways:

- **Physical characteristics.** A firm can distinguish its products from those of other firms by offering a different size, color, shape, texture, or taste. For example, toothpastes differ in flavor, color, texture, whitening capability, and alleged ability to fight decay and plaque. Some other examples of goods that are differentiated by their physical characteristics are athletic shoes, dress shirts, appliances, and pens.

- **Location.** A firm can distinguish its product by choosing a location that sets it apart from its competitors. Your city probably has several music stores that sell a particular CD at about the same price. Everything else being equal, you are likely to buy the CD from the most convenient store, but if a store across town has a lower price, you might purchase the CD there instead. Each music store has a monopoly in its own neighborhood but competes with music stores in the rest of the city. The same logic applies to grocery stores, hardware stores, and other retailers.

- **Services.** Some products are distinguished by the services that come with them. For instance, some stores provide informative and helpful salespeople, while others require consumers to make decisions on their own. Other examples of services that can differentiate products are home delivery (for appliances and pizza) and free technical assistance (for computer hardware and software).

- **Aura or image.** Some firms use advertising to make their products stand out from a group of nearly identical products. In this case, some of the product differentiation is a matter of perception and some is real. For example, brand-name aspirin is chemically identical to generic aspirin. Although designer jeans differ in fabric and design, to many consumers, these differences are small relative to the difference in price.

Short-Run and Long-Run Equilibrium

We'll use the toothbrush example to illustrate the features of monopolistic competition. The producers of toothbrushes differentiate their products with respect to color, bristle design, handle size and shape, and durability. We saw earlier that after a second firm enters the toothbrush market, both firms still make a profit. Will a third firm enter this lucrative market? The entry of a third firm will shift the demand curve facing each firm farther to the left, decreasing the market price, decreasing the quantity produced per firm, and increasing the average cost per toothbrush. If after the third firm enters the market, profit would still be positive for all three firms, then the third firm will enter the market. This entry process will continue until the entry of one more firm would make each firm lose money.

Because there are no barriers to entering the toothbrush market, firms will continue to enter the market until each firm makes zero economic profit. Figure 7.3 shows the long-run equilibrium from the perspective of the typical firm in a monopolistically competitive market. As more firms enter the market, the market share of the typical firm decreases, so its demand curve shifts to the left. The typical firm satisfies the mar-

Figure 7.3
Long-Run Equilibrium with Monopolistic Competition: Toothbrushes
In a monopolistically competitive market, new firms will continue to enter the market until economic profit is zero. The typical firm picks the quantity at which its marginal revenue equals its marginal cost (point *g*). Economic profit is zero because the price equals the average cost (shown by point *h*).

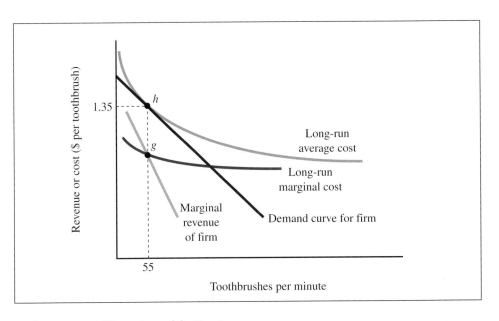

ginal principle at point *g* and sells 55 brushes per minute at a price of $1.35 (point *h*) and an average cost of $1.35. The price equals the typical firm's average cost, so the typical firm makes zero economic profit. Each firm's revenue is high enough to cover all its costs—including the opportunity cost of all its inputs—but not enough to cause additional firms to enter the market. In other words, each firm makes just enough money to stay in business.

Trade-Offs with Monopolistic Competition

From society's perspective, there are some trade-offs associated with monopolistic competition and product differentiation. Let's compare the monopolistic outcome (shown in Figure 7.1) with the long-run equilibrium under monopolistic competition (Figure 7.3). There are many more toothbrush producers with monopolistic competition, and that brings good news and bad news for consumers and society as a whole:

- **Good news.** Lower price. Competition among firms decreases the price of toothbrushes from $2 to $1.35.
- **Good news.** Greater variety. The large number of toothbrush firms—each selling a toothbrush with a unique design—means more choice for consumers.
- **Bad news.** Higher average cost. Each of the firms in the monopolistically competitive market produces less output than the monopolist and has a higher average cost of production: $1.35 per toothbrush, compared to $0.90 for the monopolist.

The same trade-offs occur with other products sold in monopolistically competitive markets. Here are some other examples:

- **Restaurants.** The typical large city has dozens of Italian restaurants, each of which has a slightly different menu and prepares its food in slightly different ways. Although a city with a single Italian restaurant would have a lower average cost of preparing Italian meals, there would be less variety of food.
- **Clothing.** Some articles of clothing such as jeans and shirts are differentiated according to their fit, color, design, durability, and the aura associated with the label. If we all wore uniforms, the average cost of producing clothing would be lower, but there would be less variety.
- **Music CDs.** Your city probably has several music stores, each of which sells a particular CD at about the same price. If a large metropolitan area had only one music store, the average cost of CDs would be lower, but travel costs for music consumers would be higher.

TEST Your Understanding

1. Complete the statement: A firm picks the quantity of output at which _____ equals _____.

2. Complete the statement with *increases* or *decreases*: The entry of an additional firm _____ the profit per unit of output because entry _____ the price and _____ the average cost of production.

3. Suppose each new firm in the bike market in Spoke's town decreases the price by $4 per bike and increases the average cost per bike by $4. How many firms will enter the market?

Chapter 7 Monopolistic Competition, Oligopoly, and Antitrust **161**

Oligopoly and Pricing Decisions

Oligopoly: A market served by a few firms.

Concentration ratio: A measure of the degree of concentration in a market; the four-firm concentration ratio is the percentage of the market output produced by the four largest firms.

In this part of the chapter, we look at an **oligopoly**, a market with just a few firms. Economists use **concentration ratios** to measure the degree of concentration in a market. For example, a four-firm concentration ratio is the percentage of total output in a market produced by the four largest firms. In Table 7.1, the four-firm concentration ratio for cigarettes is 93%, indicating that the largest four firms produce 93% of the cigarettes in the United States. According to one rule of thumb, if the four-firm concentration ratio is greater than 40%, the market is considered an oligopoly.

Most firms in an oligopoly earn economic profit, yet additional firms do not enter the market. An oligopoly—a market with just a few profitable firms—occurs for three reasons:

1. **Economies of scale in production.** As we saw in Chapter 6, a natural monopoly occurs when there are relatively large economies of scale in production, so a large firm can produce at a much lower cost than a small firm. In some cases, scale economies are not large enough to generate a natural monopoly but are large enough to generate a natural oligopoly, with a few firms serving the entire market.
2. **Government barriers to entry.** As we saw in Chapter 6, government may limit the number of firms in a market by controlling the number of business licenses.
3. **Advertising campaigns.** In some markets, a firm cannot enter without a substantial investment in advertising. The result is the same as economies of scale in production: Just a few firms will enter the market.

The key feature of an oligopoly is that firms act strategically. The firms in an oligopoly are interdependent in the sense that they sell similar products, meaning that consumers can easily switch from one firm to another. As a result, the actions of one firm affect the profits of other firms in the oligopoly. For example, if one airline cuts its fares,

Table 7.1 Concentration Ratios in Selected U.S. Manufacturing Industries

Industry	Four-Firm Concentration Ratio (%)	Eight-Firm Concentration Ratio (%)
Cigarettes	93	Not available
Guided missiles and space vehicles	93	99
Beer and malt beverages	90	98
Batteries	87	95
Electric bulbs	86	94
Breakfast cereals	85	98
Motor vehicles and car bodies	84	91
Greeting cards	84	88
Engines and turbines	79	92
Aircraft and parts	79	93

Source: U.S. Bureau of the Census, *1992 Census of Manufacturing, Concentration Ratios in Manufacturing* (Washington, DC: U.S. Government Printing Office, 1995).

the other airlines in the market will lose customers to the low-price airline unless they cut their prices, too.

Cartel Pricing and the Duopolists' Dilemma

One of the virtues of a market economy is that firms compete with one another for customers, and this leads to lower prices. But in some markets, firms cooperate instead of competing with one another. As we'll see later in the chapter, it is illegal for firms to conspire to fix prices. Adam Smith recognized the possibility that firms would conspire to raise prices: "People of the same trade seldom meet together, even for merriment and diversion, but the conversation ends in a conspiracy against the public, or in some contrivance to raise prices."[2] We'll see that raising prices is not simply a matter of firms getting together and agreeing on higher prices. An agreement to raise prices is likely to break down unless the firms find some way to punish a firm that violates the agreement.

We'll use a market with two firms—a duopoly—to explain the key features of an oligopoly. The basic insights from a duopoly also apply to oligopolies with more than two firms. Consider a duopoly in the market for air travel between two hypothetical cities. The two airlines can compete for customers on the basis of price, or they can cooperate and conspire to raise prices. To simplify matters—and to keep the numbers manageable—let's assume that the average cost of providing air travel is constant at $300 per passenger. As shown in Figure 7.4, the average cost is constant, which means that marginal cost equals average cost.

A **cartel** is a group of firms that coordinate their pricing decisions, often charging the same price for a particular good or service. Under antitrust law, cartel pricing is illegal. In our airline example, the two airlines could form a cartel and choose the price that a monopolist would choose. In Figure 7.4, the demand curve facing a monopolist is the market demand curve, and the marginal revenue curve intersects the marginal cost curve at a quantity of 150 passengers per day (point *f*). If the two airlines act as one, they will pick the monopoly price of $400 and split the monopoly output, each serving 75 passengers per day. The average cost is $300, so each airline earns a daily profit of $7,500 (a profit of $100 per passenger × 75 passengers). An arrangement under which the two

Cartel: A group of firms that coordinate their pricing decisions, often by charging the same price.

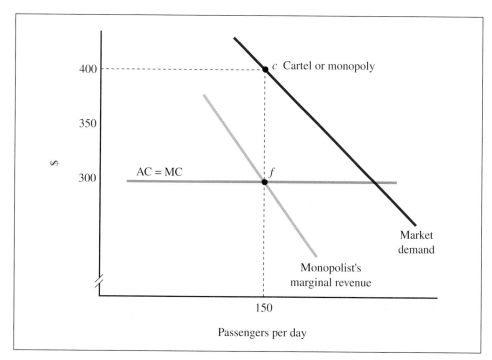

Figure 7.4
A Cartel Picks the Monopoly Price
Point *c* shows the outcome with a successful price-fixing arrangement (a cartel). The total output is 150 passengers and the price is $400 per passenger, so each firm serves 75 passengers at an average cost of $300 per passenger (shown by point *f*) and earns a profit of $7,500 per day.

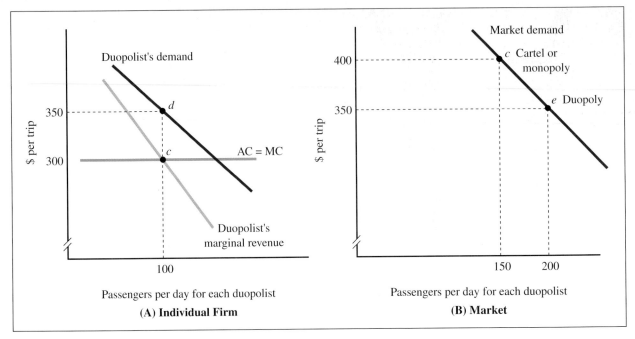

Figure 7.5

Competing Duopolists Pick a Lower Price

At the individual firm (duopolist) level, marginal revenue equals marginal cost at point *e*, so each firm serves 100 passengers at a price of $350 per passenger (shown by point *d* in panel A). Given an average cost of $300 per passenger, each duopolist earns a profit of $5,000. At the market level, the duopoly outcome has a quantity of 200 passengers (100 passengers per firm × 2 firms) at a price of $350 (point *e*).

Price fixing: An arrangement in which two firms coordinate their pricing decisions.

firms act as one, coordinating their pricing decisions, is also known as **price fixing**. As we'll see later in the chapter, cartels and price fixing are illegal under U.S. antitrust laws.

What would happen if the two firms compete against one another? If they do, each firm faces its own demand curve. The firm's demand is to the left of the market demand curve because consumers are divided between the two firms: At a given price, the number of passengers served by a single firm will be less than the number served by both firms together. In Figure 7.5, panel A shows the perspective of the individual firm. Given the firm's demand curve and marginal revenue curve, the marginal principle is satisfied at point *c*, where marginal revenue equals marginal cost. Each firm serves 100 passengers at a price of $350 (point *d*). Panel B shows the market perspective: The price is $350, and the quantity is 200 passengers. Given an average cost of $300, each firm earns a profit of $5,000 (equal to $50 per passenger × 100 passengers). When the two firms compete, each earns only $5,000, compared to $7,500 each when they conspire to fix the price at the monopoly level.

The Game Tree

Game tree: A graphical representation of the consequences of different strategies.

Each firm would earn more profit under a price-fixing agreement, but will the firms reach such an agreement? We can answer this question with the help of a **game tree**, a graphical tool that provides a visual representation of the consequences of alternative strategies. Each firm must choose a price for airline tickets, either a high price (the cartel price of $400) or a low price (the duopoly price of $350). Each firm can use the game tree to develop a pricing strategy, knowing that the other firm is also choosing a price.

Figure 7.6 shows the game tree for the price-fixing game. Let's call the managers of the airlines Jack and Jill. The game tree has three components:

1. The squares are decision nodes. For each square, there is a player (Jack or Jill) and a list of the player's options. For example, the game starts at square X, where Jill has two options: the high price or the low price.

2. The arrows show the path of the game from left to right. Jill chooses her price first, so we move from square X to one of Jack's decision nodes, either square Y or square Z. If Jill chooses the high price, we move from square X to square Y. Once we reach one of Jack's decision nodes, he chooses a price (high or low), and then we move to one of the rectangles. For example, if Jack chooses the high price, too, we move from square Y to rectangle 1.

3. The rectangles show the profits for the two firms. When we reach a rectangle, the game is over, and the players receive the profits shown in the rectangle. There is a profit rectangle for each of the four possible outcomes of the price-fixing game.

We've already computed the profits for two profit rectangles. The first rectangle shows what happens when each firm chooses the high price. This is the cartel or price-fixing outcome, with each firm earning $7,500. The fourth rectangle shows what happens when each firm chooses the low price. This is the duopoly outcome, with each firm earning $5,000.

What would happen if the two firms chose different prices? If Jill chooses the low price and Jack chooses the high price, Jill will capture a large share of the market and gain at Jack's expense. In the first column of Table 7.2, Jill serves 170 passengers at a price of $350 each and an average cost of $300 per passenger, so her profit is $8,500 (a $50 profit per passenger × 170 passengers). In the second column, Jack serves only 10 passengers at a price of $400 each and the same average cost, so his profit is $1,000 (a $100 profit per passenger × 10 passengers). This is shown by rectangle 3 in Figure 7.6: The path of the game is square X to square Z to rectangle 3. The other underpricing outcome is shown by rectangle 2. In this case, Jill chooses the high price and Jack chooses the low price, so Jack gains at Jill's expense. The roles are reversed, and so are the numbers in the profit rectangle.

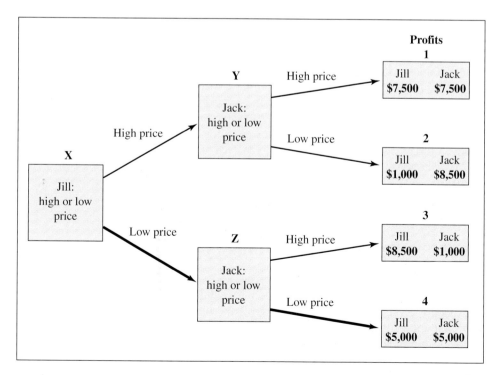

Figure 7.6

Game Tree for Price-Fixing Game
The path of the game is square X to square Z to rectangle 4: Each firm picks the low price and earns a profit of $5,000. The duopolists' dilemma is that each firm would make more profit if they both picked the high price, but neither firm will do so, fearing that the other firm would pick the low price.

Table 7.2 Prices and Profits When Firms Choose Different Prices

	Jill: Low Price	Jack: High Price
Price	$350	$400
Quantity	170	10
Average cost	$300	$300
Profit per passenger	$50	$100
Profit	$8,500	$1,000

The Outcome of the Price-Fixing Game

We can predict the outcome of the price-fixing game by a process of elimination. We'll eliminate the rectangles that would require one or both of the firms to act irrationally, leaving us with the rectangle showing the outcome of the game.

- If Jill chooses the high price, we'll move along the upper branches of the tree and eventually reach rectangle 1 or 2, depending on what Jack does. Although Jill would like Jack to choose the high price, too, this would be irrational for Jack, because he can make more profit by choosing the low price. Therefore, we can eliminate rectangle 1.

- If Jill chooses the low price, we'll move along the lower branches of the tree, eventually reaching rectangle 3 or 4, depending on Jack's choice. Jack won't choose the high price because then Jill would gain at his expense. Therefore, we can eliminate rectangle 3.

We've eliminated the two rectangles involving a high price for Jack. This means that regardless of what Jill does, Jack will choose the low price.

There are two rectangles left (2 and 4), and Jill's action will determine which rectangle we'll reach. Jill knows that Jack will choose the low price regardless of what she does, so she can either choose a high price and allow Jack to gain at her expense (rectangle 2) or choose the low price, too (rectangle 4). It would be irrational for Jill to allow herself to be underpriced, so we can eliminate rectangle 2. The remaining rectangle shows the outcome of the game: Each person chooses the low price. The thick arrows show the path of the game, from square X to square Z to rectangle 4.

Both firms will be unhappy with this outcome because each could earn a higher profit with rectangle 1. To get there, however, each firm must choose the high price. The **duopolists' dilemma** is that although both firms would be better off if they chose the high price, each firm chooses the low price. Jill won't choose the high price because Jack would underprice her and gain at her expense. Jack won't choose the high price because then Jill would gain at his expense.

Duopolists' dilemma: A situation in which both firms in a market would be better off if both chose the high price, but each chooses the low price.

Avoiding the Dilemma: Punishing a Firm That Undercuts

How might firms be able to avoid the duopolists' dilemma and get everyone to agree to the cartel price? One possibility is that the firms choose prices repeatedly and punish a firm that undercuts the cartel price.

Continuing the airline example, suppose Jack and Jill choose their prices at the beginning of each month. Jill chooses the cartel price ($400) for the first month and then waits to see what price Jack chooses. Jill could use one of the following schemes to punish Jack if he underprices her:

1. **Duopoly price.** Jill continues to choose the high price until Jack underprices her. Once that happens, she chooses the duopoly price ($350 in our example) for the remaining lifetime of her firm. Jill allows herself to be underpriced only once and then abandons the idea of cartel pricing and accepts the duopoly outcome, which is less profitable than the cartel outcome but more profitable than being underpriced by the other firm.

2. **Tit-for-tat.** Starting in the second month, Jill chooses whatever price Jack chose the preceding month. As long as Jack chooses the cartel price, the cartel arrangement will persist, but if Jack underprices Jill, the cartel will break down. In Figure 7.7, Jack underprices Jill in the second month, so Jill chooses the low price for the third month, resulting in the duopoly outcome. To restore the cartel outcome, Jack must eventually choose the high price, allowing Jill to underprice him for one month. This happens in the fourth month, so the cartel is restored in the fifth month. Although Jack can gain at Jill's expense in the second month, if he wants to restore cartel pricing, he must allow Jill to gain at his expense during the fourth month.

These three pricing schemes promote cartel pricing by penalizing the underpricer. To decide whether to underprice Jill, Jack must weigh the short-term benefit against the long-term cost:

- The short-term benefit is the increase in profit in the current period. If Jack underprices Jill, he can increase his profit from $7,500 (Jack's profit if both firms pick the high price) to $8,500 (Jack's profit if he chooses the low price and Jill chooses the high price). Therefore, the short-term benefit of underpricing is $1,000.

- The long-term cost is the loss of profit in later periods. Jill will respond to Jack's underpricing by cutting her price, and this decreases Jack's profit. For example, if Jill drops her price to $350, Jack will lose the opportunity for a monthly profit of $5,000 for the remaining lifetime of his firm.

If the two firms expect to share the market for a long time, the long-term cost of underpricing will exceed the short-term benefit, so underpricing is less likely. The threat of punishment makes it easier to resist the temptation to cheat on the cartel.

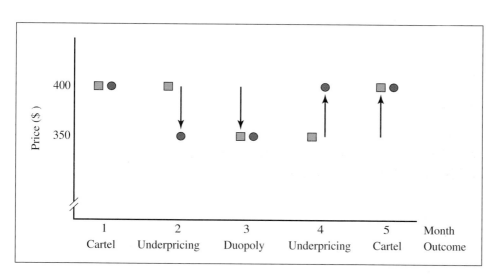

Figure 7.7
Tit-for-Tat Pricing
Under a tit-for-tat retaliation scheme, the leading firm (Jill, the square) chooses whatever price the other firm (Jack, the circle) chose the preceding month.

THE ITALIAN BREAD CARTEL

In 1993, a new bakery called Louis Basile's opened in New York City.[3] The undercover detectives operating the bakery didn't bake any bread, but instead got up every morning at 3 A.M. to drive to New Jersey to buy Italian bread from a real bakery. Soon after the detectives started selling their bread to Brooklyn grocery stores, representatives of the Association of Independent Bakers and Distributors of Italian Bread paid them a visit. Over drinks at the White Horse Tavern, the representatives told a baker/detective that if Louis Basile's didn't play by the association's price-fixing rules, people who worked at Louis Basile's would get hurt.

The association included 50 bakeries that supplied Italian bread to more than 1,000 groceries and delicatessens in the city. In 1990, the association agreed to increase the retail price of bread from $0.75 to $0.85, and all the members of the association printed the new price on their bread sleeves. In addition to fixing the price of bread, the association required each

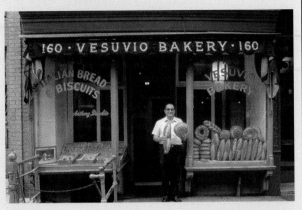

The Association of Independent Bakers and Distributors of Italian Bread enforced a price-fixing scheme among 50 bakers in New York City.

store to buy its bread from a single baker. Before a store could switch bakers, it had to pay a cash settlement to its original bakery.

We've seen that when firms have an opportunity to punish a firm that cheats on a cartel price, price fixing is more likely. For a description of how one cartel tried to enforce a price-fixing arrangement, read "A Closer Look: The Italian Bread Cartel."

Avoiding the Dilemma: Guaranteed Price Matching

The duopolists' dilemma occurs because the two firms are unable to coordinate their pricing decisions and act as one. Each firm has an incentive to underprice the other firm because the low-price firm will capture a larger share of the market and earn a larger profit. One way to avoid this dilemma is to develop a system of price matching.

To eliminate the incentive for underpricing, one firm can guarantee that it will match its competitor's price. Suppose Jill places the following advertisement in the local newspaper: "If you buy a plane ticket from me and then discover that Jack offers the same trip at a lower price, I will pay you the difference between my price and Jack's price. If I charge you $400 and Jack's price is only $350, I will pay you $50." This pricing scheme is known as **guaranteed price matching**: Jill guarantees that she will match Jack's price. It is also known as a meet-the-competition policy. Jill's promise to match Jack's lower price is credible because she announces it in the newspaper.

Guaranteed price matching: A scheme under which a firm guarantees that it will match a lower price by a competitor; also known as a meet-the-competition policy.

How will Jack respond to Jill's price-matching scheme? In effect, Jill tentatively chooses the high price but will instantly switch to the low price if Jack picks the low price. After a $50 refund, Jill's price will be $350, the same as Jack's. Jack will respond to Jill's price-matching scheme in one of two ways:

1. **Choose the high price.** If Jack matches Jill's announced high price, each firm will earn a profit of $7,500 (rectangle 1 in the game tree in Figure 7.6).

2. Choose the low price. If Jack tries to underprice Jill, she will switch to the low price, and each will earn a profit of only $5,000 (rectangle 4 in the game tree).

Jack's decision is easy: A pair of high prices is more profitable than a pair of low prices, so he will choose the high price, just like Jill.

Jill's price-matching scheme eliminates the duopolists' dilemma and makes cartel pricing possible, even without a formal cartel. The duopolists' dilemma disappears because underpricing is no longer possible. The motto of the price-matching scheme is, "High for one means high for all, and low for one means low for all." It would be irrational for Jack to choose the low price because he knows that Jill would match it. Once the possibility of underpricing has been eliminated, the duopoly will be replaced by an informal cartel, each firm charging the price that would be charged by a monopolist.

To most people, the notion that guaranteed price matching leads to higher prices is surprising. After all, Jill promises to give refunds if her price exceeds Jack's, so we might expect her to keep her price low to avoid giving out a lot of refunds. In fact, she doesn't have to worry about refunds because she knows that Jack will also choose the high price. In other words, Jill's promise to issue refunds is an empty one. Although consumers might think Jill's refund policy will protect them from high prices, the policy in fact guarantees that they will pay the high price.

TEST Your Understanding

4. Suppose Jack promises that if Jill chooses the high price, he will, too. If Jack's objective is to maximize his profit, what will he do after Jill chooses the high price?

5. If you were Jill, would you believe Jack's promise to choose the high price? Which price would you choose?

6. Complete the statement with a number: Suppose that Jack offers plane tickets for $350. Under Jill's price-matching scheme, she would give each of her customers a refund of _____.

Entry Deterrence and Limit Pricing

We've seen what happens when two duopolists try to act as one, fixing the price at the monopoly level. Now let's think about how a monopolist might try to prevent a second firm from entering its market. To explain how a monopolist tries to prevent its monopoly from becoming an oligopoly, we use the numbers from our airline example, although we look at a different city with a different cast of characters.

Suppose that Mona initially has a secure monopoly in the market for air travel between two cities. When there is no threat of entry, Mona uses the marginal principle to pick a quantity and a price. In Figure 7.8, we start at point m, with a quantity of 150 passengers per day and a price of $400 per passenger. Mona's profit per passenger is $100 ($400 − the average cost of $300), so her daily profit is $15,000. If Mona discovers that Doug, the manager of a second airline, is thinking about entering the market, what will she do? Now that she has an **insecure monopoly** or a vulnerable monopoly, she has two options: She can be passive and allow the second airline to enter the market, or she can try to prevent the second airline from entering.

The passive approach will lead to the duopoly outcome we saw earlier in the chapter. In Figure 7.8, the market will move downward along the demand curve from point m to point d (the duopoly outcome). Mona charges a price of $350 and serves 100 passengers per day (half of the quantity demanded). Her daily profit is $5,000, equal to the profit per passenger of $50 ($350 − the average cost of $300) multiplied by 100 passengers.

Insecure monopoly: A monopoly faced with the possibility that a second firm will enter the market.

Figure 7.8

Entry Deterrence and Limit Pricing

Moving downward along the demand curve, point *m* shows the secure monopoly, point *i* shows the insecure monopoly, and point *d* shows the duopoly. Point *h* shows what happens if the insecure monopolist produces a large quantity but a second firm enters anyway.

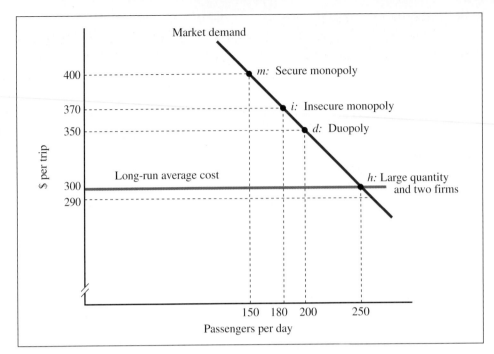

Entry Deterrence Strategy

In developing a strategy to deal with the threat of entry, Mona must answer two questions. First, what must she do to deter entry? Second, is entry deterrence more profitable than being passive and sharing the market with a second firm?

To prevent Doug from entering the market, Mona must commit herself to serving a large number of passengers. If she commits to a large passenger load, there won't be enough passengers left for a potential entrant to make a profit. How many passengers must she commit to serve? In Figure 7.8, point *z* shows the point of zero profit in the market: If the two firms serve a total of 250 passengers per day, the price ($300) equals average cost, so each firm makes zero economic profit. Suppose that because of economies of scale in providing air travel, the minimum entry quantity is 70 passengers per day: It would be impractical for any firm to serve fewer than 70 passengers. We can compute the entry-deterring quantity as follows:

$$\text{entry-deterring quantity} = \text{zero-profit quantity} - \text{minimum entry quantity}$$
$$180 = 250 - 70$$

If Mona serves 180 passengers and Doug were to enter with the minimum quantity of 70 passengers, the price would drop to average cost, making entry unprofitable.

It's important to note that Mona can't simply announce that she will serve 180 passengers. She must take actions that ensure that the most profitable quantity is 180 passengers—not the secure monopoly quantity of 150 passengers. In other words, she must commit to 180 passengers. She could commit to the larger passenger load by purchasing a large fleet of airplanes and signing labor contracts that require her to hire a large workforce. Once she makes these commitments, the most profitable passenger load will be 180.

Which is more profitable, entry deterrence or the passive duopoly outcome? The deterrence strategy, shown by point *i* in Figure 7.8, generates a price of $370 and a profit

WHAT'S THE MONOPOLY PRICE FOR MICROSOFT WINDOWS?

The Windows operating system from Microsoft, Inc., runs about 90% of the world's personal computers, so it is natural to think that Microsoft has a monopoly in the market for operating systems. According to economist Richard Schmalensee, an expert on oligopoly and monopoly, Microsoft's profit-maximizing monopoly price is between $900 and $2,000. That's the amount Microsoft would charge if it acted like a regular monopolist.[4]

So why does Microsoft charge only $99 for Windows? One possibility is limit pricing. Perhaps Microsoft's monopoly is insecure in the sense that if the price were higher, other firms would enter the market. If Microsoft charged $2,000 for its operating system, there would be a much greater incentive for other firms to develop competing operating systems. Although a price of $99 may generate less profit this year, it could ensure that Microsoft makes this profit for a long time.

per passenger of $70. Total profit is $12,600 (equal to $70 times 180 passengers). This is larger than the $5,000 profit under the passive approach, so deterrence is the best strategy.

Mona's entry deterrence strategy generates a market price between the price charged by a secure monopolist ($400) and the price charged in a market with two firms ($350). Mona can avoid sharing the market by accepting the lower price associated with an insecure monopoly ($370). The strategy of picking the price that is lower than the normal monopoly price to deter entry is known as **limit pricing**. For a discussion of limit pricing by Microsoft Corporation, read "A Closer Look: What's the Monopoly Price for Microsoft Windows?"

Limit pricing: A scheme under which a monopolist accepts a price below the normal monopoly price to deter other firms from entering the market.

The Passive Approach

Although our example shows that entry deterrence is the best strategy for Mona, it won't be the best strategy for all monopolists threatened with entry. The key variable is the minimum entry quantity. Suppose that the scale economies in air travel were relatively small, so a second firm could enter the market by serving as few as 10 passengers. In this case, if Mona commits to serving only 180 passengers, that won't be enough to deter entry: A firm entering with, say, 10, 20, or 30 passengers will make a profit. If the minimum entry quantity is 10 passengers, the entry-deterring quantity is 240 passengers:

$$\text{entry-deterring quantity} = \text{zero-profit quantity} - \text{minimum entry quantity}$$
$$240 = 250 - 10$$

The limit price associated with this entry-deterring quantity is $310. Although Mona could deter entry by committing to 240 passengers at a price of $310, her profit would be only $2,400, compared to $5,000 if she is passive and shares the market with a second firm.

The general lesson is that entry deterrence is not sensible when the minimum entry quantity is relatively low. In this case, the quantity required to deter entry is relatively large. As a result, the limit price required to deter entry is close to the average cost of production, and the profit from the insecure monopoly is less than the profit from sharing the market.

Applications: Aluminum, Campus Bookstores

Between 1893 and 1940, the Aluminum Company of America (Alcoa) had a monopoly on aluminum production in the United States.[5] During this period, Alcoa kept other firms out of the market by producing a large quantity and keeping its price low. Although a

The emergence of online textbook sellers makes the campus bookstore an insecure monopoly and could result in lower prices.

higher price would have generated more profit in the short run, other firms would have entered the market, so Alcoa's profit would have been lower in the long run.

We can apply the notion of entry deterrence to your favorite monopoly, your campus bookstore. The bookstore monopoly results from government and college rules that prohibit other organizations from selling textbooks on campus. The emergence of online textbook sellers now gives students another option, threatening the campus bookstore monopoly. Your campus bookstore could cut its prices to prevent online textbook sellers from capturing too many of its customers. If it does this, you will pay lower prices even if you don't patronize the online seller.

Economic Detective

Ballpoint Pens

In 1945, Reynolds International Pen Corporation introduced a revolutionary product—the ballpoint pen. This new type of pen could be produced with very simple technology. For three years, Reynolds earned enormous profits on this innovative product. In 1948, Reynolds stopped producing pens, dropping out of the market entirely. What happened?

The key to solving this mystery is the fact that Reynolds earned "enormous" profits for a short time. The simple technology of the ballpoint pen could be easily copied by other producers, so the price required to deter entry was very low. Indeed, this entry-deterring price was so low that it was better for Reynolds to charge a high price and squeeze out as much profit as possible from a short-lived monopoly. Reynolds sold its pens for $16, about 20 times the average production cost ($0.80). By 1948, a total of 100 firms had entered the ballpoint market, and the price had fallen close to the production cost.

Antitrust Policy

In this part of the chapter, we will explore antitrust policies, which are designed to promote competition in markets dominated by a few large firms. Antitrust policy applies to monopolies and oligopolies but not to markets that are monopolistically competitive. Under federal antitrust rules, the government can break up monopolies into several smaller companies, prevent corporate mergers that would reduce competition, and regulate business practices that tend to reduce competition. Table 7.3 provides a brief summary of the history of antitrust policy. The first legislation was the Sherman Antitrust Act of 1890, which made it illegal to monopolize a market or to engage in practices that result in a restraint of trade. Later legislation clarified some of the ambiguities of the Sherman Act and extended antitrust law.

Two government organizations, the Antitrust Division of the Department of Justice, and the Federal Trade Commission, are responsible for initiating actions against individuals or firms that may be violating antitrust laws. The courts have the power to impose penalties on the executives found to be in violation of the laws, including fines and prison sentences. In some cases, the government seeks no penalties but directs the firm to discontinue illegal practices and take other measures to promote competition.

Breaking Up Monopolies

One form of antitrust policy is to break up a monopoly into several smaller firms. A **trust** is an arrangement under which the owners of several companies transfer their decision-making powers to a small group of trustees, who then make decisions for all the participating firms. Firms in a trust act as a single firm, so an industry that appears to have many firms may in fact be a virtual monopoly.

The label *antitrust* comes from early cases that involved breaking up trusts. The classic example is John D. Rockefeller's Standard Oil Trust, which was formed in 1882 when the owners of 40 oil companies empowered nine trustees to make the decisions for all 40 companies. The trust controlled more than 90% of the market for refined petroleum products, and the trustees ran it like a monopoly. In 1911, the government ordered the breakup of the Standard Oil Trust. The Supreme Court found that Rockefeller had used "unnatural methods" to maintain his monopoly power and drive his rivals out of business. He coerced railroads to give him special rates for shipping and spied on his competitors. The government broke up Standard Oil into 34 separate companies, including the corporate ancestors to Exxon, Mobil, Chevron, and Amoco.

In 1982, the government broke up American Telephone and Telegraph (AT&T) into seven regional phone companies. AT&T had used its legal monopoly in local telephone service to prevent competition in the markets for long-distance service and communica-

Trust: An arrangement under which the owners of several companies transfer their decision-making powers to a small group of trustees, who then make decisions for all the firms in the trust.

Table 7.3   A Brief History of Antitrust Legislation

1890	Sherman Act: Made it illegal to monopolize a market or to engage in practices that result in a restraint of trade.
1914	Clayton Act: Outlawed specific practices that discourage competition, including tying contracts, price discrimination for the purpose of reducing competition, and stock-purchase mergers that would substantially reduce competition.
1914	Federal Trade Commission Act: Established to enforce antitrust laws.
1936	Robinson-Patman Act: Prohibited selling products at "unreasonably low prices" with the intent of reducing competition.
1950	Celler-Kefauver Act: Outlawed asset-purchase mergers that would substantially reduce competition.
1980	Hart-Scott-Rodino Act: Extended antitrust legislation to proprietorships and partnerships.

tions equipment. After an eight-year legal battle, AT&T agreed to form seven Regional Bell Operating Companies, transforming "Ma Bell" into seven "Baby Bells." The new AT&T was allowed to compete in the market for long-distance service, where it faced competition from newcomers MCI and Sprint. AT&T was also allowed to operate in the market for communications equipment, where it faced competition from newcomers Mitel and Northern Telecom.

In recent years, the most widely reported antitrust actions have involved Microsoft Corporation, the software giant. Microsoft receives royalties from computer makers that install the Microsoft operating software on their computers. The curious—and illegal—feature of the original arrangement was that Microsoft received a royalty for every computer made by the firm, even if the firm installed other operating systems on some of its computers. This scheme discouraged computer makers from using software from Microsoft's rivals, and the courts declared the practice illegal in 1994.

The case of *United States* v. *Microsoft Corporation* demonstrated that Microsoft stifled competition in the software industry. Under the initial ruling by Judge Jackson, the remedy was to break up the corporation into two companies, one producing the Windows operating system and a second producing application software. On appeal, this remedy was rejected, and instead Microsoft was directed to release more technical information about how its operating system works and to refrain from retaliating against computer makers that install software from other companies.

Blocking Mergers

Merger: A process in which two or more firms combine their operations.

A **merger** occurs when two firms combine their operations. A second type of antitrust policy is intended to block corporate mergers that would reduce competition and lead to higher prices. We saw earlier in this chapter that as the number of firms in a market increases, competition among firms drives down prices. Because a merger decreases the number of firms in a market, it is likely to lead to higher prices. In 1994, Microsoft tried to purchase Intuit, the maker of Quicken, a personal-finance software package that was a substitute for a similar Microsoft product. The merger would have reduced competition in the personal-finance software market, so the government blocked the merger.

Of course, the government does not oppose all corporate mergers. One possible benefit from a merger is that the new firm could combine production, marketing, or administrative operations and, thus, produce its products at a lower average cost. Under new guidelines developed in 1997, if companies involved in a proposed merger provide compelling evidence for greater efficiency, the government might allow a merger that reduces the number of firms in a market. The new guidelines will bring the U.S. antitrust rules closer to those of Europe and Canada, and could help U.S. companies compete in those markets.

In recent years, the analysis of proposed mergers has shifted from counting the number of firms in a market to predicting how a particular merger would affect prices. The data generated by retail checkout scanners provides an enormous amount of information about prices and quantities sold. Using these data, economists can determine how one firm's pricing policies affect the sales of that firm and its competitors. Economists can use this information to predict whether a merger would lead to higher prices. Two recent antitrust cases illustrate how this new approach works.

Examples: Wonder Bread and Office Depot

In 1995, Interstate Bakeries (the nation's third largest wholesale baker) tried to buy Continental Baking (the maker of Wonder Bread). From the government's perspective, the proposed merger was troublesome because the firms sold goods that were close substitutes for one another. The evidence for substitutability came from scanner data, which showed that when Interstate increased its price, many consumers switched to Wonder Bread.[6]

The Department of Justice concluded that a merger of the two bread makers would lead to higher bread prices. The government allowed the merger between the two companies but forced Interstate to sell some of its brands and bakeries. For example, Interstate sold the rights to sell its Weber brand bread to Four-S Baking Company. The idea is to ensure that other companies will compete with the newly merged company in the market for white bread.

Pricing data were also used to predict the price effects of a merger between two office supply chains, Staples and Office Depot, in 1997. Economists with the Federal Trade Commission (FTC) examined the prices and quantities of each item sold by the two chains. With the help of computers, the economists found an interesting pattern: The prices charged by Staples were lower in cities where Office Depot also had a store. This observation is consistent with the analysis of this chapter: the more firms in a market, the lower the price.

The FTC convinced the court that the proposed merger of Staples and Office Depot would lead to higher prices. The judge in the case observed that "direct evidence shows that by eliminating Staples' most significant, and in many markets, only, rival, this merger would allow Staples to increase prices or otherwise maintain prices at an anticompetitive level." Evidence from the companies' pricing data showed that the merger would have allowed Staples to increase its prices by about 13%. By blocking the merger, the FTC saved consumers an estimated $1.1 billion over five years.[7]

Regulating Business Practices: Price Fixing

Under antitrust law, it is illegal for firms to discuss their pricing strategies or their methods of punishing a firm that underprices other firms. In an early price-fixing case (*Addyston Pipe*, 1899), six manufacturers of cast-iron pipe met to fix prices in certain geographical areas. Several months after the Supreme Court ruled that their cartel pricing was illegal, the firms merged into a single firm, so instead of acting like a monopolist, which was illegal, they became a monopolist. Here are some recent examples of price fixing:

- GE/Westinghouse (1961). General Electric and Westinghouse were convicted of fixing prices for electrical generators, resulting in fines of more than $2 million and imprisonment or probation for 30 corporate executives.

- Infant formula (1993). The three major producers of infant formula (together serving 95% of the market) paid a total of $200 million to wholesalers and retailers to settle lawsuits claiming that they had conspired to fix prices.

- Plastic wrap in Japan (1993). A Tokyo court found eight Japanese companies guilty of conspiring to fix the prices of the plastic film used for wrapping food. The companies received fines of $54,000 to $73,000, and 15 executives were given suspended jail sentences of six months to one year.

- Airline pricing (1994). In an antitrust lawsuit filed in 1992, the U.S. Justice Department alleged that the nation's airlines used advance price listing to fix airline ticket prices, at a cost to consumers of about $1.9 billion. Before an airline increased its price, it could post a "suggested" price on a central computer and see whether the other airlines would increase their prices. In response to the antitrust lawsuit, the airlines agreed to drop this practice.[8]

- Carton board pricing in Europe (1994). The European Union Commission fined 19 manufacturers of carton board a total of 132 million European currency units ($165

PRICE FIXING FOR MUSIC CDS

The big-five music distributors—Universal Music, Sony Corporation, Time-Warner, EMI Music, and Bertelsmann Music Group (BMG)—collectively sell 85% of the nation's CDs. The firms subsidize the advertising campaigns of music retailers, covering a portion of retail advertising costs. In 1997, the distributors decided to tie advertising subsidies to the retailers' pricing decisions. The distributors specified a set of minimum advertised prices (MAP) and announced that any retailer that advertised a CD for less than the MAP would lose all of its "cooperative advertising" funds from the distributor. Under the MAP policy, a large retailer could lose millions of dollars in cooperative advertising funds, even if the advertisement of a sub-MAP price was funded entirely by the retailer.

In May 2000, the Federal Trade Commission reached an agreement with music distributors to end their MAP policy. Here is an excerpt from the FTC press release:

> In the 1990s, many new music retailers, including major consumer electronics stores, started to sell CDs at low prices to gain customers and market share. The more traditional music retailers also lowered their prices to compete. This retail "price war" led to lower CD prices for U.S. consumers, as prices for popular CDs fell as low as $9.99. The record companies adopted the MAP policies in 1995–96 to extinguish this "price war."
>
> The FTC alleges these MAP policies achieved their unlawful objective. The "price war" ended shortly after the policies were adopted and the

> retail price of CDs increased. The distributors increased their own prices, and since 1997 wholesale prices for music have increased.
>
> The FTC estimates that U.S. consumers may have paid as much as $480 million more than they should have for CDs and other music because of these policies over the last three years. These settlements will eliminate these policies and should help restore much-needed competition to the retail music market. Today's news should be sweet music to the ears of all CD purchasers.

Source: Federal Trade Commission, "Record Companies Settle FTC Charges of Restraining Competition in CD Music Market," Press Release, May 10, 2000.

U.S. million) for operating a cartel that fixed prices at secret meetings in luxury Zurich hotels.

- **Food additives (1996).** An employee of Archer Daniels Midland (ADM), a huge food company that likes to call itself "supermarket to the world," provided officials with audio- and videotapes of ADM executives scheming to fix prices. ADM pleaded guilty to charges of price fixing and was fined $100 million.

Review: Four Types of Markets

This is the third and last chapter on decision making by firms in different market settings. We can use Table 7.4 to review the characteristics of the four types of markets we've discussed in Chapters 5 through 7.

Table 7.4   Characteristics of Different Types of Markets

	Perfect Competition	Monopolistic Competition	Oligopoly	Monopoly
Number of firms	Very large number	Many	Few	One
Type of product	Standardized (homogeneous)	Differentiated	Standardized or differentiated	Unique
Demand faced by individual firm	Price taker: demand is perfectly elastic	Demand is price elastic but not perfectly elastic	Demand is less elastic than demand facing monopolistically competitive firm	Firm faces market demand curve
Entry conditions	No barriers	No barriers	Large barriers from economies of scale or government policies	Large barriers from economies of scale or government policies
Examples	Wheat, soybeans	Toothbrushes, music stores, clothing	Air travel, automobiles, beverages, cigarettes, long-distance phone services	Local phone service, patented drugs

1. **Perfect Competition.** There are very many firms, each selling a standardized or homogeneous product. Each firm is such a small part of the market that the firm takes the market price as given: The demand for the individual firm's product is perfectly elastic.

2. **Monopolistic competition.** There are many firms, each selling a slightly different product. Some examples are restaurants, retail stores, gas stations, and clothing. This contrasts with perfect competition, in which each firm sells a standardized product. Because the products sold by different firms in a monopolistically competitive market are not perfect substitutes, the demand for the firm's product is not perfectly elastic. There are no barriers to entering the market, so there are many firms.

3. **Oligopoly.** There are just a few firms in the market, a result of two sorts of barriers to entry: Economies of scale and government policies limit the number of firms in the market. The demand for an individual firm's product is less elastic than it would be in a monopolistically competitive market because there are fewer firms in the oligopoly. Some examples are automobiles, airline travel, and breakfast cereals.

4. **Monopoly.** A single firm serves the entire market. A monopoly occurs when the barriers to entry are very large, which could result from very large economies of scale or a government limit on the number of firms. The demand for a monopolist's product is shown by the market demand curve. Some examples of goods with large-scale economies are local phone service and electric power generation. Some examples of monopolies established by government policy are drugs covered by patents and concessions in national parks.

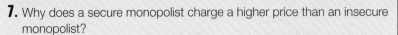

7. Why does a secure monopolist charge a higher price than an insecure monopolist?

8. Why was the federal government concerned about the merger of Interstate Bakeries and Continental Baking?

9. Under what circumstances will the government *not* block a merger that would decrease the number of firms in an already concentrated market?

Using the **TOOLS**

We've used the tools of economics to explore a firm's entry decision and to explore the incentives for firms to engage in price fixing. Here are some opportunities to use these tools to do your own economic analysis.

1. ECONOMIC EXPERIMENT: FIXED COSTS AND ENTRY

Here is an experiment that shows the implications of entry for prices and profits. Students play the role of entrepreneurs who must decide whether to enter the market for lawn cutting. If they decide to enter the market, they must then decide how much to charge for cutting lawns.

a. There are eight potential lawn-cutting firms (each represented by one to three students). There are two types of costs: a fixed cost of $14 per day, and a marginal cost of $3 for cutting each lawn. Each firm can cut up to two lawns per day.

b. There are 16 potential consumers who are willing to pay different amounts to have their lawns cut.

c. The experiment has two stages. In the first stage, each potential firm decides whether to enter the market. The entry decision is sequential: The instructor will go down the list of potential firms, one at a time, and give each firm the option of entering the market. The entry decisions are public knowledge. When a firm enters the market, it incurs a fixed cost of $14.

d. Each firm in the market posts a price for lawn cutting, and consumers shop around and decide whether to purchase lawn care at the posted prices. Each trading period lasts several minutes, and each firm can change its posted price up to three times (a total of three prices per trading period).

e. A consumer's score in a trading period equals the difference between the amount that he or she is willing to pay for lawn cutting and the price actually paid.

f. A firm's score equals its profit, which is its total revenue minus its total cost (the fixed cost of $14 plus the variable cost equal to $3 per lawn times the number of lawns cut).

2. ECONOMIC EXPERIMENT: PRICE FIXING

In this price-fixing experiment, you'll have an opportunity to conspire to fix prices in a hypothetical market with five firms. The instructor divides the class into five groups. Each group represents one of five firms that produce a particular good. Each group must develop a pricing strategy for its firm, recognizing that the other groups are choosing prices for their firms at the same time. There are only two choices: a high price (the cartel price) or a low price. The profit of a particular firm depends on the price chosen by the firm and the prices chosen by the four other firms. Here is the profit matrix:

Number of High-Price Firms	Number of Low-Price Firms	Profit for Each High-Price Firm ($)	Profit for Each Low-Price Firm ($)
0	5	—	50
1	4	20	70
2	3	40	90
3	2	60	110
4	1	80	130
5	0	100	—

From the second row, if one of the five firms chooses the high price and the other four firms choose the low price, the high-price firm earns a profit of $20, and each low-price firm earns a profit of $70. The game is played for several rounds. In the first three rounds, the firms make their choices without talking to each other in advance. In the fourth and fifth rounds, the firms discuss their strategies, disperse, and then make their choices. The group's score equals the profit earned by the firm.

3. Opposition to a New Drugstore

The city of Drugville is evaluating a request by a drugstore chain to open a new drugstore in the city. Consider the following statement from a citizen at a public hearing: "The output of the typical drugstore in our city is about 80% of the output at which its long-run average cost is minimized, so the average cost of drugs is higher than the minimum cost. The new drugstore would increase the average cost of production even further, so all our drugstores—including the new one—would be unprofitable, and consumers would pay higher prices for drugs." Assume that the citizen is correct in stating that the typical drugstore produces at 80% of the output at which average cost is minimized. Do this citizen's conclusions (all stores will be unprofitable and consumers will pay higher prices) follow logically from the facts?

4. Entry Deterrence

Your firm sells a very popular children's toy. The manager of another firm is thinking about introducing a similar toy. You have the following facts:

- Your average cost of production is constant at $2 per toy.
- At the current monopoly price of $5 per toy, you sell 120 toys per day.
- You could prevent the entry of the second firm by increasing your output to 150 toys per day and cutting your price to $4 per toy.
- If the second firm enters the market, your price would decrease to $3 per toy and you would sell only 80 toys per day.

Should you prevent entry of the second firm?

 **Summary**

This chapter is about markets ranging from those served by a few firms (oligopoly) to those served by a few dozen firms (monopolistic competition). We explored the effects of entry on prices and profit and examined the incentives for oligopolists to fix prices and discourage firms from entering the market. We also discussed antitrust policy, the purpose of which is to promote competition among the few firms in a concentrated market. Here are the main points of the chapter:

1. When a firm enters a market, the market price drops as firms compete for consumers, and the average cost of production increases as the quantity produced per firm decreases.

2. In a monopolistically competitive market, firms compete for customers by producing differentiated products, and entry continues until economic profit is zero.

3. Each firm in an oligopoly has an incentive to underprice the other firms, so price fixing (cartel pricing) will be unsuccessful unless firms have some way of enforcing a price-fixing agreement.

4. One way to maintain price fixing is a guaranteed price matching: One firm chooses the high price and promises to match any lower price.

5. To prevent a second firm from entering the market, an insecure monopolist may commit itself to producing a relatively large quantity and getting a relatively low price.

6. Under antitrust policies, the government breaks up some dominant firms, prevents some corporate mergers, and regulates business practices that reduce competition.

Key Terms

Cartel, 163
Concentration ratio, 162
Duopolists' dilemma, 166
Game tree, 164

Guaranteed price matching, 168
Insecure monopoly, 169
Limit pricing, 171
Merger, 174

Monopolistic competition, 159
Oligopoly, 162
Price fixing, 164
Trust, 173

Problems and Discussion Questions

1. Consider the city of Discville, where zoning laws limit the number of video arcades to one. The city's only video arcade has a price of $0.50 per game with an average cost of $0.34 per game. Suppose that the city eliminates its restrictions on video arcades, allowing additional firms to enter the market. According to an expert in the arcade market, "Each additional video arcade will decrease the price of games by $0.02 and increase the average cost of providing video games by $0.03." What is the equilibrium number of video arcades?

2. The city of Zoneville currently uses zoning laws to restrict the number of pizzerias. Under a proposed law, the restrictions on pizzerias would be eliminated. Consider the following statement by an expert in the pizza industry: "A pizzeria reaches the horizontal portion of its long-run average cost curve at an output of about 1,000 pizzas per day. The city's existing pizzeria sells 3,000 pizzas per day. Based on these facts, I predict that if the city eliminates the restrictions on pizzerias, we will soon have three pizzerias (3,000 pizzas/1,000 pizzas per pizzeria)." If we assume that the expert's facts about production costs are correct, is the expert's conclusion (three pizzerias) correct?

3. Consider the "Fixed Cost and Entry" experiment. Suppose the fixed cost per day is $18 per firm and the marginal cost is $4. Each firm can cut up to three lawns per day. The market demand curve is linear, with a vertical intercept of $70 and a slope of −$1 per lawn. Predict the outcome of the experiment, including the equilibrium price, quantity, and number of firms. Explain the reasoning behind your predictions.

4. Consider two firms, Speedy and Hustle, that provide land transportation from the downtown area to the airport (airporter service). The practice of guaranteed price matching is illegal.

   a. If the two firms act independently (they do not engage in price fixing or any other collusive behavior), each firm will serve 100 passengers per day at a price of $20 per passenger and an average cost of $15 per passenger.

   b. Under a price-fixing or cartel arrangement, each firm would serve 75 passengers at a price of $28 and an average cost of $18 per passenger.

   c. If one firm charges $20 and the other firm charges $28, the low-price firm will earn a profit of $900 and the high-price firm will earn a profit of $400.

   d. Speedy chooses a price first, followed by Hustle.
      Draw a game tree for the price-fixing game and predict the outcome.

5. On Wa-ki-ki Beach, there are two hotels, Weird and Bizarre. The practice of guaranteed price matching is illegal. If the two firms act independently (they do not engage in price fixing or any other collusive behavior), each firm will rent 50 rooms per day at a price of $50 per room and an average cost of $45 per room. Under a price-fixing or cartel arrangement, each hotel would rent 30 rooms per day at a price of $60 and an average cost of $48. If one firm charges $50 and the other firm charges $60, the low-price firm will earn a profit of $500 and the high-price firm will earn a profit of $150. Bizarre picks a price first, followed by Weird. Draw a game tree and predict the outcome of the pricing game.

6. Consider the market for air travel between Madison and Chicago. The long-run average cost is constant at $200 per passenger, and the demand curve is linear, with a slope of −$1 per passenger. A secure monopolist would charge a price of $280 and serve 70 passengers per day. The other possible prices are $260 for an insecure monopolist, $250 for the duopoly outcome, and $180 for the case when one firm picks a large quantity and a low price, but a second firm enters anyway.

   a. Use these numbers to draw two figures, one like Figure 7.7 and a second like Figure 7.8. Provide a complete set of numbers and briefly explain how you got them. Label any curves you draw and identify the relevant points on your graph.

   b. Use your second figure to predict the outcome of the entry deterrence game. What is the price of air travel?

7. The construction project at your city's airport is nearing completion, and your job is to decide how to use the ten new gates of the airport. The city is currently served by Gotcha Airlines, which has offered the city $20 million to help cover the cost of the airport construction project. In return, the new gates would be designated for the exclusive use of Gotcha. What are the trade-offs associated with accepting Gotcha's offer?

8. Web Exercise. Is the market for outdoor backpacks monopolistically competitive? Visit the Web site of Fog Dog Sports (*www.fogdog.com*). Click on the "Outdoor Shop" icon and check how many types of backpacks are available from this site. How are the alternative backpacks differentiated?

9. Web Exercise. Visit the Web site of the U.S. Federal Trade Commission (*www.ftc.gov/*) to get the facts on the most recent price-fixing cases. Click on the "Search" icon and do a search of news releases using the keywords "price fixing." Write a brief description of three recent price-fixing cases.

Take It to the Net

We invite you to visit the O'Sullivan/Sheffrin page on the Prentice Hall Web site at: **www.prenhall.com/osullivan/** for this chapter's World Wide Web exercises.

Model Answers to Questions

Chapter-Opening Questions

1. If Spoke enters the market, the price will drop (for example, to $140) and her average cost will be greater than $120 (for example, $125), so her profit will be less than $30 per bike (for example, $15 = $140 − $125).

2. Many firms entered the market, causing prices to drop by about 22% and profit per license to decrease significantly.

3. You benefit because competition from online sellers causes the bookstore to reduce its prices.

4. Pricing data showed that the prices charged by Staples were lower in cities where Office Depot also had a store, suggesting that competition between the two firms kept prices low. A merger would eliminate the competition, leading to higher prices.

Test Your Understanding

1. Marginal revenue, marginal cost.

2. Decreases, decreases, increases.

3. With four firms in the market, the price is $138 per bike and the average cost is $132 per bike, so profit is still positive. If a fifth firm entered the market, the price would drop to $134 and the average cost would rise to $136, so profit would be negative.

4. He will choose the low price and gain at Jill's expense.

5. Jill should ignore the incredible promise and choose the low price.

6. $50 (equal to $400 − $350).

7. To prevent the entry of a second firm, an insecure monopolist commits itself to produce a large

quantity of output and accepts a low price. A secure monopolist doesn't have to worry about other firms entering the market.

8. Scanner data showed that the bread produced by the two firms were close substitutes. An unregulated merger would have reduced competition and led to higher prices.

9. Companies that are involved in a proposed merger can present evidence that the merger would reduce costs and lead to lower prices, better products, or better service. If the evidence for this is convincing, the government might allow a merger that reduces the number of firms in a market.

Using the Tools

3. Opposition to a New Drugstore. In all the examples we have considered, the typical firm operates along the negatively sloped portion of its long-run average cost curve, yet profit is still positive. A firm will enter the market only if it expects to earn a positive profit, so the statement that the new drugstore would make profit negative for all drugstores is puzzling. We know that entry decreases prices as firms compete for customers, so the statement that consumers would pay higher prices is also puzzling.

4. Entry Deterrence. The profit from entry deterrence is $300 per day: Profit is the quantity (150) times the gap between price and average cost ($2 = $4 − $2). The profit from allowing entry is only $80 per day. The profit is the quantity (80) times the gap between price and average cost ($1 = $3 − $2). The deterrence strategy generates a higher price and a larger quantity with no change in average cost, so profits are higher.

Notes

1. Leonard W. Weiss, ed., *Concentration and Price* (Cambridge, MA: MIT Press, 1989); Timothy F. Bresnahan and Peter C. Reiss, "Entry and Competition in Concentrated Markets," *Journal of Political Economy*, vol. 99, October 1991, pp. 977–1009; Theodore E. Keeler, "Deregulation and Scale Economies in the U.S. Trucking Industry: An Econometric Extension of the Survivor Principle," *Journal of Law and Economics*, vol. 32, October 1989, pp. 229–253; Thomas Gale Moore, "Rail and Truck Reform—The Record So Far," *Regulation*, November–December 1983; Richard L. Hudson, "European Companies Speed Shift to Phone Competition," *Wall Street Journal*, June 24, 1994, p. B4.

2. Adam Smith, *Wealth of Nations* (New York: Modern Library, rev. ed. 1994).

3. Seth Faison, "Agents Turn Bakers in Battle Against Italian-Bread Cartel," *New York Times*, July 14, 1994, p. A1.

4. "Big Friendly Giant," *Economist*, January 30, 1999, p. 72.

5. Leonard W. Weiss, *Economics and American Industry* (New York: Wiley, 1963), pp. 189–204.

6. "The Economics of Antitrust: The Trustbuster's New Tools," *Economist*, May 2, 1998, pp. 62–64.

7. *Federal Trade Commission v. Staples, Inc.*, 970 F. Supp. 1066 (D.D.C. 1997, Hogan, J).

8. Sharon Walsh, "Six Airlines to Halt Advance Price Listing," *New York Times News Service*, printed in *The Oregonian*, March 18, 1994, p. B1.

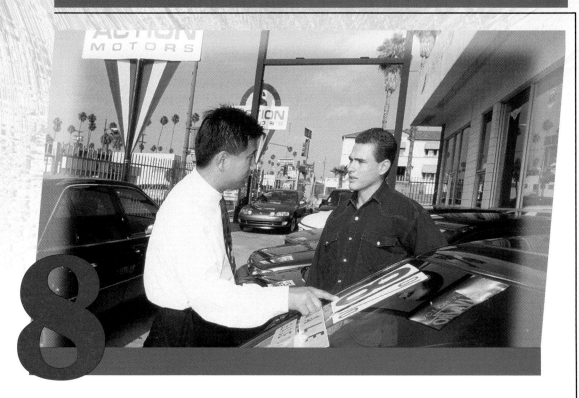

Market Failure: Spillovers and Imperfect Information

"So why are you selling this car?"

Buyers of used cars ask this question frequently and then listen carefully to the answer, checking for body language that might suggest that the seller is not being completely honest. In contrast, no one ever asks, "So why are you selling this slice of pizza?"

n this chapter we'll discuss three cases when markets fail to allocate resources efficiently. A market is efficient if it allows all the socially beneficial transactions between buyers and sellers to happen. We say that a transaction is socially beneficial if the social benefit of the transaction exceeds the social cost. A voluntary market transaction happens when the buyer's benefit exceeds the seller's cost. In a market without spillover benefits or costs, the buyer's benefit is identical to the social benefit, and the seller's cost is identical to the social cost. As a result, when there are no spillovers, buyers and sellers make socially efficient decisions: All the socially efficient transactions happen.

The first part of the chapter shows that when there are spillover benefits, some socially beneficial transactions don't happen. For example, suppose a farmer could build a dike to protect her land from flooding at a cost of $10,000. If the farmer's benefit is only $4,000, she obviously won't build the dam. But if there are two other farmers, each of whom would receive a $4,000 benefit from the dike, the social benefit of $12,000 exceeds the cost of the dam, so the dam is socially efficient. Operating on her own, an individual farmer won't execute a transaction (building the dam) that is socially efficient. As we'll see, the solution to the problem of spillover benefits is collective decision making, involving all the beneficiaries in the decision-making process.

The second part of the chapter shows that when there are spillover costs, transactions that are socially *inefficient* happen. The seller of a product charges a price high enough to cover his or her production cost (for labor, materials, capital) but ignores any spillover cost such as health costs resulting from air pollution. As a result, the seller's price is below the social cost of production, so the consumer pays an artificially low price and will purchase goods for which the social benefit (the buyer's benefit) is less than the social cost. For example, suppose that producing one unit of paper involves a production cost of $60, so the market price is $60. If a consumer is willing to pay $63 for the paper, the paper will be produced and sold. If, however, there is a spillover cost of $10 (from the health costs associated with air pollution), this transaction is not socially efficient: The social benefit ($63) is less than the social cost ($60 + $10). As we'll see, the solution to the problem of spillover cost is to impose a tax equal to the spillover cost. This tax will be built into the price of the product, allowing consumers to make socially efficient decisions.

A third cause of market failure is imperfect information. As we saw earlier in the book, the model of supply and demand is based on the assumption that buyers and sellers have enough information to make informed decisions. When buyers and sellers are fully informed about product quality, socially efficient transactions happen. In contrast, when one side of the market can't distinguish between high-quality and low-quality goods, the market for high-quality goods may be relatively small or nonexistent. For example, suppose Bianca is willing to pay $8,000 for a high-quality used car, and Owen is willing to accept $6,000 for his high-quality car. If Bianca can't tell the difference between a high-quality car and a low-quality car, she won't be willing to pay the full $8,000 for a car of unknown quality. If she figures there is a 50-50 chance that Owen's car is high quality and is willing to pay $5,000 for a 50-50 chance at a high-quality car, this socially efficient transaction won't happen because Owen isn't willing to sell his car for only $5,000. As we'll see, the problem of imperfect information isn't easily solved, but there are some ways to diminish the problem.

This chapter explores the effects of spillovers and imperfect information on several types of markets. Here are some of the practical questions that we answer:

1. Should we eliminate taxes and pay for government programs with voluntary contributions instead?
2. If a fishing firm shares a lake with a polluting steel mill, what can the government do to ensure that pollution is a the socially efficient level?

3. What is a carbon tax, and how would a tax of $100 per ton of carbon affect the equilibrium price of gasoline?
4. Why do professional baseball pitchers who switch teams spend so much time on the disabled list, nursing their injuries instead of playing?

Spillover Benefits and Public Goods

In this chapter, we'll see that if a particular good generates spillover benefits, government intervention can make beneficial transactions happen. Recall the spillover principle.

Spillover **PRINCIPLE**

For some goods, the costs or benefits associated with the good are not confined to the person or organization that decides how much of the good to produce or consume.

To illustrate the idea of spillover benefits, consider a dam built for flood-control purposes. There are 100,000 people in the valley below the dam, and each person gets a $5 benefit from the dam. The total benefit of the dam is $500,000 (equal to 100,000 people × $5 per person), which exceeds the $200,000 total cost of the dam. Because the total benefit exceeds the total cost, the dam should be built. The problem is that no single person will build the dam because the $200,000 cost exceeds his or her $5 personal benefit. In other words, if we rely on the forces of supply and demand, with each person considering only the personal benefits and costs of a dam, no dam will be built.

The government can solve this problem by collecting enough taxes to pay for the dam. Suppose the government offers to build the dam and pay for it with a tax of $2 per person. The tax raises $200,000 in tax revenue ($2 per person times 100,000 people), which is just high enough to pay the $200,000 cost of the dam. Every person will support this proposal because the $2 tax per person is less than the $5 benefit per person. The government can use its taxing power to provide a good that would otherwise not be provided.

Public Goods

The dam is an example of a **public good**, a good that is available for everyone to consume, regardless of who pays and who doesn't. In contrast, a **private good** is consumed by a single person or household. For example, only one person can eat a hot dog. If a government hands out free cheese to the poor, is the free cheese a public good or a private good? Although anyone can get in line for the cheese, only one person can actually consume a particular piece of cheese, so the free cheese is a private good that happens to be available free of charge from the government. Similarly, an apartment in a public housing project can be occupied by a single household, so it is a private good provided by the government.

Public good: A good available for everyone to consume, regardless of who pays and who doesn't.

Private good: A good consumed by a single person or household.

We can be more precise about the difference between public and private goods. Here are the formal definitions of the two types of goods:

1. Private goods are rival in consumption (only one person can consume the good) and excludable (it is possible to exclude a person who does not pay for the good).
2. Public goods are nonrival in consumption (available for everyone to consume) and nonexcludable (it is impractical to exclude people who don't pay).

Here are some other examples of public goods:

National defense   Preservation of endangered species
Law enforcement   Protecting the earth's ozone layer
Space exploration   Fireworks display

If someone refuses to pay for one of these public goods, it would be impractical to prevent that person from consuming the good. For example, a person who evades federal income taxes receives the same benefits from space exploraction and national defense as someone who pays taxes. One role of government is to use its taxing power to collect money to pay for public goods.

Application: Asteroid Diversion

We can apply the concepts of public goods to the issue of protecting the earth from catastrophic collisions with asteroids. On average, the earth is hit by a 200-meter asteroid every 10,000 years, by a 2-kilometer asteroid every million years, and by a 10-kilometer asteroid every 100 million years.[1] A collision with a 200-meter asteroid would generate a stratospheric dust cloud that would inhibit photosynthesis and retard plant growth, resulting in lower agricultural yields throughout the world. Scientists have already developed the technology to divert asteroids: Large optical telescopes would detect an asteroid on a collision course with the earth, and an orbiting gossamer mirror of coated polyester would focus a tight beam of sunlight on the asteroid, vaporizing enough of its surface to change its path.

The diversion of asteroids is a public good in the sense that it is available for everyone to consume, regardless of who pays and who doesn't. As with any public good, the key to developing an asteroid-diversion program is to collect money to pay for the program. According to NASA scientists, a diversion program would require several new telescopes, which would cost about $50 million to install and about $10 million per year to operate.[2] The cost of the gossamer mirror required to change the path of the asteroid would be $100 million to $200 million. Although it would be sensible to finance the program with contributions from all earthlings, it may be impossible to collect money from everyone. A more likely outcome is that one or more developed countries will finance their own diversion systems.

Space exploration is a public good.

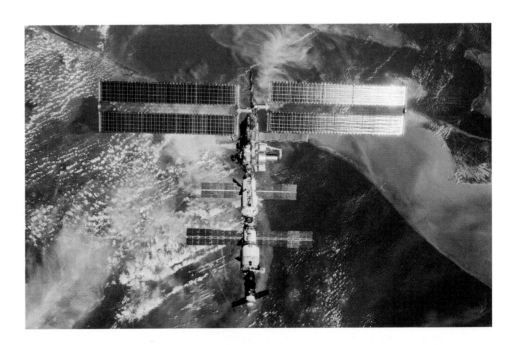

Private Goods with Spillover Benefits

There are some private goods that generate spillover benefits. One example is education, a good that generates two sorts of spillover benefits:

1. **Workplace spillovers.** In most workplaces, people work in groups, and teamwork is important. A well-educated person understands instructions readily and is more likely to suggest ways to improve the production process. When a well-educated person joins a work team, the productivity of everyone on the team increases, leading to higher wages for everyone on the team.

2. **Civic spillovers.** Citizens in a democratic society make collective decisions by voting in elections, and each citizen must live with these decisions. A well-educated person is more likely to vote intelligently, so there are spillover benefits for other citizens.

Because of these spillover benefits from education, the government uses various policies to encourage people to become educated. Local governments provide free education through high school. States subsidize students at public colleges and universities, providing college education at a fraction of its actual cost. In addition, the federal government provides financial aid to students in both public and private schools.

The government subsidizes other goods that generate spillover benefits. For example, many firms use government subsidies to support on-the-job training and education. This is sensible because some of the benefits of education and training go to other firms: When a worker trained by one firm switches to another firm, the second firm also benefits. This is the rationale for subsidizing some types of education and training programs. Another example is research at universities and other nonprofit organizations. If a research project provides knowledge or technology that leads to the development of new products or the improvement of old ones, the benefits from the project spill over onto consumers and producers. This is the rationale for subsidizing basic research in the sciences.

Voluntary Contributions and the Free-Rider Problem

Most public goods are supported by taxes. What would happen if we eliminated taxes and asked people to contribute money to pay for national defense, dams, city streets, and the police? Would people contribute enough money to support these programs at their current levels?

The problem with using voluntary contributions to support public goods is known as the **free-rider problem**. Each person will try to get the benefits of a public good without paying for it, trying to get a free ride at the expense of others who do pay. For example, only about a quarter of people who listen to National Public Radio pay the membership dues. Of course, if everyone tries to get a free ride, there will be no money to support the public good, so it won't be provided. The flip side of the free-rider problem is the chump problem: No one wants to be the chump—the person who gives free rides to other people—so no one contributes any money. The free-rider problem suggests that if taxes were replaced with voluntary contributions, the government would be forced to cut back or eliminate many programs.

Free-rider problem: Each person will try to get the benefit of a public good without paying for it, trying to get a free ride at the expense of others who do pay.

Many organizations, including public radio and television, religious organizations, and charitable organizations, raise money through voluntary contributions. So it appears that some people overcome their inclination to be free riders and contribute voluntarily to organizations that provide public goods. The successful organizations use a number of techniques to encourage people to contribute, such as the following:

- Give contributors private goods such as coffee mugs, books, musical recordings, and magazine subscriptions. People are more likely to contribute if they get something for it.

- Arrange matching contributions. You are more likely to contribute if you know that your $30 contribution will be matched with a contribution from another person.
- Appeal to people's sense of civic or moral responsibility.

It's important to note, however, that these organizations are only partly successful in mitigating the free-rider problem. Public radio is one of the success stories, but the typical public-radio station gets contributions from fewer than quarter of its listeners.

The Mystery of the Three-Clock Tower

Back in the days before the inexpensive wristwatch, most people did not carry their own timepieces. Many towns built clock towers in the center of town so that their citizens could know the time. The towns paid for the clock towers with voluntary contributions from citizens. One town in the northeastern United States built a four-sided tower but put clock faces on only three sides of the tower. To most people, this seems bizarre. If you build a clock tower, why not put clock faces on all four sides?

The key to solving this puzzle is the free-rider problem. It turns out that one of the town's wealthy citizens refused to contribute money to help build the clock tower. The town officials decided that because he did not pay, they should not put a clock face on the side of the tower facing his house. In other words, the citizen tried—unsuccessfully—to get a free ride. The problem is that other citizens on the same side of town also suffered from not seeing the clock. In this case, preventing a free ride by one citizen caused problems for other citizens.

TEST Your Understanding

1. Why does the free-rider problem occur for public goods but not for private goods?
2. Why is free cheese given to poor people not a public good?
3. Suppose there are 1,000 farmers, each of whom is willing to pay $200 for a dam. If the cost of the dam is $250,000, should it be provided?

Spillover Costs

Spillover (or externality): A cost or benefit experienced by people who are external to the decision about how much of a good to produce or consume.

We can use the paper market to illustrate the inefficiency that occurs in a market through **spillover** (or **externality**) costs. Suppose there are several paper mills along a river, and that a city downstream from the mills draws water from the river for drinking. The city's water-treatment costs depend on how much chemical waste is dumped into the river. For each gallon of chemical waste from paper mills, the city's treatment costs increase by $4. There are spillover costs because the decision makers in the paper mills ignore the costs incurred by people in the downstream city. In other words, some of the costs of producing paper are external to the firm, where decisions about how much paper to produce are made.

The economic approach to spillover costs from pollution is to force producers to pay for the pollution they generate, just as they pay for labor, raw materials, and machinery. In the paper example, the government could impose a pollution tax of $4 for each gallon of waste dumped into the river. The **pollution tax** internalizes the pollution externality: The tax means that the costs associated with the chemical waste from paper are no longer external to the firm (where decisions about how much to produce are made), but internal.

Pollution tax: A tax or charge equal to the spillover cost per unit of waste.

The Firm's Response to a Pollution Tax

Most polluting firms can control the amount of waste they dump into the environment. For example, a paper firm could install filters and other abatement equipment, or it could switch to raw materials that generate less chemical waste. The first two columns of Table 8.1 show a hypothetical relationship between the volume of waste generated and the cost of producing one ton of paper. For example, the cost per ton is $60 if the firm generates 5 gallons of waste per ton of paper but $61 if the firm generates only 4 gallons per ton of paper. In other words, when the firm decreases its waste by 1 gallon, the production cost per ton increases by $1. As the firm continues to decrease the volume of waste, it becomes progressively more expensive to decrease it further. This makes sense because the firm must use progressively more expensive abatement equipment to decrease the volume of waste. For example, the cost of eliminating the last gallon of waste is $30 ($116 minus $86).

The third and fourth columns of Table 8.1 show the tax cost per ton and the total cost per ton of paper with different volumes of waste. The tax is $4 per gallon of waste, so the tax cost is $20 if the firm generates 5 gallons of waste per ton of paper but only $16 for 4 gallons, $12 for 3 gallons, and so on. The fourth column of Table 8.1 shows the firm's total cost per ton of paper, equal to the sum of the production cost per ton and the tax cost per ton. If the firm generates 5 gallons of waste, the production cost will be $60 and the tax cost will be $20, so the total cost per ton is $80. As the firm continues to decrease the volume of waste, the production cost increases while the tax cost decreases. The total cost per ton initially decreases (from $80 to $77 to $76) but eventually increases, reaching $116 if the firm generates no waste.

How will the typical paper firm respond to a pollution tax? The question for the firm is, Should we continue to generate 5 gallons of waste per ton of paper and pay $20 in pollution taxes, or should we spend some money to reduce our waste? In Table 8.1, the total cost per ton is minimized at $76 with 3 gallons of waste. Therefore, the typical firm will decrease its waste from 5 to 3 gallons per ton of paper.

We can use the marginal principle to explain why it is sensible to generate only 3 gallons of waste.

Marginal **PRINCIPLE**

Increase the level of an activity if its marginal benefit exceeds its marginal cost; reduce the level if its marginal cost exceeds its marginal benefit. If possible, pick the level at which the marginal benefit equals the marginal cost.

Table 8.1 Cost per Ton of Paper with Varying Amounts of Pollution

Waste per Ton (Gallons)	Production Cost per Ton	Tax Cost per Ton	Total Cost per Ton
5	$60	$20	$80
4	61	16	77
3	64	12	76
2	71	8	79
1	86	4	90
0	116	0	116

In this case, the activity is reducing waste, so the firm should continue to cut its waste as long as the marginal benefit (the $4 savings in taxes) exceeds the marginal cost (the extra production cost from cutting waste by 1 gallon). Starting with 5 gallons of waste, it is sensible to cut back to 4 gallons because the $4 marginal benefit exceeds the $1 marginal cost. Similarly, it is sensible to cut back to 3 gallons because the $4 marginal benefit exceeds the $3 marginal cost. The firm will not cut back to 2 gallons, however, because the $4 marginal benefit is less than the $7 marginal cost.

The Market Effects of a Pollution Tax

We're ready to study the market effects of a pollution tax. Suppose that each firm produces 1 ton of paper per day and has the production costs shown in Table 8.1. Figure 8.1 shows the effects of the $4 pollution tax ($4 per gallon of waste) on the industry supply curve. In a perfectly competitive industry, the equilibrium price equals the average cost of production, so each firm makes just enough money to stay in the market. The original price of $60 per ton was just high enough to cover the cost of producing a ton of paper without the pollution tax. The tax increases the cost of producing paper because the typical firm pays some pollution taxes and incurs some additional costs when it cuts back its pollution from 5 gallons to 3 gallons per ton of paper. Therefore, the $60 price will not be high enough to cover the higher production costs, so some firms will leave the market. As a result, the supply curve will shift to the left: At each price, a smaller quantity of paper will be supplied.

The leftward shift of the supply curve increases the equilibrium price of paper. In Figure 8.1, the market moves from point *i* to point *f*, where the demand curve intersects the new supply curve. The price of paper increases from $60 to $68 per ton, and consumers respond to the higher price by decreasing the quantity of paper demanded, from 100 to 80 tons per day. Like other taxes, the pollution tax is partially shifted to consumers in the form of a higher price, and they respond by consuming less paper. When consumers face the full cost of producing paper, they decide to consume less of it.

As shown in Table 8.1, the pollution tax increases the unit cost of producing paper from $60 to $76. In Figure 8.1, the tax increases the equilibrium price of paper from $60 to $68. Why doesn't the price of paper rise by an amount equal to the $16 change in unit production cost, from $60 to $76?

Figure 8.1
Market Effects of a Pollution Tax

The pollution tax increases the cost of producing paper, shifting the market supply curve to the left. The equilibrium moves from point *i* to point *f*. The tax increases the equilibrium price from $60 to $68 per ton and decreases the equilibrium quantity from 100 to 80 tons per day.

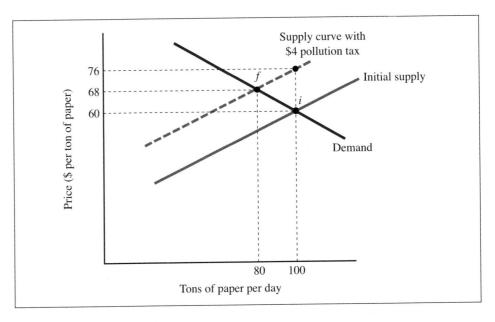

The price of paper increases by less than the change in unit production cost because the supply curve is positively sloped. As we learned in Chapter 5, the long-run supply curve is positively sloped because an increase in the total output of the industry increases the average cost of production as input prices increase and the industry relies on progressively less productive inputs. In the paper industry, the pollution tax *decreases* total output, and thus *decreases* the average cost of production. The decrease in average cost resulting from the shrinkage of the industry partly offsets the higher costs associated with the pollution tax. In Figure 8.1, the supply curve shifts upward by $16 (the increase in average production cost at the original industry output), but because the supply curve is positively sloped, the equilibrium price increases by only $8.

How does the pollution tax affect the total volume of waste dumped into the river? The volume of waste decreases for two reasons:

1. **Abatement.** There is less waste per ton of paper: 3 gallons instead of 5 gallons per ton.
2. **Lower output.** The industry produces less paper: 80 tons instead of 100 tons per day.

In this example, the volume of water pollution decreases from 500 gallons per day (100 tons of paper times 5 gallons per ton) to 240 gallons per day (80 tons of paper times 3 gallons per ton). In general, we can clean up the environment by producing less of a polluting good and generating less waste per unit of the good.

Traditional Regulation: Command and Control

An alternative to a pollution tax is a system of regulations that controls the amount of pollution generated by each firm. The label for a traditional regulatory policy is a **command-and-control policy**. The government commands each firm to produce no more than a certain volume of pollution and controls the firm's production process by forcing the firm to use a particular pollution-control technology. In our paper example, the government would tell each firm to produce no more than 4 gallons of chemical waste per ton of paper and force each firm to install a particular type of filter to meet the pollution target.

One problem with this approach is that the mandated abatement technology—the control part of the policy—is unlikely to be the most efficient technology. The regulatory policy specifies a single abatement technology for all firms. Because the producers of a polluting good often use different materials and production techniques, an abatement technology that is efficient for one firm is likely to be inefficient for others. Because a command-and-control policy causes firms to use inefficient abatement technology, the policy will increase firms' costs by a large amount. Compared to the pollution tax policy, the command-and-control policy will cause a larger shift of the market supply curve, leading to a higher price and a smaller quantity.

Global Warming and a Carbon Tax

Here is a simple experiment that explains global warming. On a warm day, park your car in a sunny spot, close the windows, and wait. Solar energy in the form of visible and ultraviolet light will come through the car windows and heat the air in the car. This is the greenhouse effect: If all the windows are closed, there is no way for the heat to escape, so the temperature in the car (or in a greenhouse) will increase. The windows of the car are like the earth's atmosphere. Solar energy comes through the atmosphere and heats the air near the earth's surface. Certain types of gases in the atmosphere (called greenhouse gases) trap this heat close to the earth's surface and are beneficial. Without these gases, the earth's surface temperature would be far below freezing, so most forms

Command-and-control policy: A pollution-control policy under which the government commands each firm to produce no more than a certain volume of pollution and controls the firm's production process by forcing the firm to use a particular pollution-control technology.

of life would die off. Unfortunately, we are pumping more of these greenhouse gases into the atmosphere, so the earth's temperature is increasing. Just as rolling up a window in a parked car increases the temperature in the car, increasing the volume of greenhouse gases increases the temperature near the earth's surface.

Scientists agree that greenhouse gases are accumulating. The volume of atmospheric carbon dioxide is now about 25% above the preindustrial level, and it is increasing at a rate of about 1.6% per year,[3] and at this rate the volume of greenhouse gases will double in about 60 years. Most scientists agree that a doubling of atmospheric carbon dioxide will increase global temperatures, but they don't agree just how large the increase in temperature will be. Because we know so little about how the earth's ecosystems will respond to a rapid increase in carbon dioxide, the actual change in temperature could be small or large. The practical policy question is, Should we do something now to reduce the accumulation of greenhouse gases or should we postpone action until we know more about the consequences of global warming and the cost of controlling it?

How would an increase in temperatures affect the earth's environment and the global economy? Most scientists expect total rainfall to increase, with some areas getting more and others getting less. The increase in carbon dioxide will make all plants—crops and weeds alike—grow faster. Overall, the net effect on agriculture is likely to be negative because scientists expect less rainfall in areas with fertile soil and more rainfall in areas with less productive soil. An increase in global temperatures would also melt glaciers and the polar ice caps, raising sea levels. As a result, a large amount of land currently used for agriculture or living space could be inundated. Of course, we could build dikes to protect low-lying areas, but such protective measures are very expensive. The Netherlands has launched a multibillion-dollar program to increase the height of its seawalls. According to a recent report from the Climate Institute, by the year 2070, much of the metropolitan area in Manila, Philippines, could be under 1 meter of water, and rising sea levels could force the relocation of 3.3 million people in Jakarta, Indonesia.[4]

The economic response to the accumulation of greenhouse gases is to impose a tax on fossil fuels. The spillover cost of a particular fuel depends on how much carbon dioxide is released into the atmosphere, so the **carbon tax for** a particular fuel would be determined by the fuel's carbon content. For example, a tax of $100 per ton of carbon would more than double the price of coal (a fuel with a high carbon content), but would increase the price of gasoline by only 23%.

A carbon tax would decrease greenhouse emissions for three reasons:

1. The tax will increase the price of energy and increase the cost of producing energy-intensive goods. Consumers will respond by demanding smaller quantities of these goods, in part by switching to goods produced with less energy.
2. Some energy producers will switch to noncarbon energy sources such as the wind, the sun, and geothermal sources.
3. Energy producers will improve the efficiency of carbon-based fuels, squeezing out more energy per ton of coal or oil.

One concern about a carbon tax is that it would impose a large burden on the poor. The revenue from a carbon tax could be used to reduce income taxes or payroll taxes, reducing the burden of the carbon tax on the poor.

Coase Bargaining

Under some circumstances, a spillover problem can be resolved through bargaining among the affected parties. The Coase bargaining solution, named after economist Ronald Coase, applies to a situation when there is a small number of affected parties, and the transactions costs of bargaining are relatively low.

Carbon tax: A tax based on a fuel's carbon content.

To illustrate the bargaining solution, consider a lake shared by a steel mill and a fishing firm. The mill initially dumps 5 tons of waste into the lake, and the pollution decreases the fish harvest. The mill can abate pollution, with the marginal cost of abatement shown in Figure 8.2. The marginal cost increases from $5 for the first ton abated (point h), to $7 for the second ton (point i), and so on up to $13 for the fifth ton (point m). As in the earlier example of the paper mill, the marginal cost of abatement increases with the level of abatement, reflecting the idea that as waste is reduced, it becomes progressively more difficult and costly to reduce waste by one more unit.

Figure 8.2 also shows the marginal benefits of abatement, which are experienced by the fishing firm in the form of a larger fish harvest. For the first unit of abatement (reducing mill waste from 5 tons to 4 tons), the marginal benefit is an additional $17 in fish harvest (point b). The marginal benefit decreases as the level of abatement increases, from $13 for the second ton abated, to $9 for the third ton abated, and so on. The first ton abated increases the fish harvest by more than the second ton abated, which increases the harvest by more than the third, and so on.

We can use the marginal principle to determine the socially efficient level of pollution abatement. In Figure 8.2, the marginal benefit is greater than or equal to the marginal cost for the first three tons of abatement, so the efficient level of abatement is 3 tons and the socially efficient level of pollution is 2 tons. For the first ton abated, the marginal benefit ($17, point b) exceeds the marginal cost ($5, point h), so abating the first ton is efficient. Similarly, the marginal benefit of the second ton exceeds the marginal cost. The marginal benefit equals the marginal cost at 3 tons of abatement, so that's the efficient level. We stop at 3 tons because for the fourth ton, the marginal benefit ($5) is less than the marginal cost ($11).

How would Coase bargaining work in this situation? Suppose the steel mill is granted the property rights to the lake: The steel firm has the right to decide how much waste is dumped into the lake. Although it is tempting to think that the mill will just dump 5 tons of waste into the lake, such a conclusion ignores the possibility of bargaining and side payments. If the mill initially dumps 5 tons, the fishing firm has an incentive to pay the mill to reduce its waste. The benefit of the first ton of abatement is an additional $17 in fish harvest. The mill would incur a cost of only $5 to abate the first

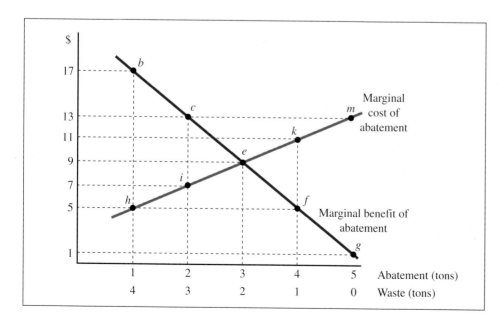

Figure 8.2
Coase Bargaining Solution to a Spillover Problem
The marginal benefit of pollution abatement equals the increase in the fish harvest, while the marginal cost equals the additional abatement cost. Using the marginal principle, the efficient level is 3 tons. Coase bargaining generates the efficient abatement level. If the steel mill owns the lake, the fishing firm will pay the steel mill to abate 3 tons. If the fishing firm owns the lake, the steel mill will pay the fishing firm not to abate the fourth and fifth tons.

ton, so there is room for bargaining. If the two firms split the difference between the $17 benefit and the $5 cost, the fishing firm would pay $11 to get a ton abated, and each firm would be better off: The fishing firm pays $11 to get an additional $17 in fish harvest, while the mill gets $11 and pays only $5 to reduce pollution. The same logic applies to the second ton of abatement, with a marginal benefit of $13, a marginal cost of $7, and a side payment of $10.

The bargaining process will generate the socially efficient level of pollution abatement (3 tons). For the third ton of abatement, the marginal benefit equals the marginal cost at $7, so a side payment of $7 will just cover the fishing firm's benefit and also cover the mill's cost. In contrast, for the fourth ton of abatement, the marginal benefit ($5) is less than the marginal cost ($11), so there is no room to negotiate a side payment. The bargaining stops at 3 tons of abatement. The lesson from this example is that if we assign property rights to the lake, bargaining between the firms generates the efficient outcome.

What would happen if we grant the property rights to the fishing firm instead of the steel mill? In this case, it is tempting to think that the fishing firm would not allow any pollution, but in fact there is an incentive to sell the rights to pollute. If we start with 5 units of abatement (zero pollution), the fishing firm would be better off arranging a side payment that allows one unit of pollution. For the first ton of pollution (reducing abatement from 5 tons to 4 tons), the fish harvest would decrease by $1 (point *g* in Figure 8.2), while the mill would save $13 in abatement cost (point *m*). Splitting the difference between the $1 cost and $13 benefit, if the steel mill paid $7 for the right to dump 1 ton of waste, both firms would be better off: The fishing firm would receive $7 to tolerate a $1 loss in harvest, while the steel mill would pay $7 to avoid $13 in abatement cost. The same logic applies to the second ton of pollution, with a $5 loss in harvest, a $11 savings in abatement cost, and an $8 side payment. This bargaining would stop at the socially efficient level of abatement (3 units) because reducing abatement further generates a cost to the fishing firm that exceeds the benefit to the steel mill.

We've seen that assigning property rights to either the steel mill or the fishing firm generates the socially efficient outcome. Once property rights are assigned, bargaining and side payments allow the firms to adjust the level of pollution as long as the marginal benefit exceeds the marginal cost. For efficiency purposes, it doesn't matter who owns the lake as long as *someone* owns it. Of course, the assignment of property rights has important equity implications: Whoever owns the lake collects the side payments from the party that doesn't.

Under what circumstances can we rely on Coase bargaining to generate the socially efficient outcome? In our example, bargaining is plausible because there are only two parties. In contrast, if there were several polluting mills and fishing firms, bargaining among all the affected parties would probably be unwieldy. In general, Coase bargaining requires a small number of affected parties and small transactions costs (the cost of arranging side payments). When the number of affected parties is large, the bargaining process won't work, and the solution to a spillover problem requires a centralized policy such as pollution taxes, regulations, or marketable permits.

Marketable Pollution Permits

Marketable pollution permits:
A system under which the government picks a target pollution level for a particular area, issues just enough pollution permits to meet the pollution target, and allows firms to buy and sell the permits.

In recent years, policymakers have developed a new approach to environmental policy. Here is how a government runs a system of **marketable pollution permits**:

- Pick a target pollution level for a particular area.
- Issue just enough pollution permits to meet the pollution target.
- Allow firms to buy and sell the permits.

For example, if the target pollution level in the paper industry is 400 gallons of waste per day, the government would issue a total of 400 permits, each of which entitles a firm to generate 1 gallon of waste per day. The key innovation is that these permits are marketable: Firms can buy and sell the permits. In fact, an environmental group could decrease the amount of pollution by purchasing a permit and then retiring it.

Marketable Permits

To explain the effects of marketable pollution permits, let's extend our example of the paper industry to include firms that have higher pollution-abatement costs. Specifically, there are two types of paper mills, each of which produces 1 ton of paper per day:

- Half the paper mills can abate pollution at a low cost, as shown in the second column of Table 8.2. For example, the production cost per ton is $61 with 4 gallons of waste, compared to $60 with 5 gallons of waste.

- Half the paper mills have high abatement costs, as shown in the third column of Table 8.2. For example, if a high-cost firm generates 4 gallons of waste, the cost per ton is $67, compared to $61 for a low-cost firm generating the same volume of waste.

The differences in abatement costs could result from differences in raw materials or production techniques. For some types of raw materials and some production techniques, the cost of abating pollution is relatively high.

Suppose the government issues four marketable permits to each paper mill. If a particular firm wants to generate 5 gallons of waste per day, it can buy a fifth permit from another firm. Of course, a firm that sells one of its permits can generate only 3 gallons of waste per day. Each firm with low abatement cost will sell a permit to a firm with high abatement cost. Such an exchange benefits both the buyer and the seller because the buyer is willing to pay more than the seller is willing to accept.

- **Willingness to pay.** Each firm with high abatement cost is willing to pay up to $7 for a permit. If such a firm gets a fifth permit, it can generate 5 gallons of waste per ton and produce a ton of paper for $60, compared to a cost of $67 per ton when the firm has only four permits. Getting a fifth permit saves the firm $7 on the ton of paper it produces, so the firm is willing to pay up to $7 for a permit.

- **Willingness to accept.** Each firm with low abatement cost is willing to accept any amount above $3 for one of its permits. If such a firm gives up one of its four permits, it could generate only 3 gallons of waste, so its production cost for the ton of paper it produces would increase by $3 (from $61 to $64). Giving up a permit costs the firm $3, so the firm is willing to accept any amount greater than $3 for a permit.

Table 8.2 Abatement Costs: Low-Cost Firm versus High-Cost Firm

Production Cost per Ton: Waste per Ton (Gallons)	Production Cost per Ton: Firm with Low Abatement Cost	Firm with High Abatement Cost
5	$ 60	$ 60
4	$ 61	$ 67
3	$ 64	$ 82
2	$ 71	$112
1	$ 86	$172
0	$116	$300

The actual price of the permit depends on the negotiating skills of the two firms. A plausible outcome of the bargaining process is a price halfway between the buyer's $7 willingness to pay and the seller's $3 willingness to accept. If the buyer and the seller split the difference, the price will be $5.

Allowing firms to sell their permits decreases the total cost of achieving any abatement target. For each permit sold, a firm with high abatement cost saves $7 in abatement costs. The firm with low abatement cost will have one less permit, so it must abate one more unit of pollution, at a cost of $3. For each permit sold, the total cost of abatement decreases by $4, the difference between the $7 cost saved by the high-cost firm and the $3 cost incurred by the low-cost firm.

Why is the total cost of abatement lower with marketable permits? By allowing firms to trade their permits, the government exploits the differences in abatement costs, relying on firms with low abatement cost to do the abatement. As a result, we can achieve the same volume of pollution abatement at a lower cost. In a perfectly competitive market, these cost savings will be passed on to consumers in the form of a lower price of paper.

Experiences with Marketable Permits

The first program of marketable pollution permits, started in 1976 by the U.S. Environmental Protection Agency, allowed limited trading of permits for several airborne pollutants. Trading was later extended to lead in gasoline (in 1985) and the chemicals that are responsible for the depletion of the ozone layer (in 1988). The 1990 Clean Air Act established a trading system for sulfur dioxide, which is responsible for acid rain. In the early 1990s, a trading system was introduced in the Los Angeles Basin for the pollutants that are responsible for urban smog.

A CLOSER LOOK | MARKETABLE POLLUTION PERMITS IN SOUTHERN CALIFORNIA

Under RECLAIM, the clean-air program implemented in Southern California in 1994, the volume of nitrogen-oxide pollution decreases by 8% per year.[5] Between 1994 and 2003, the volume of pollution decreased by 75%. Under the program, the number of marketable pollution permits (aka credits) decreases every year. In the period 1999 to 2001, a booming California economy increased production and the demand for permits. Because demand increased while supply decreased, the equilibrium price of permits increased, from $0.13 per pound of nitrogen-oxide gas to $13.

The response to the higher permit price was predictable. Large polluters like the Los Angeles Department of Water and Power developed plans to install new pollution-abatement equipment to reduce its emissions by 90%. Although the abatement equipment will cost $40 million, it is less expensive than buying pollution permits. A few years ago, Libbey Glass Company installed low-pollution burners in its plant, dropping its emissions below the volume allowed by its permits. The company sold its extra permits to other firms, generating income for Libbey and allowing other firms with more expensive abatement technology to continue production.

The first pollution permit was sold in 1977, and thousands of exchanges have occurred since then. Here are some examples:

- Duquesne Light Company paid $3,750,000 to Wisconsin Power and Light for the rights to dump 15,000 tons of sulfur dioxide. In this transaction, the price of a ton of sulfur dioxide emissions was $250.

- Mobil Oil Corporation paid $3,000,000 for the rights to dump 900 pounds of reactive vapors per day. Mobil paid this sum to the city of Torrance, California, which had earlier acquired the pollution rights from General Motors.

- A firm in Los Angeles installed a new incinerator that decreased its hydrocarbon emissions by 100 tons per year and offered to sell the rights to emit 100 tons of hydrocarbons for $400,000.

A system of marketable permits may lead to severe pollution in some areas. For example, if you live in Torrance, California, you probably don't like the idea that Mobil Oil will use a marketable permit to generate more pollution at its refinery. You probably don't care that the marketable permit system is more efficient than a command-and-control system that would limit the refinery's pollution to its current level. This "hot spot" problem suggests that the marketable permit system may be inappropriate for pollutants that generate large local effects. Alternatively, the number of permits issued for a particular geographical area could be limited to prevent severe pollution.

The government can use marketable permits to reduce air and water pollution over time. A common practice is to issue marketable permits with a one-year life and then decrease the number of permits issued each year. For example, under an air-quality management plan for the Portland, Oregon, metropolitan area, the number of permits will decrease by 10% each year. This approach was also used by the Environmental Protection Agency to phase out lead in gasoline and the chemicals that are responsible for the depletion of the ozone layer. For an example of a permit policy that decreases pollution over time, read "A Closer Look: Marketable Pollution Permits in Southern California."

TEST Your Understanding

4. Why does a command-and-control policy increase production costs by a relatively large amount?

5. Use a supply and demand diagram to show the effects of a carbon tax on the market for an energy-intensive good such as aluminum or steel.

6. Explain how a carbon tax would decrease the total volume of greenhouse gases.

Imperfect Information and Disappearing Markets

As we saw at the beginning of the chapter, the model of supply and demand is based on the assumption that buyers and sellers have enough information to make informed choices. The classic example of a market with imperfect information is the market for used cars. Suppose prospective buyers cannot distinguish between low-quality cars (lemons) and high-quality cars (plums). Although a buyer can get some information about a particular car by looking at the car and taking it for a test drive, the information gleaned from this kind of inspection is not enough to determine whether the car is a lemon or a plum. In contrast, the seller (the current owner of a used car) knows from experience whether the car is a lemon or a plum.

Asymmetric information: One side of the market—either buyers or sellers—has better information about the good than the other.

We say that there is **asymmetric information** in a market if one side of the market—either buyers or sellers—has better information than the other. For example, the sellers of used cars know more about the cars being sold than buyers do. Because buyers cannot distinguish between lemons and plums, there will be a single market: Lemons and plums will be sold together in a mixed market for the same price.

Ignorant Consumers and Knowledgeable Sellers

We begin our discussion with an extreme case, a market in which all the cars on the market will be lemons. This extreme case is unrealistic, but it provides a useful starting point for a discussion of the implications of asymmetric information. This extreme case shows that one possibility is the disappearance of the market for the high-quality good. As we'll see later, a more realistic case is a situation in which most—but not all—the used cars are lemons, so there is a small chance that a buyer will get a high-quality car.

How much is a consumer willing to pay for a used car that could be either a lemon or a plum? To determine the price in a mixed market—with both high-quality and low-quality goods—we must answer three questions:

1. How much is the consumer willing to pay for a plum (a high-quality car)?
2. How much is the consumer willing to pay for a lemon (a low-quality car)?
3. What is the chance that a used car purchased in the mixed market will be a lemon?

Suppose the typical buyer is willing to pay $4,000 for a plum and $2,000 for a lemon. In addition, the consumer has neutral expectations about the used-car market. That means that the consumer assumes half the used cars are lemons and the other half are plums, so there is a 50% chance of getting a lemon. How much is the consumer willing to pay for a car that has a 50% chance of being a lemon? Suppose that she or he is willing to pay the average value of the two types of cars, or $3,000. (The analysis wouldn't change if we instead assumed that the consumer is willing to pay less than the average value, say, $2,600.)

Sellers of used cars know what they are selling. The current owner of a used car knows from everyday experience whether the car is a lemon or a plum. Given a single market price for all used cars, lemons and plums alike, each current owner must decide whether or not to sell his or her car. We can use the supply curves for lemons and plums to show how many plums and lemons will be supplied at a particular price.

Figure 8.3 shows two hypothetical supply curves: one for plums and another for lemons. The minimum price for plums is $2,500: At any price less than $2,500, no plums will be supplied. As shown by the plum supply curve, the number of plums supplied increases with the price of used cars. For example, 4 plums will be supplied at a price of $3,000 (point n). The minimum price for lemons is $500: At any price less than $500, no lemons will be supplied. Lemons have a lower minimum price because they are worth less to their current owners. As shown by the lemon supply curve, the number of lemons supplied increases with the price of used cars. For example, 16 lemons will be supplied at a price of $3,000 (point m).

Equilibrium in the Mixed Market

Table 8.3 shows two scenarios for our hypothetical used-car market, with numbers consistent with the supply curves shown in Figure 8.3. In the first column, we assume that buyers have neutral expectations about the chance of getting a lemon. If buyers assume that half the used cars on the market are lemons and half are plums, the typical buyer will be willing to pay $3,000 for a used car. At this price, 4 plums and 16 lemons will be supplied, so 80% of the used cars (16 of 20) will be lemons. In this case, consumers underestimate the chance of getting a lemon.

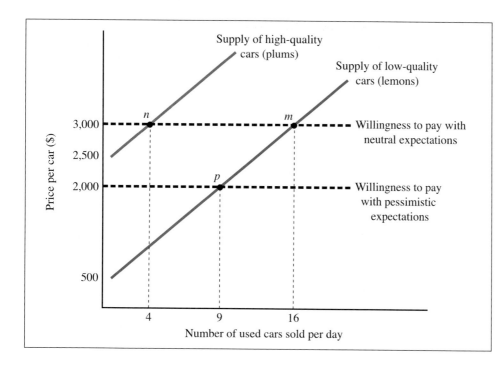

Figure 8.3
Market for Used Cars
Suppose buyers have neutral expectations (assume that there is a 50% chance of getting a lemon), and are willing to pay $3,000 for a used car. At this price, the supply of plums is 4 (point *n*) and the supply of lemons is 16 (point *m*). At a price of $2,000, only lemons will be supplied (9 lemons, as shown by point *p*).

What will consumers do when they realize that they've underestimated the chance of getting a lemon? They certainly won't be willing to pay $3,000 for a used car. In general, the greater the chance of getting a lemon, the smaller the amount that consumers are willing to pay. As a result, the price of used cars will decrease. As was explained earlier in the book, a market reaches an equilibrium when there is no pressure to change the price. Therefore, the scenario represented by the data in the first column is not an equilibrium.

Suppose that after observing the outcome in the first column, buyers become very pessimistic. They assume that all the used cars on the market are lemons. Under this assumption, the typical buyer will be willing to pay only $2,000 (the value of a lemon) for a used car. This price is less than the $2,500 minimum price for supplying plums, so plums will disappear from the used-car market. This is shown in Figure 8.3: At a price of

Table 8.3   All Used Cars Are Lemons

	Neutral Expectations	Pessimistic Expectations
Assumed chance of lemon	50%	100%
Willingness to pay for lemon	$2,000	$2,000
Willingness to pay for plum	$4,000	$4,000
Willingness to pay for used car	$3,000	$2,000
Number of lemons supplied	16	9
Number of plums supplied	4	0
Total number of used cars	20	9
Actual chance of lemon	80%	100%

$2,000, the quantity of plums supplied is zero, but the quantity of lemons is 9 (point p). In other words, all the used cars will be lemons, so consumers' pessimism is justified. Because consumers' expectations are consistent with their actual experiences in the market, the equilibrium price of used cars is $2,000. The equilibrium in the used-car market is shown in the second column of Table 8.3.

In this equilibrium, no plums are bought or sold, so every buyer will get a lemon. The domination of the used-car market by lemons is an example of the **adverse-selection problem**. The uninformed side of the market (buyers, in this case) must choose from an undesirable or adverse selection of goods (used cars, in this example). The asymmetric information in the market generates a downward spiral of price and quantity: A decrease in price decreases the quantity of plums supplied, decreasing the price further when buyers realize that most of the cars on the market are lemons, which leads to even fewer plums on the market. In the extreme case, this downward spiral continues until all the cars on the market are lemons, so every buyer will get a lemon.

Adverse-selection problem: The uninformed side of the market must choose from an undesirable or an adverse selection of goods.

Reviving the High-Quality Market: Thin Markets and Warranties

The disappearance of high-quality cars from our hypothetical market is an extreme—and unrealistic—case. In most used-car markets, some high-quality cars are offered for sale even when the price of used cars is low, so there is at least a small chance that a buyer will get a high-quality car. Some people sell high-quality used cars when a change in circumstances forces them to switch to a different car. For example, a person who switches to a job farther from home might switch to a car that is more fuel-efficient. A growing family might switch to a bigger car. Some people buy a new car every few years, and the decision to replace an old car with a new one is unaffected by the resale price of used cars. Some of these people sell high-quality cars, so there will be some high-quality cars sold even at low prices.

In our earlier example, the market for high-quality used cars disappears because informed suppliers refuse to participate in the mixed market for used cars. Specifically, the $2,500 minimum price for high-quality cars is so high that no plums are supplied at the equilibrium price of $2,000. If the minimum price for plums is lower—say, $1,800—some plums will be supplied when the market price is $2,000. Although most of the used cars will be lemons, some lucky buyers will get plums. In this case, we say that asymmetric information generates a **thin market**: Some high-quality goods are sold but fewer than would be sold in a market with perfect information.

Thin market: A market in which some high-quality goods are sold but fewer than would be sold in a market with perfect information.

We can use a simple example to show how we get a thin market for plums. In Table 8.4, consumers assume that there is a 90% chance of getting a lemon (worth $2,000 to the consumer) and a 10% chance of getting a plum (worth $4,000 to the consumer). Let's assume that each consumer is willing to pay $2,200 for a used car under these circumstances. Consumers are willing to pay a little more than the value of a lemon because there is a small chance of getting a plum. Figure 8.4 shows the supply curves for this example: At a price of $2,200, there will be 2 plums (shown by point s) and 18 lemons (shown by point t). In this case, consumers accurately assess the chance of getting a lemon: 90% of the used cars sold (18 of 20) turn out to be lemons. Therefore, the equilibrium price of used cars is $2,200 and the equilibrium quantity is 20 cars, 10% of which are plums.

The domination of the used-car market by lemons provides an opportunity for clever sellers. Buyers are willing to pay $4,000 for a plum, and some plum owners would gladly sell their cars if they could get more than $2,200 for them. This large gap between the willingness to pay and the willingness to accept provides a profit opportunity for clever entrepreneurs who can somehow persuade a skeptical consumer that a particular used car is a plum, not a lemon.

Table 8.4   Thin Market for Plums

Assumed chance of lemon	90%
Willingness to pay for lemon	$2,000
Willingness to pay for plum	$4,000
Willingness to pay for used car	$2,200
Number of lemons supplied	18
Number of plums supplied	2
Total number of used cars	20
Actual chance of lemon	90%

A supplier could identify a particular car as a plum in a sea of lemons by offering one of the following guarantees:

- **Money-back guarantee.** The seller could promise to refund the $3,500 price if the car turned out to be a lemon. Because the car is in fact a plum—a fact known by the seller—the buyer will not ask for a refund, and buyer and seller will be happy with the transaction.

- **Warranties and repair guarantees.** The seller could promise to cover any extraordinary repair costs for one year. Because the car is a plum, there won't be any extraordinary repair costs, so buyer and seller will be happy with the transaction.

Car consumers also have an incentive to get information about the quality of used cars. A consumer who identified a plum could buy the high-quality car for a price below his or her willingness to pay ($4,000). There is a big payoff from information that enables the consumer to distinguish between lemons and plums. It may be rational for a car consumer to hire a mechanic to inspect a particular car for defects.

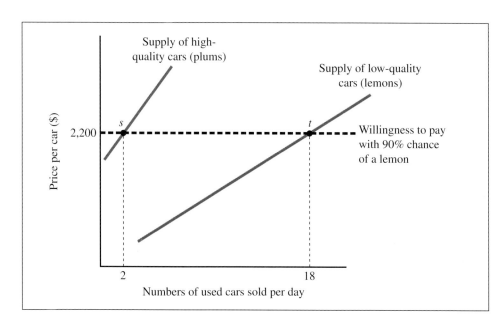

Figure 8.4
Thin Market for Plums
If buyers assume that there is a 90% chance of getting a lemon, they are willing to pay $2,200 for a used car. At this price, the supply of plums is 2 (point *s*) and the supply of lemons is 18 (point *t*), so the actual chance of getting a lemon is 90%, the same as the assumed chance of getting a lemon.

USED BASEBALL PLAYERS

Professional baseball teams compete with each other for players. After six years of play in the major leagues, a player has the option of becoming a free agent and offering his services to the highest bidder. A player is likely to switch teams if the new team offers him a higher salary than does his original team. One of the puzzling features of the free-agent market is that pitchers who switch teams are more prone to injuries than pitchers who don't. On average, pitchers who switch teams spend 28 days per season on the disabled list; pitchers who do not switch teams spend only 5 days per season on the disabled list.[6] This doesn't mean that all the switching pitchers are lemons: Many of them are injury-free and are terrific additions to their new teams. But on average, the switching pitchers spend five times longer recovering from injuries.

This puzzling feature of the free-agent market for baseball players is explained by asymmetric information and adverse selection. Because the coaches, physicians, and trainers from the player's original team have interacted with the player on a daily basis for several years, they know from experience whether he is likely to suffer from injuries that prevent him from playing. In contrast, the new team has much less information: Its physicians can examine the pitcher, but a single exam is not the same as several years of daily experience with the pitcher. Suppose the market price for pitchers is $1 million per year and a pitcher who is currently with the Chicago Cubs is offered this salary by another team. If the Cubs think the pitcher is likely to spend a lot of time next season recovering from injuries, they won't try to outbid another team for the pitcher; they will let the pitcher switch teams. But if the Cubs think the pitcher will be injury-free and productive, he will be worth more than $1 million to the Cubs, so they will outbid other teams and keep the pitcher. In general, an injury-prone pitcher is more likely to switch teams: As with the used-car market, there are many "lemons" on the used-pitcher market. The market for baseball players playing other positions (outfield, infield) does not suffer from adverse selection, perhaps because the injuries that affect their performance are easier for a potential new team to detect.

Although you may think it's bizarre to compare baseball pitchers to used cars, people in baseball don't think so. They recognize the similarity between the two markets. Jackie Moore, who manages a free-agent camp where teams looking for players can see free agents in action, sounds like a used-car salesman.[7] "We want to get players off the lot. We want to cut a deal. How many camps can you go into where you can look at a player and take him home with you?"

Adverse Selection in Insurance Markets

So far, we've discussed markets in which sellers have better information than buyers, but what happens when buyers are better informed than sellers? Consider the market for insurance. A person who buys an insurance policy knows much more about his or her risks and needs for insurance than the insurance company does. For example, when you buy an auto insurance policy, you know more than your insurance company about your driving habits and your chances of getting into an accident. We'll see that insurance markets suffer from the adverse-selection problem: Insurance companies must pick from an adverse or undesirable selection of customers.

Let's look at the market for malpractice insurance. To keep things simple, suppose there are only two types of physicians: careful and reckless. On average, the cost of settling malpractice suits against careful doctors is $4,000 per doctor per year, while the cost of settling malpractice suits against reckless doctors is $30,000 per doctor per year. If the doctor is insured, these costs are paid by an insurance company. Uninsured physicians will have to pay these costs themselves. Suppose insurance companies cannot distinguish between careful doctors and reckless doctors, but each doctor knows whether he or she is careful or reckless. This means that there is asymmetric information in the insurance market: Buyers (physicians) have better information than sellers (insurance companies).

If insurance companies cannot distinguish between careful doctors and reckless doctors, there will be a mixed market and a single price for malpractice insurance. Suppose all insurance companies are initially neutral in their expectations about what type of doctors will buy malpractice insurance. Insurance companies assume that half the doctors who buy insurance are careful and half are reckless. If the typical insurance company gets equal numbers of careful doctors and reckless doctors, the average cost of providing insurance will be $17,000 per doctor. Therefore, if the insurance company charges $17,000 per year for insurance and its expectations about the mixture of careful doctors and reckless doctors are correct, the company's total revenue will cover its total cost. In other words, the company will earn zero economic profit.

The expectations of the insurance company are unlikely to be realized, however. At a price of $17,000, few if any of the careful physicians will buy malpractice insurance. The premium is more than four times the average cost of settling malpractice suits against a careful doctor, so malpractice insurance is not a very good deal for them. Most careful doctors would rather take the risk, knowing that they will pay an average of $4,000 per year to settle malpractice suits. This is the adverse-selection problem: Insurance companies get an undesirable (adverse) selection of doctors. To ensure zero economic profit, the price of insurance must increase to $30,000, the average cost of serving the reckless physicians.

In this example, most careful physicians do not buy malpractice insurance because insurance companies are unable to distinguish between careful doctors and reckless doctors. The reckless doctors in the mixed market increase the cost of providing insurance and increase the price of insurance. In fact, insurance companies try to identify careful doctors and offer them lower insurance rates. When a doctor applies for an insurance policy, the insurance company gathers information about the doctor and the history of his or her medical practice. Although these actions help insurance companies distinguish between careful and reckless physicians, they are by no means perfect, so the adverse-selection problem persists.

Moral Hazard

Does insurance affect people's risk-taking behavior? Insurance causes people to take greater risks because part of the cost of an undesirable outcome will be borne by the insurance company. Here are some examples of people taking greater risks because they have insurance:

- Irma could buy a fire extinguisher for her kitchen. If she had to pay for any property damage caused by a fire, she would definitely buy a fire extinguisher. But because her homeowner's insurance covers property damage from fires, she doesn't buy a fire extinguisher.

- Harry decides how carefully to drive his car. If he had to pay for any repairs resulting from a collision, he would drive very carefully. But his auto insurance covers all repair costs, so he drives recklessly.

- Flo can either fly on a commercial airline or hitch a ride with her pilot friend in a four-seat airplane. Traveling in small airplanes is much riskier, and if Flo dies in an airplane crash, her family would lose the income she would otherwise earn. If she didn't have life insurance to offset these income losses, she wouldn't take the risk of harming her family in that way. But because her family would collect $1 million in life insurance, she is willing to take the risk.

Moral hazard problem:
Insurance encourages risky behavior.

The **moral hazard problem** is that insurance encourages risky behavior. More precisely, moral hazard occurs when an insured party takes an unobserved action (not observed by the insurer) that affects the probability of the event that triggers payment from the insurer. For example, Harry's unobserved action is reckless driving, which increases the probability of a collision, an event that triggers payment from his auto insurance company.

The moral hazard problem is pervasive. The availability of fire insurance decreases investment in fire-prevention programs and other investments that reduce the risk of fire. Collision insurance increases risky behavior on the roads. The availability of life insurance encourages risky activities such as flying small airplanes, parachuting, and bungee jumping.

Economic Detective

Bicycle Theft Insurance

At Wheeler State University, 1 out of every 10 bicycles was stolen in 1998. When a group of young entrepreneurs discovered that no one on campus had bicycle-theft insurance, they decided to go into the insurance business, offering one-year theft insurance for $15 per bike. They sold 100 policies in 1999 and expected 10 of their 100 customers (10% of them) to lose their bicycles to theft. The entrepreneurs figured that their total revenue would more than cover the cost of replacing 10 bicycles, leaving a tidy profit. By the end of 1999, a total of 20 insured bicycles had been stolen, and the students lost a bundle of money on their little enterprise. What happened?

The key to solving this puzzle is the fact that the 10% theft rate occurred in 1998, when no one had theft insurance. When the entrepreneurs offered theft insurance, they expected the same theft rate. Because of moral hazard, however, the students who bought theft insurance were less careful in protecting their bikes from theft, perhaps using less secure locks or leaving their bikes on campus overnight. As a result, the theft rate for insured bikes was 20%, not 10%. The entrepreneurs lost money because they did not anticipate that insurance would increase risk taking.

People who buy bicycle theft insurance are less careful in protecting their bikes from theft.

7. Complete the statement with *buyers* or *sellers*: There is asymmetric information in the used-car market because _____ cannot distinguish between low-quality cars and high-quality cars, but _____ can.

8. Suppose the typical consumer is willing to pay $3,000 for a plum and $1,000 for a lemon. If there is a 50% chance of getting a lemon, how much is the consumer willing to pay for a used car?

9. Buyers assume that there is a 70% chance of getting a lemon; seven lemons and three plums are supplied. Is this an equilibrium? Explain.

10. Complete the statement with numbers: Suppose that the average annual malpractice cost is $40,000 for reckless doctors and $2,000 for careful doctors. If half the insured doctors are reckless, the insurance company will earn zero economic profit if the price of insurance is _____. If careful doctors are not willing to pay any more than $5,000 for insurance, the price required for zero economic profit is _____.

Using the **TOOLS**

In this chapter, we explain why the government provides public goods, and how government can respond to the spillover costs from pollution. We've seen what happens when one side of the market—either buyers or sellers—has better information than the other side. Here are some opportunities to do your own economic analysis of markets with spillovers and imperfect information.

1. ECONOMIC EXPERIMENT: FREE RIDING

This experiment demonstrates some of the features of the free-riding problem. Here is how it works:

a. The instructor selects 10 students at random and gives each student 10 dimes (or play money).

b. Each student can contribute money to support a public good by dropping one, two, or three dimes into a public-good pot. Each student has the option of keeping all the dimes and not contributing anything. The contributions are anonymous; none of the students knows how much the other students contribute.

c. For each dime in the pot, the instructor adds two dimes. For example, if the students contribute a total of 40 dimes, the instructor adds 80 dimes, for a total of 120 dimes in the pot. The 2-for-1 match represents the idea that the benefits of public goods exceed the costs. In this case, the benefit-cost ratio is 3 to 1.

d. The instructor divides the money in the public-good pot equally among the 10 students. For example, if there are 120 dimes in the pot, each student receives 12 dimes.

e. Steps 2 through 4 can be repeated four or five times.

We can extend the experiment to mimic the compulsory tax system. The instructor could require each student to contribute three dimes, the maximum amount, each round. Would a switch to a compulsory tax system make the students better off or worse off?

2. Stream Preservation

Consider a trout stream that is threatened with destruction by a nearby logging operation. Each of the 10,000 local fishers would be willing to pay $5 to preserve the stream. The owner of the land would incur a cost of $20,000 to change the logging operation to protect the stream.

a. Is the preservation of the stream efficient from the social perspective?

b. If the landowner has the right to log the land any way he or she wants, will the stream be preserved?

c. Propose a solution to this problem. Describe a transaction that would benefit the fishers and the landowner.

d. Will your proposed solution work?

3. Market Effects of a Carbon Tax

Consider the market for gasoline. In the initial equilibrium, the price is $2 per gallon and the quantity is 100 million gallons. The price elasticity of demand is 1.0 and the price elasticity of supply is 2.0. Suppose the government imposes a carbon tax, which is expected to shift the gasoline supply curve to the left by 24%.

a. Use a supply–demand diagram to show the market effects of the carbon tax.

b. Predict the new equilibrium price and quantity of gasoline.

4. ECONOMIC EXPERIMENT: LEMONS

In this experiment, students play the role of consumers purchasing used cars. More than half the used cars on the road (57%) are plums, and the remaining cars (43%) are lemons. Each consumer offers a price for a used car and then rolls a pair of dice to find out whether he or she gets a lemon or a plum. In general, rolling a big number is good news: To get a plum, you need to roll a big number. The higher the price you offer, the smaller the number you must roll to get a plum. Here is how the experiment works:

a. Each consumer tells the instructor how much he or she is offering for a used car and then rolls the dice.

b. The instructor tells the consumer whether the number she rolled is large enough to get a plum. If the number is not large enough, she gets a lemon.

c. The consumer's score equals the difference between the maximum amount she is willing to pay for the type of car she got ($1,200 for a plum and $400 for a lemon) and the price she actually paid. For example, if Otto offers $500 and gets a plum, his score is $700. If Carla offers $600 and gets a lemon, her score is −$200.

d. The instructor announces the result of each transaction to the class.

e. There are three to five buying periods. At the end of the last trading period, each consumer adds up his or her surpluses.

5. State Auto Insurance Pool

Consider a state in which automobile drivers are divided equally into two types of drivers: careful and reckless. The average annual auto insurance claim is $400 for a careful driver and $1,200 for a reckless driver. Suppose the state adopts an insurance system under which all drivers are placed in a common pool and allocated to insurance companies randomly. An insurance company cannot refuse coverage to any driver it is assigned, but a driver who is unhappy with the insurance company has the option of being reassigned (randomly) to another insurance company. By law, each insurance company must charge the same price to all its customers. Predict the price of auto insurance under two alternative policy scenarios: (1) auto insurance is mandatory; (2) auto insurance is voluntary.

Summary

In this chapter, we've seen that governments can solve the problems caused by spillover benefits and costs. We also explored the effects of imperfect information on the markets for used goods and insurance. Here are the main points of the chapter:

1. If the cost of a particular good exceeds its per capita benefit, that good will not be provided by a market, even if the total benefit of the good exceeds its total cost. We can use government—with its taxing authority—to make a collective decision about whether to provide such a good.

2. A system of voluntary contributions suffers from the free-rider problem: People will voluntarily contribute only a small fraction of the amount that would be generated under a compulsory taxation to pay for the public good.

3. A pollution tax, which forces firms to pay for pollution, decreases the total volume of pollution because firms produce less of the polluting good and generate less pollution for each unit produced.

4. Under Coase bargaining, two parties affected by spillovers use side payments to reach the socially efficient outcome.

5. If one side of the market cannot distinguish between high-quality and low-quality goods, both types of goods will be sold in a mixed market at the same price.

6. Insurance markets suffer from adverse selection because buyers have better information than sellers.

7. Insurance encourages risky behavior because part of the cost of an unfavorable outcome will be paid by an insurance company.

Key Terms

adverse-selection problem, 200
asymmetric information, 198
carbon tax, 192
command-and-control policy, 191

free-rider problem, 187
marketable pollution permits, 194
moral hazard problem, 204
pollution tax, 188

private good, 185
public good, 185
spillover (or externality), 188
thin market, 200

Problems and Discussion Questions

1. A three-person city is considering a fireworks display. Bertha is willing to pay $100 for the proposed fireworks display; Marian is willing to pay $30; Sam is willing to pay $20. The cost of the fireworks display is $120.

    a. Will any single citizen provide the display on his or her own?

    b. If the cost of the fireworks display is divided equally among the citizens, will a majority vote in favor of the display?

    c. Describe a transaction that would benefit all three citizens.

2. Each of the 80,000 citizens in a particular county would be willing to pay $0.10 to increase the number of wolf litters by one. Each litter of wolves imposes costs on ranchers (from livestock losses) of $5,000.

    a. Is the provision of an additional litter of wolves efficient from the social perspective?

    b. If ranchers have the right to kill any wolves on their property, will an additional litter be provided?

    c. Propose a solution to this problem. Describe a transaction that would benefit both the wolf lovers and ranchers.

3. Use a supply–demand graph to show a situation in which the equilibrium quantity of a polluting good is 20 tons, but a pollution tax decreases the equilibrium quantity of the good to zero. Is this situation likely to occur?

4. Suppose the government adopts a zero-tolerance pollution policy, meaning that paper mills are required to eliminate all water pollution. Suppose the paper firms have access to the abatement technology shown in the first two columns of Table 8.1.

    a. What is the production cost per ton under the zero-tolerance policy?

    b. If the government uses a pollution tax to implement this policy, what is the smallest tax that would cause the typical firm to voluntarily pick zero pollution?

5. Use the notion of adverse selection to explain a classic quip from Groucho Marx: "I won't join any club that is willing to accept me as a member."

6. The following table shows some scenarios for different used-car markets. Which markets are in equilibrium? Graph each equilibrium, using Figure 8.4 as a model.

	Scenario A	Scenario B	Scenario C
Assumed chance of lemon	60%	80%	95%
Willingness to pay for used car	$6,000	$5,000	$4,500
Number of lemons supplied	70	40	90
Number of plums supplied	30	10	10
Total number of used cars	100	50	100

7. You are thinking about buying a used camera at a price of $60. You are willing to pay $20 for a lemon and $100 for a plum. Under what circumstances would it be wise to buy a used camera? Are these circumstances likely to occur? Explain.

8. Scientists have recently developed new genetic tests that could be used by an insurance company to determine whether a potential customer is likely to develop certain diseases. Discuss the trade-offs associated with allowing insurance companies to use these tests.

9. On the campus of Bike University, half the bikes are expensive (replacement value = $100), and half are cheap (replacement value = $20). There is a 50%

chance that any particular bike—expensive or cheap—will be stolen in the next year. Suppose a firm offers bike-theft insurance for $40 per year: The firm will replace any insured bike that is stolen. If the firm sells 20 insurance policies, will the firm make a profit? Explain.

10. As Kira tries to decide whether or not to do a bungee jump, she asks to make one phone call. If there is a moral hazard problem, whom will she call?

11. Many professional athletes purchase insurance against career-ending injuries. Would you expect the insured players to act differently from those who don't have insurance?

12. Consider the example of marketable pollution permits discussed in this chapter. Suppose that instead of issuing four permits to each firm, the government issues only three permits to each firm.
   a. How much money is a high-cost firm willing to pay to get one additional permit?
   b. How much money is a low-cost firm willing to accept in exchange for one of its permits?
   c. If firms split the difference between the willingness to pay and the willingness to accept for a permit, what will be the price of a permit?

13. Web Exercise. Visit the Web site of Carfax (*www.carfax.com*) and check out the sample reports. What sort of deception occurs in the market for used cars? How much does it cost to get a report on a used car you are considering buying? Do you think the information is worth the price?

14. Web Exercise: Visit the Web site for the U.S. Environmental Protection Agency (*www.epa.gov*) and search the site for information on electric vehicles. How do the costs of electric cars compare to the costs of gas-powered vehicles? What about performance?

Take It to the Net

We invite you to visit the O'Sullivan/Sheffrin page on the Prentice Hall Web site at: **www.prenhall.com/osullivan** for this chapter's World Wide Web exercise.

Model Answers to Questions

Chapter-Opening Questions

1. A system based on voluntary contributions would suffer from the free-rider problem with few people contributing money to support the public good.

2. Grant the property rights for the lake to either the fishing firm or the steel mill.

3. As discussed in the section on Global Warming, a $100 tax on carbon would increase the price of gasoline by about 23%.

4. Like the used-car market, the used-pitcher market has asymmetric information: The pitcher's original team has more information than the new team. A team is more likely to be outbid by another team for a pitcher's services if the pitcher has health problems that make him worth less to the original team.

Test Your Understanding

1. The producer of a private good collects money from each consumer—if you don't pay, you don't get the good. In contrast, it is impossible to prevent people who don't pay from consuming a public good.

2. Although free cheese comes from the government, it is a private good because only one person can consume a piece of cheese.

3. The total benefit is $200,000, which is less than the $250,000 cost, so the dam should not be built.

4. A command-and-control policy causes firms to use inefficient abatement technology, leading to higher costs.

5. The tax will increase production costs, shifting the supply curve to the left. The new supply curve will intersect the demand curve at a higher price and a smaller quantity.

6. Consumers will buy a smaller quantity of taxed goods. Energy producers will switch to noncarbon energy sources and improve the efficiency of carbon fuels.

7. Buyers, sellers.

8. $2,000, the average value of the two types of cars.

9. Yes: 70% of the cars are lemons.

10. $21,000 (the average of the two cost figures), $40,000 (the cost for reckless doctors).

Using the Tools

2. Stream Preservation

  a. The benefit is $50,000 (10,000 fishers × $5 per fisher), which exceeds the cost of ending the logging ($20,000). Because the benefit exceeds the cost, the preservation of the stream is socially efficient.

  b. No. If the landowner is one of the fishers, the $20,000 cost exceeds the $5 benefit.

  c. The citizens could contribute to a stream-preservation fund to cover the landowner's cost. If each fisher contributed $3 (60% of his or her benefit), together they could raise a total of $30,000. The landowner would be better off by $10,000, and each fisher would be better off by $2.

  d. The free-rider problem may make it difficult to raise enough money to pay off the landowner.

3. Market Effects of a Carbon Tax. See Figure 8.A. Using the price-change formula from Chapter 3, the percentage change in price is 8%—that is, % change in demand / $(E_s + E_d)$ = 24% / (2.0 + 1.0). Therefore, the price increases from $2 to $2.16 per gallon. The tax causes the market to move upward along the demand curve, so we can use the formula for the price elasticity of demand to predict the change in quantity: E_d = % change in quantity / % change in price. The percentage change in

Figure 8.A
Market Effects of a Carbon Tax

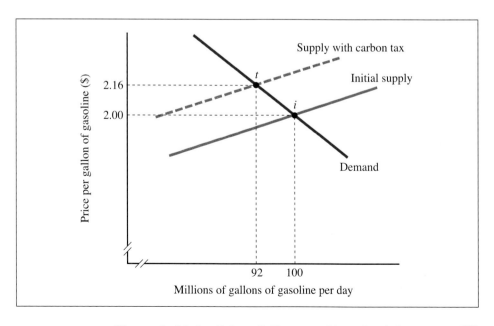

quantity is 8%: 1.0 = 8% / 8%. Therefore, the quantity decreases from 100 million gallons to 92 million gallons.

5. State Auto Insurance Pool. Under the pooling policy, there will be a single mixed market and a single price for auto insurance. If auto insurance is mandatory, the pooling policy will increase the price to $800—the average cost per driver for each insurance company. If auto insurance is voluntary, the long-run equilibrium price will exceed $800 and may even approach $1,200. If insurance companies initially have neutral expectations about the mixture of careful drivers and reckless drivers, the price of insurance will be $800 per driver. If this price exceeds the maximum price of some careful drivers, they will drop out of the market, so more than 50% of the insured drivers are reckless. Given the larger percentage of reckless (high-cost) drivers, insurance companies will lose money at a price of $800 per driver, so they will increase the price. The price of insurance will increase until the insurance company's expectations about the mixture of careful drivers and reckless drivers are realized. If all the careful drivers drop out of the market, the price of insurance will increase to $1,200, the cost per reckless driver.

Notes

1. Carl Sagan, "A Warning for Us?" *Parade*, June 5, 1994, p. 8; John Boudreau, "Collision Course: Scientists Say There's a Big Asteroid Bang in Our Future," *Washington Post*, April 6, 1994, p. C1.

2. "Mirror Beam Could Deflect Killer Asteroid, Theory Says," *New York Times*, November 9, 1994, p. C6.

3. Andrew R. Solow, "Is There a Global Warming Problem?" in *Global Warming: Economic Policy Responses*, edited by Rudiger Dornbush and James M. Poterba (Cambridge, MA: MIT Press, 1991).

4. Eduardo Lachica, "Asia Faces Increasing Pressure to Act as Global Warming Threatens Its Coasts," *Wall Street Journal*, August 22, 1994, p. A5C.

5. Gary Polakovic, "Cost of Clean Air Credits Soars in Southland," *Los Angeles Times*, September 5, 2000, B2.

6. Kenneth Lehn, "Information Asymmetries in Baseball's Free Agent Market," *Economic Inquiry*, vol. 22, January 1984, pp. 37–44.

7. Chris Sheridan, "Free Agents at End of Baseball's Earth," Associated Press, printed in *Corvallis Gazette-Times*, April 15, 1995, p. B1.

The Labor Market

Recent reports on the earnings of college graduates have made the jobs of college recruiters easier:[1]

- In 1972, the typical college graduate earned 43% more than a high school graduate.
- In 2001, the typical male college graduate earned 76% more than a male high school graduate, while the college premium for females was 98%.

These facts raise two questions: First, why do college graduates earn so much more than high school graduates? Second, why did the earnings gap almost double during the last 25 years?

p to this point in the book, we have discussed the markets for final goods and services. In this chapter, we switch to the market for one of the factors of production: labor. We use a model of supply and demand to see how wages are determined and why wages differ between college graduates and high school graduates, for men and women, and for different occupations. Here are some of the practical questions we answer.

1. If the wage increases, will an individual work more hours or fewer hours?
2. If a worker switches from a relatively safe factory job to a job in a steel mill, by how much will his or her wage increase?
3. Why do women, on average, earn only about 75% as much as men?
4. How have companies such as Nike and Disney responded to allegations that their products are produced in foreign sweatshops with dreadful working conditions and low wages?
5. In 1913, Henry Ford increased the wage of his autoworkers from $3 per day (the wage paid by other automakers) to $5. Was he being generous or was he trying to maximize his profit?

The Demand for Labor

We can use supply and demand curves to show how wages are determined and show how public policies affect wages and employment. We'll start with the demand side of the labor market, looking first at how an individual firm can use the key principles of economics to decide how many workers to hire.

Labor Demand by an Individual Firm in the Short Run

Consider a perfectly competitive firm that produces rubber balls. Because this firm is perfectly competitive, it takes the price of its output and the prices of its inputs as given. Because it hires a tiny fraction of the workers in the labor market, it takes the market wage as given and can hire as many workers as it wants at that wage. In addition, the firm produces a tiny fraction of the rubber balls sold in the market, so it takes the price of its output as given. Let's say the price of rubber balls is $0.50.

Consider the firm's hiring decision in the short run, defined as the period during which at least one input—for example, the factory—cannot be changed. We can use two of the key principles of economics to explain the firm's hiring decision. Recall the marginal principle:

Marginal **PRINCIPLE**

> **Increase the level of an activity if its marginal benefit exceeds its marginal cost but reduce the level if the marginal cost exceeds the marginal benefit. If possible, pick the level at which the marginal benefit equals the marginal cost.**

This firm's activity is hiring labor, one of inputs used, to produce rubber balls, and the firm will pick the quantity of labor at which the marginal benefit of labor equals the marginal cost of labor. The firm can hire as many workers as it wants at the market wage, so the marginal cost of labor equals the hourly wage. If the wage is $8 per hour, the extra cost associated with one more hour of labor—the marginal cost—is $8, regardless of how many workers the firm hires.

What is the marginal benefit of labor? The firm hires labor to produce balls, so the marginal benefit equals the monetary value of the balls produced with an additional hour of labor. Table 9.1 shows how to compute the marginal benefit associated with dif-

Table 9.1 The Marginal Principle for Labor Decision

Number of Workers	Balls per Hour	Marginal Product	Price per Ball	Marginal Benefit = Marginal Revenue Product	Marginal Cost When Wage = $8
1	26	26	$0.50	$13	$8
2	50	24	0.50	$12	$8
3	72	22	0.50	$11	$8
4	92	20	0.50	$10	$8
5	108	16	0.50	$8	$8
6	120	12	0.50	$6	$8
7	128	8	0.50	$4	$8
8	130	2	0.50	$1	$8

ferent quantities of labor. The first two columns show a hypothetical relationship between the number of workers and the quantity of balls produced. As the number of workers increases, the number of balls increases but at a decreasing rate, which is consistent with the principle of diminishing returns.

PRINCIPLE of Diminishing Returns

> **Suppose that output is produced with two or more inputs and we increase one input while holding the other inputs fixed. Beyond some point—called the point of diminishing returns—output will increase at a decreasing rate.**

Because of diminishing returns, the **marginal product of labor** (the change in output from one additional worker) decreases as the number of workers increases, from 26 for the first worker, to 24 for the second worker, and so on. To simplify matters, we assume that diminishing returns begin with the second worker, but as we saw earlier in the book, the marginal product of labor typically rises for the first few workers and then eventually decreases.

The marginal benefit of labor equals the **marginal revenue product of labor (MRP)**, defined as the extra revenue generated by one additional worker. To compute the MRP, we multiply the marginal product of labor by the price of output ($0.50 per ball, in this example):

$$\text{MRP} = \text{price of output} \times \text{marginal product}$$

Figure 9.1 shows the marginal revenue product curve. Because the marginal product drops as the number of workers increases, the MRP curve is negatively sloped, falling from $11 for the third worker (point n) to $8 for the fifth worker (point m), and so on.

A firm can use its MRP curve to decide how much labor to hire at a particular wage. In Figure 9.1, the marginal cost curve is horizontal at the market wage ($8). The perfectly competitive firm takes the wage as given, so the marginal cost curve is also the labor supply curve faced by the firm. The marginal principle is satisfied at point m, where the marginal cost equals the marginal revenue product. The firm will hire five workers because for the first five workers, the marginal benefit (the MRP) is greater than or equal to the marginal cost (the $8 wage). It would not be sensible to hire another worker because the additional revenue from the sixth worker ($6) would be less than the $8 additional cost of that worker. If the wage increases to $11, the firm will satisfy the marginal principle at point n, hiring only three workers.

Marginal product of labor: The change in output from one additional laborer.

Marginal revenue product of labor (MRP): The extra revenue generated from one more unit of labor; equal to the price of the output times the marginal product of labor.

Figure 9.1

The Marginal Principle and the Firm's Demand for Labor

Using the marginal principle, the firm picks the quantity of workers at which the marginal benefit (the marginal revenue product of labor) equals the marginal cost (the wage). The firm's short-run demand curve for labor is the marginal revenue product curve.

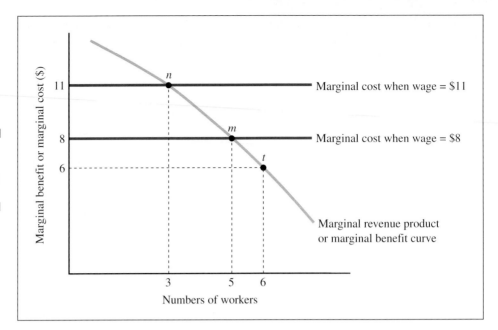

Short-run demand curve for labor: A curve showing the relationship between the wage and the quantity of labor demanded over the short run, the period when the firm cannot change its production facility.

Long-run demand curve for labor: A curve showing the relationship between the wage and the quantity of labor demanded over the long run, when the number of firms in the market can change and firms already in the market can modify their production facilities.

The MRP curve is also the firm's **short-run demand curve for labor**, which shows the relationship between the wage and the quantity of labor demanded in the short run, the period when the firm cannot change its production facility. The demand curve answers the following question: At each wage, how many hours of labor does the firm want to hire? We've already used the MRP curve to answer this question for two different wages ($11 and $8), and we can do the same for any other wage. Because the MRP curve is a marginal benefit curve and the firm uses the marginal principle to decide how much labor to hire, the MRP curve is the same as the firm's demand curve. If you pick a wage, the MRP curve tells you exactly how much labor the firm will demand.

What sort of changes would cause the demand curve to shift? To draw the labor demand curve, we hold fixed the price of the output and the productivity of workers. Therefore, an increase in the price of output will increase the MRP of workers, shifting the entire demand curve to the right: At each wage, the firm will hire more workers. Similarly, if workers become more productive, the increase in the marginal product of labor will increase the MRP and shift the demand curve to the right. Conversely, a decrease in price or labor productivity would shift the demand curve to the left.

Market Demand in the Short Run

To draw the short-run market demand curve for labor, we add the labor demands of all the firms that use a particular type of labor. In the simplest case, all firms are identical, and we simply multiply the number of firms by the quantity of labor demanded by the typical firm. If there were 100 firms and each hired 5 workers at a wage of $8, the market demand for labor would be 500 workers. Similarly, if the typical firm hired 3 workers at a wage of $11, the market demand would be 300 workers.

What about Labor Demand in the Long Run?

Recall that in the long run, firms can enter or leave the market and firms already in the market can change all their inputs, including their production facilities. The **long-run demand curve for labor** shows the relationship between the wage and the quantity of labor demanded over the long run, when the number of firms in the market can change and firms in the market can modify their production facilities.

Although there are no diminishing returns in the long run, the market demand curve is still negatively sloped. As the wage increases, the quantity of labor demanded decreases for two reasons:

1. The **output effect**. An increase in the wage will increase the cost of producing balls, and firms will pass on at least part of the higher labor cost to their consumers: Prices will increase. According to the law of demand, firms will sell fewer balls at the higher price, so they will need less of all inputs, including labor.

2. The **input-substitution effect**. An increase in the wage will cause the firm to substitute other inputs for labor. At a wage of $4, it may not be sensible to use much machinery in the ball factory, but at a wage of $20, it may be sensible to mechanize the factory, using more machinery and fewer workers.

Output effect: The change in the quantity of labor demanded resulting from a change in the quantity of output produced.

Input-substitution effect: The change in the quantity of labor demanded resulting from a change in the relative cost of labor.

The output effect reinforces the input-substitution effect, so the market demand curve is negatively sloped.

The notion of input substitution applies to other labor markets as well. For the most graphic examples of factor substitution, we can travel from a developed country such as the United States, Canada, France, Germany, or Japan to a less developed country in South America, Africa, or Asia. Wages are much lower in the less developed countries, so production tends to be more labor intensive. In other words, labor is less costly relative to machinery and equipment, so labor is substituted for these other inputs. Here are some examples:

- **Mining**. U.S. firms use huge earth moving equipment to mine for minerals, while many firms in less developed countries use thousands of workers, digging by hand.

- **Furniture**. Firms in developed countries manufacture furniture with sophisticated machinery and equipment, while many firms in less developed countries make furniture by hand.

- **Accounting**. Accountants in developed countries use computers and sophisticated software programs, while some accountants in less developed countries use simple calculators and ledger paper.

Short-Run Versus Long-Run Demand

How does the short-run demand curve for labor compare to the long-run demand curve? There is less flexibility in the short run because firms cannot enter or leave the market, and firms in the market cannot modify their production facilities. As a result, the demand for labor is less elastic in the short run. That means the short-run demand curve is steeper than the long-run demand curve. You may recall that we used the same logic to explain why the short-run supply curve for a product (lawn rakes) was steeper than the long-run supply curve for the product.

TEST Your Understanding

1. The coach of a professional basketball team wants to hire a new player for $3 million per year. Under what circumstances would it be sensible to hire the player?

2. Complete the statement with *increase* or *decrease*: According to the output effect, a decrease in the wage will _____ production costs, so the price of output will _____. The quantity of output produced will _____, so the demand for labor will _____.

3. Explain the input-substitution effect associated with a decrease in the wage.

The Supply of Labor

The labor supply curve answers the following question: How many hours of labor will be supplied at each wage? When we speak of a labor market, we are referring to the market for a specific occupation in a specific geographic area. Consider the supply for nurses in the city of Florence. The supply question is, How many hours of nursing services will be supplied at each wage? To answer, we must think about how many nurses are in the city and how many hours each nurse works.

The Individual Decision: How Many Hours?

Let's start with an individual's decision about how many hours to work. The decision to work is a decision to sacrifice some leisure time: Each hour of work reduces leisure time by one hour. Therefore, the demand for leisure is the flip side of the supply of labor. The price of leisure time is the income sacrificed for each hour of leisure, that is, the hourly wage.

We know from Chapter 2 that an increase in the price of a good has two effects: a substitution effect and an income effect. An increase in the wage—the price of labor—has the following effects on the demand for leisure:

1. **Substitution effect.** The worker faces a trade-off between leisure time and consumer goods such as music, books, food, and entertainment. For each hour of leisure time Leah takes, she loses one hour of work time, and her income drops by an amount equal to the wage. Therefore, she has less money to spend on consumer goods. For example, if the wage is $8 per hour, each hour of leisure decreases the amount of income available to spend on consumer goods by $8. When the wage increases to (say) $10, Leah will sacrifice more income—and consumer goods—for each hour of leisure. Given the larger sacrifice of consumer goods per hour of leisure time, she will demand less leisure time. That means that she will work more hours and earn more money for consumer goods. In other words, as the wage increases, she will substitute income—and the consumer goods it buys—for leisure time.

2. **Income effect.** For most people, leisure is a normal good in the sense that the demand for leisure increases as real income increases. An increase in the wage increases Leah's real income in the sense that she can afford more of all goods, including leisure time. Suppose Leah has a total of 100 hours per week to divide between leisure and work. At a wage of $10, she works 36 hours and has 64 hours of leisure. She also earns $360 ($10 per hour × 36 hours of work) and spends that amount on consumer goods. If her wage increases to $15, her real income increases because she can have more consumer goods *and* more leisure time. For example, if she worked only 30 hours, she could buy $450 worth of consumer goods ($15 per hour × 30 hours) and have 70 hours of leisure (100 hours per week − 30 hours of work). The increase in real income causes Leah to consume more of all goods, including leisure time. That means that an increase in real income causes her to demand more leisure and supply less labor.

For the demand for leisure, the income and substitution effects of an increase in the wage work in opposite directions: The substitution effect decreases the desired leisure time, while the income effect increases the desired leisure time. Therefore, we can't predict whether an increase in the wage will cause Leah to demand more leisure time (supply less labor) or less leisure (supply more labor).

A simple example will show why we can't predict a worker's response to an increase in the wage. Suppose each nurse initially works 36 hours per week at an hourly wage of

$10, and the wage increases to $12. Here are three reasonable responses to the higher wage:

1. **Lester works fewer hours.** If Lester works 30 hours instead of 36 hours, he gets 6 hours of extra leisure time and still earns the same income per week ($360 = 30 hours × $12 per hour).

2. **Sam works the same number of hours.** If Sam continues to work 36 hours per week, he gets an additional $72 of income ($2 per hour × 36 hours) and the same amount of leisure time.

3. **Maureen works more hours.** If Maureen works 43 hours instead of 36 hours, she sacrifices 7 hours of leisure time but earns a total of $516, compared to only $360 at a wage of $10 per hour.

Empirical studies of the labor market confirm that each of these responses is reasonable. When the wage increases, some people work more, others work less, and others work about the same amount.[2] In most labor markets, the average number of hours per worker doesn't change very much as the wage changes because the increases in work hours from people like Maureen are nearly offset by decreases in work hours from people like Lester.

The Market Supply Curve

Now that we know how individual workers respond to changes in wages, we're ready to consider the supply side of the labor market. The **market supply curve for labor** shows the relationship between the wage and the quantity of labor supplied. In Figure 9.2, the market supply curve for labor is positively sloped, consistent with the law of supply: The higher the wage (the price of labor), the larger the quantity of labor supplied. An increase in the wage affects the quantity of nursing supplied in three ways:

Market supply curve for labor: A curve showing the relationship between the wage and the quantity of labor supplied.

1. **Change in hours per worker.** When the wage increases, some nurses will work more hours, while others will work fewer hours, and others will work the same number of hours. We don't know for certain whether the average number of work hours will increase, decrease, or stay the same, but the change in the average number of hours is likely to be relatively small.

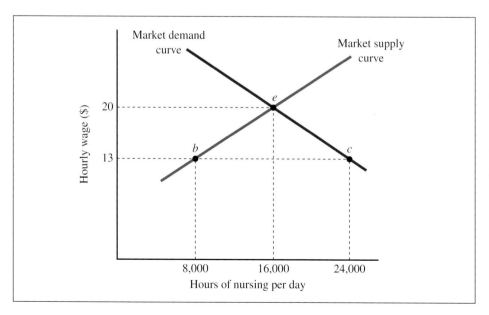

Figure 9.2
Supply, Demand, and Market Equilibrium
At the market equilibrium (point *e*, with wage = $20 per hour and quantity = 16,000 hours), the quantity supplied equals the quantity demanded, so there is neither excess demand for labor nor excess supply of labor.

2. **Occupational choice.** An increase in the nursing wage will cause some workers to switch from other occupations to nursing and motivate more new workers to pick nursing over other occupations.
3. **Migration.** Some nurses in other cities will move to Florence to earn the higher wages offered there.

The second and third effects reinforce one another, so an increase in the wage causes movement upward along the market supply curve. If the wage of Florence nurses increases from $13 to $20 per hour, the quantity of nurses supplied increases from 8,000 hours per day (point *b*) to 16,000 hours per day (point *e*). Although individual workers may not work more hours as the wage increases, the supply curve is positively sloped because an increase in the wage changes workers' occupational choices and causes migration.

Market Equilibrium

We're ready to put supply and demand together to think about equilibrium in the labor market. A market equilibrium is a situation in which there is no pressure to change the price of a good or service. Figure 9.2 shows the equilibrium in the market for nurses. The supply curve intersects the demand curve at point *e*, so the equilibrium wage is $20 per hour, and the equilibrium quantity is 16,000 hours of nursing per day. At this wage, there is neither an excess demand for labor nor an excess supply of labor, so the market has reached an equilibrium.

How would a change in the demand for nurses affect the equilibrium wage of nurses? We know from Chapter 2 that a change in demand causes the equilibrium price and the equilibrium quantity to move in the same direction: An increase in demand increases the equilibrium price and quantity, while a decrease in demand decreases the equilibrium price and quantity. For example, suppose that the demand for medical care increases. Nurses help provide medical care, so an increase in the quantity of medical care demanded will shift the demand curve for nurses to the right: At each wage, firms will demand more hours of nursing services. As shown in Figure

Figure 9.3
Market Effects of an Increase in Demand for Labor

An increase in the demand for nursing services shifts the demand curve to the right, moving the equilibrium from point *e* to point *f*. The equilibrium wage increases from $20 to $22 per hour, and the equilibrium quantity increases from 16,000 hours to 19,000 hours.

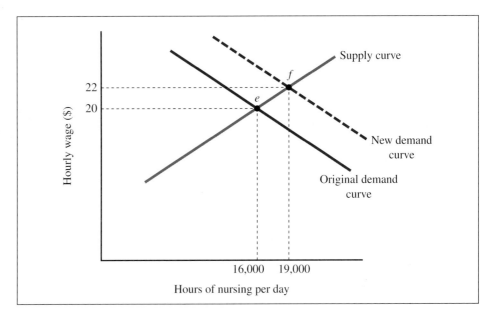

9.3, an increase in demand increases the equilibrium wage and the equilibrium quantity of nursing services.

How would a change in supply of nurses affect the equilibrium wage of nurses? We know from Chapter 2 that a change in supply causes price and quantity to move in opposite directions: An increase in supply decreases the equilibrium price but increases the equilibrium quantity, while a decrease in supply increases the equilibrium price but decreases the equilibrium quantity. Suppose a new television program makes nursing look like an attractive occupation, causing a large number of youngsters to become nurses rather than accountants, lawyers, or doctors. The supply curve for nurses will shift to the right: At each wage, more nursing hours will be supplied. The equilibrium wage will decrease, and the equilibrium quantity will increase. For another example of the market effects of a change in supply, read "A Closer Look: Nannies Versus Au Pairs."

TEST Your Understanding

4. Your objective is to earn exactly $120 per week. If your wage decreases from $6 to $4 per hour, how will you respond?

5. Each worker in a certain occupation works exactly 40 hours per week, regardless of the wage. Does this mean that the market supply curve for the occupation is vertical (a fixed quantity, regardless of the wage)?

6. Complete the following: A decrease in the supply of nurses will _____ the equilibrium wage and _____ the equilibrium quantity of nursing services.

Explaining Differences in Wages and Income

Now that we know how the equilibrium wage for a particular occupation is determined, we're ready to explain why wages vary from one job to another. Let's think about why some occupations pay more than others, why women earn less than men, and why college graduates earn more than high school graduates.

A CLOSER LOOK   NANNIES VERSUS AU PAIRS

In 1992, the Network of American Nanny Agencies (NANA) asked the U.S. Congress to impose strict limits on the number of European women participating in cultural exchange programs. Why? Each year about 8,000 European women participate in the au pair program, coming to the United States for one-year stints to learn about the country, improve their English, and provide child care. NANA claimed the au pairs provide unfair competition and depress the wages of domestic nannies.[3]

How would the elimination of the au pair program affect the wage of nannies? As shown in the figure, the supply curve for child-care services would shift to the left: At each wage, fewer workers would provide child-care services. As a result, the equilibrium wage for

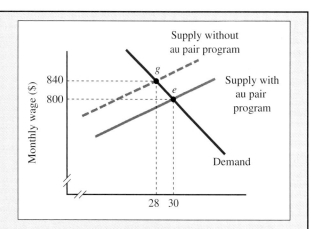

child-care workers would increase, from $800 per month to $840 per month in this example.

Why Do Wages Differ Across Occupations?

There is substantial variation in wages across occupations. Most professional athletes earn more than medical doctors, who earn more than college professors, who earn more than janitors. We'll see that the wage for a particular occupation will be high if the supply of workers in that occupation is small relative to the demand for those workers. This is shown in Figure 9.4, where the supply curve intersects the demand curve at a high wage.

The supply of workers in a particular occupation could be small for four reasons:

1. **Few people with the required skills.** To play professional baseball, people must be able to hit balls thrown at them at about 90 miles per hour. The few people who have this skill are paid a lot of money because baseball team owners compete with one another for skillful players, bidding up the wage. The same logic applies to other professional athletes, musicians, and actors. The few people who have the skills required for these occupations are paid high wages.

2. **High training costs.** The skills required for some occupations can only be acquired through education and training. For example, the skills that are required of a medical doctor can be acquired in medical school, and legal skills can be acquired in law school. If it is costly to acquire these skills, a relatively small number of people will become skilled, and they will receive high wages. The higher wage compensates workers for their training costs.

3. **Undesirable job features.** Some occupations are dangerous, and only a relatively small number of people are willing to work in dangerous occupations. The workers with the greatest risk of losing their lives on the job are lumberjacks, boilermakers, taxicab drivers, and mine workers. The workers who choose dangerous occupations receive high wages so they are compensated for the danger associated with their jobs. The same logic applies to other undesirable job features. For example, wages are higher for jobs that are stressful or dirty or that force people to work at odd hours.

4. **Artificial barriers to entry.** As we'll see later, government and professional licensing boards restrict the number of people in certain occupations, and labor unions restrict their membership. These supply restrictions increase wages.

Figure 9.4

Supply Is Low Relative to Demand

If supply is low relative to demand—because few people have the skills, training costs are high, or the job is undesirable—the equilibrium wage will be high.

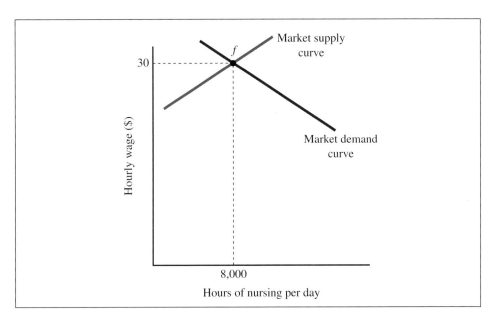

HIGH WAGES FOR STEELWORKERS

Why do steelworkers earn more than other manufacturing workers? Studies of the labor market have shown that more dangerous jobs pay higher wages.[4] Let's compare the wage for a very safe manufacturing job to the wage in a steel mill. Each year, 1 in 10,000 steelworkers is killed on the job. To compensate for the higher risk of getting killed on the job, steelworkers receive a wage premium of 3.7%, or about $700 per year.

For some facts on wages in dangerous jobs, read "A Closer Look: High Wages for Steelworkers."

Gender and Racial Discrimination

Why do women, on average, earn less than men? In the United States, the typical woman earns about 75% as much as the typical man. The gender gap is smaller in European nations but much larger in Japan.

Why is the gender gap so large? Part of the gender gap is caused by differences in education. Although women get about half of all college degrees, they are overrepresented in majors such as general liberal arts and health sciences and underrepresented in more lucrative majors such as physics, chemistry, computer science, and engineering. Similarly, although women get about half of all master's degrees, they are overrepresented in education programs and underrepresented in engineering and other more lucrative fields. In terms of professional degrees, women are underrepresented in law and medical schools.

Another reason for the wage gap is occupational discrimination: Women have been denied access to many occupations, causing them to flood a small number of female-dominated occupations such as teaching, nursing, and clerical work. Given the plentiful supply of workers in these female-dominated occupations, wages are low compared to the wages in male-dominated occupations. Given the distribution of men and women in different occupations in the 1990s, about half of female workers would have to change occupations to achieve equal gender representation in all occupations.[5]

What about differences in earnings by race? In 1995, black males who worked full time earned 73% as much as their white counterparts, while black females earned 86% as much as their white counterparts. Hispanic males earned 62% as much as white males, while Hispanic females earned 73% as much as white females.[6] For both males and females, part of the earnings gap is caused by differences in productivity: On average, whites have more education and work experience, so they are paid higher wages. Part of the wage gap is caused by racial discrimination. Some black and Hispanic workers are paid lower wages for similar jobs, and others are denied opportunities to work in some high-paying jobs.

Economists disagree in their assessment of how much of the earnings gap is caused by labor-market discrimination. A recent study suggests that racial discrimination decreases the wages of black men by about 13 percent.[7] Another study shows that black–white earnings differences have decreased over the last few decades and that the differences are now small enough that "most of the disparity in earnings between blacks and whites in the labor market of the 1990s is due to the differences in skills they bring to the market, and not to discrimination within the labor market."[8] The differences in skills brought to the labor market are caused by a number of factors, including past discrimination that has inhibited the acquisition of job skills and differences in educational opportunities. For example, in urban areas, only about one-third of black high school students have above-average scores on reading and math exams, compared to about two-thirds of white students.

Why Do College Graduates Earn Higher Wages?

In 2001, the typical male college graduate earned 76% more than the typical high school graduate and the college premium for females was 98%. Over the last 25 years, this wage gap, or "college premium," has almost doubled. There are two explanations for the college premium.

The first explanation is based on supply and demand analysis. A college education provides the skills necessary to enter certain occupations, so a college graduate has more job options than a high school graduate. Both high school grads and college grads can fill jobs that require only a high school education, so the supply of workers for these low-skilled jobs is plentiful, and the equilibrium wage for these jobs is low. In contrast, there is a smaller supply of workers for jobs that require a college education, so the wages in these high-skill jobs are higher than the wages for low-skill jobs. This is the **learning effect** of a college education: College students learn the skills required for certain occupations.

Learning effect: The increase in a person's wage resulting from the learning of skills required for certain occupations.

The second explanation of the college premium requires a different perspective on college and its role in the labor market. Suppose certain skills are required for a particular job but an employer cannot determine whether a prospective employee has these skills. For example, most managerial jobs require the employee to manage his or her time efficiently, but it is impossible for an employer to determine whether a prospective employee is a good manager of time. Suppose that these skills are also required to complete a college degree. For example, to get passing grades in all your classes, you must be able to use your time efficiently. When you get your college degree, firms will conclude that you have some of the skills they require, so they may hire you instead of an equally skilled high school graduate. This is the **signaling effect** of a college education: A person who completes college provides a signal to employers about his or her skills. This second explanation suggests that colleges simply provide a testing ground where students can reveal their skills to potential employers.

Signaling effect: The increase in a person's wage resulting from the signal of productivity provided by completing college.

The most important factor in doubling the college premium over the last 25 years is technological change. Changes in technology have increased the demand for college graduates relative to the demand for other workers. In all sectors of the economy, firms are switching to sophisticated machinery and equipment that require highly skilled workers. The share of jobs that require the skills of a college graduate has increased steadily, increasing the demand for college graduates and increasing their wages. Another factor in the growing college premium is the pace of technological change. Workers with more education can more easily learn new skills and new jobs, so firms are willing to pay more for college graduates.

TEST Your Understanding

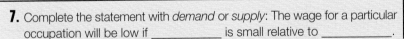

7. Complete the statement with *demand* or *supply*: The wage for a particular occupation will be low if _____ is small relative to _____.

8. The wages of police officers vary from city to city. What could explain the wage differences?

9. In some countries, it is customary to tip restaurant waiters. What are the implications for the wages paid to waiters?

10. Would you expect people who work between midnight and 8 A.M. to earn higher or lower wages than people who work from 9 A.M. to 5 P.M.? Explain.

Public Policy and Labor Markets

We can use the model of the labor market to show the effects of public policies on wages and employment. We'll look at two policies: the minimum wage and occupational licensing. Each of these policies affects one side of the labor market—supply or demand—leading to changes in the equilibrium wage and total employment.

Effects of the Minimum Wage

The current federal minimum wage is $5.15 per hour, and several states have higher minimum wages. In the United States, about 5% of workers are paid the minimum wage. Figure 9.5 shows the effects of a minimum wage on the market for restaurant workers. The market equilibrium is shown by point *e*: The supply of restaurant workers equals demand at a wage of $4.70 and a quantity of 50,000 worker hours per day. At the minimum wage of $5.15 per hour, the quantity of labor demanded is only 49,000 hours (point *d* on the demand curve). In other words, the minimum wage decreases the quantity of labor used by restaurants by 1,000 hours per day. The minimum wage also increases the quantity supplied to 51,000 hours (point *f*), so there is an excess supply of 2,000 hours.

What are the trade-offs associated with the minimum wage? From the perspectives of restaurant workers and restaurant diners, there is good news and bad news:

- **Good news for some restaurant workers.** Some workers keep their jobs and receive a higher wage ($5.15 per hour instead of $4.70 per hour).

- **Bad news for some restaurant workers.** Some workers lose their jobs. If the typical workday for restaurant workers is 5 hours, the loss of 1,000 hours of restaurant work per day translates into a loss of 200 jobs.

- **Bad news for diners.** The increase in the wage increases the cost of producing restaurant meals, increasing the price of meals.

There are winners and losers from the minimum wage: Workers who keep their jobs gain at the expense of other workers and at the expense of diners. A recent study suggests that

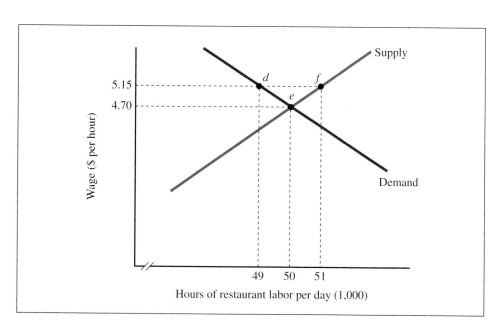

Figure 9.5

The Market Effects of a Minimum Wage
The market equilibrium is shown by point *e*: The wage is $4.70 per hour, and the quantity of labor is 50,000 labor hours per day. A minimum wage of $5.15 per hour decreases the quantity of labor demanded to 49,000 hours per day. Although some workers receive a higher wage, others lose their jobs or work fewer hours.

a 10% increase in the minimum wage decreases the number of minimum-wage jobs by about 1%.[9]

In recent years, there has been growing concern in the United States about poor working conditions and low wages for foreign workers who produce products for U.S. consumers. For a discussion of this issue, read "A Closer Look: Foreign Sweatshops and Codes of Conduct."

A CLOSER LOOK — FOREIGN SWEATSHOPS AND CODES OF CONDUCT

Several widely publicized reports have documented poor working conditions and low wages in foreign factories that produce shoes, clothing, and toys for U.S. corporations. In 1996, a report revealed that part of Wal-Mart's Kathie Lee Collection was produced in Honduras by people working 20 hours per day for $0.31 per hour.[10] Similar reports suggested that goods sold by Nike, Disney, and Mattel were produced in overseas sweatshops. Some human-rights activists have organized protests to publicize what they consider unethical business practices and have organized consumer boycotts.

The corporations have responded to the uproar by monitoring the firms that produce their goods and establishing codes of conduct for foreign suppliers.[11] The Council on Economic Priorities, an interest group in New York, inspects workplaces and awards the "Social Accountability 8000" to businesses that meet its criteria for wages and working conditions. The Apparel Industry Partnership, a group that includes social activists and apparel firms, is developing a code of conduct for apparel producers. The group was pleased to see the results of a survey suggesting that three-fourths of America's shoppers would be willing to pay higher prices for clothes and shoes bearing a "No Sweat" label. Some companies have hired accounting firms such as Price Waterhouse Coopers to audit their foreign suppliers. On campus, the United Students Against Sweatshops is developing a code of conduct for companies that produce products bearing university logos.

The efforts to monitor the labor practices of foreign suppliers raise several questions:

- How will better working conditions and higher wages affect the cost of producing the products and their prices?
- How will consumers respond to the higher prices?
- How much more are consumers willing to pay for "No Sweat" products?
- Will firms selling "No Sweat" products lose customers to firms selling products produced in factories that don't meet the codes of conduct?

Corporations with overseas production facilities responded to the uproar over sweatshops by monitoring the foreign firms that produce the goods for the corporations and establishing codes of conduct for foreign suppliers.

Occupational Licensing

In some occupations, the number of workers is limited by government-sanctioned licensing boards. A licensing board establishes requirements for working in a particular occupation. For example, a person may be prohibited from working in an occupation unless she or he (1) completes a given educational program, (2) passes an examination, (3) has a certain amount of work experience, and/or (4) has lived in a particular area for some time. Among the workers who are subject to occupational licensing are physicians, dentists, beauticians, plumbers, and pharmacists. In the United States, there are more than 1,500 occupational licensing boards.[12]

Occupational licensing is controversial. In principle, the licensing requirements are designed to protect consumers from incompetent workers. However, occupational licensing has been criticized on three grounds:

1. **Weak link between performance and licensing requirements.** In many cases, the licensing requirements seem arbitrary, and there is a weak link between the requirements and the likely performance of the worker.

2. **Alternative means of protection.** There are other ways to protect consumers from incompetent workers. The government could provide consumers with information about the past performance of workers. Or consumers can spread the word about workers' performance, just as they spread the word for other goods and services. Of course, the dissemination of information will work better for some occupations (for example, plumbers and beauticians) than it would for others (such as doctors).

3. **Entry restrictions.** The licensing requirements increase the cost of entering the occupation, decreasing the supply of workers and increasing the wage paid to workers subject to occupational licensing.

Figure 9.6 shows the market effects of occupational licensing for retail pharmacists. Most of the drugs dispensed by retail pharmacists have already been prepared for use by drug companies, so the principal tasks for a retail pharmacist are counting pills and pasting labels on bottles. To be licensed as a retail pharmacist, a worker can complete a five-year baccalaureate or a six-year doctorate. The market equilibrium with this educational requirement is shown by point e in Figure 9.6: The wage of retail pharmacists is $15 per hour.

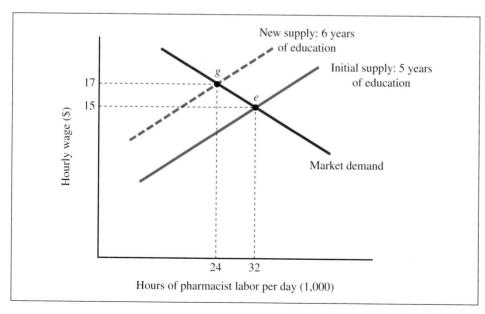

Figure 9.6

The Market Effects of Occupational Licensing

Occupational licensing increases the cost of entering an occupation, shifting the supply curve to the left. An increase in the required education for pharmacists increases the equilibrium wage from $15 to $17 and decreases the equilibrium quantity from 32,000 to 24,000 hours of pharmacist labor.

What would be the market effects of increasing the educational requirement for retail pharmacists? In 1991, three labor organizations representing more than 170,000 pharmacists proposed changes in the licensing of pharmacists, changes that would force all new pharmacists to complete the six-year doctorate program.[13] The increase in the education requirement (from five years to six) would increase the cost of entering the occupation, shifting the supply curve to the left: At every wage, fewer pharmacist hours would be supplied. In Figure 9.6, the market would move from point e to point g, increasing the equilibrium wage to $17. In addition, the increase in the wage would increase the cost of producing and selling drugs, increasing the price of drugs. The general lesson is that occupational licensing increases wages, increases production costs, and increases prices.

If occupational licensing leads to higher prices, why does it persist for workers such as plumbers, beauticians, and retail pharmacists? Perhaps it persists because consumers believe that licensing protects them from incompetent and unscrupulous workers and because consumers are willing to pay higher prices for this perceived protection. Or perhaps the workers who receive higher wages are better organized than consumers and are therefore more effective in influencing public policy.

TEST Your Understanding

11. Imelda works 20 hours per week in a shoe store and is paid the minimum wage. When the government increases the minimum wage by $1, she rejoices, saying, "I will be better off by $20 per week." Is her calculation correct?

12. Comment on the following statement: "It's silly to suggest that an increase in the minimum wage will decrease the quantity of labor demanded by fast-food restaurants. It's impossible to substitute machines for workers, so the restaurants will hire the same number of workers at the higher wage."

13. Complete this statement with *increases* or *decreases*: Occupational licensing increases the cost of entering an occupation, so it _____ supply, _____ the wage, and _____ the price of goods produced by the licensed occupation.

Labor Unions

Labor union: An organized group of workers; the objectives of the organization are to increase job security, improve working conditions, and increase wages and fringe benefits.

We've used a simple model of labor supply and labor demand to explain differences in wages. Our analysis is based on the assumption that workers take the market wage as given. A **labor union** is an organized group of workers, the objectives of which are to increase job security, improve working conditions, and increase wages and fringe benefits.

A Brief History of Labor Unions in the United States

Craft union: A labor organization that includes workers from a particular occupation, for example, plumbers, bakers, or electricians.

As shown in Figure 9.7, about one-sixth of all workers in the United States belong to a union, down from about one-third of workers 40 years ago. Among private-sector workers, the unionization rate is less than 10%, while more than 37% of public-sector workers belong to unions. There are two types of labor unions:

1. A **craft union** includes workers from a particular occupation, for example, plumbers, bakers, or electricians.

Industrial union: A labor organization that includes all types of workers from a single industry, for example, steelworkers or autoworkers.

2. An **industrial union** includes all types of workers from a single industry, for example, steelworkers or autoworkers.

There are also umbrella organizations that include many individual unions. The largest of these "unions of unions" is the AFL-CIO (the American Federation of Labor–Congress of Industrial Organizations).

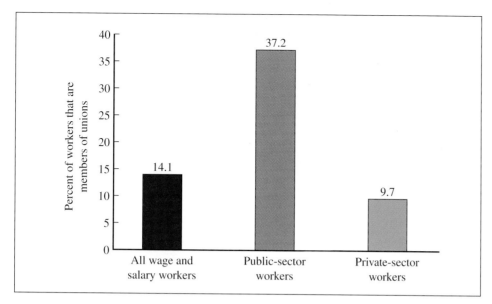

Figure 9.7
**Unionization Rates
in the United
States, 1997**
Overall, 14% of all wage and
salary workers are members
of unions. More than 37% of
public-sector workers are
members of unions.

*Source: Statistical Abstract of
the United States, 1998.*

Let's take a brief look at the history of labor organizations in the United States. In the 19th century, there were all sorts of craft unions, and the main umbrella organizations were the Knights of Labor (founded in 1869) and the AFL (founded in 1881). The CIO (formed in 1931) was a collection of industrial unions that represented semiskilled workers in mass production, including workers in the automobile, rubber, and steel industries. The CIO merged with the AFL in 1955. The most important recent trend has been the expansion of unions serving workers in the public sector. In the last 30 years, the number of government workers in unions and employee associations has more than doubled.

Labor unions get their power to influence labor markets from the states and the federal government. Let's take a brief look at the most important pieces of union legislation:

- The Wagner Act (1935) guaranteed workers the right to join unions and required each firm to bargain with a union formed by a majority of its workers. The National Labor Relations Board (NLRB) was established to enforce the provisions of the Wagner Act.

- The Taft-Hartley Act (1947) gave government the power to stop strikes that "imperiled the national health or safety" and gave the states the right to pass right-to-work laws. These laws, which are currently in force in 21 states, outlaw union shops, defined as workplaces where union membership is required as a condition of employment.

- The Landrum-Griffin Act (1959) was a response to allegations of corruption and misconduct by union officials. This act guaranteed union members the right to fair elections, made it easier to monitor union finances, and made the theft of union funds a federal offense.

Labor Unions and Wages

One goal of a union is to increase the wages of its members, and there is evidence that unions do raise the wages of union workers. One study of unions concluded that unionized workers earn 20% to 30% more than nonunion workers doing the same work.[14] Let's look at three ways in which a union could try to increase the wages of its members.

One approach is to organize workers and negotiate a higher wage. Suppose workers in a particular industry form an industrial union and agree on a union wage that exceeds the equilibrium wage. Like a minimum wage imposed by a government, a wage negotiated by a union means that some workers will earn higher wages but other workers who are willing to work will not have the opportunity to do so. To deal with this problem, the union can reduce the number of workers by restricting membership or can share the smaller number of jobs among its members.

Another way in which a union can increase the wage of its members is to promote the products produced by union workers. You've probably seen advertisements encouraging people to buy products with the union label. An increase in the demand for a final good will increase the demand for labor used to produce that good, increasing the equilibrium wage. This approach can be used together with a negotiated union wage to prevent an excess supply of labor at the union wage.

A third approach—which may or may not increase wages—is to impose work rules that increase the amount of labor required to produce a given quantity of output, which is sometimes called "featherbedding." One example of featherbedding is a minimum crew size, which forces a firm to hire more workers than it needs to perform a particular task. For example, the typical unionized airline hires three workers to guide an airplane into the gate, while nonunion airlines use only two workers. In the past, railroad unions forced railroads to use firemen (whose job is to shovel coal) on diesel-powered engines, which don't use coal.

Featherbedding may or may not increase the demand for labor. Although featherbedding forces the firm to use more labor per unit of output, it also decreases the quantity of output. A firm suffering from featherbedding hires workers it doesn't need, so its production costs will be higher than it would be without featherbedding. Firms increase their prices to cover these extra production costs, and consumers respond by purchasing less output. Therefore, the direct effect of featherbedding (that is, the increase in the amount of labor required for a given quantity of output) will be at least partly offset by a decrease in output. The demand for labor is derived from the demand for the final good, so featherbedding may actually decrease the demand for labor, decreasing the wage and total employment.

A different approach to managing union employment comes from Volkswagen AG, Europe's largest automaker. In 1993, Volkswagen got its labor unions to switch to a four-day, 28-hour workweek, down from a five-day, 36-hour workweek. If workers hadn't accepted the shorter workweek and lower pay, Volkswagen would have eliminated 30,000 of its 100,000 jobs in Germany. In other words, the switch to the shorter workweek preserved 30,000 union jobs in the automobile industry.[15] Some analysts suggest that shorter workweeks for union workers will become more common as European unions grapple with lower demand for their workers.

Do Labor Unions Increase Productivity?

We've seen that unions lead to higher wages and work rules that are designed to decrease labor productivity. In other words, there are some costs associated with labor unions. Could unions increase productivity?

Unions may increase productivity by facilitating communication between workers and managers. If a worker is unhappy with his or her job, one option is to quit. From the firm's perspective, this is costly because the firm loses an experienced worker and must train a new one. A dissatisfied worker who belongs to a union has a second option: The worker can use the union as an intermediary to discuss job issues with managers. This sort of communication can solve problems before they become so severe that the worker quits. There is evidence that firms whose workers are in unions have lower turnover rates, in part because they facilitate communication between workers and managers.[16] These lower turnover rates lead to lower training costs and a more experienced workforce.

Imperfect Information and Efficiency Wages

So far, our analysis of the labor market has been based on the assumption that there is perfect information in the labor market. What happens when workers have better information than their employers? Workers differ in their skill levels and the amount of effort they exert on the job. Employers cannot always distinguish between skillful and unskillful workers or between hard workers and lazy workers. In other words, there is asymmetric information in the labor market.

We know from our discussion of the market for used cars that asymmetric information causes high-quality and low-quality goods to be sold in a mixed market at a single price. Suppose there are two types of workers:

1. Low-skill workers, whose marginal revenue product equals $100 per day
2. High-skill workers, whose marginal revenue product equals $200 per day

The employer cannot distinguish between these two types of workers and offers a single wage, realizing that it will probably hire some workers of each type.

What is the appropriate wage? Suppose the opportunity cost of high-skill workers is $130, and a firm offers a wage of $110. Because the wage is less than the opportunity cost of high-skill workers, only low-skill workers will apply for jobs. The firm will lose money because the $110 wage exceeds the $100 marginal revenue product of the low-skill workers. To get some high-skill workers, the employer must pick a wage that exceeds the $130 opportunity cost of high-skill workers. As the firm increases its wage, it will attract more high-skill workers, and the average productivity of its workforce will increase. Depending on the responses of the two types of workers to the higher wage, a firm could make more profit by offering a higher wage. This is known as **paying efficiency wages**: The firm pays a higher wage to increase the average productivity of its workforce.

> **Paying efficiency wages:** The practice of a firm paying a higher wage to increase the average productivity of its workforce.

Another reason for paying relatively high wages is to encourage employees to work hard. Firms realize that their employees can vary their work efforts, from working hard to hardly working (shirking). To encourage their employees to work hard, employers fire workers who are caught shirking. The penalty associated with being fired will be much greater if the firm pays a wage above the worker's opportunity cost. For example, suppose a worker could earn $80 per day in another job. If the firm pays its workers $100 per day, a worker who is fired—and then immediately gets a job with another firm—would take a pay cut of $20 per day. This is another example of paying efficiency wages: By increasing the wage, the firm increases the work effort of its employees and increases the average productivity of its workforce.

Another reason for paying efficiency wages is to reduce turnover in the workforce. If one firm pays a higher wage than its competitors, that discourages workers from switching employers. The firm paying the higher wage will have lower turnover and thus incur smaller costs in hiring and training workers.

Higher Wages at Ford Motor Company

Economic Detective

In the early days of the automobile industry, the prevailing wage for autoworkers was $3 per day. The assembly-line jobs were repetitive and tedious, and the turnover rate of workers was very high. When Henry Ford decided to increase the daily wage for his workers from $3 to $5, most observers were baffled. They figured that Ford's labor costs would be almost twice as high as those of his rivals, so he would lose a lot of money and quickly go out of business. The wage hike appeared to be a great act of generosity but very bad business. You can imagine their surprise when Ford's profit doubled from $30 million to $60 million. How was this possible? How can higher wages lead to higher profits?

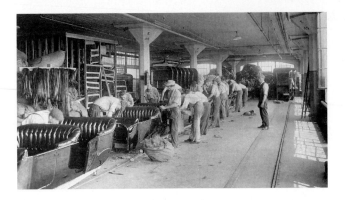

People were baffled when Henry Ford increased the daily wage for his assembly workers from $3 to $5.

The key to solving this puzzle is the concept of efficiency wages. When Ford raised the wage, the average productivity of Ford workers increased by about 50%, a result of several changes in the workforce[17]:

- The pool of job applicants improved, so Ford could choose better workers.
- Fewer workers were fired for shirking.
- Fewer workers quit voluntarily.
- The rate of absenteeism was cut in half.

In the words of Henry Ford, "There was no charity in any way involved. . . . The payment of five dollars a day for an eight-hour day was one of the finest cost cutting moves we ever made."

The Distribution of Income

In 2001, the median household income in the United States was $42,228, but this simple average tells only part of the income story. Some households earn much more income, and others earn much less. In this part of the chapter, we'll discuss the extent of income inequality in the United States and explore some of the reasons why the households with the highest income are receiving a larger and larger share of total income.

Income Distribution Facts

Table 9.2 shows the distribution of income without considering the effects of taxes or noncash transfers such as food stamps, public housing, or medical care. To compute the numbers in the table, we take four steps.

Table 9.2 Shares of Income Earned by Different Groups, 2001

Income Group	Income Range	Percent of Total Income
Lowest Fifth	0 to $17,970	3.5
Second Fifth	$17,971 to $33,314	8.7
Middle Fifth	$33,315 to $53,000	14.6
Fourth Fifth	$53,001 to $83,500	23.0
Highest Fifth	$83,501 and greater	50.1

Source: *Money Income in the United States: 2001*, Table A-2.

1. Rank the nation's households according to income: the household with the lowest income is at the top of the list, and the household with the highest income is at the bottom of the list.

2. Divide the households into five groups: the lowest fifth includes the poorest 20% of the households (the top 20% of the list); the second fifth is the next poorest 20% (the next 20% of the list), and so on. The second column of the table shows the income ranges for each of the five groups: The lowest fifth includes households with income up to $17,970, the second fifth includes households with income between $17,971 and $33,314, and so on.

3. Compute each group's income by adding up the income received by all the households in the group.

4. Compute each group's percentage of total income (the number in the table) by dividing the group's income by the nation's total income.

What explains the differences in the incomes of U.S. households? There are five key factors.

1. *Differences in labor skills and effort.* Some people have better labor skills than others, so they earn higher wages. Labor skills are determined by innate ability and education. In addition, some people work longer hours or at more demanding jobs, so they earn more income.

2. *Inheritances.* Some people inherit large sums of money and earn income by investing this money.

3. *Luck and misfortune.* Some people are luckier than others in investing their money, starting a business, or picking an occupation. Among the unlucky people are those who develop health problems that make it difficult to earn an income.

4. *Discrmination.* Some people are paid lower wages or have limited opportunities for education and work because of their race or gender.

5. *Redistribution programs.* The government uses various redistribution programs (Social Security, AFDC, SSI) to give money to individual households. These cash transfers are included in the computations of income in Table 9.2.

How does government policy affect the distribution of income? In the absence of government cash transfers, the share of the lowest quintile would be 0.90% (compared to 3.5% with the transfers included), while the share of the highest quintile would be 55.6%. With these numbers as starting points, the inclusion of cash transfers, taxes, and the value of noncash transfers, the share of the lowest quintile rises to 4.7%, and the share of the highest quintile drops to 46.5%.

Recent Changes in the Distribution of Income

Table 9.3 shows the changes in the distribution of income between 1970 and 2001. The share of the top fifth rose from 43.3% to 50.1%, while the share of every other group dropped. By historical standards, these changes in the distribution of income were very rapid. What caused these changes in the distribution in income?

It appears that the most important reason for growing inequality is what labor economists call an increase in the demand for skill.[18] In the labor market, the demand for highly skilled (highly educated) workers has increased relative to the demand for less skilled (less educated) workers. As a result, wages increase more rapidly with skills and education, widening the gap between the least skilled and the most skilled. As we saw at the beginning of the chapter, in the last three decades, the college premium has increased significantly. At the same time, the premium for advanced degrees increased.

1. The wage in a particular occupation will be relatively high if supply is small relative to demand. This will occur if (a) few people have the skills required for the occupation, (b) training costs are high, or (c) the job is dangerous or stressful.

2. College graduates earn more than high school graduates because a college education provides new skills and allows people to reveal their skills to employers.

3. There are trade-offs with a minimum wage or a union wage: Some workers earn higher income, but others lose their jobs.

4. Occupational licensing increases the wage of the licensed occupation and increases the price of the good produced by that occupation.

5. A firm that increases its wage may increase the average productivity of its workers and increase its profit.

Key Terms

craft union, 226
industrial union, 226
input-substitution effect, 215
labor union, 226
learning effect, 222

long-run demand curve for labor, 214
marginal product of labor, 213
marginal revenue product of labor (MRP), 213
market supply curve for labor, 217

output effect, 215
paying efficiency wages, 229
short-run demand curve for labor, 214
signaling effect, 222

Problems and Discussion Questions

1. You are an economic consultant to a city that just imposed a payroll tax of $1 per hour of work. This payroll tax is paid by workers through a payroll deduction: For each hour of work, the employer deducts $1 and sends the money to the city government. The initial wage (before the tax) is $10, and total employment is 20,000 hours per day. Use a graph to show the effect of the tax on the equilibrium wage and employment.

2. We discussed the response of Lester, Sam, and Maureen to an increase in the wage. Which person's response is closest to your own? If your wage increased, would you work more hours, fewer hours, or about the same number of hours?

3. Critically appraise the following statement from Mr. Chuckles: "The law of supply says that an increase in price increases the quantity supplied. A decrease in the income tax rate will increase the worker's net wage, so each worker will work more hours. As a result, the revenue from the income tax will increase."

4. Consider two markets for carpenters: the city of Portland and the United States. Draw two supply curves for carpenters: one for the city of Portland and one for the United States. In which market would you expect a more elastic supply of carpenters?

5. The advocates of higher salaries for teachers point out that most teachers have college degrees and that teaching children is an important job.
   a. Why aren't teachers' salaries higher, given the importance of the job and the education required?
   b. Suppose a new law requires that teachers are paid the same hourly wage as college graduates who work in business. Predict the effects of this law on the market for teachers.

6. Comment on the following: "There is no substitute for an airline pilot: Someone has to fly the plane. Therefore, an increase in the wage of airline pilots will not change the number of pilots used by the airlines."

7. Suppose a new government program improves worker safety in coal mines. Use a graph to predict the effect of the program on the equilibrium wage for coal workers.

8. Under some occupational licensing laws, licensed members of an occupation write licensing exams. An example is the bar exam for licensing lawyers. How might this practice limit entry into an occupation?

9. One response to the gap in wages between men and women is a policy called comparable worth, under which the government specifies a minimum wage for some occupations, typically the occupations with a disproportionate number of women.

Evaluate the merits of a such policy. What are the trade-offs?

10. Web Exercise. Visit the Web site of the U.S. Census Bureau (*www.census.gov*), and download the report "Money Income in the United States." How do the average earnings of women with bachelor's degrees compare to those of female high-school dropouts and women with master's degrees? Do the same comparisons for men.

11. Web Exercise. Visit the Web site of the U.S. Bureau of Labor Statistics (*www.bls.gov/*). Do a keyword search of the site to get some information on the bureau's projections of employment in different occupations. Try the following: "occupational + employment + projections." Which occupations are expected to grow most rapidly in coming years? Which are expected to grow slowly?

Take It to the Net

We invite you to visit the O'Sullivan/Sheffrin page on the Prentice Hall Web site at: **www.prenhall.com/osullivan/** for additional World Wide Web exercises for this chapter.

Model Answers to Questions

Chapter-Opening Questions

1. When the wage increases, some people work more hours, others work fewer hours, and others work about the same number of hours.

2. As shown in "A Closer Look: High Wages for Steelworkers," the worker's income would increase by about 3.7%.

3. The gender gap results from differences in skills and productivity as well as occupational discrimination.

4. As shown in "A Closer Look: Foreign Sweatshops and Codes of Conduct," U.S. corporations have developed codes of conduct and hired firms to audit their foreign suppliers.

5. Henry Ford described the wage hike as "one of the finest cost cutting moves we ever made."

Test Your Understanding

1. If the marginal revenue product of the new player exceeds $3 million. If the player increased attendance and increased the revenue from ticket sales by $4 million, for instance, it would be sensible to hire the player.

2. Decrease, decrease, increase, increase.

3. As the wage decreases, labor will become less expensive relative to other inputs, so the firm will substitute labor for other inputs.

4. You will work 30 hours per week instead of 20 hours.

5. No. An increase in the wage will increase the number of workers because of changes in occupational choices and migration.

6. Decrease, increase.

7. Demand, supply.

8. Wages are higher in cities where police officers face a greater chance of being killed on the job.

9. Waiters in tipping countries will have lower wages than waiters in nontipping countries.

10. Working between midnight and 8 A.M. disrupts sleeping and eating patterns and a person's social life. Because of these undesirable consequences, we expect workers on the midnight-to-8-A.M. shift to receive higher wages than workers on the day shift.

11. Imelda's statement could be incorrect for three reasons: (1) She may lose her job as a result of the higher minimum wage; (2) if she keeps her job, her employer may ask her to work fewer hours per week; (3) as a consumer, she will pay higher prices for the goods produced by minimum-wage workers, partly offsetting any increase in income she may receive.

12. There are opportunities to substitute machinery for workers, as shown by the switch to "smart" cash registers (the pictures on the buttons speed up money collection; beaming the information to the kitchen speeds up the process of filling orders and collecting money) and automated cooking machines (burgers on tracks). In addition, there is

the output effect: The increase in cost will increase price, so restaurants will sell less food and thus need fewer workers.

13. Decreases, increases, increases.

14. The firm will attract better applicants, and workers are less likely to shirk.

15. Total employment is maximized at the intersection of supply and demand, so the union should do nothing, letting the market reach the equilibrium.

16. If demand is elastic, a decrease in price will increase total expenditures (total revenue, total income). Therefore, the union should decrease its wage.

Using the Tools

1. **Market Effects of Immigration.** Immigration will shift the supply curve to the right, decreasing the equilibrium wage. We can use the price-change formula for an increase in supply (explained in Chapter 3) to predict the change in the equilibrium wage (the price of labor):

    a. The wage will decrease from $5 to $4.80 per hour.

    b. The cost of producing food will decrease, so the price of food will decrease.

2. **Effects of a Nurses' Union**

    a. The union causes movement upward along the market demand curve as the number of nurses decreases by 3% per year.

    b. The quantity of labor decreases by 3% per year. To compute the resulting change in price, we can use the formula for price elasticity of demand. To be consistent with an elasticity of 1.5, a 3% decrease in quantity generates a 2% increase in the wage.

3. **Demand for Newskids.** The elasticity of demand is 2.0, so a 20% increase in price will decrease the quantity demanded by 40%: A price elasticity of 2.0 means the percentage change in quantity is two times the percentage change in price. In other words, the number of subscribers per newskid will decrease from 100 to 60. The income of the typical newskid will decrease from $200 ($2 per subscriber × 100 subscribers) to $180 ($3 per subscriber × 60 subscribers). This is the output effect in action.

4. **Equilibrium with Efficiency Wages**

    a. Wage = $90. Each firm will get all low-skill workers, each with marginal revenue product (MRP) = $100. Each firm will make a profit, so this is not an equilibrium. Competition among the firms will bid up the wage.

    b. Wage = $100. Each firm will get all low-skill workers, each with MRP = $100. Each firm will make zero economic profit, so this is an equilibrium wage.

    c. Wage = $140. Each firm will get half low-skill workers and half high-skill workers, so the average MRP = $150. Each firm will make a profit, so this is not an equilibrium. Competition among the firms will bid up the wage.

    d. Wage = $150. Each firm will get half low-skill workers and half high-skill workers, so the average MRP = $150. Each firm will make zero economic profit, so this is an equilibrium.

    e. Wage = $170. Each firm will get half low-skill workers and half high-skill workers, so the average MRP = $150. Each firm will lose money, so this is not an equilibrium.

Notes

1. W. Michael Fox and Beverly J. Fox, "What's Happening to Americans' Income?" *The Southwest Economy*, Federal Reserve Bank of Dallas, Issue 2, 1995, pp. 3–6; U.S. Bureau of the Census, Current Population Reports, P60–218, *Money Income in the United States: 2001* (Washington, DC: U.S. Government Printing Office, 2002).

2. Mark Killingsworth, *Labor Supply* (New York: Cambridge University Press, 1983).

3. Brent Bowers, "Nanny Agencies Say Threat from 'Au Pairs' Isn't Kid Stuff," *Wall Street Journal*, May 28, 1992, p. B1.

4. Craig Olson, "An Analysis of Wage Differentials Received by Workers on Dangerous Jobs," *Journal of Human Resources*, vol. 16, spring 1981, pp. 167–185.

5. Suzanne Bianchi and Daphne Spain, "Women, Work, and Family in America," *Population Bulletin*, vol. 51, no. 3, 1998, pp. 2–48.

6. U.S. Department of Labor, *Employment and Earnings* (Washington, DC: U.S. Government Printing Office, 1996).

7. William Darity and Patrick Mason, "Evidence on Discrimination in Employment: Codes of Color,

Codes of Gender," *Journal of Economic Perspectives*, vol. 12, no. 2, 1998, pp. 63–90.

8. James Heckman, "Detecting Discrimination," *Journal of Economic Perspectives*, vol. 12, no. 2, 1998, pp. 101–116.

9. Victor R. Fuchs, Alan B. Krueger, and James M. Poterba, "Economists' Views about Parameters, Values, and Policies: Survey Results in Labor and Public Economics," *Journal of Economic Literature* vol. 36, 1998, pp. 387–425.

10. "Stamping Out the Sweatshops: Dress Code," *Economist*, April 19, 1997.

11. "Sweatshop Wars," *Economist*, February 27, 1999.

12. Werner Hirsch, *Law and Economics: An Introductory Analysis*, 2nd ed. (San Diego, CA: Academic Press, 1988), pp. 347–350.

13. Lawrence J. McQuillan, "Pharmacists' Proposal Will Raise Costs of Medicine," *The Margin*, spring 1993, p. 52.

14. Richard B. Freeman and James Medoff, *What Do Unions Do?* (New York: Basic Books, 1985).

15. Ferdinand Protzman, "VW Plan for 4-Day Workweek Is Adopted," *New York Times*, November 26, 1993, p. D11; Tyler Marshall, "VW, Unions, OK 20% Reduction in Work Week," *Los Angeles Times*, November 26, 1993, p. A1; "Worldwire," *Wall Street Journal*, July 8, 1994, p. A5.

16. Freeman and Medoff.

17. J. R. Lee, "So-Called Profit Sharing System in the Ford Plant," *Annals of the American Academy of Political and Social Science*, May 1915, pp. 297–310; David Halberstam, *The Reckoning* (New York: William Morrow, 1986), pp. 91–92; Daniel M. G. Graff and Lawrence H. Summers, "Did Henry Ford Pay Efficiency Wages?" *Journal of Labor Economics*, vol. 5, 1987, pp. 557–586.

18. Finis Welch, "In Defense of Inequality," *American Economic Review*, vol. 89, no. 2, 1999, pp. 1–17.

Measuring a Nation's Production and Income

In late 1999, the United States Department of Commerce announced its "achievement of the century." What could be the highlight of a century that could rival other great U.S. accomplishments such as providing electricity to homes and businesses throughout the country, completing the interstate highway system, and landing a man on the moon? The Department of Commerce chose, as its great achievement, the development of the National Income and Product Accounts.

How can a mere system of accounting compare to the other great feats of the century? The Department of Commerce noted the role of the National Income and Product Accounts in winning World War II, providing a basis for understanding the economy, and allowing policymakers to stabilize the economy and promote economic growth. An accounting system can indeed be powerful.

This chapter begins your study of **macroeconomics**: the branch of economics that deals with any nation's economy as a whole. Macroeconomics focuses on the economic issues—unemployment, inflation, growth, trade, and the gross domestic product—that are most often discussed in newspapers, on the radio, and on television.

Macroeconomics: The branch of economics that looks at the economy as a whole.

Macroeconomic issues are at the heart of political debates. All presidential candidates must learn a quick lesson in macroeconomics. Once elected, a president learns that the prospects for reelection will depend on how well the economy performs during his or her term of office. If the voters believe that the economy has performed well, the president will be reelected; otherwise, the president will not likely be reelected. Democrats such as Jimmy Carter, as well as Republicans such as George H. W. Bush, have failed in their bids for reelection because of the voters' economic concerns. Bill Clinton survived a personal scandal in part because of the superb performance of the U.S. economy while he was president.

Macroeconomic events profoundly affect our everyday lives. For example, if the economy fails to create enough jobs, workers will become unemployed throughout the country, and millions of lives will be disrupted. Similarly, slow economic growth will mean that living standards will not increase rapidly in the future. In contrast, if prices for all goods start increasing rapidly, some people will find it difficult to maintain their lifestyles.

This chapter and the next will introduce you to the concepts you need to understand macroeconomics. In this chapter, we will explain how economists and government statisticians measure the income and production for an entire country. The next chapter will discuss unemployment and inflation. Both chapters will explain the terms that are often used when economics is reported in the media.

Macroeconomics focuses on two basic issues. One focus is on long-run economic growth. We need to understand what happens during the long run to understand what factors are behind the rise in living standards in modern economies. Today, in the United States, living standards are much higher than they were for our grandparents, and our living standards are much higher than those of millions of people throughout the globe.

The other focus of macroeconomics is fluctuations in economic performance. Although living standards have improved over time, the economy has not grown smoothly. There are periods when the economy appears to malfunction and no longer grow as rapidly. A recession is a period when the economy fails to grow for at least six consecutive months. During these periods, not enough jobs are created, and large numbers of workers become unemployed. At other times, unemployment may not be a problem, but we become concerned that the prices of everything that we buy seem to increase rapidly.

Before we can study growth and fluctuations, we need to have a basic vocabulary and understanding of some key concepts. We begin with production and income because these are the most fundamental concepts. Every day, men and women go off to work, where they produce or sell merchandise or provide services, then return home with paychecks at the end of the week or month. The income that they earn allows them to purchase the goods and services necessary to conduct modern life. This chapter steps back from these individual details and looks at the economy as a whole. From the perspective that looks at the entire economy, we will be able to construct measures that can tell us how quickly the entire economy is growing or whether it has failed to grow. We will also be able to measure the total income generated in the economy and how this income flows back to workers and investors. These measures are critical for understanding how many people find jobs and whether their living standards are rising or falling.

After reading this chapter, you will be able to answer the following questions:

1. How are production and income related?
2. What is the gross domestic product?

3. When prices change, how do we measure real income?

4. Do increases in gross domestic product necessarily translate into improvements in the welfare of citizens?

As we learn the answers to these questions, we will build the necessary foundation for studying macroeconomics.

Production, Income, and the Circular Flow

Let's begin with a simple diagram called the circular flow. We use the circular flow to make a very simple but fundamental point: Production generates income.

In the simple economy depicted in Figure 10.1, there are only households and firms, which make transactions in both factor markets and product markets. In the factor markets, the households supply inputs to production. The primary inputs are labor and capital—what economists call factors of production. Households supply labor by working for firms, and households supply capital—buildings, machines, and equipment—to the firms. In the factor markets, households are paid by the firms for supplying these factors: wages for their work, and interest, dividends, and rents for supplying capital. The households then take their income and purchase the goods and services produced by the firms in the product markets. The payments the firm receives from the sale of its products are used to pay for the factors of production. The important part of this diagram is that production generates income; corresponding to the production of goods and services in the economy are flows of income to households.

For example, consider a manufacturer of computers. At the same time the computer manufacturer produces and sells new computers, it also generates income through its production. The computer manufacturer pays wages to workers, perhaps pays rent on office and factory buildings, and pays interest on borrowed money.

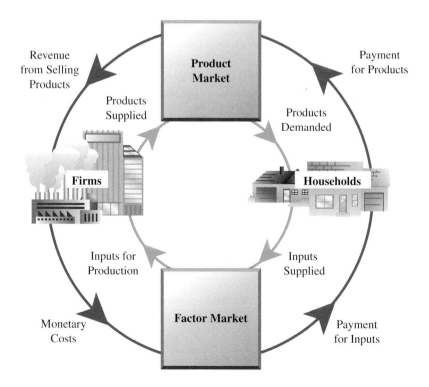

Figure 10.1

Circular Flow
The circular flow diagram shows how production of goods and services generates income for households and how households purchase goods and services produced by firms.

Whatever is left over after paying for the cost of production is the firm's profit, which is income to the owners of the firm. Wages, rents, interest, and profits are all different forms of income.

In another example, your taxes pay for a school district to hire principals, teachers, and other staff to provide educational services to the students in your community. These educational services are considered production in the modern economy. At the same time, the principals, teachers, and staff all earn income through their employment with the school district. The school district may also rent buildings where classes are held and pay interest on borrowed funds.

Our goal is to understand both sides: the production in the economy and the generation of income in the economy. We begin with understanding how to measure the production for the entire economy.

Measuring Gross Domestic Product

To measure the production of the entire economy, we need to combine an enormous array of goods and services, from new computers to professional basketball games. We can add computers to basketball games, much as we can really add apples and oranges if we are interested in the total monetary value of an apple harvest and an orange harvest. Our goal is to summarize the total production of an entire economy into a single number, which we call the gross domestic product.

Gross domestic product (GDP): The total market value of all the final goods and services produced within an economy in a given year.

The most common measure of the total output of an economy is **gross domestic product (GDP)**, the total market value of all the final goods and services produced within an economy in a given year. All the words in this definition are important. Let's analyze each part of this definition.

"Total market value" means that we take the quantity of goods produced and multiply them by their respective prices and then add up the totals. If an economy produced two cars at $15,000 per car and three computers at $3,000 per computer, the total value of these goods and services would be

$$(2 \text{ cars} \times \$15,000/\text{car}) + (3 \text{ computers} \times \$3,000/\text{computer}) = \$39,000$$

The reason we multiply the goods by their prices is that we cannot simply add together the number of cars and the number of computers. Using prices allows us to express the value of everything in a common unit of measurement—in this case dollars. (In countries other than the United States, we would express the value in terms of the local currency.) This is how we add apples and oranges together: by finding out what is the value of both the apples and the oranges (as measured by what you would pay for them) and adding them up in terms of their prices.

"Final goods and services" in the definition of GDP means those goods and services that are sold to ultimate, or final, purchasers. For example, the two cars that were produced would be final goods whether they were sold to households or to a business. However, in producing the cars, the automobile manufacturer bought steel that went into the body of the cars. This steel would not be counted as a final good or service in GDP. It is an example of an **intermediate good**, a good that is used in the production process; therefore it is not a final good or service.

Intermediate goods: Goods used in the production process that are not final goods or services.

The reason we do not count intermediate goods as final goods is to avoid double-counting. The price of the car already reflects the price of the steel that is contained in it. We do not want to count the steel twice. Similarly, the large volumes of paper used by an accounting firm are also intermediate goods because they become part of the final product delivered by the accounting firm to its clients.

The final words in our definition of GDP are "in a given year." GDP is expressed as a rate of production, that is, as so many dollars per year. In 2001, for example, GDP in the

United States was $10,082 billion. Goods produced in prior years, such as used cars, are not included in GDP this year.

Because we measure GDP using the current prices for goods and services, GDP will increase if prices increase, even if the physical amount of goods that are produced remains the same. Suppose that next year, the economy again produces two cars and three computers, but in the following year, all the prices in the economy have doubled: The price of cars is $30,000, and the price of computers is $6,000. GDP in the following year will also be twice as high, or $78,000—(2 cars × $30,000/car) + (3 computers × $6,000/computer)—even though the quantity produced is the same as during the prior year.

Let's apply the reality principle, one of our five basic principles of economics:

Reality **Principle**

What matters to people is the real value of money or income—its purchasing power—not the face value of money or income.

We would like to have another measure of total output in the economy that does not increase just because prices increase. For this reason, economists have developed the concept of **real GDP**, a measure of GDP that takes into account price changes.

Later in this chapter, we explain how real GDP is calculated. The basic idea is simple. When we use current prices to measure GDP, that is what we call **nominal GDP**. Nominal GDP can increase for one of two reasons: Either the production of goods and services has increased or the prices of those goods and services have increased.

To explain real GDP, we need first to look at a simple example. Suppose an economy produced a single good: computers. In year 1, 10 computers were produced, and each sold for $1,000. In year 2, 12 computers were produced, and each sold for $1,100. Nominal GDP would be $10,000 in year 1 and $13,200 in year 2. Nominal GDP would have increased by a factor of 1.32.

We can measure real GDP by calculating GDP using year 1 prices as a measure of what was produced in year 1 *and* also what was produced in year 2. In year 1, real GDP would be 10 computers × $1,000/computer = $10,000; and in year 2, it would be 12 computers × $1,000/computer = $12,000. Real GDP in year 2 is greater than real GDP in year 1 by a factor of 1.2. The key idea is that we construct a measure using the same prices for both years and thereby take price changes into account.

Figure 10.2 plots real GDP for the U.S. economy for the years 1930–2001. The data for real GDP are constructed so that nominal GDP and real GDP are set equal for a single year, in this case 1992. For both earlier and later years, the data for real GDP take into account changes in prices and, thus, measure movements in real output only.

The graph shows that real GDP has grown substantially over this period. This is what economists call **economic growth**: sustained increases in the real production of an economy over a long time. Later, in Chapter 12, we will study economic growth in detail. We will also look carefully at the behavior of real GDP over shorter periods, during which real GDP can rise and fall. Decreases in real GDP cause great disruption and lead to a loss of jobs and unemployment.

Real GDP: A measure of GDP that adjusts for changes in prices.

Nominal GDP: The value of GDP in current dollars.

Economic growth: Sustained increases in the real production of an economy over a period of time.

Who Purchases GDP?

To gain further insight into gross domestic product, let's look at its components. Economists divide GDP into four broad categories, each corresponding to different types of purchasers represented in GDP:

1. Consumption expenditures: purchases by consumers.
2. Private investment expenditures: purchases by firms.

Figure 10.2
**U.S. Real GDP,
1930–2001**

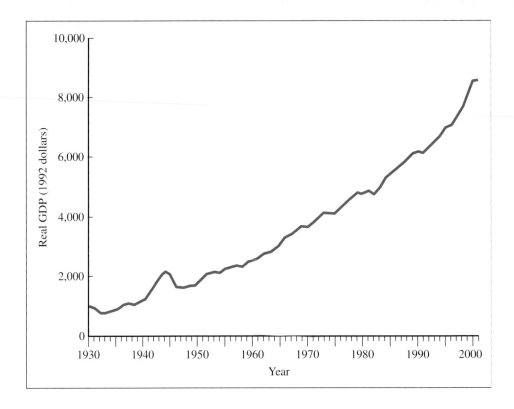

3. Government purchases: purchases by federal, state, and local governments.
4. Net exports: net purchases by the foreign sector, or domestic exports minus domestic imports.

Before discussing these categories, let's look at some data for the U.S. economy to get a sense of the size of each of these four components. Table 10.1 shows the figures for GDP for the third quarter of 2002. (A quarter is a three-month period; the third quarter runs from July through September.) In the third quarter of 2002, GDP was $10,506 billion, or approximately $10.5 trillion. To get a sense of the magnitude, consider that the U.S. population is approximately 281 million people, making GDP per person approximately $37,387.

Consumption Expenditures

Consumption expenditures:
Purchases of newly produced goods and services by households.

Consumption expenditures are purchases by consumers of currently produced goods and services, either domestic or foreign. These purchases include TV sets, VCRs, automobiles, clothing, hairstyling services, jewelry, movie tickets, food, and all other consumer items. We can break down consumption into durable goods, nondurable goods, and services.

**Table 10.1   Composition of U.S. GDP, Third Quarter 2002
(Billions of Dollars Expressed at Annual Rates)**

GDP	Consumption Expenditures	Private Investment Expenditures	Government Purchases	Net Exports
10,506	7,361	1,597	1,981	−433

Source: U.S. Department of Commerce.

Durable goods last for a long time, such as automobiles or refrigerators. **Nondurable goods**, such as food, last for a short time. **Services** reflect work done in which people play a prominent role in delivery (such as a dentist filling a cavity); they range from haircutting to health care. Services are the fastest-growing component of consumption. Overall, consumption spending is the most important component of GDP, constituting about 70% of total purchases.

Private Investment Expenditures

Private investment expenditures in GDP consist of three components:

1. First, there is spending on new plants and equipment during the year. If a firm builds a new factory or purchases a new machine, that is included in GDP. Purchasing an existing building or buying a used machine does not count in GDP because the goods were not produced during the current year.

2. Second, newly produced housing is included in investment spending. The sale of an existing home to a new owner is not counted because the house was not built in the current year.

3. Finally, if firms add to their stock of inventories, the increase in inventories during the current year is included in GDP. If a hardware store had $1,000 worth of nuts and bolts on its shelves at the beginning of the year and $1,100 at the year's end, its inventory investment would be $100 ($1,100 − $1,000). The $100 increase in inventory investment is included in GDP.

We call the total of new investment expenditures **gross investment**. During the year, some of the existing plant, equipment, and housing will deteriorate or wear out. This wear and tear is called **depreciation**. If we subtract depreciation from gross investment, we obtain **net investment**. Net investment is the true addition to the stock of plant, equipment, and housing in a given year.

Make sure you understand this distinction between gross investment and net investment. Consider the $1,597 billion in total investment spending for third quarter of 2002, a period in which there was $1,175 billion in depreciation. That means that there was only ($1,597 − $1,175) = $422 billion in net investment by firms in that year. Seventy-four percent of gross investment went to make up for depreciation of existing capital.

Warning: When we discuss measuring production in the GDP accounts, we use *investment* in a different way than when we use *investment* in the sense we have come to understand it. For an economist, investment in the GDP accounts means purchases of new final goods and services by firms. In everyday conversation, we may talk about investing in the stock market or investing in gold. Buying stock for $1,800 on the stock market is a purchase of an existing financial asset; it is not the purchase of new goods and services by firms. So that $1,800 does not appear anywhere in GDP. The same is true of purchasing a gold bar. In GDP accounting, *investment* denotes the purchase of new capital. Be careful not to confuse the common usage of *investment* with the definition of *investment* as we use it in the GDP accounts.

Government Purchases

Government purchases are the purchases of newly produced goods and services by federal, state, and local governments. They include any goods that the government purchases plus the wages and benefits of all government workers (paid when the government purchases their services as employees). The majority of spending in this category actually comes from state and local governments: $1,283 billion of the total $1,981 billion in 2002.

Durable goods: Goods that last for a long period of time, such as appliances.

Nondurable goods: Goods that last for a short period of time, such as food.

Services: Work done in which people play a prominent role in delivery, ranging from haircutting to health care.

Private investment expenditures: Purchases of newly produced goods and services by firms.

Gross investment: Actual investment purchases.

Depreciation: The wear and tear of capital as it is used in production.

Net investment: Gross investment minus depreciation.

Government purchases: Purchases of newly produced goods and services by all levels of government.

Transfer payments: Payments to individuals from governments that do not correspond to the production of goods and services.

This category does not include all the spending by governments. It excludes **transfer payments**; these are funds paid to individuals but are not associated with the production of goods and services. For example, payments for Social Security, welfare, and interest on government debt are all considered transfer payments and are not included in government purchases in GDP. The reason they are excluded is that nothing is being produced in return for the payment. But wage payments to the police, postal workers, and the staff of the Internal Revenue Service are all included because they do correspond to services that are currently being produced.

Because transfer payments are excluded from GDP, a vast portion of the budget of the federal government is not part of GDP. In 2002, the federal government spent approximately $2,011 billion, of which only $698 billion (about one-third) was counted as federal government purchases. Transfer payments are important, however. They affect both the income of individuals and their consumption and savings behavior. They also affect the size of the federal budget deficit. At this point, keep in mind the distinction between government purchases—which are included in GDP—and total government spending or expenditure—which may not be included.

Net Exports

Net exports: Exports minus imports.

The United States has an open economy; that means that the United States trades with other economies. Imports are goods we buy from other countries; exports are goods made here and sold to other countries. **Net exports** are total exports minus total imports. In Table 10.1, we see that net exports in the third quarter of 2002 were −$433 billion. Net exports were negative because our imports exceeded our exports.

In creating a measure of GDP, we try to measure the goods produced in the United States. Consumption, investment, and government purchases include all purchases by consumers, firms, and the government, whether or not the goods were produced in the United States. But purchases of foreign goods by consumers, firms, or the government should be subtracted when we calculate GDP because these goods were not produced in the United States. At the same time, we must add to GDP any goods produced here and sold abroad. For example, supercomputers made in the United States and sold in Europe should be added to GDP. By including net exports as a component of GDP, we correctly measure U.S. production by adding exports and subtracting imports.

For example, suppose someone in the United States buys a $25,000 Toyota made in Japan. If we look at final purchases, we will see that consumption spending rose by

Spending on new bridges, such as San Francisco's Golden Gate Bridge (1937), is included as government purchases in the National Income Accounts.

$25,000 because a consumer made a purchase of a consumption good. Net exports fell by $25,000, however, because the value of the import was subtracted from total exports. Notice that total GDP did not change with the purchase of the Toyota. This is exactly what we want in this case, because there was no U.S. production.

Now suppose that the United States sells a car for $18,000 to a resident of Spain. In this case, net exports would increase by $18,000 because the car was a U.S. export. GDP would also be a corresponding $18,000 higher because this sale represents U.S. production.

For the United States in the third quarter of 2002, net exports were −$433 billion. In other words, in that quarter, the United States bought $433 billion more goods from abroad than it sold abroad. When we buy more goods from abroad than we sell, we have a **trade deficit**. A **trade surplus** occurs when our exports exceed our imports.

Figure 10.3 shows the U.S. trade surplus as a share of GDP from 1960 to 2001. While at times the United States had a trade surplus, in the 1980s and late in the 1990s the United States ran a trade deficit that often exceeded 3% of GDP. What are the consequences of such large trade deficits?

When the United States runs a trade deficit, U.S. residents are spending more on goods and services than they are currently producing. Although the United States does sell many goods abroad (such as supercomputers, movies, records, and CDs), it buys even more goods and services from abroad (such as Toyotas, VCRs, and German machine tools).

The result is that the United States is forced to sell some of its assets to individuals or governments in foreign countries. Here is how it works: When U.S. residents buy more goods abroad than they sell, they give up more dollars for imports than they receive in dollars from the sale of exports. These dollars given up to purchase imports end up in the hands of foreigners, who can use them to purchase U.S. assets such as stocks, bonds, or real estate. In the early 1990s, Japanese investors bought many assets

Trade deficit: An excess of imports over exports.

Trade surplus: An excess of exports over imports.

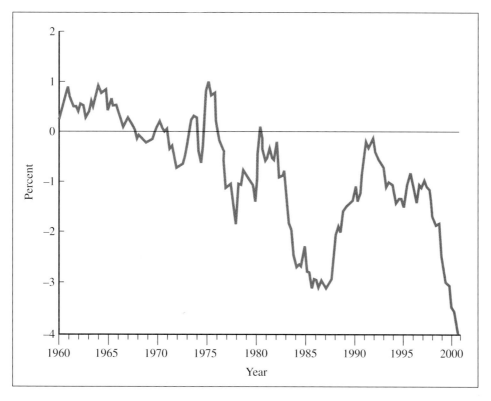

Figure 10.3

U.S. Trade Balance as a Share of GDP, 1960–2001

Table 10.3 Composition of U.S. National Income, Third Quarter 2002 (Billions of Dollars)

National income	8,388
Compensation of employees	6,027
Corporate profits	771
Rental income	144
Proprietor's income	759
Net interest	687

Source: U.S. Department of Commerce.

Real Versus Nominal GDP

Output in the economy can increase from one year to the next. And prices can rise from one year to the next. Realizing that, we need a measure of output that reflects actual increases in production, separate and apart from any price changes that may have occurred in the economy during the year. Recall that we defined nominal GDP as GDP measured in current prices, and we defined real GDP as GDP adjusted for price changes. Now we take a closer look at how real GDP is measured in modern economies.

Let's start with a simple economy in which there are only two goods, cars and computers, produced in the years 2004 and 2005. The data for this economy, the prices and quantities produced for each year, are shown in Table 10.4. The production of cars and the production of computers increased, but the production of computers increased more rapidly. The price of cars rose, while the price of computers remained the same.

Let's first calculate nominal GDP for this economy in each year. Nominal GDP is the total value of goods and services produced in each year. Using the data in the table, we can see that nominal GDP for the year 2004 is:

$$(4 \text{ cars} \times \$10,000/\text{car}) + (1 \text{ computer} \times \$5,000/\text{computer}) = \$45,000$$

Similarly, nominal GDP for 2005 is $75,000.

Table 10.4 GDP Data for a Simple Economy

Year	Quantity Produced		Price	
	Cars	Computers	Cars	Computers
2004	4	1	$10,000	$5,000
2005	5	3	12,000	5,000

Now we'll find real GDP. To compute real GDP, we calculate GDP using constant prices. What prices should we use? For the moment, let's use the prices for the year 2004. Because we are using 2004 prices, real GDP and nominal GDP for 2004 are both equal to $45,000. For 2005, real GDP is

$$(5 \text{ cars} \times \$10,000/\text{car}) + (3 \text{ computers} \times \$5,000/\text{computer}) = \$65,000$$

Note that real GDP for 2005, which is $65,000, is less than nominal GDP for 2005, which is equal to $75,000. The reason real GDP is less than nominal GDP here is because prices of cars rose between 2004 and 2005, and we are measuring GDP using 2004 prices. We can measure real GDP for any other year simply by calculating GDP using constant prices.

We now calculate the growth in real GDP for this economy between 2004 and 2005. Because real GDP was $45,000 in 2004 and $65,000 in 2005, real GDP grew by

$$(\$65,000 - \$45,000)/\$45,000 = 0.444$$

which equals 44.4%. This is an average of the growth rates for both goods, cars and computers.

We can also use the data in Table 10.4 to measure the changes in prices for this economy. The basic idea is that the differences between nominal GDP and real GDP for any year arise only because of changes in prices. Thus, by comparing real GDP and nominal GDP, we can measure the changes in prices for the economy. In practice, we do this by creating an index, called the **GDP deflator**, which measures how prices change over time. Because we are calculating real GDP using year 2004 prices, we will set the value of this index equal to 100 in the year 2004, which we call the base year. To find the value of the GDP deflator for the year 2005 (or other years), we use the following formula:

> **GDP deflator:** An index that measures how the price of goods included in GDP change over time.

value of GDP deflator in 2005 = $100 \times [(\text{nominal GDP in 2005})/(\text{real GDP in 2005})]$

Using this formula, we find that the value of the GDP deflator for 2005 is

$$100 \times (\$75,000/\$65,000) = 100 \times 1.15 = 115$$

Since the value of the GDP deflator is 115 in 2005 and was 100 in the base year of 2004, this means that prices rose by 15% ($[(115 - 100)/100] = 0.15$ or 15%) between the two years. Note that this 15% is an average of the price changes for the two goods, cars and computers.

Up until 1996, the Department of Commerce, which produces the GDP figures, used these methods to calculate real GDP and measure changes in prices. Today the Department of Commerce uses a slightly different method. Instead of picking just one year as the base year and calculating price changes from that year, it takes an average of price changes using different base years. It produces what is called a **chain price index**. If you look in the newspapers today or at the data produced by the Department of Commerce, you will see GDP measured in chained dollars with a chain-type price index for GDP. In practice, we can use the chain price index just as we did the GDP deflator— as a measure of price changes for GDP.

> **Chain price index:** A method for calculating changes in prices that includes an average of price changes using different base years.

GDP as a Measure of Welfare

GDP is our best measure of the value of output produced by an economy. But it is not a perfect measure. There are several recognized flaws in the construction of GDP of which you need to be aware. Because of these flaws, we should be cautious if we want to interpret GDP as a measure of our economic well-being. First, GDP ignores transactions that

The growth in GDP is exaggerated because the cost of restaurant meals includes cooking services that were previously performed at home and not counted in GDP.

do not take place in organized markets. The most important example is services, such as cleaning, cooking, and providing free child care, that are performed in the home. Because these services are not transferred through markets, GDP statisticians cannot measure them. This has probably led us to overestimate the growth in GDP. In the last three decades, there has been a big increase in the percentage of women in the labor force. Since more women are now working outside the home, there is naturally a demand for more meals in restaurants, more cleaning services, and more paid child care. All this new demand shows up in GDP, but the services that were provided earlier—when they were provided free—did not show up in earlier GDP. This naturally overstates the true growth in GDP.

Second, GDP ignores the underground economy, where transactions are not reported to official authorities. These transactions can be legal, but people don't report the income they have generated because they want to evade paying taxes on that income. For example, waiters and waitresses may not report all their tips, and owners of flea markets may make under-the-table cash transactions with their customers. There are also illegal transactions that result in unreported income, such as profits from the illegal drug trade.

In the United States, the Internal Revenue Service estimated in the early 1990s that about $100 billion in federal income taxes from the underground economy were not collected each year. If the average federal income tax rate in the country is about 20%, this means approximately $500 billion ($100/0.20) in income escapes the GDP accountants from the underground economy every year, about 7% of GDP at the time.

Third, GDP does not value changes in the environment that arise through the production of output. Suppose a factory produces $1,000 of output but pollutes a river and lowers the river's value by $2,000. Instead of recording a loss to society of $1,000, GDP will show a $1,000 increase. This is an important limitation of GDP accounting as a measure of our economic well-being because changes in the environment are important. In principle, we can make adjustments to try to correct for this deficiency.

A very important question is whether GDP, even correcting for some of its limitations, provides a good measure of economic welfare. Most of us would prefer to live in a country with a high standard of living and few of us would want to experience poverty up

Two economists, David G. Blanchflower of Dartmouth College and Andrew J. Oswald of Warwick University in the United Kingdom, have systematically analyzed surveys over nearly a 30-year period that ask individuals to describe themselves as "happy, pretty happy, or not too happy." The results of their work are provocative. Over the last 30 years, reported levels of happiness have actually declined in the United States and remained relatively flat in the United Kingdom, despite very large increases in income per person in both countries. Could it be the increased stress of everyday life has taken its toll on our happiness despite the increase in income?

At any point in time, however, money does appear to buy happiness. Holding other factors constant, individuals with higher incomes do report higher levels of

personal satisfaction. These "other factors" are quite important. Unemployment and divorce lead to sharply lower levels of satisfaction. Blanchflower and Oswald calculate that a stable marriage is worth $100,000 in terms of reported satisfaction.

Perhaps most interesting are their findings about trends in happiness for different groups in our society. Although whites report higher levels of happiness than blacks, the gap has decreased over the last 30 years. Men's happiness has risen relative to that of women over the last 30 years. What economic and social factors do you think account for these trends?

Source: David G. Blanchflower and Andrew J. Oswald, National Bureau of Economic Research Working Paper 7847, January 2000.

close. But does a higher level of GDP really lead to more satisfaction? As "A Closer Look: Does Money Buy Happiness?" explores, higher income does not necessarily lead to higher levels of perceived happiness.

Using the TOOLS

In this chapter, we looked closely at how we measure a nation's production and how we measure its income. Here's an opportunity to test your understanding of the key concepts.

1. Nominal GDP Versus Real GDP
Economists observed that in one country, nominal GDP increased two years in a row but real GDP fell over the same two years. How can this have occurred? Construct a numerical example to illustrate this possibility.

2. Fish and National Income
Suppose you were worried that national income did not adequately take into account the depletion of the stock of fish in the economy. Describe how you would advise the Commerce Department to take this into account in its calculations.

3. Transfer Payments Versus Government Employment
In Economy A, the government puts on the payroll as government employees workers who cannot find jobs for long periods, but these "employees" do no work. In Economy B, the government does not hire any long-term unemployed workers; instead, it just gives them cash grants. How do the GDP statistics compare between the two otherwise identical economies?

11

Unemployment and Inflation

Could the World Wide Web solve all our unemployment problems? Imagine a nonprofit firm called Employment.com. Here is how the firm operated: Every employer posted every job vacancy on this firm's Web site, along with the range for the starting salary. Everyone seeking a job filled out a detailed online résumé and also posted his or her preferred type of employment and acceptable salary range. The postings were organized by the required qualifications for the job, the salary range, the geographic area, and the type and nature of the job, including the starting date. Information was provided free to all firms and job seekers—the nonprofit company sold advertising on its Web site to pay for its services.

Would information made available in this way change how labor markets operate? Could it reduce the unemployment rate to zero? Do you think this scheme could really work?

n this chapter, we look at unemployment and inflation, two key concepts in macroeconomics. Unemployment and inflation are at the heart of all macroeconomic policy. Losing a job is one of the most stressful experiences a person can suffer. For the elderly, the fear that the purchasing power of their wealth will evaporate with inflation is also a source of deep concern.

In this chapter, we examine how economists define unemployment and inflation and the problems in measuring them. Once we have a basic understanding of what unemployment is and what inflation is, we will be able to investigate further their causes, consequences, and their social costs.

After studying this chapter, you will be able to answer the following questions:

1. What is unemployment? Why can't it be driven down to zero?
2. What demographic groups suffer the most unemployment? Can the unemployment statistics tell us the answer?
3. What is the consumer price index and how is it related to the cost of living?
4. How accurately can we measure inflation in the economy? If we don't do a good job, what impact does our inaccuracy have?
5. What are the costs of unemployment and inflation?

What Is Unemployment?

One of the reasons we want to avoid poor economic performance is that it imposes costs on individuals and society. If the economy fails to create enough jobs, many individuals will not find work, causing hardship for them and their families. Recall from Chapter 10 that one of the key issues for macroeconomics is understanding economic fluctuations—the ups and downs of the economy. During periods of poor economic performance, such as economic recessions when real GDP declines, unemployment rises sharply and becomes a cause of public concern. During times of good economic performance and rapid economic growth, unemployment is reduced but does not disappear. Our first task is to understand how economists and government statisticians measure unemployment and then learn to interpret what they measure.

Definitions

Let's begin with some definitions.

Unemployed: People who are looking for work but do not have jobs.

The **unemployed** are those individuals who do not currently have a job but who are actively looking for work. The phrase *actively looking* is critical. Individuals who looked for work in the past but are not looking currently are not counted as unemployed. The **employed** are individuals who currently have jobs. Together, the unemployed and employed comprise the **labor force**.

Employed: People who have jobs.

Labor force: The employed plus the unemployed.

labor force = employed + unemployed

The unemployment rate is the number of unemployed divided by the total labor force; it represents the percentage of the labor force unemployed and looking for work:

unemployment rate = unemployed/labor force

Labor force participation rate: The fraction of the population that is over 16 years of age that is in the labor force.

Finally, we need to understand what is meant by the **labor force participation rate**, defined as the labor force divided by the population 16 years and older. It represents the fraction of the population 16 years and older that is in the labor force:

labor force participation rate = labor force/population age 16 and over

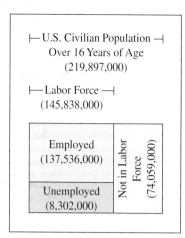

Figure 11.1
Unemployment Data, January 2003
Source: Bureau of Labor Statistics, U.S. Department of Labor, 2003.

To illustrate these concepts, suppose that an economy consists of 200,000 individuals 16 years and older, of whom 122,000 are employed and 8,000 are unemployed. In this example, the labor force is 130,000 (122,000 + 8,000) people. The labor force participation rate is 0.65, or 65% (130,000/200,000). The unemployment rate is 0.0615, or 6.15% (8,000/130,000).

Figure 11.1 helps to put these definitions into perspective for the U.S. economy. The large box is the total population 16 years and older, which in January 2003 was comprised of 219,897,000 individuals. This population is divided into two groups: those in the labor force and those outside the labor force. For this year, the labor force participation rate was 64.1%. Within the labor force, there were 137,536,000 employed and 8,302,000 unemployed.

Table 11.1 contains some international data on unemployment for 2003. Notice the sharp differences between countries; for example, the Netherlands had a 4.3% unemployment rate, while Spain had an unemployment rate of 12.1%.

Issues in Measuring Unemployment

Recall that we defined the unemployed as those people who are looking for work but do not currently have jobs. With that in mind, let's take a closer look at our measures of unemployment.

Table 11.1   Unemployment Rates Around the World, 2003

Country	Unemployment Rate (%)
United States	5.7
Belgium	10.8
Sweden	5.1
France	9.1
Italy	8.9
Spain	12.1
United Kingdom	5.1
Netherlands	4.3
Japan	5.5
Australia	6.1

Source: Economist, March 8, 2003.

It is relatively straightforward in principle to determine who is employed: Just count the people who are working. What is more difficult is to distinguish between those who are unemployed and those who are not in the labor force. How are these two groups distinguished? Each month, the Bureau of Labor Statistics directs its staff to interview a large sample of households. It asks about the employment situation of all members of households 16 years and older. If someone in a household is not working, the interviewer asks whether the person is actively looking for work. If so, he or she is classified as unemployed; but if the unemployed person is not actively looking for work, that person is classified as not being in the labor force.

Obviously, it is difficult for an interviewer to determine whether someone is truly looking for work. Without knowing whether someone in the household actually made any effort to look for a job during the time before the interview, the interviewer must rely on good-faith responses to the questions.

What about those people who were looking for work sometime in the recent past but did not find any opportunities and have stopped looking? These people are considered **discouraged workers**. They are not included in the official count of the unemployed.

To add to difficulties in measurement and interpreting what is measured, some workers may hold a part-time job but prefer to work full time. Other workers may hold jobs far below their capabilities. Workers in either of these situations are called **underemployed**. It is very difficult for the government to distinguish between employed and underemployed workers.

Another fact about unemployment that we have to understand is that different groups of people suffer more unemployment than other groups. Table 11.2 contains some unemployment statistics for selected groups for January 2003. Adults have substantially lower unemployment rates than teenagers. Minorities have higher unemployment rates, African American teenagers having extremely high unemployment rates. On average, men and women have roughly the same unemployment rates, but the unemployment rates for married men and married women are lower than unemployment rates of women who maintain families alone.

These relative differentials among unemployment rates do vary somewhat as GDP rises and falls. Teenage and minority unemployment rates often rise very sharply during

Discouraged workers: Workers who left the labor force because they could not find jobs.

Underemployed: Workers who hold a part-time job but prefer to work full time or who hold jobs that are far below their capabilities.

Table 11.2   Selected U.S. Unemployment Statistics, Unemployment Rates for January 2003 (Percent)

Total	5.7
Males 20 years and older	5.4
Females 20 years and older	4.7
Both sexes, 16–19 years	16.8
White	5.1
African American	10.3
White, 16–19 years	15.2
African American, 16–19 years	30.4
Married men	3.5
Married women	3.8
Women maintaining families	8.0

Source: Bureau of Labor Statistics, U.S. Department of Labor, 2003.

poor economic times. In better times, there is typically a reduction of unemployment for all groups. Nonetheless, teenage and minority unemployment remains high at all times.

Types of Unemployment

We can divide unemployment into three basic types. By studying each type separately, we can gain insight into some of the causes of each type of unemployment.

The unemployment rate is closely tied to the overall fortunes of the economy. Unemployment rises sharply during periods when real GDP falls and decreases when real GDP grows rapidly. During periods of falling GDP, firms will not want to employ as many workers as they do in good times because they are not producing as many goods and services. Firms will lay off or fire some current workers and will be more reluctant to add new workers to their payrolls. The result will be fewer workers with jobs and rising unemployment. Economists call the unemployment that accompanies fluctuations in real GDP **cyclical unemployment**. Cyclical unemployment rises during periods when real GDP falls or grows at a slower than normal rate and decreases when the economy improves.

Unemployment occurs even during periods when the economy is growing. Since 1970, for example, the unemployment rate in the United States has not fallen below 4% of the labor force. Unemployment that is not associated with economic fluctuations is either frictional unemployment or structural unemployment.

Frictional unemployment is the unemployment that occurs naturally during the normal workings of an economy. It can occur for a variety of reasons. People change jobs, move across the country, get laid off from their current jobs and search for new opportunities, or take their time after they enter the labor force to find an appropriate job. Suppose that when you graduate from college, you take six months to find a job that you like. During the six months in which you are looking for a good job, you are among those unemployed who make up frictional unemployment. Searching for a job, however, makes good sense. It would not be wise to take the first job you were offered if it had low wages, poor benefits, and no future.

The chapter opening story raised the possibility that the Internet could help reduce unemployment to zero: Firms could post help-wanted advertisements and workers could indicate interest in seeking employment. As we think about the nature of search and frictional unemployment, we can see that mere exchanges of information would not reduce frictional unemployment to zero. Some workers, for example, would prefer to continue searching for jobs in their own area rather than moving across country to seek another job. Firms would also want to scrutinize employees very carefully because hiring and training a worker is costly. Improving information flows could even have the perverse effect of informing workers of other opportunities in the economy and thereby lead to more workers quitting their current jobs and seeking other employment.

Structural unemployment occurs because of a mismatch between the jobs that are available and the skills of workers who are seeking jobs. Workers with low skills may not find opportunities for employment. If the government requires employers to pay wages, taxes, and benefits that exceed the contribution of these workers, firms will not be likely to hire them. Similarly, workers whose skills do not match the employment opportunities in their area may be unemployed. Aerospace engineers in California will not find jobs in their area if the aerospace industry relocates to Alabama.

The line between frictional unemployment and structural unemployment is sometimes hard to draw. Suppose a highly skilled steelworker is laid off because his company shuts down its plant in his area and moves to a new plant overseas. The worker would like to find a comparable job, but only low-wage, unskilled work is available in his town. Jobs are available but not his kind of job, and the steel company will never return. Is this person's unemployment frictional or structural? There really is no correct answer. You

Cyclical unemployment: The component of unemployment that accompanies fluctuations in real GDP.

Frictional unemployment: The part of unemployment associated with the normal workings of the economy, such as searching for jobs.

Structural unemployment: The part of unemployment that results from the mismatch of skills and jobs.

might think of the steelworker as experiencing either frictional or structural unemployment. In practice, it does not matter, either to the steelworker or to the economist, whether this episode of unemployment is frictional or structural.

Suspicious Unemployment Statistics

Economic Detective

Suppose that after a long period of high unemployment, government statisticians noticed that the labor force was smaller than it was before the spell of unemployment. Is there any reason you might be suspicious of these numbers? As an economic detective, you may have good reasons to question them. During the period of high unemployment, some workers may have become discouraged and dropped out of the labor force. They may return to the labor force when economic conditions improve.

Total unemployment in an economy is composed of cyclical, frictional, and structural unemployment. The level of unemployment at which there is no cyclical unemployment is called the **natural rate of unemployment**. The natural rate of unemployment consists of only frictional unemployment and structural unemployment. The natural rate of unemployment is the economist's notion of the appropriate unemployment rate when there is **full employment**. It may seem strange to think that workers can be unemployed when the economy is at full employment. But economists choose to consider the economy to be at full employment when there is no cyclical unemployment, although there is frictional and structural unemployment. The economy needs some frictional unemployment to operate efficiently: It is the unemployment that exists so that workers and firms find the right matches.

In the United States today, economists estimate that the natural rate of unemployment is between 4.0% and 5.5%. The natural rate of unemployment can vary over time and will differ across countries. In Europe, for example, estimates of the natural rate of unemployment place it between 7% and 10%.

The actual unemployment rate can be higher or lower than the natural rate of unemployment. During a period in which the real GDP fails to grow at its normal rate, there will be positive cyclical unemployment, and actual unemployment can far exceed the natural rate of unemployment. For example, in the United States in 1983, unemployment exceeded 10% of the labor force. A more extreme example occurred in 1933 during the Great Depression, when the unemployment rate reached 25%. On the other hand, when the economy grows very rapidly for a long period, actual unemployment can fall below the natural rate of unemployment. With sustained rapid economic growth, employers will be aggressive in hiring workers. During the late 1960s, unemployment rates fell below 4%; the natural rate of unemployment was estimated to be more than 5% at that time. In this case, cyclical unemployment was negative.

Just as a car will overheat if the engine is overworked, so the economy will overheat if economic growth is too rapid. At low unemployment rates, firms will find it difficult to

Natural rate of unemployment: The level of unemployment at which there is no cyclical unemployment.

Full employment: The level of employment that occurs when the unemployment rate is at the natural rate.

The desperate economic times of the Great Depression drove many of the unemployed to sell apples on the street, as this man did in "Hobo Jungle" in New York City.

recruit workers, and competition among firms will lead to increases in wages. As wages increase, increases in prices soon follow. The sign of this overheating will be a general rise in prices for the entire economy, which we commonly call inflation. As we discuss in later chapters, when the actual unemployment rate falls below the natural rate of unemployment, inflation will increase.

The Costs of Unemployment

When there is excess unemployment, both society and individuals suffer economic loss. From a social point of view, excess unemployment means that the economy is no longer producing at its potential. The resulting loss of resources can be very large. For example, in 1983, when the unemployment rate averaged 9.6%, typical estimates of the shortfall of GDP from the level it would be at full employment were near 6%. Simply put, this meant that society was wasting 6% of the total resources at its disposal.

That social loss translates into reduced income and lower employment for individuals. When unemployment increases, more workers are fired or laid off from their existing jobs, and individuals seeking employment find fewer opportunities available. To families with fixed obligations such as mortgage payments, the loss in income can bring immediate hardships. Unemployment insurance, payments received from the government on becoming unemployed, can cushion the blow to some degree, but unemployment insurance is typically only temporary and does not replace a worker's full earnings.

The effects of unemployment can also linger into the future. Workers who suffer from a prolonged period of unemployment are likely to lose some of their skills. For example, an unemployed stockbroker might be unaware of the latest developments and trends in financial markets. This will make it more difficult for him or her to find a job in the future. Economists who have studied the high rates of unemployment among young people in Europe point to the loss of both skills and good work habits (such as coming to work on time) as key factors leading to long-term unemployment.

The costs of unemployment are not simply financial. In our society, a person's status and position are largely associated with the type of job the person holds. Losing a job can impose severe psychological costs. Some studies, for example, have found that increased crime, divorce, and suicide rates are associated with increased unemployment.

TEST Your Understanding

1. How do economists define the unemployed?
2. Previously unemployed individuals who have stopped looking for work are called _____ workers.
3. The three types of unemployment are cyclical, frictional, and _____.
4. The natural rate of unemployment consists solely of _____ and _____ unemployment.

The Consumer Price Index and the Cost of Living

Suppose you moved to France and began to work. You received your first paycheck, which was in euros, the currency now used in France. The actual number of euros written on the check would not mean much to you initially. What you would like to know is what goods and services your paycheck could buy. Was this a fat paycheck or a thin one? Should you celebrate your first paycheck with a five-course gourmet dinner or head for the nearest inexpensive café?

Even in our own country, where we feel we have a reasonable sense of what a dollar can buy, we do know that the value of a dollar—what it purchases—varies over time. In 1976, a new starting professor of economics was paid $15,000. In 2000, a new starting professor at the same university was paid $55,000. Prices, of course, had risen in those 24 years. Which starting professor had the better deal?

These examples are illustrations of one of our five principles of economics, the reality principle:

Reality **PRINCIPLE**

What matters to people is the real value of money or income—its purchasing power—not the face value of money or income.

Consumer price index (CPI): A price index that measures the cost of a fixed basket of goods chosen to represent the consumption pattern of individuals.

Economists have developed a number of different measures to track the cost of living over time. The best known of these measures is the **consumer price index (CPI)**.

The CPI is widely used by both government and the private sector to measure changes in prices facing consumers. The CPI is an index that measures changes in a fixed basket of goods—a collection of items chosen to represent the purchasing pattern of a typical consumer. We first find out how much this basket of goods costs in a given year, called the base year. We then ask how much it costs in other years and measure changes in the cost of living relative to this base year. The CPI for a given year, say year K, is defined as

$$\text{CPI in year } K = (\text{cost of basket in year } K / \text{cost of basket in base year}) \times 100$$

Suppose a basket of goods costs $200 in the base year of 1992 and $250 in 1997. First, the value for the CPI in 1992 (the base year) is

$$\text{CPI in 1992} = (200/200) \times 100 = 100$$

The CPI in 1992 is 100. The way that the CPI is constructed, its value in a base year will always be 100. Now let's calculate the value of the CPI for 1997:

$$\text{CPI in 1997} = (250/200) \times 100 = 125$$

The CPI in 1997 is 125. The CPI rose from 100 in 1992 to 125 in 1997 in this example, a 25% increase in average prices over this five-year period.

Here is how you would use this information. Suppose you had $300 in 1992. How much would you need to be able to have the same standard of living in 1997? The answer is given by multiplying the $300 by the ratio of the CPI in 1997 to the CPI in 1992:

$$\$300 \times (125/100) = \$375$$

You need $375 in 1997 just to maintain what was your standard of living in 1992. This is the type of calculation that economists do to evaluate changes in living standards over time.

How do we actually calculate the CPI in practice? Each month, the Bureau of Labor Statistics sends its employees out to sample prices for more than 90,000 specific items around the entire country. Figure 11.2 shows the broad categories that are used in the CPI and the importance of each category in household budgets. Rent and food and beverages account for 44% of total spending by households.

The CPI Versus the GDP Deflator

In Chapter 10, we discussed nominal GDP and real GDP. We defined the GDP deflator and showed how it was used to measure changes in the prices of goods and services in the economy. The GDP deflator (including the more recent chain price index for GDP)

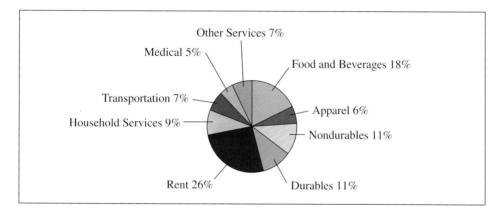

Figure 11.2
**Components
of the CPI**

*Source: Bureau of Labor
Statistics Handbook*
(Washington, DC: U.S.
Government Printing Office,
1992).

and the CPI are both measures of average prices for the economy. Yet, these measures differ in several ways.

First, the CPI measures the costs of a typical basket of goods for consumers. It includes goods produced in prior years (such as older cars) as well as imported goods. The GDP deflator does not measure price changes from either used goods or imports. The reason that the GDP deflator does not include used or imported goods is that it is based on the calculation of GDP, which measures only goods and services produced currently in the United States.

Second, unlike the GDP deflator, the CPI asks how much a fixed basket of goods costs in the current year compared to the cost of those same goods in a base year. Because consumers will tend to buy less of goods whose prices have risen, the CPI will tend to overstate true changes in the cost of living. For example, if the price of steak rises, consumers may switch to chicken and spend less on steak. But if the current basket of goods and services in the CPI includes steak, the CPI thinks the share of higher-priced steak in the basket is the same as the share of steak before its price increase; the CPI does not allow the share of steak in the index to decrease.

Problems in Measuring Changes in Prices

Most economists believe that in reality all the indexes—the GDP deflator and the CPI—overstate actual changes in prices. In other words, the increase in prices is probably less than the reported indexes tell us. The principal reason for this overstatement is that we have a difficult time measuring quality improvements. Suppose that the new computers sold to consumers become more powerful and more efficient each year. Further, suppose that the dollar price of a new computer remains the same each year. Even though the prices remain the same, the computers in later years are of much higher quality. If we looked simply at the prices of computers and did not take into account the change in quality, we would say there was no price change for computers. But in later years we are getting more computer power for the same price. If we failed to take the quality change into account, we would not see that the price of computer power has fallen.

Government statisticians do try to adjust for quality when they can. But quality changes are so common in our economy and products evolve so rapidly that it is impossible to keep up with all that is occurring. As a result, most economists believe that we overestimate the inflation rate by between 0.5% and 1.5% each year. This overstatement has important consequences. Some government programs, such as Social Security, automatically increase payments when the CPI goes up. Some union contracts also have **cost-of-living adjustments** or automatic wage changes based on the CPI. If the CPI overstates increases in the costs of living, the government might be overpaying Social

Cost-of-living adjustments:
Automatic increases in wages
or other payments that are tied
to a price index.

Security recipients. If the CPI overstates the increase in the cost of living by 1% a year, the Congressional Budget Office estimates that this would lead to approximately $50 billion in extra payments—beyond inflation protection—to Social Security recipients. Defenders of the elderly dispute this argument. Although the CPI probably does overstate overall increases in the cost of living, they point out that the elderly spend a higher fraction of their income on health care, whose costs have risen faster than the CPI. Regardless of which side is correct in this debate, it is clear that many tax dollars are at stake in this debate.

Inflation and Its Costs

Inflation rate: The percentage rate of change of the price level in the economy.

We have now looked at two different price indexes: the GDP deflator used for calculating real GDP and the consumer price index. Using either price index, we can calculate the percentage rate of change of the index. The percentage rate of change of a price index is the **inflation rate**:

$$\text{inflation rate} = \% \text{ rate of change of a price index}$$

Here is an example. Suppose that a price index in a country was 200 in 1998 and 210 in 1999. Then the inflation rate between 1998 and 1999 was

$$\text{inflation rate} = (210 - 200)/200 = 0.05 = 5\%$$

The country experienced a 5% inflation rate.

It is important to distinguish between the price level and the inflation rate. In everyday language, people sometimes confuse the *level of prices* with inflation. You might hear someone say that inflation is high in San Francisco because rents on apartments are high, but this is not a correct use of the term *inflation*. Inflation refers not to the level of prices, whether they are high or low, but to their percentage change. If rents were high in San Francisco but remained constant between two years, there would be no inflation in rents there during that time.

Taking a look at the period following World War II, Figure 11.3 plots the inflation rate, the percentage change in the price index, for 1950–2001 for the United States. In the 1950s and 1960s, the inflation rate was frequently less than 2% a year. The inflation rate was a lot higher in the 1970s, reaching nearly 12% per year. In recent years, the inflation rate has subsided, and it has been near 2% in recent years. The inflation rates today are close to the low levels that prevailed nearly 40 years ago. Prices rarely fall today, but as "A Closer Look: Deflations and Depressions" shows, prices have actually fallen quite sharply at times in U.S. history.

What are the costs of inflation? Economists typically separate the costs of inflation into two categories. One includes costs associated with fully expected or **anticipated inflation**. The other includes the costs associated with unexpected or **unanticipated inflation**.

Anticipated inflation: Inflation that is expected.

Unanticipated inflation: Inflation that is not expected.

Let's consider the costs of anticipated inflation first. Suppose the economy had been experiencing 4% annual inflation for many years and everyone was fully adjusted to it.

Even if everyone has adjusted to inflation, it still has some costs. First, there are the actual physical costs of changing prices, which economists call *menu costs*. Restaurant owners, catalog producers, and any other businesses that must post prices will have to incur costs to change their prices because of inflation. Economists believe that these costs are relatively small for the economy.

Second, people will hold less money when there is inflation. Inflation makes it more expensive to hold money because the purchasing power of money will decrease as prices rise. People will respond by holding less cash at any one time. If they hold less cash, they

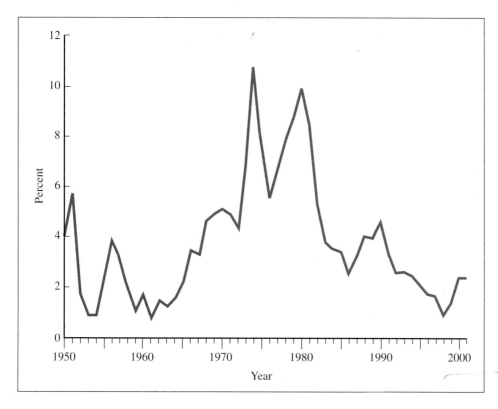

Figure 11.3
**U.S. Inflation Rate,
1950–2001**
Source: U.S. Department of
Commerce based on chain
price index.

must visit the bank or their ATM more frequently because they will run out of cash sooner. Economists use the term *shoe-leather costs* to refer to the additional wear and tear necessary to hold less cash. Economists who have estimated these costs find that they can be large, as much as 1% of GDP.

Finally, our tax system and financial system do not completely adjust even to fully anticipated inflation. It is difficult for the government and businesses to change their

A CLOSER LOOK   DEFLATIONS AND DEPRESSIONS

If you were born after 1952, you have never lived in a year without the price level rising, that is, without inflation. You might think it would be great if prices fell and we experienced what economists call a deflation. It may surprise you that we think you should hope that never happens.

During the Great Depression, the United States underwent a deflation, with the average level of prices falling 33% between 1929 and 1933. Wages fell along with prices during this period. The biggest problem caused by a deflation is that people cannot pay their debts. Imagine that you owe $40,000 for your education and expect to be able to pay it off over several

years if you earn $20,000 a year. If a massive deflation caused your wages to fall to $10,000, you might not be able to pay your $40,000 debt, which doesn't fall with deflation. You would be forced to default on your loan, as millions of people did during the Great Depression.

When people fail to pay interest and principal on their loans, banks get into trouble because they are no longer earning any money. In the 1930s, banks failed in the United States and throughout the world, including Austria, Hungary, Czechoslovakia, Romania, Poland, and Germany. These bank failures helped make the Great Depression a worldwide phenomenon.

normal rules of operation when inflation changes. For example, you pay taxes when you sell a stock whose price has increased solely because of inflation even if the real value of the stock did not increase. Many financial markets are also not fully adjusted for inflation. For example, some states have usury laws, or ceilings on interest rates. At times of high inflation, some lenders may require interest rates above the usury ceilings to provide them with an adequate return. If they cannot lend at rates above the ceiling, the market may actually disappear.

When there is unanticipated inflation, there are winners and losers. For example, suppose inflation was higher than everyone expected. In this case, anyone making a contract in dollar terms to sell a product would lose. For example, workers who agreed to a wage rate in dollar terms would earn less than they anticipated. However, buyers with fixed dollar contracts, such as firms hiring workers, would gain. They would be paying less to hire workers than they had anticipated. Unanticipated inflation causes unfair redistributions or transfers of income between parties.

These redistributions eventually impose real costs on the economy. Consider an analogy. Suppose you live in a very safe neighborhood where no one locks their doors. If a rash of burglaries (transfers between you and the crooks) starts to occur, people will invest in locks, alarms, and more police. You and your community will incur real costs to prevent these arbitrary redistributions. The same is true for unanticipated inflation. As inflation became more volatile in the late 1970s in the United States, many people devoted their time to speculation in real estate and commodity markets to try to beat inflation. An economy becomes less efficient when people take actions based on beating inflation. Latin American countries that have experienced high and variable inflation rates know all too well these costs from inflation.

TEST Your Understanding

5. The value of a price index in the base year is _____.

6. Economists believe that the CPI tends to underestimate the increase in the cost of living over time. True or false? Explain.

7. Unlike the CPI, the chain price index for GDP does not include used goods or _____ goods.

8. If a price index is 50 in 1998 and 60 in 1999, the rate of inflation between the two years is _____.

Using the **TOOLS**

1. Government Employment and the Unemployment Rate

Suppose the government hires workers who are currently unemployed but does not give them any work to do. What will happen to the measured unemployment rate? Is this an accurate reflection of the underlying economic situation?

2. Starting Salaries for Young Professors

The starting salary for a new assistant professor was $15,000 in 1976 and $55,000 in 2000. The value of the CPI for 2000 was 168.8 compared to 55.6 in 1976. In which year did a newly hired professor earn more in real terms?

3. Interpreting World Unemployment Statistics

A student looking at Table 11.1 argues that Spain must have very high cyclical unemployment compared to Japan because Spain's unemployment rate is so high. Explain why the student may not be correct.

4. Apartment Vacancies and Unemployment

In a major city, the vacancy rate for apartments was approximately 5%, yet substantial numbers of individuals were searching for new apartments. Can you explain why this occurs and relate it to unemployment?

Summary

In this chapter, we continued our introduction to the basic concepts of economics and explored the definition and nature of both unemployment and inflation. We also looked at the complex issues involved in measuring unemployment and inflation. Here are some of the key points to remember:

1. The unemployed are individuals who do not have jobs but are actively seeking employment.

2. The three types of unemployment are cyclical, frictional, and structural.

3. Unemployment rates vary across groups. It is often difficult to distinguish between the unemployed and discouraged workers who were once unemployed but stopped looking for work.

4. Economists measure changes in the cost of living through the consumer price index, which is based on the cost of purchasing a standard basket of goods and services.

5. We measure inflation as the percentage change in the price level.

6. Economists believe that most price indices overstate true inflation because they fail to capture quality improvements.

7. Both anticipated and unanticipated inflation impose costs on the economy.

Key Terms

Problems and Discussion Questions

1. Here are some data for an economy:
   - 10 million individuals 16 years and older
   - 5.5 million employed
   - 0.5 million unemployed

   Calculate the labor force, the labor force participation rate, and the unemployment rate for this economy.

2. Sometimes at the beginning of an economic boom, total employment increases sharply but the unemployment rate does not fall. Why might this occur?

3. In inner cities, minority youths have high unemployment rates. Many economists believe that the unemployment picture is worse than the statistics portray. What could be the basis for this belief?

4. Suppose the government decided that homemakers should be counted as employed because they perform important services. How do you think this change would affect our measure of the labor force, the labor force participation rate, and the unemployment rate? (You may want to construct a numerical example.)

5. Why is the natural rate of unemployment always positive?

6. When oil prices increased sharply in the 1970s, some businesses were affected more adversely than others. Explain why some economists believe that the oil price increase led to higher frictional unemployment.

7. A country reports a price index of 55 in 1990 and 60 in 1991. What is the inflation rate between 1990 and 1991?

8. A job paid $3,000 in 1960. The CPI in 1960 was 29.3, compared to 164 in 1999. In 1999, what salary would be comparable to 1960's $3,000 in real terms?

9. An economy has 100 million people employed, 8 million unemployed, and 4 million discouraged workers. What is the conventional measure of the unemployment rate? What would be the best alternative measure that takes into account discouraged workers?

10. Critically evaluate the following statement: "Tokyo is an expensive place to live. They must have a high inflation rate in Japan."

11. Web Exercise. Go to the data section of the Web site for the Bureau of Labor Statistics (*stats.bls.gov*). Contrast the change in the price indexes from 1960 to the present for the overall CPI with the change in some of its components such as food and beverages and medical care. What are some of your findings?

12. Web Exercise. Use the Web to find articles about the difficulties in precisely measuring changes in prices in the economy. You might want to start with the Boskin report, which can be found on the history page of the Social Security Administration (*www.ssa/gov/history/repstud.html*). On the basis of your reading, what do you consider to be the most important problem?

Take It to the Net

We invite you to visit the O'Sullivan/Sheffrin page on the Prentice Hall Web site at: **www.prenhall.com/osullivan/** for additional World Wide Web exercises for this chapter.

Model Answers to Questions

Chapter-Opening Questions

1. The unemployed are individuals without jobs and actively seeking work. The unemployment rate cannot be driven down to zero because of natural frictions in the labor market.

2. Teenagers and minorities have the highest unemployment rates.

3. The consumer price index is a price index that is used to measure changes in the cost of living.

4. Because of changes in the quality of goods and other factors, we cannot measure inflation perfectly and probably tend to overestimate the true inflation rate. This will have financial implications if payments are linked to changes in measured prices.

Test Your Understanding

1. The unemployed are individuals who are not employed but are actively looking for work.

2. Discouraged.

3. Structural.

4. Frictional, structural.

5. 100.

6. False. The CPI overestimates the increase in the cost of living over time for two reasons. It does not fully take into account technological change, and it assumes that the quantities of goods consumed do not decrease as prices increase.

7. Imported.

8. 20%.

Using the Tools

1. Government Employment and the Unemployment Rate. If the government hires an individual, that individual is an employee and no longer unemployed. The unemployment rate would fall. But the underlying economic reality has not changed: The individual is not producing any goods or services.

2. Starting Salaries for Young Professors. Starting salaries were higher in 2000. The 2000 equivalent of the 1976 salary of $15,000 is $15,000 (168.8/55.6) = $45,539, which is less than the actual salary of $55,000 for 2000.

3. **Interpreting World Unemployment Statistics.** Spain could have higher frictional unemployment or structural unemployment than Japan. Without detailed knowledge of an economy, we cannot tell how much of unemployment is cyclical, frictional, or structural.

4. **Apartment Vacancies and Unemployment.** Owners of apartments naturally want to choose reliable renters, while at the same time, prospective tenants want to find the best apartments. This results in a process of search, just like in the labor market. Apartment vacancies are analogous to job vacancies; apartment seekers are analogous to the unemployed.

Why Do Economies Grow?

To understand what economic growth means, consider how the typical American lived in 1783, seven years after the Declaration of Independence was written. According to economic historian Stanley Lebergott, an average U.S. home at that time had no central heat, one fireplace, no plumbing, no hot water, and toilets that were outdoor shacks surrounding a hole in the ground. The lack of plumbing meant that hygiene was not what it is today: Well into the 19th century, a typical farmer took a bath once a week. Houses had no electricity or gas; a solitary candle provided light at night. There were no refrigerators, no toasters, or any appliances. Bedrooms contained no furniture other than a bed (with no springs); two people slept in what we now consider a single bed. For women, things were particularly hard. They were expected to bake more than half a ton of bread a year, kill chickens, and butcher hogs, as well as prepare all vegetables. Canned foods were not readily available until a century later. And you really don't want to hear about medical "science" in those days.[1]

ur living standards are dramatically different today because there has been a remarkable growth in GDP per person. Growth in GDP is perhaps the most critical aspect of a country's economic performance. Over long periods, there is no other way to raise the standard of living in an economy.

With the tools developed in this chapter, here are some questions we can answer:

1. What countries have the highest living standards today?
2. Do countries with high savings rates have faster rates of GDP growth?
3. Do trade deficits help or hinder economic growth?
4. What factors determine technological progress?

The chapter begins by looking at some data from both rich and poor countries over the last 30 years. We will see how GDPs per capita (meaning per person—every man, woman, and child) compare over this period.

We then look at how growth occurs. Economists believe that there are two basic mechanisms that increase GDP per capita over the long term. One is **capital deepening**, increases in an economy's stock of capital—its total stock of plant and equipment—relative to its workforce. **Technological progress** is the other mechanism by which economies can grow. To economists, technological progress specifically means that an economy operates more efficiently, producing more output, but without using any more inputs. In other words, the economy gets more output without any more capital or labor. Technological progress does occur and is a key element of economic growth. We examine different theories of the origins of technological progress and discuss how to measure its overall importance for the economy.

Finally, we discuss in detail the role of education and investments in human beings in fostering economic development.

Capital deepening: Increase in the stock of capital per worker.

Technological progress: An increase in output without increasing inputs.

The Diversity of Economic Experience

Throughout the world, there are vast differences in standards of living and in rates of economic growth. To understand these differences, we first need to look at the concepts and the tools economists use to study economic growth. With these concepts and tools, we will be equipped to understand the data that measures economic growth.

Measuring Economic Growth

From earlier chapters, we know that real GDP measures in constant prices the total value of final goods and services in a country. Since countries differ in the size of their populations, we want to know what is a country's real GDP per person, or its **real GDP per capita**.

Real GDP per capita typically grows over time. A convenient way to describe the changes in real GDP per capita is growth rates. The **growth rate** of a variable is the percentage change in that variable from one period to another. For example, calculate the growth rate of real GDP from year one to year two. Suppose real GDP was 100 in year one and 104 in year two. The growth rate of real GDP is

Real GDP per capita: Gross domestic product per person adjusted for changes in prices. It is the usual measure of living standards across time and between countries.

Growth rate: The percentage change of a variable.

growth rate, **in percent** = [(GDP in year 2 − GDP in year 1) / GDP in year 1] × 100
$$= [(104 - 100) / 100] \times 100$$
$$= [4 / 100] \times 100$$
$$= [0.04] \times 100 = 4\% \text{ per year}$$

Real GDP grew by 4% per year.

Small growth rates can have very powerful effects in the long run. Here's a rule of thumb to help you understand the power of growth rates. Suppose you know the growth rate of real GDP and it is constant, but you want to know how many years it will take until the level of real GDP doubled. The answer is given by the **rule of 70**:

Rule of 70: If an economy grows at x percent per year, output will double in 70/x years.

$$\text{years to double} = 70/(\% \text{ growth rate})$$

Example: For an economy that grew at 5% a year, it would take

$$70/5 = 14 \text{ years}$$

for real GDP to double. (In case you are curious, the rule of 70 is derived by using the mathematics of logarithms.)

Making comparisons of real GDP across countries is difficult. Not only do countries have their own currencies, but also patterns of consumption and prices can differ sharply between countries. Two examples can illustrate this point. First, because land is scarce in Japan, people live in smaller spaces than do residents of the United States and the price of housing is higher (relative to other goods) than in the United States. Second, developing countries (such as India or Pakistan) have very different price structures than developed countries. In particular, as compared to developed countries, in developing countries the prices of goods that are not traded—such as household services or land—are relatively cheaper than goods that are traded in world markets. In other words, although all residents of the world may pay the same price for gold jewelry, hiring a cook or household helper is considerably less expensive in India or Pakistan than in the United States.

In making accurate comparisons of GDP across countries, it is important to take these differences into account. Fortunately, a team of economists led by Robert Summers and Alan Heston of the University of Pennsylvania has devoted decades to developing methods for measuring real GDP across countries. Their procedures are based on gathering extensive data on prices of comparable goods in each country and making adjustments for differences in relative prices and consumption patterns. These methods are now officially used by the World Bank and the International Monetary Fund in making cross-country comparisons of real GDP. Most economists view this approach as the best way to make accurate comparisons of living standards across countries.

According to these methods, the country with the highest level of income in 1999 was Luxembourg; its real income per capital was $41,230. The United States was second at $31,910, and Switzerland was third at $28,760.

Growth Rates and Patterns of Growth

Table 12.1 lists real GDP per capita for 1999 and average annual growth rate of real GDP per capita between 1960 and 1999 for 11 countries. Japan, with a GDP per capita of $25,170, follows the United States. Not far behind are France, the United Kingdom, and Italy. More representative of typical countries were Mexico and Costa Rica, with GDPs per capita in 1999 of $8,070 and $7,880, respectively. This is about one-fourth of GDP per capita in the United States. The very poor countries have extremely low GDP per capita. India, for example, had a GDP per capita of $2,230—7% of the GDP per capita of the United States.

In the third column of Table 12.1, notice the differences in growth rates. Consider Japan. In 1960, Japan had a GDP per capita that was one-half France's and one-fourth the United States' GDP per capita. But Japan's GDP per capita grew at 4.43% per year, compared to 2.13% for the United States and 2.76% for France. To place Japan's growth rate for this period into perspective, recall the rule of 70. If an economy grows at an average annual rate of x percent a year, it takes $70/x$ years for output to double. In Japan's case,

Table 12.1   GDP per Capita and Economic Growth

Country	GDP per Capita in 1999 Dollars	Average per Capita Growth Rate, 1960–1999 (%)
United States	$31,910	2.13
Japan	25,170	4.43
France	23,020	2.76
United Kingdom	22,200	2.07
Italy	22,000	3.00
Mexico	8,070	2.36
Costa Rica	7,880	2.23
Zimbabwe	2,610	1.28
India	2,230	1.98
Pakistan	1,860	1.04
Zambia	720	−1.31

Source: World Bank Development Indicators, 2001 and the Penn World Tables.

per capita output was doubling every 70/4.43 years, or approximately every 16 years. At this rate, from the time someone is born to the time that person reaches the age of 32, living standards have increased by a factor of four—an extraordinary rate of growth.

Convergence: The process by which poorer countries catch up with richer countries in terms of real GDP per capita.

One question economists ask is whether poorer countries can close the gap between their level of GDP per capita and the GDP per capita of richer countries. Closing this gap is called **convergence**. To converge, poorer countries have to grow at more rapid rates than richer countries are growing. Since 1960, Japan, Italy, and France all have grown more rapidly than the United States and have narrowed the gap in per capita incomes.

Cell phones are a sign of economic growth throughout the entire world.

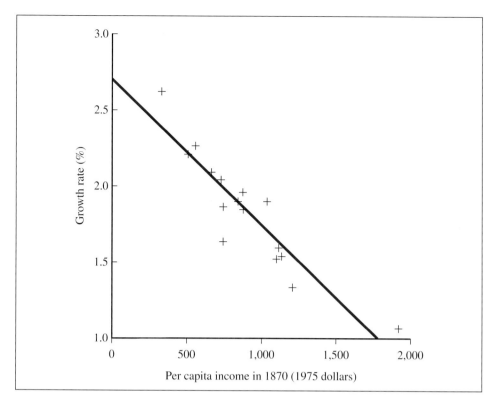

Figure 12.1

Countries with Lower Income in 1870 Grew Faster

Source: M. Obstfeld and K. Rogoff, *Foundation of International Macroeconomics* (Cambridge, MA: MIT Press, 1996), Table 7.1.

For a more extensive look at the evidence, Figure 12.1 plots for 16 currently developed countries the average growth rate from 1870 to 1979 versus the level of GDP in 1870. The line through the points slopes downward, which means that countries with higher levels of GDP in 1870 grew more slowly than countries with lower levels of GDP; in other words, there was a tendency for countries with lower levels of initial income to grow faster and thus catch up. Depending on which countries we look at, there seems to have been convergence among the currently developed countries.

If we compare the less developed countries to the advanced industrial countries, the picture is not so clear. While Costa Rica grew at a faster rate than the United States, India grew only 1.98% per year and fell farther behind advanced economies. In Africa, GDP per capita fell substantially in Zambia, while in Zimbabwe, GDP per capita grew at a slower rate than the U.S. rate.

Economists who have studied the process of economic growth in detail find weak evidence that poorer countries are closing the gap in per capita income with richer countries. On average, it does not appear that poorer countries grow at substantially higher rates than richer countries are growing. Although there are some success stories, such as Japan and other Asian economies, including Hong Kong and Singapore, there are also economies such as Zambia's that have regressed.

The rule of 70 reinforces how important are small differences in economic growth. A per capita GDP growth rate of 5% a year means that the living standard doubles in 14 years. With only 1% growth, doubling would take 70 years.

TEST Your Understanding

1. What measure of output do we use to measure living standards across countries with populations of different sizes?

Capital Deepening

One of the most important mechanisms of economic growth economists have identified is increases in the amount of capital per worker: capital deepening.

As capital—machines, equipment, and structures—is added to an economy, the workers in the economy will become more productive. In the simplest example, if workers have more or better machines at their disposal, they will be able to produce more output. A worker in the United States using sophisticated equipment in a modern factory, for example, will typically be able to produce much more output per day than a worker in a developing country who must use less sophisticated equipment. The ability to produce additional output with the added capital will benefit the workers. Firms, which own the capital, will find that workers can produce more output and will compete with other firms to hire these workers. This competition among firms will raise the wages of workers to reflect their increased productivity. The final result will be that wages for workers will increase as capital per worker increases.

An economy is better off with an increase in the stock of capital. With additions to the stock of capital, workers will enjoy higher wages, and total GDP in the economy will increase. Workers are more productive because each worker has more capital at his or her disposal.

But how does an economy increase its stock of capital per worker?

Saving and Investment

Saving: Total income minus consumption.

Let's begin with the simplest case: an economy with a constant population, producing at full employment, that has no government or foreign sector. In this simple economy, output can be purchased only by consumers or by firms. In other words, output consists solely of consumption and investment. At the same time, this output generates an amount of income that is equivalent to the amount of output. Any income that is not consumed we call **saving**. In this economy, saving must equal investment. Here's why: By definition, consumption plus saving equals income

$$C + S = Y$$

but at the same time, income—which is equivalent to output—also equals consumption plus investment:

$$C + I = Y$$

Thus, saving must equal investment:

$$S = I$$

This means that whatever consumers decide to save goes directly into investment.

Next, we need to link the level of investment in the economy to the stock of capital in the economy. The stock of capital depends on two factors. The stock of capital increases with any gross investment spending but decreases with any depreciation.

(Recall that *gross* means "before taking depreciation into account.") For example, suppose the stock of capital at the beginning of the year is $100. During the year, if there were $10 in gross investment and $4 in depreciation, the capital stock at the end of the year would be $106 (equal to $100 + $10 − $4).

It may be helpful to picture this as being like a bathtub. The level of water in a bathtub (the stock of capital) depends on the flow of water into the bathtub through the input faucet (gross investment) minus the flow of water out of the bathtub down the drain (depreciation). As long as the flow in exceeds the flow out, the water level in the bathtub (the stock of capital) will increase.

Higher saving, which leads to higher gross investment, will therefore tend to increase the stock of capital available for production. As the stock of capital grows, however, there typically will be more depreciation, because there is more capital to depreciate. It is the difference between gross investment and depreciation, which is net investment, that ultimately determines the change in the stock of capital for the economy and therefore the level of real wages and real output. In our example, net investment is $10 − $4 = $6.

Population Growth, Government, and Trade

So far we've considered the simplest economy. Let's consider a more realistic economy with population growth, government, and trade.

First, consider the effects of population growth. A larger labor force will allow the economy to produce more total output. However, with a fixed amount of capital and an increasing labor force, the amount of capital per worker will be less. With less capital per worker, output per worker will also tend to be less because each worker has fewer machines to use. This is an illustration of the principle of diminishing returns.

PRINCIPLE of Diminishing Returns

Suppose that output is produced with two or more inputs and that we increase one input while holding the other inputs fixed. Beyond some point—called the point of diminishing returns— output will increase at a decreasing rate.

Consider India, which has the world's second largest population, with over 1 billion people. Although India has a large labor force, the amount of capital per worker is low. With sharp diminishing returns to labor, per capita output in India will tend to be low.

The government can affect the process of capital deepening in several ways through its policies of spending and taxation. Suppose the government taxed its citizens so that it could fight a war, pay its legislators higher salaries, or give foreign aid to needy countries. The higher taxes will reduce total income. If consumers save a fixed fraction of their income, total private saving (savings from the nongovernmental sector) will fall. In these cases, the government is not investing the funds it collects, putting those funds into capital formation. Instead, it is draining from the private sector saving that would have been used for capital deepening. The overall result is a reduction of total investment in the economy and less capital deepening. In these examples, the government is taxing the private sector to engage in consumption spending, not investment.

Now suppose the government took all the tax revenues and invested them in valuable infrastructure such as roads, buildings, and airports. Suppose consumers were saving 20% of their incomes. If the government took a dollar in taxes, private saving would fall by 20 cents, but government investment would increase by $1. The net result is an increase in total social saving (private plus government) of 80 cents. This would promote capital deepening: In this case, the government is taxing its citizens to provide investment.

Finally, the foreign sector can affect capital deepening. An economy can run a trade deficit and import investment goods to aid capital deepening. The United States, Canada, and Australia built their vast railroad systems in the 19th century by running trade deficits (selling less goods and services to the rest of the world than they were buying, financing this gap by borrowing) to enable them to purchase the large amount of capital needed to build their rail networks. In these cases, the large trade deficits were valuable for the economy. They enabled growth to occur at more rapid rates through the process of capital deepening. Eventually, these economies had to pay back the funds that were borrowed from abroad by running trade surpluses, selling more goods and services to the rest of the world than they would buy. But since economic growth raised GDP and the wealth of the economy, they could afford to pay back the borrowed funds. Therefore, this was a reasonable strategy for these countries to follow.

Not all trade deficits promote capital deepening, however. Suppose a country ran a trade deficit because it wanted to buy more consumer goods. The country would be borrowing from abroad, but there would be no additional capital deepening, just additional consumption spending. When the country was forced to pay back the funds, there would be no additional GDP to help foot the bill. Society will be poorer in the future when it must pay the bill for what it consumes now—its current consumption.

There are natural limits to capital deepening. Capital is subject to diminishing returns just as labor. With a given labor force, increases in capital will lead to increases in output but at a diminishing rate. Capital deepening can be important for many countries, but it is only one important factor that leads to economic growth.

TEST Your Understanding

5. Explain why saving must equal investment if we are not taking into account the government sector or the foreign sector.

6. If everything else is held equal, how does an increase in the size of the population affect total and per capita output?

7. If the private sector saves 10% of its income and the government raises taxes by $200 to finance public investments, by how much will total investment—private and public—increase?

8. If a country runs a trade deficit to finance increased current consumption, it will have to reduce consumption in the future to pay back its borrowings. True or false? Explain.

The Key Role of Technological Progress

The other mechanism affecting economic growth is technological progress. Economists use the term *technological progress* in a very specific way: It means that an economy operates more efficiently by producing more output without using any more inputs.

In practice, technological progress can take many forms. The invention of the lightbulb made it possible to read and work indoors at night; the invention of the thermometer assisted doctors and nurses in their diagnoses; and the invention of disposable diapers made life easier at home. All these examples—and you could provide many more—enable society to produce more output without more labor or more capital. With higher output per person, we enjoy a higher standard of living.

Technological progress can be thought of as the birth of new ideas. These new ideas enable us to rearrange our economic affairs and make us more productive. Not all tech-

Table 12.2 Sources of Real GDP Growth, 1929–1982 (Average Annual Percentage Rates)

Due to capital growth	0.56
Due to labor growth	1.34
+ technological progress	1.02
Output growth	2.92

Source: Edward F. Denison, *Trends in Economic Growth 1929–82* (Washington, DC: The Brookings Institution, 1985).

nological innovations are necessarily major scientific breakthroughs; some are much more mundane. Good commonsense ideas from the workers or managers of a business allow it to make more effective use of its capital and labor and to deliver a better product to its consumers at the current price—this is also technological progress. As long as there are new ideas, inventions, and new ways of doing things, the economy can become more productive and per capita output can increase.

How Do We Measure Technological Progress?

If someone asked you how much of the increase in your standard of living were due to technological progress, how would you answer?

Robert Solow, a Nobel laureate in economics from the Massachusetts Institute of Technology, developed a method for measuring technological progress in an economy. As is usual with good ideas, his theory was simple.

Other economists had previously developed methods to measure how the total output in an economy—its real GDP—could be determined by the amount of inputs that were used in that economy, labor and capital, given the current state of technology. Solow recognized that real GDP could increase in an economy for two basic reasons. First, there could be increases in the total amount of labor or capital in the economy. Second, given technology could improve, allowing the economy to produce more output from the same levels of inputs.

Solow noted that over any period, we can observe increases in capital, labor, and output. Using these, we can measure technological progress indirectly. We first ask how much of the change in output can be explained by contributions from the changes in the amount of inputs—capital and labor—that are used. Whatever growth we cannot explain must have been caused by increases in technological progress. The method that Solow developed for determining the contributions to economic growth from increased capital, labor, and technological progress is called **growth accounting**.

Following this basic approach, Table 12.2 contains a breakdown of the sources of growth for the U.S. economy for 1929 to 1982. Figure 12.2 shows the relative contributions of the sources of growth based on these data. Over 1929 to 1982, total output grew at a rate of nearly 3%. Because capital and labor growth are measured at 0.56% and 1.34%, respectively, the remaining portion of output growth, 1.02%, must be due to technological progress. That means that approximately 35% of output growth comes directly from technological progress.

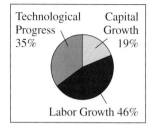

Figure 12.2
Percentage Contributions to Real GDP Growth

Source: Data from Edward F. Denison, *Trends in Economic Growth 1929–82* (Washington, DC: The Brookings Institution, 1985).

Growth accounting: A method to determine the contribution to economic growth from increased capital, labor, and technological progress.

Growth Accounting: Three Examples

Growth accounting is a useful tool for understanding different aspects of economic growth. Here are three examples of how economists use growth accounting.

Singapore and Hong Kong

Singapore and Hong Kong have both had phenomenal post–World War II economic growth. From 1980 to 1985 each grew at a rate of approximately 6% a year. But a closer examination, by Alwyn Young of the University of Chicago, revealed that the sources of growth in each were very different.[2] In Singapore, nearly all the growth was accounted for by increases in labor and capital. In particular, the ratio of investment to GDP reached as high as 43% in 1983.

Hong Kong had a much lower investment rate—approximately 20% of GDP—and technological progress made an important contribution. This meant that the residents of Hong Kong could enjoy the same level of GDP but consume, not save, a higher fraction of GDP. Residents of Hong Kong were enjoying higher consumption than residents of Singapore were, despite the similarity in growth rates.

The difference in the sources of economic growth between Singapore and Hong Kong may also have important implications for future growth. Singapore increased its GDP by increasing its labor inputs and increasing its stock of capital. Eventually, Singapore will find it difficult to keep increasing inputs to production. Economic leaders became concerned that unless they managed to increase their rate of technological progress, their long-term growth prospects would not be strong.

In Hong Kong, there is a different concern. Now that Hong Kong is part of China, residents hope the Chinese will allow them to continue to maintain their free and open economy in which technological progress has flourished. Technological progress has been the driving force for growth in Hong Kong, where there is a strong desire to maintain the system that produced technological innovation.

Understanding Labor Productivity

Labor productivity: Output per hour of work.

One of the common statistics reported about the U.S. economy is **labor productivity**. Defined as output per hour of work, labor productivity is a simple measure of how much a typical worker can produce given the amount of capital in the economy and the state of technological progress. Since 1973, there has been a slowdown in the growth of labor productivity in the United States and other countries in the world. Table 12.3 shows U.S. productivity growth for different periods since World War II. The table shows that productivity growth was extremely high during the 1960s. It slowed a bit in the late 1960s and then slowed dramatically after the oil shocks in the 1970s. In recent years, there has been a resurgence in productivity growth, which reached 2.5% from 1994 to 2000.

Table 12.3   U.S. Annual Productivity Growth, 1959–2000

Years	Annual Growth Rate (%)
1959–1968	3.5
1968–1973	2.5
1973–1980	1.2
1980–1986	2.1
1986–1994	1.4
1994–2000	2.5

Source: Economic Report of the President (Washington, DC: U.S. Government Printing Office, 2000) and Bureau of Labor Statistics.

Similar patterns have been observed in other countries. Zvi Grilliches, a Harvard economist and expert on productivity, compared the growth of output per hour in the manufacturing for 12 countries over different periods.[3] If we use his data and compare the periods 1960 to 1973 and 1979 to 1986, we find that productivity growth slowed in 11 of 12 countries. In Japan, it fell from 10.3% to 5.6%; in Canada, it fell from 4.5% to 1.4%. Only the United Kingdom exhibited any increase in productivity growth over those periods, and that increase was only from 4.3% to 4.4%.

The slowdown in productivity growth has also meant slower growth in real wages and in GDP in the United States since 1973. Figure 12.3 plots real hourly earnings for U.S. workers; it shows that real hourly earnings have fallen since 1973. Total compensation, which includes employee benefits such as health insurance, did continue to rise through the 1980s: Employees received lower wages but higher benefits. But the rate of growth of total compensation was less than the growth of real hourly earnings in the pre-1973 period.

The decrease in the growth of labor productivity was the primary factor behind this pattern of real wages, because wages can rise with a growing labor force only if output per worker continues to increase. What can explain this decrease in the growth rate? Economists are not short of possible answers. The factors, they say, are declines in the education and skills of the workforce, lower levels of investment and, thus, a lower level of capital, less spending on infrastructure (such as highways and bridges), and the belief that managers of companies are more concerned with producing short-term profits than long-term profits, among lots of other economic and sociological factors as well.

Growth accounting has been used to narrow the range of plausible explanations. Using growth accounting methods, economists typically find that the slowdown in labor productivity, in the United States and abroad, cannot be explained by reduced rates of capital deepening. Nor can it be explained by changes in the quality or experience of the labor force. Either a slowdown in technological progress or other factors that are not directly included in the analysis, such as higher worldwide energy prices, must be responsible for the slowdown. Moreover, since the slowdown has been worldwide, it's possible that factors that affect all countries (such as higher energy prices) are responsi-

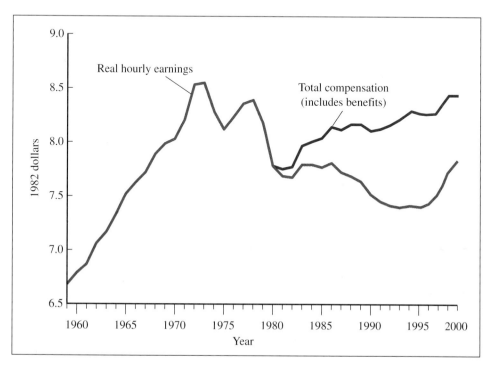

Figure 12.3
Real Hourly Earnings and Total Compensation in the United States

Source: Economic Report of the President (Washington, DC: U.S. Government Printing Office, 2000).

For many years, international organizations such as the World Bank have tried a variety of diverse methods to assist developing countries. These have included increases in foreign aid, infusions of new machinery, promotion of universal education, and efforts to stem population growth. Despite these efforts, some areas of the world, such as Sub-Sahara Africa, have failed to grow at all.

A former World Bank economist, William Easterly, believes that the World Bank and other international organizations have failed to take into account one of the basic laws of economics: individuals and firms respond to incentives.[4] Accordingly to Easterly, governments in developing countries have failed to provide the proper economic environment that would motivate individuals and firms to take actions that promote economic development. As an example, providing free schooling is not enough—individuals need to know that their investments in education will pay off in the future in terms of higher incomes or better jobs. Governments in developing countries often adopt policies that effectively tax exports, pursue policies that lead to rampant inflation, and enforce laws that inhibit the growth of the banking and financial sectors. The results are predictable: fewer exports, an uncertain financial environment, and reduced savings and investment. Sometimes these actions are simply based on bad economic advice. Other times, racial or ethnic groups in polarized societies use the economic system to take advantage of their rivals.

In Easterly's view, the World Bank and other international organizations need to stop searching for the magic bullet for development. Instead, they should hold governments responsible for creating the proper economic environment. With the right incentives, individuals and firms in developing countries will take actions that promote economic growth.

ble rather than factors specific to a single country. Dale Jorgenson, a Harvard economist, has conducted extensive research attempting to link higher energy prices to the slowdown in productivity growth. Not all economists accept this view, however, and the productivity slowdown remains a bit of a mystery.

A New Economy?

As Table 12.3 shows, productivity growth climbed in the last half of the 1990s. Proponents of a "new economy" claimed that the computer and Internet revolution had led to a permanent increase in productivity growth. Skeptics wondered whether this increase in productivity growth was truly permanent or just temporary. Investment in computer technology had proceeded rapidly since the mid-1980s, but until recently there was little sign of increased productivity growth. Had the investment in information technology finally paid off?

Robert J. Gordon of Northwestern University used growth accounting methods to shed light on this issue. After making adjustments for the lower unemployment rate and high GDP growth rate in the late 1990s, he found that there had been increases in technological progress. But he found that these increases were confined to just 12% of the economy, the durable goods manufacturing industry, including the production of computers. Because the increase in technological progress was confined to a relatively small portion of the economy, Gordon was skeptical that we were now operating in a "new economy" with permanently higher productivity growth.

Other economists, also using growth accounting methods, came to different conclusions as they analyzed the data. A study by the President's Council of Economic Advisors found that the increase in technological progress was more widespread throughout the economy, suggesting that more of the increase was likely to be permanent. Unfortunately, economic growth slowed sharply in the United States beginning in 2000. Productivity growth also fell, as customary during slowdowns. Economists will have to wait a number of years until the economy fully recovers to determine if the long-run productivity growth rate has permanently increased.

Although capital deepening and technological progress are keys to growth, other factors are important as well. As "A Closer Look: Getting the Incentives Right" explains, economic growth depends on providing proper incentives for both firms and individuals.

What Causes Technological Progress?

Because technological progress is an important source of growth, we want to know how it occurs and what government policies can do to promote it. Economists have identified a variety of factors that may influence the pace of technological progress in an economy.

Research and Development in Fundamental Science

One way to induce more technological progress in an economy is to pay for it. If the government or large firms employ workers and scientists to advance the frontiers in physics, chemistry, and biology, their work can lead to technological progress in the long run. Figure 12.4 presents data on the spending on research and development as a percent of GDP for each of seven major countries for 1998. Although the United States spends the most in total on research and development, as a percent of GDP it spends less than Japan. Moreover, a big part of U.S. spending on research and development is in defense-related areas, unlike in Japan. The United States has the highest percentage of scientists and engineers in the labor force in the world.

But not all technological progress is "high tech." An employee of a soft-drink company who discovers a new and popular flavor for a soft drink is engaged in technological progress, just as scientists and engineers are.

Monopolies That Spur Innovation

The radical notion that monopolies spur innovation was put forth by economist Joseph Schumpeter. In his view, a firm will try to come up with new products and more efficient ways to produce products only if it reaps a reward. The reward a firm seeks is high profit from its innovations. And high profit can be obtained only if the firm is the sole seller or monopolist for the product. Other firms will try to break its monopoly through more inno-

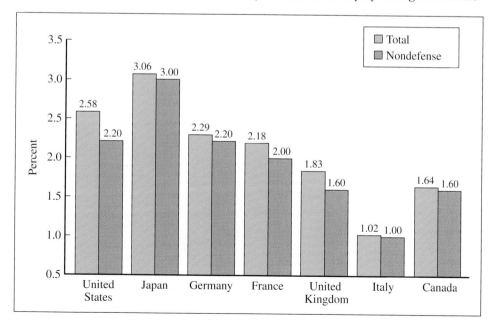

Figure 12.4
Research and Development as a Percentage of GDP, 1998

Source: National Patterns of R&D Resources, 2001, Washington, DC.

Creative destruction: The process by which competition for monopoly profits leads to technological progress.

vation, a process Schumpeter called **creative destruction**. By allowing firms to compete to be monopolies, society benefits from increased innovation.

Governments do allow temporary monopolies for new ideas by issuing patents. A patent allows the inventor of a product to have a monopoly until the term of the patent expires, which in the United States is now 20 years. With a patent, we tolerate some monopoly power (the power to raise prices that comes with limited competition) in the hope of spurring innovation.

A related idea, which is becoming increasingly important in modern society, is the need to protect intellectual property rights. Publishers of both books and computer software face problems of unauthorized copying, particularly in some developing countries. While the residents of those countries clearly benefit from inexpensive copied software or books, the producers of the software and books in the developed countries will face reduced incentives to enter the market. Large and profitable firms with secure domestic markets may continue to produce despite unauthorized copying, but other firms may be discouraged. The United States has put piracy and unauthorized reproduction among its top agenda items in recent trade talks with several countries.

The Scale of the Market

Adam Smith stressed that the size of a market was important for economic development. In larger markets, there are more incentives for firms to come up with new products and new methods of production. Just as Schumpeter suggested, the lure of profits guides the activities of firms, and larger markets enable firms the opportunity to make larger profits. This provides another rationale for free trade. With free trade, markets are larger, and there is more incentive to engage in technological progress.

Induced Innovations

Some economists have emphasized that innovations come about through inventive activity designed specifically to reduce costs. This is known as induced innovation. For example, during the 19th century in the United States, the largest single cost in agriculture was wages. Ingenious farmers and inventors thus came up with many different machines and methods to cut back on the amount of labor required.

Education and the Accumulation of Knowledge

Education can contribute to economic growth in two ways. First, increased knowledge and skills can be a form of investment in human beings that complements our investments in physical capital, as we will see in the next section. Second, education can enable the workforce in an economy to use its skills to develop new ideas or to copy ideas

The rate of return to elementary school education in Africa probably exceeds the rate of return to investment in machines and buildings.

or import them from abroad. Consider a developing country today. In principle, it has at its disposal the vast accumulated knowledge of the developed economies. If it could find a way to tap into this knowledge, it could more quickly and easily adapt their technological progress to its own economies. But this probably requires a broad and skilled workforce—one reason why many developing countries send their best students to educational institutions in developed countries.

For many years, economists who studied technological progress typically did so independently of economists who studied models of economic growth. But starting in the mid-1980s, several economists, including Nobel laureate Robert E. Lucas of the University of Chicago and Paul Romer, now of Stanford University, began to develop models of growth that contained technological progress as an essential feature. Their work helped initiate what is known as **new growth theory**, which accounts for technological progress within a model of economic growth. In this field, economists study, for example, how incentives for research and development, new product development, or international trade interact with the accumulation of physical capital. It enables economists to address policy issues, such as whether subsidies for research and development are socially justified and whether policies that place fewer taxes on income earned from investment will spur economic growth or increase economic welfare. Current research in economic growth now takes place within a broad framework that includes explanation of technological progress.

New growth theory: Modern theories of growth that try to explain the origins of technological progress.

All growth theory today is "new growth theory."

Human Capital

Increasing knowledge and skills can be considered a form of **human capital**—an investment in human beings. Many economists, including Nobel laureate Gary Becker of the University of Chicago, have studied this in detail.

Human capital: Investment in education and skills.

A classic example of human capital is the investment a student makes to attend college. The costs of attending college consist of the direct out-of-pocket costs (tuition and fees) plus the opportunity costs of forgone earnings. The benefits of attending college are the higher wages and more interesting jobs offered to college graduates as compared to high school graduates. Individuals decide to attend college because these benefits exceed the costs, and it is a rational economic decision. A similar calculation faces a newly graduated doctor who must decide whether to pursue a specialty. Will the forgone earnings of a general physician (which are quite substantial) be worth the time spent learning a specialty that will eventually result in extra income? Investments in health and nutrition can be analyzed within the same framework.

Human capital theory has two implications for understanding economic growth.

First, not all labor is equal. When economists measure the labor input in a country, they must adjust for differing levels of education. These levels of education reflect past investments in education and skills; individuals with higher educational levels will, on average, be more productive.

Second, health and fitness also affect productivity. In developing countries, economists have found that there is a strong correlation between the height of individuals and the wages that they can earn in the farming sector. At the same time, increases in income through economic growth have led to sharp increases in height and weight, as "A Closer Look: Our Tiny Ancestors" explains.

Human capital theory can also serve as a basis for important public-policy decisions. Should a developing country invest in capital (either public or private) or in education? The poorest developing countries lack many things: good sanitation systems, effective transportation systems, and capital investment for agriculture and industry. However, the best use of investment funds may be not for bridges, sewer systems, and roads but for human capital and education. Studies demonstrate that the returns from investing

As you may have seen in a museum, men and women have grown taller and heavier in the last 300 years. As an example, an average American male adult today stands at approximately 5'10", nearly 4.5 inches taller than the typical Englishman in the late 18th century. Body weights are also substantially higher today. According to Nobel laureate Robert Fogel of the University of Chicago, the average weight of English males in their 30s was about 134 pounds in 1790— 20% below today's average. A typical Frenchman in his 30s at that time weighed only 110 pounds!

Fogel has argued that these lower weights and heights reflected inadequate food supplies and chronic malnutrition. Not only did lower food supplies lead to smaller physical stature, but they also led to a higher incidence of chronic disease. Fogel estimated that the chronic malnutrition caused by limited food supplies at those times limited labor productivity. In France, 20% of the labor force lacked enough physical energy to put in more than three hours of light work a day. A high percentage of workers in the society were too frail and ill to contribute much to national output.

Economic growth produced a "virtuous" circle. It increased food supplies, enabling workers to become more productive and increase GDP even more.

in education are extremely high in developing countries. The gains from elementary and secondary education, in particular, often exceed the gains from more conventional investments. In developing countries, a person having an extra year in school can often raise his or her wages by 15% to 20% a year.

The returns for investing in the education of females in developing countries are often higher than those for men. This is particularly true in the poorest countries, where female literacy rates are often less than 10%. Women's health in developing countries is closely tied to their education. Education promotes not only productivity but basic social development as well. For these reasons, the World Bank has focused attention on the crucial role that increased female education can play in promoting economic development.

As you see, human capital analysis is a valuable tool for understanding economic growth.

TEST Your Understanding

9. Technological progress means that we produce more output without using any additional inputs. True or false? Explain.

10. Explain how economists estimate the contribution of technological change to the growth of output.

11. Who invented the theory of creative destruction?

12. Define human capital.

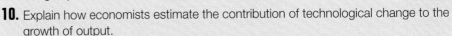

Using the TOOLS

In this chapter, we studied what affects economic growth. Here are some opportunities to do your own economic analysis.

1. Shorten the Length of Patents?

A group of consumer activists claims that drug companies earn excessive profits because of the patents they have on drugs. The activists advocate cutting to five years the length of time that a drug company can hold a patent. They argue this will lead to lower prices for drugs because competitors will enter the market after the five-year period. Do you see any drawbacks to this proposal?

2. Capital Deepening
Which of the following will promote economic growth through capital deepening?

a. Higher taxes used to finance universal health care

b. Increased imports to purchase new VCRs for consumers

c. Increased imports to purchase supercomputers for industry

3. Future Generations
Some economists say that economic growth involves a trade-off between current generations and future generations. If a current generation raises its saving rate, what does it sacrifice? What will be gained for future generations?

4. Will the Poorer Country Catch Up?
Suppose one country has a GDP that is one-eighth the GDP of its richer neighbor. But the poorer country grows at 10% a year, while the richer country grows at 2% a year. In 35 years, which country will have a higher GDP? (Hint: Use the rule of 70.)

Summary

In this chapter, we explored the mechanisms of economic growth. Although economists do not have a complete understanding of what leads to growth, they regard increases in capital per worker, technological progress, and human capital as key factors. In this chapter, we discussed these factors in detail. Here are the main points to remember:

1. There are vast differences in per capita GDP throughout the world. There is debate about whether poorer countries in the world are converging in per capita incomes with richer countries.

2. Economies grow through two basic mechanisms: capital deepening and technological progress.

Capital deepening is an increase in capital per worker. Technological progress is an increase in output with no additional increases in inputs.

3. Ongoing technological progress will lead to sustained economic growth.

4. A variety of theories try to explain the origins of technological progress and determine how we can promote it. They include spending on research and development, creative destruction, the scale of the market, induced inventions, and education and the accumulation of knowledge.

5. Investments in human capital are an important component of economic growth.

Key Terms

capital deepening, 274
convergence, 276
creative destruction, 286
growth accounting, 281

growth rate, 274
human capital, 287
labor productivity, 282
new growth theory, 287

real GDP per capita, 274
rule of 70, 275
saving, 278
technological progress, 274

Problems and Discussion Questions

1. If a country's GDP grows at 3% per year, how many years will it take for GDP to increase by a factor of four?

2. The growth rate of real GDP per capita equals the growth rate of real GDP minus the growth rate of the population. If the growth rate of population is

1% per year, how fast must real GDP grow for real GDP per capita to double in 14 years?

3. True or False: There is very strong evidence that poor countries are closing the gap with rich countries.

4. Explain why the expansion of markets from free trade can lead to increased technological innovation.

5. If we cannot measure every invention or new idea, how can we possibly measure the contribution to growth of technological progress?

6. Some economists argue that we have entered a "new economy" with permanently higher productivity growth. How can growth accounting be used to evaluate this claim?

7. Suppose a government places a 10% tax on incomes and spends half of the money from taxes on investment and half on a public consumption good such as military parades. Individuals save 20% of their income and consume the rest. Does total investment (public and private) increase or decrease in this case?

8. The United States ran large trade deficits during the 1980s and 1990s. How would you determine whether these trade deficits led to increased or decreased capital deepening?

9. Economic historians have found that the average height of individuals in both the United States and the United Kingdom fell during the mid-19th century before rising again. This was a period of rapid industrialization as well as migration into urban areas and foreign immigration. Incomes appeared to continue to rise. What factors do you think might account for this fall in height and how would it affect your evaluation of economic welfare during the period?

10. Most law students tend to be in their 20s and 30s, rather than in their 40s. Explain this phenomenon, using the idea of investment in human capital.

11. Web Exercise. The Web site for the National Bureau of Economic Research (*www.nber.org*) contains links to online data, including the Penn World Tables. Using these links, compare the relative growth performance for real GDP of Italy, Great Britain, and France (or other countries) over a period of your choice.

12. Web Exercise. Using the Web site for the World Bank (*www.worldbank.org*), prepare a short paper on prospects and barriers for economic growth in Africa.

Take It to the Net

We invite you to visit the O'Sullivan/Sheffrin page on the Prentice Hall Web site at: **www.prenhall.com/osullivan/** for additional World Wide Web exercises for this chapter.

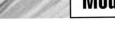

Model Answers to Questions

Chapter-Opening Questions

1. Countries with the highest standard of living today include the United States, Luxembourg, Japan, and Germany.

2. Countries with higher savings rates can grow faster for some period of time, although the growth of per capita income in the long run is determined by the rate of technical progress.

3. A trade deficit that is used to finance investment can lead to higher growth; however, a trade deficit that is used to finance consumption will allow higher consumption now but will reduce consumption in the future.

4. Technological progress depends on a number of factors, including research and development, the process of creative destruction, the scale of the market, induced innovations, and education and the accumulation of knowledge.

Test Your Understanding

1. We use per capita real GDP.

2. Nontraded goods are relatively cheaper in developing countries.

3. True. Developing countries have not caught up to developed countries.

4. It would take 35 years (70/2).

5. Output is divided into consumption and investment. Output also equals income. Income is either consumed or saved. Therefore, saving must equal investment.

6. Total output increases, while per capita output falls.

7. $180. Government investment is $200; but with a saving rate of 10%, the $200 in taxes reduces private saving (and private investment) by $20.

8. True. Without using the trade deficit to increase investment, consumption must fall in the future.

9. True. Technological progress means more output without additional inputs.

10. The contribution from technological progress is estimated by determining how much of the growth in output cannot be explained by the growth in inputs.

11. Joseph Schumpeter.

12. Human capital includes investments in education and skills.

Using the Tools

1. Shorten the Length of Patents? The drawback to the proposal is that the shorter patent life will reduce the incentive of drug companies to invest in the discovery of new drugs. As Schumpeter emphasized, firms need incentives in the form of monopoly profits to engage in long-term research. However, prices are clearly higher as long as a single firm has a patent.

2. Capital Deepening. Only c, increased imports to purchase supercomputers for industry, adds to capital deepening. The others will not increase the stock of capital.

3. Future Generations. A country that increases its saving rate must cut back on its consumption. The long-run benefit will be a higher stock of capital for future generations. The current generation, however, will have to make a sacrifice, in terms of reduced consumption, to provide the additional capital. Therefore, there will be a trade-off in consumption between the present generation and future generations.

4. Will the Poorer Country Catch Up? After 35 years, GDP in the initially poorer country will exceed the GDP of its slower-growing neighbor. Because the poorer country grows at 10% a year, the rule of 70 implies that its GDP doubles every seven years. In 35 years, its GDP will have doubled five times. This means that its GDP will have grown by a factor of 32 over the 35-year period. According to the rule of 70, the richer country, growing at 2% a year, will only double its GDP in 35 years. This implies that the country that was poorer initially will have a higher level of GDP after 35 years, even though it started at one-eighth the level of the richer country. To see this, suppose that the poorer country had a GDP of one and the richer country had a GDP of eight. After 35 years, the initially poorer country would now have a GDP of 32, while the initially richer country would have a GDP of 16.

Notes

1. Stanley Lebergott, *The Americans* (New York: W. W. Norton, 1984), pp. 65–68.

2. Alwyn Young, "A Tale of Two Cities: Factor Accumulation and Technical Change in Hong Kong and Singapore," in *NBER Macroeconomic Annual 1992*, edited by Olivier Blanchard and Stanley Fischer (Cambridge, MA: MIT Press 1992); pp. 1–53.

3. Zvi Grilliches, "Productivity Puzzles and R&D: Another Nonexplanation," *Journal of Economic Perspectives*, vol. 2, fall 1988, pp. 9–21.

4. William Easterly, *The Elusive Quest for Growth: Economists' Adventures and Misadventures in the Tropics* (Cambridge, MA: MIT Press, 2002).

Aggregate Demand and Aggregate Supply

Economic times were good in the 1990s in the United States. But the 1930s were a different story. During the Great Depression, nearly one-fourth of the labor force was unemployed. Unemployed workers could not buy goods and services. Factories were shut down because there was little or no demand for their products. As factories shut down, more workers became unemployed. How could this destructive chain of cause and effect be stopped and turned around? Why were the 1930s so different from the 1990s? What steps can we take to prevent the first decade of the twenty-first century from resembling the 1930s?

conomies do not always operate at full employment, nor do they always grow smoothly. At times, real GDP grows at a rate below its long-run trend or falls steeply, as it did in the Great Depression. Recessions and excess unemployment occur when real GDP falls. At other times, GDP grows too rapidly, and unemployment falls below the natural rate of unemployment. When real GDP grows too fast, the result is an increase in the rate of inflation. Real GDP growth that is too slow and real GDP growth that is too fast are examples of **economic fluctuations**, movements of GDP away from full employment. Economic fluctuations, also called **business cycles**, are the focus of this chapter.

Economic fluctuations: Movements of real GDP above or below normal trends.

Business cycles: Another name for economic fluctuations.

After studying this chapter, you will be able to answer the following questions:

1. How do we define a recession?
2. Why doesn't the economy always operate at full employment?
3. Why can a sharp decrease in government spending cause a recession?
4. How do changes in the demand for goods and services affect prices and output in the short run and in the long run?

Let's begin by getting familiar with the terms we use when we talk about economic fluctuations.

During the Great Depression, there was a failure in coordination. Factories would have produced more output and hired more workers if there had been more demand for their products. If that had happened, the additionally employed workers would have been able to demand and afford to buy the additional goods that the factories produced.

Insufficient demand for goods and services was a key problem, identified by John Maynard Keynes, during the Great Depression. Since then, economists have viewed real GDP as determined by demand in the short run, when these coordination problems are most pronounced. We will make clear that the short run in macroeconomics is the time when prices do not fully adjust to changes in demand. In the next several chapters, we will be analyzing models based on the idea that demand determines output in the short run.

In the long run, underlying economic forces push the economy back toward full employment. When the economy is at full employment, that does not mean there are no unemployed workers. Recall the distinction between frictional, structural, and cyclical unemployment in Chapter 11. Full employment means that there is no cyclical unemployment, only frictional and structural unemployment.

The level of output in the economy when it operates at full employment is called **potential output**. Later in this chapter, we describe the economic forces that bring the economy back to full employment and potential output in the long run.

Potential output: The level of output in the economy when it is at full employment.

In this chapter, we develop tools for analyzing economic fluctuations in both the short run and the long run. We introduce the aggregate demand and aggregate supply curves, which will assist us in understanding some aspects of business cycles. The aggregate demand and aggregate supply curves will set the stage for our investigations of economic fluctuations in later chapters.

Business Cycles and Economic Fluctuations

To begin our study of economic fluctuations, let's look at data on real GDP at the end of the 1980s and the early 1990s. Figure 13.1 plots real GDP for the United States from 1988 to 1992. Notice that in mid-1990, real GDP begins to fall. A **recession** is a period when real GDP falls for six or more consecutive months. Economists talk more in terms of quarters of the year—consecutive three-month periods—than in terms of months. So they would say that when real GDP falls for two consecutive quarters, that's a recession. The date at which the recession starts, when output starts to decline, is called the **peak**; and the date

Recession: Six consecutive months of negative economic growth.

Peak: The time at which a recession begins.

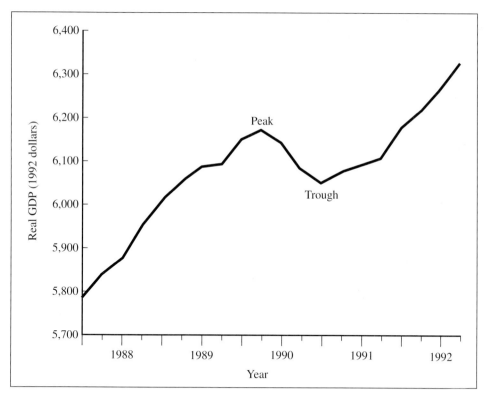

Figure 13.1
**The 1990
Recession**

Source: U.S. Department of
Commerce.

at which the recession is considered to have begun to end, when output starts to increase again, is called the **trough**. In Figure 13.1, we see the peak and trough of the recession. After a trough, the economy enters a recovery period, or period of **expansion**.

Since World War II, the United States has experienced ten recessions. Table 13.1 contains the dates of the peaks and troughs of each recession as well as the percent decline in real GDP from each peak to each trough. The sharpest decline in output

Trough: The time at which output stops falling in a recession.

Expansion: The period from a trough to the next peak of a business cycle.

Table 13.1   Ten Postwar Recessions

Peak	Trough	Percent Decline in Real GDP
November 1948	October 1949	1.5
July 1953	May 1954	3.2
August 1957	April 1958	3.3
April 1960	February 1961	1.2
December 1969	November 1970	1.0
November 1973	March 1975	4.9
January 1980	July 1980	2.5
July 1981	November 1982	3.0
July 1990	March 1991	1.4
March 2001	November 2001	1.6

occurred during the recession from 1973 to 1975, which started as a result of a sharp rise in worldwide oil prices. In the last two decades of the twentieth century, there were two recessions—one starting in 1981 and the other in 1990.

The twenty-first century started off with a recession. Economic growth slowed considerably in 2001 and employment began to fall in March. With the economy already in a weakened state, the terrorist attack on September 11, 2001, disrupted economic activity, damaged producer and consumer confidence, and plunged the economy into a recession.

Throughout the broader sweep of U.S. history, there have been other periods of downturns—20 of them from 1860 up to World War II. Not all of these were particularly severe, and in some, unemployment hardly changed. However, there were economic downturns, such as those in 1893 and 1929, that were severe.

Depression: The common name for a severe recession.

Depression is the common term for a severe recession. In the United States, the Great Depression refers to 1929 through 1933, the period when real GDP fell by more than 33%. It created the most severe disruptions to ordinary economic life in the United States during the twentieth century. Throughout the country and in much of the world, banks closed, businesses failed, and many people lost their jobs and their life savings. Unemployment rose sharply. In 1933, more than 25% of people who were looking for work failed to find jobs.

Although the United States has not experienced a depression since that time, other countries have. During the late 1980s and 1990s, several Asian countries and several Latin American countries suffered severe economic disruptions that were true depressions.

Although the definition of recessions focuses on the behavior of real GDP, other important economic measures follow the behavior of output. In particular, unemployment rises sharply during recessions. Figure 13.2 plots the unemployment rate for 1965 to 1996. The periods of recessions are marked on the graph with shaded bars. As you can see in the graph, unemployment rises sharply during recessions. For example, during the 1990 recession, the unemployment rate rose from 5.5% to 7.5% before beginning to turn downward.

Figure 13.2
The Unemployment Rate During Recessions
Shaded bars are recessions according to NBER (National Bureau of Economic Research) business cycle reference dates.

Source: Bureau of Labor Statistics, Department of Labor.

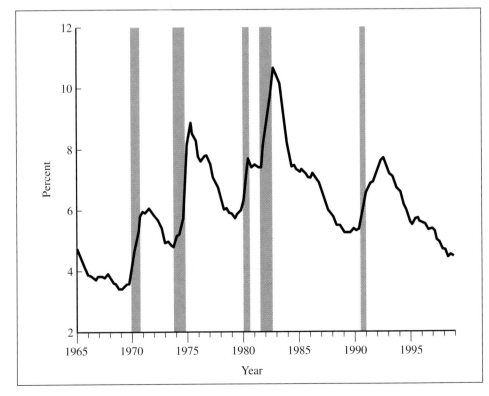

The relationship between changes in real GDP and corresponding changes in unemployment is called **Okun's law**. To understand Okun's law, we first need to remember that potential GDP typically grows over time. The average rate of potential GDP growth is called the trend rate of growth. Okun's law states that for every percentage point that real GDP grows faster than the normal rate of increase in potential output, the unemployment rate falls by 0.5 percentage point. For example, suppose the trend rate of growth of real GDP is 3% per year and the current unemployment rate is 5% of the total labor force. If real GDP then grows at 4% for a year (1 percentage point above trend), the unemployment rate will fall by 0.5 percentage point, to 4.5%. If real GDP grew at only 2% per year (1 percentage point below trend), the unemployment rate would rise to 5.5%. Okun's law provides a link between real GDP growth and the unemployment rate.

Other economic measures also rise and fall along with real GDP. Both investment spending and consumption spending rise and fall along with increases and decreases in real GDP. The prices of shares of stocks also tend to rise and fall as real GDP goes up and down. We use the term **procyclical** to describe economic measures that move in conjunction with real GDP. Thus, investment spending, consumption spending, and prices of stocks are all procyclical. Economic measures that fall as real GDP rises are known as **countercyclical**. Unemployment, for example, is countercyclical.

Be sure you understand that when economists say "business cycle," they are not referring to a regularly recurring cycle, such as phases of the moon, the rotation of the seasons, or the appearance of 17-year locusts. There are no fixed time intervals between recessions, as you can see in Table 13.1. During the 1960s and the 1990s, there were long periods without economic downturns. Yet there were two back-to-back recessions in the early 1980s.

Moreover, recessions tend to be unpredictable. After a recession has occurred, we can sometimes pinpoint its possible causes: either external shocks to the economy (such as sharp increases in the world price of oil) or changes in economic policy (such as sharp decreases in government spending). And the stock market always plunges sharply during recessions. But the wise men and women of Wall Street never anticipate the precise timing of an economic downturn.

Although we have focused on recessions, don't forget that a sustained period during which economic growth is too rapid can also damage the economy. Whereas an economy can operate for a time beyond its level of potential output, if output stays above potential output for too long a time, it will also be disruptive to the economy. When real GDP grows faster than its trend rate of growth, unemployment will fall. When the unemployment rate falls sufficiently below the natural rate of unemployment, the result will be an increase in the inflation rate for the economy.

This is why good economic policy tries to avoid both unnecessary downturns and recessions as well as prolonged booms that reduce unemployment below the natural rate. Whether we have become more successful in recent years in reducing economic fluctuations is a subject of current debate, as we discuss in "A Closer Look: Is the Economy More Stable Today?"

Okun's law: A relationship between changes in real GDP and the unemployment rate.

Procyclical: Economic measures moving in the same direction as real GDP.

Countercyclical: Economic measures moving in the opposite direction of real GDP.

TEST Your Understanding

1. A recession occurs when growth is negative for _____ months in a row.

2. Since the unemployment rate rises when output falls, we say that unemployment is _____.

3. The highest level of output before a recession is known as the _____.

4. After a business cycle trough, the _____ phase begins.

Sticky Prices and Demand-Side Economics

Economic fluctuations can occur for a variety of reasons. One reason is that large shocks sometimes hit the economy. Consider a few examples. A developing country that is highly dependent on agriculture can suffer a loss of its cash crop if there is prolonged drought. Sharp increases in the price of oil can hurt modern economies that use oil in production, as was the case in both 1973 and 1979. Wars can devastate entire regions of the world, and natural disasters, such as earthquakes or floods, can cause sharp reductions in GDP.

Economic fluctuations can also occur because a number of small shocks all hit the economy at the same time. For example, a country that primarily produces tea might face a sudden shift of consumer preferences throughout the world to coffee. Or a series of small improvements to technology in a variety of industries could cause output to rise. One school of thought known as **real business cycle theory** emphasizes the role that shocks to technology can play in causing economic fluctuations.

Real business cycle theory: An economic theory that emphasizes how shocks to technology can cause fluctuations in economic activity.

But other economists suggest that recessions may not be simply caused by bad luck or external shocks. John Maynard Keynes and many economists since have identified difficulties in coordinating economic affairs as providing the starting point for understanding fluctuations in economic activity.

Normally, the price system is the mechanism that coordinates what goes on in an economy, even in a complex economy. In microeconomics, we learn that the price system helps coordinate who does what, what resources to use, how much to make, from whom to buy, and so on, so that the economy produces as efficiently as possible. Prices give the correct signals to all producers in the economy so that resources are used efficiently and without waste. If consumers decide to consume fresh fruit rather than chocolate, the price of fresh fruit will rise and the price of chocolate will fall. The economy will produce more fresh fruit and less chocolate on the basis of these price signals.

On a day-to-day basis, the price system works silently in the background, matching the desires of consumers with the output from producers.

But the price system does not always work instantaneously. If prices are slow to adjust, then the proper signals are not given quickly enough to producers and consumers. Demands and supplies will not be brought immediately into equilibrium, and coordination can break down.

In modern economies, some prices are very flexible, while others are not. Arthur Okun, the economist who came up with Okun's law, distinguished between auction prices, prices that adjust on a nearly daily basis, and custom prices, prices that adjust slowly. Prices for fresh fish, vegetables, and other food products are examples of auction prices—they are typically very flexible and adjust rapidly. Prices for industrial commodities such as steel rods or machine tools are custom prices and tend to adjust slowly to changes in demand. As shorthand, economists often refer to slowly adjusting prices as sticky prices (just like a door that won't open immediately but sometimes gets stuck).

Wages, the price of labor, adjust very slowly. Workers often have long-term contracts that do not allow employers to change workers' wages at all during a given year. Union workers, university professors, high-school teachers, and employees of state and local governments are all groups whose wages adjust very slowly. As a general rule, there are very few workers in the economy whose wages change quickly. Perhaps movie stars, athletes, and rock stars are the exceptions; their wages rise and fall with their popularity. But they are far from the typical worker in the economy. Even unskilled, low-wage workers are often protected from decreases in their wages by minimum-wage laws.

Because prices and wages are sticky over short periods, prices do not fully do the job of bringing demands and supplies into balance over short periods of time.

Typically, firms such as automobile manufacturers and steel firms let demand determine the level of output in the short run. To understand this idea, consider an automobile firm that buys material from a steelmaker on a regular basis. Because the auto firm and the steel producer have been in business with one another for a long time and have an ongoing relationship, they have negotiated a contract that keeps steel prices fixed in the short run.

Suppose that the automobile company's cars suddenly become very popular. The firm needs to expand production, so it needs more steel. Under their agreement, the steel company would meet this higher demand for its product and sell more steel—without raising its price—to the automobile company. So the production of steel is totally determined in the short run by the demand from automobile producers, not by price.

But what if the automaker discovered that it had produced an unpopular car and needed to cut back on its planned production? The firm would require less steel. Under the agreement, the steelmaker would supply less steel but not reduce its price. Again, demand, not price, determines steel production in the short run.

Similar agreements between firms, both formal and informal, exist throughout the economy. Typically, in the short run, firms will meet changes in the demand for their products by adjusting production with only small changes in the prices they charge their customers.

What we have just illustrated for an input such as steel applies in the same way to workers as inputs to production. Suppose that the automobile firm hires union workers under a contract that fixes their wages for a specific period. If the economy suddenly thrives at some point during that period, the automobile company will employ all the workers and perhaps require some to work overtime. If the economy stagnates at some point during that period, the firm will lay off some workers, using only part of the union labor force. In either case, wages will not change during the period of the contract.

Over longer periods of time, prices do change. Suppose the automobile company's car remains popular for a long time. The steel company and the automobile company will adjust the price of steel on their contract to reflect this increased demand. These price adjustments occur only over long periods; in the short run, demand, not prices, determines output, and prices are slow to adjust. The **short run in macroeconomics** is the period when prices do not change or don't change very much. In the macroeconomic short run, demand determines output.

In the long run, prices adjust fully to changes in demand. But over short periods, both formal and informal contracts between firms mean that changes in demand will be reflected primarily in changes in output, not prices.

Short run in macroeconomics: The period of time in which prices do not change very much.

Aggregate Demand and Aggregate Supply

We now develop the graphical tool known as the aggregate demand and aggregate supply model. We consider aggregate demand and aggregate supply to understand how output and prices are determined in both the short run and the long run. We will be able to do that because we will consider two types of aggregate supply curves: one for the long run and one for the short run.

Aggregate Demand

The **aggregate demand curve** plots the total demand for GDP as a function of price level. The **price level** is the average level of prices in the economy as measured by a price index, such as the GDP deflator or the CPI. For each price level, we ask what the total quantity demanded will be for all goods and services in the economy. In Figure 13.3, the aggre-

Aggregate demand curve: The relationship between the level of prices and the quantity of real GDP demanded.

Price level: The average level of prices in the economy as measured by a price index, such as the GDP deflator or the CPI.

Prices for industrial commodities adjust slowly to changes in demand.

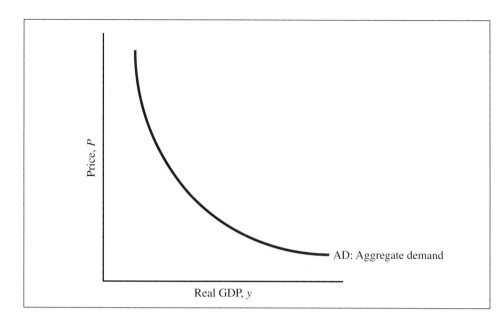

Figure 13.3
Aggregate Demand
The aggregate demand curve plots the total demand for real GDP as a function of the price level. The aggregate demand curve slopes downward, indicating that aggregate demand increases as the price level falls.

gate demand curve is downward sloping. As the price level falls, the total quantity demanded for goods and services increases. To understand what the aggregate demand curve represents, we must first learn the components of aggregate demand, why the aggregate demand curve is downward sloping, and the factors that can shift the aggregate demand curve.

Components of Aggregate Demand

In our study of GDP accounting, we divided GDP into four components: consumption spending, investment spending, government purchases, and net exports. These four components are also the four parts of aggregate demand. Because the aggregate demand curve describes the demand or desired spending for total GDP, we can, therefore, think of the demand for total GDP as coming from four basic sources.

Sources of Aggregate Demand—Desired Spending By:

consumers (consumption spending)

firms (investment spending)

government (government purchases of goods and services)

foreign sector (net exports)

As we will see, changes in the demand coming from any of these four sources will shift the aggregate demand curve.

The Slope of the Aggregate Demand Curve

To understand the slope of the aggregate demand curve, let's consider the supply of money in the economy. We discuss the supply of money in detail in later chapters, but for now, just think of the supply of money as being the total amount of currency (cash plus coins) held by the public and the value of all deposits in checking accounts in the economy. If you have $100 in cash and $900 in your checking account, you have $1,000 of money.

As the price level or average level of prices in the economy changes, so does the purchasing power of your money. This is an example of the reality principle:

Reality **PRINCIPLE**

What matters to people is the real value or purchasing power of money or income, not the face value of money or income.

The change in the purchasing power of money will affect aggregate demand—or total demand for all goods and sevices in the economy. As the price level falls, the purchasing power of money will increase, and your $1,000 can purchase more goods and services. As the price level falls, increasing the purchasing power of money, people find that they are wealthier. With increased wealth, people want to increase their spending on goods and services. And so the quantity demanded for goods and services will increase as the price level falls. This means that the aggregate demand curve is downward sloping.

When the price level increases, the real value of money decreases, reducing wealth and, thus, reducing the total demand for goods and services. And so as the price level increases, total demand for goods and services in the economy decreases.

The increase in spending that occurs when the real value of money increases when the price level falls is known as the **wealth effect**. This is one reason the aggregate demand curve slopes downward. Lower prices lead to higher levels of wealth. Higher levels of wealth increase spending on total goods and services.

There are two other reasons why the aggregate demand curve is downward sloping: one has to do with interest rates, and the other has to do with international trade.

First, consider the interest rate effect. With a given supply of money in the economy, a lower price level will lead to lower interest rates. As interest rates fall, the demand for investment goods in the economy (both investment by firms and consumer durables by households) will increase. We'll explain this in detail in later chapters.

Second, consider the effects from international trade. In an open economy, a lower price level will mean that domestic goods become cheaper relative to foreign goods, so the demand for domestic goods will increase. Moreover, as we will see, lower interest rates will affect the exchange rate to make domestic goods become relatively cheaper than foreign goods. The wealth effect, the interest rate effect, and the effects from international trade reinforce one another, leading to the downward sloping aggregate demand curve in Figure 13.3.

Wealth effect: The increase in spending because the real value of money increases when the price level falls.

Factors That Shift the Aggregate Demand Curve

Different factors can shift the aggregate demand curve. At any price level, an increase in aggregate demand means that total demand by all sectors of the economy for all the goods and services contained in real GDP has increased, and the curve shifts to the right. Factors that decrease aggregate demand will shift the aggregate demand curve to the left. At any price level, a decrease in aggregate demand means that total demand for the goods and services contained in real GDP has decreased.

Let's look at the key factors that shift the aggregate demand curve:

- Changes in the supply of money. An increase in the supply of money in the economy will increase aggregate demand and shift the aggregate demand curve to the right. We know that an increase in the supply of money will lead to higher demand by both consumers and firms. At any given price level, a larger supply of money will mean more consumer wealth and an increased demand for goods and services. A decrease in the supply of money will decrease aggregate demand and shift the aggregate demand curve to the left. (We will discuss the money supply and aggregate demand further in later chapters.)

- Changes in taxes. A decrease in taxes will increase aggregate demand and shift the aggregate demand curve to the right. Lower taxes will increase income available to households and increase their spending on goods and services. Aggregate demand will increase as taxes are decreased. For opposite reasons, increases in taxes will decrease aggregate demand and shift the aggregate demand curve to the left. (We will discuss taxes and aggregate demand further in the next chapter.)

- Changes in government spending. An increase in government spending will increase aggregate demand and shift the aggregate demand curve to the right. Because the government is a source of demand for goods and services, higher government spending naturally leads to an increase in total demand for goods and services. Similarly, decreases in government spending will decrease aggregate demand and shift the curve to the left. (We will discuss government spending and aggregate demand further in the next chapter.)

- Other factors. Any change in demand from households, firms, or the foreign sector will also change aggregate demand. For example, if the Japanese economy expands very rapidly and the Japanese buy more U.S. goods, our aggregate demand will increase. Similarly, if firms become optimistic about the future and increase their investment spending, aggregate demand will also increase.

When we discuss factors that shift aggregate demand, we must not include any changes in the demand for goods and services that arise from movements in the price level. Changes in aggregate demand that accompany changes in the price level are already included in the curve and do not shift the curve. The increase in consumer spending that occurs from the wealth effect when the price level falls is included in the curve and does not shift the curve.

Both Figure 13.4 and Table 13.2 summarize our discussion. Decreases in taxes, increases in government spending, and increases in the supply of money all shift the aggregate demand curve to the right. Increases in taxes, decreases in government spending, and decreases in the supply of money shift it to the left. In general, any increase in demand (not brought about by a change in the price level) will shift the curve to the right. Decreases in demand shift it to the left.

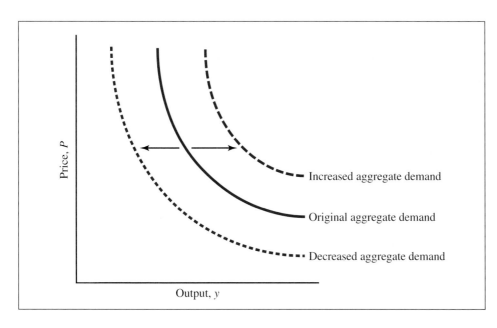

Figure 13.4

Shifting Aggregate Demand

Decreases in taxes, increases in government spending, and an increase in the supply of money all shift the aggregate demand curve to the right. Higher taxes, lower government spending, and a lower supply of money shift the curve to the left.

Table 13.2 Factors That Shift Demand

Factors That Increase Aggregate Demand	Factors That Decrease Aggregate Demand
Decrease in taxes	Increase in taxes
Increase in government spending	Decrease in government spending
Increase in money supply	Decrease in money supply

Aggregate Supply

Aggregate supply curve: The relationship between the level of prices and the quantity of output supplied.

The **aggregate supply curve** depicts the relationship between the level of prices and real GDP. We will develop two different aggregate supply curves: one corresponding to the long run and one to the short run.

The Long-Run Aggregate Supply Curve

Long-run aggregate supply curve: A vertical aggregate supply curve. It reflects the idea that in the long run, output is determined solely by the factors of production.

First we'll consider the aggregate supply curve for the long run, that is, when the economy is at full employment; we call it the **long-run aggregate supply curve**. The level of full-employment output, which we denote by y^*, depends solely on the supply factors—capital and labor—and the state of technology. Once the economy is at full employment, the level of output that can be produced with the workers who are employed just depends on the amount of capital that is available in the economy and the state of technology. These are precisely the factors we highlighted in our discussion of long-run economic growth in the last chapter. Capital and technology are the fundamental factors that determine output in the long run, that is, when the economy operates at full employment.

The level of full-employment output does not depend on the level of prices in the economy, just on the supply factors and the state of technology. Because the level of full-employment output does not depend on the price level, we can plot the long-run aggregate supply curve as a vertical line (unaffected by the price level), as in Figure 13.5.

We combine the aggregate demand curve and the long-run aggregate supply curve in Figure 13.6. Given an aggregate demand curve and an aggregate supply curve, their

Figure 13.5
Long-Run Aggregate Supply
In the long run, the level of output y^* is independent of the price level.

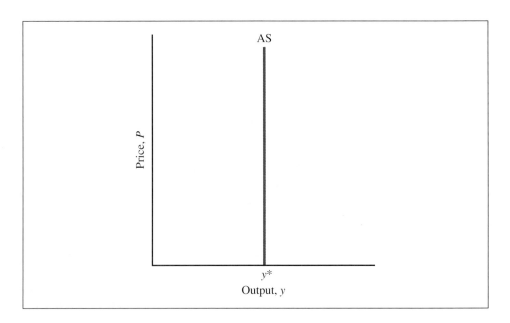

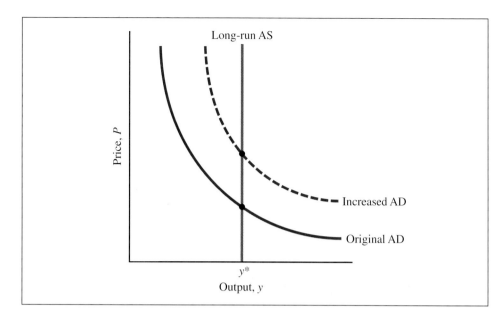

Figure 13.6
Aggregate Demand and Long-Run Aggregate Supply
Output and prices are determined at the intersection of AD and AS. An increase in aggregate demand leads to a higher price level.

intersection determines the price level and level of output. At that intersection point, the total amount demanded will just equal the total amount supplied. The position of the aggregate demand curve will depend on the level of taxes, government spending, and the supply of money. The level of full-employment output determines the long-run aggregate supply curve.

An increase in aggregate demand (perhaps brought about by a tax cut or an increase in the supply of money) will shift the aggregate demand curve to the right, as in Figure 13.6. With a long-run aggregate supply curve, the increase in aggregate demand will raise prices but leave the level of output unchanged. In general, shifts in the aggregate demand curve when we have a long-run supply curve do not change the level of output in the economy but only change the level of prices. That is, an increase in demand when we have a long-run supply curve will only raise the average level of prices in the economy but not change the level of real output.

In the long run, output is determined solely by the supply of capital and the supply of labor. As our model of the aggregate demand curve with the long-run aggregate supply curve indicates, changes in demand will affect only prices, not the level of output.

This result has important implications. In particular, in the long run, increases in government spending do not increase the level of output. But if the level of output remains the same and government spending increases, some other component of demand (consumption, investment, or net exports) must decrease. (Recall that GDP is the sum of consumption, investment, government purchases, and net exports.) The term **crowding out** refers to any decrease in consumption, investment, or net exports that occurs when there is an increase in government spending. In the long-run model, government spending will crowd out one of these components of demand.

Crowding out in the long-run model is an example of the principle of opportunity cost:

Crowding Out: The reduction in consumption, investment, or net exports caused by an increase in government spending.

PRINCIPLE of Opportunity Cost

The opportunity cost of something is what you sacrifice to get it.

For example, if government spending increases, the society will enjoy the benefits of the spending. But if it crowds out investment spending, the society will also be investing less

Figure 13.7

Increased Government Spending Crowds Out Consumption

Source: U.S. Department of Commerce.

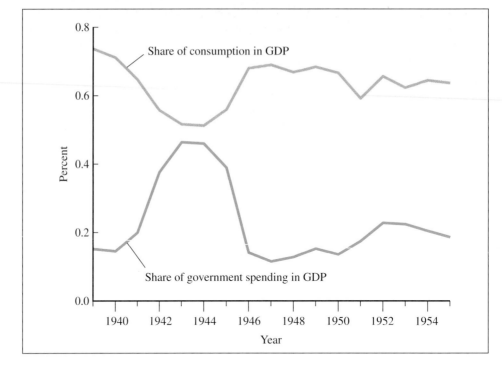

for the future. If the increase in government spending crowds out private consumption, then consumers will sacrifice their own private consumption goods.

As a historical example of crowding out, consider World War II. As Figure 13.7 indicates, as the share of government spending increased sharply during the war, the share of consumption spending fell as well. A similar pattern occurred for investment spending.

Short-run aggregate supply curve: A relatively flat supply curve. It reflects the idea that prices do not change very much in the short run and that firms adjust production to meet demand.

The Short-Run Aggregate Supply Curve

In the short run, prices are sticky (slow to adjust), and output is determined primarily by demand. We can use the aggregate demand curve combined with a **short-run aggregate supply curve** to illustrate this idea. Figure 13.8 shows a relatively flat short-run aggregate sup-

Figure 13.8

Aggregate Demand and the Short-Run Aggregate Supply

With a short-run aggregate supply curve, shifts in aggregate demand lead to changes in output but small changes in prices.

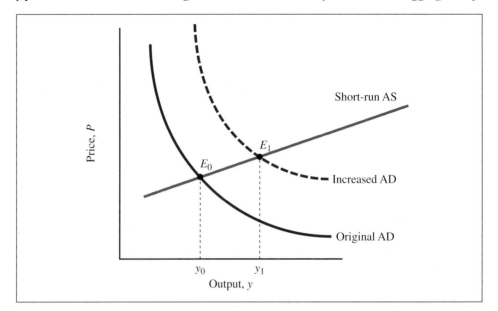

ply curve (AS). The short-run aggregate supply curve is relatively flat because in the short run, firms are assumed to supply all the output demanded, with small changes in prices. We previously discussed that with formal and informal contracts, firms will supply all the output that is demanded with only relatively small changes in prices. The short-run aggregate supply curve has a small upward slope. As they supply more output, firms may have to increase prices somewhat if, for example, they have to pay higher wages to obtain more overtime from workers or pay a premium to obtain some raw materials.

As we just explained, the short-run aggregate supply curve is relatively flat because at any point in time, firms are assumed to supply all the output demanded with relatively small changes in prices. However, the entire short-run aggregate supply curve can shift upward or downward as prices adjust to their long-run levels, as we shall see later in this chapter. Our description of the aggregate supply curve is consistent with evidence about the behavior of prices in the economy. Most studies find that changes in demand have relatively little effect on prices within a few quarters. Thus, the aggregate supply curve can be viewed as relatively flat within a limited time. However, changes in aggregate demand will ultimately have an effect on prices.

The intersection of the AD and AS curves at point E_0 determines the price level and the level of output. Because the aggregate supply curve is flat, aggregate demand primarily determines the level of output. In Figure 13.8, as aggregate demand increases, the new equilibrium will be at a slightly higher price, and output will increase from y_0 to y_1.

It is important to realize and understand that the level of output where the aggregate demand curve intersects the short-run aggregate supply curve need not correspond to full-employment output. Firms will produce whatever is demanded. If demand is very high, output may exceed full-employment output; if demand is very low, output will fall short of full-employment output. Because prices do not adjust fully over short periods of time, the economy need not always remain at full employment or potential output. Changes in demand will lead to economic fluctuations with sticky prices and a short-run aggregate supply curve. Only in the long run, when prices fully adjust, will the economy operate at full employment.

Supply Shocks

Up to this point, we have been exploring how changes in aggregate demand affect output and prices in the short run and in the long run. However, even in the short run, it is possible for external disturbances to hit the economy and cause the short-run aggregate

A CLOSER LOOK | FAVORABLE SUPPLY SHOCKS

During the 1970s, the world economy was hit with a series of unfavorable supply shocks, raising prices and lowering output. These shocks included a spike (a sudden steep increase) in the price of oil in 1973, another in 1979 when producers of oil reduced their supplies to the market, and still another when the prices of many agricultural commodities increased.

In the 1990s, things were different—pleasantly different. Between 1997 and 1998, the price of oil on the world market fell from $22 a barrel to less than $13 a barrel. The result was that gasoline prices, adjusted for inflation, were lower than they had ever been in our lifetimes. This not only meant cheaper vacations and commuting but also had positive macroeconomic effects. Favorable supply shocks allowed output to rise and prices to fall simultaneously—the best of all worlds. These favorable shocks allowed the U.S. economy to grow rapidly and reduced unemployment without incurring risks of increased inflation.

Figure 13.9

Supply Shock
An adverse supply shock, such as an increase in the price of oil, will shift up the AS curve. The result will be higher prices and a lower level of output.

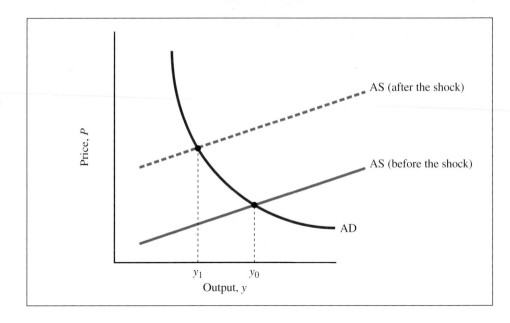

Supply shocks: External events that shift the aggregate supply curve.

supply curve to move. **Supply shocks** are external events that shift the aggregate supply curve.

The most important illustrations of supply shocks for the world economy are the sharp increases in the price of oil that occurred in 1973 and again in 1979. When oil prices increased sharply, firms no longer sold all the goods and services that were demanded at the current price—meaning the price before the increases in oil prices. Because oil was a key input to production for many firms in the economy, the additional costs of oil reduced the profits of firms. To maintain their profit levels, firms raised the prices of their products.

Figure 13.9 illustrates a supply shock that raises prices. The short-run aggregate supply curve shifts up with the supply shock because firms will supply their output only at a higher price. The shift of the AS curve raises the price level and lowers the level of output from y_0 to y_1. Adverse supply shocks can therefore cause a recession (a fall in output) with increasing prices. This situation corresponds closely to the events of 1973, when higher oil prices led to both a recession and rising prices for the economy.

Favorable supply shocks, such as falling prices, are also possible. In this case the short-run aggregate supply curve will shift down. As "A Closer Look: Favorable Supply Shocks" indicates, this happened to the United States in the 1990s.

Economic
Detective

Did Higher Taxes Cause the Recession?

The economy went into a recession. The political party that was in power blamed increases in the world prices of oil and food. Opposing politicians blamed a tax increase that the party in power had enacted. On the basis of aggregate demand and aggregate supply analysis, what evidence should you look at to try to determine what caused the recession?

To determine whether increases in world prices for oil and food or tax increases caused the recession, you need to look at what happened to domestic prices in the economy. If prices rose sharply while output fell, then supply shocks (increases in world oil and food prices) caused the recession. However, if prices fell while output fell, tax increases probably were the culprit.

Output and Prices in the Short Run and in the Long Run

Up to this point, we have examined how aggregate demand and aggregate supply determine output and prices both in the short run and in the long run. You may be wondering how long is the short run and how short is the long run. Here is the story of how the short run and the long run are connected.

In Figure 13.10, we show the aggregate demand curve intersecting the short-run aggregate supply curve at E_0 at an output level y_0. We also depict the long-run aggregate supply curve in this figure. The level of output in the economy, y_0, exceeds the level of potential output, y_p. In other words, this is a boom economy: Output exceeds potential. What happens when an economy is producing at a level exceeding potential output?

If the economy is producing at a level above full employment, firms will find it increasingly difficult to hire and retain workers. Unemployment will be below its natural rate. Workers will find it easy to obtain a job and easy to change jobs. To attract workers to their firms and to prevent their own workers from quitting, firms will have to raise wages to try to outbid other firms looking to hire workers. As one firm raises its wage, others will have to raise their wages even higher to attract workers.

For most firms, wages are the largest cost of production. As their labor costs increase, they have no choice but to increase the prices of their products. As prices rise, workers know that they need higher dollar or nominal wages to maintain their real wage. This is an illustration of the reality principle:

Reality **PRINCIPLE**

What matters to people is the real value of money or income—its purchasing power—not the face value of money or income.

This process by which rising wages cause higher prices and higher prices feed higher wages is known as a **wage–price spiral**. It occurs when the economy is producing at a level of output that exceeds the potential output of the economy.

Wage–price spiral: Changes in wages and prices causing more changes in wages and prices.

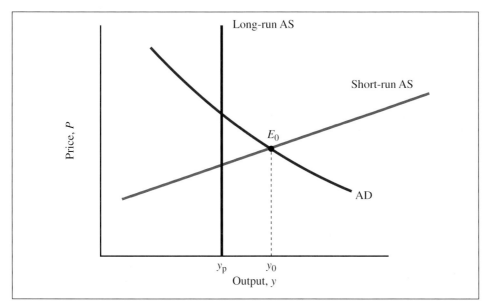

Figure 13.10
The Economy in the Short Run
In the short run, the economy produces at y_0, which exceeds potential output y_p.

When current output exceeds potential and unemployment is below the natural rate, increasing wages and prices will shift the short-run aggregate supply curve upward. Figure 13.11 illustrates this graphically; the dashed lines indicate how the short-run aggregate supply curve shifts upward over time. As long as the economy is producing at a level of output that exceeds potential output, there will be continuing competition for labor and raw materials that will lead to continuing increases in wages and prices. In the long run, the short-run aggregate supply curve will keep rising until it intersects the aggregate demand curve at E_1. At this point, the economy reaches the long-run equilibrium—precisely the point where the aggregate demand curve intersects the long-run aggregate supply curve.

When the economy is producing below full employment or potential output, the process works in reverse. Unemployment will exceed the natural rate, and there will be excess unemployment. Firms will find that it is easy to hire and retain workers and that they can offer less than other firms to hire skilled workers. As all firms cut wages, the average level of wages in the economy falls. Because wages are the largest component of costs, prices start to fall as well. In this case, the wage–price spiral works in reverse.

We illustrate this case in Figure 13.12. In this case, unemployment exceeds the natural rate, and with high unemployment, workers would find it difficult to find jobs. As a consequence, wages begin to fall; soon prices fall as well. As prices fall, the aggregate supply curve will move downward until it intersects the aggregate demand curve at the level of full employment or potential output.

The lesson here is that adjustments in wages and prices take the economy from the short-run equilibrium to the long-run full-employment level of output. Changes in wages and prices steer the economy back to full employment in the long run. How long does this adjustment process take? On this key point, there is disagreement among economists. Some believe that the economy returns to full employment rather rapidly—within one or two years. Others believe that it is a much more extended process, perhaps taking as long as five years. These differences in perspective are important for understanding whether economic policies can improve the performance of the economy.

Figure 13.11

Adjusting to the Long Run

With output exceeding potential, the AS curve shifts upward, as depicted by the dotted lines. The economy adjusts to the long-run equilibrium at E_1.

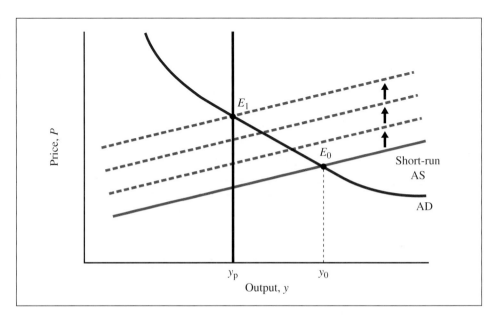

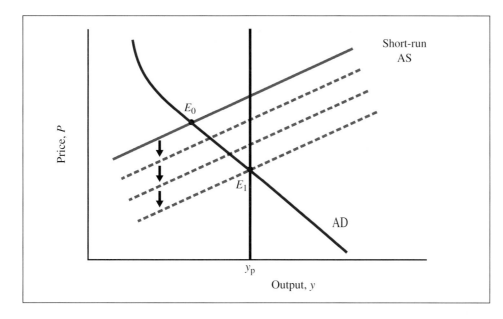

Figure 13.12
Adjusting to an Economic Downturn
With output less than potential, the AS curve shifts downward, as depicted by the dotted lines. The economy adjusts to the long-run equilibrium at E_1.

TEST Your Understanding

5. Name three factors that shift the aggregate demand curve to the right.

6. A decrease in the price level shifts the aggregate demand curve to the right. True or false? Explain.

7. Complete the statement with *vertical* or *horizontal*: The long-run aggregate supply curve is _____.

8. Suppose the supply of money increases. How do prices and real GDP change in both the short run and the long run?

Using the TOOLS

In this chapter, we explored the nature of economic fluctuations and developed the tools of aggregate demand and aggregate supply. Take this opportunity to test your skills using the tools we developed in this chapter.

1. Counting Recessions
Consider the data for the fictitious economy of Euroclive:

Year and Quarter	2000:1	2000:2	2000:3	2000:4	2001:1	2001:2	2001:3
Real GDP	195	193	195	196	195	194	198

How many recessions occurred in the economy over the time indicated?

2. Rationales for Sticky Wages
Think of some group of workers (for example, federal workers) that has sticky wages. Explain why sticky wages may provide economic benefits for both workers and employers.

3. Frugal Consumers

Suppose households become nervous about the future and decide to increase their saving and decrease their consumption spending. How will this shift the aggregate demand curve? Use the short-run aggregate supply curve to figure out what will happen to prices and output in the short run. Use the long-run aggregate supply curve to determine what will happen to prices and output in the long run.

4. Stagflation

Suppose oil prices suddenly increase and the economy is hit by an adverse supply shock. What will happen to the price level and real GDP? Why is this sometimes called stagflation?

Summary

We examined the nature of business cycles and economic fluctuations and provided the foundation for studying short-run, demand-side economics. We also developed aggregate demand and aggregate supply as tools to help us analyze what is happening or has happened in the economy. Here are the main points to remember in this chapter:

1. Recessions occur when real output falls for two quarters.

2. Unemployment rises during recessions; other economic measures rise and fall with real GDP.

3. Economists think of GDP as being determined primarily by demand factors in the short run.

4. The aggregate demand curve depicts the relationship between the price level and total demand for real output in the economy. The aggregate demand curve is downward sloping because of the wealth effect, an interest rate effect, and an international trade effect.

5. Decreases in taxes, increases in government spending, and increases in the supply of money all increase aggregate demand and shift the aggregate demand curve to the right. Increases in taxes, decreases in government spending, and decreases in the supply of money all decrease aggregate demand and shift the aggregate demand curve to the left. In general, anything (other than price movements) that increases the demand for total goods and services will increase aggregate demand.

6. The aggregate supply curve depicts the relationship between the price level and the level of output firms supply in the economy. Output and prices are determined at the intersection of the aggregate demand and aggregate supply curves.

7. The long-run aggregate supply curve is vertical because, in the long run, output is determined by the supply of factors of production. The short-run aggregate supply curve is fairly flat because, in the short run, prices are largely fixed and output is determined by demand.

8. Supply shocks can shift the short-run aggregate supply curve even in the short run.

9. The short-run aggregate supply curve shifts in the long run, restoring the economy to the full-employment equilibrium.

Key Terms

aggregate demand curve, 300
aggregate supply curve, 304
business cycles, 294
countercyclical, 297
crowding out, 305
depression, 296
economic fluctuations, 294
expansion, 295

long-run aggregate supply curve, 304
Okun's law, 297
peak, 294
potential output, 294
price level, 300
procyclical, 297
real business cycle theory, 298
recession, 294

short-run aggregate supply curve, 306
short run in macroeconomics, 300
supply shocks, 308
trough, 295
wage–price spiral, 309
wealth effect, 302

Problems and Discussion Questions

1. What can be misleading about the term *business cycle*?

2. Explain intuitively why the unemployment rate is countercyclical.

3. To compare how deeply recessions affected the economies of two different countries, we might use the following measures:
   a. The number of recessions
   b. The proportion of time each economy was in a recession
   c. The magnitude of the worst recession
   Draw several diagrams that show economies experiencing recessions. Use these diagrams to illustrate how these measures convey different features of recessions.

4. Explain why the aggregate demand curve is downward sloping.

5. Give an example of a good or service whose prices are sticky. What factors tend to make its price sticky?

6. Explain why the long-run aggregate supply curve is vertical and why the short-run supply curve is close to horizontal.

7. Suppose that in the long-run, there was a new higher level of full-employment output. What would happen to the level of prices in the economy?

8. In the short run, what happens to the unemployment rate if aggregate demand suddenly falls?

9. Suppose the economy is at full employment and aggregate demand falls. Show the effects on output and prices in the short run. Also show how the short-run aggregate supply curve adjusts over time to bring the economy to the long-run equilibrium.

10. Use aggregate demand and aggregate supply diagrams to show the effects of "favorable" supply shocks.

11. Web Exercise. Is the U.S. trade balance (export minus imports) procyclical or countercyclical? Use the World Wide Web to find data of the trade balance and GDP to explore this answer. A good place to start might be the Web site of the Federal Reserve Bank of St. Louis (*www.stls.frb.org/fred/*). You might also want to explore this issue for other countries.

12. Web Exercise. How are movements in the stock market related to business cycles? Use the Web site in question 11 or your own source to answer this question.

Take It to the Net

We invite you to visit the O'Sullivan/Sheffrin page on the Prentice Hall Web site at: **www.prenhall.com/osullivan/** for additional World Wide Web exercises for this chapter.

Model Answers to Questions

Chapter-Opening Questions

1. A recession occurs when real GDP declines for two consecutive quarters.

2. Because wages and prices are slow to adjust, the economy may not always operate at full employment.

3. In the short run, output is largely determined by demand. Therefore, a sharp decrease in government spending could cause a recession.

4. In the short run, changes in the demand for goods and services primarily affect output. In the long run, changes in demand for goods and services primarily affect prices.

Test Your Understanding

1. Six.

2. Countercyclical.

3. Peak.

4. Recovery.

5. Increases in government spending, decreases in taxes, and increases in the supply of money.

6. False. Changes in prices are movements along the aggregate demand curve, not shifts of the curve.

7. Vertical.

8. In the long run, an increase in the money supply will raise prices but not change output. In the short run, an increase in the supply of money will increase output but not change prices very much.

Using the Tools

1. **Counting Recessions.** There was only one recession in Euroclive, the peak of which was in 2000:4. Although output did fall in 2000:2, the decline was only for one quarter. The decline beginning in 2001:1 lasted for two quarters.

2. **Rationales for Sticky Wages.** It would be inconvenient and costly for employers and employees to renegotiate wages every day. Conflicts over wages would certainly arise. To keep the peace, wages are adjusted only periodically.

3. **Frugal Consumers.** The decrease in consumption spending is a decrease in the demand for total goods and services—therefore, a decrease in aggregate demand. The aggregate demand curve shifts to the left. In the short run, output falls and prices decrease slightly. In the long run, prices fall and output returns to full employment.

4. **Stagflation.** If the short-run aggregate supply curve shifts upward, the result will be a lower level of output and higher prices. This is sometimes called stagflation because the falling output means that the economy is stagnating and the rising prices mean that the inflation rate will rise.

14

Aggregate Demand and Fiscal Policy

During the decade of the 1990s, the Japanese economy was in a prolonged recession. Economists and journalists put forward many different suggestions for jump-starting the economy. One idea was that the government issue everyone in the economy a certificate entitling him or her to the equivalent of $200 in yen. However, these yen certificates would only be valid for purchases for one month; after that time, the certificates would be worthless.

　　The logic behind issuing these time-dated certificates was straightforward. Individuals would feel compelled to rush out and use the certificates within the month. They would, therefore, immediately purchase goods and services and stimulate demand. Firms would increase production to meet the increased demand, thereby creating more jobs and lifting the economy out of the recession. This is an example, although an unusual one, of policies designed to shift the aggregate demand curve.

Fiscal policy: The use of taxes and transfers to affect the level of aggregate demand.

N ewspaper and television stories about the economy tend to focus on what causes the changes in short-term real GDP. For example, it is common to read about how changes in economic conditions in Europe or Asia or changes in government spending or taxation will affect near-term economic growth. To understand these stories, we need to understand the behavior of the economy in the short run. To do that, we will explore in more detail the aggregate demand curve and how the government can use **fiscal policy**—changes in taxes and spending that affect the level of GDP.

In this chapter, we emphasize that shifts in aggregate demand determine the level of output or GDP, at least over short periods of time. In macroeconomics, the short run is the period during which prices do not change or change very little. Until prices adjust in the long run, the aggregate demand for goods and services determines the level of GDP. Producers will supply, in the short run, the level of output that is demanded.

With the tools developed in this chapter, you will be able to answer the following questions:

1. Why do governments cut taxes to increase economic output?
2. Why is the U.S. economy more stable today than it was prior to World War II?
3. If consumers become more confident about the future of the economy, can that confidence lead to faster economic growth?
4. If a government increases spending by $10 billion, could total GDP increase by more than $10 billion?

Behind the Aggregate Demand Curve

In the last chapter, we discussed how output and prices are determined where the aggregate demand curve intersects the short-run aggregate supply curve. Over time, we also saw that the aggregate supply curve will shift to bring the economy back to full employment.

In this chapter, we will focus on the short run. We will look more closely at some of the underlying factors that shift the aggregate demand curve and the variety of policy tools that governments have to change GDP in the short run. In Figure 14.1, we review how a shift in aggregate demand can increase the level of GDP in the short run. As the aggregate demand curve shifts from AD^0 to AD^1, the level of output increases from y_0 to y_1.

Let's take a closer look at the shift in the aggregate demand curve. Suppose that the government increases spending on goods and services by $10 billion. You might think that the aggregate demand curve would shift to the right by $10 billion, reflecting the increased demand for goods and services by the government of $10 billion. Initially, the shift will be precisely $10 billion. In Figure 14.2, this is depicted by the shift (at a given price level) from A to B. But after a brief period of time, total aggregate demand will increase by *more* than $10 billion. In Figure 14.2 the final shift in the aggregate demand curve is shown by the larger movement from A to C. The ratio of the final shift in aggregate demand to the initial shift in aggregate demand is known as the **multiplier**.

Multiplier: The ratio of the final shift in aggregate demand to the initial shift in aggregate demand.

Why does the aggregate demand curve shift more than the initial increase in desired spending? The logic goes back to the ideas of the economist John Maynard Keynes. Here's how it works: As government spending increases and the aggregate demand curve shifts to the right, output will increase as well. Increased output, however, also means increased income—workers and consumers now will have higher incomes. They typically will wish to spend part of that income, which will further increase aggregate

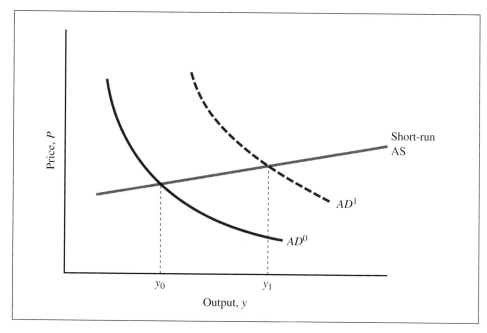

Figure 14.1
**A Shift in
Aggregate Demand**

The shift in the aggregate
demand curve from AD^0 to
AD^1 increases output from y_0
to y_1.

demand. It is the additional spending by consumers that causes the further shift in the
aggregate demand curve.

We will now start to take a closer look at this process. To explore these ideas, we first
need to look more carefully at the behavior of consumers and how their behavior helps
to determine the level of aggregate demand. We then will be able to understand how
governments can use fiscal policy to shift the aggregate demand curve and thereby influence the level of GDP in the short run.

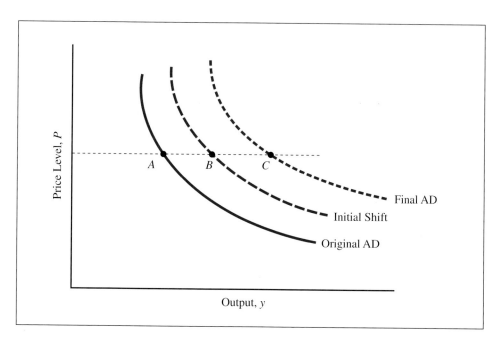

Figure 14.2
**Initial and Final
Shift in Aggregate
Demand**
Initially an increase in desired
spending will shift the aggregate demand curve horizontally to the right from A to B.
The final shift from A to C
will be larger. The ratio of the
final shift to the initial shift is
known as the
multiplier.

The Consumption Function and the Multiplier

Consumer Spending and Income

Economists have found that consumer spending depends on the level of income in the economy. When consumers have more income, they want to purchase more goods and services. The relationship between consumer spending and income is known as the **consumption function**:

$$C = C_a + by$$

where consumption spending C has two parts. The first part, C_a, is a constant and is independent of income. This means that much of consumption spending does not depend on the level of income. For example, all consumers, regardless of their current income, will have to purchase some food. Economists call this **autonomous consumption spending**. The second part, by, represents the part of consumption that is dependent on income. It is the product of a fraction b, called the **marginal propensity to consume (MPC)**, and the level of income y in the economy. The MPC (or b in our formula) tells us how much consumption spending will increase for every dollar that income increases. For example, if $b = 0.6$, then for every \$1 that income increases, consumption increases by \$0.60.

We will initially be considering a very simple economy without government or the foreign sector—just firms and households. In this simple world, output (or real GDP) is also equal to the income that flows to the households. As firms produce output, it is paid to the households as income (wages, interest, profits, and rents). We can, therefore, use the symbol y to represent both output and income.

We plot a consumption function in Figure 14.3. The consumption function is a line that intersects the vertical axis at C_a, the level of autonomous consumption spending; autonomous consumption must be greater than zero, so the line does not pass through the zero point on the origin. Its slope equals b, the marginal propensity to consume. Although output is plotted on the horizontal axis, remember that it is also equal to income, so income rises dollar for dollar with output. The marginal propensity to consume (the slope of the line) is always less than one. A consumer who receives a dollar of income will spend part of it and save the rest. The fraction that the consumer spends is given by his or her MPC. The fraction that the consumer saves is determined by his or

Consumption function: The relationship between the level of income and consumption spending.

Autonomous consumption spending: The part of consumption that does not depend on income.

Marginal propensity to consume (MPC): The fraction of additional income that is spent.

Figure 14.3
Consumption Function
The consumption function relates desired consumer spending to the level of income.

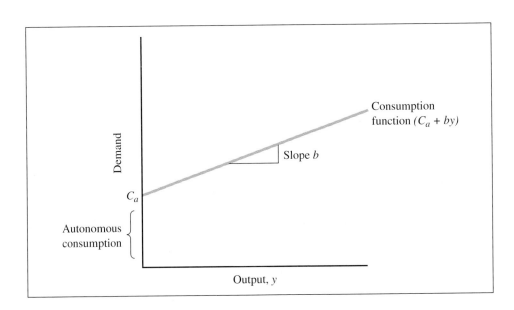

her **marginal propensity to save (MPS)**. The sum of the marginal propensity to consume and the marginal propensity to save is always equal to one. For example, if the MPC is 0.8, then the MPS must be 0.2. When a consumer receives an additional dollar, he or she spends $0.80 and saves the remaining $0.20.

Marginal propensity to save (MPS): The fraction of additional income that is saved.

Changes in the Consumption Function

The consumption function is determined by the level of autonomous consumption and by the MPC. The level of autonomous consumption can change, and so can the MPC. Changes in either shift the consumption function to another position on the graph. A higher level of autonomous consumption but no change in MPC will shift the entire consumption function upward and parallel to its original position. Why it shifts upward should be clear: Increased autonomous consumption is represented as a higher intercept on the vertical axis. We show an increase in autonomous consumption in panel A of Figure 14.4.

A number of factors can cause autonomous consumption to change. Here are two:

1. Increases in consumer wealth will cause an increase in autonomous consumption. (Wealth consists of the value of stocks, bonds, and consumer durables—consumer goods that last a long time, such as automobiles and refrigerators. Wealth is not the same as income; income is the amount of money earned during a period, such as in a given year.) Nobel laureate Franco Modigliani has emphasized that increases in stock prices, which raise consumer wealth, will lead to increases in autonomous consumption. Conversely, a sharp fall in stock prices would lead to a decrease in autonomous consumption.

2. Changes in consumer confidence will shift the consumption function. Increases in consumer confidence will increase autonomous consumption. Forecasters pay attention to consumer confidence, based on household surveys; consumer confidence is reported regularly in the financial press.

A change in the marginal propensity to consume will cause a change in the slope of the consumption function. We show an increase in the MPC in panel B of Figure 14.4, where we assume that autonomous consumption is fixed. As the MPC increases, the consumption function rotates upward, counterclockwise; that means that the consumption function line gets steeper.

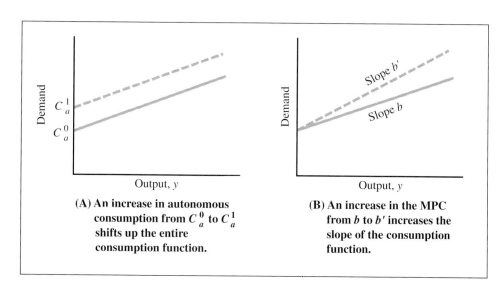

Figure 14.4
Movements of the Consumption Function

(A) An increase in autonomous consumption from C_a^0 to C_a^1 shifts up the entire consumption function.

(B) An increase in the MPC from b to b' increases the slope of the consumption function.

Several factors can change the MPC. Here are two:

1. Consumers' perceptions of changes in their income affect their MPC. If consumers believe that an increase in their income is permanent, they will consume a higher proportion of the increased income than they would if they believed the increase was temporary. As an example, consumers will spend a higher proportion of a permanent salary increase than they would spend of a one-time bonus. Similarly, studies have shown that consumers save—not spend—a high proportion of one-time windfall gains, such as lottery winnings.

2. A change in the tax rate will change the slope of the consumption function, as we will see later in this chapter.

Determining Aggregate Demand

Now that we have developed the consumption function, we can show how the aggregate demand curve is determined and how the aggregate demand curve can shift to the left or right. To simplify our task, we first look at the level of aggregate demand for a given level of prices in the economy—that is, we look at a single point on the aggregate demand curve at a constant price level, such as point A in Figure 14.2. Holding the price level constant will enable us to understand more fully the factors that shift the aggregate demand horizontally to the left or to the right.

In an economy without government or the foreign sector, aggregate demand will be determined by consumption and investment spending. To simplify, let's assume that a firm wishes to invest a fixed amount, I. In Figure 14.5, we first plot the consumption function. The vertical axis represents the demand for goods and services while the horizontal axis represents output. Although the horizontal axis is labeled "output," recall that in our simple economy output is equal to income. We add the desired level of investment, I, vertically to the consumption function. Since desired investment spending is a constant level I, it just increases the consumption function by a fixed amount. At any level of output, total demand for goods and services can be read off the $C + I$ line.

Figure 14.5

Determining Aggregate Demand

Aggregate demand is determined where the $C + I$ line intersects the 45° line. At that level of output, y^*, desired spending equals output.

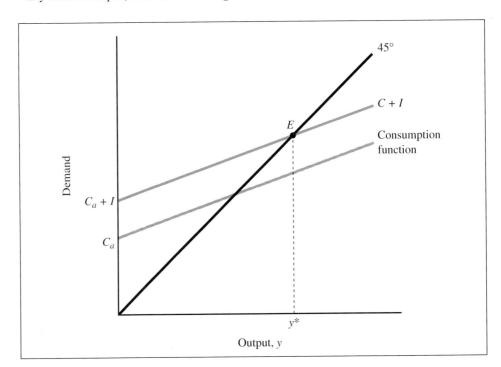

The other straight line in the figure is a 45° diagonal line. From any point on the 45° diagonal line, the distance leftward over to the vertical axis is equal to the distance downward to the horizontal axis. That's simple graphical math: From any point on the diagonal, the horizontal and vertical distances are equal.

Aggregate demand is determined where the $C + I$ line intersects the 45° diagonal line. The level of output on the aggregate demand curve is given by y^*. At that point, the total demand for goods and services—the vertical distance—is equal to the level of output—the horizontal distance. What this means is that at the level of output y^*, firms are producing precisely the level of total output necessary to meet the consumption and investment demands by households and firms. At any other level of output, firms would be producing either too many goods or too few goods to be consistent with the demands generated by households and firms.

We have just developed a simple model to understand a point on the aggregate demand curve, such as point A in Figure 14.2. We will use the model throughout this chapter to discuss factors that shift the aggregate demand curve. Sometimes the model in Figure 14.5 is called the **Keynesian cross**, in recognition that some of the underlying ideas stem from the work of John Maynard Keynes. However, it is important to always remember that the Keynesian cross is simply a model to help us understand aggregate demand.

Keynesian cross: A simple model of aggregate demand based on ideas from Keynes.

The Multiplier

In all economies, investment spending fluctuates. We can use the model of aggregate demand we have developed to see what happens if there are changes in investment spending. Suppose investment spending originally was I_0 and increased to I_1, an increase that we will call ΔI (the symbol Δ, the greek capital letter delta, is universally used to represent change). What happens to aggregate demand?

Figure 14.6 shows how output is determined at the original level of investment and at the new level of investment. The increase in investment spending shifts the $C + I$ curve upward by ΔI. The intersection of the $C + I$ curve with the 45° line shifts from E_0 to E_1. Aggregate demand increased from y_0 to y_1 by the amount Δy.

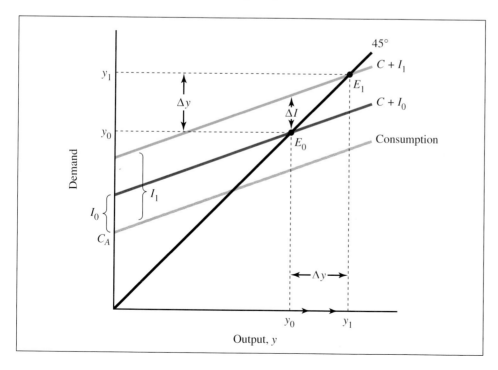

Figure 14.6
Multiplier
When investment increases by ΔI from I_0 to I_1, aggregate demand increases by Δy from y_0 to y_1. The change in output (Δy) is greater than the change in investment (ΔI).

The figure shows that the increase in aggregate demand—that is, the amount Δy—is greater than the increase in investment—the amount ΔI—or $\Delta y > \Delta I$.

This is a general result; the increase in output—or aggregate demand—always exceeds the increase in investment. This explains the multiplier—why the final shift in the aggregate demand curve in Figure 14.2 is greater than the initial shift in aggregate demand. The initial shift in aggregate demand just reflects the increase in desired investment spending. The final shift reflects the full increase in aggregate demand caused by the initial increase in investment, including the additional demand by consumers.

The basic idea of how the multiplier works in an economy is simple. Let's say that a computer firm invests $10 million in building a new plant. Initially, total spending in the economy increases by the $10 million paid to a construction firm. The construction workers and owners of the construction firm then spend part of the income they are paid. Suppose the owners and workers spend $8 million on new automobiles. Producers of these automobiles will expand their production because of the increase indicated by this demand. In turn, workers and owners in the automobile industry will earn an additional $8 million in wages and profits. They, in turn, will spend part of this additional income, let's say $6.4 million, on televisions and other goods and services. And the workers in the production of the televisions and those other goods and services will earn additional income, and so on, and so on.

Table 14.1 shows how the multiplier works in detail. In the first round, there is an initial increase of investment spending of $10 million. This additional demand leads to an initial increase in GDP and income of $10 million. Assuming that the MPC is 0.8, the $10 million of additional income will increase consumer spending by $8 million. Round 2 begins with the $8 million increase in consumer spending. Because of this increase in demand, GDP and income increase by $8 million. At the end of round 2, consumers will have an additional $8 million; with an MPC of 0.8, consumer spending will, therefore, increase by $0.8 \times \$8$ million, or $6.4 million. The process continues in round 3 with an increase in consumer spending of $6.4 million. It continues, in diminishing amounts, through subsequent rounds. If we add up the spending in all the (infinite) rounds, we will find that the initial $10 million of spending leads to a $50 million increase in GDP and income. In this case, the multiplier is 5.

The multiplier also works in reverse. Suppose that consumers become pessimistic, cutting back on autonomous consumption by $10 million. Demand for GDP falls by $10 million, which means that output and income fall by $10 million. Consumers then cut

Table 14.1   The Multiplier in Action

Round of Spending	Increase in Demand	Increase in GDP and Income	Increase in Consumption
1	$10	$10	$ 8
2	8	8	6.4
3	6.4	6.4	5.12
4	5.12	5.12	4.096
5	4.096	4.096	3.277
.	.	.	.
.	.	.	.
.	.	.	.
Total	50 million	50 million	40 million

Note: All figures for increases indicate millions of dollars.

back their spending further because their incomes have fallen. What happens is the reverse of what we just described for the multiplier working in the positive direction. If the MPC were 0.8, total spending would fall by $50 million.

In our very simple economy without the government or the foreign sector, there is a simple formula that links the multiplier to the marginal propensity to consume:

$$\text{multiplier} = 1/(1 - \text{MPC})$$

Suppose the MPC = 0.8; then the multiplier would be $1/(1 - 0.8)$ or 5.

Notice that the multiplier increases as the MPC increases. If MPC = 0.4, the multiplier = 1.67; if the MPC = 0.6, the multiplier = 2.5. To see why the multiplier increases as the marginal propensity to consume increases, think back to our examples of the multiplier. The multiplier occurs because the initial increase in investment spending increases income, which leads to higher consumer spending. With a higher MPC, the increase in consumer spending will be greater, since consumers will spend a higher fraction of the additional income they receive as the multiplier increases. With this extra spending, the eventual increase in output will be greater and, therefore, so will the multiplier.

Now you should clearly understand why the final shift in the aggregate demand curve from A to C in Figure 14.2 is greater than the initial shift in the curve from A to B. This is the multiplier in action.

TEST Your Understanding

1. What is the slope of the consumption function called?

2. Complete the statement with *upward* or *downward*: An increase in autonomous consumption will shift the consumption function _____.

3. If the MPC is 0.7, the marginal propensity to save must be _____.

4. Explain why aggregate demand is determined where the $C + I$ line crosses the 45° diagonal line.

5. If the MPC is 0.6, the multiplier is _____.

Government Spending and Taxation

Fiscal Policy

We now make our model more realistic, bringing in government spending and taxation, therefore making the model useful for understanding economic-policy debates. In those debates, we often hear recommendations for increasing government spending to increase GDP or cutting taxes to increase GDP. As we will explain, both the level of government spending and the level of taxation, through their influence on aggregate demand, affect the level of GDP in the short run. Using taxes and spending to shift the aggregate demand curve and influence the level of GDP in the short run is known as fiscal policy.

Let's look first at the role government spending plays in determining aggregate demand. Government purchases of goods and services are a component of spending:

$$\text{total spending including government} = C + I + G$$

Increases in government purchases, G, shift the $C + I + G$ line upward, just as increases in investment I or autonomous consumption do. If government spending increases by $1, the $C + I + G$ line will shift upward by $1.

Panel A of Figure 14.7 shows how increases in government spending affect aggregate demand. The increase in government spending from G_0 to G_1 shifts the $C + I + G$ line upward and increases the level of output from y_0 to y_1.

Figure 14.7
Fiscal Policy

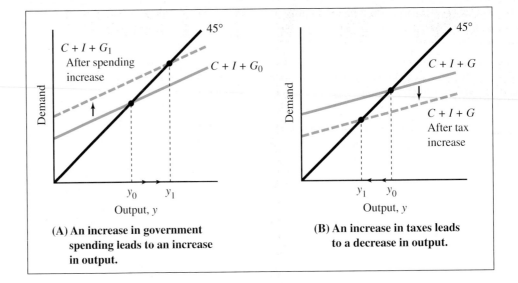

(A) An increase in government spending leads to an increase in output.

(B) An increase in taxes leads to a decrease in output.

As you can see, changes in government purchases have exactly the same effects as changes in investment or changes in autonomous consumption. The multiplier for government spending is also the same as for changes in investment or autonomous consumption:

$$\text{multiplier for government spending} = 1/(1 - \text{MPC})$$

For example, if the MPC were 0.6 and the multiplier were 2.5, a $10 billion increase in government spending would increase GDP by $25 billion. The multiplier for government spending works just like the multiplier for investment or consumption. An initial increase in government spending raises GDP and income. The increase in income, however, generates further increases in demand as consumers increase their spending.

Now let's consider taxes. We need to take into account that government programs affect households' **disposable personal income**—income that ultimately flows back to households and to consumers after subtraction from their income of any taxes paid and after addition to their income of any transfer payments they receive (such as Social Security, unemployment insurance, or welfare). If the government takes $10 net out of every $100 you make, your income after taxes and transfer payments is only $90.

Here's how we include taxes and transfers into the model: We make consumption spending depend on income after taxes and transfers, or $y - T$, where T is net taxes (taxes paid to government minus transfers received by households). For simplicity, we'll just refer to T as taxes, but remember that it is taxes less transfer payments. The consumption function with taxes is

$$C = C_a + b(y - T)$$

If taxes increase by $1, after-tax income will decrease by $1. Since the marginal propensity to consume is b, this means that consumption will fall by $b \times \$1$, and the $C + I + G$ line will shift downward by $b \times \$1$. For example, if b is 0.6, a $1 increase in taxes will mean that consumers will have a dollar less of income and will, therefore, decrease consumption spending by $0.60.

Panel B of Figure 14.7 shows how an increase in taxes will decrease the level of GDP. As the level of taxes increases, the demand line will shift downward by $b \times$ (the increase in taxes). Output, or aggregate demand, will fall from y_0 to y_1.

The multiplier for taxes is less than the multiplier for government spending. If we cut government spending by $1, the $C + I + G$ will shift downward by $1. However, if we

Disposable personal income:
The income that flows back to households, taking into account transfers and taxes.

increase taxes by \$1, consumers will cut back their consumption by only $b \times \$1$. Thus, the $C + I + G$ line will shift downward by slightly less than \$1, or $b \times \$1$. For example, if $b = 0.6$, the demand line would shift down vertically only by \$0.60. Because the initial shift is less for taxes than for government spending, the multiplier is smaller.

The models that we are using are very simple and leave out important factors. Nonetheless, the same basic principles apply in real situations. Here are five examples of fiscal policy from recent years.

1. In 1993, the three members of the president's Council of Economic Advisers wrote a letter to President Clinton stating that they thought the cuts in government spending being proposed at the time were \$20 billion too large. The economic model the council members used had a multiplier for government spending of approximately 1.5. With this multiplier, the decrease in GDP from the \$20 billion spending cut would be (\$20 billion $\times$ 1.5) = \$30 billion. This was approximately 0.5% of GDP. If, in the absence of these cuts, GDP was expected to grow at 3% a year, the president's advisers estimated that with these cuts, GDP would grow at only 2.5% a year. However, the advice of the council members came too late to influence the policy decisions.

2. During 1994, the U.S. government urged the Japanese to increase public spending and cut taxes to stimulate their economy. The Japanese came up with a plan and presented it to U.S. policymakers. U.S. policymakers evaluated the effects of this plan by using multiplier analysis. The United States thought that this plan did not provide enough fiscal stimulus and urged the Japanese to take more aggressive actions. Several years later, the Japanese did adopt a more aggressive plan.

3. During the late 1990s, the Chinese economy came under pressure from the economic downturn in Asia and its own attempts to reform and restructure the economy. To prevent a severe economic slowdown, the Chinese engaged in active fiscal policy. The government decided to increase its spending on domestic infrastructure, including roads, rails, and urban facilities.

4. In 2001, President George W. Bush led the effort for a tax cut that would be phased in over 10 years. In the first year, however, all taxpayers would receive a one-time cut of up to a maximum of \$600. This was designed to provide direct stimulus to a sluggish economy.

5. After the September 11, 2001, terrorist attack, the government increased spending for disaster relief in New York. In addition, President George W. Bush and Congress immediately began to work on additional spending programs and tax relief programs to stimulate the economy.

We use special terminology to describe government actions taken to effect changes in the economy. Government policies that increase total demand and GDP are called **expansionary policies**. Government policies that decrease total demand and GDP are **contractionary policies**. Tax cuts and government spending increases are examples of expansionary policies. Tax increases and government spending cuts are examples of contractionary policies.

When a government increases its spending or cuts taxes to stimulate the economy, it will increase the government's **budget deficit**, the difference between its spending and its tax collections. For example, suppose the budget were initially balanced (government spending equaled taxes received) and the government increased its spending. The government would then be running a budget deficit—government spending exceeding taxation. To pay for its additional spending, the government would have to borrow money by selling government bonds, which are government IOUs, to the public. Traditional models assume that this borrowing has no significant effects on the economy. Although

Expansionary policies:
Government policy actions that lead to increases in output.

Contractionary policies:
Government policy actions that lead to decreases in output.

Budget deficit: The difference between a government's spending and revenues.

these models of aggregate demand are very simple and leave out many factors, like all models, they illustrate some important lessons:

- An increase in government spending will increase the total demand for goods and services.
- Cutting taxes will increase the after-tax income of consumers and will also lead to an increase in the total demand for goods and services.

With these tools, the government can change aggregate demand in the short run.

TEST Your Understanding

6. If the MPC is 0.4, what is the government-spending multiplier?
7. Using taxes and government spending to control the level of aggregate demand is known as _____ policy.
8. True or false and why. To slow economic growth, governments should cut taxes.
9. An increase in government spending of $10 billion will shift the $C + I + G$ line up by _____ and increase GDP by this amount times the government-spending multiplier.
10. If economic advisers fear that the economy is growing too rapidly, what fiscal policies should they recommend?

Fiscal Policy in U.S. History

The elements of modern fiscal policy were developed in the 1930s, but it took a long time before economic policy decisions were based on Keynesian principles. Many people associate active fiscal policy in the United States with actions taken by President Franklin Roosevelt during the 1930s. But this is a misleading view, as "A Closer Look: Fiscal Policy in the Great Depression" explains.

Although modern fiscal policy was not deliberately used during the 1930s, the growth in military spending at the onset of World War II increased total demand in the

A CLOSER LOOK — FISCAL POLICY IN THE GREAT DEPRESSION

The Great Depression in the United States lasted throughout the 1930s and did not really end until the beginning of World War II in the early 1940s. It was during this period that the modern theory of fiscal policy was developed. According to this theory, expansionary fiscal policy—tax cuts and increased government spending—could pull the economy out of recession or depression. Was fiscal policy actually used during the Great Depression?

According to E. Cary Brown, a former economics professor at the Massachusetts Institute of Technology, "Fiscal policy, then, seems to have been an unsuccessful recovery device in the thirties—not because it did not work, but because it was not tried." During the

1930s, politicians did not believe in modern fiscal policy, largely because they feared the consequences of government budget deficits. According to Brown, fiscal policy was expansionary only during two years of the Great Depression in 1931 and 1936. In those years, Congress voted for substantial payments to veterans, over the objections of Presidents Herbert Hoover and Franklin Roosevelt. Although government spending increased during the 1930s, so did taxes, resulting in no net fiscal expansion.

Source: Adapted from E. Cary Brown, "Fiscal Policy in the Thirties: A Reappraisal," *American Economic Review*, vol. 46, December 1956, pp. 863–868.

economy and helped to pull the economy out of its long decade of poor performance. But to see fiscal policy in action, we need to turn to the 1960s. It was not until the presidency of John F. Kennedy during the early 1960s that modern fiscal policy came to be accepted.

Walter Heller, the chairman of the president's Council of Economic Advisers under John F. Kennedy, was a forceful advocate of active fiscal policy. From his perspective, the economy was operating far below its potential, and a tax cut was the perfect medicine to bring the economy back to full employment. When Kennedy entered office, the unemployment rate was 6.7%. Heller believed that the unemployment rate at full employment was approximately 4%. He convinced Kennedy of the need for a tax program to stimulate the economy, and Kennedy put forth an economic program that was based largely on Keynesian principles.

Two other factors led the Kennedy administration to support the tax cut: First, tax rates were extremely high at the time. The top individual tax rate was 91%, compared to about 40% today. The corporate tax rate was 52%, compared to 35% today. Second, Heller convinced Kennedy that even if a tax cut led to a federal budget deficit (the gap between federal spending and taxes), it was not a problem. In 1961, the federal deficit was less than 1% of GDP, and future projections indicated that the deficit would disappear as the economy grew because of higher tax revenues.

The tax cuts were enacted into law in February 1964, after Lyndon Johnson became president following Kennedy's assassination. The tax cuts included permanent cuts in tax rates for both individuals and corporations. Estimating the actual effects that the tax cuts had on the economy is difficult; to have a valid comparison, we need to estimate how the economy would have behaved without the tax cuts. However, the economy grew at a rapid rate following the tax cuts. From 1963 to 1966, both real GDP and consumption grew at rates exceeding 4%. We cannot rule out the possibility that the economy could have grown this rapidly without the tax cuts. Nonetheless, the rapid growth during this period suggests that the tax cuts had the effect, predicted by our theory, of stimulating economic growth. (Some economists would argue that supply-side factors, such as lower marginal tax rates, could also have stimulated growth.)

The next major use of modern fiscal policy occurred in 1968. As the Vietnam War began and military spending increased, unemployment fell to very low levels. From 1966 to 1969, the overall unemployment rate fell below 4%. Policymakers became concerned that the economy was overheating and that this would lead to a higher inflation rate for the economy. In 1968, a temporary tax surcharge of 10% was enacted to reduce total demand for goods and services. The 10% surcharge was a tax on a tax, so it raised the taxes paid by households by 10%. The surcharge was specifically designed to be temporary and was scheduled to expire within a year.

The surcharge did not decrease consumer spending as much as economists had initially estimated. Part of the reason was that the tax increase was temporary. Economists who have studied consumption behavior have noticed that consumers often base their spending on an estimate of their long-run average income or **permanent income**, not on their current income.

Permanent income: An estimate of a household's long-run average level of income.

For example, consider a salesman who usually earns $50,000 a year, although his income in any single year might be higher or lower than $50,000. On the basis of his permanent income, he consumes $45,000, for an MPC of 0.9 of his permanent income. If his income in one year is higher than average, say $55,000, he may still consume $45,000, as if he earned his normal $50,000, and save the rest.

The temporary, one-year tax surcharge did not have a major effect on the permanent income of households. Because their permanent income was not decreased very much by the tax surcharge, households that based their consumption decisions on their permanent income would be expected to maintain their prior level of consumption. Instead of reducing consumption, they would simply reduce their saving for the period that the surcharge was in effect. It appears that this is what consumers did, resulting in a smaller decrease in demand for goods and services than economists anticipated.

President George W. Bush signed a major tax cut into law in 2001.

TAX RELIEF FOR AMERICA

During the 1970s, there were many changes in taxes and spending but no major changes in overall fiscal policy. There was a tax rebate and other tax incentives in 1975 following the recession in 1973. However, these tax changes were mild.

The tax cuts enacted during 1981 at the beginning of the first term of President Ronald Reagan were significant. However, they were not proposed to increase aggregate demand. Instead, the tax cuts were justified on the basis of improving economic incentives and increasing the supply of output. Taxes can have important effects on the supply of labor, saving, and economic growth. Proponents of the 1981 tax cuts emphasized these effects and not increases in aggregate demand. Nonetheless, the tax cuts did appear to increase consumer demand and helped the economy recover from the back-to-back recessions in the early 1980s.

By the mid-1980s, large government budget deficits began to emerge. Policymakers became concerned with those growing budget deficits. As deficits grew and became the focus of attention, there was no longer interest in using fiscal policy to manage the economy. Although there were government spending and tax changes in the 1980s and 1990s, few of them were justified solely as policies to change aggregate demand.

At the beginning of his administration, President Bill Clinton proposed a "stimulus package" but it was defeated in Congress. He later successfully passed a major tax increase to bring the budget into balance. By the year 2000, the federal budget began to show surpluses rather than deficits, setting the stage for tax cuts. During his first year in office, President George W. Bush passed a 10-year tax cut plan that decreased tax rates. Although the justification for his plan was largely based on improved incentives from lower tax rates, the first year of the tax cut featured tax refunds of up to $600 per married couple. The justification for the refunds was to increase aggregate demand.

After the September 11, 2001, terrorist attack, the focus of fiscal policy began to change again. The president and the Congress became less concerned with balancing the federal budget in a period of economic distress and authorized new spending programs to provide relief to victims and to stimulate the economy. Most of the discussion was phrased in terms of aggregate demand. What policies and actions would be the most effective in providing the needed stimulus to the economy?

Automatic Stabilizers

With a slight addition to our basic model, we can explain one of the important facts in U.S. economic history. Figure 14.8 plots the rate of growth of U.S. real GDP from 1871 to 2000. It is apparent from the graph that the U.S. economy has been much more stable after World War II than before. The reason is that government taxes and transfer pay-

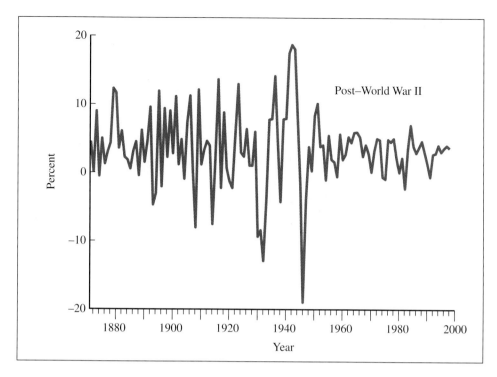

Figure 14.8
Growth Rate of U.S. GDP, 1871–2000

Source: Angus Maddison, *Dynamic Forces in Capitalist Development* (New York: Oxford U. Press, 1991); Bureau of Economic Analysis, Department of Commerce, 2000.

ments (such as unemployment insurance and welfare payments) grew sharply after the war. These taxes and transfer payments can automatically reduce fluctuations in real GDP and thereby stabilize the economy. We say that taxes and transfers act as **automatic stabilizers** for the economy.

Here is how the automatic stabilizers work. When income is high, the government collects more taxes and pays out less in transfer payments. Because the government is taking funds out of the hands of consumers, there will be reduced consumer spending. On the other hand, when output is low (such as during recessions), the government collects less taxes and pays out more in transfer payments, increasing consumer spending because the government is putting funds into the hands of consumers. The automatic stabilizers prevent consumption from falling as much in bad times and from rising as much in good times. This stabilizes the economy without any need for decisions from Congress or the White House.

Another way to think about automatic stabilizers is to recognize that taxes effectively reduce a household's marginal propensity to consume. Suppose that a household normally has an MPC of 0.8 from disposable income. However, if a household faces a tax rate of 25%, it only gets to keep 75% of any income. The MPC out of disposable income will be 0.75×0.8 or 0.6. Thus, instead of an MPC of 0.8, the MPC, taking into account the taxes, will be only 0.6.

Remember that a smaller marginal propensity to consume also leads to a lower value for the multiplier. As tax rates increase and the adjusted MPC out of disposable income falls, the multiplier will decrease. A smaller multiplier means that any shocks, such as shocks to investment, will have less of an impact on the economy.

Now that we have introduced income taxes into our model, we can see how automatic stabilizers work. Since World War II, taxes and transfer payments in the United States have increased sharply. As we have seen, higher tax rates will lower the multiplier and make the economy less susceptible to shocks. With higher taxes and transfer payments, there is a much looser link between fluctuations in disposable personal income and fluctuations in

Automatic stabilizers: Taxes and transfer payments that stabilize GDP without requiring policymakers to take explicit action.

This Internal Revenue Service worker in Austin, Texas, is an integral part of a process to stabilize the U.S. economy.

GDP. Because disposable personal income is more stable, consumption spending is also more stable. Thus, there is a smaller multiplier, and the economy is more stable.

It is important to emphasize that automatic stabilizers work silently in the background, doing their job without requiring explicit action by policymakers. Total tax collections rise and fall with GDP without requiring that policymakers change tax rates. The fact that the automatic stabilizers work without any laws being enacted is particularly important at times when it is difficult to obtain a political consensus for taking any action and policymakers are reluctant to use fiscal policy as a deliberate policy tool.

Other factors contribute to the stability of the economy. We explained how consumers base their spending decisions in part on their permanent income, not just on their current level of income. If households base their consumption decisions partly on their permanent or long-run income, they will not be very sensitive to changes in their current income. If their consumption does not change very much with current income, the marginal propensity to consume out of current income will be small, which will make the multiplier small as well. When consumers base their decisions on long-run factors, not just on their current level of income, the economy tends to be stabilized.

Exports and Imports

With international trade becoming an increasingly important economic and political issue, it is critical to understand how exports and imports affect the level of GDP. Two simple modifications of our model will allow us to understand how exports and imports affect aggregate demand.

Exports and imports affect aggregate demand through their influence on how the world beyond the United States demands goods and services produced in the United States. An increase in exports means that there's an increase in the demand for goods produced in the United States. An increase in imports means that there's an increase in foreign goods purchased by U.S. residents. Importing goods rather than purchasing them from our domestic producers reduces the demand for U.S. goods. For example, if we in the United States spend a total of $10 billion on all automobiles but we import $3 billion in automobiles, then only $7 billion is spent on U.S. automobiles.

To get a clearer picture of the effects on GDP from exports and imports, let's for the moment ignore government spending and taxes. To modify our model of aggregate demand to include the effects of exports and imports, we need to take two steps:

1. Add exports, X, to other sources of spending as another source of demand for U.S. goods and services. We assume that the level of exports (foreign demand for U.S. products) is given.

2. Subtract imports, M, from total spending by U.S. residents. We will assume that imports, like consumption, increase with the level of income.

Consumers will import more goods as income rises. We can write this as

$$\text{imports} = M = my$$

where m is a fraction known as the **marginal propensity to import**. We subtract this fraction from b, the overall marginal propensity to consume, to obtain the MPC for spending on domestic goods, $b - m$. For example, if $b = 0.8$ and $m = 0.2$, then for every $1 that GDP increases, total consumption increases by $0.80 but spending on domestic goods increases only by $0.60 because $0.20 is spent on imports. The MPC in this example, adjusted for imports, is $(0.8 - 0.2) = 0.6$.

Figure 14.9 shows how equilibrium output is determined in an open economy, that is, an economy that engages in trade with the rest of the world. We plot total demand for U.S. goods and services on our graph and find the level of equilibrium income where it intersects the 45° line. The total demand line has an intercept on the vertical axis of $C_a + I + X$, which is the sum of autonomous consumption, investment, and exports. The slope of the line is $b - m$, which is the MPC adjusted for imports. Aggregate demand is determined at the value of output where the demand line for U.S. goods crosses the 45° line.

Let's examine an application of the model that we just developed. Suppose the Japanese decide to buy another $5 billion worth of goods from the United States. What will happen to U.S. domestic output? Panel A of Figure 14.10 shows the effect of an increase in exports. The demand line will shift vertically upward by the increase in

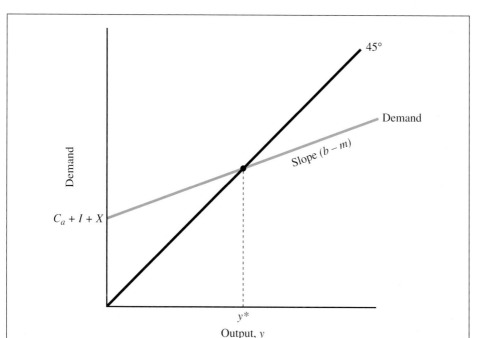

Figure 14.9

Determining Output in an Open Economy
Aggregate demand is determined where the demand for domestic goods equals output.

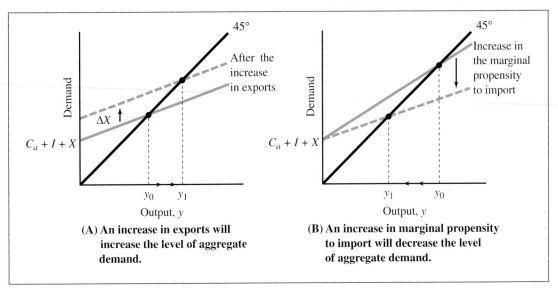

45°

After the
increase
in exports

Demand

ΔX ↑

$C_a + I + X$

y_0 y_1

Output, y

**(A) An increase in exports will
increase the level of aggregate
demand.**

45°

Increase in
the marginal
propensity
to import

Demand

$C_a + I + X$

y_1 y_0

Output, y

**(B) An increase in marginal propensity
to import will decrease the level
of aggregate demand.**

Figure 14.10
Increase in Exports and Imports

exports (ΔX). This will increase output or aggregate demand from y_0 to y_1. The increase in income will be larger than the increase in exports because of the multiplier effect. This multiplier is based on the MPC adjusted for trade. For example, if $b = 0.8$ and $m = 0.2$, the adjusted MPC ($b - m$) is 0.6 and the multiplier will be $1/(1 - 0.6) = 2.5$. Therefore, a \$5 billion increase in exports will lead to a \$12.5 billion shift in aggregate demand.

Now, suppose that U.S. residents become more attracted to foreign goods, and as a result, our marginal propensity to import increases. What happens to aggregate demand? Panel B of Figure 14.10 depicts the effect of an increase in imported foreign goods. The adjusted MPC ($b - m$) will fall as the marginal propensity to import increases. This reduces the slope of the demand line, and output will fall from y_0 to y_1.

We can now understand why our domestic political leaders are eager to sell our goods abroad. Whether it is electronics or weapons, increased U.S. exports will increase aggregate demand and reduce unemployment in the short run. At the same time, we can also understand why politicians will find "buy American" policies attractive in the short run. To the extent that U.S. residents buy U.S. goods rather than imports, aggregate demand will be higher.

Economic
Detective

The Netherlands' Multiplier

Some economists have argued the multiplier for government spending in the Netherlands is smaller than the multiplier for government spending in the United States. As an economic detective, can you explain this difference? (*Hint:* Imports and exports are a higher fraction of GDP in the Netherlands.)

The Netherlands is a small country and highly dependent on foreign trade. It has a high marginal propensity to import, which makes its adjusted MPC ($b - m$) low. A low adjusted MPC will make the multiplier low as well. Thus, the multiplier for fiscal policy is less in the Netherlands than the United States because the Netherlands has a higher marginal propensity to import.

A Final Reminder

It is important to emphasize that all the models in this chapter are based on shifting the aggregate demand curve. They are useful to understand how policy can be used in the short run. Policies appropriate for the short run are not necessarily appropriate for the long run. In this chapter, we have seen that an increase in desired consumption spending will raise aggregate demand and output in the short run. But in our chapter on long-run growth, we saw that higher saving (lower consumption) would increase output in the long run. The models in this chapter are designed only to analyze changes in aggregate demand and short-run fluctuations in output. They are not designed for advising what should be long-run policy.

Using the **TOOLS**

In this chapter, we developed the graphical tools and the mathematical formulas to analyze Keynesian economics. Here is an opportunity to do your own economic analysis.

1. ECONOMIC EXPERIMENT: ESTIMATING THE MARGINAL PROPENSITY TO CONSUME

For this experiment, each class member is asked to fill out the following table. Given a certain monthly income, how would you spend it and how much would you save? The top row of each column gives you the monthly disposable income. How would you allocate it each month among the various categories of spending in the table and savings? Complete each column in the table. The sum of your entries should equal your disposable income at the top of each column.

Monthly Disposable Income	$1,250	$1,500	$1,750	$2,000
Expenditures and Savings				
Food				
Housing				
Transportation				
Medical				
Entertainment				
Other expenses				
Savings				

After you have filled out the chart, compute the changes in your savings and total consumption as your income goes up. What is your marginal propensity to save (MPS)? What is your marginal propensity to consume (MPC) over your total expenditures? Graph your consumption function.

2. Using Multipliers

a. Suppose the MPC is equal to 0.8. Government spending increases by $20 billion. By how far does the aggregate demand curve shift to the right?

b. Now suppose that the MPC is 0.8 and the marginal propensity to import is 0.2. How far to the right will the $20 billion in government spending now shift the aggregate demand curve?

3. A Shock to Consumption

We can think of a shock to consumption as a change in autonomous consumption C_a. Economic historian Peter Temin argued that the Great Depression was caused by a

Test Your Understanding

1. It is the MPC.
2. Upward.
3. 0.3.
4. At that point, total demand is equal to the level of output produced.
5. 2.5
6. 1.67.
7. Fiscal.
8. False. Cutting taxes will increase aggregate demand and output.
9. $10 billion.
10. Either government spending should be cut or taxes increased.

Using the Tools

2. Using Multipliers
   a. In this case, the multiplier is $1/(1 - 0.8) = 5.0$. Therefore, the aggregate demand curve will shift to the right by $100 billion.
   b. Now the MPC adjusted for imports is $0.8 - 0.2 = 0.6$. The multiplier will be $1/(1 - 0.6) = 2.5$. Thus, the aggregate demand curve will shift to the right by $50 billion.

3. A Shock to Consumption. A decrease in autonomous consumption will shift down the vertical intercept of the $C + I + G$ line. This will lead to a fall in output. A large enough fall could cause a major fall in output.

4. Tax Refunds and Consumer Spending
   a. If the tax refunds were not expected and consumers base their spending on current income, then consumer spending should increase, increasing GDP.
   b. The same would be true if they anticipated the refund but still based their spending on the current value of income (which was increased by the refund).
   c. If they had anticipated the refund and also based their spending on their long-run income, there would be no change in consumption spending. In this case, the tax refund would not change their long-run income and, thus, would not change their spending decisions.

15

Money, the Banking System, and the Federal Reserve

As long as there has been paper money, there have been counterfeiters. In 1023, China formed a government agency to print paper money; by 1107, it had begun to print money in three colors to thwart counterfeiters. In 1998, the U.S. Treasury introduced a new $20 bill, using modern technology to make life difficult for counterfeiters. The portrait of Andrew Jackson is slightly off-center, and embedded in the paper is a plastic thread, invisible to the unaided human eye, that glows green under ultraviolet light. The new $20 bills are also printed with a special ink that looks green when viewed directly but changes to black when viewed from side to side. These are ingenious technological marvels. But the institution of money is an even greater marvel.

he term *money* has a special meaning for economists, so we'll look carefully at how they define money and the role that it plays in the economy.

The supply of money in the economy is determined primarily by the banking system and the actions of the Federal Reserve, our nation's central bank. We will see how the Federal Reserve, operating through the banking system, can create and destroy money. We will also study how the Federal Reserve operates and who controls it.

The supply of money is very important for the economy's performance. In our discussion of aggregate demand, we indicated how increases in the supply of money increase aggregate demand. In the short run, when prices are largely fixed, increases in the money supply will raise total demand and output. In the long run, continuing money growth leads to inflation. Therefore, changes in the supply of money have important effects on both output and prices: how much is produced, the cost of producing output, and what will be the prices of what is produced. In this chapter, we explain in detail how the supply of money in the economy is determined.

After reading this chapter, you should be able to answer the following questions:

1. Why do all societies have some form of money?
2. Why do banks play a special role in our economy?
3. Can banks really create money through computer entries?
4. When the Federal Reserve uses its special powers to buy and sell government bonds, how do buying and selling government bonds affect the supply of money in the economy?
5. Why is the chairman of the Federal Reserve one of the most powerful people in the country?

What Is Money?

Let's first discuss the definition and role of money and then see how it is measured in the U.S. economy.

Definition of Money

Money: Anything that is regularly used in exchange.

Economists define **money** as anything that is regularly used in economic transactions or exchanges. Let's consider some examples of money used in that way.

We use money regularly, every day. In an ice cream store, we hand the person behind the counter some dollar bills and coins, and we receive an ice cream cone. This is an example of an economic exchange: One party hands over currency—the dollar bills and the coins—and the other party hands over goods and services (the ice cream cone). Why do the owners of ice cream stores accept the dollar bills and coins in payment for the ice cream? The reason is that they will be making other economic exchanges with the dollar bills and coins they accept. Suppose they take the currency they receive from selling the ice cream and pay their supplier with it. The ice cream cones cost $1.50 each, and 100 ice cream cones are sold in a day. The seller then has $150 in currency. If the ice cream costs the seller $100, the seller pays $100 of the currency received and keeps $50 for other expenses and profits.

In the real world, transactions are somewhat more complicated. The ice cream store will take the currency it receives each day and deposit it into an account at its local bank. It will typically pay its suppliers with a check drawn on its account at that local bank. This is another example of an economic exchange: The ice cream supplier sells ice cream to the store in exchange for a check.

Why does the supplier accept a check? The supplier can use the check to make further transactions. The supplier can deposit the check in his or her own bank account and then either withdraw currency from this account or write checks on it.

In these examples, what is money? Recall the definition of money: anything that is regularly used in economic transactions or exchanges. Clearly, currency is money because it was used to purchase ice cream. Checks are also money because they are used to pay the supplier.

At other times and in other societies, different items have been used as money. In some ancient cultures, precious stones were used in exchanges; therefore, those stones constituted money. In more recent times, gold bars have served as money. During World War II, prisoners of war did not have currency, but they did have rations of cigarettes. The cigarettes began to be used for exchanges among the prisoners and played the role of money in the prison camps.

Three Properties of Money

Regardless of what money is in a particular society, it serves several functions, all related to making economic exchanges easier. Here we discuss three key properties of money.

1. Money Serves as a Medium of Exchange

As our examples illustrate, money is accepted in economic exchanges; that is, it serves as a **medium of exchange**. Suppose money did not exist and you had a car you wanted to sell to buy a boat. You could look for a person who had a boat and wanted to buy a car and then trade your car directly for a boat. This would be an example of **barter**: trading goods directly for goods.

But there are obvious problems with barter. Suppose local boatbuilders were interested in selling boats but not interested in buying your car. Unless there were a **double coincidence of wants**—that is, unless you wanted to trade a car for a boat and the boat owner wanted to trade a boat for your car—this economic exchange could not occur. The probability of a double coincidence of wants occurring is very, very tiny. Even if a boat owner wanted a car, he or she might want a different type of car than yours.

By serving as a medium of exchange, money solves this problem. A car owner can sell the car to anyone who wants it and receive money in return. With that money, the car owner can then find someone who owns a boat and purchase the boat for money. The boat owner can use the money in any way he or she pleases. With money, there is no need for a double coincidence of wants. This is why money exists in all societies: It makes economic transactions much easier.

2. Money Serves as a Unit of Account

Money also provides a convenient measuring rod when prices for all goods are quoted in money terms. A boat may be listed for sale at $5,000, a car at $10,000, and a movie ticket at $5. All these prices are quoted in money. We could in principle quote everything in terms of movie tickets. The boat would be worth 1,000 tickets, and the car would be worth 2,000 tickets. But since we are using money (and not movie tickets) as a medium of exchange, it is much easier if all prices are expressed in terms of money. We say that money is used as a **unit of account**, and all we mean by that is that prices are quoted in terms of money. This also makes it easier to conduct economic transactions, since there is a standard unit—whether that unit is movie tickets or the more convenient unit of dollars—in which to do so.

3. Money Serves as a Store of Value

If you sell your car to purchase a boat, you may not be able to purchase the boat immediately. In the meantime, you will be holding the money you received from the sale of the car. Ideally, during that period, the value of the money should not change. What we are referring to here is the function of money to be a **store of value**.

Medium of exchange: The property of money that exchanges are made through the use of money.

Barter: Trading goods directly for goods.

Double coincidence of wants: The problem in a system of barter that one person may not have what the other desires.

Unit of account: The property of money that prices are quoted in terms of money.

Store of value: The property of money that it preserves value until it is used in an exchange.

Money is actually a somewhat imperfect store of value because of inflation. Suppose inflation is 10% a year, which means that all prices rise 10% each year. Let's say you sold a tennis racket for $100 to buy 10 CDs worth $100 but that you waited a year to buy them. Unfortunately, at the end of the year, during which there was 10% inflation, the 10 CDs now cost $110 ($100 × 1.10), or $11 each. With your $100, you can now buy only 9 CDs and get $1 in change. Money has lost some of its stored value.

As long as inflation is low and you do not hold money for a long time, the loss in the purchasing power of money will not be a major problem. But as inflation rates increase, money becomes less useful as a store of value.

TEST Your Understanding

1. Money solves the problem of double coincidence of wants that would regularly occur under a system of _____.

2. Why is money only an imperfect store of value?

3. What is the problem associated with the double coincidence of wants?

4. Because we measure all prices in monetary units, money serves as a unit of account. True or false? Explain.

5. Why are checks included in the definition of money?

Measuring Money in the U.S. Economy

In the United States and other modern economies, there are typically several different ways in which economic transactions can be carried out. In practice, this leads to different definitions of money.

The most basic measure of money in the United States is called **M1**. Table 15.1 contains the components of M1 and their size for January 2003, and Figure 15.1 shows their relative percentages.

M1: The sum of currency in the hands of the public plus demand deposits plus other checkable deposits.

The first part of M1 is currency that is held by the public, that is, all currency held outside of bank vaults. The next two components are deposits in checking accounts, called demand deposits. Until the 1980s, checking accounts did not pay interest, and a new category, titled other checkable deposits, was introduced in the early 1980s to describe checking accounts that did pay interest. Today, this distinction is not as meaningful because many checking accounts pay interest if the account balance is sufficiently high. Finally, traveler's checks are included in M1 because they are regularly used in economic exchanges.

Let's take a closer look at the amount of currency in the economy. Since there are approximately 280 million people in the United States, the $630 billion of currency

Table 15.1   Components of M1, January 2003

Currency held by the public	$630 billion
Demand deposits	$295 billion
Other checkable deposits	$279 billion
Traveler's checks	$8 billion
Total of M1	$1,212 billion

Source: Federal Reserve Bank of St. Louis.

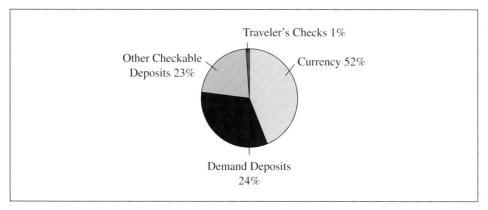

Figure 15.1

Components of M1 for the United States

- Traveler's Checks 1%
- Other Checkable Deposits 23%
- Currency 52%
- Demand Deposits 24%

amounts to more than $2,250 in currency for every man, woman, and child in the United States. Do you and your friends each have $2,250 of currency?

Most of the currency in the official statistics is not used in ordinary commerce in the United States. Much of it is held abroad by wealthy people who want U.S. currency in case of emergencies or who use it to keep their wealth out of sight of their own governments and tax authorities. Some of it circulates in other countries along with their local currencies. Currency is also used in illegal transactions such as the drug trade. Few dealers of illegal drugs open bank accounts that could be inspected by international law authorities.

The United States is not the only country that has a large amount of currency per capita outstanding, as "A Closer Look: Lots of Currency" explains.

M1 does not include all the assets that are used to make economic exchanges. Economists also use a somewhat broader definition of money known as **M2**, which includes assets that are sometimes used in economic exchanges or can be readily turned into M1. M2 consists of all the assets in M1 plus several other assets such as deposits in money market mutual funds. These are funds in which individuals can invest; they earn

M2: M1 plus other assets, including deposits in savings and loans and money market mutual funds.

Currency held by the public is part of the official money supply.

A CLOSER LOOK | LOTS OF CURRENCY

The economist Case M. Sprenkel has noted that other developed countries besides the United States have large amounts of currency per capita outstanding. In 1992, for example, while the United States had $1,096 of currency per person, measured in dollars, the Japanese had $2,228 per person and the Swiss had $3,116 per person. Austria, Belgium, Germany, Spain, and Sweden all had per capita currency holdings larger than those of the United States. British currency holdings per person, by contrast, were less than half of per capita money holdings in the United States.

What can explain these differences? There probably are some cultural differences. The Japanese traditionally carry more currency and use it frequently for gifts. There are even automated teller machines in Japan that press money to remove its wrinkles. But cultural preferences are not sufficient explanation. After all, why should the British hold so much less currency than the Belgians?

Sprenkel believed that much of the currency of the countries with large currency holdings per capita was actually held abroad, in developing countries whose domestic currencies did not provide good stores of value. As he put it, "The Argentinean taxi driver or the Algerian bellhop would like to have the American tourist or businessman's dollars, but would also appreciate the Italian's lire or the Japanese's yen if that is who is arriving." Currencies from developed countries are likely to be better stores of value than currencies in many developing countries.

Source: Case M. Sprenkel, "The Case of the Missing Money," *Journal of Economic Perspectives*, Fall 1993, pp. 175–184 (quotation from p. 177).

interest and can be used to write checks over some minimum amount. Deposits in savings accounts are also included in M2. While deposits in savings accounts cannot generally be used directly in exchanges, they can be converted to M1 and then used in exchanges. In January 2003, M2 totaled $5,826 billion.

Economists use different definitions of money because it is not always clear which assets are used primarily as money—that is, which assets are used for economic exchanges—and which are used primarily for saving and investing. For example, consider money market mutual funds, which came into existence only in the late 1970s. Although people can use these funds to write checks and engage in economic transactions, many people use them in other ways. Some may have their wealth temporarily invested in these funds in anticipation of moving their wealth into the stock market. Others may use them to earn interest while avoiding the risks of the stock market or bond market. Sometimes money market mutual funds are used like regular checking accounts; at other times, they are used like savings accounts. If they are used like checking accounts, they should be in M1; but if they are used like savings accounts, they should be part of M2. Economists keep an eye on both M1 and M2 because they often do not know precisely how money market accounts are used.

TEST Your Understanding

6. About one-third of M1 consists of _____.

7. Complete the statement with *M1* or *M2*: Economists use _____ to measure the amount of money that is regularly used in transactions.

8. Which is greater: M1 or M2?

9. How do you explain the fact that the total amount of currency divided by the U.S. population is approximately $2,250?

10. Why are money market mutual funds hard to classify?

Banks as Financial Intermediaries

Now let's see what part banks play in the creation of the supply of money. Financial intermediaries help to bring savers and investors together. By using their expertise and the powers of diversification, financial intermediaries reduce risk to savers and allow investors to obtain funds on better terms. Commercial banks operate precisely in this manner.

A typical commercial bank will accept funds from savers in the form of deposits—for example, in a checking account. The bank does not leave all these funds idle; if it did, it could never make a profit. Instead, the bank turns the money around and makes loans to businesses. A local hardware store might need a $100,000 loan to purchase its inventory. To make this loan, the bank would pool deposits from many savers. It will make other loans as well, reducing its risk through diversification.

It will be easier to understand how banks work if we examine a simplified **balance sheet** for a commercial bank. A balance sheet shows how banks raise money and where the money goes.

Balance sheets have two sides: one for assets and one for liabilities. **Liabilities** are the source of funds for the bank. If you open a checking account and deposit your funds in that account, the bank is liable for returning these funds to you. Your deposits are liabilities to the bank.

Assets are the uses of these funds. Assets generate income for the bank. Loans are examples of a bank's assets because a borrower must pay interest to the bank.

The difference between a bank's assets and its liabilities is its **net worth**:

$$\text{net worth} = \text{assets} - \text{liabilities}$$

If a bank has $1,000 of assets and $900 of liabilities, it has a net worth of $100. When a bank is started, its owners must place their own funds into the bank. These funds are the bank's initial net worth. If a bank makes profits, its net worth increases; if it loses money, its net worth decreases.

In Figure 15.2, we show the assets and liabilities of a hypothetical bank. On the liability side, the bank has $2,000 of deposits. The net worth of the bank is $200. This is entered on the liability side of the balance sheet because it is also a source of funds. The total source of funds is therefore $2,200—the deposits in the bank plus its net worth.

On the asset side, the bank holds $200 in **reserves**; these are assets that are not lent out. Banks are required by law to hold a specific fraction of their deposits as reserves and not make loans with it; this fraction of deposits is called **required reserves**. Banks may choose to hold additional reserves beyond what is required; these are called **excess reserves**. A bank's reserves are the sum of its required and excess reserves. Reserves can be either cash kept in a bank's vaults or deposits with the Federal Reserve. Banks do not earn any interest on these reserves.

In our example, the bank is holding 10% of its deposits, or $200, as reserves. The remainder of the bank's assets consists of loans. In this case the bank makes $2,000 in loans.

By definition, total assets will always equal liabilities plus net worth. Balance sheets must always balance.

Balance sheet: An account for a bank that shows the sources of its funds (liabilities) as well as the uses for the funds (assets).

Liabilities: The sources of funds for a bank, including deposits.

Assets: The uses of the funds of a bank, including loans and reserves.

Net worth: The difference between assets and liabilities.

Reserves: The fraction of banks' deposits that are set aside in either vault cash or as deposits at the Federal Reserve.

Required reserves: The fraction of banks' deposits that banks are legally required to hold in their vaults or as deposits at the Fed.

Excess reserves: Any additional reserves that a bank holds above its required reserves.

Assets	Liabilities
$ 200 Reserves	$2,000 Deposits
$2,000 Loans	$ 200 Net Worth
Total: $2,200	Total: $2,200

Figure 15.2
Balance Sheet for a Bank

The Process of Money Creation

To understand the role that banks play in determining the supply of money, let's suppose that someone walks into the First Bank of Hollywood and deposits $1,000 in cash to open a checking account. Because currency held by the public and checking deposits are both included in the supply of money, the total money supply has not changed. The money supply did not change because the cash deposit of currency into the checking account reduced the currency held by the public by precisely the amount that the deposit in the checking account increased.

However, banks do not keep in their vaults all the cash they receive. For a bank to make a profit, it must make loans. Let's assume that banks are required to keep 10% of deposits as reserves and hold no excess reserves. That means that the **reserve ratio**—the ratio of reserves to deposits—will be 0.1. The First Bank of Hollywood will keep $100 in reserves and make loans totaling $900. The top panel in Figure 15.3 shows the change in the bank's balance sheet after it has made its loan.

Reserve ratio: The ratio of reserves to deposits.

Suppose the First Bank of Hollywood loaned the funds to an aspiring movie producer. The bank opens a checking account, with a balance of $900, for the producer, who needs the funds to buy equipment. The producer buys the equipment from a supplier who accepts payment in the form of a $900 check, and deposits the check in the Second Bank of Burbank. The next panel in Figure 15.3 shows what happens to the balance sheet of the Second Bank of Burbank. Liabilities increase by the deposit of $900. The bank must hold $90 in reserves (10% of the $900 deposit) and can lend out $810. Suppose that it lends the $810 to an owner of a coffeehouse and opens a checking account with a balance of $810 for her. She then purchases coffee costing $810, paying with a check to the supplier, who deposits the $810 check into the Third Bank of Venice.

Figure 15.3

Process of Deposit Creation: Changes in Balance Sheets

The Third Bank of Venice receives a deposit of $810. It must keep $81 in reserves and can lend out $729. This process continues throughout the Los Angeles area with new loans and deposits. The Fourth Bank of Pasadena will receive a deposit of $729, hold $72.90 in reserves, and lend out $656.10. The Fifth Bank of Compton will receive a deposit of $656.10 as the process goes on.

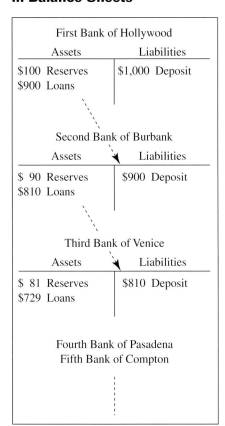

The original $1,000 cash deposit has created checking account balances throughout Los Angeles. What total amount of checking account balances has been created? Adding up the new accounts in all the banks (even the ones we have not named), we have

$$\$1,000 + \$900 + \$810 + \$729 + \$656.10 + \ldots = \$10,000$$

There is a simple formula that relates the total reserves in checking balances to the initial deposit:

total increase in checking account balance throughout all banks
= (initial cash deposit) × (1/reserve ratio)

In our example, the reserve ratio is 0.1, so the increase in checking account balances is 1/0.1, or 10 times the initial cash deposit. The initial $1,000 deposit led to a total increase in checking account balances throughout all banks of $10,000.

Recall that the money supply, M1, is the sum of deposits at commercial banks plus currency held by the public. Therefore, the change in the money supply, M1, will be the change in deposits in checking accounts plus the change in currency held by the public. Notice that we referred to "change," meaning increase or decrease. Here's why: In our example, deposits increased by $10,000, but the public (as represented by the person who made that first deposit at the First Bank of Hollywood) holds $1,000 less of currency because the person deposited the currency in the bank. Therefore, the money supply, M1, increased by $9,000 ($10,000 − $1,000). No single bank lent out more than it had in deposits. Yet for the banking system as a whole, the money supply expanded by a multiple of the initial cash deposit.

The term *1/reserve ratio* in the formula is called the **money multiplier**. It tells us what the total increase in checking account deposits would be for any initial cash deposit. Recall the multiplier for government spending in the last chapter: An increase in government spending led to larger increases in output through the multiplier. The government-spending multiplier arose because additional rounds of consumption spending were triggered by an initial increase in government spending. In the banking system, an initial cash deposit triggers additional rounds of deposits and lending by banks. This leads to a multiple expansion of deposits.

Money multiplier: An initial deposit leads to a multiple expansion of deposits. In the simplified case, increase in deposits = (initial deposit) × (1/reserve ratio).

As of 2003 in the United States, banks were required to hold 3% reserves against checkable deposits up to $42.1 million and 10% on all checkable deposits exceeding $42.1 million. Since large banks would face a 10% reserve requirement on any new deposits, you might think, on the basis of our formula, that the money multiplier would be approximately 10.

However, the money multiplier for the United States is between 2 and 3, much smaller than the value of 10 implied by our simple formula. The primary reason is that our formula assumed that all loans made their way directly into checking accounts. In reality, people hold part of their loans as cash. The cash that people hold is not available for the banking system to lend out. The more money people hold in cash, the lower the amount of money they deposit, creating fewer deposits, thus decreasing the money multiplier. The money multiplier would also be less if banks held excess reserves. We can represent these factors in a money multiplier ratio, but it will not be as simple as the one we introduced here.

The money creation process also works in reverse. Suppose you go to your bank and ask for $1,000 in cash from your checking account. The bank must pay you the $1,000. Its liabilities fall by $1,000, but its assets must also fall by $1,000. Withdrawing your $1,000 means two things at the bank: First, if the reserve ratio is 0.1, the bank will reduce its reserves by $100. Second, your $1,000 withdrawal minus the $100 reduction in reserves means that the bank has $900 less to lend out; hence, it will reduce its loans by $900. With fewer loans, there will be fewer deposits in other banks. The money multiplier working in reverse decreases the money supply.

You may wonder how a bank goes about reducing its outstanding loans. If you had borrowed from a bank to invest in a project for your business, you would not want the bank phoning you, asking for its funds, which are not lying idle but are invested in your business. Banks do not typically call in loans from outstanding borrowers. Instead, if banks cannot tap into their excess reserves when their customers want to withdraw cash, they would have to make fewer new loans. In these circumstances, a new potential borrower would find it harder to obtain a loan from the bank.

Up to this point, our examples have always started with an initial cash deposit. However, suppose that Paul receives a check from Freda and Paul deposits it into his bank. Paul's bank will eventually receive payment from Freda's bank. When Paul's bank does receive payment, the bank will initially have an increase in both deposits and reserves, just as if a cash deposit were made. Because Paul's bank has to hold only a fraction of the deposits as reserves, it will be able to make loans with the remainder.

However, there is one crucial difference between this example in which one individual writes a check to another and our earlier example in which an individual makes a cash deposit: When Paul receives the check from Freda, the money supply will not be changed. Here's why it won't: When Freda's check is deposited in Paul's bank, the money supply will begin to expand, but when Freda's bank loses its deposit, the money supply will start to contract. The expansions and contractions offset each other when private citizens and firms write checks to one another.

TEST Your Understanding

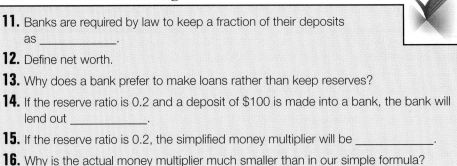

11. Banks are required by law to keep a fraction of their deposits as _____.

12. Define net worth.

13. Why does a bank prefer to make loans rather than keep reserves?

14. If the reserve ratio is 0.2 and a deposit of $100 is made into a bank, the bank will lend out _____.

15. If the reserve ratio is 0.2, the simplified money multiplier will be _____.

16. Why is the actual money multiplier much smaller than in our simple formula?

The Role of the Federal Reserve in the Money Creation Process

Banks can expand the money supply only if new reserves come into the banking system. When private citizens and firms write checks to one another, there will be no net change in the supply of money in the system. Because the total amount of reserves in the system is unchanged, the money supply cannot expand. There is one organization, however, that has the power to change the total amount of reserves in the banking system: the Federal Reserve.

Open Market Operations

The Federal Reserve (the Fed) can increase or decrease the total amount of reserves in the banking system through either of the following operations:

Open market purchases: The Fed's purchase of government bonds, which increases the money supply.

Open market sales: The Fed's sale of government bonds to the public, which decreases the money supply.

- In **open market purchases**, the Federal Reserve buys government bonds from the private sector.
- In **open market sales**, the Fed sells government bonds to the private sector.

To understand how the Fed can increase the supply of money, let's trace what happens after an open market purchase. Suppose the Federal Reserve purchases $1 million worth of government bonds from the private sector. The Fed writes a check for $1 million and presents it to the party who sold the bonds. The Federal Reserve now owns those bonds.

The party who sold the bonds has a check written on the Federal Reserve for $1 million. He deposits this check in his bank. The bank credits his account in the amount of $1 million because it has the check for $1 million written against the Federal Reserve.

Here is the key to how that increases the supply of money: Checks written against the Federal Reserve count as reserves for banks. As soon as the bank presents the check to the Federal Reserve, the bank will have $1 million in new reserves. If the reserve requirement is 10%, the bank must keep $100,000 in reserves, but it can make loans for $900,000. And so the process of money creation begins. Open market purchases increase the money supply.

The Federal Reserve has powers that ordinary citizens and even banks do not have. The Fed can write checks against itself to purchase government bonds without having any explicit "funds" in its account for the purchase. Banks accept these checks because they count as reserves for the bank.

As you might expect, open market sales will decrease the supply of money. Suppose the Federal Reserve sells $1 million worth of bonds to a Wall Street firm. The firm will pay for the bonds with a check for $1 million drawn on its bank and give this check to the Federal Reserve. The firm now owns the bonds.

The Federal Reserve presents this check to the Wall Street firm's bank. The bank must either hand over $1 million in cash or, more likely, reduce its reserve holding with the Federal Reserve by $1 million. (Banks keep accounts with the Fed, and in this case, the Fed would reduce the bank's account balance by $1 million.) Because the bank's reserves have fallen, it must decrease its loans to increase reserves to their required levels. And so, the process of money destruction begins. Open market sales decrease the money supply.

In summary, if the Federal Reserve wishes to increase the money supply, it buys government bonds from the private sector—called open market purchases. If the Fed wishes to decrease the money supply, it sells government bonds to the private sector—called open market sales.

Other Tools

Open market operations are by far the most important way in which the Federal Reserve changes the supply of money. There are two other ways in which the Fed can change the supply of money:

1. Change the reserve requirement.
2. Change the discount rate.

If the Fed wishes to increase the supply of money, it can reduce banks' reserve requirements. Banks would then only need to hold a smaller fraction of their deposits as reserves and could make more loans, expanding the money supply. To decrease the supply of money, the Federal Reserve could raise reserve requirements.

Although changing reserve requirements can be a strong tool, the Federal Reserve does not use it very often because it is disruptive to the banking system. Suppose a major bank whose clients were multinational corporations held exactly 10% of its deposits as reserves and the remainder as loans. If the Federal Reserve suddenly increased its reserve requirement to 20%, the bank would be forced to call in or cancel many of its loans. Its multinational clients would not like this! For these reasons, the Fed today does not make sharp changes in reserve requirements. In the past, the Fed did change reserve requirements sharply; when it did, the results were extremely disruptive to banks and their customers.

The Fed will lend banks reserves at an interest rate called the **discount rate**. Suppose a major customer comes to the bank and asks for a loan. Unless the bank could find an additional source of funds, it would have to refuse to make the loan. Banks are reluctant to turn away major customers. They first try to borrow reserves from other banks through the **federal funds market**, a market in which banks borrow or lend reserves to each other. If the federal funds rate seemed too high to the bank, it could borrow directly from the Federal Reserve at the discount rate.

Discount rate: The interest rate at which banks can borrow from the Fed.

Federal funds market: The market in which banks borrow and lend reserves to one another.

By changing the discount rate, the Federal Reserve can influence the amount of borrowing by banks. If the Fed raised the discount rate, banks would be discouraged from borrowing reserves because it has become more costly to borrow. Lowering the discount rate will induce banks to borrow additional reserves.

In principle, the Federal Reserve could use the discount rate as a tool independent of monetary policy: lowering the discount rate to expand the money supply and raising the discount rate to reduce the money supply. In practice, the Fed keeps the discount rate close to the federal funds rate to avoid large swings in borrowed reserves by banks. Changes in the discount rate, however, are quite visible to financial markets. Participants in the financial markets often interpret these changes as revealing clues about the Fed's intentions for future monetary policy.

The media typically describes the Federal Reserve as setting the federal funds rate. In fact, the Fed does conduct monetary policy by setting targets for the federal funds rate. Once it has set those targets, it uses open market operations to keep the actual funds rate on target.

TEST Your Understanding

17. Complete the statement with *increases* or *decreases*: When the Federal Reserve buys bonds, it _____ the money supply.

18. Complete the statement with *sale* or *purchase*: An open market _____ will lead to a reduction of reserves in banks.

19. Who borrows and lends in the federal funds market?

20. What is the discount rate?

The Structure of the Federal Reserve

The Federal Reserve System was created in 1913 after a series of financial panics in the United States. Financial panics can occur when there is bad news about the economy or about the health and vitality of financial institutions that causes concern among individuals doing business in the financial markets. During these panics, depositors became fearful that they would not be able to withdraw their account balances if they delayed, so they started to withdraw their funds immediately. This meant that banks could no longer make loans to businesses, resulting in severe economic downturns. Congress created the Federal Reserve System to be a **central bank**, serving as a banker's bank. One of the Fed's primary jobs was to serve as a **lender of last resort**. If there was a panic in which depositors wanted to withdraw their funds, the Federal Reserve would be there to lend funds to banks, thereby reducing some of the adverse consequences of the panic.

The Federal Reserve's important role as a lender of last resort came into play immediately following the September 11, 2001, terrorist attack. "A Closer Look: The Fed Responds to the Terrorist Attack" outlines the key steps that the Federal Reserve took to ensure the continuing operation of the financial system.

Congress was aware that it was creating an institution with vast powers, so it deliberately created a structure in which, at least on paper, it attempted to disperse power away from the financial centers (such as New York) to the rest of the country. To understand the structure of the Federal Reserve today, keep in mind it has three distinct subgroups: Federal Reserve Banks, the Board of Governors, and the Federal Open Market Committee.

The United States was divided into 12 Federal Reserve districts, each of which has a **Federal Reserve Bank**. These district banks provide advice on monetary policy, take part in decision making on monetary policy, and provide a liaison between the Fed and the banks in their districts.

Figure 15.4 is a map of the United States, identifying geographically each of the 12 Federal Reserve Banks. At the time the Fed was created, economic and financial power in this country was concentrated in the East and the Midwest. This is no longer true. What major western city does not have a Federal Reserve Bank?

The **Board of Governors of the Federal Reserve** is the true seat of power over the monetary system. Headquartered in Washington, D.C., the seven members of the board are

Central bank: A banker's bank; an official bank that controls the supply of money in a country.

Lender of last resort: A central bank is the lender of last resort, the last place, having failed all others, that banks in emergency situations can obtain loans.

Federal Reserve Bank: One of 12 regional banks that are an official part of the Federal Reserve System.

Board of Governors of the Federal Reserve: The seven-person governing body of the Federal Reserve system in Washington, D.C.

THE FED RESPONDS TO THE TERRORIST ATTACK

When the financial markets closed after September 11, 2001, many firms that borrowed funds regularly in the markets did not have sufficient cash on hand to meet their ongoing bills and obligations. Unless some actions were taken quickly, these firms would default on their debts, leading to payment problems for other firms and further defaults. To prevent this avalanche of defaults, the Federal Reserve immediately took a number of steps to provide additional funds to the financial system.

The first tool that the Federal Reserve used was to allow banks to borrow more from the Federal Reserve itself at the discount rate. In regular times, the volume of these direct loans from the Federal Reserve is not very large. On Wednesday, September 12, 2001, total lending to banks rose to $45.5 billion, up from just $1 billion the week before.

The Federal Reserve System routinely acts as a clearinghouse for checks. A bank will bring checks it receives from customers to the Federal Reserve and receive immediate credit on its accounts. The Federal Reserve then debits the account of the bank on which the check was written. The difference between the credits and debits extended by the Federal Reserve is called the Federal Reserve float. Immediately following September 11, the Federal Reserve allowed this float to increase sharply from $2.9 billion to $22.9 billion. These actions effectively put an additional $20 billion into the banking system.

The Federal Reserve also increased its open market purchases of government securities in the market by nearly $30 billion. It also arranged to provide dollars to foreign central banks that needed funds for their own needs and the needs of the banks in their countries. Taking all these actions together, the Federal Reserve extended an additional $90 billion in credit following September 11. This massive response by the Federal Reserve prevented a major financial panic.

Source: William Poole, "The Role of Government in U.S. Capital Markets," paper delivered at UC Davis, October 8, 2001.

appointed for staggered 14-year terms by the president and must be confirmed by the Senate. The chairperson of the Board of Governors serves a four-year term. As the principal spokesperson for monetary policy in the United States, what the chairperson says, or might say, is carefully observed or anticipated by financial markets throughout the world.

Decisions on monetary policy are made by the **Federal Open Market Committee (FOMC)**. The FOMC is a 12-person board consisting of the seven members of the Board of

Federal Open Market Committee (FOMC): The group that decides on monetary policy; it consists of the seven members of the Board of Governors plus 5 of 12 regional bank presidents on a rotating basis.

Figure 15.4

Federal Reserve Banks of the United States

Governors, the president of the New York Federal Reserve Bank, and the presidents of four other regional Federal Reserve Banks. (Presidents of the regional banks other than New York serve on a rotating basis; the seven nonvoting bank presidents attend the meetings and provide their views.) The chairperson of the Board of Governors also serves as the chairperson of the FOMC. The FOMC makes the actual decisions on changes in the money supply. Its members are assisted by vast teams of professionals at the Board of Governors and at the regional Federal Reserve Banks. The structure of the Federal Reserve System is depicted in Figure 15.5.

The chairperson of the Board of Governors is also required to report to Congress on a regular basis. Although the Federal Reserve operates with independence from the U.S. Treasury, it is a creation of Congress. The U.S. Constitution gives Congress the power to "coin money and regulate the value thereof." In practice, the Fed takes its actions first and later reports its actions to Congress. The chairperson of the Federal Reserve often meets with members of the executive branch to discuss economic affairs.

On paper, the powers of monetary policy appear to be spread throughout the government and the country. In practice, however, the Board of Governors and especially the chairperson have the real control. The Board of Governors operates with considerable independence. Presidents and members of Congress can bring political pressures on the Board of Governors, but 14-year terms provide some insulation from external pressures.

Countries differ in the degree to which the central bank is independent of political authorities. In both the United States and the United Kingdom, the central banks operate with considerable independence of elected officials. In other countries, the central bank is part of the treasury department of the government and potentially subject to more direct political control.

There is a lively debate among economists and political scientists as to whether more independent central banks (with less external political pressure) have less inflation. Even if there is an advantage to an independent central bank, there still is an important issue: In a democratic society, why should we allow there to be an important and powerful institution that is not directly subject to the control by the people or our elected officials?

Why should we care about the Fed and the supply of money? In this chapter, we have discussed the role that money plays in the economy, how commercial banks play a key role in the creation of money, and how the Fed exercises ultimate control over the money supply. In the next chapter, we will see that the Fed can also determine short-

Figure 15.5
Structure of the Federal Reserve System

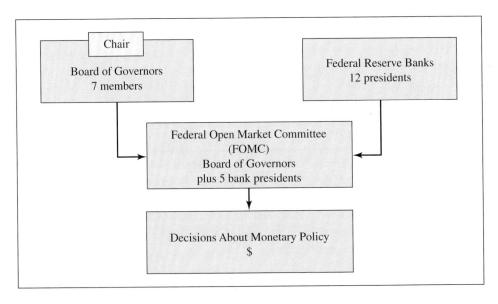

term interest rates and thereby influence the level of economic activity. It is precisely this power over the economy that makes the Fed such a subject of public interest.

Using the **TOOLS**

In this chapter, we studied the money creation process as it works through the banking system. Take this opportunity to do your own economic analysis.

1. ECONOMIC EXPERIMENT: MONEY AND THE STORE OF VALUE

This experiment demonstrates that goods that are more effective stores of value can become the medium of exchange. There are three types of individuals (A, B, C) and three types of goods in the economy (1, 2, 3). Type A consumes good 1; Type B consumes good 2; and Type C consumes good 3. No type produces the good it consumes: Type A produces good 2; Type B produces good 3; and Type C produces good 1. Here is how the game works: In the first period, individuals start with one unit of the good they produce and are randomly paired with other individuals. They can either engage in trade or not. If they successfully trade for the good they are allowed to consume, they consume it immediately and earn 100 points. At that time, they also costlessly produce one unit of their good for the next round of play. If individuals do not trade, they must store their goods. They lose 10 points for storing good 1, lose 20 points for storing good 2, and lose 30 points for storing good 3. The game proceeds for several periods, and the individual with the most points wins. What good do you think emerges as the medium of exchange?

2. Bad Loans to South America

During the 1980s, U.S. banks made loans to South American countries. Many of these loans turned out to be worthless. How did this affect the assets, liabilities, and net worth of these banks?

3. Reserve Requirements as a Tax

Left on their own, most banks would reduce their reserve requirements far below 10%. Consequently, banks view reserve requirements as a "tax" on their holdings of deposits. Explain how a 10% reserve requirement could be viewed as a 10% tax.

4. High-Powered Money

Economists define high-powered money as the reserves at banks plus the currency held by the public. The Federal Reserve is often said to control the stock of high-powered money. Does the stock of high-powered money change when:

a. Currency is deposited into a bank?

b. A bank makes a loan?

c. The Federal Reserve buys government bonds?

Summary

We began this chapter examining the role money plays in the economy and how economists define money. We then took a closer look at banks as financial intermediaries. We saw how banks can create money through deposit creation. And we learned how the Federal Reserve can control the supply of money through open market purchases and sales and other policies. Here are the main points you should remember from this chapter:

1. Money consists of anything that is regularly used in making exchanges, that is, buying and selling goods and services. In modern economies, money consists primarily of currency and deposits in checking accounts.

2. Banks are financial intermediaries that earn profits by accepting deposits and making loans. Deposits, which are liabilities of banks, are included in the money supply.

3. Banks are required by law to hold a fraction of their deposits as reserves, either in cash or in deposits with the Federal Reserve. Total reserves consist of required reserves plus excess reserves.

4. If there is an increase in reserves in the banking system, the supply of money will expand by a multiple of the initial deposit. This multiple is known as the money multiplier.

5. the Federal Reserve's primary tool for increasing or decreasing the total amount of reserves in the banking system is through open market purchases of government bonds (which increase reserves) or open market sales (which decrease reserves).

6. The Federal Reserve can also change the supply of money by changing reserve requirements or changing the discount rate.

7. Decisions about the supply of money are made at the Federal Open Market Committee (FOMC), which includes the seven members on the Board of Governors and the president of the New York Federal Reserve Bank, as well as 4 of the 11 other regional bank presidents, who serve on a rotating basis.

Key Terms

assets, 343
balance sheet, 343
barter, 339
Board of Governors of the Federal Reserve, 348
central bank, 348
discount rate, 347
double coincidence of wants, 339
excess reserves, 343
federal funds market, 347

Federal Open Market Committee (FOMC), 349
Federal Reserve Bank, 348
lender of last resort, 348
liabilities, 343
M1, 340
M2, 341
medium of exchange, 339
money, 338
money multiplier, 345

net worth, 343
open market purchases, 346
open market sales, 346
required reserves, 343
reserve ratio, 344
reserves, 343
store of value, 339
unit of account, 339

Problems and Discussion Questions

1. Why are traveler's checks classified as money?

2. Both insurance companies and banks are financial intermediaries. Why do macroeconomists study banks more intensively than insurance companies?

3. What is the opportunity cost to a bank of holding excess reserves?

4. If a customer took $2,000 in cash from a bank and the reserve ratio was 0.2, by how much would the supply of money be eventually reduced?

5. If the Federal Reserve undertakes an open market sale of $2 million and the reserve ratio is 0.15, by how much will the money supply decrease?

6. If banks hold excess reserves, how will this affect the money multiplier?

7. Explain the mechanism through which an increase in the discount rate affects the money supply.

8. Occasionally, some economists or politicians suggest that the Secretary of Treasury become a member of the Federal Open Market Committee. How do you think this would affect the independence of the Federal Reserve?

9. Suppose the Federal Reserve purchased gold or foreign currency. How would this purchase affect the domestic money supply? (*Hint:* Think about open market purchases of government bonds.)

10. The Federal Reserve has traditionally conducted its open market operations through the purchase and sale of government bonds. In principle, could the

Federal Reserve conduct monetary policy through the purchase and sale of stocks on the New York Stock Exchange? Do you see any potential drawbacks to such a policy?

11. In 1992, the state of California ran out of funds and could not pay its bills. It issued IOUs, called warrants, to its workers and suppliers. Only large banks and credit unions accepted the warrants. Should these warrants be viewed as money?

12. Web Exercise. Go to the Web site of the Federal Reserve (*www.federalreserve.gov*) and read the minutes from the last Open Market Committee meeting. What decisions did it make with regard to open market operations? What other items of business were on its agenda that day?

13. Web Exercise. Go to the data Web site of the Federal Reserve Bank of St. Louis (*www.stls.frb.org/fred*). Look carefully at the components of M1 and M2 over the last 10 years. What trends do you see?

Take It to the Net

We invite you to visit the O'Sullivan/Sheffrin page on the Prentice Hall Web site at: **www.prenhall.com/osullivan/** for additional World Wide Web exercises for this chapter.

Model Answers to Questions

Chapter-Opening Questions

1. All societies have money because it makes it much easier to conduct trade.

2. Banks play a special role in our economy because the liabilities of banks are part of the supply of money.

3. The banking system as a whole can create money through the process of multiple expansion. However, this depends on the actions of the Federal Reserve.

4. When the Federal Reserve purchases bonds from the public, it increases reserves in banks and leads to an increase in the supply of deposits and loans. When the Federal Reserve sells bonds to the public, the supply of loans and deposits decreases.

5. The chairman of the Federal Reserve is the most powerful person in the Federal Reserve System, which determines the supply of money in the economy.

Test Your Understanding

1. Barter.

2. Inflation makes money an imperfect store of value.

3. Without money, you would need to find someone who had the good that you wanted to buy and also wants to trade for the good that you have.

4. True. Money serves as a unit of account because prices are quoted in terms of money.

5. Checks are counted as money because they are regularly used in economic exchanges.

6. Currency held by the public.

7. M1.

8. M2 is greater.

9. A "typical" person in the United States does not hold this amount of currency. Some currency is held abroad, and some is held for illegal purposes.

10. Money market mutual funds are used both for making transactions and for savings.

11. Reserves.

12. Net worth is assets minus liabilities.

13. Banks do not earn interest on reserves, but they do on loans.

14. $80.

15. 5.

16. The simplified formula does not take into account that individuals hold some cash from their loans.

17. Increases.

18. Sale.

19. Banks borrow and lend.

20. The discount rate is the interest rate at which banks can borrow from the Fed.

Using the Tools

1. Economic Experiment: Money and the Store of Value. As the experiment should reveal, good 1 should emerge as the most likely medium of exchange.

2. **Bad Loans to South America.** Bad loans will reduce the assets of a bank. Because they do not change the liabilities of a bank (its deposits), the net worth of the bank must also fall along with the value of its assets. If the net worth of a bank falls too far, the bank can be closed.

3. **Reserve Requirements as a Tax.** Because a bank earns no interest on reserves, the reserve requirement acts as a tax. Suppose the bank held no reserves at all and could earn 20% interest on loans. A 10% reserve requirement means that the bank could only earn 20% interest on 90% of its deposits. This is equivalent to a tax of 10%.

4. **High-Powered Money.** The stock of high-powered money changes only when the Federal Reserve buys a government bond. In this case, the total of reserves plus currency increases. If the public deposits currency in the bank, currency held by the public falls but the currency held by the bank (which counts as reserves) increases. When a bank makes a loan, the total reserves in the banking system do not change.

Monetary Policy and Inflation

A phone call is made from Washington, D.C., to the Federal Reserve Bank of New York. Traders at the New York Federal Reserve Bank proceed to the market in which U.S. bonds are traded and purchase bonds in the market on their account. Within minutes, interest rates and exchange rates start to move; months and even years later, the effects of the interest rate and exchange rate changes are felt in cities, counties, and states throughout this country and abroad. Economic livelihoods—jobs and profits—are altered by these actions. How can simple transactions in our financial market lead to dramatic changes across the globe?

n this chapter, we will learn why everyone is so interested in what the Federal Reserve is about to do. In the short run, when prices don't have enough time to change, and we consider them temporarily fixed, the Federal Reserve can influence the level of interest rates in the economy. When the Federal Reserve lowers interest rates, investment spending and GDP increase. When the Fed increases interest rates, it reduces investment spending and GDP. In the long run, when prices fully adjust, changes in the money supply affect prices, not output. Thus, the actions taken by the Federal Reserve to control the supply of money also control the rate of inflation in the economy in the long run.

After reading this chapter, you will be able to answer the following questions:

1. Why does investment spending depend on interest rates?
2. Why do short-term interest rates rise after the Federal Reserve makes open market sales?
3. How do the housing and construction industries respond after the Federal Reserve decides to increase the money supply?
4. Why do countries with lower rates of money growth have lower interest rate levels than countries with higher rates of money growth?

We begin the chapter with a discussion of investment spending and interest rates. A key point is that the level of investment spending in the economy will depend on the level of interest rates. Since the Federal Reserve controls the level of interest rates in the short run, it also will be able to affect the level of investment spending in the economy.

The Federal Reserve influences the level of interest rates in the short run by changing the supply of money through open market operations: selling or buying bonds in the open market. We will explain in this chapter how interest rates are determined in the short run by the supply and demand for money.

In the long run, the economy returns to full employment and changes in aggregate demand (including changes in the supply of money) will affect only prices, not output. Thus, the effects of money on output and employment are temporary, but the effects on prices and the rate of inflation are permanent.

Investment: A Plunge into the Unknown

Investments are actions taken today that have costs today and provide benefits in the future. Firms or individuals incur costs today in the hope of future gain. The phrase *hope of* is an important aspect of investment decisions. That simply means that payoffs occurring in the future cannot be known with certainty. Investments are a plunge into the unknown.

Consider a few examples: When an automobile firm builds a new plant because it anticipates increased future demand for its cars, it is taking a gamble. Suppose the model in the future proves to be unpopular, or the economy goes into a recession and consumers cut back their purchases of all cars? By building a new plant when it was not needed, the firm will have made an investment decision that didn't pay off in the future. Suppose a government builds nuclear plants, then citizens decide that they are unsafe and force the plants to be closed. The government would have wasted resources on this investment.

Firms and individuals regularly revise their estimates of the future—because it is uncertain. Sometimes they're optimistic, deciding to increase their investment spending; at other times, they're pessimistic, cutting back on investment spending. These changes in outlook can occur suddenly and may lead to sharp swings in investment spending. John Maynard Keynes said these sharp swings were often irrational, reflect-

A high-rise building is a risky venture for its investors, who are betting that the office space will be needed in the future.

ing, perhaps, our most basic, primal instincts. He often referred to what he called the animal spirits of investors.

To estimate future events, firms will look carefully at current developments. If economic growth is currently sluggish, firms may project that it will be sluggish in the future as well. If there is an upsurge in economic growth, firms may become optimistic, increasing their investment spending. Investment spending tends to be closely related to the current pace of economic growth. One theory of investment spending, known as the **accelerator theory**, emphasizes the role of expected growth in real GDP on investment spending. When real GDP growth is expected to be high, firms anticipate that their investments in plant and equipment will be profitable and therefore increase their total investment spending.

Projections for the future and investors' current animal spirits are both likely to move in conjunction with real GDP growth. For these reasons, we would expect that investment spending would be a volatile component of GDP. As Figure 16.1 indicates, this is the case. Figure 16.1 plots total investment spending as a share of U.S. GDP from 1970 to 2002. There are two things you need to see in this figure:

1. Over this period, the share of investment in GDP ranged from a low of 11% to a high of 19%—a dramatic difference of 8 percentage points of GDP.

2. These swings in investment spending often occur over short periods. During periods of recessions, investment spending falls sharply. Investment spending is highly **procyclical**, meaning that investment spending increases during booms and falls during recessions.

Accelerator theory: The theory of investment that says that current investment spending depends positively on the expected future growth of real GDP.

Procyclical: A component of GDP is procyclical if it rises and falls with the overall level of GDP.

Figure 16.1

Investment Spending as a Share of U.S. GDP, 1970–2002

Shaded areas indicate recessions according to NBER business cycle reference dates.

Source: Department of Commerce.

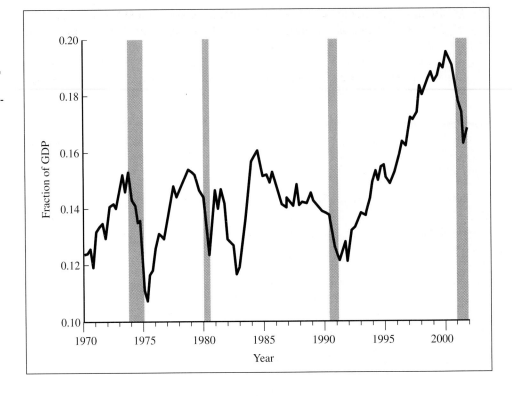

Although investment spending is a much smaller component of GDP than consumption, it is much more volatile than consumption. It is, therefore, important for understanding fluctuations in real GDP. Recall that changes in investment are amplified by the multiplier. If the multiplier is 1.5 and investment spending initially falls by 1% of GDP, then GDP will fall by 1.5%. If the fall in GDP makes firms more pessimistic, they may cut investment even further. This further cut in investment will lead to still further reductions in GDP. A small initial fall in investment can trigger a much larger fall in GDP. Nobel laureate Paul Samuelson expressed these interactions with his **multiplier-accelerator model**. In this model, a downturn in real GDP leads to a sharp fall in investment, which further reduces GDP through the multiplier for investment spending.

Multiplier-accelerator model: A model in which a downturn in real GDP leads to a sharp fall in investment, which triggers further reductions in GDP.

Investment spending is not affected only by psychology or expectations about real GDP growth in the future. Because investments are really trade-offs—something in the present traded for something in the future—the terms affecting what is the trade-off between the present and the future are also important. The terms affecting trade-offs between the present and the future are interest rates, as we shall see next.

Nominal Interest Rates and Real Interest Rates

If you deposit $100 in a bank and the interest rate the bank pays is 6% a year, at the end of one year you will have $106 ($100 × 1.06). Here are some other familiar examples of interest rates: If you borrow money for college tuition from a bank, the bank will require you to pay the funds back with interest. If a hardware store borrows money from a bank to purchase its inventory, the store will have to pay the funds back to the bank with interest. If you buy from the government or a corporation a $1,000 bond for one year at a 6% annual interest rate, you will receive $1,060 ($1000 × 1.06) next year from the issuer. A **bond** is a promise to pay money in the future. In buying the bond, you have loaned your $1,000 to the issuer, who has promised to repay it with interest.

Bond: A promise or IOU to pay money in the future in exchange for money now.

The interest rates quoted in the market—that is, at savings and loans, or banks for bonds—are called **nominal interest rates**. These are the actual rates that individuals and firms pay or receive when they borrow money or lend money.

Nominal interest rate: Interest rates quoted in financial markets.

When there is inflation, the dollar costs of borrowing or lending will not reflect the true costs. To provide an accurate measure of the costs of borrowing or lending, we need to apply the reality principle and make adjustments for changes in prices.

Reality **PRINCIPLE**

What matters to people is the real value of money or income—its purchasing power—not the face value of money or income.

Distinguishing between nominal interest rates and real interest rates is how economists account for inflation in their measurements of the costs of borrowing and lending. The **real rate of interest** is defined as the nominal interest rate minus the inflation rate:

Real rate of interest: The nominal rate minus the inflation rate.

$$\text{real rate} = \text{nominal rate} - \text{inflation rate}$$

If the nominal rate of interest is 6% per year and the inflation rate is 4% during the year, the real rate of interest is 2% (6% − 4% = 2%) over that year.

To understand what the real rate of interest means, consider this example. You have $100, and there is 4% annual inflation. It's not hard to figure out that next year you will need $104 to have the same purchasing power then that you have today. Let's say you deposit today $100 in a bank that pays 6% annual interest. At the end of the year, you have $106 ($100 × 1.06).

Let's calculate your real gain. After one year, you have increased your holdings by $6, starting with $100 and ending with $106. But taking into account the $4 you need to keep up with inflation, your gain is only $2 ($6 − $4). The real rate of interest you earned, the nominal rate adjusted for inflation, is 2%—or $2 on the original $100 deposit.

A similar calculation applies to firms or individuals who borrow money. Suppose a firm borrows $100 at a 10% annual interest rate when there is 6% inflation during the year. The firm must pay back $110 at the end of the year ($100 × 1.10). But the borrower will be paying back the funds with dollars whose value has been reduced because of inflation. Since there was 6% inflation during the year, the lender would have to receive $106 (or $6 extra) just to keep up with inflation over the year. There is only a $4 gain ($10 − $6). Thus, the real rate of interest to the borrower is just 4%, or $4 on the original $100 loan, correcting for the effects of inflation.

We defined the real interest rate as the nominal interest rate minus the actual inflation rate. When firms or individuals borrow or lend, they do not know what the rate of inflation will actually be. Instead, they must form an expectation—an estimate—of what they believe the inflation rate will be in the future. For a given nominal interest rate, we can define the **expected real interest rate** as the nominal rate minus the expected inflation rate. The expected real interest rate is the rate at which borrowers or lenders expect to make transactions.

Expected real interest rate: The nominal rate minus the expected inflation rate.

Investment Spending and Interest Rates

To understand the link between investment spending and interest rates, here's a simple example. A firm can invest $100 today in a project and receive $104 one year from today. There is no inflation: A dollar today and a dollar next year have the same purchasing power. Figure 16.2 depicts this investment. A cost is incurred today and the return occurs one year later. Should the firm make this investment?

Figure 16.2

Typical Investments
A typical investment, in which a cost of $100 incurred today yields a return of $104 next year.

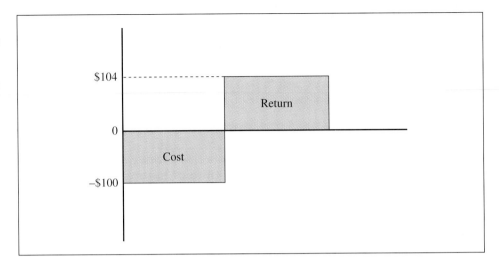

To decide whether to invest the $100, the firm should take into account the principle of opportunity cost.

PRINCIPLE of Opportunity Cost

The opportunity cost of something is what you sacrifice to get it.

We have to look at the $100 the firm would give up today to get $104 one year from today. What we look at is how that $100 could have been used for other purposes. Suppose the annual interest rate in the economy is 3%. The firm could lend the $100 at 3% and receive $103 in one year. The interest rate prevailing in the economy provides a measure of the opportunity cost of the investment.

In this case, the firm would not be too smart lending the $100 at 3% annual interest return. The investment is the smart thing to do. The firm will earn a net return of $4 ($104 − $100) from the investment project, whereas the return from lending the $100 would have been only $3. Because the net return from the investment exceeds the opportunity cost of the funds, the firm is better off investing.

What if the annual interest rate in the economy were 6%? Lending the $100 would return $6—the opportunity cost that could be earned by lending instead of investing in the project. The return on the investment of $4 would be less than the opportunity cost of $6. The firm would be better off making a loan of the $100, not investing it. The higher lending interest rate makes the difference as to which is the more profitable use of the $100.

There are millions of investment projects that can be undertaken, nearly all providing different returns from any other. Consider the array of investments A through E in Table 16.1. At a market interest rate of 2% per year, only investment A is unprofitable. All the other investments have a return greater than the opportunity cost of the funds. If the interest rate in the market increased to 4%, both A and B would be unprofitable. Investment C would join A and B as being unprofitable at an interest rate of 6%; D would become unprofitable if the market interest rate increased to 8%. If interest rates exceeded 9%, all the investments would become unprofitable.

Firms will compare the net return on an investment with the opportunity cost of that investment, and they will invest as long as the net return exceeds the opportunity cost. As market interest rates rise, there will be fewer profitable investments. The total level of investment spending in the economy will decline as market interest rates

Table 16.1   Returns on Investment

Investment	Cost	Return
A	$100	$101
B	$100	$103
C	$100	$105
D	$100	$107
E	$100	$109

increase. Figure 16.3 depicts the negative relationship—graphically represented as the downward-sloping line—between interest rates and investment.

Real investment spending is inversely related to the real interest rate. To understand why, let's return to our example in which a $100 investment today would yield a $104 return in one year, the interest rate is 3%, and there is no inflation. Because there is no inflation, nominal interest rates and real interest rates are the same. In this case, the firm looked at the real net return on the investment of $4, which is a real return of 4% from the investment; compared it to the real rate of interest of 3%; and decided that the investment was profitable. Now suppose that the return from the investment project and the real interest rate in the economy are the same—3% per year—but there is 2% annual inflation. Also suppose that the inflation rate increases to 5%: the real rate of interest of 3% plus the inflation rate of 2%. The investment project will still cost $100, but it will pay a return of $100 plus $6, or $106, in one year. The extra $2 arises because of the 2% inflation: When the firm sells its product on the market, it will earn 2% more because of the rise in prices in the economy.

The firm will compare its nominal or dollar net return of 6% to the opportunity cost of 5% and find that the investment will be more profitable than making the loan. Because both the nominal net return and nominal interest rates in the economy increase by the rate of inflation of 2%, the firm faces the identical situation as if there were no inflation.

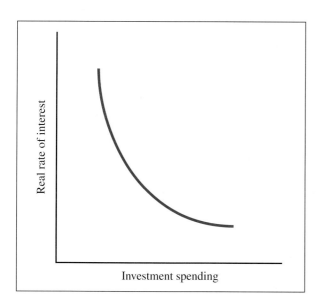

Figure 16.3

Interest Rates and Investment

As the real interest rate declines, investment spending in the economy increases.

You can see now that investment spending is negatively related to real interest rates. That's why nominal interest rates are not a good indicator of the true cost of investing. If nominal interest rates are 10% but inflation is 9%, the real rate of interest is 1%. If a firm had a project that paid a real net return greater than 1%, it would want to undertake this investment. Inflation would increase the nominal net return and the nominal interest rate equally. The firm makes its investment decisions by comparing its expected real net return from investment projects to the real rate of interest.

Economic Detective

The Case of High Interest Rates and Investment

Some journalists were puzzled that a country with high inflation had high interest rates but also high levels of investment spending. As an economic detective, can you explain this phenomenon?

To resolve the mystery, you need to distinguish between real and nominal interest rates. Investment spending depends negatively on real interest rates. However, if there are high levels of inflation, real interest rates could be low, while nominal interest rates remain high.

TEST Your Understanding

1. Investment spending is very procyclical, moving in conjunction with GDP. True or false? Explain.

2. Complete the statement with *real* or *nominal*: The rate of interest you earn in the bank is known as a _____ or dollar rate of interest.

3. Complete the statement with *increases* or *decreases*: As real rates of interest increase in the economy, real investment spending _____.

4. The _____ cost of funds is the interest rate that can be earned by lending the funds.

5. If a project costs $100 today and pays a nominal return of $107 next year, what is the nominal annual interest rate at which the project should still be undertaken?

Model of the Money Market

Now we turn to how the Federal Reserve can determine interest rates and thereby affect investment spending. We begin by learning the factors that determine the public's demand for money. Once we understand what affects the demand for money, we can see how actions taken by the Federal Reserve determine interest rates in the short run.

The Demand for Money

Let's think of money as simply one part of wealth. Suppose your total wealth is valued at $1,000. In what form will you hold your wealth? Should you put all your wealth into the stock market? Or perhaps into the bond market? Or should you hold some of your wealth in money, that is, currency and checking accounts?

If you invest your wealth in assets such as stocks or bonds, you earn income on your investment. Stocks pay dividends and increase in value; bonds pay interest. If you hold your wealth in currency or a checking account, you receive either no interest or very low interest. Holding your wealth in the form of money means that you sacrifice some potential income.

Money does, however, provide valuable services. It facilitates transactions. If you go to a grocery store to purchase some cereal, the store will accept currency or a check, but you won't be able to pay for your cereal with your stocks and bonds. People hold money primarily for this basic reason: Money makes it easier to conduct transactions. Economists call this reason for holding money the **transactions demand for money**.

To understand the demand for money, we rely on the principle of opportunity cost:

Transactions demand for money: The demand for money based on the desire to facilitate transactions.

PRINCIPLE of Opportunity Cost

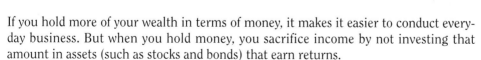

The opportunity cost of something is what you sacrifice to get it.

If you hold more of your wealth in terms of money, it makes it easier to conduct everyday business. But when you hold money, you sacrifice income by not investing that amount in assets (such as stocks and bonds) that earn returns.

The opportunity cost of holding money is the return that you could have earned by holding your wealth in other assets. We measure the opportunity cost of holding money by the interest rate. Suppose that the interest rate available to you on a long-term bond is 6% per year. If you hold $100 of your wealth in the form of this bond, you earn $6 a year. If you hold currency instead, you earn no interest. So the opportunity cost of holding $100 in currency is $6 per year or 6% per year.

As interest rates increase in the economy, the opportunity cost of holding money also increases. Economists have found that as the opportunity cost of holding money increases, the public demands less money. The quantity demanded of money will decrease with an increase in interest rates.

In Figure 16.4, we draw a demand for money curve, M^d, as a function of the interest rate. At higher interest rates, individuals will want to hold less money than they will at lower interest rates because the opportunity cost of holding money is higher. As interest rates rise from r_0 to r_1, the quantity demanded of money falls from M_0 to M_1.

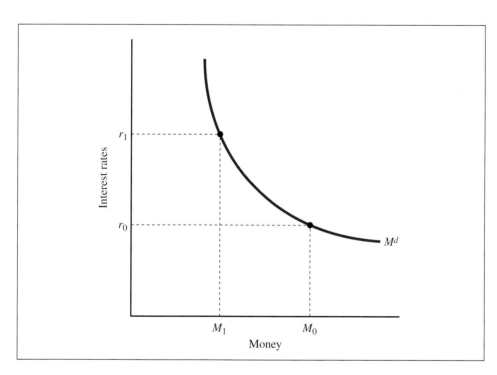

Figure 16.4
Demand for Money
As interest rates increase from r_0 to r_1, the quantity of money demanded falls from M_0 to M_1.

The demand for money also depends on two other factors. One is the overall price level in the economy. The demand for money will increase as the level of prices increases. If prices for your groceries are twice as high, you will need twice as much money to purchase them. The amount of money people typically hold during any time period will be closely related to the dollar value of the transactions that they make. This is an example of the reality principle in action:

Reality **PRINCIPLE**

What matters to people is the real value of money or income—its purchasing power—not the face value of money or income.

The other factor that influences the demand for money is the level of real GDP or real income. It seems obvious that as income increases, individuals and businesses will make more purchases. As real GDP increases, individuals and businesses will be making more transactions. To facilitate these transactions, they will want to hold more money. Increases in prices or income will shift the demand curve to the right.

Traditionally, economists have identified other motives besides transactions for individuals or firms to hold money. If you hold your wealth in the form of property, such as a house or a boat, it is costly to sell the house or boat on short notice if you need to obtain funds. These forms of wealth are illiquid, meaning that they are not easily transferable into money. If you hold your wealth in currency or checking accounts, you do not have this problem. Economists recognize that individuals have a **liquidity demand for money**: People want to hold money to be able to make transactions on quick notice.

Individuals may also wish to hold some types of money—particularly savings accounts and assets contained in M2—that pay interest but are less risky than holding stocks or bonds. Over short periods, individuals may not wish to hold stocks or bonds because prices of stocks and bonds might fall. Holding your wealth in a savings account avoids the risk of falling stock or bond prices. The demand for money that arises because it is safer than other assets is called the **speculative demand for money**.

The demand for money, in practice, will be the sum of transactions, liquidity, and speculative demands. As we continue, keep in mind that the demand for money will depend positively on the level of income and prices and negatively on interest rates.

Liquidity demand for money: The demand for money that represents the needs and desires of individuals or firms to make purchases on short-term notice without incurring excessive costs.

Speculative demand for money: The demand for money that reflects the fact that holding money over short periods is less risky than holding stocks or bonds.

Interest Rate Determination

Combining the supply of money, determined by the Fed, with the demand for money, determined by the public, we can see how interest rates are determined in the short run in a demand and supply model of the money market.

Figure 16.5 depicts a model of the money market. The supply of money is determined by the Federal Reserve, and we assume for simplicity that it is independent of interest rates. We represent this independence by a vertical supply curve for money, M^s. In the same graph, we draw the demand for money M^d. Market equilibrium occurs where the demand for money equals the supply of money, at an interest rate of r^*.

At this equilibrium interest rate, r^*, the quantity of money demanded by the private sector equals the quantity of money supplied by the Federal Reserve. What happens if the interest rate is higher than r^*? At a higher interest rate, the quantity of money demanded would be less than the fixed quantity supplied; the result would be an excess supply of money. In other markets, excess supplies cause the price to fall. It's the same here. The "price of money" in the market for money is the interest rate. The interest rate would fall and return to the equilibrium value, r^*. If the interest rate were below r^*, the demand for money would exceed the fixed supply: There would be an excess demand for

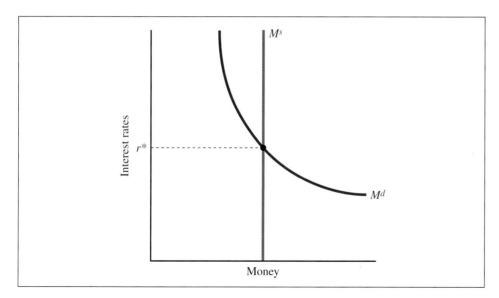

Figure 16.5
Equilibrium in the Money Market
Equilibrium in the money market occurs at an interest rate of r^* at which the quantity of money demanded equals the quantity of money supplied.

money. As in other markets when there are excess demands, the price rises. Here, the "price of money," or the interest rate, would rise until it reached r^*.

As you see, money market equilibrium follows the same logic as any other economic equilibrium.

We can use this simple model of the money market to understand the power of the Federal Reserve. Suppose the Federal Reserve increased the money supply through an open market purchase of bonds. In panel A of Figure 16.6, an increase in the supply of money shifts the money supply curve to the right, leading to lower interest rates. A decrease in the money supply through the Fed's open market sale of bonds, as depicted in panel B of Figure 16.6, will decrease the supply of money, shifting the money supply curve to the left, increasing interest rates.

We can also think of the process from the perspective of banks. Recall our discussion of money creation through the banking system. After the Fed's open market purchase of bonds, banks will find that they have additional reserves and will want to make loans. To entice businesses to borrow, banks will lower the interest rates they charge on their loans. After an open market purchase of bonds by the Fed, interest rates will fall throughout the entire economy.

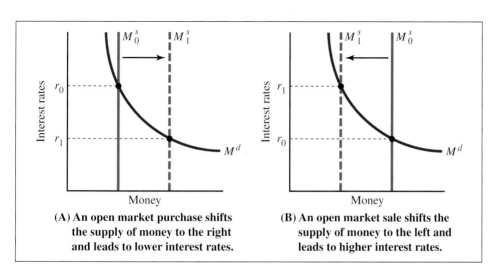

(A) An open market purchase shifts the supply of money to the right and leads to lower interest rates.

(B) An open market sale shifts the supply of money to the left and leads to higher interest rates.

Figure 16.6
Federal Reserve and Interest Rates
Changes in the supply of money will change interest rates.

6. How do we measure the opportunity cost of holding money?

7. Complete the statement with *increase* or *decrease*: The quantity of money demanded will _____ as interest rates increase.

8. What will happen to interest rates if the Fed sells bonds on the open market?

Interest Rates, Investment, and Output

To show how the Fed's actions affect the economy, we first combine our model of the money market with the curve that shows how investment spending is related to interest rates. In Figure 16.7, the graph on the left shows how interest rates are determined by the demand and supply for money. At the equilibrium interest rate r^*, we can see from the graph on the right that the level of investment in the economy will be given by I^*.

We will use this simple model to illustrate the effects of monetary policy on the economy. But before we do so, we should note that consumption as well as investment can depend on interest rates. Spending on consumer durables, such as automobiles and refrigerators, will also depend negatively on the rate of interest. Consumer durables are really investment goods for the household. If you buy an automobile, you incur the cost today and receive benefits (the ability to use the car) in the future. As interest rates rise, the opportunity costs of investing in the automobile will rise. Consumers will respond to the increase in the opportunity cost by purchasing fewer cars. In this chapter, we discuss how changes in interest rates affect investment, but keep in mind that purchases of consumer durables will be affected as well.

Monetary Policy

Through its actions, the Federal Reserve can change the level of output in the short run. How does it do so? Consider an open market purchase. The Fed buys government bonds from the public, increasing the supply of money. With an increase in the supply of money, interest rates fall.

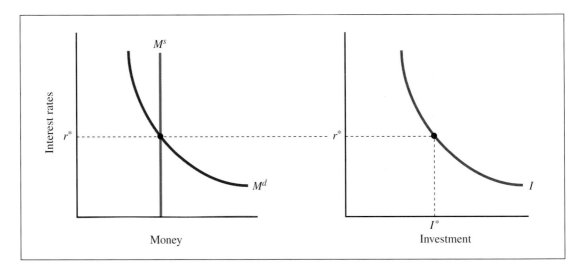

Figure 16.7
The Money Market and Investment Spending
The equilibrium interest rate r^* is determined in the money market. At that interest rate, investment spending is given by I^*.

In Figure 16.8, we show the effects of an increase in the money supply through an open market purchase using our money market and investment graphs. As the supply of money increases, interest rates will fall from r_0 to r_1. With the decrease in interest rates, investment spending will increase from I_0 to I_1. Thus, the effects of the open market purchase will be to increase investment spending.

The increase in investment spending will increase aggregate demand—total demand for goods and services in the economy—and shift the aggregate demand curve to the right. With the increase in aggregate demand, both output and prices will increase in the short run. Thus, the Fed's open market purchase ultimately has the effect of increasing output and prices in the economy.

An open market sale of bonds by the Fed works precisely in reverse. In an open market sale, the Fed sells bonds to the private sector, reducing the money supply. Interest rates increase in the money market. With higher interest rates, firms reduce their investment spending. The decrease in investment spending decreases the total demand for goods and services in the economy. The reduced demand for goods and services leads to a reduction in GDP. We can represent this entire sequence of events:

open market sale →	decrease in money supply →	rise in interest rates →	fall in investment spending →	decrease in GDP

Stop here for a moment and think of the sequence of events by which the Federal Reserve can affect the level of GDP in the short run. It all starts in the financial markets. By buying and selling government bonds, the Federal Reserve can change the supply of money and the level of interest rates. In making their investment decisions, firms and individuals are influenced by the level of interest rates. Finally, changes in the demand for goods and services will affect the level of GDP in the short run. The sequence of events may be a bit indirect, but it is powerful.

The Federal Reserve can also influence the level of output through other tools, such as changes in reserve requirements or changes in the discount rate, discussed in

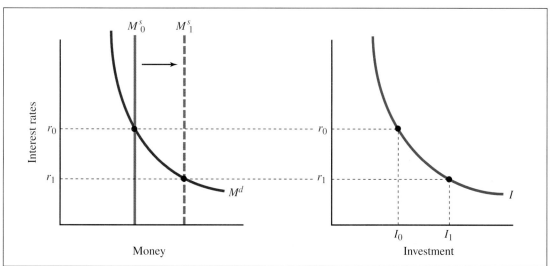

Figure 16.8

Monetary Policy and Interest Rates

As the money supply increases, interest rates fall from r_0 to r_1. Investment spending increases from I_0 to I_1.

Actions that the Federal Reserve takes to influence the level of GDP are known as **monetary policy**. Monetary policy does not take instantaneously. There are significant delays in the process, as we explain in "A Closer Look: Lags in Monetary Policy."

Monetary policy: The range of actions taken by the Federal Reserve to influence the level of GDP or the rate of inflation.

Monetary Policy in an Open Economy

We have been discussing monetary policy without taking into account international trade or international movements of financial funds across countries. Once we bring in these considerations, we will see that monetary policy operates through an additional route.

Suppose the Federal Reserve conducts an open market purchase of bonds, lowering U.S. interest rates. As a result, investors in the United States will be earning lower interest rates and will seek to invest some of their funds abroad. To invest abroad, they will need to sell dollars and buy foreign currency of the country where they intend to invest. This will affect the **exchange rate**: the rate at which one currency trades for another. As investors sell their dollars to buy foreign currency, the exchange rate, which is the value of the dollar from the perspective of the U.S. investor, will fall. A fall in the exchange rate or a decrease in the value of a currency is called **depreciation**. Lower U.S. interest rates will cause the dollar to depreciate, which means that it declines in value.

Exchange rate: The rate at which one currency trades for another in the market.

Depreciation: A fall in the exchange rate or a decrease in the value of a currency.

The lower value of the dollar will mean that U.S. goods become cheaper on world markets. Suppose that the exchange rate were two Swiss francs to the dollar, meaning you received two Swiss francs for every dollar. If a U.S. machine tool sold for $100,000, the machine tool would cost the Swiss 200,000 francs. Suppose the value of the dollar fell, so you received only one franc for each dollar. The same machine tool would then cost the Swiss only 100,000 francs. The lower value of the dollar makes U.S. goods cheaper to foreigners. Foreign residents will want to buy more U.S. goods as they become less expensive to foreign residents. So the U.S. exports more to foreign countries.

That's the good news about the lower value of the U.S. dollar. The bad news is that the lower value of the dollar will make it more expensive for U.S. residents to buy foreign goods. If the exchange rate were two Swiss francs to the dollar and Swiss chemicals cost 60,000 francs, the chemicals would cost a U.S. resident $30,000. If the exchange depreciates to one franc per dollar, the same chemical will cost $60,000. As the U.S. exchange rate falls, imports become more expensive, and U.S. residents tend to import fewer goods.

A CLOSER LOOK   LAGS IN MONETARY POLICY

Monetary policy takes time to operate because there are lags in the process. Economists recognize two broad classes of lags: inside lags and outside lags. Inside lags are the lags in implementing policy; outside lags refer to the time it takes for policies to actually work. To help you understand them, imagine that you are steering a large ocean liner and looking out for possible collisions with hidden icebergs. The time it takes you to spot an iceberg, communicate this information to the crew, and initiate the process of changing course is the inside lag. Because ocean liners are large and have lots of momentum, it will take a long time before your ocean liner begins to turn; this is the outside lag.

How long are these lags in practice? Inside lags can easily take as long as six months before policymakers fully recognize that the economy is heading in the wrong direction. Outside lags are even longer and more uncertain. Economists differ in their estimates of outside lags; it may take from two to five years before the full effect of Federal Reserve actions are felt. Because it takes so long for policies to work, policymakers are typically very cautious before making substantial changes.

In an open economy, monetary policy will affect the level of imports, such as these cars.

As we have seen, as the U.S. dollar exchange rate falls, U.S. goods become cheaper and foreign goods become more expensive. The United States will export more goods and import fewer goods. Because exports increase and imports decrease, net exports will increase. The increase in net exports increases the demand for U.S. goods and increases GDP in the short run. We can represent this sequence of events:

open market →	increase in money supply →	fall in interest rates →	fall in exchange rate →	increase in net exports →	increase in GDP
purchase					

The three new links in the sequence are from interest rates to exchange rates, from exchange rates to net exports, and from net exports to GDP.

This sequence also works in reverse. If the Fed raises interest rates, investors from around the world will want to invest in the United States. As they buy dollars, the U.S. dollar exchange rate will increase, and the dollar will increase in value. An increase in the value of a currency is called **appreciation**. The appreciation of the dollar will make U.S. goods more expensive to foreigners and make imports cheaper for U.S. residents. Suppose the exchange rate appreciates to three francs to the dollar. That machine tool will increase in price to the Swiss to 300,000 francs, while the Swiss chemicals will fall in price to U.S. residents to $20,000.

Appreciation: An increase in the exchange rate or an increase in the value of a currency.

When U.S. interest rates increase, we expect exports to decrease and imports to increase, decreasing net exports. The decrease in net exports will decrease the demand for U.S. goods and lead to a fall in output in the short run.

Here is the expanded sequence of events:

open market →	decrease in money supply →	rise in interest rates →	rise in exchange rate →	decrease in net exports →	decrease in GDP
sale					

To summarize, an increase in interest rates will reduce both investment spending (including consumer durables) and net exports. A decrease in interest rates will increase investment spending and net exports. Monetary policy is even more powerful in an open economy than in a closed economy.

TEST Your Understanding

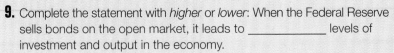

9. Complete the statement with *higher* or *lower*: When the Federal Reserve sells bonds on the open market, it leads to _____ levels of investment and output in the economy.

10. What are all the events in the sequence from an open market purchase to a change in output in a closed economy?

11. Explain how monetary policy works in an economy that is open to trade.

Money and Inflation in the Long Run

An economy can, in principle, produce at full employment with any inflation rate. There is no "magic" inflation rate that is necessary to sustain full employment. To understand this point, consider the long run when the economy operates at full employment. As we discussed in Chapter 13, in the long run changes in aggregate demand, including changes in the supply of money, change only prices, not output. Economists believe that, in the long run, changes in the supply of money have no effect on any real variables in the economy, such as employment, output, or real interest rates in the long run. Economists call this the **long-run neutrality of money**.

As a consequence of the long-run neutrality of money, changes in the money supply will be fully reflected in prices. If the Federal Reserve increases the money supply at 5% a year, there will be 5% annual inflation; that is, prices in the economy will rise by 5% a year.

Let's think about how this economy looks. The **nominal wages**—wages in dollars—of workers are all rising at 5% a year. However, because prices are also rising at 5% a year, **real wages**—wages adjusted for changes in purchasing power—remain constant.

Some workers may feel cheated by the 5% inflation. They might believe that without the inflation they would experience real wage increases, because their nominal wages are rising by 5% a year. Unfortunately, they are wrong. They suffer from what economists call **money illusion**, a confusion of real and nominal magnitudes. Here's the source of the illusion: The only reason their nominal wages are rising by 5% a year is the general 5% inflation. If there were no inflation, their nominal wages would not increase at all.

After a time, everyone in the economy would begin to expect that the 5% annual inflation would continue. Economists say that in this situation, individuals hold **expectations of inflation**. These expectations affect all aspects of economic life. For example, automobile producers will on average expect their prices to be 5% higher next year. They will also expect their costs—labor and steel, for example—to increase by 5% a year. Workers would begin to understand that their 5% increases in wages would be matched by a 5% increase in the prices of the goods they buy. Continued inflation becomes the normal state of affairs. Expectations of inflation become ingrained in decisions made in all aspects of life.

When the public holds expectations of inflation, real and nominal rates of interest will differ. Recall that the nominal interest rate—the rate quoted in the market—is equal to the real rate of interest plus the expected inflation rate. So if inflation is 5% a year, nominal rates will exceed real rates by 5%.

In the long run, the real rate of interest does not depend on monetary policy because money is neutral; that is, changes in the supply of money do not affect real variables in the long run. However, nominal rates of interest depend on the rate of inflation, which in the long run is determined by the growth of the money supply. Monetary policy therefore does affect the nominal interest rate in the long run. If Country A and

Long-run neutrality of money: An increase in the supply of money has no effect on real interest rates, investment, or output in the long run.

Nominal wages: Wages in dollars.

Real wages: Nominal or dollar wages adjusted for changes in purchasing power.

Money illusion: Confusion of real and nominal magnitudes.

Expectations of inflation: The beliefs held by the public about the likely path of inflation for the future.

Country B had the same real rate of interest but Country A had a higher inflation rate, then Country A would also have a higher nominal interest rate. As Nobel laureate Milton Friedman pointed out, countries with higher money growth typically have higher nominal interest rates than the nominal interest rates in countries with lower money growth rates—and that's because of the differences in inflation across the countries.

Using the **TOOLS**

1. Brazilian Economics
During the early 1990s, interest rates in Brazil were typically at double-digit levels, but firms were investing in a large number of projects. Does this make economic sense? If so, in what way?

2. Interest Rates on Checking Accounts
During the 1980s, banks started to pay interest (at low rates) on checking accounts for the first time. Given what you know about opportunity costs, how would interest rates on checking accounts affect the demand for money?

3. Nominal Interest Rates and the Demand for Money
We know that investment spending depends on real interest rates. Yet the demand for money depends on nominal interest rates, not on real interest rates. Can you explain why money demand should depend on nominal interest rates?

4. World Trade and Monetary Policy
The last three decades have witnessed a large increase in the volume of world trade. Do you think that this increase in trade has strengthened or weakened the monetary policy in terms of its short-term effects on employment and output?

Summary

This chapter explained how changes in the supply of money could affect output and employment in the short run and inflation in the long run. We began with a discussion of investment and interest rates and then turned to the determination of interest rates and the channels through which monetary policy works in both a closed and open economy. The last part of the chapter discussed the effects of monetary policy in the long run. Here are the main points of this chapter:

1. Investments incur costs today to provide benefits in the future.

2. Investment spending depends inversely on real interest rates.

3. The demand for money depends negatively on the interest rate and positively on the level of prices and real GDP.

4. The level of interest rates is determined in the money market by the demand and supply of money.

5. To increase the level of GDP, the Federal Reserve buys bonds on the open market. To decrease the level of GDP, the Federal Reserve sells bonds on the open market.

6. An increase in the money supply will decrease interest rates, increase investment spending, and increase output. A decrease in the money supply will increase interest rates, decrease investment spending, and decrease output.

7. In an open economy, a decrease in interest rates will depreciate the exchange rate and lead to an increase in net exports. An increase in interest rates will appreciate the exchange rate and lead to a decrease in net exports.

8. In the long run, higher money growth leads to higher inflation and higher nominal interest rates.

Key Terms

Problems and Discussion Questions

1. "When real interest rates are high, so is the opportunity cost of funds." What does this statement mean?

2. "If the real interest rate were zero, it would be a financially sound decision to level the Rocky Mountains so that automobiles and cars would save on gas mileage." Putting aside ecological concerns, why is this statement true?

3. If the inflation rate is 10% over the year and annual interest rates are 9%, would you invest in a project that only paid an annual real return of 1%?

4. Explain why interest rates are sometimes called the price of holding money.

5. If investment spending became less sensitive to interest rates, how would this reduced sensitivity affect the strength of monetary policy?

6. Refrigerators and clothing are, to some extent, durable. Explain why the decision to purchase a refrigerator is likely to be more sensitive to interest rates than the decision to buy clothing.

7. In an open economy, changes in the money supply affect both interest rates and exchange rates. Comparing the United States and the Netherlands, in which country would monetary policy have a more significant effect on GDP through changes in exchange rates?

8. The demand for money will decrease as income falls. Use this fact to explain why interest rates usually fall in a recession.

9. Interpret the following statement: "High interest rates are the evidence of loose monetary policy, not tight monetary policy."

10. Are workers or firms more likely to have accurate information about the future course of inflation?

11. Web Exercise. The Federal Reserve uses both econometric models as well as other more general information about the economy to make decisions about monetary policy. To see what some of this information looks like, go to the Web site for the Federal Reserve Open Market Committee (*www.federalreserve.gov/fomc*) and read the report of the Beige Book (a briefing book named for the color of its cover). What type of information is provided in the Beige Book?

12. Web Exercise. Have international factors become more important in monetary-policy considerations? Got to the Web page of the Federal Reserve (*www.federalreserve.gov*) and read some recent speeches given by Fed officials. Do international considerations seem to affect policymakers in the United States?

Take It to the Net

We invite you to visit the O'Sullivan/Sheffrin page on the Prentice Hall Web site at: **www.prenhall.com/osullivan/** for additional World Wide Web exercises for this chapter.

Model Answers to Questions

Chapter-Opening Questions

1. Interest rates represent the opportunity cost of an investment. The higher the opportunity cost, the less investment.

2. When the Federal Reserve sells bonds on the open market, the money supply decreases. Given the demand for money, this raises interest rates.

3. If the Federal Reserve increases the supply of money, interest rates will fall. Lower interest rates will lead to more production of housing and increased construction.

4. Countries with lower rates of money growth will have lower inflation rates than countries with higher money growth. Nominal interest rates (which reflect inflation) will also be lower.

Test Your Understanding

1. True. Investment rises and falls with GDP.
2. Nominal.
3. Decreases.
4. Opportunity.
5. 7%.
6. We use nominal interest rates to measure the opportunity costs of holding money because the alternative to holding money is holding assets that pay interest.
7. Decrease.
8. Interest rates will rise if the Federal Reserve sells bonds.
9. Lower.
10. An open market purchase will lower interest rates, leading to increased investment and higher output as demand increases.
11. An increase in the money supply will lower interest rates, depreciate the exchange rate and lead to an increase in net exports and higher output as demand increases.

Using the Tools

1. **Brazilian Economics.** While nominal interest rates were at double-digit levels, inflation was also at double-digit rates. Real interest rates were substantially lower, which is why firms still wanted to undertake investment projects.

2. **Interest Rates on Checking Accounts.** When interest is paid on checking accounts, it lowers the opportunity cost of holding wealth in these accounts, since you earn interest on the checking account. With a lower opportunity cost, the demand for money will increase.

3. **Nominal Interest Rates and the Demand for Money.** The nominal interest rate measures the opportunity cost of holding money. If you hold money, you earn no interest. If you invest in a bond, you earn the nominal rate of interest.

4. **World Trade and Monetary Policy.** Monetary policy is more powerful if it can operate both through the traditional closed economy channel as well as the open economy channel. Thus, as trade becomes more important to economies around the world, monetary policy will become more powerful.

International Trade and Finance

In November 1999, large numbers of colorful protestors gathered in Seattle, Washington, at a meeting of world leaders to discuss international trade and to express their indignation about recent developments in international trade, multinational corporations, and international organizations. Protestors carried signs denouncing the WTO, or World Trade Organization, a recently created and relatively obscure international agency.

The protest at times turned violent, and protestors smashed windows in downtown Seattle. Protestors returned to their homes fondly remembering the "spirit of Seattle." The intensity of the protest took many observers by surprise. Since World War II, trade has grown steadily and the world has become more interdependent. Were the protestors just expressing discontent about modern life or are there fundamental problems with our system of international trade and finance?

this chapter explores the world of international trade and finance. We begin by exploring the basic question of why nations trade and what principles govern trade. A good deal of our public policy debate today centers on issues directly relating to trade. Nation-states play a critical role in international trade—they can promote or discourage trade. We explore in detail the methods that nations use to restrict trade, the rationale for these restrictions, and recent policy debates, including those that inflamed some of the Seattle protestors.

International trade differs in one important respect from domestic trade within a country. Countries use different currencies. To conduct international trade, it is necessary to exchange one currency for another. We will see how the **exchange rate**, the rate at which one currency trades for other, is determined in markets and the role that governments can play in influencing the exchange rate or designing a system of exchange rates. And we will look at some of the difficult policy issues we face as the world financial system becomes increasingly interdependent.

Exchange rate: The rate at which one currency can be exchanged for another.

After reading this chapter, you should be able to answer the following questions:

1. Why does trade exist?
2. Why do both rich and poor countries benefit from trade?
3. Do trade laws inhibit environmental protection?
4. If the dollar increases in value against the Japanese yen, how will this affect the balance of trade between the United States and Japan?
5. Why has a group of European countries adopted a common currency?

Markets and Trade

A market is an arrangement that allows buyers and sellers to exchange things. A buyer exchanges money for a product (a good or service), while a seller exchanges a product for money. Before we explore how a market operates, let's think about why markets exist in the first place.

In the words of Adam Smith, "Man is the only animal that makes bargains; one dog does not exchange bones with another dog." We use markets to make our bargains,

The typical person is not self-sufficient but instead specializes by working at a particular job and using his or her income to purchase goods and services.

exchanging what we have for what we want. If each person were self-sufficient, producing everything he or she consumed, there would be no need for markets. Markets exist because we aren't self-sufficient but instead consume many products produced by other people. To get the money to pay for these products, each of us produces something to sell. Some people grow food; others produce goods such as clothing and bicycles; and others provide services such as medical care or legal advice. Because each of us specializes in one or two products, we need markets to sell what we produce and to buy other products. Most of us use the labor market to sell our work time to employers and then use our labor income to buy food, housing, appliances, and other products.

Specialization and the Gains from Trade

Why do people specialize and trade? We can explain the rationale for specialization and trade with an example involving two people and two products: bread and shirts. The first two rows of Table 17.1 show how much of each good Brenda and Sam can produce in one hour. Brenda can produce either six loaves of bread or two shirts, while Sam can produce either one loaf of bread or one shirt.

We can use the principle of opportunity cost to explain the benefits from specialization and trade. Opportunity cost is defined in terms of one unit of the good or, in our example, in terms of one shirt or one loaf of bread. The opportunity costs are shown in the third and fourth rows of Table 17.1.

1. Brenda's opportunity cost of one shirt is three loaves of bread; that's how many loaves of bread she could produce in the time it takes her to produce one shirt. She needs half an hour to produce a shirt, and during that half hour, she could produce three loaves of bread instead.

2. Brenda's opportunity cost of a loaf of bread is one-third of a shirt; that's how many shirts she could produce in the time it takes her to produce a loaf of bread. She needs one-sixth of an hour to produce a loaf of bread, and during that one-sixth of an hour, she could produce one-third of a shirt instead.

3. Sam's opportunity cost of a shirt is one loaf of bread.

4. Sam's opportunity cost of a loaf of bread is one shirt.

Each person could be self-sufficient. Brenda could produce all the bread and shirts she wants to consume, and Sam could produce everything for himself, too. But what would happen if they decided to specialize and trade? Suppose they agree to trade at the rate of two loaves of bread for each shirt.

• Brenda could specialize in bread and trade for shirts. Instead of producing one shirt for herself, Brenda could use the time it would take to produce one shirt to produce three loaves of bread; that's her opportunity cost of a shirt. If she then trades two loaves of bread for one shirt, she will have one loaf of bread left over. Specialization

Table 17.1 Production per Hour and Opportunity Cost

	Brenda	Sam
Bread produced per hour	6	1
Shirts produced per hour	2	1
Opportunity cost of one loaf of bread	one-third shirt	1 shirt
Opportunity cost of one shirt	3 loaves of bread	1 loaf of bread

and trade make Brenda better off because she gets the same number of shirts and one extra loaf of bread.

- Sam could specialize in shirts and trade for bread. Instead of producing one loaf of bread for himself, Sam could use the time it would take to produce a loaf of bread to produce one shirt; that's his opportunity cost of a loaf of bread. If he trades the shirt for two loaves of bread, he will have two loaves of bread instead of the one he could have produced himself. Specialization and trade make Sam better off because he gets the same number of shirts and one extra loaf of bread.

The example shows the benefit of specialization and trade. By specializing and trading, each person can consume more.

Opportunity Cost and Comparative Advantage

Comparative advantage: The ability of one person or nation to produce a good at an opportunity cost that is lower than the opportunity cost for another person or nation.

We say that a person has a **comparative advantage** in producing a particular good if he or she has a lower opportunity cost than another person in producing that good. It is sensible for each person to produce the good for which he or she has a comparative advantage.

- Shirts. Sam's opportunity cost for shirts (one loaf) is lower than Brenda's (three loaves), so it is sensible for Sam to specialize in shirts and trade for bread.
- Bread. Brenda's opportunity cost for bread (one-third shirt) is lower than Sam's (one shirt), so Brenda should specialize in bread and trade for shirts.

Specialization and trade—with each person producing the good for which he or she has a comparative advantage—allows each person to consume more.

Absolute advantage: The ability of one person or nation to produce a particular good at a lower absolute cost than that of another person or nation.

You may have noticed that Brenda is more productive than Sam in producing both goods. Economists say that she has an **absolute advantage** in producing both goods. Despite her absolute advantage, Brenda gains from specializing in bread and trading some of her bread for shirts produced by Sam. In an hour Brenda can produce twice as many shirts as Sam, but she can produce six times as many loaves of bread. Brenda relies on Sam to make some of her shirts because that frees her to spend more time producing bread, the good for which she has the greater productivity advantage over Sam and therefore a comparative advantage. The lesson is that trade results from comparative advantage (lower opportunity costs), not from absolute advantage.

TEST Your Understanding

1. Tim's opportunity cost of producing one chair is five tables, while Carla's opportunity cost of producing one chair is one table. Compute each person's opportunity cost of tables. Which person should produce chairs and which person should produce tables?
2. Wally is the manager of a car wash and is more productive at washing cars than any of the potential workers he could hire. Does that mean he should wash all the cars himself?

Markets and International Trade

Export: A good produced in the "home" country (for example, the United States) and sold abroad.

In today's global economy, many products are produced in one country and sold in another. International trade is one component of the global economy. To understand international trade, we first need some basic terminology. From the perspective of the United States, an **export** is a good produced in the United States and sold in another country. An **import** is a good produced elsewhere and purchased in the United States. Now let's apply the principle of comparative advantage to international trade.

Recall how Brenda and Sam benefited from specialization and trade. We saw that specialization and trade are beneficial if there are differences in opportunity costs that generate comparative advantages. Although our example consisted of two individuals, the same ideas apply to nations, which differ in their natural resources, climate, public infrastructure, physical capital, and labor forces. The resulting differences in productivity mean that, like an individual, a nation has a comparative advantage in the production of particular products. When a nation specializes in production and engages in trade, it gives its citizens an opportunity to consume larger quantities of goods and services.

A nation will specialize in the product for which it has a comparative advantage. Like trade between individuals, international trade results from comparative advantage, not absolute advantage. This explains why a rich nation trades with a poor nation, even though a rich nation is more productive and has an absolute advantage in all products. For example, suppose the United States is more efficient than India in producing both computers and clothing, but the United States has a comparative advantage in computers whereas India has a comparative advantage in clothing. Both countries would be better off if each country specialized—the United States in computers and India in clothing—and traded. Remember, it is comparative advantage that matters. Even if the United States were absolutely more efficient in producing clothing, both countries would still benefit from specialization and trade. Thus, the United States should export computers to India and import clothing from India, and India should import computers from and export clothing to the United States. Of course, this is just a hypothetical example—indeed, at the current time, India does export some computer programs to the United States based on its comparative advantage in this activity.

Import: A good produced in a foreign country and consumed in the "home" country (for example, the United States).

Protectionist Policies

Despite the advantages from global specialization, most nations use trade barriers to restrict international trade. Why? Trade barriers are often designed to protect domestic firms from competition from foreign firms and to protect the jobs of workers in industries that would be adversely affected by trade. These industries are often very successful in lobbying politicians to obtain protections from trade. Policies that restrict trade are known as **protectionist policies**.

Protectionist policies: Rules that restrict the free flow of trade between nations.

The Variety of Protectionist Policies

There are three common forms of protection:

1. A **quota** is an absolute limit on the volume of a particular good that can be imported into a country. If a country imposed a quota on steel imports of 200,000 tons, only 200,000 tons of steel could enter that country.

2. Under a **voluntary export restraint** (VER), one country agrees to limit the volume of exports to another country. For example, the Japanese government agreed to limit the number of Japanese cars sold in the United States and Europe. Many nations use voluntary export restraints to avoid explicit quotas, which are often prohibited by treaties.

3. A **tariff** is a special tax on imported goods. For example, a 10% tariff on imported television sets means that the tax on a $300 imported TV set is $30.

Quota: A limit on the amount of a good that can be imported.

Voluntary export restraint: A scheme under which an exporting country voluntarily decreases its exports.

Tariff: A tax on an imported good.

There are other ways a nation can limit imports without an official trade barrier. One way is to target imports for extra-strict enforcement of health and safety laws. A foreign firm that is faced with stricter standards than domestic firms may decide to stay out of the market. Another way a country can restrict imports is to design or allow its customs system to be inefficient and sluggish. If it takes a lot of time and effort to pass imported goods through customs, foreign firms may drop out of the market. These are examples of nontariff trade barriers, practices that do not show up as official laws but have the same effects as tariffs and quotas.

We can illustrate the effects of trade restrictions with a simple supply and demand diagram. Figure 17.1 shows the domestic demand for shirts, a good that the country typically imports. There are three different supply curves in the diagram. The lower supply curve shows the total supply of shirts when there is free trade. With free trade, the price of shirts is $12. The top supply curve represents a complete ban on imported shirts—with a total ban on imports, the price of shirts will be $23. The middle curve shows the effects of trade barriers (either an import quota, tariff, or voluntary export restraint). In this case, there is still some trade, and the price of shirts is $20. As you can see, restraints on imports raise the domestic price of shirts to consumers. However, domestic producers benefit because they receive a higher price for their products.

Rationales for Protectionist Policies

What are the rationales for protectionist policies such as an import ban, an import quota, a voluntary restraint, or a tariff? We will discuss three possible motivations for policies that restrict trade:

1. To shield workers from foreign competition
2. To nurture infant industries until they mature
3. To help domestic firms establish monopolies in world markets

1. To Shield Workers from Foreign Competition

One of the most basic arguments for protectionism is that it protects workers in industries that would be hurt by trade. Suppose that relative to the United States nations in the Far East have a comparative advantage in producing textiles. If the United States reduced existing tariffs for the textile industry, domestic manufacturers could not compete. They would have to close their factories and lay off workers. In an ideal world, the laid-off workers would take new jobs in other sectors of the economy. In practice, this is

Figure 17.1

Market Effects of a Quota, a VER, or a Tariff

An import quota shifts the supply curve to the left. The market moves upward along the demand curve to point *q*, which is between points *x* (free trade) and *c* (an import ban). We can reach the same point with a tariff that shifts the total supply curve to the same position.

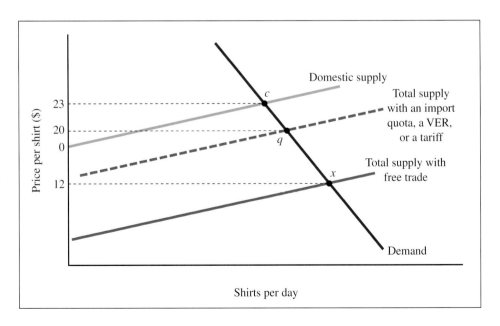

difficult. Many workers don't have the skills to work in other sectors, and obtaining these skills takes time. Moreover, the textile industry is heavily concentrated in the southeastern part of the United States. Politicians from that region will try to keep tariffs in place to prevent the temporary unemployment and changes in employment patterns that free trade would cause. The result of this protection is less efficient production, higher prices, and lower consumption for the United States. These costs can be significant. For example, economists have estimated that protectionist policies for textiles and apparel imposed costs of $10 billion. Although some jobs in the industry were preserved, the cost of saving each job was over $170,000.

2. To Nurture Infant Industries

During World War II, the United States built hundreds of boats, called Liberty ships, for the navy. As more and more of these ships were built, each required fewer hours to complete because workers learned from their experiences, acquiring knowledge during the production process. Engineers and economists call this phenomenon **learning by doing**. To learn a new game, such as Ping-Pong, you learn by doing. At first, you may find it difficult to play, but your skills improve as you go along.

Learning by doing: Knowledge gained in production, resulting in increases in productivity.

Tariffs and other protectionist policies are often defended on the grounds that they protect new industries, or **infant industries**, that are in the early stages of learning by doing. A tariff shields a young industry from the competition of its more mature rivals. After the infant industry grows up, the tariff can be eliminated because the industry is able to compete.

Infant industry: A new industry that is protected from foreign competition.

In practice, infant industries rarely become competitive with their foreign rivals. During the 1950s and 1960s, many Latin American countries used tariffs and other policies to protect their young manufacturing industries from foreign competition. Unfortunately, the domestic industries never became as efficient as foreign suppliers, and the Latin American countries that tried this policy suffered. Another problem with protecting an infant industry is that once an industry is given tariff protection, it is difficult to take such protection away.

3. To Help Domestic Firms Establish Monopolies in World Markets

If the production of a particular good has very large-scale economies, the world market will support only a few firms. A nation might be tempted to adopt policies to capture the monopoly profits for itself. Suppose the commercial aircraft industry can support only one large firm; if two firms enter the industry, both will lose money. A nation that decides to get into this industry could agree to provide financial support to a domestic firm to guarantee that the firm will make a profit. With such a guarantee, the domestic firm will enter the industry. Knowing this, a foreign firm will be reluctant to enter, so the domestic firm will capture the monopoly profit.

One example of this is the Airbus, an airplane that is produced in Europe. Several European countries provided large subsidies for firms producing the Airbus. These subsidies allowed the Airbus firms to underprice some of their rivals in the United States, and at least one U.S. manufacturer of commercial airplanes was forced out of business. What could go wrong with these monopoly creation policies? If both nations subsidize their domestic firms, both firms will enter the market and lose money. The taxpayers in both countries will then have to pay for the subsidies. And there is the possibility a nation may pick the wrong industry to subsidize. Together, the British and French subsidized an airplane known as the Concorde to provide supersonic travel between Europe and the United States. Although the Concorde captured the market, the market was not worth capturing. The Concorde lost money because it was very costly to develop, and people are not willing to pay a very large premium for supersonic travel. The Concorde stopped flying in 2003.

A proposal to lift trade restrictions is often met with opposition from people employed in protected domestic industries. French farmers protested against GATT.

International Trade Agreements

Since 1980, the average U.S. tariff has been about 5% of the value of imported goods, a rate that is close to the average tariffs in Japan and most European nations but very low by historical standards. Under the Smoot-Hawley tariffs of the 1930s, the average tariff in the United States was a whopping 59% of value. Tariffs are lower today because of several international agreements that reduce tariffs.

The first major trade agreement following World War II was the **General Agreement on Tariffs and Trade (GATT)**. This agreement was initiated in 1947 by the United States and 23 other nations and now has more than 100 member nations. There have been eight rounds of GATT negotiations over tariffs and trade regulations, resulting in progressively lower tariffs for the member nations. The last set of negotiations, the Uruguay Round, completed in 1994, decreased tariffs by about one-third of the previous level.

In the last few decades, there has been considerable progress in lowering the barriers to international trade. Here are some examples of international trade agreements:

General Agreement on Tariffs and Trade (GATT): An international agreement that has lowered trade barriers between the United States and other nations.

North American Free Trade Agreement (NAFTA): An international agreement that lowers barriers to trade among the United States, Canada, and Mexico.

World Trade Organization (WTO): An organization that oversees GATT and other international trade agreements.

European Union (EU): An organization of European nations that has reduced trade barriers in Europe.

Asian Pacific Economic Cooperation (APEC): An organization of 18 Asian nations that attempts to reduce trade barriers among its members.

- **North American Free Trade Agreement (NAFTA)**. Took effect in 1994 and is being implemented over the following 15 years. The agreement will eventually eliminate all tariffs and other trade barriers among Canada, Mexico, and the United States. NAFTA may soon be extended to other nations in the Western Hemisphere.

- **World Trade Organization (WTO)**. Has more than 130 member nations and oversees the General Agreement on Tariffs and Trade and other international trade agreements. There have been eight rounds of tariff negotiations, lowering tariffs among the member nations. WTO promotes trade in other ways: It has eliminated many import quotas, reduced agricultural subsidies, and outlawed restrictions on international trade in services such as banking, insurance, and accounting.

- **European Union (EU)**. Designed to remove all trade barriers within Europe and create a single market. Fifteen nations have joined.

- **Asian Pacific Economic Cooperation (APEC)**. In 1994, the leaders of 18 Asian nations signed a nonbinding agreement to reduce trade barriers among themselves.

In 2001, a new round of negotiations began in Doha, Qatar, on a wide range of issues.

Recent Trade Controversies

Let's take a look at two recent trade controversies that were in the minds of some of the Seattle protestors.

Trade and the Environment

In recent trade negotiations, a new player—environmental groups—appeared on the scene. Starting in the early 1990s, environmentalists began to question whether policies that liberalized trade could harm the environment. The issue that attracted their attention was the killing of dolphins by tuna fishers. Anyone who catches tuna with a large net will also catch the dolphins that swim with the tuna, and most of the captured dolphins will die. In 1972, the United States outlawed the use of tuna nets by U.S. ships. A short time later, ships from other nations, including Mexico, began netting tuna and killing dolphins. The United States responded with a boycott of Mexican tuna caught with nets, and the Mexican government complained to an international trade authority that the tuna boycott was an unfair trade barrier. The trade authority agreed with Mexico and forced the United States to remove the boycott.

Under current World Trade Organization (WTO) rules, a country can adopt any environmental standard it chooses, as long as it does not discriminate against foreign producers. For example, the United States can limit the exhaust emissions of all cars that operate in the United States. As long as emissions rules apply equally to all cars, domestic and imports, the rules are legal according to the WTO. An international panel upheld U.S. fuel-efficiency rules for automobiles on this principle.

The tuna boycott was a violation of WTO rules because killing dolphins does not harm the U.S. environment directly. For the same reason, the United States could not ban imported goods that are produced in factories that generate air or water pollution in other countries. It is easy to understand why WTO rules do not allow countries to restrict trade on the basis of the methods that are used to produce goods and services. Countries differ in the value they place on the environment. For example, a poor nation may be willing to tolerate more pollution if it means attaining a higher standard of living.

If trade restrictions cannot be used to protect the dolphins and deal with other global environmental problems, what else can we do? International agreements have been used for a variety of different environmental goals, from limiting the harvest of whales to eliminating the chemicals that deplete the ozone layer. These agreements are difficult to reach, and some nations will be tempted to use trade restrictions to pursue environmental goals. If they do, they will encounter resistance because WTO rules mean that a nation can pursue its environmental goals only within its own borders.

Trade disputes about environmental issues are part of a larger phenomenon of trade issues intersecting with national regulations. At one time, most trade disputes were simply matters of protecting domestic industries from foreign competition. The agriculture, textile, and steel industries were frequently beneficiaries of protection in many different countries throughout the world. But in recent years, a new breed of trade disputes has revolved around social issues and the role of government regulation.

As an example, the European Union has banned hormone-treated beef. While this was motivated in part by a desire to keep out U.S. imports and protect European farmers, it also reflects the nervousness of European citizens about technology. After all, Europe banned all hormone-treated beef, not just imports from the United States. Shouldn't a country have the right to pursue this policy, even if it is not based on the best science?

While the costs of the policy would be fairly straightforward in terms of higher prices for beef products, the benefits, in terms of potential safety, are much more difficult to ascertain. Similar issues arise as genetically modified crops become more commonplace. As a world trading community, we will have to decide at what point we allow national policy concerns to override principles of free trade.

Does Trade Cause Inequality?

Inequality in wages has been growing in the United States since 1973. Wages of skilled workers have risen faster than the wages of unskilled workers. World trade has also boomed since 1973. Could there be a connection between increased world trade and income inequality?

Trade theory suggests a link between increased trade and increased wage inequality. Here is how they might be linked: Suppose the United States produces two types of goods: one using skilled labor (say, airplanes) and one using unskilled labor (say, textiles). The United States is likely to have a comparative advantage in products that use skilled labor; developing countries are likely to have a comparative advantage in products that use unskilled labor. An increase in world trade will increase both exports and imports. An increase in U.S. exports means that we'll produce more goods requiring skilled labor, so the domestic demand for skilled labor will increase, pulling up the wage of skilled labor in the United States. At the same time, an increase in U.S. imports means that we'll import more goods produced by unskilled labor, so the domestic demand for unskilled labor will decrease, pulling down the wage of unskilled labor in the United States. As a result, the gap between the wages of the two types of workers will increase.

Economists have tried to determine how much trade has contributed to growing wage inequality. As usual, there are other factors that make such a determination difficult. It is difficult, for example, to distinguish between the effects of trade and the effects of technical progress. Technical change, such as the rapid introduction and use of computers, will also tend to increase the demand for skilled workers and decrease the demand for unskilled workers. Economists have noted, however, that the exports of goods using skilled labor and the imports of goods using unskilled labor have both increased, just as the theory predicts. At least some of the increased wage inequality is caused by international trade.

One response to this undesirable side effect of trade is to use trade restrictions to protect industries that use unskilled workers. Another approach is to ease the transition to an economy with a larger fraction of skilled jobs. In the long run, workers will move to industries that use skilled workers, so they will eventually earn higher wages. The government could facilitate this change by providing assistance for education and training.

TEST Your Understanding

3. Match each trade restriction with its description.

Restriction	Description
A. Tariffs	1. Limits on total imports
B. Quotas	2. Hidden impediments to trade
C. Voluntary export restraint	3. Agreement between nations to restrict trade
D. Nontariff trade barriers	4. Taxes on imports

4. Complete the statement with *GATT* or *NAFTA*: _____ is a worldwide trade agreement, while _____ applies to a single continent.

5. What restrictions do WTO rules place on a nation's environmental policies?

How Exchange Rates Are Determined

Up to this point, we have discussed the determinants of trade and national policies that can affect the flow of trade across countries. However, just as our domestic production and consumption are truly made possible by our domestic banking and financial systems, international trade is also facilitated through a complex international financial system. In the remainder of this chapter, we will explore the workings of this international financial system.

In this section, we begin our discussion of international finance by examining how the value of a currency is determined in world markets. We then look at the factors that can change the value of a currency.

What Are Exchange Rates?

To conduct international transactions between countries with different currencies, it is necessary to exchange one currency for another. The exchange rate is defined as the rate at which we can exchange one currency for another. Suppose a U.S. songwriter sells the rights to a hit song to a Japanese producer. The U.S. songwriter agrees to accept $50,000. If the exchange rate between U.S. dollars and Japanese yen is 100 yen per dollar, it will cost the Japanese producer 5 million yen to purchase the rights to the song. Because international trade occurs between nations with different currencies, the exchange rate—the price at which one currency trades for another currency—is a crucial determinant of the trade in goods and assets.

An increase in the value of a currency is called an **appreciation**. If the exchange rate between the dollar and the yen increases from 100 yen per dollar to 110 yen per dollar, one dollar will purchase more yen. Because the dollar has increased in value, we say that the dollar has appreciated against the yen. A **depreciation** is a reduction in the value of a currency. If the exchange rate falls to 90 yen per dollar, we get fewer yen for each dollar, so we say that the dollar has depreciated against the yen.

Appreciation: An increase in the value of a currency.

Depreciation: A decrease in the value of a currency.

In this chapter, we measure the exchange rate in units of foreign currency per dollar, that is, as 100 yen per dollar or two francs per dollar. We can think of the exchange rate as the price of dollars in terms of foreign currency. If the dollar appreciates from 100 yen per dollar to 110 yen per dollar, the price of dollars in terms of yen has increased—that is, the dollar has become more expensive in terms of yen. An appreciation of the dollar, therefore, is an increase in the price of dollars in terms of yen. Similarly, a depreciation of the dollar against the yen is a decrease in the price of dollars in terms of yen.

Be sure you understand that if the dollar appreciates against the yen, the yen must depreciate against the dollar. If we get more yen in exchange for the dollar, each yen will trade for fewer dollars. If the dollar appreciates from 100 to 110 yen per dollar, 100 yen will exchange for $0.91 rather than $1. Similarly, if the dollar depreciates against the yen, the yen must appreciate against the dollar. If we get fewer yen per dollar, each yen will exchange for more dollars. If the dollar depreciates from 100 yen to 90 yen per dollar, 100 yen will exchange for $1.11 rather than $1.

The exchange rate enables us to convert prices in one country to values in another country. A simple example illustrates how an exchange rate works. If you want to buy a watch from Switzerland, you need to know what the watch would cost. You call the store in Switzerland; you are told that the watch sells for 300 Swiss francs. The store owners live in Switzerland and want to be paid in Swiss francs. To figure out what it will cost you in dollars, you need to know the exchange rate between francs and dollars. If the exchange rate is two francs per dollar, the watch would cost you $150. If the exchange rate is three francs per dollar, however, the watch would cost only $100. The exchange rate allows you to convert the value of the watch (or any other good or service) from francs (or any other currency) to dollars.

Supply and Demand

How are exchange rates determined? The exchange rate between U.S. dollars and Swiss francs is determined in the foreign exchange market, the market in which dollars trade for Swiss francs. To understand this market, we can use simple supply and demand analysis.

In Figure 17.2, we plot the demand and supply curves for dollars in exchange for Swiss francs. On the vertical axis, we have the exchange rate, e, in francs per dollar: e will measure how many francs trade for one dollar. For example, if you receive two francs per dollar, then $e = 2$ francs/dollar. If e increases, one dollar buys more francs, and the price of dollars in terms of francs has increased. For example, if e increases from 2 francs/dollar to 2.5 francs/dollar, the dollar has become more valuable—meaning that it has appreciated—against the franc. Similarly, if the exchange rate falls to 1.5 francs/dollar, the dollar has depreciated in value against the franc, and the price of dollars in terms of francs has decreased.

Be sure you see both sides of the same exchange coin: If the dollar appreciates against the franc, then the franc depreciates against the dollar. If the exchange rate increases from 2 to 2.5 francs/dollar, a single franc falls in value from $0.50/franc to $0.40/franc:

$$2.5 \text{ francs/dollar} = 1/(2.5) \text{ dollars/francs} = 0.4 \text{ dollars/franc} = \$0.40/\text{franc}$$

Figure 17.2 shows the supply and demand curves for dollars in exchange for francs. The supply curve is the quantity supplied of dollars in exchange for francs. Individuals or firms that want to buy Swiss goods or assets will need to exchange dollars for francs. For example, to invest in the Swiss stock market, a U.S. investor must first trade dollars for francs because Swiss sellers of stocks or bonds want to be paid in their own currency. We have defined the exchange rate as francs per dollar, so an increase in the exchange rate means that each dollar exchanges for more francs and francs become cheaper relative to dollars. The supply curve is drawn under the assumption that as francs become cheaper, total spending on Swiss goods and assets will increase. Therefore, the supply curve is

Figure 17.2

Demand for and Supply of Dollars
Market equilibrium occurs where demand equals supply.

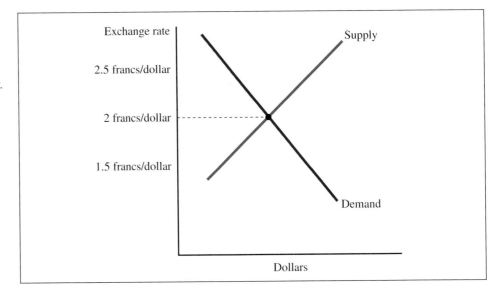

upward sloping: As the value of the dollar increases, more dollars will be supplied to the currency market in exchange for francs.

The demand curve represents the quantity demanded of dollars in exchange for francs. Individuals or firms in Switzerland that want to buy U.S. goods or assets must trade francs for dollars. For example, to visit Disneyland, a Swiss family must exchange francs for dollars. As the exchange rate falls, dollars become cheaper in terms of francs. This makes U.S. goods and assets less expensive for Swiss residents because each Swiss franc buys more U.S. dollars. As U.S. goods and assets become cheaper, we assume that more Swiss residents will want to trade francs for dollars. Therefore, the demand curve is downward sloping: Total demand for dollars will increase as the price of the dollar falls, or depreciates, against the franc.

Equilibrium in the market for foreign exchange occurs where the demand curve intersects the supply curve. In Figure 17.2, this occurs at an exchange rate of 2 francs/dollar. At this price, the willingness to trade dollars for francs just matches the willingness to trade francs for dollars. The foreign exchange market is in balance.

Changes in Demand or Supply

Changes in demand or changes in supply will change equilibrium exchange rates. In Figure 17.3, we show how an increase in demand, a shift of the demand curve to the right, will increase, or appreciate, the exchange rate. U.S. dollars will become more expensive relative to Swiss francs as the price of U.S. dollars in terms of francs increases.

Two factors will shift the demand curve for dollars: First, higher U.S. interest rates will lead to an increased demand for dollars. With higher returns in U.S. markets, investors throughout the world will want to buy dollars to invest in U.S. assets. The other factor, lower U.S. prices, will also lead to an increased demand for dollars. For example, if prices at Disneyland fell, there would be an overall increase in the demand for dollars because more tourists would want to visit Disneyland.

Figure 17.4 shows the effects of an increase in the supply of dollars, a shift in the supply curve to the right. An increase in the supply of dollars will lead to a fall, or depreciation, of the value of the dollar against the franc. What will cause the supply of dollars to increase? Again, the same two factors: interest rates and prices. Higher Swiss interest rates will lead U.S. investors to purchase Swiss bonds or other interest-paying assets. Purchasing Swiss bonds will require U.S. investors to supply dollars for francs, which

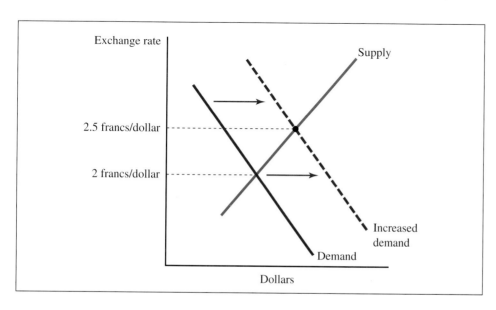

Figure 17.3

Shifts in Demand for Dollars

An increase in the demand for dollars will increase (appreciate) the exchange rate. Higher U.S. interest rates or lower U.S. prices will increase the demand for dollars.

Figure 17.4

Shifts in the Supply of Dollars

An increase in the supply of dollars will decrease (depreciate) the exchange rate. Higher Swiss interest rates or lower Swiss prices will increase the supply of dollars.

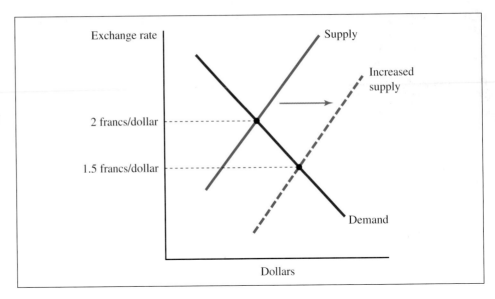

will drive down the exchange rate for dollars. Lower Swiss prices will also lead to an increase in the supply of dollars for francs.

Let's summarize the key facts about the foreign exchange market, using Swiss francs as our example:

1. The demand curve for dollars represents the demand for dollars in exchange for francs. It is downward sloping. As the dollar depreciates, there will be an increase in the quantity demanded of dollars in exchange for francs.

2. The supply curve for dollars is the supply of dollars in exchange for francs. It is upward sloping. As the dollar appreciates, there will be an increase in the quantity supplied of dollars in exchange for francs.

3. Increases in U.S. interest rates and decreases in U.S. prices will increase the demand for dollars, leading to an appreciation of the dollar.

4. Increases in Swiss interest rates and decreases in Swiss prices will increase the supply of dollars in exchange for francs, leading to a depreciation of the dollar.

Real Exchange Rates and Net Exports

As our examples of Swiss watches and Disneyland indicate, changes in market exchange rates can affect the demand for a country's goods and services. However, we have been assuming that the prices of watches and trips to Disneyland do not change. In general, prices change over time, and we need to adjust the exchange rate determined in the foreign exchange market to take into account changes in prices. This is an application of the reality principle:

Reality PRINCIPLE

What matters to people is the real value of money or income—its purchasing power—not the face value of money or income.

Real exchange rate: The market exchange rate adjusted for prices.

Economists have developed a concept that adjusts the market exchange rates for changes in prices. It is called the **real exchange rate**. The real exchange rate is defined as the price of all U.S. goods and services relative to all foreign goods and services, expressed in a common currency. We measure it by expressing U.S. prices for goods and services in foreign currency and comparing them to foreign prices. Here is the formula for the real exchange rate:

real exchange rate = (exchange rate × U.S. price index)/foreign price index

We can use this formula to help us understand the factors that change the real exchange rate. First, an increase in U.S. prices will raise the real exchange rate. When foreign prices and the exchange rate are held constant, an increase in U.S. prices will raise the relative price of U.S. goods. Second, an appreciation of the dollar, when prices are held constant, will also raise the price of U.S. goods relative to foreign goods. And if foreign prices fall, U.S. goods will become more expensive as well.

Be sure to understand the real exchange rate because it takes into account changes in a country's prices. Suppose that Country A had an inflation rate of 20% while Country B had no inflation. Moreover, the exchange rate of Country A fell, or depreciated, 20% against the currency of Country B. In this case, there would be no change in the real exchange rate between the two countries. Although prices in Country A would have increased by 20%, its currency would be 20% cheaper. From the point of view of residents of Country B, nothing has changed at all; it would still cost them the same price in their currency to buy goods in Country A.

Economists have found that a country's net exports (exports minus its imports) will decrease when its real exchange rate increases. For example, if the U.S. real exchange rate increases, the prices of U.S. goods will increase relative to foreign goods. This will reduce U.S. exports because our goods will have become more expensive; it will also increase imports to the United States because foreign goods will have become cheaper. As a result of the decrease in U.S. exports and the increase in U.S. imports, net exports will decline.

Figure 17.5 plots an index of the real exchange rate for the United States against net exports for 1980 to 2000, a period in which there were large changes in net exports and in the real exchange rate. The index is based on an average of real exchange rates with all U.S. trading partners; it's called a **multilateral real exchange rate**. As you can see in the figure,

Multilateral real exchange rate: An index of the real exchange rate with a country's trading partners.

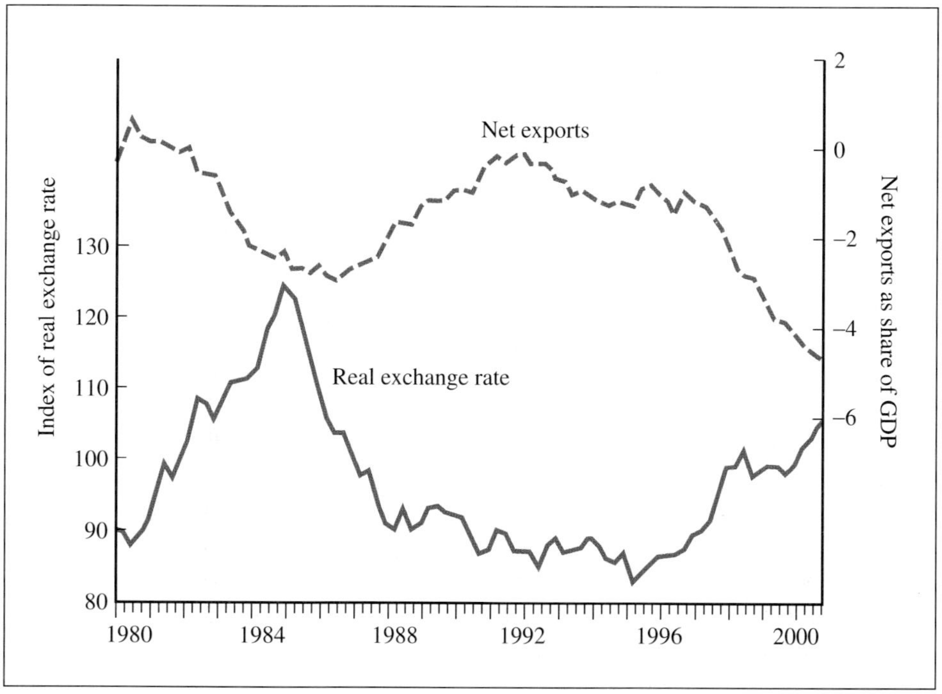

Figure 17.5
Real Exchange Rate and Net Exports as Share of GDP 1980–2000

Source: Department of Commerce and Federal Reserve.

both in 1984 and 1996 the real exchange rate increased sharply. Subsequently, net exports as a share of GDP fell. The relationship between the real exchange rate and net exports is not perfect—other factors also affect net exports.

TEST Your Understanding

Use demand and supply analysis to determine whether the dollar will appreciate or depreciate against the franc in each of these cases:

6. Banks cut interest rates in Switzerland.

7. Interest rates fall in the United States.

8. Annual inflation in the United States increases from 4% to 6%.

9. The Swiss inflation rate falls from 5% to 3% per year.

The Global Financial System Today

Movements in exchange rates have consequences for countries. For example, when a country's exchange rate appreciates—increases in value—it has two distinct effects.

1. The increased value of the exchange rate makes imports less expensive for the residents of the country where the exchange rate appreciated. For example, if the U.S. dollar appreciates against the Swiss franc, Swiss watches will become less expensive for U.S. consumers. U.S. consumers would like an appreciated dollar, because it would lower their cost of living.

2. The increased value of the exchange rate makes U.S. goods more expensive on world markets. A U.S. exchange appreciation will increase imports, such as Swiss watches, but decrease exports, such as California wine.

Since exports decrease and imports increase, net exports (exports minus imports) will decrease.

When a country's exchange rate depreciates, there are two distinct effects:

1. For example, if the U.S. dollar depreciated against the Japanese yen, Japanese imports would become more expensive in the United States, thereby raising the U.S. cost of living.

2. At the same time, U.S. goods would become cheaper on world markets. With exports increasing and imports decreasing, net exports would increase.

Sometimes countries do not want their exchange rate to change. They may want to avoid sharp increases in their cost of living from an exchange rate depreciation, or they may want to avoid a reduction in net exports through an exchange rate appreciation. To prevent the value of the currency from changing, governments can enter the foreign exchange market to try to influence the price of foreign exchange. Economists call these efforts to influence the value of foreign exchange **foreign exchange market intervention**.

Foreign exchange market intervention: The purchase or sale of currencies by a government to influence the market exchange rate.

In the United States, the Treasury Department has the official responsibility for foreign exchange intervention, though in conjunction with the Federal Reserve. In other countries, governments also intervene in the foreign exchange market.

To influence the price at which one currency trades for another, governments have to affect the demand or supply for that currency. For example, to increase the value of its currency, a government must increase the demand for its currency; to decrease the value of its currency, a government must increase the supply of its currency.

In Figure 17.6, we show how governments can fix, or peg, the price of a currency. Suppose the U.S. and Swiss governments want the exchange rate to be 2 francs/dollar.

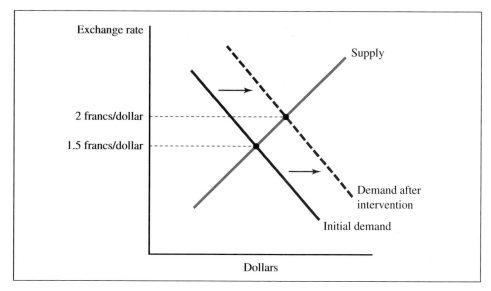

Figure 17.6
Intervention to Raise the Price of Dollars
To increase the price of dollars, the U.S. government sells francs in exchange for dollars. This shifts the demand curve for dollars to the right.

The price at which demand and supply are equal, however, is currently 1.5 francs/dollar. To raise the price of dollars, the governments need to increase the demand for dollars. To do this, either government—the United States or Switzerland—or both can go into the market for foreign exchange and sell francs in exchange for dollars. This will shift the demand curve for dollars to the right until the price of dollars rises to 2 francs/dollar.

Should governments peg foreign exchange rates? This question leads us directly to the consideration of two types of exchange rate systems: fixed exchange rates and flexible exchange rates.

Fixed Exchange Rates

Whether you are in California, New York, or Indiana, all prices are quoted in dollars. No one asks whether your dollar came from San Francisco or Miami. Within the United States, a dollar is a dollar. Suppose, though, that every state in the United States had its own currency. There might be a California dollar (with a picture of the Golden Gate Bridge), an Oregon dollar (showing pictures of tall trees), and a Florida dollar (showing Disney World, of course). In principle, these dollars might trade at different rates, depending on the supply and demand of one state's dollar relative to the supply and demand for another state's dollar. For example, in one year, the Texas dollar might be worth more than the Michigan dollar, trading for 1.2 Michigan dollars.

Think how much more complicated it would be to do business if each state had different currencies. To buy goods from a mail-order company in Maine, you would have to find out the exchange rate between your state's dollar and the Maine dollar. Any large business operating in all 50 states would be overwhelmed by trying to keep track of all exchange rate movements across the states. The economy would become less efficient as individuals and businesses focused all their attention on exchange rates.

These same ideas apply across nations. Wouldn't it be nice if all countries either used the same currency or fixed their exchange rates against one another so that no one would have to worry about exchange rate movements? Currency systems in which governments try to keep constant the values of their currencies against one another are called **fixed exchange rate systems**.

In a typical fixed exchange rate system, one country stands at the center, and other countries fix, or peg, their exchange rates to the currency of this center country. Each other country must intervene in the foreign exchange market, if necessary, to keep its

Fixed exchange rates: A system in which governments peg exchange rates between currencies.

exchange rate constant. A government will have to intervene if, at the fixed exchange rate, the private demand and supply for its currency are not equal.

Suppose the supply of a country's currency exceeds the demand at the fixed exchange rate. An excess supply of a country's currency at the fixed exchange rate is known as a **balance of payments deficit**. A balance of payments deficit will occur whenever there is a trade deficit (an excess of imports over exports) that is not matched by net sales of assets to foreigners by the private sector. (For example, a trade deficit of $100 billion with net sales of assets to foreigners of only $80 billion would mean that there is an excess supply of $20 billion.) With an excess supply of a country's currency in the currency market, that currency would fall in value without any intervention. To prevent the currency from depreciating in value and to maintain the fixed exchange rate, the government must sell foreign exchange—that means sell foreign currency—and buy its own currency. If a country sells foreign exchange, its holdings of foreign exchange will fall. So you can see that when a country runs a balance of payments deficit, it will decrease its holdings of foreign exchange.

It's also very possible that the demand for a country's currency exceeds the supply of its currency at the fixed exchange rate. An excess demand for a country's currency at the fixed exchange rate is known as a **balance of payments surplus**. A balance of payments surplus arises when there is a trade surplus (excess of exports over imports) that is not matched by net purchases of foreign assets by the private sector. With an excess demand for a country's currency, it would rise in value without any intervention. To prevent the currency from appreciating in value and to maintain the fixed exchange rate, the government must buy foreign exchange—buy foreign currency—and sell its own currency. Because it is buying foreign exchange, its holdings of foreign exchange will increase. From this discussion, you should be able to see that when a country runs a balance of payments surplus, it will increase its holdings of foreign exchange.

Under a fixed exchange rate system, countries that run persistent balance of payments deficits or balance of payments surpluses must take corrective actions. If domestic policy actions—such as changing taxes, changing spending, or changing the supply of money—do not cure the problem, it will eventually become necessary to change the level at which the exchange rate is fixed. A country that faces a balance of payments deficit can lower the value at which the currency is pegged to increase its net exports; this is called a **devaluation**. Conversely, a country that faces a balance of payments surplus can increase the value at which its currency is pegged and reduce its net exports; this is called a **revaluation**.

The U.S. Experience with Fixed and Flexible Exchange Rates

After World War II, the countries of the world operated under a fixed exchange system known as Bretton Woods, after the town in New Hampshire where the representatives of each nation met and agreed to adopt this system. The United States operated at the center of this system: All countries fixed or pegged their currencies against the U.S. dollar.

The Bretton Woods system lasted until the early 1970s, when the world abandoned it and went to the current system—a **flexible exchange rate** system in which free markets primarily determine exchange rates. What that means is that the exchange rate of a currency is determined by the supply and demand for it. If a fixed exchange rate system makes it easier to trade, why did it break down in the early 1970s? Fixed exchange rate systems provide benefits, but they require countries to maintain similar economic policies—especially to maintain similar inflation rates and interest rates.

To understand this, suppose the exchange rate between the United States and Switzerland were fixed, but the United States had an annual inflation rate of 6% com-

Balance of payments deficit: Under a fixed exchange rate system, a situation in which the supply of a country's currency exceeds the demand for its currency at the current exchange rate.

Balance of payments surplus: Under a fixed exchange rate system, a situation in which the demand for a country's currency exceeds the supply of its currency at the current exchange rate.

Devaluation: A decrease in the exchange rate in a fixed exchange rate system.

Revaluation: An increase in the exchange rate in a fixed exchange rate system.

Flexible exchange rate: A currency system in which exchange rates are determined by free markets.

pared to 0% inflation in Switzerland. Because prices in the United States would be rising by 6% per year, the U.S. real exchange rate against Switzerland would also be increasing at 6% per year. This difference in their real exchange rates over time would cause a trade deficit to emerge in the United States as U.S. goods became more expensive on world markets. As long as the differences in inflation continued and the exchange rate remained fixed, the U.S. real exchange rate would continue to appreciate, and the U.S. trade deficit would grow even worse. Clearly, this course of events could not continue.

In the late 1960s, inflation in the United States began to exceed inflation in other countries, and a U.S. balance of payments deficit emerged. In 1971, President Richard Nixon surprised the world and devalued the U.S. dollar against the currencies of all the other countries. This was a sharp departure from the rules underlying Bretton Woods, in which the United States was at the center of the system and other countries were supposed to make adjustments, if necessary, against the dollar. President Nixon hoped that a one-time devaluation of the dollar would alleviate the U.S. balance of payments deficit and maintain the underlying system of fixed exchange rates. However, the U.S. devaluation did not stop the U.S. balance of payments deficit, and the Bretton fixed exchange rate system soon collapsed.

Exchange Rate Systems Today

The flexible exchange rate system has worked well enough since the breakdown of Bretton Woods. World trade has grown at a rapid rate. Moreover, the flexible exchange rate system has managed to handle many diverse situations, including two major oil shocks, large U.S. budget deficits in the 1980s, and large current account surpluses by the Japanese.

During the Bretton Woods period, many countries placed restrictions on flows of financial capital—for example, by not allowing their residents to purchase foreign assets or by limiting foreigners' purchases of domestic assets. By the 1970s, these restrictions began to be eliminated, and private-sector transactions in assets grew rapidly. With massive amounts of funds being traded in financial markets, it becomes very difficult to fix, or peg, an exchange rate.

Nonetheless, countries whose economies are closely tied together might want the advantages of fixed exchange rates. One way to avoid some of the difficulties of fixing exchange rates between countries is to abolish individual currencies and establish a single currency. This is precisely what a group of European countries did. They developed a single currency throughout Europe and a single central bank to control the supply of the currency. The common currency has been named the **euro**. "A Closer Look: The Euro," provides more details on this system. With a single currency, European countries hope to capture the benefits of a large market, such as the market within the United States.

Euro: The common currency in Europe.

The United Kingdom initially decided to remain outside this European single-currency system. Its currency, like the U.S. dollar, the Swiss franc, and the Japanese yen, will float against each of those currencies and the euro. Many other countries have tied their exchange rate to either the dollar or the yen. Some economists believe that the world will eventually settle into three large currency blocs: the euro, the dollar, and the yen.

Financial Liberalization and Financial Crises

The economies of the world are linked through the financial system as well as through trade in goods and services. One of the most important developments of the last decade has been the increase in the financial linkages among countries. For example, the residents of the United States can now routinely invest in firms in Asia and Latin America. A

A CLOSER LOOK | THE EURO

January 1, 1999, was the day that the euro, the new common European currency, made its debut. On that day, Austria, Belgium, Finland, France, Switzerland, Ireland, Italy, Luxembourg, the Netherlands, Portugal, and Spain irrevocably fixed their exchange rates to the euro. On July 1, 2002, national currencies disappeared. French francs, German marks, Italian lire, and other currencies have ceased to exist.

A European central bank manages the monetary affairs for the single currency. It plays a role similar to the role the Federal Reserve Bank plays in the United States. The countries in the European Union no longer conduct their own independent monetary policy. With monetary policy gone, fiscal policy is their only remaining tool for macroeconomic stabilization.

Not all the European Union countries joined this system. Fearing a possible loss of independence, the United Kingdom, Denmark, and Sweden decided not to join this system initially. Greece would have liked to join, but it did not meet some of the EU's fiscal criteria necessary to join. Economists will carefully watch this experiment unfold in the twenty-first century.

Financial liberalization: The opening of financial markets to participants from foreign countries.

firm in Thailand that wants to undertake a major new venture might borrow funds in Western Europe, Japan, or the United States. Large banks in Japan have routinely made loans to firms throughout the world. In the past, many governments limited the ability of their citizens and businesses to borrow or lend in foreign countries. But in recent years, many economies have undergone a process of **financial liberalization**, opening up their financial markets to participants from foreign countries.

Financial liberalization creates many new opportunities for countries. They no longer need to rely on their own residents to finance important projects but instead can tap the resources from the entire world. Similarly, financial liberalization allows investors to scout the world for new and profitable investment opportunities and does not restrict them to their own country. In general, financial liberalization facilitates global specialization and leads to a more efficient world economy.

Because of the tighter linkages in product and financial markets, the economies of the world are becoming more and more interdependent. The greater flow of products across national boundaries and the increases in international financial transactions have increased the need for international institutions to help make the system work. The **International Monetary Fund (IMF)**, headquartered in Washington, D.C., works closely with the governments of the world to promote efficient and effective financial policies to facilitate the growth in world trade and commerce.

International Monetary Fund (IMF): An organization that works closely with national governments to promote financial policies that facilitate world trade.

Nonetheless, despite international institutions, increased economic interdependence can make the global system more fragile. In particular, major financial crises do occur that can potentially affect many countries. In 1994, Mexico experienced a severe financial crisis. In 1997, it was Asia's turn. How do these crises originate? What policies can be taken to prevent or alleviate them?

Let's examine the Asian financial crisis. Economic growth had been remarkable in Asia for over 20 years, improving to a great extent the standard of living of millions of people. In the early 1990s, several Asian countries began to open up their capital markets to foreign investors and began to borrow extensively from abroad. Billions of dollars poured into Asia. In many cases, there was little financial supervision, and many of the investments proved to be unwise. Companies in both Thailand and South Korea began to lose money. Domestic investors and world investors suddenly became pessimistic and began pulling their funds out of South Korea and Thailand, among other Asian countries. The withdrawal of funds forced devaluations of currencies throughout Asia. Because many businesses had borrowed in dollars, the devaluations raised the burden of the debt and further deepened the crisis, taking its toll on other countries, including Indonesia, Malaysia, and Hong Kong. The International Monetary Fund attempted to help restore the health of these economies' financial systems, but in many cases, their policies were ineffective. The countries that undertook fiscal reforms were the quickest to recover.

These examples highlight many of the ingredients of a financial crisis. With our vast global capital markets, funds can move quickly from country to country, and economic policies sometimes do not keep pace with changing political and economic developments. It can be extremely difficult to maintain a fixed exchange rate in this environment. The flow of funds, moreover, is often so large that financial failures could cause major global disruptions in trade and commerce. The major countries of the world are searching for a reliable set of rules and institutional mechanisms to assist in financial crises. Historically, the International Monetary Fund has played a key role in assisting countries that run into financial difficulties. However, in Mexico, the sums were so large that the United States was forced to take the lead in resolving its situation. In Asia, the International Monetary Fund did not have this backing from the United States, and it was less successful. As world capital markets continue to grow, governments throughout the world will almost surely be tested through new and often unpredictable financial crises. They will need to anticipate and react to rapid changes in the economic and political environment to maintain a stable financial environment for trade.

Using the **Tools**

This chapter explored the origins of international trade and provided an overview of the international financial system necessary for trade. Take this opportunity to use the tools you developed in this chapter to do your own economic analysis.

1. ECONOMIC EXPERIMENT: PROTECTIONIST POLICIES
Review the market equilibrium experiment from Chapter 2. We can modify the experiment to show the effects of protectionist policies on equilibrium prices and quantities. On the supply side of the market, there are domestic apple producers and foreign apple producers; the domestic producers have higher unit costs. After several trading periods without any government intervention, you can change the rules as follows.

a. Apple imports are banned: Foreign producers cannot participate in the market.

b. There is a tariff (a tax on imports) of $5 per bushel.

2. Ban on Shoe Imports
Consider a country that initially consumes 100 pairs of shoes per hour, all of which are imported. The price of shoes is $40 per pair before a ban on importing them is imposed. Use a graph to explain what happens to the price of shoes and the quantity of shoes consumed after a total ban on imports.

3. The Real Exchange Rate Between Germany and the United States
Consider the following data for the United States and Germany:

Year	Germany GDP Deflator	U.S. GDP Deflator	Market Exchange Rate
1980	85.7	76.0	2.49 marks/dollar
1990	113.4	119.6	2.12 marks/dollar

a. By what percent did the dollar depreciate against the mark over this period?

b. Using the formula for the real exchange rate

real exchange rate = (exchange rate × U.S. price index)/foreign price index

compute the real exchange rate for 1980 and 1990.

c. By how much did the real exchange rate change over this period? Compare your answer to part a.

4. Exchange Rate Depreciation and the Returns from Investing

A newspaper headline said, "Foreign Investors Fear Dollar Depreciation: U.S. Interest Rates Rise."

a. Suppose you were a Swiss citizen and had invested in a one-year U.S. bond that yielded 6% per year. The bond cost $1,000 and paid $1,060 at the end of the year. At the time you bought the bond, the exchange rate was 2 francs/dollar. How many francs did the bond cost? If the exchange rate remained at 2 francs/dollar when you received your payment, how many francs would you have? What would be your percentage return in francs for the year?

b. Suppose the dollar fell against the franc during the year from 2 francs to 1.5 francs/dollar. At the end of the year, how many francs would you have? What would be your percentage return in francs for the year?

c. Using your answers to parts a and b, explain the newspaper headline.

Summary

In this chapter, we examined the logic of international trade, the actions that nation-states take to promote or discourage trade, and the world of international finance. Here are some of the key ideas of this chapter:

1. Most people are not self-sufficient but instead specialize to earn income, which they use to buy goods and services from others.

2. If one country has a comparative advantage vis-á-vis another country in producing a particular good (a lower opportunity cost), specialization and trade will benefit both countries.

3. The free flow of goods can be hampered by barriers to trade, including tariffs, quotas, voluntary export restraints, and nontariff trade barriers. There are many international agreements designed to reduce trade barriers, including GATT, NAFTA, and the European Union.

4. Exchange rates are currently determined in foreign exchange markets by supply and demand.

5. The real exchange rate—the market exchange rate adjusted for prices—is the relative price of a country's goods and services on world markets.

6. Governments can attempt to change the value of currencies by buying or selling currencies in the foreign exchange market. Purchasing a currency will raise its value; selling a currency will decrease its value.

7. A system of fixed exchange rates can provide a better environment for business but requires that countries keep their inflation rates and interest rates within narrow limits.

Key Terms

absolute advantage, 378
appreciation, 385
Asian Pacific Economic Cooperation (APEC), 382
balance of payments deficit, 392

balance of payments surplus, 392
comparative advantage, 378
depreciation, 385
devaluation, 392
euro, 393

European Union (EU), 382
exchange rate, 376
export, 378
financial liberalization, 394
fixed exchange rate, 391

Problems and Discussion Questions

1. Recall the example of Brenda and Sam shown in Table 17.1. Suppose a technological innovation increases the shirt productivity of both people: Brenda can now produce three shirts per hour while Sam can now produce two shirts per hour. Their productivity for bread has not changed. Suppose they agree to trade one shirt for each loaf of bread. Will both people still gain from specialization and trade?

2. Consider two financial planners, Phil and Frances. In an hour, Phil can either produce one financial statement or answer 10 phone calls while Frances can either produce three financial statements or answer 12 phone calls. Does either person have an absolute advantage in producing both products? Should the two planners be self-sufficient (each producing statements and answering phones), or should they specialize?

3. Professor A is a better teacher than Professor B for both an undergraduate course (U) and a graduate course (G). As the chair of the department, you measure teaching performance as the average grade received by students on standardized exams. How would you decide which course the professors should teach? Assume that students in course G will get 90 points if Professor A teaches it or 45 if Professor B teaches it. Students in course U will get 90 points if Professor A teaches it or 60 if Professor B teaches it.

4. Use the notion of comparative advantage to explain why two countries, one of which is less efficient in producing all products, will still find it advantageous to trade.

5. Some studies have suggested that industries in countries that receive protection from foreign trade are less efficient than the same industries in other countries that do not receive protection. Can you explain this finding?

6. The European Union is committed to eliminating most of the trade barriers among its member nations. What types of people benefit from these barriers? Which types will lose?

7. Using demand and supply analysis to assist you, what are the effects on the exchange rate between the British pound and the Japanese yen from:
   a. An increase in Japanese interest rates
   b. An increase in the price of British goods
   c. An increase in British interest rates

8. Suppose that a South American country saw its exchange rate depreciate 10% against the dollar, and that prices in that country rose 12% while prices in the United States did not change. What happened to the real exchange rate between the South American country and the United States?

9. There are rumors that there is about to be a military coup in an Eastern European country. Explain what you think will happen to the country's exchange rate.

10. What would be required before all the countries of the world could enter into a fixed exchange rate system? Do you think it is feasible?

11. Web Exercise. Go to the Web site for the World Trade Organization (*www.wto.gov*) and explore some of the ongoing trade disputes. Pick one or two of these disputes and find additional background information, such as newspaper stories, on the Web. Use this information to understand the nature of the controversy.

12. Web Exercise. What are the key policy issues facing the European Central Bank? Go to the Web site of the European Central Bank (*www.ecb.int/about/about.htm*). Outline the three most important issues that are currently being debated.

Take It to the Net

We invite you to visit the O'Sullivan/Sheffrin page on the Prentice Hall Web site at: **www.prenhall.com/osullivan/** for additional World Wide Web exercises for this chapter.

Model Answers to Questions

Chapter-Opening Questions

1. Trade exists because it is more efficient to specialize in the production of goods and services and then trade goods and services with others.

2. Comparative advantage makes trade between rich and poor nations beneficial to both.

3. Under current WTO rules, a country cannot adopt any environmental standard that discriminates against foreign producers. For example, the United States cannot impose an import ban of goods that are produced in polluting factories in other nations. This rule means that global environmental issues must be resolved with international agreements, not trade restrictions.

4. If the dollar increases in value against the Japanese yen, it will make our exports more expensive and our imports less expensive. This dollar increase against the yen will reduce our trade balance with Japan.

5. Many European countries have adopted a single currency because they believe that a single large market with no worries of exchange rate changes will reduce the costs of trade.

Test Your Understanding

1. Tim's opportunity cost of one table is one-fifth of a chair, while Carla's opportunity cost of one table is one chair. Carla has a lower opportunity cost of chairs, so she should produce chairs. Tim has a lower opportunity cost of tables, so he should produce tables.

2. No. If he has a comparative advantage at managerial tasks such as doing the books or marketing, he should hire some workers to wash the cars, allowing him to specialize in the tasks for which he has a comparative advantage.

3. A4, B1, C3, D2.

4. GATT, NAFTA

5. A nation's environmental laws must not discriminate against imported goods. The laws must apply equally to imports and domestic goods.

6. The dollar will appreciate.

7. The dollar will depreciate.

8. The dollar will depreciate.

9. The dollar will depreciate.

Using the Tools

2. **Ban on Shoe Imports.** Banning imports will shift the supply curve up and to the left. As a result, the price of shoes will rise above $40 per pair, and the consumption of shoes will be less than 100 pairs of shoes per hour.

3. **The Real Exchange Rate Between Germany and the United States**

   a. The dollar fell by 14.8% [$(2.12 - 2.49)/2.49 = 0.148$].

   b. The real exchange rate increased from 2.208 to 2.236.

   c. Using the formula for the real exchange rate, we find that the real exchange rate was 2.208 in 1980 and 2.236 in 1990. That is an increase of 1.3% from 1980 to 1990. Although the dollar depreciated, prices rose more in the United States than in Germany, so the real exchange rate actually increased.

4. **Exchange Rate Depreciation and the Returns from Investing**

   a. At 2 francs/dollar, the bond costs 2,000 francs and pays 2,120 francs, for a 6% return.

   b. If the dollar fell to 1.5 francs/dollar, at the end of the year you would only have $(1,060)(1.5) = 1,590$ francs, and your return on your 2,000-franc investment would be -20.5%.

   c. If the dollar falls, returns measured in francs will decrease and foreign investors will find dollar investments less attractive. To keep investors from withdrawing funds from the United States, interest rates would have to increase.

Glossary

Accelerator theory: The theory of investment that says current investment spending depends positively on the expected future growth of real GDP.

Adverse-selection problem: The uninformed side of the market must choose from an undesirable or adverse selection of goods.

Aggregate demand: The relationship between the level of prices and the quantity of real GDP demanded.

Aggregate supply: The relationship between the level of prices and the quantity of output supplied.

Anticipated inflation: Inflation that is expected.

Appreciation: An increase in the value of a currency.

Asian Pacific Economic Cooperation (APEC) organization: An organization of 18 Asian nations that attempts to reduce trade barriers between their nations.

Assets: The uses of the funds of a bank, including loans and reserves.

Asymmetric information: One side of the market—either buyers or sellers—has better information about the good than the other.

Automatic stabilizers: Taxes and transfer payments that stabilize GDP without requiring policymakers to take explicit action.

Autonomous consumption spending: The part of consumption that does not depend on income.

Average cost pricing policy: A regulatory policy under which the government picks the lowest price at which the market demand curve intersects the long-run average cost curve.

Average fixed cost (AFC): Fixed cost divided by the quantity produced.

Balance of payments deficit: Under a fixed exchange rate system, a situation in which the supply of a country's currency exceeds the demand for the currency at the current exchange rate.

Balance of payments surplus: Under a fixed exchange rate system, a situation in which the demand for a country's currency exceeds the supply of the currency at the current exchange rate.

Balance sheet: An account for a bank that shows the sources of its funds (liabilities) as well as the uses for the funds (assets).

Barter: Trading goods directly for other goods.

Board of Governors of the Federal Reserve: The seven-person governing body of the Federal Reserve System in Washington, D.C.

Budget deficit: The difference between a government's spending and its revenues from taxation.

Business cycles: Another name for economic fluctuations.

Capital: See *physical capital*; see *human capital*.

Capital deepening: Increases in the stock of capital per worker.

Carbon tax: A tax based on a fuel's carbon content.

Cartel: A group of firms that coordinate their pricing decisions, often by charging the same price.

Central bank: A banker's bank; an official bank that controls the supply of money in a country.

Ceteris paribus: Latin meaning "other things being equal."

Chain price index: A method for calculating changes in prices that uses data from different base years.

Change in demand: A change in the amount of a good demanded resulting from a change in something other than the price of the good; represented graphically by a shift of a demand curve.

Change in quantity demanded: A change in the amount of a good demanded resulting from a change in the price of the good; represented graphically by a movement along a demand curve.

Change in quantity supplied: A change in the amount of a good supplied resulting from a change in the price of the good; represented graphically by a movement along a supply curve.

Change in supply: A change in the amount of a good supplied resulting from a change in something other than the price of the good; represented graphically by a shift of the supply curve.

Command-and-control policy: A pollution-control policy under which the government commands each firm to produce no more than a certain volume of pollution and controls the firm's production process by forcing the firm to use a particular pollution-control technology.

Complements: Two goods for which an increase in the price of one good decreases the demand for the other good.

Concentration ratio: A measure of the degree of concentration in a market; the four-firm concentration ratio is the percentage of output produced by the four largest firms.

Constant-cost industry: An industry in which the average cost of production is constant, so the long-run supply curve is horizontal.

Consumer price index (CPI): A price index that measures the cost of a fixed basket of goods chosen to represent the consumption pattern of individuals.

Consumer surplus: The difference between the maximum amount a consumer is willing to pay for a product and the price that he or she pays for the product.

Consumption expenditures: Purchases of newly produced goods and services by households.

Consumption function: The relationship between the level of income and consumption spending.

Contractionary policies: Government policy actions that lead to decreases in output.

Convergence: The process by which poorer countries "catch up" with richer countries in terms of real GDP per capita.

Cost-of-living adjustments: Automatic increases in wages or other payments that are tied to a price index.

Countercyclical: Moving in the opposite direction of real GDP.

Craft union: A labor organization that includes workers from a particular occupation, for example, plumbers, bakers, or electricians.

Creative destruction: The process by which competition for monopoly profits leads to technological progress.

Cross elasticity of demand: A measure of the responsiveness of the quantity demanded to changes in the price of a related good; computed by dividing the percentage change in the quantity demanded of one good (X) by the percentage change in the price of another good (Y).

Crowding out: The reduction in investment (or other component of GDP) in the long run caused by an increase in government spending.

Cyclical unemployment: The component of unemployment that accompanies fluctuations in real GDP.

Deadweight loss from monopoly: A measure of the inefficiency from monopoly; equal to the difference between the consumer surplus loss from monopoly pricing and the monopoly profit.

Demand curve: See *individual demand curve; see market demand curve*.

Demand schedule: A table of numbers that shows the relationship between price and quantity demanded by a consumer, ceteris paribus (other things being equal).

Depreciation: The wear and tear of capital as it is used in production.

Depression: The common name for a severe recession.

Devaluation: A decrease in the exchange rate to which a currency is pegged in a fixed rate system.

Diminishing returns: As one input increases while the other inputs are held fixed, output increases but at a decreasing rate.

Discount rate: The interest rate at which banks can borrow from the Fed.

Discouraged workers: Workers who left the labor force because they could not find jobs.

Diseconomies of scale: A situation in which an increase in the quantity produced increases the long-run average cost of production.

Disposable personal income: The income that flows back to households, taking into account transfers and taxes.

Double coincidence of wants: The problem in a system of barter that one person may not have what the other desires.

Duopolists' dilemma: A situation in which both firms would be better off if they both choose a high price but each chooses a low price.

Durable goods: Goods that last for a long period of time, such as household appliances.

Economic cost: Explicit costs plus implicit costs.

Economic fluctuations: Movements of GDP above or below normal trends.

Economic growth: Sustained increases in the real production of an economy over a period of time.

Economic profit: Total revenue minus the total economic cost.

Economics: The study of the choices made by people who are faced with scarcity.

Economies of scale: A situation in which an increase in the quantity produced decreases the long-run average cost of production.

Elastic demand: The price elasticity of demand is greater than one.

Employed: People who have jobs.

Entrepreneur: A person who has an idea for a business and coordinates the production and sale of goods and services, taking risks in the process.

Entrepreneurship: Effort used to coordinate the production and sale of goods and services.

Euro: The common currency in Europe.

European Union (EU): An organization of European nations that has reduced trade barriers within Europe.

Excess reserves: Any additional reserves that a bank holds above required reserves.

Exchange rate: The rate at which currencies trade for one another in the market.

Expansion: The period from a trough to the next peak of a business cycle.

Expansionary policies: Government policy actions that lead to increases in output.

Expectations of inflation: The beliefs held by the public about the likely path of inflation for the future.

Expected real interest rate: The nominal interest rate minus the expected inflation rate.

Export: A good produced in the home country (for example, the United States) and sold in another country.

External benefit: Another term for spillover benefit.

External cost: Another term for spillover cost.

Factors of production: Labor and capital used to produce goods and services.

Federal funds market: The market in which banks borrow and lend reserves to and from one another.

Federal Open Market Committee (FOMC): The group that decides on monetary policy; it consists of the 7 members of the Board of Governors plus 5 of 12 regional bank presidents on a rotating basis.

Federal Reserve Banks: One of 12 regional banks that are an official part of the Federal Reserve System.

Financial intermediaries: Organizations that receive funds from savers and channel them to investors.

Financial liberalization: The opening of financial markets to participants from foreign countries.

Fiscal policy: The use of taxes and transfers to affect the level of aggregate demand.

Fixed exchange rates: A system in which governments peg exchange rates.

Flexible exchange rates: A currency system in which exchange rates are determined by free markets.

Foreign exchange market intervention: The purchase or sale of currencies by governments to influence the market exchange rate.

Franchise or licensing scheme: A policy under which the government picks a single firm to sell a particular good.

Free-rider problem: Each person will try to get the benefit of a public good without paying for it, trying to get a free ride at the expense of others who do pay.

Frictional unemployment: The part of unemployment associated with the normal workings of the economy, such as searching for jobs.

Full employment: The level of employment that occurs when the unemployment rate is at the natural rate.

Game tree: A graphical representation of the consequences of different strategies.

GDP deflator: An index that measures how the price of goods included in GDP changes over time.

General Agreement on Tariffs and Trade (GATT): An international agreement that has lowered trade barriers between the United States and other nations.

Government purchases: Purchases of newly produced goods and services by all levels of government.

Gross domestic product (GDP): The total market value of all the final goods and services produced within an economy in a given year.

Gross investment: Actual investment purchases.

Gross national product (GNP): GDP plus net income earned abroad.

Growth accounting: A method to determine the contribution to economic growth from increased capital, labor, and technological progress.

Growth rate: The percentage rate of change of a variable.

Guaranteed price matching: A scheme under which a firm guarantees that it will match a lower price by a competitor; also known as a meet-the-competition policy.

Household: A group of related family members and unrelated individuals who live in the same housing unit.

Human capital: The knowledge and skills acquired by a worker through education and experience and used to produce goods and services.

Import: A good produced in a foreign country and purchased by residents of the home country (for example, the United States).

Income effect for price change: The change in consumption resulting from an increase in the consumer's real income.

Income effect for wage change: An increase in the wage rate raises a worker's real income, increasing the demand for leisure.

Income elasticity of demand: A measure of the responsiveness of the quantity demanded to changes in consumer income; computed by dividing the percentage change in the quantity demanded by the percentage change in income.

Increasing-cost industry: An industry in which the average cost of production increases as the industry grows, so the long-run supply curve is positively sloped.

Indirect taxes: Sales and excise taxes.

Individual demand curve: A curve that shows the relationship between price and quantity demanded by an individual consumer, ceteris paribus (everything else held fixed).

Individual supply curve: A curve that shows the relationship between price and quantity supplied by an individual firm, ceteris paribus (everything else held fixed).

Indivisible input: An input that cannot be scaled down to produce a small quantity of output.

Industrial union: A labor organization that includes all types of workers from a single industry, for example, steelworkers or autoworkers.

Inelastic demand: The price elasticity of demand is less than one.

Infant industry: A new industry that is protected from foreign competitors.

Inferior good: A good for which an increase in income decreases demand.

Inflation rate: The percentage rate of change of the price level in the economy.

Input-substitution effect: The change in the quantity of labor demanded resulting from a change in the relative cost of labor.

Insecure monopoly: A monopoly faced with the possibility that a second firm will enter the market.

Intermediate good: Goods used in the production process that are not final goods or services.

International Monetary Fund: An organization that works closely with national governments to promote financial policies that facilitate world trade.

Invisible hand: The term that economists use to describe how the price system can efficiently coordinate economic activity without central government intervention.

Keynesian cross: A simple model of aggregate demand based on ideas from Keynes.

Labor: Human effort, including both physical and mental effort, used to produce goods and services.

Labor force: The employed plus the unemployed.

Labor-force participation rate: The fraction of the population over 16 years of age that is in the labor force.

Labor productivity: Output produced per hour of work.

Labor union: An organized group of workers; the objectives of the organization are to increase job security, improve working conditions, and increase wages and benefits.

Law of demand: The lower the price, the larger the quantity demanded, ceteris paribus (other things being equal).

Law of supply: The higher the price, the larger the quantity supplied, ceteris paribus (other things being equal).

Learning by doing: Knowledge gained during production that increases productivity.

Learning effect: The increase in a person's wage resulting from the learning of skills required for certain occupations.

Lender of last resort: A central bank is the lender of last resort, the last place, all others having failed, from which banks in emergency situations can obtain loans.

Liabilities: The sources of funds for a bank, including deposits of a financial intermediary.

Limit pricing: A scheme under which a monopolist accepts a price below the normal monopoly price to deter other firms from entering the market.

Liquidity demand for money: The demand for money that represents the needs and desires individuals or firms can fill on short notice without incurring excessive costs.

Long run: A period of time long enough that a firm can change all the factors of production, meaning that a firm can modify its existing production facility or build a new one.

Long-run aggregate supply curve: A vertical aggregate supply curve. It reflects the idea that, in the long run, output is determined solely by the factors of production.

Long-run average cost (LAC): Long-run total cost divided by the quantity of output produced.

Long-run demand curve for labor: A curve showing the relationship between the wage and the quantity of labor demanded over the long run, when the number of firms in the market can change and firms already in the market can modify their production facilities.

Long-run market supply: A curve showing the relationship between the market price and quantity supplied by all firms in the long run.

Long-run neutrality of money: An increase in the supply of money has no effect on real interest rates, investment, or output in the long run.

Long-run total cost: The total cost of production in the long run when a firm is perfectly flexible in its choice of all inputs and can choose a production facility of any size.

M1: The sum of currency in the hands of the public plus demand deposits plus other checkable deposits.

M2: M1 plus other assets, including deposits in savings and loans and money market mutual funds.

Macroeconomics: The branch of economics that looks at a nation's economy as a whole.

Marginal benefit: The extra benefit resulting from a small increase in some activity.

Marginal change: A small change in value.

Marginal cost: The additional cost resulting from a small increase in some activity.

Marginal product of labor: The change in output from one additional worker.

Marginal propensity to consume (MPC): The fraction of additional income that is spent.

Marginal propensity to import: The fraction of additional income that is spent on imports.

Marginal propensity to save (MPS): The fraction of additional income that is saved.

Marginal rate of substitution (MRS): The rate at which a consumer is willing to substitute one good for another.

Marginal revenue: The change in total revenue from selling one additional unit.

Marginal revenue product of labor (MRP): The extra revenue generated from one more unit of labor; equal to price of output times the marginal product of labor.

Market: An arrangement that allows buyers and sellers to exchange things. A buyer exchanges money for a product, while a seller exchanges a product for money.

Marketable pollution permits: A system under which the government picks a target pollution level for a particular area, issues just enough pollution permits to meet the pollution target, and allows firms to buy and sell the permits.

Market demand curve: A curve showing the relationship between price and quantity demanded by all consumers together, ceteris paribus (other things being equal).

Market equilibrium: A situation in which the quantity of a product demanded equals the quantity supplied, so there is no pressure to change the price.

Market supply curve: A curve showing the relationship between price and quantity supplied by all producers together, ceteris paribus (other things being equal).

Market supply curve for labor: A curve showing the relationship between the wage and the quantity of labor supplied.

Medium of exchange: The property of money that exchanges are made through the use of money.

Merger: A process in which two or more firms combine their operations.

Microeconomics: The study of the choices made by consumers, firms, and government, and how these decisions affect the market for a particular good or service.

Minimum efficient scale: The output at which the long-run average cost curve becomes horizontal.

Monetary policy: The range of actions taken by the Federal Reserve to influence the level of GDP or the rate of inflation.

Money: Anything that is regularly used in exchange.

Money illusion: Confusion of real and nominal magnitudes.

Money multiplier: An initial deposit leads to a multiple expansion of deposits. In the simplified case increase in deposits = (initial deposit) × (1/reserve ratio).

Monopolistic competition: A market served by dozens of firms selling slightly different products.

Monopoly: A market in which a single firm serves the entire market.

Moral hazard problem: Insurance encourages risky behavior.

Multilateral real exchange rate: An index of the real exchange rate with a country's trading partners.

Multiplier: The ratio of the final shift in aggregate demand to the initial shift in aggregate demand.

Multiplier-accelerator model: A model in which a downturn in real GDP leads to a sharp fall in investment, which triggers further reductions in GDP through the multiplier.

National income: Net national product less indirect taxes.

Natural monopoly: A market in which the entry of a second firm would make price less than average cost, so a single firm serves the entire market.

Natural rate of unemployment: The level of unemployment at which there is no cyclical unemployment.

Natural resources: Things created by acts of nature and used to produce goods and services.

Negative relationship: A relationship in which an increase in the value of one variable decreases the value of the other variable.

Net exports: Exports minus imports.

Net investment: Gross investment minus depreciation.

Net national product (NNP): GNP less depreciation.

Net worth: The difference between assets and liabilities.

New growth theory: Modern theories of growth that try to explain the origins of technological progress.

Nominal GDP: The value of GDP in current dollars.

Nominal rates of interest: Interest rates quoted in the market.

Nominal wages: Wages in dollars.

Nondurable goods: Goods that last for short periods of time, such as food.

Normal good: A good for which an increase in income increases demand.

Normative economics: Analysis that answers the question, What ought to be?

North American Free Trade Agreement (NAFTA): An international agreement that lowers barriers to trade between the United States, Mexico, and Canada (signed in 1994).

Oligopoly: A market served by a few firms.

Open market purchases: The Fed's purchase of government bonds, which increases the money supply.

Open market sales: The Fed's sales of government bonds to the public, which decreases the money supply.

Opportunity cost: What you sacrifice to get something.

Output effect: The change in the quantity of labor demanded resulting from a change in the quantity of output.

Patent: The exclusive right to sell a particular good for some period of time.

Paying efficiency wages: The firm's practice of paying wages to increase the average productivity of its workers.

Peak: The time at which a recession begins.

Perfectly competitive market: A market with a very large number of firms, each of which produces the same standardized product and takes the market price as given.

Permanent income: An estimate of a household's long-run average level of income.

Personal disposable income: Personal income after taxes.

Personal income: Income (including transfer payments) received by households.

Physical capital: Objects made by human beings and used to produce goods and services.

Pollution tax: A tax or charge equal to the spillover cost per unit of waste.

Positive economics: Analysis that answers the question, What is or what will be?

Positive relationship: A relationship in which an increase in the value of one variable increases the value of the other variable.

Potential output: The level of output in the economy when it is at full employment.

Poverty budget: The minimum amount the government estimates that a family needs to avoid being in poverty; equal to three times the minimum food budget.

Predatory pricing: A pricing scheme under which a firm decreases its price to drive a rival out of business, and increases the price when the other firm disappears.

Price ceiling: A maximum price; transactions above the maximum price are outlawed.

Price change formula: A formula that shows the percentage change in equilibrium price resulting from a change in demand or supply, given the values for the price elasticity of demand and the price elasticity of supply.

Price elasticity of demand: A measure of the responsiveness of the quantity demanded to changes in price;

computed by dividing the percentage change in quantity demanded by the percentage change in price.

Price elasticity of supply: A measure of the responsiveness of the quantity supplied to changes in price; computed by dividing the percentage change in quantity supplied by the percentage change in price.

Price fixing: An arrangement in which two firms coordinate their pricing decisions.

Price floor: A minimum price; transactions below the minimum price are outlawed.

Price level: An average of all the prices in the economy as measured by a price index.

Price-support program: A policy under which the government specifies a minimum price above the equilibrium price.

Principle: A simple truth that most people understand and accept.

Private good: A good that is consumed by a single person or household.

Private investment expenditures: Purchases of newly produced goods and services by firms.

Procyclical: Moving in same direction as real GDP.

Production possibilities curve: A curve showing the combinations of two goods that can be produced by an economy, assuming that all resources are fully employed.

Protectionist policies: Rules that restrict the free flow of goods between nations, including tariffs (taxes on imports), quotas (limits on total imports), voluntary export restraints (agreements between governments to limit exports), and nontariff trade barriers (subtle practices that hinder trade).

Public good: A good that is available for everyone to consume, regardless of who pays and who doesn't.

Quotas: A limit on the amount of a good that can be imported.

Real business cycle theory: The economic theory that emphasizes how shocks to technology can cause fluctuations in economic activity.

Real exchange rate: The market exchange rate adjusted for prices.

Real GDP: A measure of GDP that controls for changes in prices.

Real GDP per capita: Gross domestic product per person adjusted for changes in prices. It is the usual measure of living standards across time and between countries.

Real rate of interest: The nominal interest rate minus the inflation rate.

Real wages: Nominal or dollar wages adjusted for changes in purchasing power.

Recession: Six consecutive months of negative economic growth.

Rent control: A policy under which the government specifies a maximum rent that is below the equilibrium rent.

Rent seeking: The process under which a firm spends money to persuade the government to erect barriers to entry and pick the firm as the monopolist.

Required reserves: The fraction of banks' deposits that banks are legally required to hold in their vaults or as deposits at the Fed.

Reserve ratio: The ratio of reserves to deposits.

Reserves: The fraction of banks' deposits set aside in either vault cash or as deposits at the Federal Reserve.

Revaluation: An increase in the exchange rate in a fixed exchange system.

Rule of 70: If an economy grows at x percent per year, output will double in $70/x$ years.

Saving: Total income minus consumption.

Scarcity: A situation in which resources are limited and can be used in different ways, so we must sacrifice one thing for another.

Services: Reflect work done in which people play a prominent role in delivery, ranging from haircutting to health care.

Short run: A period of time over which one or more factors of production is fixed; in most cases, a period of time over which a firm cannot modify an existing facility or build a new one.

Short-run aggregate supply curve: A relatively flat supply curve. It reflects the idea that prices do not change very much in the short run and that firms adjust production to meet demand.

Short-run average total cost (SATC): Short-run total cost divided by the quantity of output, equal to AFC plus AVC.

Short-run average variable cost (SAVC): Variable cost divided by the quantity produced.

Short-run demand curve for labor: A curve showing the relationship between the wage and the quantity of labor demanded in the short run, the period when the firm cannot change its production facility.

Short run in macroeconomics: The period of time that prices do not change very much.

Short-run marginal cost (SMC): The change in total cost resulting from producing one more unit of the good in the short run.

Short-run market supply curve: A curve showing the relationship between price and the quantity of output supplied by all firms in the short run.

Short-run production function: Shows how much output is produced from varying amounts of labor, holding the capital stock constant.

Short-run supply curve for a firm: A curve showing the relationship between the price of a product and the quantity of output supplied by a firm in the short run.

Shut-down price: The price at which the firm is indifferent between operating and shutting down.

Signaling effect: The increase in a person's wage resulting from the signal of productivity provided by completing college.

Slope: The change in the variable on the vertical axis resulting from a one-unit increase in the variable on the horizontal axis.

Speculative demand for money: The demand for money that reflects holding money over short periods is less risky than holding stocks or bonds.

Spillover (or externality): A cost or benefit experienced by people who are external to the decision about how much of a good to produce or consume.

Store of value: The property of money that it preserves value until it is used in an exchange.

Structural unemployment: The part of unemployment that results from the mismatch of skills and jobs.

Substitutes: Two goods related in such a way that an increase in the price of one good increases the demand for the other good.

Substitution effect for price changes: The change in consumption resulting from a change in the price of one good relative to the price of other goods.

Substitution effect for wage changes: An increase in the wage rate increases the opportunity cost of leisure and leads workers to demand less leisure and supply more labor.

Sunk cost: The cost a firm has already paid—or has agreed to pay some time in the future.

Supply curve: See *individual supply curve*; see *market supply curve*.

Supply schedule: A table of numbers that shows the relationship between price and quantity supplied, ceteris paribus (other things being equal).

Supply shocks: External events that shift the aggregate supply curve.

Tariffs: A tax on an imported good.

Taxi medallion: A license to operate a taxi.

Technological progress: An increase in output without increasing inputs.

Thin market: A market in which some high-quality goods are sold, but fewer than would be sold in a market with perfect information.

Total product curve: A curve showing the relationship between the number of workers and the quantity of output produced.

Total revenue: The money the firm gets by selling its product; equal to the price times the quantity sold.

Total variable cost (TVC): Cost that varies as the firm changes the quantity produced.

Trade deficit: The excess of imports over exports.

Trade surplus: The excess of exports over imports.

Transactions demand for money: The demand for money based on the desire to facilitate transactions.

Transfer payments: Payments to individuals from governments that do not correspond to the production of goods and services.

Trough: The time at which output stops falling in a recession.

Trust: An arrangement under which the owners of several companies transfer their decision-making powers to a small group of trustees, who then make decisions for all the firms in the trust.

Unanticipated inflation: Inflation that is not expected.

Underemployed: Workers who hold a part-time job but prefer to work full time or hold jobs that are far below their capabilities.

Unemployed: People who are looking for work but do not have jobs.

Unit of account: The property of money that prices are quoted in terms of money.

Variable: A measure of something that can take on different values.

Variable costs: Costs that vary as the quantity produced changes.

Voluntary export restraint (VER): A scheme under which an exporting country voluntarily decreases its exports.

Wage–price spiral: Changes in wages and prices causing more changes in wages and prices.

Wealth effect: The increase in spending that occurs because the real value of money increases when the price level falls.

World Trade Organization (WTO): An organization that oversees GATT and other international trade agreements.

Answers to Odd-Numbered Problems and Discussion Questions

Appendix to Chapter 1

1. a. See Figure S.1.
   b. The slope is $5.
   c. The monthly bill will increase by $15.
3. 10%, −2%, 6%.
5. The number of burglaries will decrease by 4.

Chapter 1

1. The statement ignores the opportunity cost of the time spent in college.
3. The marginal cost is the cost of equipping and paying one more officer. The officer would presumably decrease crime, and the marginal benefit is determined by the reduction in crime resulting from the additional officer. If you can measure the marginal cost and the marginal benefit, you should continue to hire officers until the marginal benefit equals the marginal cost.
5. In the long run, the firm can modify its production facility or build a new one.
7. Eventually, we expect output to increase at a decreasing rate because more and more workers share the espresso machine.

Figure S.1 Relationship Between Hours of Tennis and the Monthly Tennis Club Bill

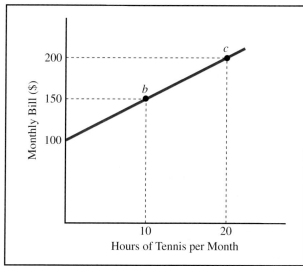

9. Salaries increased faster than the price of consumer goods.

Chapter 2

1. a. w, $150, 200 per day.
   b. demand, increase.
   c. supply, decrease.
3. a. The cost of producing computers will decrease, so the production of computers will be more profitable, so firms will supply more of them. The supply curve will shift to the right, decreasing the equilibrium price.
   b. The tax increases the production cost, shifting the supply curve to the left and increasing the equilibrium price.
5. Education at private and public schools are substitutes, so the tuition hike will shift the demand for private education to the right, increasing the equilibrium price and quantity.
7. If price and quantity both increase, we know from Table 4.1 that demand has increased. We shift the demand curve to the right, increasing the price and quantity.
9. How many people switch to automobile travel as a result of the higher cost of air travel? How does the shift to automobile travel affect the number of injuries and deaths on the highways? Does the airport security system reduce the number of injuries and deaths related to air travel? If so, how many lives are saved and how many injuries are avoided?
11. The supply curve for shirts shifts to the left, increasing the equilibrium price and decreasing the equilibrium quantity.

Chapter 3

1. The price elasticity is 1.30 = the percentage change in quantity (13%) divided by the percentage change in price (10%). Demand is elastic.
3. Each brand has many substitute goods (all the other brands), so the demand for a specific brand will be more elastic than the demand for running shoes in general.
5. Inelastic: An increase in price increases total revenue, while a decrease in price decreases total revenue.
7. Use the elasticity formula: The 10% increase in the price of beer will decrease the quantity of beer consumed by 13%, decreasing the highway death rate by the same percentage. Therefore, the number of highway deaths will decrease by 13 (13% of 100).

9. Use the price-change formula: The predicted change in price is 1% = 4%/(1 + 3). In the graph, we shift the supply curve to the left, so the restrictions increase the price from $100,000 to $101,000 and decrease the equilibrium quantity.

Chapter 4

1. The average cost is $15 for 40 shirts, $9 for 100 shirts, $7 for 200 shirts, and $6 for 400 shirts.

3.

Labor	Output	Marginal product
0	0	
1	5	5
2	11	6
3	15	4
4	18	3
5	19	1

5. There are no diminishing returns, so marginal cost is constant.

7. The $12,500 figure includes some of the fixed cost of production (design and tooling costs), so it is an average cost, not a marginal cost.

9. As shown in Figure 4.6, the average cost for the large generator is $4.60 (point *b*), compared to an average cost of $5.00 for the small generator (point *c*).

Chapter 5

1.

Tables per hour	Total cost	Marginal cost
3	120	—
4	155	35
5	200	45
6	270	70

3. If the firm continues to operate its facility, its total revenue will be $9,000 = $30 times 300 units of output. This is the benefit of operating the facility. The cost of operating the facility is the variable cost, which equals labor cost ($7,000 = the $100 wage times 700 workers). Total revenue exceeds variable cost, so it is sensible to continue operating the facility, even though it is losing money.

5. The manager is bluffing. His total revenue ($35,000) exceeds the *variable cost* ($30,000 for the farm workers). The $20,000 paid for seed and fertilizer was incurred months ago, and it is a sunk cost that will be ignored in the decision about whether to harvest the crop. Because his total revenue exceeds his variable cost, the farmer will harvest the crop even if the workers don't accept a wage cut.

7. We cannot draw a supply curve or complete the price elasticity of supply because we cannot be certain that the other variables that affect the supply of gasoline (the price of inputs, technology) did not change over this period.

9.

Number of firms	Industry output	Total cost for typical firm	Average cost per lamp
40	400	$300	$30
80	800	$360	$36
120	1,200	$420	$42

We have 3 points on the long-run supply curve: At a price of $30, the quantity is 400 lamps; at a price of $36, the quantity is 800 lamps; at a price of $42, the quantity is 1,200 lamps.

11. Because the industry uses such tiny amounts of the relevant inputs, the prices of these inputs won't change as the industry grows. Therefore, the average cost per haircut does not depend on the quantity of haircuts. The long-run supply curve is horizontal, for example, at a constant cost of $10 per haircut.

Chapter 6

1. To maximize profit, the restaurant will pick the quantity at which marginal revenue equals marginal cost. Using the marginal-revenue formula, we can compute the marginal revenue at each price and quantity:

Price	$10	$9	$8	$7
Quantity	30	40	50	60
Marginal revenue	$7	$5	$3	$1

Marginal revenue equals marginal cost at a price of $8 and a quantity of 50 meals.

3. On average, the payback per dollar spent on these lottery games is about 50¢. In other words, for every $100 spent by players, the state pays $50 in prizes. The commercial gambling games have much higher paybacks: The payback per dollar is 81¢ for horse racing and 89¢ for slot machines. The lottery games have lower paybacks because each state has a monopoly on lottery games: The state outlaws commercial lotteries. If the state allowed other organizations to offer lottery games, the competition between commercial and state lottery games would increase the payback from lottery games.

5. The artificial barrier to entry will generate higher prices and a smaller quantity demanded. If we eliminated the barriers, there would be more teams, and ticket prices would fall, increasing total attendance.

7. A decrease in demand shifts the demand curve to the left, and the new demand curve will intersect the negatively sloped long-run average-cost curve at a smaller quantity and a higher average cost (price). The loss of scale economies will cause the regulated price to rise.

9. Monopoly power increases prices in the game of Monopoly, consistent with the conclusions in this chapter.

11. The consumer advocate is assuming that the demand for the drug is perfectly inelastic, so an increase in price does

not have any effect on the quantity demanded. This is unrealistic and is inconsistent with the law of demand.

Chapter 7

1. The following table shows price and average cost for different numbers of arcades. Price exceeds average cost for the first 4 arcades, so the equilibrium number of arcades is 4.

Number of arcades	1	2	3	4	5
Price	50¢	48¢	46¢	44¢	42¢
Average cost	34¢	37¢	40¢	43¢	46¢

3. A firm that cuts 3 lawns will have a total cost of $30 ($18 in fixed cost + $12 in variable cost (3 lawns times $4 per lawn), or an average cost of $10 per lawn. In equilibrium, the price will be equal to average cost, which happens with a quantity of 60 lawns. Dividing the 60 lawns cut by 3 lawns per firm, there will be 20 firms in equilibrium.

5. If both firms pick the high price, each will get a profit of $360. If both pick the low price, each will get a profit of $250. For each firm, picking the low price is the dominant strategy.

   If firms pick prices each day, Bizarre weighs the benefit of undercutting ($140 on the day of undercutting) against the cost (the difference between the high-price profit [$360] and the low-price profit [$250] times the number of days remaining after the undercutting). On the first day, the cost is $220, which exceeds the benefit of $140. Assuming that Bizarre is not savvy enough to think about the end game (the last day), she will not undercut Weird.

7. By accepting the offer, the city gives up an opportunity to increase competition and reduce prices.

Chapter 8

1. a. No. Bertha is willing to pay the most ($100), but she is willing to pay less than the cost ($120).

   b. No. The cost per citizen will be $40, so Bertha is the only one who is willing to pay more than the cost per capita.

   c. Suppose each citizen pays $10 less than his or her willingness to pay: Bertha pays $90; Marian pays $20; Sam pays $10. This scheme raises $120 and benefits each citizen.

3. See Figure S.2. The market equilibrium is shown by point *i*: The demand curve intersects the supply curve at 20 units per day. The pollution tax shifts the supply curve by such a large amount that the supply curve lies entirely above the demand curve. For this to occur, the spillover cost from the pollutant must be very high, the cost of abatement must be very high, and the demand for good must be relatively low.

5. Suppose Groucho wants to join a social club to associate with people who are richer than he is, and he assumes that other people join clubs for the same reasons. A club will invite him to join only if he would increase the average income of the club. In other words, Groucho will be

Figure S.2 Pollution Tax Makes the Equilibrium Quantity of a Polluting Good Zero

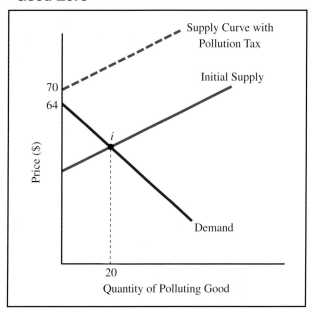

invited to join only groups in which most people are poorer than he is, clubs with an adverse selection of people. The same reasoning applies if Groucho wants to associate with people who are wittier than he is and he assumes that other people feel the same way. A club that asks him to join will have an average wit level that is less than his, so he will be forced to interact with dimwits.

7. Suppose you're willing to pay the average value of the two types of cameras ($60) for a 50% chance of getting a plum. If you expect a greater than 50% chance of getting a plum, it will be wise to buy a used camera. Given the adverse-selection problem, your chance of getting a plum is likely to be less than 50%.

9. No one with a $20 bike will buy a $40 insurance policy, so all of the insured bikes will be expensive ones. Total revenue will be $800 (equal to 20 times $40), while total cost for replacing the 10 stolen bikes will be $1,000 (equal to 10 times $100). The firm will lose $200.

11. Insured athletes may spend less effort in avoiding injuries, knowing that the insurance company will compensate them for a career-ending injury.

Chapter 9

1. The payroll tax shifts the supply curve to the left: At every price, a smaller quantity is supplied. The leftward shift of the supply curve increases the equilibrium wage to a wage above $10.

3. Some people will work fewer hours, so they will pay less in taxes: They pay a lower rate on fewer hours. Other people will work the same number of hours and pay less in taxes too: They pay a lower rate on the same number of hours.

Even a person who works more hours could pay less in taxes: If the increase in hours is small relative to the decrease in the hourly tax rate, the tax bill (hours times the tax rate) will actually decrease. The only people who will pay more in taxes are the workers who increase their hours by an amount that is large relative to the decrease in the hourly rate.

5. a. The supply of teachers is large relative to demand, so wages are relatively low. This could result from the psychological rewards from teaching, the work hours, or the free summer time.

   b. This is effectively a minimum wage for teachers, and it has the same effect as a minimum wage for any occupation: The increase in the wage will decrease the quantity demanded, so some teachers will lose their jobs.

7. Let's assume that the program is paid for by government, not coal companies. The program will increase the supply of coal workers, shifting the supply curve to the right. The equilibrium wage will decrease.

9. Like a minimum wage, a comparable-worth policy that increases wages in some occupations will decrease the quantity of labor demanded, so fewer workers will be hired. In addition, higher wages lead to higher production costs and output prices, so consumers will be harmed. An alternative policy is to break down the barriers that have discouraged women from choosing certain occupations.

Chapter 10

1. If we are interested in the increase in the production of goods and services, we should be interested in the growth of real GDP. If we also care about the increase in prices, we should be interested in the growth of nominal GDP.

3. We calculate the value of the goods produced in 2004 using the prices in 2004 and 2005. For 2004, the value of production is $24,000. For 2005, the value of production is $26,200. The value of production (attributable all to price changes) rose by 9.2%. If the price index for 2004 was 100, the price index for 2005 would be 1.092.

5. No, because you need to compare the price index in one year to a value in another year.

7. Refrigerators are an example of a good that depreciates. If a refrigerator costs $2,000, lasts for 10 years, and depreciates evenly over 10 years, the yearly depreciation would be $200.

9. Deterioration in air quality should be subtracted from NNP to arrive at national income. Improvements to air quality should be added.

11. At any point in time, individuals may base their happiness *relative* to others.

Chapter 11

1. The labor force is 6 million (employed plus unemployed); the labor force participation rate is 60% (labor force divided by population 16 years and older); the unemployment rate is 8.3% (unemployed divided by labor force).

3. This belief is based on the idea that with high unemployment rates, there are likely to be discouraged workers.

5. There will always be frictional and structural unemployment.

7. The inflation rate is 11% [(60 − 55)/55].

9. The conventional unemployment rate is 7.4% (8 million/108 million). An alternative measure would add the discouraged workers to total unemployment. This would also increase the labor force by the same amount. The alternative unemployment measure would be 10.7% (12 million/112 million).

Chapter 12

1. It will double in 23.3 years (70/3) and increase by a factor of 4 in 46.6 years.

3. False. The evidence is actually very weak.

5. We measure it through growth accounting. We ask how much growth can be explained by increases in labor and capital. The remainder is attributed to technological progress.

7. Public investment increases by 5% (one-half of 10%). Private savings and investment falls by 2% (20% of 10%). Thus, total investment (public and private) increases.

9. Although income may have been increasing during this period, the fall in height suggests that basic nutrition and overall welfare may have been decreasing. This perhaps could be accounted for by rapid increases in the population of cities and the stresses of urban life in this period.

Chapter 13

1. The term *cycle* could be misleading if we think of regular, reoccurring cycles. Business cycles do not fit this pattern.

3. Draw a line representing the trend in output. Then draw a pattern of actual output. The number of recessions will be the number of times the output line falls below the trend line. The proportion of the time the economy is in a recession will be the fraction of time the output line is below trend. The magnitude of the worst recession is the farthest the output line falls below trend.

5. Rents on apartments are sticky with month-long or year-long leases. They are sticky because it is costly to move and change apartments.

7. As the long-run aggregate supply curve moved to the right, prices would fall.

9. When aggregate demand falls, the aggregate demand curve shifts to the left, and prices and output fall. In the long run, the short-run aggregate supply curve falls to restore the economy to full employment.

Chapter 14

1. They shift the aggregate demand curve to the right.

3. The multiplier is 2.04. Therefore, investment spending needs to rise by 73.5.

5. No. Raising tax rates will also lower GDP.

7. a. GDP will rise.

   b. No. Inventories could rise because demand falls short of the expectations of producers.

9. GDP will fall because the multiplier for spending is greater than the multiplier for taxes.

11. More generous unemployment insurance programs put more funds into the economy in bad times and less in good times. This stabilizes consumption spending and output.

Chapter 15

1. They are accepted in exchange.
3. The opportunity cost of excess reserves is the income that could be earned by lending the reserves.
5. $13.3 million (the multiplier is 1/0.15 = 6.6).
7. An increase in the discount rate will lead banks to reduce their borrowed reserves from the Fed, and the supply of money will fall.
9. It would increase the supply of money. Any purchases by the Fed will increase reserves in banks and lead to an expansion of the supply of money.
11. They were not fully equivalent to money because they were accepted in exchange only by large banks and credit unions and not, for example, by stores or by individuals.

Chapter 16

1. The real interest rate measures the opportunity cost of funds. Thus, a high real interest rate translates into high opportunity costs for investment.
3. Yes. With an inflation rate of 10% and a nominal interest rate of 9%, the real rate of interest on funds is −1%. This is less than the real return on the project.
5. Monetary policy would become weaker since a decrease in interest rates would have less of an effect on investment.
7. The Netherlands has a higher ratio of exports (and imports) to GDP than the United States. Thus, we would expect that monetary policy would have more of an effect through exchange rates in the Netherlands than in the United States.

9. Nominal interest rates are equal to the real rate plus the expected inflation rate. High rates of money growth ("loose monetary policy") will lead, in the long run, to high rates of actual inflation and expected inflation and, thus, ultimately to high nominal interest rates.

Chapter 17

1. Brenda could specialize in bread. Instead of producing one shirt for herself, Brenda could use the time to produce two loaves of bread. If she then trades one loaf of bread for one shirt, she will have one loaf of bread left over. Sam could specialize in shirts. Instead of producing one loaf of bread for himself, he could use the time to produce two shirts. If he trades one shirt for one loaf of bread, he will have the same amount of bread but one extra shirt. Both Brenda and Sam benefit from specialization and trade.
3. Professor A has a comparative advantage in the graduate course: He is twice as productive as Professor B (90/45), but only 1.5 times as productive in the undergraduate course (90/60). Comparative advantage is always based on relative productivity.
5. Industries which receive protection from trade have less of an incentive to reduce their costs or to engage in innovations to improve their productivity.
7. a. appreciate the yen against the pound
   b. depreciate the pound against the yen
   c. appreciate the pound against the yen
9. With a rumor of a coup, a country's exchange rate will depreciate. Fearing economic instability and the possibility of controls being imposed in the market for currency and other assets, foreign investors will want to sell the country's currency to buy foreign assets. The result of the sales would be a currency depreciation.

Index

Wages
    for college graduates, 222
    differences in income and, 219–22
    at Ford Motor Company, 229
    gender discrimination and, 221–22
    imperfect information and efficiency, 229
    labor unions and, 227–28
    nominal, 370
    racial discrimination and, 221–22
    real, 370
    for steelworkers, 221
    sticky, 299
Wagner Act (1935), 227
Wal-Mart, 224
Warranties, 201
Wealth effect, 302
Wealth of Nations (Smith), 5, 6
Weather, effects of, on change in supply, 52–53
Welfare, gross domestic product as measure of, 251–53
Wind power
    increasing supply of, 54
    scale economies in, 96

Wireless women, 115
Wisconsin Power and Light, 197
Wolfram, supply of, during World War II, 119
Wonder bread, 174–75
Workers, shielding, from foreign competition, 380–81
Workforce turnover, 229
Workplace spillovers, 187
World Bank, 275, 288
    assistance of developing countries by, 284
World Trade Organization (WTO), 375, 382
    environment and, 383
World War II
    growth of trade since, 375
    supply of wolfram during, 119

X

XM Satellite Radio, 147

Y

Young, Alwyn, 282

Photo Credits

Chapter 1: Page 1, Bob Daemmrich/Stock Boston; page 12, © Danny Lehman/CORBIS BETTMANN; page 19, Mark Richards/PhotoEdit.

Chapter 2: Page 33, Walter H. Hodge/Peter Arnold, Inc.; page 54, Glen Allison/Getty Images, Inc.—Photodisc.

Chapter 3: Page 63, Jonathan Novrok/PhotoEdit; page 68, IPA/Chapman Parry/The Image Works; page 70, Les Stone/Corbis/Sygma.

Chapter 4: Page 81, © Owen Franken/CORBIS BETTMANN; page 93, Jonathan Nourok/PhotoEdit; page 94, Marilyn Kazmers-SharkSong/ Dembinsky Photo Associates; page 96, California Department of Water Resources.

Chapter 5: Page 105, Spencer Grant/PhotoEdit; page 112, Michael Newman/PhotoEdit; page 115, © Roger Wood/CORBIS BETTMANN; page 118, David Young-Wolff/PhotoEdit.

Chapter 6: Page 131, Barry Schwartz/Oregon State University; page 133: Myrleen Ferguson/PhotoEdit; page 143, R. Valladares; page 147, ESA/Photo Researchers, Inc.

Chapter 7: Page 155, John Coletti/Stock Boston Inc./PictureQuest; page 168, Michael Melford/Getty Images, Inc.— Image Bank; page 172, Bill Aron/PhotoEdit; page 176, Beaura Kathy Ringrose/Michael Tobin.

Chapter 8: Page 183, Michael Newman/PhotoEdit; page 186, NASA/Johnson Space Center; page 196, Malcolm Fife/Getty Images, Inc.— Photodisc; page 204, Deborah Davis/PhotoEdit.

Chapter 9: Page 211, David Young-Wolff/PhotoEdit; page 224, © Catherine Karnow/CORBIS BETTMANN; page 230, Ford Motor Company.

Chapter 10: Page 239, Pat Lacroix/Getty Images, Inc.—Image Bank; page 246, AP/Wide World Photos; page 252 (left), © Hulton-Deutsch Collection/CORBIS BETTMANN; page 252 (right), Getty Images, Inc.—Image Bank.

Chapter 11: Page 257, Peter D. Byron/ PhotoEdit; page 262, Culver Pictures, Inc.

Chapter 12: Page 273, © Wolfgang Kaehler/CORBIS BETTMANN; page 276, David Young-Wolff/PhotoEdit; page 286, Florent Flipper/Unicorn Stock Photos.

Chapter 13: Page 293, Tony Freeman/PhotoEdit; page 300, Spencer Grant/PhotoEdit.

Chapter 14: Page 315, Getty Images, Inc./Stone Allstock; page 328, Stockphoto.com; page 330, Bob Daemmrich/Stock Boston.

Chapter 15: Page 337, Myrleen Ferguson/PhotoEdit; page 341, PhotoAventurier/Getty Images, Inc.— Liaison.

Chapter 16: Page 355, Crandall/The Image Works; page 357, Tony Freeman/PhotoEdit; page 369, Paul Conklin/PhotoEdit.

Chapter 17: Page 375, Steven Rubin/The Image Works; page 376, Ronnie Kaufman/Corbis/Stock Market; page 382, Y. Forestier/Corbis/Sygma.